Transforming the Workforce for Children Birth Through Age 8: A Unifying Foundation

D0745949

Committee on the Science of Children Birth to Age 8:
Deepening and Broadening the Foundation for Success

Board on Children, Youth, and Families

LaRue Allen and Bridget B. Kelly, *Editors*

INSTITUTE OF MEDICINE *AND*
NATIONAL RESEARCH COUNCIL
OF THE NATIONAL ACADEMIES

THE NATIONAL ACADEMIES PRESS
Washington, D.C.
www.nap.edu

THE NATIONAL ACADEMIES PRESS   500 Fifth Street, NW   Washington, DC 20001

NOTICE: The project that is the subject of this report was approved by the Governing Board of the National Research Council, whose members are drawn from the councils of the National Academy of Sciences, the National Academy of Engineering, and the Institute of Medicine. The members of the committee responsible for the report were chosen for their special competences and with regard for appropriate balance.

This activity was supported by contracts between the National Academy of Sciences and The Bill & Melinda Gates Foundation (OPP1088695); the David and Lucile Packard Foundation (2013-38717); the U.S. Department of Education and U.S. Department of Health and Human Services (Administration for Children and Families and Health Resources and Services Administration) (HHSH25034019T); the Robert R. McCormick Foundation (unnumbered); and the W.K. Kellogg Foundation (460007972). The views presented in this publication do not necessarily reflect the views of the organizations or agencies that provided support for the activity.

Library of Congress Cataloging-in-Publication Data

National Research Council (U.S.). Committee on the Science of Children Birth to Age 8: Deepening and Broadening the Foundation for Success, Board on Children, Youth, and Families, author.
   Transforming the workforce for children birth through age 8 : a unifying foundation / Committee on the Science of Children Birth to Age 8: Deepening and Broadening the Foundation for Success, Board on Children, Youth, and Families ; LaRue Allen and Bridget B. Kelly, editors ; Institute of Medicine and National Research Council of the National Academies.
       p. ; cm.
   Includes bibliographical references.
   ISBN 978-0-309-32485-4 (pbk.) — ISBN 978-0-309-32486-1 (pdf)
   I. Allen, LaRue, 1950- , editor. II. Kelly, Bridget Burke, 1973- , editor. III. Title.
   [DNLM: 1. Child Development. 2. Occupations. 3. Child Care. 4. Child Welfare. 5. Child. 6. Education.
   7. Infant. 8. Learning. WS 105]
   RJ102
   362.196892—dc23
                                    2015020477

Additional copies of this report are available for sale from the National Academies Press, 500 Fifth Street, NW, Keck 360, Washington, DC 20001; (800) 624-6242 or (202) 334-3313; http://www.nap.edu.

For more information about the Institute of Medicine, visit the IOM home page at: www. iom.edu.

The serpent has been a symbol of long life, healing, and knowledge among almost all cultures and religions since the beginning of recorded history. The serpent adopted as a logotype by the Institute of Medicine is a relief carving from ancient Greece, now held by the Staatliche Museen in Berlin.

Suggested citation: Institute of Medicine (IOM) and National Research Council (NRC). 2015. *Transforming the workforce for children birth through age 8: A unifying foundation.* Washington, DC: The National Academies Press.

THE NATIONAL ACADEMIES
Advisers to the Nation on Science, Engineering, and Medicine

The **National Academy of Sciences** is a private, nonprofit, self-perpetuating society of distinguished scholars engaged in scientific and engineering research, dedicated to the furtherance of science and technology and to their use for the general welfare. Upon the authority of the charter granted to it by the Congress in 1863, the Academy has a mandate that requires it to advise the federal government on scientific and technical matters. Dr. Ralph J. Cicerone is president of the National Academy of Sciences.

The **National Academy of Engineering** was established in 1964, under the charter of the National Academy of Sciences, as a parallel organization of outstanding engineers. It is autonomous in its administration and in the selection of its members, sharing with the National Academy of Sciences the responsibility for advising the federal government. The National Academy of Engineering also sponsors engineering programs aimed at meeting national needs, encourages education and research, and recognizes the superior achievements of engineers. Dr. C. D. Mote, Jr., is president of the National Academy of Engineering.

The **Institute of Medicine** was established in 1970 by the National Academy of Sciences to secure the services of eminent members of appropriate professions in the examination of policy matters pertaining to the health of the public. The Institute acts under the responsibility given to the National Academy of Sciences by its congressional charter to be an adviser to the federal government and, upon its own initiative, to identify issues of medical care, research, and education. Dr. Victor J. Dzau is president of the Institute of Medicine.

The **National Research Council** was organized by the National Academy of Sciences in 1916 to associate the broad community of science and technology with the Academy's purposes of furthering knowledge and advising the federal government. Functioning in accordance with general policies determined by the Academy, the Council has become the principal operating agency of both the National Academy of Sciences and the National Academy of Engineering in providing services to the government, the public, and the scientific and engineering communities. The Council is administered jointly by both Academies and the Institute of Medicine. Dr. Ralph J. Cicerone and Dr. C. D. Mote, Jr., are chair and vice chair, respectively, of the National Research Council.

www.national-academies.org

CHERYL POLK, President, HighScope Educational Research Foundation, Ypsilanti, Michigan

P. FRED STORTI, Executive Director (Retired), Minnesota Elementary School Principals' Association, St. Paul

ROSS A. THOMPSON, Distinguished Professor, Department of Psychology, University of California, Davis

ALBERT WAT, Senior Policy Analyst, Education Division, National Governors Association, Washington, DC

Study Staff

BRIDGET B. KELLY, Study Director
SHEILA A. MOATS, Program Officer
WENDY E. KEENAN, Program Associate
SARAH M. TRACEY, Research Associate
ALLISON L. BERGER, Senior Program Assistant
FAYE HILLMAN, Financial Associate
CRISTINA NOVOA, Christine Mirzayan Science and Technology Policy Graduate Fellow (*January to June 2014*)
PAMELLA ATAYI, Administrative Assistant, Board on Children, Youth, and Families
KIMBER BOGARD, Director, Board on Children, Youth, and Families

Consultants

RONA BRIERE, Consultant Editor
SRIK GOPAL, FSG, Inc.
DAVID PHILLIPS, FSG, Inc.
HALLIE PRESKILL, FSG, Inc.
LAUREN SMITH, FSG, Inc.
LAUREN TOBIAS, Maven Messaging & Communications

Practitioner Advisors

ANNA ARLOTTA-GUERRERO, Clinical Assistant Professor, School of Education, University of Pittsburgh, Pennsylvania

FAITH ARNOLD, Owner and Director, Sun Children's, Inc., Bellwood, Illinois

CELIA C. AYALA, Chief Executive Officer, Los Angeles Universal Preschool, Los Angeles, California

REBECCA LYNNE DOW, Founder and Director, Appletree Education, Truth or Consequences, New Mexico

SAUNDRA HARRINGTON, Program Supervisor, Infant & Toddler Connection of Norfolk, Virginia

ELIZABETH HEIDEMANN, Kindergarten Teacher, Cushing Community School, Rockland, Maine

MICHELLE N. HUTSON, Center Designee/Lead Teacher, Gulf Coast Community Action Agency Head Start, D'Iberville, Mississippi

BETTE M. HYDE, Director, Washington State Department of Early Learning, Olympia, Washington

MELINDA LANDAU, Manager, Health/Family Support Programs, San Jose Unified School District, San Jose, California

DINA LIESER, Co-Director, Docs For Tots, Melville, New York

CARRIE A. NEPSTAD, Associate Professor of Child Development, Harold Washington College, City Colleges of Chicago, Illinois

VALERIE A. PRESTON, School Social Worker, New York City Department of Education, New York

MALIK J. STEWART, Manager, Federal and Regulated Programs, Red Clay Consolidated School District, Wilmington, Delaware

HEIDI SULLIVAN, Supervisor and Family Support Worker, Life Point Solutions-Every Child Succeeds, Cincinnati, Ohio

MAURICE TOME, Second Grade Teacher, School Within School, District of Columbia Public Schools, Washington, DC

Reviewers

This report has been reviewed in draft form by individuals chosen for their diverse perspectives and technical expertise, in accordance with procedures approved by the National Research Council's Report Review Committee. The purpose of this independent review is to provide candid and critical comments that will assist the institution in making its published report as sound as possible and to ensure that the report meets institutional standards for objectivity, evidence, and responsiveness to the study charge. The review comments and draft manuscript remain confidential to protect the integrity of the deliberative process. We wish to thank the following individuals for their review of this report:

Ashaunta Tumblin Anderson, University of California, Riverside
Sally Atkins-Burnett, Mathematica Policy Research, Inc.
Susan Bredekamp, Early Childhood Education Consultant
Esther R. Buch, Early Childhood Education Consultant
Theresa Canada, Western Connecticut State University
Linda M. Espinosa, University of Missouri–Columbia
Rochel Gelman, Rutgers, The State University of New Jersey
James J. Lesko, AEM Corporation
David Osher, American Institutes for Research
Marti T. Rosa, Wheelock College
Allan N. Schore, University of California, Los Angeles
Ruby Takanishi, New America
Steve Tozer, University of Illinois at Chicago
Claudia Walker, Murphey Traditional Academy

Although the reviewers listed above have provided many constructive comments and suggestions, they were not asked to endorse the conclusions or recommendations nor did they see the final draft of the report before its release. The review of this report was overseen by **Bernard Guyer,** Bloomberg School of Public Health, Johns Hopkins University, and **Greg J. Duncan,** University of California, Irvine. Appointed by the National Research Council and the Institute of Medicine, they were responsible for making certain that an independent examination of this report was carried out in accordance with institutional procedures and that all review comments were carefully considered. Responsibility for the final content of this report rests entirely with the authoring committee and the institution.

Acknowledgments

The committee and project staff are deeply appreciative of the diverse and valuable contributions made by so many who assisted with this study.

First, we are grateful for the support of the number of sponsors who funded this study, listed in full at the front of this report.

Throughout this process, we benefited from the insights of many individuals with a range of experiences related to the work of the committee. Their willingness to take the time to share their perspectives were essential to the committee's work. We offer our profound thanks to the Practitioner Advisors, named at the front of this report, for their ongoing generosity with their time and insights. It was a privilege and an inspiration to benefit from their experiences and perspectives. We also thank the many stakeholders who offered input and shared information and documentation with the committee over the course of the study. We very much appreciate and value the contributions of the individuals who participated in public information-gathering sessions (see Appendix B) and interviews (see Appendix C). In addition, we appreciate the generous hospitality of the institutions and organizations that hosted us and provided space to us on our site visits and regional public information-gathering sessions. In particular, we are immensely grateful for the planning assistance and logistical support for site visits provided to us by Betsy Coleman, Diane Horm, Sharon Phillips, Elizabeth Sullins, Lori Kelly, Kristie Kauerz, and Jasmiine Bacu.

We thank Cristina Novoa, who ably assisted the committee as a Mirzayan Fellow and graciously continued to provide valuable support beyond the initial period of her fellowship. We are also grateful to Lauren

Tobias of Maven Messaging & Communications and to Srik Gopal, David Phillips, Lauren Smith, and Halle Preskill of FSG, Inc., for their valuable and thoughtful work as consultants for this study. We thank Mardel Asbury Crandall, Jennifer Henk, and Zina Conley at the University of Arkansas for their commissioned work. We also appreciate the contributions of the following individuals who assisted with research support for this study: Carrie Germeroth, University of Denver; Julie Russ Harris, Harvard University; Christina Rucinski, Fordham University; Julia Sarama, University of Denver; and Brittany A. Sovran, Denver University.

We thank Rona Briere and Alisa Decatur at Briere Associates, Inc., for diligently editing this report. We also appreciate the creativity and effort of Jay Christian and LeAnn Locher for their design work.

For help with scheduling and communication for committee members, we thank Shirley Archer-Fields, Ben Barrett, Anne Blevins, Betsy Coleman, Jessica Craig, Aldine Harmon, Melanie Kellogg, Cynthia Kendall, Rina Plotkin, Allegra Pocinki, Juliana Shadlen, Jacqueline Wellington, and Marge Yahrmatter. We are also grateful to the staff at Kentlands Travel for their assistance with the travel needs of this project.

Finally, we convey our deep gratitude and appreciation for the hard work of the many staff in various offices of the National Academies who provided their support to the project.

Contents

PART IV: DEVELOPING THE CARE AND EDUCATION
WORKFORCE FOR CHILDREN BIRTH THROUGH AGE 8

PART V: BLUEPRINT FOR ACTION

APPENDIXES

Summary

Children are already learning at birth, and they develop and learn at a rapid pace in their early years, when the environments, supports, and relationships they experience have profound effects. Their development is not only rapid but also cumulative. Children's health, development, and early learning provide a foundation on which later learning—and lifelong progress—is constructed. Young children thrive when they have secure, positive relationships with adults who are knowledgeable about how to support their development and learning and responsive to their individual progress. Thus, the adults who provide for their care and education bear a great responsibility. Indeed, the science of child development and early learning makes clear the importance and complexity of working with young children from infancy through the early elementary years, or birth through age 8. It also illuminates the essential need for consistency and continuity in early care and education both over time as children develop and across systems and services. Yet just when children would benefit most from high-quality experiences that build on each other consistently over time, the systems with which they interact are fragmented.

The current state of the care and education workforce for these children is one of the most telling indicators of this fragmentation. Despite their shared objective of nurturing and securing the future success of young children, these professionals are not acknowledged as a cohesive workforce, unified by their shared contributions and the common knowledge base and competencies needed to do their jobs well. They work in disparate systems, and the expectations and requirements for their preparation and credentials have not kept pace with what the science of child development and early learning indicates children need. Care and education for young children take place in many different programs and settings, with different practitioner traditions and cultures; funded through multiple governmental and nongovernmental sources; and operating under the management or regulatory oversight of diverse agencies with varying policies, incentives, and constraints. Strengthening the workforce to better reflect the science is challenging given this complex, and often decentralized, oversight and influence.

Better support for care and education professionals will require mobilizing local, state, and national leadership; building a culture in higher education and ongoing professional learning that reflects the importance of establishing a cohesive workforce for young children from birth through age 8; ensuring practice environments that enable and reinforce the quality of their work; making substantial improvements in working conditions, well-being, compensation, and perceived status or prestige; and creating consistency across local, state, and national systems, policies, and infrastructure. This report offers a blueprint for action to connect what is *known* about how to support children to what is *done* in the settings where children grow and develop.

STUDY CHARGE AND SCOPE

Young children experience many important influences, including their parents or other primary caregivers;[1] their siblings and other family members; their peers; members of their communities; and the adults who work with them to provide for their care and education, health, and security. These professionals represent one of the most important channels available for improving the quality of early care and education.

To that end, this study was commissioned to focus on the implications of the science of development and early learning for care and education professionals who work with children from birth through age 8. This age span is not a developmental period with discrete boundaries; rather, it falls on a continuum that encompasses individual variations in development and that begins before birth and continues after age 8 into the rest of childhood and beyond. It is, however, an important window for children because of the troubling disconnect between the particularly disjointed nature of the systems that serve them and the rapid pace of their development as their experiences profoundly shape their long-term trajectories.

---

[1] An ongoing study and forthcoming report of the Institute of Medicine and the National Research Council will focus on strengthening the capacity of parents of young children from birth through age 8. More information can be found at www.iom.edu/activities/children/committeeonsupportingtheparentsofyoungchildren.

The major focus of this report is on those professionals who are responsible for regular, daily care and education of young children from birth through age 8, working in settings such as homes, childcare centers, preschools, educational programs, and elementary schools. Many of the report's messages are also applicable to closely related care and education professionals who see these children somewhat less frequently or for periodic or referral services, such as home visitors, early intervention specialists, and mental health consultants. The report also encompasses professionals in leadership positions and those who provide professional learning for the care and education workforce. In addition, the report includes considerations for the interactions among care and education professionals and practitioners in the closely related health and social services sectors who also work with children and their families. Finally, findings presented in this report regarding foundational knowledge and competencies are applicable broadly for all adults with professional responsibilities for young children.

This report's focus is on the competencies and professional learning that need to be shared among care and education professionals across professional roles and practice settings in order to support greater consistency. Although further specialized competencies and professional learning experiences differentiated by age, setting, and role are also important, this committee's task was to bridge those competencies and experiences in ways that will enable these professionals to contribute collectively and more effectively to greater consistency in practices that support development and high-quality learning for young children.

A UNIFYING FOUNDATION

The foundation for a workforce that can truly meet the needs of children from birth through age 8 is based on essential features of child development and early learning and on principles that guide support for high-quality professional practice with respect to individual practitioners, leadership, systems, policies, and resource allocation.

Essential Features of Child Development and Early Learning

Several essential features of child development and early learning inform not only what children need but also how adults can meet those needs, with support from the systems and policies that define and support their work:

- Children are already learning actively at birth, and the early foundations of learning inform and influence future development and learning continuously as they age.

- A continuous, dynamic interaction among experiences (whether nurturing or adverse), gene expression, and brain development underlies the capacity for learning, beginning before birth and continuing throughout life.
- Young children's development and early learning encompass cognitive development; the acquisition of subject-matter knowledge and skills; the development of general learning competencies; socioemotional development; and health and physical well-being. Each of these domains is crucial to early learning, and each has specific developmental paths. They also are overlapping and mutually influential: building a child's competency in one domain supports competency-building in the others.
- Stress and adversity experienced by children can undermine learning and impair socioemotional and physical well-being.
- Secure and responsive relationships with adults (and with other children), coupled with high-quality, positive learning interactions and environments, are foundational for the healthy development of young children. Conversely, adults who are underinformed, underprepared, or subject to chronic stress themselves may contribute to children's experiences of adversity and stress and undermine their development and learning.

Principles to Support Quality Professional Practice

These principles are based on what the science of child development and early learning reveals about the necessary competencies and responsibilities of practitioners in meeting the needs of young children. They encompass the high-quality professional learning and supports needed for practitioners to acquire, sustain, and update those competencies. Yet adults who master competencies can still be constrained in applying them by the circumstances of their settings and by the systems and policies of governance, accountability, and oversight that affect their practice. Thus, the following principles also apply to the characteristics of practice environments, settings, systems, and policies that are needed to ensure quality practice and to support individual practitioners in exercising their competencies:

- Professionals need foundational and specific competencies.
- Professionals need to be able to support diverse populations.
- Professional learning systems need to develop and sustain professional competencies.
- Practice environments need to enable high-quality practice.
- Practice supports need to facilitate and sustain high-quality practice.

- Systems and policies need to align with the aims of high-quality practice.
- Professional practice, systems, and polices need to be adaptive.

AREAS OF RECOMMENDATION

Drawing on the unifying foundation of the science of child development and early learning and principles for quality professional practice, the committee's recommendations support a convergent approach to caring for and educating young children—one that enables continuity across settings from birth through elementary school. The recommendations address qualification requirements for professional practice, higher education and ongoing professional learning during practice, evaluation and assessment of professional practice, the critical role of leadership, interprofessional practice, support for implementation, and improvement of the knowledge base. The following is a brief summary of the committee's major areas of recommendation. Detailed recommendations, with specified actors and actions as well as extensive discussion of considerations for implementation, can be found in Chapter 12.

The committee recognizes the challenges of the complex, long-term systems change that will be required to implement its recommendations. Full implementation of some of these recommendations could take years or even decades; at the same time, the need to improve the quality, continuity, and consistency of professional practice for children from birth through age 8 is urgent. Balancing this reality and this urgent need will require strategic prioritization of immediate actions as well as long-term goals with clearly articulated intermediate steps as part of pathways over time. The pace of progress will depend on the baseline status, existing infrastructure, and political will in different localities. Significant mobilization of resources will be required, and therefore assessments of resource needs, investments from government at all levels and from nongovernmental sources, and financing innovations will all be important.

The collective insight, expertise, and action of many stakeholders will also be needed. Important work related to the recommendations in this report is currently being carried out by many strong organizations, yet the persistently diffuse nature of the numerous systems and institutions that serve children from birth through age 8 calls for approaches that are increasingly collaborative and inclusive. Many of the committee's recommendations rely on a collective approach of this kind, and features of a framework for collaborative systems change for early care and education are described in Chapter 12.

Qualification Requirements for Professional Practice

All care and education professionals have a similarly complex and challenging scope of work. Yet practices and policies regarding requirements for qualification to practice vary widely for different professionals based on their role, the ages of the children with whom they work, their practice setting, and what agency or institution has jurisdiction or authority for setting qualification criteria. Greater coherence in qualification requirements across professional roles would improve the consistency and continuity of high-quality learning experiences for children from birth through age 8.

> **Recommendation 1: Strengthen competency-based qualification requirements for all care and education professionals working with children from birth through age 8.**

A review process guided by mutual alignment with the principles set forth in this report across agencies and organizations and across the national, state, and local levels would lay the groundwork for greater coherence in the content of and processes for qualification requirements, such as those for credentialing and licensure. As a result, even when different systems or localities have policies that are organized differently by age ranges and roles, those policies could still work in concert to foster quality practice across professional roles and settings that supports more consistent high-quality learning experiences for children from birth through age 8.

> **Recommendation 2: Develop and implement comprehensive pathways and multiyear timelines at the individual, institutional, and policy levels for transitioning to a minimum bachelor's degree qualification requirement, with specialized knowledge and competencies, for all lead educators[2] working with children from birth through age 8.**

Currently, most lead educators in care and education settings prior to elementary school are not expected to have the same level of education—a bachelor's degree—as those leading elementary school classrooms. Policy decisions about qualification requirements are complex, as is the relationship among level of education, high-quality professional practice, and outcomes for children. Given that empirical evidence about the effects of a bachelor's degree is inconclusive, a decision to maintain the status quo

---

[2] Lead educators are those who bear primary responsibility for children and are responsible for planning and implementing activities and instruction and overseeing the work of assistant teachers and paraprofessionals. They include the lead educator in classroom and center-based settings, center directors/administrators, and owner/operators and lead practitioners in home-based or family childcare settings.

and a decision to transition to a higher level of education as a minimum requirement entail similar uncertainty and as great a potential consequence for outcomes for children.

The committee therefore makes the recommendation to transition to a minimum expectation of a bachelor's degree for lead educators working with young children on several grounds. The current differential in education requirements lags behind the science of child development and early learning, which clearly indicates that the work of lead educators for young children of all ages is based on the same high level of sophisticated knowledge and competencies. It follows that they should be on an equal footing in their preparation for practice. Furthermore, holding lower educational expectations for early childhood educators than for elementary school teachers perpetuates the perception that educating children before kindergarten requires less expertise than educating early elementary students, which in turn helps justify policies that make it difficult to maximize the potential of young children and the early learning programs that serve them. Disparate degree requirement policies also create a bifurcated job market, both between elementary schools and early care and education and within early care and education as a result of degree requirements in Head Start as well as other settings and publicly funded prekindergarten programs. This situation potentially perpetuates a cycle of disparity in the quality of learning experiences for young children.

Most important for this recommendation is that simply instituting policies requiring a minimum bachelor's degree is not sufficient, and this recommendation is closely interconnected with those that follow. A degree requirement will be feasible and its potential benefits fully realized only if it is implemented carefully over time and in the context of efforts to address interrelated factors that affect the quality of professional practice and with supportive federal, state, and local policies and informed, supportive leadership. Pathways and timelines will be needed to improve quality, availability, and access for both high-quality higher education and ongoing professional learning; to implement systems and policy changes to licensure and credentialing; and to effect parity across professional roles in compensation, workplace policies, and working conditions. Pathways and timelines for individuals will need to be differentiated for currently practicing professionals and prospective educators, and recruitment plans will be needed to engage a new, diverse generation of care and education professionals who will be incentivized to give equal consideration to roles across the birth through age 8 continuum.

Assessments of resource needs will be important, followed by resource mobilization plans and innovative financing strategies for scholarships and stipends for individuals, subsidies for higher education programs, and adjustments to the increased labor costs that will result from parity in compensation and benefits in the care and education sector. Strategies will also be needed to assess, monitor, and mitigate possible negative consequences, such as workforce shortages, reduced diversity in the professions, increased disparities among current and future professionals, upward pressure on out-of-pocket costs to families, and disruptions to the sustainability of operating in the for-profit and not-for-profit care and education market.

Recommendation 3: Strengthen practice-based qualification requirements, including a supervised induction period, for all lead educators working with children from birth through age 8.

The opportunity for supervised practice is important to ensure that practitioners have mastered the competencies necessary to work with children from birth through age 8, yet many professional roles in care and education currently are not required to have a supervised induction period as a transition to autonomous practice. In introducing this requirement, it will be necessary in parallel to consider and develop strategies for the significant investment needed to develop a greater number and diversity of field placements capable of providing this kind of professional learning with appropriately qualified supervisors and mentors. It will also be necessary to consider how to differentiate and apply this requirement for experienced practitioners who are acquiring this level of qualification while already practicing.

Higher Education and Ongoing Professional Learning

Recommendation 4: Build an interdisciplinary foundation in higher education for child development.

The goal of this recommendation is for higher education to foster a fundamental shared knowledge base and competencies around child development for professionals in all sectors who work with young children, based on requirements for core coursework, other learning activities, and field-based learning experiences. Guided by the science of child development, this could serve as a baseline prerequisite for further study or as a child specialization enhancement. This would support preparation for various professional roles working with children from birth through age 8 in education, social services, and health/allied health professions. Additional coursework, learning, and practicum requirements would be differentiated according to the specific professional pathway students follow.

Recommendation 5: Develop and enhance programs in higher education for care and education professionals.

Building on the cross-disciplinary foundation described in Recommendation 4, high-quality programs in higher education are needed that further ensure and document the acquisition of the knowledge and competencies needed for quality professional practice in care and education for children from birth through age 8. These programs need to provide a formally defined, accredited course of study in child development, early learning, and instruction. Such a course of study needs to provide students with coursework in development, subject-matter content, and instructional and other practices to foster development and early learning; field experiences; and methods to document demonstrated mastery of practice. In some cases this defined, accredited course of study could be a specified degree or major, but it could also be a concentration or certificate in child development, early learning, and instruction that a student would complete alongside another major or as a postbaccalaureate program.

Programs that are differentiated for specific age ranges, subject-matter specialization, or responsibilities should also ensure adequate knowledge of the development and learning of children across the birth through age 8 continuum so that care and education professionals will be prepared to support consistent learning experiences for children.

Recommendation 6: Support the consistent quality and coherence of professional learning supports during ongoing practice for professionals working with children from birth through age 8.

The goal of this recommendation is to incentivize greater quality, consistency, and parity in learning opportunities across settings and roles for care and education professionals who work with children from birth though age 8 through technical assistance; funding mechanisms such as interagency pooling of resources; and support for clearinghouses, quality assurance systems, and other means of better coordinating professional learning systems. Support of this kind should promote joint professional learning opportunities among care and education professionals across roles, age groups, and settings; provide a forum to facilitate collaborations; and provide guidance for individuals and employers on how to set professional learning objectives; select and prioritize sequenced, high-quality professional learning activities; and access financial and other supports.

Evaluation and Assessment of Professional Practice

Based on the science of child development and early learning and its implications for professional competencies, current systems for measuring the performance of educators—and even current reforms to those systems—are not sufficient for those who work with children in the early elementary years and younger; indeed, they may produce unreliable data about children's learning and development and the quality of instruction. Current reforms focus on student outcomes and instructional practices in one or two areas instead of capturing the developmental nature of early learning and the full range of domains that are important. In addition, evaluation and assessment systems fail to capture important competencies such as trauma-informed practice, family engagement, and collaboration and communication with other professionals. As a result, current evaluation and assessment policies and systems may reinforce and reward a narrow view of effectiveness while missing best practices that should be fostered and recognized in professionals working with children from birth through age 8.

Recommendation 7: Develop a new paradigm for evaluation and assessment of professional practice for those who work with children from birth through age 8.

Developing and implementing more appropriate systems for evaluating and assessing the performance of care and education professionals in elementary schools and early care and education settings will require a shift from the current paradigm. Because of the variable nature of children's learning and development from birth through age 8, considering multiple sources of evidence derived with multiple methods and at multiple times is important when evaluating and assessing educator performance. A continuous improvement system of evaluation and assessment should align with research on the science of how young children develop and learn, be comprehensive in its scope of early developmental and learning objectives, reflect day-to-day practice competencies and not just single-point assessments, reflect what professionals do in their practice settings and also how they work with professional colleagues and with families, be tied to access to professional learning, and account for setting-level and community-level factors beyond the control of practitioners that affect their capacity to practice effectively (such as overcrowded classrooms, poorly resourced settings, lack of access to professional learning supports, community factors, and home environments).

The Critical Role of Leadership

Elementary school principals, early care and education center directors or program directors, and other administrators are an important factor in the quality of early learning experiences for the children in the settings they oversee. These leaders play an instrumental role in helping care and education professionals strengthen their core competencies and in creating a work environment in which they can fully use their knowledge and skills. Principals and directors often take a lead role in selecting content and activities for professional learning. In addition, leaders have a major influence because they are responsible for workforce hiring practices and for the systems used for evaluating the performance of the professionals they oversee. They need to have the knowledge and competencies to hire and supervise educators who are capable of working with children in the settings they lead.

> **Recommendation 8: Ensure that policies and standards that shape the professional learning of care and education leaders encompass the foundational knowledge and competencies needed to support high-quality practices for child development and early learning in their organizations.**

Statements about what these leaders should know and be able to do should be aligned in both specific competencies and the general principles on which they are based, including the science of early childhood development. States and organizations that issue statements of core competencies and other policies related to professional learning and qualifications for leadership in elementary education would benefit from a review to ensure that the scope of instructional leadership is inclusive of the early elementary years, including prekindergarten as it increasingly becomes included in public school systems. States and organizations that issue statements of core competencies and other policies related to professional learning and qualifications for leadership in centers, programs, family childcare, and other settings for early childhood care and education would benefit from a review to ensure that competencies related to instructional leadership are emphasized alongside administrative and management competencies. In addition, both types of leaders need specific competencies for collaboration and communication because of their important role in bridging systems to support greater continuity in early learning experiences before and after young children enter school systems, as well as to support linkages with other sectors such as health and social services.

Interprofessional Practice

A critical factor in providing consistent support for children from birth through age 8 is the ability of care and education professionals to work in synergy with other professionals both across settings within the care and education sector and in other closely related sectors, especially health and social services.

Recommendation 9: Improve consistency and continuity for children from birth through age 8 by strengthening collaboration and communication among professionals and systems within the care and education sector and with closely related sectors, especially health and social services.

Continuity across care and education settings and among diverse services and agencies is important not only to provide more consistent and better-coordinated services for individual children and their families but also to create shared understanding of the interconnected quality of developmental processes that each practitioner, focused on a specialized scope of practice, may see only in part. In this area of recommendation, the committee emphasizes the important need for consultation between educators and infant and child mental health professionals, with a focus on improving the availability of mental health services and consultation.

Support for Implementation

Implementing the preceding recommendations will require better alignment, more inclusive coordination, and support for collaborative efforts among the multiple stakeholders that influence children from birth through age 8.

Recommendation 10: Support workforce development with coherent funding, oversight, and policies.

This recommendation calls for national, state, and local governmental and nongovernmental agencies and organizations to review and revise their policies, guidelines, programmatic portfolios, oversight provisions, and incentives for professional learning and quality professional practice to ensure that they are oriented to the primary aim of optimal support for child development and early learning and aligned with the unifying foundation set forth in this report. These efforts should include revision of categorical policies and funding streams to identify and remove barriers to continuity across practice settings, professional roles, and age ranges from birth through age 8.

Recommendation 11: Collaboratively develop and periodically update coherent guidance that is foundational across roles and settings for care and education professionals working with children from birth through age 8.

This recommendation calls for national nongovernmental organizations that currently offer resources and support for the care and education workforce to engage in a collaborative effort to provide and periodically update shared, coherent foundational guidance for care and education professionals working with children from birth through age 8. The aim is to promote consistency among the various entities with oversight and influence over the many professional roles that entail working with these young children. Providing comprehensive guidelines based in evidence and drawing on collective expertise in the field will improve the availability of high-quality, continuous developmental support and learning experiences for children as they age.

This collaborative effort will be most effective if it draws and builds on the existing resources of participating organizations to create both a robust and coherent platform for what is common across professional roles and a shared foundation to consistently inform the work of collaborating organizations in their specialized areas of workforce development. The success of this effort will depend on balanced representation among professional roles and settings involved in care and education across the birth through age 8 continuum, from infancy through early elementary school. Representation will also need to reflect practice communities, the research community, policy research and analysis, policy makers and government leadership, higher education, agencies that oversee licensure and credentialing as well as accreditation, and organizations that provide ongoing professional learning. Another key consideration for participating organizations is to reflect the racial, ethnic, and linguistic diversity of the workforce itself and the children and families served, as well as geographic diversity to represent the varied circumstances in different local contexts.

Recommendation 12: Support comprehensive state- and local-level efforts to transform the professional workforce for children from birth through age 8.

This recommendation calls for support of collaborative efforts at the state and local levels. To this end, federal and state government agencies and national nongovernmental resource organizations should provide technical support and cross-sector financial resources, including public–private partnerships, that can be combined with local resources. To model this approach, the committee calls for national governmental and nongovernmental funders to jointly support at least 10 local or state coalitions to undertake 10-year initiatives to review, assess, and improve professional learning and workforce development for the care and education workforce for children from birth through age 8. Guided by the science of child development and early learning, these initiatives should implement a collective effort to build a more coherent infrastructure of professional learning supports; improve the quality, availability, and accessibility of professional learning activities; and revise and align policies, incentives, and financial and technical support. To that end, these state or local coalitions should be supported in carrying out the following efforts:

- Ascertain the current status of the local care and education workforce for children from birth through age 8 across professional roles, settings, and age ranges (including demographics, practice settings, qualification requirements, salaries, and participation in current professional learning systems).
- Map the local landscape of stakeholders with a role in professional learning and workforce development, including the activities they are undertaking.
- Identify the strengths, gaps, unmet needs, and fragilities in current systems.
- Estimate resource needs, and develop a plan for financing and resource mobilization to increase, diversify, and strategically allocate funding that takes into account public investments at the federal, state, and local levels; investments from private philanthropic and corporate sources; and out-of-pocket spending by families.
- Establish and clearly articulate an organizational and decision-making structure, priorities, goals, planned activities and policy changes, timelines, and benchmarks for progress.
- Facilitate ongoing stakeholder coordination and sharing of information related to funding, activities, and data collection and use.
- Document and share actions undertaken and lessons learned.

Improvement of the Knowledge Base

Several of the preceding recommendations for workforce development hinge on the ability of local, state, and national stakeholders and policy makers to understand the current status, characteristics, and needs of the workforce across professional roles and settings that serve children from birth through age 8; to monitor progress over time; and to draw on research findings regarding effective policies and practices. This information also is essential for mobilizing resources and galvanizing public support for new initiatives.

Recommendation 13: Build a better knowledge base to inform workforce development and professional learning services and systems.

An important component of the knowledge base for workforce development and professional learning is the dynamic cycle of continuously learning about child development and best practices and translating that knowledge into widespread professional practice. This is a shared responsibility: support is required to advance the research itself, and mechanisms are also needed to connect that research to the practice community. The latter might include involving the practice community in research, as well as making research findings and their implications more timely, accessible, and available to practicing professionals. Professionals in turn need to understand the importance of continuously updating their knowledge and competencies and to have the motivation and incentives to do so. In the course of reviewing the existing knowledge base, the committee identified several ongoing research and evaluation needs, which are listed in Chapter 12.

A CALL TO ACTION

Many of the challenges discussed in this report are not new. For too long, the nation has been making do with the systems and policies that *are* rather than envisioning the systems and policies that are *needed*, and committing to the strategies necessary to achieve them. Implementing the committee's recommendations will produce substantive changes that elevate the perception of the professionals who work with children from birth through age 8 and improve the quality of professional practice, the quality of the practice environment, and the status and well-being of the workforce—and ultimately, outcomes for children. Comprehensive implementation of these recommendations will not happen quickly and will not come cheaply. It will require a strategic, progressive trajectory of change over time to transform the professional landscape, accompanied by significant commitment and investment of financial and other resources.

The committee expects that building on a unified foundation, driven by the science of child development and early learning, will introduce a self-perpetuating cycle of excellence, supported by policy makers and a society that recognize the complex and important role of early care and education professionals; the intellectually, physically, and emotionally challenging nature of their work; and the deep, extensive, and ongoing professional learning required for them to be successful. These changes hold promise for helping to retain highly effective practitioners in these professional roles and to bolster the recruitment of a robust and viable pipeline of new professionals. It is through the quality work of these adults that the nation can make it right from the very beginning for all of its children.

Part I

Introduction and Context

1

Introduction

Children are already learning at birth, and they develop and learn at a rapid pace in their early years, when the environments, supports, and relationships they experience have profound effects. Children's development from birth through age 8 is not only rapid but also cumulative. Early learning and development provide a foundation on which later learning is constructed, and consistency in high-quality learning experiences as children grow up supports continuous developmental achievements. The adults who provide for the care and education of young children bear a great responsibility for their health, growth, development, and learning, building the foundation for lifelong progress. Young children thrive and learn best when they have secure, positive relationships with adults who are knowledgeable about how to support their health, development, and learning and are responsive to their individual progress. Indeed, the science of child development and of how best to support learning from birth through age 8 makes clear what an important, complex, dynamic, and challenging job it is for an adult to work with young children in each of the many professional roles and settings where this work takes place.

Even though they share the same objective—to nurture young children and secure their future success—the various professionals who contribute to the care and education of children from birth through age 8 are not perceived as a cohesive professional workforce. Those who care for and teach young children do so in disparate systems with a variety of backdrops and circumstances. The requirements for their preparation and credentials often depend on the setting where they work rather than on the needs of children. They work in homes, childcare centers, preschools, educational programs, and elementary schools. Their work relates directly to those who provide services such as home visiting, early intervention, and special education, and is also closely connected to the work of pediatric health professionals and social services professionals who work with children and families.

Growing public understanding of the importance of early childhood is reflected by an increased emphasis on this age group in policy and investments. Yet the sophistication and complexity of the professional roles that entail working with children from infancy through the early elementary years are not recognized and reflected consistently in practices and policies regarding education and other expectations for qualification to practice, professional learning expectations and supports, and compensation and other working conditions. Those who care for and educate young children currently are not acknowledged as a workforce unified by their common objective and shared contributions to the development and early learning of young children and the common knowledge base and competencies needed to do their jobs well.

STUDY CHARGE, SCOPE, AND APPROACH

Over the past several decades, much has been learned about the rapid development of critical neurological and biological systems in the earliest years and about the important foundation that is laid through the early experiences of children. Considerable work also has been done to examine the interventions, programs, policies, and systems that have been implemented or are needed to have a positive influence on young children in early life and for the long term. Over time, these efforts increasingly have addressed important topics related to early childhood in a frame that is inclusive of children from birth through age 8. This age span is not a discrete developmental period with precise boundaries at its margins; indeed, it falls on a developmental continuum that encompasses individual variations and that begins before birth and continues after age 8 into the rest of childhood, through adolescence, and throughout the life course. Nonetheless, focusing on this specific age span within this continuum is important because it is a range in which a troubling disconnect currently exists.

This age span is a window during which development is progressing at a particularly rapid pace, and experiences during the first 8 years of life shape a child's long-term trajectory. In this window, children benefit from consistent, cumulative learning experiences and other influences that build on each other and evolve as children age. Yet just when children would benefit most from consistency and continuity, the systems with which they interact and the professionals who work with them are particularly fragmented and disjointed. By third grade, a child has entered the education system that will guide her or him for nearly the next decade, having previously been prepared by formal and informal learning opportunities beginning from birth. However, both early learning opportunities and the education system that most commonly follows often fail to support children seamlessly, on a consistent, cumulative trajectory free from disruptive transitions, to position them for their future academic achievements and success in life.

Many factors influence child development during this window of time, including, for example, the availability of and equitable access to the wide range of services and programs that are or could be provided for children and their families; the funding and financing that affect the allocation of resources to and among those services and programs; the quality of their implementation on a large scale; the policies for their oversight, evaluation, and accountability; and the degree to which they are coordinated and interact across settings and sectors. Improvements and progress across all of these factors will be important to promote the development and early learning of all children from birth through age 8. However, none of these improvements will be truly effective without concerted attention to the adults who work with children. Effort in this area is one of the most important mechanisms available for improving the quality of the care and education received by young children; providing information, support, and links to resources as these professionals interact with families and with each other; and ultimately, improving outcomes for children. This study was commissioned specifically to focus on the science of development and early learning not just for what it reveals about children, but in particular for its implications for the professionals who work with children during this critical period. These implications apply to the knowledge and competencies these professionals need; their systems for professional learning; and other supports that contribute to improving the quality of professional practice and developing an excellent, robust, and stable workforce across the many professional roles that relate to children from birth through age 8. This dual focus on the science of learning and the development of the workforce is central to ensuring that all children get a good start in life.

Study Charge

The full statement of task for the Committee on the Science of Children Birth to Age 8: Deepening and Broadening the Foundation for Success is presented in Box 1-1. In summary, the committee was charged with examining how the science of children's health, learning, and development can inform how the workforce supports children from birth through age 8. Areas of emphasis included the influence of neurobiology, health, and development on learning trajectories and educational achievement, as well as on workforce considerations such as standards, expectations, and

BOX 1-1
Statement of Task

An ad hoc committee will conduct a study and prepare a consensus report on how the science of children's health, learning, and development from birth through age 8 can be employed to inform how we prepare a workforce to seamlessly support children's health, development, learning, and school success from birth through age 8, including standards and expectations, instructional practices, preparation and professional development, and family engagement across diverse contexts (e.g., rural/urban) and populations (e.g., special education, immigrant, dual language learners, sub-threshold children). The committee will address the following questions:

1. What do we know about the influence of neurobiology, health, and development (e.g., emotion regulation, executive functioning, psychosocial) on learning trajectories and educational achievement for children from birth through age 8, including typical and atypical pathways?
2. What generalized and specialized knowledge, skills, and abilities do adults, working with children across the birth through age 8 continuum and across infant, toddler, preschool-aged, and K-3 settings (for example, home visitors, childcare workers, early childhood educators, health professionals, center directors, elementary school teachers, principals) need to seamlessly support children's health, learning, development, and school success?
3. What staff development structure and qualifications are necessary for educators at each level (e.g., entry level, full professional, etc.) to support children's learning across the continuum of development from birth through age 8? This should be linked to question 2.

qualifications; generalized and specialized knowledge and competencies; instructional practices; professional learning; leadership; and family engagement. The committee was tasked with looking across diverse contexts and populations and across professional roles and settings to draw conclusions and make recommendations about how to reenvision professional learning systems and inform policy decisions related to the workforce in light of the science of child development and early learning and the knowledge and competencies needed by the adults who work with children from birth through age 8. The statement of task specifies a wide range of audiences for the report, such as federal funding agencies, state and local agencies, regulatory agencies, federal and state legislatures, institutions of higher education, and programs and practitioners that serve children birth through age 8.

As noted above, one critical factor that influences child development from birth through age 8 is the availability of resources to invest in any

4. How can the science from questions 1 and 2 be employed to reenvision preparation and professional development programs across infant, toddler, preschool-aged, and K-3 settings, including how to assess children and use data to inform teaching and learning from birth through age 8?
5. How can the science on children's health, development, learning, and educational achievement, and the skills adults need to support them, inform policy decisions conducive to implementing the recommendations?

Based on currently available evidence, the report could include findings, conclusions, and recommendations on the above, paying particular attention to research on (1) poverty, racial inequities, and disadvantage; (2) learning environments in the home and in schools; (3) adult learning processes as they relate to teaching children; and (4) leadership/management skills as they relate to developing the skills of a highly effective workforce designed to support children's learning, growth, and development from birth through age 8. The report will provide research and policy recommendations to specific agencies and organizations (governmental and nongovernmental) as well as inform institutions serving children birth through age 8. Recommendations will be geared toward the following, including recommendations for joint actions among agencies, institutions, and stakeholders: federal funding agencies, including the Administration for Children and Families, the Maternal and Child Health Bureau of the Health Resources and Services Administration, the National Institutes of Health, the U.S. Department of Education, with a particular emphasis on Title II of the Elementary and Secondary Education Act (Title II), which focuses on improving teacher and principal quality; legislatures (Congress, state legislatures); higher education institutions; state and local education agencies; state early childhood care and education agencies; family childcare programs; regulation agencies; and practitioners that provide health, education, and care services to children birth through age 8.

potential changes, most of which will require significant allocation of new or reallocation of existing resources. While acknowledging that the availability of resources is an important reality that would affect the feasibility of the committee's recommendations, the sponsors specified in clarifying the study charge that this committee not conduct analyses or develop consensus conclusions and recommendations addressing funding and financing. The sponsors did not want the committee to be swayed by foregone conclusions about the availability of resources in interpreting the evidence and the current state of the field and in carrying out deliberations about its recommendations. The sponsors also recognized that the breadth of expertise required to fulfill such a broad and comprehensive charge precluded assembling a committee with sufficient additional breadth and depth of expertise in economics, costing and resource needs assessment, financing, labor markets, and other relevant areas to address funding and financing issues.[1]

Study Scope

The landscape of influences on and opportunities for a child's development and early learning is complex and encompasses many interrelated settings, services, and stakeholders. Figure 1-1 shows illustrative examples within the main categories of care and education; health; parents, family, and community; and other influences. While overwhelming and perhaps even intimidating, this is nonetheless the reality of the environment in which efforts to improve the quality of professional practice and support for the workforce will be implemented. This landscape is explored in greater depth in Chapter 2, with a focus on the care and education sector.

Many adults interact with children within this complex landscape, and every interaction a child has with an adult is an opportunity for a learning experience. Yet it was not possible for a single consensus study to cover in depth every adult role with the potential to influence child development and early learning within this landscape. The emphasis specified in the committee's statement of task is on learning and educational achievement, instructional practices, and educators. Therefore, the committee chose to focus on professionals who work in the care and education sector, and to a lesser extent on those in the health and social services sectors who intersect closely with the care and education sector. That said, the findings and conclusions in this report about foundational knowledge and competencies are applicable broadly for all adults with professional responsibilities for young children.

When this report delves into specialized competencies and the implications for professional learning and workforce development, the major focus is on those professionals who are responsible for regular, daily care and education. In many cases, the committee's review was also inclusive of or applicable to closely related care and education professions who see children somewhat less frequently or for periodic or referral services, such as home visitors, early intervention specialists, and mental health consultants. In addition, it encompassed considerations for professionals in leadership positions and those who work in the training, education, and professional development of the care and education workforce, as well as for the interactions of care and education professionals with closely related practitioners

---

[1] Personal communications between sponsor representatives and Institute of Medicine (IOM)/National Research Council (NRC) staff during contract negotiations and between sponsors and committee members during a public information-gathering session held on December 19, 2013.

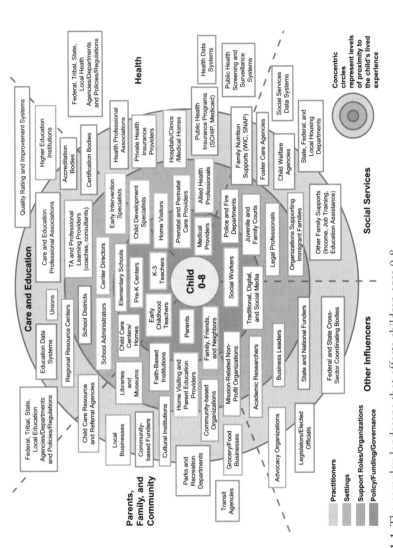

FIGURE 1-1 The complex landscape that affects children ages 0-8.

NOTE: SCHIP = State Children's Health Insurance Program; SNAP = Supplemental Nutrition Assistance Program; WIC = Special Supplemental Nutrition Program for Women, Infants, and Children.

who work with children aged 0-8 and their families in the health and social services sector. Figure 1-2 summarizes the study's scope of inclusion for different professional roles.

Finally, as specified in the statement of task, the committee's major focus was on the competencies and professional learning that, to support greater consistency in high-quality learning experiences for children, need to be shared among care and education professionals across the birth through age 8 continuum and across professional roles and practice settings. This focus included areas in which care and education professionals will benefit from understanding the scope of learning—and the scope of educational practices—for the settings and ages that precede or follow them within the birth through age 8 range. Although further specialized competencies and professional learning differentiated by age, setting, and/or role are important, this study was not intended to duplicate or supplant existing infrastructure or processes for articulating, reviewing, and guiding

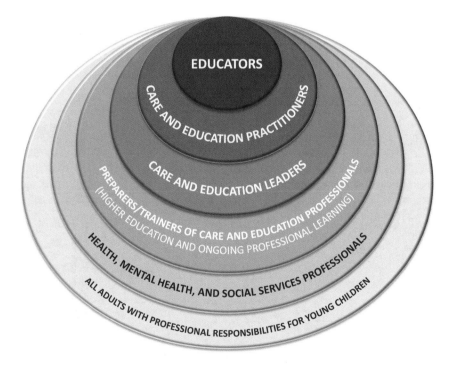

FIGURE 1-2 Illustration of the study's scope of inclusion for different professional roles, with the specificity and depth of focus decreasing from the innermost/darkest rings to the outermost/lightest rings.

those competencies. Those further competencies require greater depth of representation for each age range and professional role than was feasible with a committee composed to be broadly representative in its expertise across the entirety of its broad charge. Rather, this committee's task was to bridge those efforts by providing information and recommendations to assist each such effort in contributing collectively and more effectively to greater consistency and continuity for children.

It is important to acknowledge that parents (or other designated primary caretakers or guardians) and other family members are the most important adults in the life of most young children, with the potential to make the largest contribution to the child's future success. Given the study charge to focus on the professional workforce, this report does not cover interventions to support or educate parents, but it does cover the role of care and education professionals in engaging and collaborating with families. An ongoing study and forthcoming report of the Institute of Medicine (IOM) and the National Research Council (NRC) will focus on strengthening the capacity of parents of young children from birth through age 8.[2]

Terminology

Selected key terms used broadly throughout this report are described here. Other terms that appear less frequently in the report that may be ambiguous or used in different ways in different fields are explained when first introduced in the chapter in which they appear.

Professional roles The terminology used to describe professional roles within the care and education sector varies widely based on setting, tradition, and emerging—but not always consistent—preferences from within the field itself. For this report, the committee selected some terms to use consistently whenever possible, with the aim of using terms that would be generally inclusive across subspecialized roles and reflect the shared value and importance across roles, and avoiding terms that sometimes are perceived as implying differing value for different roles.

To refer inclusively and collectively to the overall care and education workforce, this report uses the term "care and education professionals." To refer to professionals with regular (daily or near-daily), direct responsibilities for the care and education of young children, this report uses the terms "educators," which includes educators in childcare settings and centers that span ages 0 through 8, as well as preschools and elementary schools. To refer to closely related professions such as home visitors, early intervention

---

[2] More information about this study can be found at www.iom.edu/activities/children/committeeonsupportingtheparentsofyoungchildren.

specialists, and mental health consultants, who may not have the same frequency of direct interaction with a child as educators but are closely linked to the professional practice of the educators who do, the report uses either the term used for the specific role or, collectively with educators, "care and education practitioners." The term "practitioners" also is used broadly to denote professional roles in the health and social services sectors.

As noted above, this report encompasses those in leadership roles, such as center directors, principals, and administrators, as an important part of the care and education workforce, and therefore includes some review of implications for their professional practice, professional learning, and workforce development. These roles are generally referred to as "leaders" or, collectively with the overall care and education workforce, as "care and education professionals."

Professional learning This report uses the term "professional learning" to describe all of the various mechanisms that can contribute to ensuring that the early care and education workforce has what it needs to gain and reinforce necessary knowledge and competencies for quality practice that will foster continuous progress in the development and early learning of children from birth through age 8. Chapter 8 provides a detailed overview of this conceptualization of professional learning.

Systems This report uses the term "systems" to describe the many interrelated elements—such as institutions, organizations, stakeholder groups, and policies—that contribute to services for young children and affect the adults who work with them. The term encompasses both "systems" as complex wholes and specified subsets (such as "professional learning systems" or "licensure systems").

Finally, it should be noted that this report uses terms consistently whenever possible. However, there are some exceptions. In some cases, for example, where a finding or discussion is specific to a more narrow professional role, the specific term for that role is used (e.g., "home visitor"). In other cases, where a source document uses a different term from that selected by the committee and it is not clear whether the committee's term would accurately reflect the intent of the authors, the source term is retained.

Study Approach

The committee met five times to deliberate in person, and conducted additional deliberations by teleconference and electronic communications. Public information-gathering sessions were held in conjunction with the committee's first, second, and third meetings and in three locations across the country; the complete agendas for these sessions can be found in Appendix B. The committee also conducted interviews and site visits in three locations. Additional interviews were conducted by a consultant team to inform a mapping of systems and stakeholders in the care and education and related sectors and to explore professional learning in greater depth with relevant stakeholders. Interview participants and themes from the interviews and site visits are listed in Appendix C. The committee also had the opportunity to gather information from and engage in discussions with practitioner advisors who served as consultants for this study; these individuals are listed in the front of this report.

The committee reviewed literature and other documents from a range of disciplines and sources.[3] Comprehensive systematic reviews of all primary literature relevant to every aspect of the study's broad charge was not within the study scope. To avoid replication of existing work, the committee sought relevant high-quality reviews and analyses. Where these were available, the report includes summaries of their key findings, but otherwise refers the reader to the available resources for more detailed information. In specific topic areas where existing reviews and analyses were insufficient, the committee and staff conducted targeted or systematic literature and document searches. This report therefore builds on a large body of previous work. Indeed, several prior reports of the IOM and the NRC provide more detailed review and analysis specific to subcomponents of what is covered in this report (see Box 1-2).

Applying this approach to review the existing body of work revealed some gaps in the evidence base and led to the identification of some important research areas, which are listed in Chapter 12. However, the committee does not intend its highlighting of ongoing research needs to be taken as suggesting inaction; rather, the report provides a framework for immediate actions that are sound and well supported based on the available research findings. The committee's aim is to offer an ambitious yet pragmatic analysis and agenda for action with real potential for implementation in the

---

[3] In developing the statement of task for this study, the sponsors elected to manage the already broad scope of work and range of required expertise by limiting the study's consideration of programs and policies for workforce development and support for young children to the United States, given that this is the policy and implementation environment for the committee's recommendations. However, there is also much relevant research and practice-based experience from international settings outside the United States. Of direct relevance to the topic of this report, for example, the interested reader is referred to *Preparing Teachers and Developing School Leaders for the 21st Century: Lessons from Around the World*, a report of the Organisation for Economic Co-operation and Development (http://www.oecd.org/site/eduistp2012/49850576.pdf, accessed March 24, 2015). In addition, readers may be interested in following the work of the IOM's ongoing Forum on Investing in Young Children Globally. More information can be found at www.iom.edu/activities/children/investingyoungchildrenglobally.

BOX 1-2
Related Reports of the Institute of Medicine
and the National Research Council

Eager to Learn: Educating Our Preschoolers (2000)
Educating Teachers of Science, Mathematics, and Technology: New Practices for the New Millennium (2000)
From Neurons to Neighborhoods: The Science of Early Childhood Development (2000)
How People Learn: Brain, Mind, Experience, and School: Expanded Edition (2000)
Early Childhood Development and Learning: New Knowledge for Policy (2001)
Knowing What Students Know: The Science and Design of Educational Assessment (2001)
Testing Teacher Candidates: The Role of Licensure Tests in Improving Teacher Quality (2001)
Learning and Instruction: A SERP Research Agenda (2003)
Strategic Education Research Partnership (2003)
Early Childhood Assessment: Why, What, and How (2008)
Mathematics Learning in Early Childhood: Paths Toward Excellence and Equity (2009)
Preparing Teachers: Building Evidence for Sound Policy (2010)
Incentives and Test-Based Accountability in Education (2011)
Education for Life and Work: Developing Transferable Knowledge and Skills in the 21st Century (2012)
Improving Measurement of Productivity in Higher Education (2012)

NOTE: All reports are available for free download at www.nap.edu.

---

context of the complexities of the heterogeneity and variability of different communities.

BACKGROUND AND CONTEXT

The various professionals who care for and teach young children from birth through age 8 currently do so in disparate settings and systems under a variety of circumstances while coming from different backgrounds. The expectations and requirements for their professional practice vary depending on their practice setting. Each of these professional roles and settings has variations in pathways for training, professional learning systems, requirements and systems for licensure and credentialing, and other policies for oversight and accountability. The implications of this varied and complex landscape are discussed in greater depth throughout this report.

To provide an overview here as context for the report, this section briefly reviews the historical origins of different workforce roles and some of the major challenges that must be met to arrive at a more convergent approach to caring for and teaching young children, one that allows for greater consistency and continuity from birth through elementary school settings.

The current professions, settings, and systems that contribute to the care and education of children from birth through age 8 in the United States have their roots in five distinct traditions: (1) childcare, (2) nursery schools, (3) kindergartens, (4) compensatory education, and (5) compulsory education at the primary level (see Table 1-1). For many years, these traditions

TABLE 1-1 Historical Traditions in the United States for Professions, Systems, and Settings for the Care and Education of Children from Birth Through Age 8

Childcare	Childcare centers were established in the United States primarily to provide safe and secure settings for young children while their parents are at work. Childcare practices are historically grounded more in public health and child protection traditions than in education traditions. Many federal funding streams and state licensing for childcare programs still reflect this historical aim of subsidizing safe childcare to enable adult workforce participation rather than orienting primarily to providing an early learning environment for children (Kostelnik and Grady, 2009).
Nursery Schools	Historically, nursery schools in the United States were established to provide supplemental early learning experiences to children below school age. Children attending nursery schools were primarily from middle- and upper-class families. The aim was to nurture children's social, emotional, physical, and intellectual development, and nursery school teachers were responsible for engaging children in activities that aligned with their interests and provided opportunities for creative expression, project work, and the use of natural materials (Kostelnik and Grady, 2009).
Kindergartens	In its early history in the United States, kindergarten, funded through philanthropy, was primarily intended to provide classroom learning, health services, home visits, and other assistance to children living in poverty and their families. Although kindergarten has moved over time into elementary schools, originally it functioned as a transition between home-based care and formal schooling and focused on play, self-expression, social cooperation, and independence. While the original emphasis was on development in social and emotional domains, over time, kindergarten began also to incorporate content-based learning as well as mathematics and literacy skill development (Kostelnik and Grady, 2009).

continued

TABLE 1-1 Continued

Compensatory Education	Compensatory programs provide services to children and their families who experience developmental, socioeconomic, or environmental circumstances that can negatively affect child development, such as poverty or disability. Examples in the United States include federally mandated programs under the Individuals with Disabilities Education Act as well as Head Start, which provides prekindergarten for young children from low-income families. The learning environments in these programs are influenced by other care and education traditions, and as they have become well established, these programs have also influenced other settings and services (Kostelnik and Grady, 2009).
Compulsory Education	Originally schooling in the United States varied greatly, including private institutions, church-sponsored schools, charity schools for low-income families, local schools created by parents, private tutors, and boarding schools for children from wealthy families, among others. Due to the disjointed and uncoordinated approach, schooling was inconsistent and inequitable, with some children having limited access to opportunities to learn. A publicly funded, locally governed, universal system was established as a result of education reform movements. As described by Kostelnik and Grady (2009, pp. 48-49), the purpose of this compulsory education was • to prepare children for citizenship in a democratic society, • to help students acquire knowledge and skills to become economically self-sufficient, • to unify a diverse population, and • to help the nation address social problems related to poverty, violence, class conflict, and ethnic differences. At present, about half of states require children to attend school by age 6, while for some the minimum age is 5 and for others is it as old as 8 (ECS, 2005; Snyder and Dillow, 2011, Tables 174, 175, and 176).

proceeded along relatively separate paths, which led to different roles, different entry points for working in those roles, and different pathways and modes of professional preparation and ongoing professional learning. As efforts emerge to help these traditions converge, the different philosophies and historical perspectives associated with each may complement one another or clash, and in any case they all influence today's dialogue about the care and education of young children and the role of the workforce that provides it.

Although the care and education traditions described in Table 1-1 each have their own histories, philosophies, and perspectives, they often are thought of in two major categories: preprimary education and elementary education. As summarized by Kostelnik and Grady (2009, p. 57), each of these brings different assets and qualities that can strengthen a convergent approach for the birth through age 8 continuum, and there are also many shared assets across the traditions:

- Preprimary education has a long history of
  - working with very young children,
  - educating the whole child,
  - working in teams,
  - working with families,
  - identifying children with special needs early on,
  - integrating children with special needs into classrooms with typically developing children, and
  - deriving programs and curricula based on studies of child development.
- Elementary education has a long history of
  - providing access to all children regardless of race, income, ability, or language;
  - providing auxiliary services to supplement children's educational needs;
  - rallying the community to come together on behalf of children;
  - aligning curriculum from one level to the next;
  - addressing issues of accountability;
  - helping children and families make the transition from kindergarten to first grade; and
  - deriving programs and curricula, typically organized by distinct subject-matter content, based on studies of pedagogy and teacher practice.
- Both preprimary education and elementary education have a long history of
  - public service,
  - working with multiple funding streams,
  - working with community partners,
  - drawing on research to shape professional practice, and
  - professional organizations that support their members.

A more recent development is the growing emergence of preschool in public education. Head Start, created in 1965, is the first publicly funded preschool program for children from low-income families. Because there was much interest in but a lack of funding for Head Start, a few states started similar programs for students from low-income families during the

1980s (K-12 Academics, 2014). The first National Education Goal[4] and the three accompanying objectives acknowledged that "the well-being of young children is a shared responsibility of family and society" and stated that "all children will have access to high-quality and developmentally appropriate preschool programs that help prepare them for school" (Kagan et al., 1995, p. 1).

Since then, publicly funded universal preschools have been emerging, although tuition remains the primary source of funding for most preschool programs. As of 2008, 38 states and the District of Columbia financed some prekindergarten programs, while many school districts used local and federal funds to implement preschool services (Barnett et al., 2009; Wat and Gayl, 2009). Currently, several states, including Florida, Georgia, Illinois, New York, Oklahoma, and West Virginia, are considering legislation to provide or already have universal preschool for all 4-year-olds. Illinois has a universal preschool program that also serves 3-year-olds. For children not in public preschools, there are multiple options: federally funded Head Start for eligible families; for-profit and not-for-profit providers, some of which accept government subsidies for low-income families; and government-funded special education programs (K-12 Academics, 2014).

Major Challenges to Navigate[5]

The field of early care and education has experienced a number of sometimes divisive issues. Following is a sample of some of the major challenges that must be navigated to promote a more unified workforce with a more convergent approach to caring for and teaching young children from birth through age 8, an approach that allows for greater consistency and continuity from birth through elementary school settings.

Differential Realities Related to Resources

Limited resources can be a challenge in all education settings. Public education has the stability of public financing, but resources are not always adequate to the need and are not distributed evenly. In particular, when public education is funded by property taxes, families living in poverty will most likely have schools with fewer resources, meaning lower-quality public schools and lower-quality learning experiences in the early elementary years, contributing to a cycle of disparity in education and achievement.

---

[4] The National Education Goals were established in 1990 by the president and state governors.
[5] The discussion in this section is based in part on Kostelnik and Grady, *Getting It Right from the Start—the Principal's Guide to ECE.*

In early childhood settings outside of public school systems, the variability in funding streams and the lack or unpredictability of sustained funding mean that resource limitations are even more problematic. These other settings for educating young children rely on a multitude of sources, including federal, state, and local governments; nongovernmental funds such as private business and philanthropic resources; and out-of-pocket payments for childcare and education. As a result, there are disparities in the level of funding available among counterparts within the field.

One consequence of divergent financing mechanisms is that programs sometimes view each other as competitors for limited resources. For example, both Head Start and school-based preschool programs are required to demonstrate enrollment numbers in order to receive funding, and they are often in competition for the same population of students. Private providers and programs, which often rely heavily on out-of-pocket payments and in some cases subsidies, may feel that their role in the community and their client base is undermined by the emerging availability of public programs. The sense of a competitive care and education environment hinders the development of a system that fosters coordination and collaboration to ease transitions among settings and support continuity of high-quality learning experiences for children (Kostelnik and Grady, 2009).

Historical Schism Between Childcare and Early Education

Although it is common to group the workforce as preprimary and elementary education, it is important to recognize the challenges that have resulted as childcare and other forms of preprimary early childhood education have developed relatively independently of one another and with different purposes in mind (see Table 1-1). Policies for education programs and childcare, with their differing origins, often lack coordination and alignment around a comprehensive vision that encompasses the multiple aims of keeping children safe and healthy, providing them with high-quality learning experiences, and enabling their parents to be available to work. The disconnect among systems affects elements associated with the quality of learning experiences, such as teacher and administrator qualifications and standards for program quality and oversight. It also poses a challenge to developing mutual understanding and cooperation among professionals across systems (Kostelnik and Grady, 2009).

Differences in Professional Learning, Compensation, and Status

Those care and education professionals who work in early childhood settings outside of elementary schools and those who work in public and other school systems experience major differences in educational expectations as well as in the available systems for both preparation and professional learning during ongoing practice. The preprimary workforce has still nascent and highly diffuse professional learning systems, whereas the early elementary workforce is part of a much more regulated and established system for preparing and licensing K-12 teachers. In addition, many of the same issues that divide the workforce also divide those who provide their professional learning.

Discrepancies among compensation for different kinds of educators can lead to "informal (but powerful) hierarchies in which some individuals clearly have lower status than others," which can create contention in working environments and hinder professionalism, respect, and collaboration among colleagues with an otherwise common purpose of supporting children's early learning (Kostelnik and Grady, 2009, p. 55).

Assumptions and Perceptions of Divergence in Philosophies About Appropriate Instructional Practices and Outcomes for Children

There are some divisive issues related to educational philosophies and instructional practices among the different historically defined education traditions. These issues sometimes reflect actual differences in professional practices, but in some cases are also fueled by assumptions or misperceptions. These assumptions and misperceptions are compounded by the lack of mutual understanding and collaborative relationships across settings or the fact that various groups in the field tend not to see one another as colleagues with common purposes. Three examples are presented below:

- **Many preprimary educators fear that preschools located in the public schools will place too great an emphasis on a narrow range of academic skills, will lose their focus on whole-child learning, and will reduce or eliminate time for play.** Over the years, kindergarten has transformed from a "children's garden" for play, learning, and discovery to a "mini-first grade." This shift involves stricter schedules with long periods for group instruction, reducing or eliminating recess and play time, and removing play equipment (Kostelnik and Grady, 2009). Many early childhood educators are concerned that preschool will experience a similar transformation. Currently, many kindergarten teachers expect their students to enter the classroom knowing letters, numbers, and colors, and believe that literacy and mathematics instruction should begin in preschool or kindergarten. A major concern voiced by early childhood educators is that school-based preprimary programs will move in directions they consider developmentally inappropriate and inconsistent with high-quality programming for young children (Bassok and Rorem, 2014; Elkind, 2007; Kostelnik and Grady, 2009; Wien, 2004).

- **Many educators of elementary-grade children aged 6-8 believe that programs for younger children pay inadequate attention to literacy and numeracy or to learning outcomes and K-12 standards.** These worries have several sources: concern about children entering elementary school not adequately prepared for academic learning and ready to progress through the next grade levels and perceived differences in perspectives on appropriate learning and instructional practices, including the perception among many that the early childhood field provides passive support for development, rather than active promotion of learning and skill development driven by learning standards and student outcomes. Although these perspectives are changing, there is ongoing debate over the best method for implementing early learning standards into early learning curricula and how to align these standards with K-12 standards. Similar divisions and perceptions exist not just between early childhood education and elementary education, but also between the early and later grades within K-12 systems (Kostelnik and Grady, 2009).

- **Debates over adult-led versus child-initiated learning experiences can be contentious.** For some in education, a philosophical divide exists about whether early learning experiences are best when mainly child-initiated or when primarily adult-led instruction is used. This can be a contentious issue in which both sides are driven by concerns about the ramifications for children and find it challenging to find common ground (Kostelnik and Grady, 2009). However, although some tend to treat these as mutually exclusive, research findings actually support a mix of these approaches (see the discussion of false dichotomies in instructional approaches in Chapter 6).

Kindergarten Teachers Getting Lost in the Middle

In the context of the differences between preprimary and elementary education, kindergarten teachers often are in the middle, not really part of either group when it comes to communities of practitioners who share a work environment. In many states, even if there is a commitment to making kindergarten, and increasingly prekindergarten, universally available, they are often voluntary rather than part of compulsory education. Whether and how kindergarten and prekindergarten are offered often is left to the discretion of the locality, and they often differ from the rest of the public school system in various ways. In some school systems, for example, kindergarten and prekindergarten are only a half-day. Some programs also are funded through a different mechanism than the regular public school funding stream. Thus, in some states and districts, the "K-12 system" is in reality a grade 1-12 system, leaving kindergarten teachers outside of the established structure.

Systems Capacity to Improve Continuity in Care and Education for Young Children

Currently, the work of bridging early childhood and early elementary education to increase continuity of care and education for children from birth through age 8 rarely is the purview of a single entity at the local, state, or national level. Typically, one or more agencies oversee early childhood programs for young children before entry into kindergarten, while a public education system oversees K-12 education. (In a few states, such as New Jersey and North Carolina, the departments of education have small "P-3" offices that are charged with promoting greater coordination between early childhood and early elementary initiatives.) While interagency collaboration sometimes occurs, it usually does so in a piecemeal fashion, focusing on one specific topic (e.g., aligning learning standards), rather than taking a more systemic approach. Also, the extent to which agencies serving children from birth through third grade come together often relies on the priorities and interests of the agency leaders and value they place on alignment and coordination. In short, early childhood and public education leaders work largely in separate circles (even if they are in the same agency), and often lack formal, systematic opportunities to ensure that their goals, strategies, and policies are mutually reinforcing and supportive. Given this context, the work required to increase continuity becomes no one's official job. Local, state, and federal systems lack the organizational leadership to develop comprehensive strategies, manage their execution, and monitor their progress.

In addition, even if both early childhood and K-12 leaders understand the importance of increasing continuity across the 0-8 age span, they may struggle to be able to take this work on. The recent increased attention to both early childhood and K-12 education has resulted in a myriad of reforms in both sectors. The expansion of quality rating and improvement systems, the greater focus on standards and assessments, and the pressure to help the early childhood workforce attain higher education and more training experiences are just a few priorities that early childhood program and policy leaders need to address. In the meantime, K-12 educators and leaders are implementing more rigorous college- and career-ready standards and assessments; revamping their human capital policies, from recruitment to compensation to teacher evaluation; and responding to pressures to improve test scores and other performance metrics. Arguably, there has been more activity within the early childhood community to assume continuity as a goal, but helping both sectors understand how this work can advance their existing priorities and then finding the capacity (time, staffing, financial resources) to take it on is an important challenge to tackle.

In summary, the ultimate goal for this committee was to contribute to a more coherent care and education continuum for children through the infant-toddler years, preschool ages, and early grades across all settings, including the home, family childcare homes, childcare centers, preschools, and elementary schools, as well as across home visiting, early intervention, and other consultative services and across referrals to and linkages with the health and social services sectors. These different settings and the professionals who work within them are characterized by differences in terminology, expectations, approaches to teaching and learning, accountability policies, relationships with families and the community, funding, and system priorities and pressures. Bringing these multiple different systems together will require coordination and alignment across multiple interconnected moving parts and will entail significant conceptual and logistical challenges for the stakeholders involved: care and education practitioners; leaders, administrators, and supervisors; those who provide professional learning for the care and education workforce; policy makers; health, mental health, and social services providers; and parents and other adults who spend time with young children. The aim of this report is to navigate these challenges by identifying the areas of convergence that can be leveraged to build and sustain a strong foundation for providing high-quality, consistent early learning opportunities for children as they grow.

ORGANIZATION OF THE REPORT

The committee was tasked with applying what is known about child development and early learning to inform how the early care and education workforce can support children from birth through age 8. This report presents the committee's findings, conclusions, and recommendations. The report is divided into five parts. After this introductory chapter, Part I continues with Chapter 2, which describes in greater detail the current landscape of care and education for children from birth through age 8.

Part II focuses on the science of child development and early learning in two chapters. Chapter 3 describes interactions between the biology of development, particularly brain development, and the environmental influences experienced by a child. Chapter 4 then summarizes what is known about the various elements of child development and early learning in four domains: cognitive development, general learning competencies, socioemotional development, and health and physical well-being.

Part III turns to the implications of the science for the care and education of children from birth through age 8. Chapter 5 draws on the science of child development and early learning, as well as the realities of the landscape described in Chapter 2, to establish the critical need—and the opportunities—for continuity in care and education across the birth through age 8 continuum. Chapter 6 then explores in depth the educational practices that, when applied with consistency and high quality over time for children as they age, can continuously support development and early learning. Chapter 7 considers the knowledge and competencies needed by professionals with responsibilities for the education of young children to implement these practices.

Part IV focuses on the development of the care and education workforce. Chapter 8 presents a framework for considering the key factors that contribute to workforce development and quality professional practice for care and education professionals who work with children from birth through age 8. Chapter 9 covers higher education programs and professional learning during ongoing practice. Chapter 10 considers current qualification requirements for educators who work with young children and systems and processes for evaluating educators, as well as program accreditation and quality improvement systems. Chapter 11 turns to factors that contribute to the work environment and the status and well-being of educators, such as compensation and benefits, staffing structures and career advancement pathways, retention, and health and well-being.

Ultimately in Chapter 12, the committee offers a blueprint for action based on a unifying foundation for the development of a workforce capable of providing more consistent and cumulative support for the development and early learning of children from birth through age 8. This foundation encompasses: essential features of child development and early learning, shared knowledge and competencies for care and education professionals, principles for high-quality professional practice at the level of individuals and the systems that support them, and principles for effective professional learning. This foundation is intended to inform coordinated and coherent changes across systems for individual practitioners, leadership, organizations, policies, and resource allocation. Chapter 12 also provides a framework for the inclusive and collaborative systems transformation that will be needed to carry out these changes. Finally, the committee offers recommendations for specific action in the areas of qualification requirements for professional practice, higher education, professional learning during ongoing practice, evaluation and assessment of professional practice, the role of leadership, interprofessional practice, improvement of the knowledge base, and support for implementation. Accompanying these recommendations is extensive discussion of considerations for their implementation.

REFERENCES

Barnett, W. S., D. J. Epstein, A. H. Friedman, J. Stevenson-Boyd, and J. T. Hustedt. 2009. *The state of preschool 2008: State preschool yearbook.* New Brunswick, NJ: National Institute for Early Education Research.

Bassok, D., and A. Rorem. 2014. *Is kindergarten the new first grade? The changing nature of kindergarten in the age of accountability.* Working Paper Series No. 20. Charlottesville: EdPolicyWorks, University of Virginia.

ECS (Education Commission of the States). 2005. *Attendance: Compulsory school age requirements.* http://www.ecs.org/clearinghouse/50/51/5051.htm (accessed March 22, 2015).

Elkind, D. 2007. *The power of play: How spontaneous, imaginative activities lead to happier, healthier children.* Cambridge, MA: Da Capo Lifelong.

K-12 Academics. 2014. *Preschool education.* http://www.k12academics.com/systems-formal-education/preschool-education (accessed December 18, 2014).

Kagan, S. L., E. Moore, S. Bredekamp, M. E. Graue, L. M. Laosa, E. L. Boyer, L. F. Newman, L. Shepard, V. Washington, and N. Zill. 1995. *Reconsidering children's early development and learning: Toward common views and vocabulary.* Washington, DC: National Education Goals Panel.

Kostelnik, M. J., and M. L. Grady. 2009. *Getting it right from the start: The principal's guide to early childhood education.* Thousand Oaks, CA: Corwin.

Snyder, T. D., and S. A. Dillow. 2011. *Digest of education statistics 2010.* Washington, DC: National Center for Education Statistics, Institute of Education Sciences, U.S. Department of Education.

Wat, A., and C. Gayl. 2009. *Beyond the school yard: Pre-K collaborations with community-based partners.* Washington, DC: Pew Center on the States.

Wien, C. A. 2004. *Negotiating standards in the primary classroom: The teacher's dilemma.* New York: Teachers College Press.

2

The Care and Education Landscape for Children from Birth Through Age 8

To provide context for the environment in which the professionals who are the focus of this report work, this chapter describes the complex landscape of systems that provide or support services for young children and their families, including practice settings, professional roles, and funding streams. Professional learning systems, also a key part of this landscape, are discussed in Part IV.

PRACTICE SETTINGS

Early childhood services, programs, and interventions for children and their families are delivered or provided in a number of different settings in both the care and education and the health and social services sectors. These settings are summarized in Figure 2-1. This figure shows, within each setting (single band), how children are served over different age spans as they grow up. It also shows the junctions within a sector (represented by bands of the same shade) at which children tend to cross over from one setting to another over time; for example, a child may cross over from center-based childcare or Head Start to elementary school. These junctions illustrate the need for continuity along two dimensions. Continuity over time is essential to help provide consistent, high-quality experiences for children as they age, especially as they transition to different settings. Continuity across settings and sectors is vital as well. At any given age, a child may spend time in multiple settings. For example, a 6-year-old child may attend an elementary school, be in a family childcare setting after school, participate in a community-based program once per week at the local li-

43

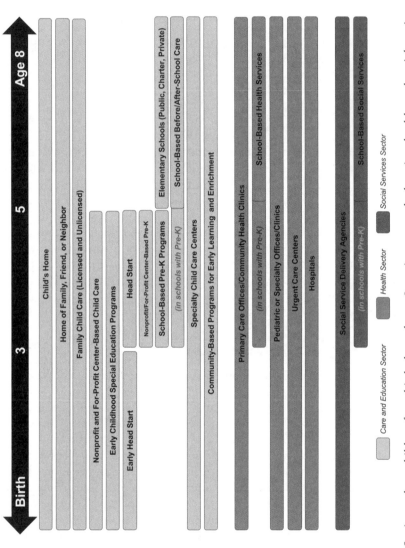

FIGURE 2-1 Settings where children from birth through age 8 receive care and education, health, and social services.

brary, receive health screenings in school, go to a pediatric health clinic, and participate in programs or receive services administered by a social service agency. (See also the discussion of continuity in Chapter 5.)

PROFESSIONAL ROLES

A variety of different professional roles contribute to the development and early learning of young children across sectors and settings. Roles in the care and education sector are summarized in Figure 2-2, while Figure 2-3 captures some of the major roles in the health and social services sectors. Note that while this report focuses on the professional workforce for young children, families are included among the adult roles in care and education in the overview presented here because they are the most important adults in the life of most young children, with the potential to make the greatest contribution to determinants of the child's future success. An ongoing study and forthcoming report of the Institute of Medicine and the National Research Council will focus on strengthening the capacity of parents of young children from birth through age 8.[1]

Collectively, Figures 2-1 through 2-3 illustrate how, depending on the practice setting, different professional roles may interact with varying age ranges and therefore may require different specialized skills building on knowledge and competencies shared among all care and education professionals. For example, an educator in a family childcare center that provides after-school care may work with children from birth through age 8 and beyond. Conversely, an educator in a center-based preschool may work only with children aged 3-5, and in any given year, an educator in an elementary school typically works with only one grade. In the health and social services sectors, many professionals work with children across the entire 0-8 age span.

Conclusion About Settings and Professional Roles

Children between birth and age 8 spend time in a variety of settings, both informal and formal, and interact with a wide range of professionals and other adults. All of these settings and interactions offer the potential to support healthy development and early learning, and children can meet developmentally informed expectations for early learning when they are immersed in high-quality environments with professionals who are promoting their progress and working in positive ways with their families.

---

[1] More information about this study can be found at www.iom.edu/activities/children/committeeonsupportingtheparentsofyoungchildren.

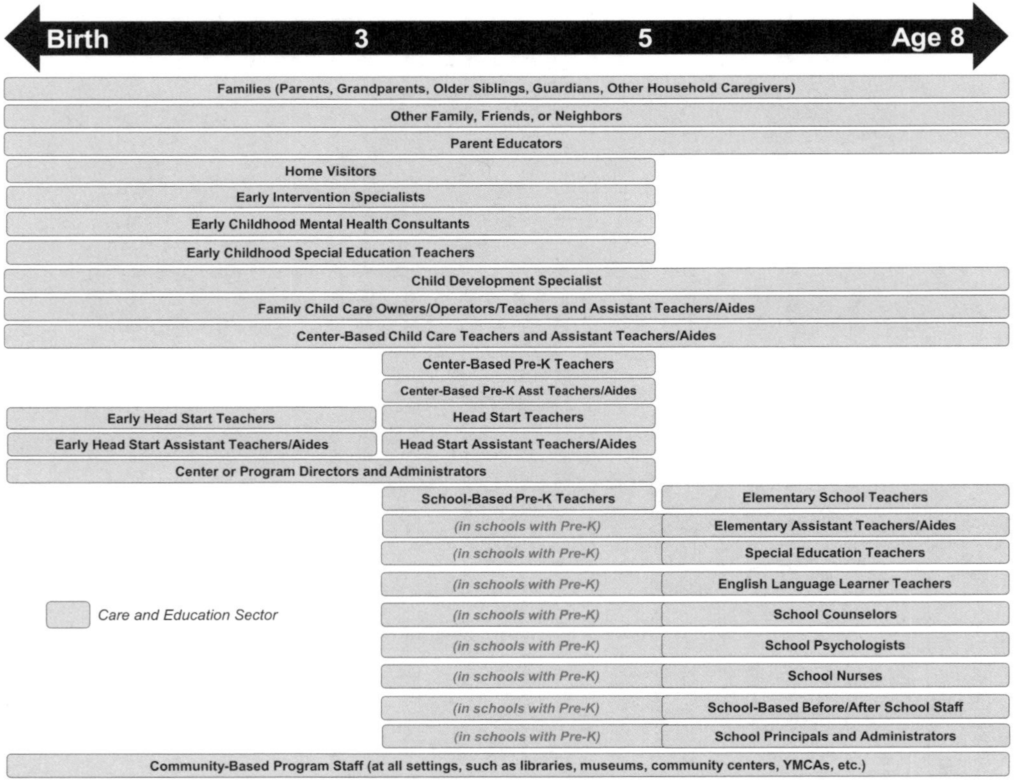

FIGURE 2-2 Adults who support children from birth through age 8 in the care and education sector.

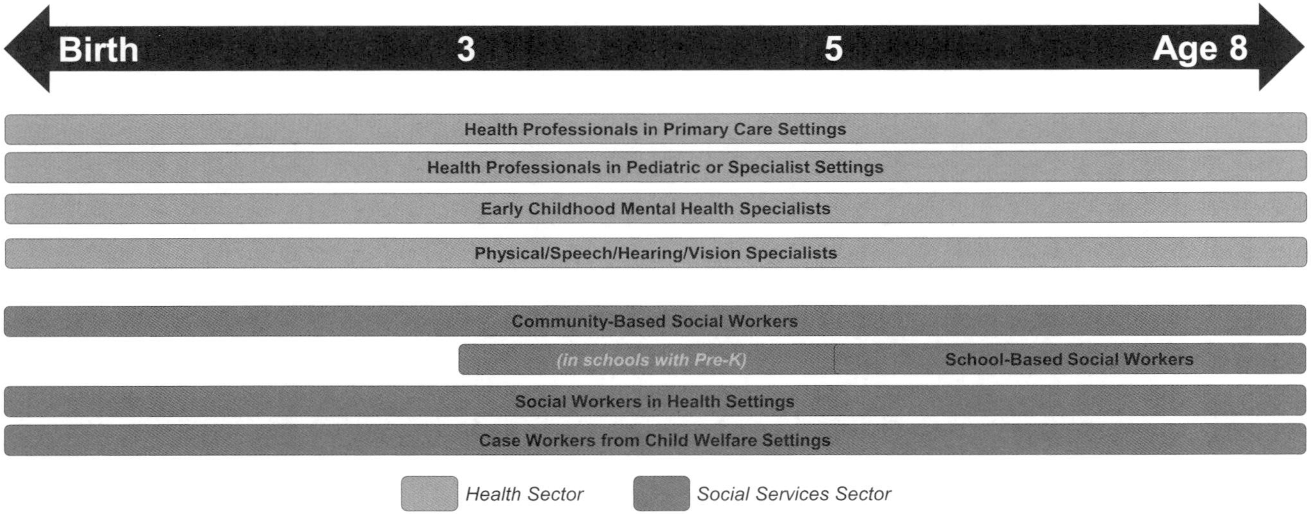

47

FIGURE 2-3 Major categories of adults who support children from birth through age 8 in the health and social services sectors.

FUNDING STREAMS

Numerous funded programs and other sources of funding contribute to services that support the development and early learning of children from birth through age 8 across the care and education, health, and social services sectors. These include federal, state, and local governmental sources as well as nongovernmental sources of funds such as private businesses and philanthropic organizations and out-of-pocket payments for childcare and education. Historically, different programs and funding streams may have been initiated with different purposes in mind—for example, public school to provide equal access to education, childcare subsidies to enable adults to work, and Head Start and other prekindergarten programs to equalize access to early childhood education and reduce disparities in academic and other outcomes. Regardless of their original intent, most of the programs that serve young children are increasingly recognizing their potential to contribute to comprehensive development across domains, and as a result are adopting shared long-term goals for school success and health (Bartik, 2011; Partnership for America's Economic Success, 2010).

Government Funding

Child development and early learning and health are recognized on many levels as a public good with benefits for society as a whole, and there is a long tradition of public investments in achieving these benefits, especially for children and families who are disadvantaged. Many different avenues of public investment exist through federal programs as well as state and local initiatives. Revenues for these investments derive not just from general funds but also from designated allocations based on voter referenda in some states.

Federal expenditures for children include education, health, income security, early care and education, nutrition, tax provisions, and housing and social services (Hahn et al., 2014). More than 80 federal programs and tax provisions benefit children. The 10 largest programs and tax provisions for children accounted for more than three-quarters (77 percent) of the total $664 billion spent on children in 2013. Of these, Medicaid is the single largest program, spending $72 billion on children in 2013. The next three largest federal expenditures on children are tax provisions: the earned income tax credit, the child tax credit, and the dependent exemption. These are followed by the Supplemental Nutrition Assistance Program, the tax exclusion for employer-sponsored health insurance, social security benefits for dependents and survivors under 18, child nutrition programs, Title I funding for educating disadvantaged children, and the Temporary Assistance for Needy Families block grant (Hahn et al., 2014).

For care and education for children from birth through age 8, there are major federal funding programs in the U.S. Departments of Education and Health and Human Services, such as the Maternal and Child Health Services Block Grant Program; the Child Care and Development Fund; Head Start/ Early Head Start; Maternal, Infant, and Early Childhood Home Visiting Programs; Preschool Development Grants; Race to the Top funds; and grants through the Individuals with Disabilities Education Act and the Elementary and Secondary Education Act. The U.S. Department of Defense is another source of federal funding for care and education, providing prekindergarten through grade 12 education programs for children of active duty military and U.S. Department of Defense civilian families (U.S. Department of Defense, n.d.) as well as childcare, including Child Development Centers, Family Child Care, and School Age Care (Military One Source, n.d.).

While federal funding represents a large public investment in children, state and local government funding sources also make a major contribution. Education and health expenditures account for nearly all (96 percent) of state and local spending on children (Hahn et al., 2014). State and local sources for expenditures on early care and education include state general funds; dedicated funds, which include tobacco and lottery-specific taxes; and tobacco funds (National Conference of State Legislatures, 2011). Property taxes support most of the funding provided for education by local government (New America Foundation, 2014). Other local sources include miscellaneous charges and receipts and other local tax initiatives (Tax Policy Center, 2013).

Federal, state, and local government investments in children vary by age. A study examining 2011 federal spending and 2008 total government spending found that state and local governments provide the majority of total public investments in children aged 6 and older, while the majority of public investments in children aged 0-2 comes from the federal government, which also provides about half of public investments in children aged 3-5. School-aged children receive the highest total public spending, while the youngest children receive the highest federal spending (Edelstein et al., 2012).

Nongovernmental Funding

Outside government, philanthropic organizations are one source of private funds for care and education programs and other services for children from birth through age 8 (Mitchell et al., 2001). With business leaders increasingly concerned about the available pipeline of skilled workers, especially for jobs requiring strong technological, mathematical, literary, or information-processing skills, the business community has shown some interest in investing in education, including early learning. One avenue to this end is investment in early childhood care and education through childcare benefits or subsidies for employees or through direct provision of childcare services. Another avenue is through the engagement of business leaders in advocacy to foster greater government investment. Although not as widespread, in some cases businesses and corporations invest directly to improve the availability and quality of care and education programs in their communities (Mitchell et al., 2001).

Public–Private Partnerships

Private investments of philanthropies or business and corporate sponsors are sometimes paired with public action and funding for initiatives to improve the availability and quality of early care and education programs and services. Such partnerships can occur on a statewide level but are more commonly local, resulting from the direct collaboration of local business leaders, public officials, and local and national philanthropies in pooling resources to effect changes that none would be capable of accomplishing alone. Several examples of these partnerships are included in Chapter 5 and Appendix G.

Out-of-Pocket Payments

Another nongovernmental, noninstitutional funding stream is out-of-pocket payment for services. Across the entire socioeconomic distribution of families in the United States, a large burden of the costs of early care and education is borne directly by families themselves through fees and tuition. Children from low-income families are eligible for government-funded programs, as eligibility for enrollment is based on family income. Families who are ineligible for these programs and lack employer-based childcare benefits must pay for these services out of pocket. Furthermore, in states in which state-funded full-day kindergarten is not compulsory, some families pay for kindergarten tuition costs directly (Guernsey and Holt, 2012). Some families make additional direct, out-of-pocket investments in education through out-of-pocket tuition for private elementary schools.

Many families whose income is above the level that would qualify for public programs nonetheless do not earn enough to afford out-of-pocket tuition expenses for prekindergarten and childcare programs (Guernsey and Holt, 2012; Wat, 2008). Fees have increased significantly: families were paying $94 per week in 1997, and this number had increased to nearly $180 by 2011 (Whitebook et al., 2014). These costs can exceed college tuition fees (Wat, 2008). Families earning $30,000 to $60,000 are less likely to enroll their children in center-based programs, and often choose less expensive programs in which quality often suffers. Enrollment in accredited, high-quality programs tends to increase for families with annual salaries above $60,000 (Wat, 2008).

Implications of Funding Diversity for Continuity in Care and Education for Children Aged 0-8

The number and diversity of funding streams for care and education reflect a range of investments in early childhood, but they also are one reason why, as discussed below and in detail in Chapter 5, continuity in care and education for children from birth through age 8 is challenging. Each funding stream is subject to the policies of the agency or institution from which it derives. For the most part, each has its own requirements as to scope of services allowed, quality standards (or lack thereof), eligibility criteria (including ages served), and reporting and accountability. Some states and federal agencies are experimenting with harmonizing some of these requirements to promote greater continuity and provide families with easier access, or are changing governance structures to facilitate these experiments. As discussed in Chapter 1, this committee was not charged with conducting a review of financing, but as detailed in Part V, the reality is that the commitment of significant resources will be necessary to effect the comprehensive changes in workforce development required to achieve the quality of professional practice that is needed. Therefore, some examples of innovative and alternative funding approaches for improving care and education for young children are provided in Appendix G.

Conclusion About Funding

A wide range of resources contribute to supporting the health, well-being, and education of children from birth through age 8. Many federal programs support child development and early learning. In addition, many funds invested in children come from state and local sources and from sources outside of government, including philanthropy, the business sector, and out-of-pocket payments by families. Therefore, avenues for oversight and accountability reside at the national, state, and local levels and both within and outside of government.

IMPLICATIONS OF THE CURRENT LANDSCAPE FOR THE CARE AND EDUCATION WORKFORCE

The number of settings and variety of professional roles with which a child interacts over time represent a wide array of opportunities for exerting positive influence on a child's development and early learning. However, the landscape of services, settings, and funding streams described in this chapter clearly illustrates how complex a challenge it is to ensure that the quality and developmentally informed progression of services remains consistent across standards, professional practices, professional learning supports, policies, governance, funding, and continuous improvement and accountability systems.

At a fundamental level, although they have been grouped in this report as care and education professionals to reflect the aspiration of continuity and consistency, not all of the various professionals who work with young children are seen or see themselves as part of the same professional landscape. Educators in elementary schools are embedded in systems whose scope extends through high school, with a perceived identity that often inclines to the later grades and does not lend itself easily to a primary identity as a professional with a role in early learning. At the same time, "early childhood education" systems and professionals tend to encompass primarily the preschool years and center-based programs. Center-based care does sometimes start in the infant-toddler years, but many of the professionals in settings that serve infants and toddlers, as well as professionals in family childcare, who span multiple age ranges, have a much more diffuse identity that is matched by much less well-defined infrastructure across all aspects of systems and supports. Other professionals, such as home visitors, early intervention specialists, and mental health consultants, have a clear role in the early learning of children, yet they occupy a space that cuts across—or drifts within—the care and education, health, and social services sectors depending on how implementation is organized in a given state or municipality. In keeping with this range of identities, numerous and varied organizations and institutions—including national- and state-level professional associations as well as research, policy, and advocacy organizations—provide guidance and set standards.

The result is that—although the science of development and early learning indicates that every environment can be a learning environment for young children and that everyone who works in that environment has a role as an educator—there currently are very different systems and expectations for different settings and professionals. Therefore, silos among funding sources and levels, policies, professional learning systems, professional expectations and requirements to be qualified to practice, and compensation and benefits challenge the central goal this report is intended to advance: the achievement of greater continuity and coherence in high-quality care and education for children from birth through age 8. The remainder of this report presents the committee's findings, conclusions, and recommendations with respect to meeting this challenge.

REFERENCES

Bartik, T. J. 2011. *Investing in kids early childhood programs and local economic develop-ment*. Kalamazoo, MI: Upjohn Institute.

Edelstein, S., J. Isaacs, H. Hahn, and K. Toran. 2012. *How do public investments in children vary with age?: A kids' share analysis of expenditures in 2008 and 2011 by age group*. Washington, DC: Urban Institute.

Guernsey, L., and A. Holt. 2012. *Counting kids and tracking funds in pre-K and kindergarten: Falling short at the local level. Issue brief*. Washington, DC: New America Foundation.

Hahn, H., J. Isaacs, S. Edelstein, E. Steele, and C. E. Steuerle. 2014. *Kids' share 2014: Report on federal expenditures on children through 2013*. Washington, DC: Urban Institute.

Military One Source. n.d. *Military child care programs*. http://www.militaryonesource.mil/cyt/child-care-options?content_id=267339 (accessed January 23, 2015).

Mitchell, A., L. Stoney, and H. Dichter. 2001. *Financing child care in the United States: An ex-panded catalog of current strategies*. North Kansas City, MO: Ewing Marion Kauffman Foundation.

National Conference of State Legislatures. 2011. *Early care and education state budget actions FY 2011: Summary of findings*. Denver, CO: National Conference of State Legislatures.

New America Foundation. 2014. *Federal, state, and local K-12 school finance overview*. http://febp.newamerica.net/background-analysis/school-finance (accessed September 23, 2014).

Partnership for America's Economic Success. 2010. *Early childhood finance: Meeting notes and initial findings of a conference convened by the Kauffman Foundation and the Partnership for America's Economic Success*. http://readynation.org/uploads/20101124_KauffmanPAESConferenceReport101026FINAL.pdf (accessed August 18, 2014).

Tax Policy Center. 2013. *State and local tax policy: What are the sources of revenue for local governments?* http://www.taxpolicycenter.org/briefing-book/state-local/revenues/local_revenue.cfm (accessed September 23, 2014).

U.S. Department of Defense. n.d. *About Department of Defense Education Activity (DoDEA)*. http://www.dodea.edu/aboutDoDEA/index.cfm (accessed January 23, 2015).

Wat, A. 2008. *The pre-K pinch: Early education and the middle class*. Washington, DC: Pre-K Now.

Whitebook, M., D. Phillips, and C. Howes. 2014. *Worthy work, still unlivable wages: The early childhood workforce 25 years after the National Child Care Staffing Study*. Berke-ley, CA: Center for the Study of Child Care Employment, Institute for Research on Labor and Employment.

Part II

The Science of Child Development and Early Learning

The committee was tasked with applying what is known about child development and early learning to inform how the workforce can more seamlessly support children from birth through age 8. This part of the report summarizes key findings and the committee's conclusions based on the science of early child development and learning, focusing in particular on those areas with implications for the workforce.

Chapter 3 describes interactions between the biology of development, particularly brain development, and the environmental influences experienced by a child. Chapter 4 examines child development and early learning in the areas of cognitive development, learning of specific subjects, general learning competencies, socioemotional development, and physical development and health—and the interrelationships among them. Chapter 4 also addresses the critical overarching issue of the effects of chronic stress and adversity on child development and early learning.

Throughout these chapters, the implications of the findings for adults with responsibilities for young children are highlighted. The messages in these chapters thus form a foundation that, together with the context described in Chapter 2 of the settings and institutional systems in which adult professionals work with children, informs the subsequent discussion in Part III of the knowledge, skills, and abilities that adults working with children across the birth through age 8 continuum need and that need to be supported by the systems in which they are educated, trained, and work. This in turn informs the discussion of the development of the early care and education workforce in Part IV.

3

The Interaction of Biology and Environment

Among the most compelling stories emerging in the early 21st century from the science of child development have been the extraordinary developmental processes by which a microscopic assembly of embryonic neural cells gives rise to the human brain—the most complex physical object in the known universe (Fox et al., 2010; IOM and NRC, 2009; National Scientific Council on the Developing Child, 2004). These remarkable developmental events contribute to the entire, elaborate array of individual life attributes and trajectories, from personality, intelligence, and individual achievement to lifelong risks for disease, disorder, and criminality. The course of brain development also shapes a child's growing capacities (or incapacities) for learning; complex thought; and supportive, empathic involvement with others—capacities that powerfully influence life chances for success, productivity, and satisfaction. The profusion of *possible* futures and life paths grounded in the character, course, and timing of early brain development is guided and sustained by continuous, bidirectional interactions between human biology and social and educational environments. Such interactions, strongly influenced by the quality of the care and teaching and the learning environments that families and societies provide, co-determine over time the developmental, educational, biological, and health outcomes that progressively characterize individual lives. Although much complexity—at the behavioral, neurobiological, cellular, and molecular levels—awaits further elucidation, much has already been learned about the nature, timing, and consequences of neurodevelopmental events and how they interact with the environments in which children develop, learn, and engage with adults and peers. New knowledge of these developmental processes has yielded a rich and useful harvest of insights for those who care for, teach, protect, and support young children.

THE DEVELOPING BRAIN, THE DEVELOPING SCIENCE

The publication of *From Neurons to Neighborhoods: The Science of Early Childhood Development* (NRC and IOM, 2000) proved a pivotal moment in the integration and dissemination of the insights gained from new knowledge of developmental processes. That report assembles and compellingly presents the evidence that early child development is critically dependent upon relationships with caring and teaching adults, that individual biology and social experiences are equally influential in determining developmental outcomes, and that infants are born able and ready to learn. The report also made clear that growing children's social experiences of adversity and stress—experiences disproportionately prevalent in impoverished communities of low socioeconomic status—have direct effects on the structure and function of the developing brain. Emotion and the social experiences of early life are deeply and enduringly represented within behavioral development and are "biologically embedded" in the anatomic structure and function of the growing brain (Hertzman, 2012).

In the decade and a half since *From Neurons to Neighborhoods* was published, enormous strides have been taken toward a neurobiological accounting of how young brains develop and how both perturbations of experience and support can fundamentally alter the trajectories of normative and maladaptive development. Four broad categories of insight have emerged in developmental neuroscience with specific implications for learning, care, and behavior in early childhood.

First, the past decade of research has converged on an understanding that in many or perhaps even most instances, causality with respect to disease, disorders, and maladaptive development—as well as the preservation of health and maintenance of normative, adaptive development—is best viewed as an *interplay between genome-based biology and environmental exposures.* This understanding represents a clear departure from the historical views that human morbidities are attributable to *either* pathogenic environments or faulty genes. Thus whereas it was once viewed as sufficient to ascertain, through genetically informed (e.g., twin) studies, the proportion of variation in an individual's observable characteristics, or "phenotype," attributable to genes and to environments, it is now generally accepted that the key to a deeper, richer understanding of pathogenesis and adaptive development is elucidation of how genes and environments work together.

Second, the role of *developmental time* in the dramatic unfolding of brain structure and function and the acquisition of concomitant human capacities has become increasingly important in explaining early development.

Critical and sensitive periods—time windows in which experience-related developmental transitions must or can most readily occur—create a temporal mapping of anticipated early childhood exposures that guide the timing and sequencing of developmental change. As the molecular substrates for such critical periods and events have become known and tractable, altering their timing and manipulating the opening and closing of specific developmental windows have become increasingly plausible (Greenough and Black, 1992; Greenough et al., 1987; NRC and IOM, 2000).

Third, there is now strong evidence that *early psychosocial adversities*—beginning even during fetal development—can have important short- and long-term effects on the brain's development, the regulation of stress-responsive hormone systems, and the calibration of stress reactivity at a variety of levels from behavioral to gene expression responses. Stress triggers activation of the hypothalamic–pituitary–adrenocortical (HPA) axis, which results in cortisol secretion from the adrenal gland, as well as activation of the autonomic nervous system (ANS), which ignites the so-called fight or flight sequence of physiologic changes, including increases in blood pressure and heart rate, sweating, and pupil dilation. Together, these two systems exert important effects on the cardiovascular and immune systems that anticipate and prepare the individual for stress or challenge, including affecting the regulation of glucose levels and altering the activation levels for a variety of genes.

Fourth, inquiry into the sources of special vulnerability and resilience with respect to early adversity has led to the discovery of substantial *individual differences in children's susceptibilities to both negative and positive environmental exposures*. This discovery has reinforced the unique character of each child's responses to the physical and social worlds, has offered perspectives on why some children thrive within environments of great adversity, and has illuminated seemingly contradictory findings about how social conditions affect health and development. It also has informed a better understanding of children's differential responsiveness to interventions (Belsky and van Ijzendoorn, 2015). These individual differences in context sensitivity, like health and developmental outcomes, are likely due to the joint, interactive effects of nature and nurture.

Taken together, these four broad categories of insights have reshaped understanding of the formative experiences of early life—in families, communities, health care settings, childcare centers, and schools—and are changing societal approaches to crafting, managing, and monitoring those experiences. Following a synopsis of the emerging neuroscience of childhood learning and development, each of these new groups of insights is considered in turn, along with its implications for those who raise, teach, and care for young children. Given the foundational and rapid processes of brain development during foundational periods of early development, this is a window of both great risk of vulnerability to developmental disruption and great potential for receptivity to positive developmental influences and interventions.

THE NEUROSCIENCE OF LEARNING AND DEVELOPMENT

The fundamental insights derived from developmental and educational psychology about child development from birth through age 8 are enhanced by an increasingly elegant neuroscience defining the cerebral, neural circuit, cellular, and molecular processes that attend early learning, cognition, and socioemotional development. Even greater insight into these processes will inevitably result from innovative approaches to imaging the growing brain and from federal investments in collaborative scientific projects such as the National Institutes of Health's BRAIN Initiative.[1] This section summarizes some of the major recent advances in brain science of relevance to this report. For a more comprehensive review, the interested reader is referred to previous National Research Council reports (see IOM and NRC, 2009; NRC and IOM, 2000), as well as overviews appearing in the developmental neuroscience literature (e.g., Bloom et al., 2001; Boyce and Kobor, 2015; Fox et al., 2010).

Early Brain Development

The early central nervous system appears in **embryologic development** at 2 to 3 weeks postconception. Over the remaining weeks of gestation, primitive cells differentiate into specialized cells and brain regions with distinctive forms and functions. Precursor neural cells differentiate into neurons and glia cells; the former appear at 5 to 25 weeks of gestation and play key roles in the execution of brain functions, while the latter appear later in prenatal development and have key structural and functional supportive functions in the brain and nervous system.

New neurons must **migrate** to new locations within the developing brain to serve specific roles within particular functional regions, such as the motor cortex, which coordinates bodily movement, or the auditory cortex, which serves hearing. In moving from their site of origin to their precise correct position in the brain, neurons are guided along structural "maps" created by molecular signals from neighboring cells. Failures of neuronal migration have now been implicated in the genesis of neurological and psychiatric disorders, such as some seizure disorders and intellectual deficits.

As neurons move toward their final brain positions, they grow long, tubular extensions called **axons** along which an electrical signal can be

---

[1] See http://www.nih.gov/science/brain/index.htm (accessed March 24, 2015).

propagated to another neuron. They also develop branched projections from the neuronal cell body called **dendrites,** which are capable of receiving such signals from other neurons (see Figure 3-1). The point of physical communication between neurons is the **synapse,** a microscopic cleft across which a chemical signal—a neurotransmitter—is released, resulting in the activation of the downstream neuron. Many of the psychotropic medications currently used for disorders such as depression and anxiety act upon the molecular mechanisms involved in synaptic communication.

The rate of formation of both new neurons and new synapses during prenatal brain development is staggering. As shown in Figure 3-2, during a period of **neuronal proliferation** between 5 and 25 weeks of gestation, new neurons are generated from neural stem cells at a rate as high as 250,000 per minute. In a slightly later but overlapping period, synapses are produced at a rate of 40,000 per second. Both periods are followed by a systematic pruning of both neurons and synapses, the former through a phase of programmed cell death called apoptosis, and the latter through attrition of the least utilized synaptic connections. Both the striking overproduction of neurons and synapses and the subsequent, rapid elimination of those that are underutilized must occur in sequence and to the proper

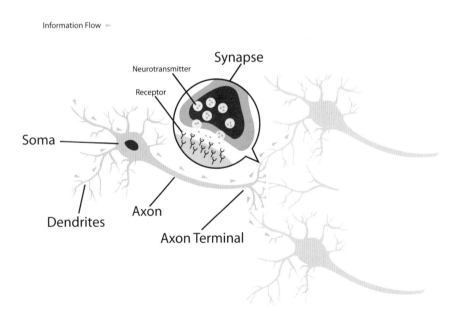

FIGURE 3-1 The structure of neurons and neuronal connections.
SOURCE: Kellett, 2015.

62

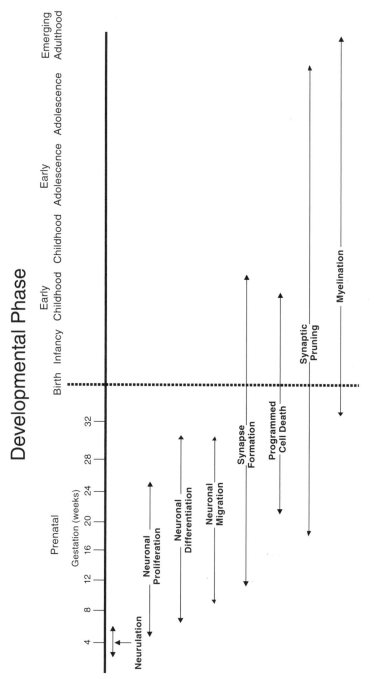

FIGURE 3-2 Developmental phases of neural development.
SOURCE: IOM and NRC, 2009, p. 122.

degree for normal intellectual and socioemotional development to occur. Schizophrenia has been linked, for example, to abnormal synaptic pruning during the adolescent years of development.

Myelination—the progressive "insulation" of the neuronal axons with a myelin sheath produced by specialized neural cells—increases the speed and efficiency of neuronal activation. Myelination occurs at different developmental rates in different areas of the brain; the prefrontal cortex, responsible for the slowly acquired "executive" functions of reasoning, decision making, and attentional skills, becomes fully myelinated as late as early adulthood. It is the white myelin sheath, with its cholesterol and lipoprotein components, that is responsible for the increasing, maturational presence of "white matter" in the developing brain.

The early development of the brain also progresses at the level of cortical and subcortical organization and signaling circuits that are integrated into networks with similar functions. The cortical structures and signaling circuitry of the brain underlie neural systems for complex cognitive and socioemotional functions such as learning and memory, self-regulatory control, and social relatedness (IOM and NRC, 2009). During this development, specialization occurs with different anatomical regions of the brain involved in different functions, including both those that are explicit and conscious, which have been the focus of much developmental science research to understand cognitive development, as well as those that are implicit and automatic or unconscious, which are increasingly being studied for their foundational importance for socioemotional development (Schore, 2010).

A related feature of brain development is lateralization, in which specialized functions are predominant in one hemisphere, or side, of the brain. For example, growing evidence points to the specialized dominance of the right side of the brain in processing social and emotional information, including nonverbal information, which are the foundation of important functions such as interpreting social stimuli, understanding the emotions and intentions of others, and engaging in social interactions, including the important development of attachment in very young children (De Pisapia et al., 2014; Decety and Lamm, 2007; Hecht, 2014; Schore, 2014; Semrud-Clikeman et al., 2011).

Although structural specialization does develop in the brain, it is also becoming increasingly well understood that brain functioning is more complex than discretely assigned anatomical areas. Language, for example, has been tied to the left hemisphere, in what are known as Broca's and Wernicke's areas. However, there is emerging recognition that aspects of communicating through language, which requires nonverbal information and interpretation of meaning and inference, are also linked to right hemisphere functions (Ross and Monnot, 2008). Similarly, cortical functions are also interconnected with subcortical systems that underlie arousal systems and autonomic function. Developmental neuroscience has also been increasingly focused on the importance of the maturation of these brain systems prenatally and early in life, which like the cortical regions, undergo a rapid growth in the first year of life (Knickmeyer et al., 2008).

The brain has capacity for change in anatomy and function as a result of experience and stimulation, a function known as neural plasticity. Such plasticity takes place at multiple levels of organization and scale, ranging from synaptic changes in neurotransmitter production and release to regional increases in the size of a specific cortical region following the acquisition of new skills. For example, the cortical area controlling the fingers of the left hand expands in students of the violin at a level commensurate with their years of study and increasing virtuosity. Learning and mastery thus are physically represented, at both the micro and macro levels, in the changes in brain structure and function resulting from neural plasticity.

As a consequence of the exquisite precision of the timing, spatial resolution, and sequencing of brain development, enriching experiences in the early years will support healthy brain development, while conversely, a variety of disturbances or deficiencies prenatally or in early childhood can interrupt or perturb the growing brain, resulting in functional changes that range from subtle incapacities to generalized developmental disabilities. Prenatally, such disturbances can include, for example, deficiencies in folate in the maternal diet, which can result in severely disordered formation of the brain and spine, and infection with such organisms as toxoplasmosis or cytomegalovirus, which can produce severe forms of psychopathology such as schizophrenia or autism. In early childhood, one perturbation that occurs with great prevalence in human populations is the developing brain's exposure, directly or indirectly through the parents' experiences, to substantial psychosocial adversity and stress, such as abuse or neglect, the death of a parent, or exposure to violence in the home or neighborhood. Because of its early sensitivity to such adversity, the developing brain can sustain profound effects on structure; function; and capacities for learning, cognition, and adaptive behavior. Although children across populations and socioeconomic levels can experience these kinds of stressors, exposure to many of them is unevenly distributed within populations, which can result in disproportionate risk for the marginalized and the poor.

GENE–ENVIRONMENT INTERPLAY AND DEVELOPMENT

As noted earlier, poor health and maladaptive development have historically been attributed to either experiential or heritable causes, depending on the prevailing scientific and cultural view. Proponents of environmental determinism, the predominant view in the 1960s and 1970s, claimed that, with few heritable exceptions, aspects of context and environmental exposure were the principal forces shaping developmental outcomes. In other periods, such as that following the Human Genome Project in the 1980s and 1990s, proponents of genetic determinism alleged that all the major determinants of disease and developmental disorder were single-gene or polygenic variations. Based on more recent research, however, it is now understood that the interaction of genes and experiences guides development and that the key to a richer understanding of pathogenesis is an elucidation of how genes and environments work together to produce—or to protect from—illness and disorder, i.e., *gene–environment interplay* (Boyce et al., 2012; Rutter, 2010).

The Interplay of Genetic and Environmental Variation

Gene–environment interplay is a category of interactive processes comprising gene–environment correlation (rGE), gene–environment interaction (GxE), and epigenetic modification of the DNA packaging that regulates gene expression. The first of these, rGE, denotes the influence of genetic variation on environmental exposures, referring to how individuals may select, alter, and generate experiences that are in keeping with their own genetic proclivities. For example, a child who has a more inhibited temperament will be inclined toward less intensive social environments. The second, GxE, describes genetic or environmental effects that are conditional upon each other—for example, the effects of genetic variation that become apparent only in the presence of specific environmental conditions, or the effects of social contexts that are more or less potent depending on the underlying genotype of the individual who experiences them. Third, epigenetic processes that stem from environmental exposures modify chromatin—the structural packaging of the genome—through the chemical "tagging" of DNA or the histone proteins around which it is wound. These chromatin modifications or "marks" alter gene activity, control the production of the protein for which the gene codes, and thereby modify the observable, phenotypic characteristics of the child—all without affecting the DNA sequence itself (Boyce and Kobor, 2015).

The exploration of these domains of gene–environment interplay has become one of the most prolific, engaging, and controversial areas of biomedical and social science research. On the one hand, such research holds promise for illuminating how differences in individual susceptibility and environmental conditions operate together to initiate disorders of development, behavior, and health or to sustain health, resilience, and adaptive well-being. On the other hand, this arena of biomedical research also is marked by ongoing, sometimes divisive, controversies over methods and the interpretation of findings.

Initial reports of GxE interaction in developmental psychopathology (Caspi et al., 2002, 2003), now a decade past, revealed for the first time the potential and long-theorized capacity for DNA sequence variants to amplify or constrain the health and developmental risks of disadvantaged or abusive early environments. In the decade that followed, a large number of scientific papers reported GxE interaction in which DNA sequence variations (called single nucleotide polymorphisms, or SNPs) statistically moderated the influence of risky social contexts on the incidence of disordered development and psychopathology. Studies of both human children (see, e.g., Dunn et al., 2011; Molenaar et al., 2013) and animal species (see, e.g., Barr et al., 2004; Burns et al., 2012) continue to identify statistical interactions between variation in genotype and aspects of the rearing environment, although ongoing, legitimate concerns remain about the reliability of findings on GxE interaction (Manuck and McCaffery, 2014).

How GxE interaction exerts effects on developmental and behavioral outcomes has been explained in part by studies showing how variations in DNA sequence are linked to connectivity in specific brain regions (Thompson et al., 2010). Recent functional magnetic resonance imaging studies, for example, have demonstrated the heritability of task-related brain region activation and shown how a functional mutation in an important gene is associated with differences in the function of the prefrontal cortex, where executive skills reside (Egan et al., 2001). Such studies of GxE interaction have employed "candidate" SNPs in genes relevant to brain development and psychopathology or in genes sharing candidate biological pathways (e.g., pathways involved in inflammation). Other researchers have developed experimental animal models for testing the effects of GxE interaction on cognitive and behavioral outcomes (Koch and Britton, 2008; Turner and Burne, 2013) or focused on families of environment-responsive intracellular molecules, called "transcription factors," that control the activation or expression of multiple genes (Slavich and Cole, 2013).

Epigenetics

Among the most compelling, emergent stories in developmental biology is the discovery of the molecular, *epigenetic* processes by which environmental conditions can regulate the activation or deactivation of genes. It is increasingly understood that development is driven not only by the joint, additive, or interactive effects of genetic and contextual variation but also by the direct regulation of gene expression by environmental events and experiences (see, e.g., Lam et al., 2012; Pezawas et al., 2005; Rutter, 2012). Research in epigenetics has shown that experiences can alter gene expression through their effects on molecular regulators that interact with the DNA molecule.

As described earlier, an epigenetic mark is a chemical change in DNA packaging, or chromatin, that affects gene transcription (i.e., the decoding of the gene) without changing the DNA sequence itself. Chromatin modifications that occur as a result of experiences and exposures in an individual's social and physical environments constitute a molecular pathway by which context can influence gene expression and phenotype. This physical conformation of chromatin, which resembles "beads on a string" (see Figure 3-3), allows or disallows access to gene coding regions by RNA polymerase, the enzyme that decodes DNA sequences. Which chromatin conformation exists at a given time depends on epigenetic processes of chemical modification or "marking" that modifies either the DNA itself or the histone proteins around which the DNA is wrapped.

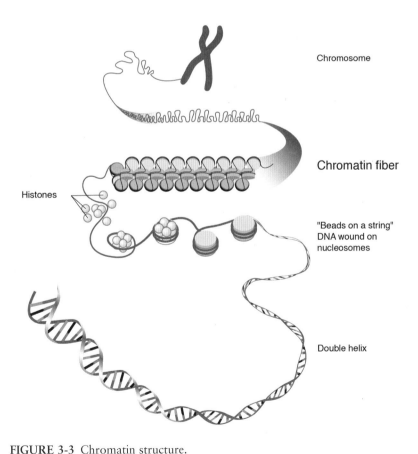

FIGURE 3-3 Chromatin structure.
SOURCE: Leja and NHGRI, 2010.

Early in development, the maturation of the embryo itself depends upon epigenetic programming that shapes cell differentiation and development (Strachan and Read, 2011). The early embryonic genome undergoes several phases of genome-wide epigenetic change that establish and maintain the distinctive, somatic cell lines that make up specific tissues. These early modifications create a kind of genetic *tabula rasa* for the epigenetic reprogramming of cellular diversity (Boyce and Kobor, 2015). Because the body's approximately 200 different cell types contain the same genomic DNA sequence, epigenetic processes must control the tracking of primitive, undifferentiated cells into distinctive cell types through differential expression of each cell's approximately 20,000 genes. Only by such divergent activation of genes could so many tissue types emerge from a single, common genome and ensure the stability of each cell type over generations of cell division. Differential gene expression also guides the differentiation of cellular functions, for example, the development of neurons into unique subsets, the guidance of axon growth, and the spatial organization of brain development (Fox et al., 2010).

At the same time, epigenetic processes also are called upon for adaptive, dynamic responses later in development, such as those a child makes to changing environmental conditions like exposures to severe adversity and stress. In research entailing the calibration of rat pups' stress reactivity, for example, high levels of maternal care resulted in increased production of the glucocorticoid receptor in pups' brains through an epigenetic change in chromatin structure (Weaver et al., 2004). This epigenetic modification of a regulatory region in the glucocorticoid receptor gene increases its expression, thereby blunting cortisol reactivity. Thus, a single set of molecular processes serve both stability and change—an "epigenetic paradox" of the same molecular mechanisms providing for contrasting cellular needs.

Paradoxical though they may be, the uses and functions of epigenetic processes play critically important roles in the successful emergence of social, educational, and biological capacities. A new body of research addressing the genomic and neurobiological bases for complex social cognitions, for example, has shown how inferences about others' thoughts and emotions, the processing of facial information, and control of socially evoked emotion all require functional connectivity between a variety of brain structures, including the amygdala, hippocampus, and prefrontal cortex (Adolphs, 2009; Blakemore, 2010, 2012; Lesch, 2007; Norman et al., 2012; Robinson et al., 2005, 2008). There is evidence that perturbations in such brain circuits are related to genetic and epigenetic processes (Lesch, 2007; Norman et al., 2012). Environmental conditions produce patterns of cellular signals in the brain, and these neural signals remodel epigenetic marks, which modify the expression of genes controlling brain development. Because some of these epigenetic marks are chemically stable, environmental influences during childhood can become "biologically embedded" within the genome of the growing child (Hertzman, 2012).

Further, the processes that influence postnatal development, learning, and health also can be mediated by epigenetic events controlling neuro-regulatory genes. Social dominance and rearing conditions in nonhuman primates, for example, are associated with epigenetic variation in the immune system (Cole et al., 2012; Provencal et al., 2012; Tung et al., 2012). In human research, epigenetic changes in the glucocorticoid receptor gene in brain cells have been identified in suicide victims with a history of child abuse (McGowan et al., 2009; Sasaki et al., 2013), and longitudinal associations have been found between socioeconomic disadvantage and stress in early life and both genome-wide and gene-specific epigenetic changes in later life (Borghol et al., 2012; Essex et al., 2013; Lam et al., 2012).

Most recently, new research has revealed that epigenetic, molecular processes may sometimes underlie GxE interactions (Klengel et al., 2013; Mehta et al., 2013). Specifically, an epidemiologically observed interaction between childhood trauma and an SNP in a cortisol response-regulating gene predicts symptoms of posttraumatic stress disorder in adulthood. Laboratory investigation of this GxE interaction revealed that the effect is mediated through epigenetic changes in a cortisol response element in the gene. This observation shows how chromatin modification and epigenetic marks may be a molecular mechanism for GxE interactions.

**Interplay of Genes and Environment:
Implications for Adults**

For adults who work with children, it is important to recognize that "nature" and "nurture" are not parallel tracks. Instead, the tracks are woven together and influence each other's pathways in ways that may vary greatly depending on the individual child. The adaptations that occur as a result of these mutual interactions mean that the early experiences and early learning environments that adults provide can affect all domains of human development.

In sum, a new and promising body of research is producing evidence, in both animal and human studies, that many variations in human developmental and educational trajectories have early origins in early childhood (Shonkoff and Garner, 2012); are the products of gene–environment interplay (Rutter, 2006); and influence developing neural circuits and processes that are directly linked to long-term trajectories of health, disease, and life achievement (Fox et al., 2010). This research may signal a period of remarkable progress in understanding the extensive interplay among social environments, genes, and epigenetic processes and how genetic and environmental variations converge in typical and atypical development (Boyce and Kobor, 2015).

DEVELOPMENTAL TIME

The central role of time is a recurrent theme in developmental science. The effects of experience change dynamically across the life span, as critical and sensitive periods open and close, especially in the early years. During critical periods of development, important experiences or exposures result in irreversible changes in brain circuitry. During sensitive periods, the brain is especially responsive to such experiences (Fox et al., 2010). These are defined windows of early life when there is plasticity highly dependent on experience (Takesian and Hensch, 2013). In a classic example of this, when children lack patterned visual stimulation because of cataracts, strabismus, or other occlusions of vision during the early development of the brain's visual circuitry (i.e., birth to 7-8 years of age), the result is deprivation amblyopia (dimness of sight). The developing brain is also especially vulnerable to the effects of physical and social environmental exposures during early developmental periods. For example, during critical periods of neurodevelopment children are more prone than adults to toxic chemical injury (Nelson et al., 2014; Zeanah et al., 2011). In a random-assignment trial of children in orphanages, neurobiological and developmental outcomes were dramatically improved for children whose foster care placements occurred prior to 2 years of age (Nelson et al., 2014; Zeanah et al., 2011).

The molecular mechanisms for such critical and sensitive periods are being studied in animal models involving experimental manipulations at the neuronal and molecular levels. Recent research has shown how plasticity in the brain over time is initiated and constrained by molecular "triggers" and "brakes" (Takesian and Hensch, 2013). Such findings have led to a fundamental shift from assuming that brain plasticity *arises* during sharply defined critical periods to a new understanding that the brain is instead intrinsically plastic and normal development requires a timed, molecular *suppression* of that plasticity. The onset and offset of critical periods are due to epigenetic molecular mechanisms (Fagiolini et al., 2009). These discoveries together reveal a complex time sensitivity within development that is initiated, guided, and curtailed by epigenetic, molecular events affecting the neuroregulatory genes that govern brain development (Boyce and Kobor, 2015).

BIOLOGICAL CONSEQUENCES OF PSYCHOSOCIAL ADVERSITIES IN EARLY LIFE

As discussed earlier, there is now strong evidence that psychosocial and other stressors in early life—beginning even in the prenatal period—can have important effects on development. This section focuses in depth on the biological consequences of these stressors. Chapter 4 places those biological consequences in the context of broader considerations and consequences having to do with chronic stress and adversity, focusing in particular on the stressors associated with economic adversity; social buffering of stress; and the relationships among stress, learning, and mental health. Importantly, children experience stress—and the biological dysregulation that can occur—not only as a result of the active stressors of chronic threat or danger but also because of the unavailability of nurturing, supportive care on which children rely, especially early in life. Both conditions appear to constitute significant stressors for young children.

Multiple biological systems are affected by chronic adversity because these systems are activated by stressful events and their persistence. As noted earlier, adverse early experiences can have significant consequences for a child's brain development through the "biological embedding" of such experiences in the stress response systems of the child's brain (Hertzman, 1999). In studies of children who have a depressed parent, live in poverty, witness persistent conflict, are abused or neglected, are in foster care, or experience other kinds of significant chronic stress, developmental researchers have documented important consequences for neurocognitive development (for reviews, see Blair and Raver, 2012; Hertzman and Boyce, 2010; Lupien et al., 2009; Thompson, 2014). The biological effects of chronic stress, especially when it occurs early in life, influence not only brain development but also immunologic functioning; autonomic reactivity; the development of stress reactivity and coping; and memory, learning, and thinking (McEwen, 2012; Ulrich-Lai and Herman, 2009).

The specific effects of early stressors depend critically upon the timing, intensity, and duration of the exposure. Chronic stressors are characterized by prolonged activation of the physiologic stress response systems and are particularly harmful when experienced in the absence of the protection afforded by stable, responsive relationships (Garner and Shonkoff, 2012). Evidence that early adverse experiences can have lasting effects on multiple biological systems helps explain the well-documented association between early adversity and later problems in physical and mental health in adulthood (Boyce et al., 2012; Danese and McEwen, 2012; Edwards et al., 2005). Chronic adversity has these effects because of the cumulative biological "wear and tear" that results from the prolonged activation and overburdening of biological systems that are designed primarily for short-term activation (Geronimus et al., 2006; McEwen, 2012).

Effects on the Neuroendocrine Stress Response System

The HPA axis both contributes to coping with stress and is affected by chronic stress. The HPA axis is activated when the brain detects threatening events, leading to the production of cortisol, which mobilizes energy, enhances cardiovascular tone, alters immune functioning, and orients an individual to danger attentionally and cognitively. These biological responses have important psychological consequences that together provide immediate resources for coping with adversity, including heightened motivation for self-defense, threat vigilance, and motivational and emotional arousal. Over time, however, chronic stress and repeated exposures to adversity can alter the brain centers and neuroendocrine circuitry that underlie the regulation of stress responses and change the functioning of the HPA axis (Ulrich-Lai and Herman, 2009).

Considerable variability in stress reactivity is observed in children facing adversity (see, e.g., Essex et al., 2011). The HPA system is altered in two ways through experiences of adversity (Bruce et al., 2013; Hertzman and Boyce, 2010), and both reflect poor regulation of HPA responses as the result. One is when the HPA axis becomes *hyperresponsive* to perceived threats, so that cortisol levels rise quickly and are slow to decline, as the result of repeated shocks to the stress system. Children who are hyper-responsive may show heightened vigilance to threat, greater reactivity and poorer self-regulation when challenges ensue, and difficulties maintaining cognitive and attentional focus (Blair and Raver, 2012; Evans and Kim, 2013). This heightened reactivity has been observed in children who have been maltreated (Cicchetti and Rogosch, 2001), in infants and toddlers growing up in poverty (Blair et al., 2008, 2011), and in the young children of chronically depressed mothers (Essex et al., 2002).

Another way in which the HPA system can be dysregulated is when stress reactivity becomes blunted or *underresponsive*. In this case, cortisol levels are low, and the typical daily rhythm of cortisol secretion that regulates physiologic functioning is diminished or absent, as if the system is beginning to shut down. This pattern has been observed in young children living within deprived, institutional care (Carlson and Earls, 1997); neglected children placed in foster care (Dozier et al., 2006); and young children living in homes characterized by domestic violence and maternal emotional unavailability (Sturge-Apple et al., 2012). Thus, the effects of chronic, severe deprivation produce a dampening of the HPA axis, possibly due to changes in the hormonal feedback system by which cortisol production is controlled (Bruce et al., 2013; Nelson et al., 2014).

Chronic dysregulation of the HPA axis also alters the immune system, increasing vulnerability to infections, boosting levels of the cytokines by which immune cells communicate with each other, and embedding a biological "bias" toward inflammatory responses (Miller et al., 2011). The effects of HPA dysregulation contribute to the well-known association between stressors and both acute and chronic illness.

Chronic cortisol output also alters the functioning of other brain systems that help regulate HPA activity, including the prefrontal cortex (the seat of executive functions such as planning and emotion regulation), hippocampus (memory and learning), amygdala (emotion activation and regulation), and hypothalamus (multiple neuroendocrine functions) (Lupien et al., 2009; Ulrich-Lai and Herman, 2009). These linkages of stress exposure with brain areas that influence self-regulation, memory, emotion, and behavioral motivation help explain the associations between chronic stress and impairments in focused attention, learning, memory, and self-regulation in children and adults.

Stress also is associated with acute increases in ANS reactivity. The stress effects of ANS activation can result in elevated blood pressure (El-Sheikh and Erath, 2011); poor control of blood sugar levels; and immune system and inflammation dysregulation, through the effects of ANS molecular signals on white blood cell functions.

Prenatal Stressors

Although this report focuses on children beginning at birth rather than on the prenatal period, it is important to note in some depth that child development and early learning also are affected by prenatal exposures. There is growing evidence that the biological embedding of chronic stress begins prenatally because fetal development is affected by the hormonal, autonomic, and other physiologic correlates of maternal stress. Prenatal exposure to cortisol, for example, can have profound influences on the developing brain, as some portion of maternally secreted cortisol moves through the placenta and affects the fetus's neurodevelopment. In animal models, treating the pregnant mother with corticosterone (the rodent equivalent of cortisol) delays the maturation of neurons, myelination, glia cell formation, and blood supply to brain structures (Lupien et al., 2009). In humans, observed effects of prenatal stressors, including maternal depression and anxiety, include smaller birth weights, perturbations in postnatal development and behavior, and increased reactivity of the HPA axis. Heightened prenatal exposure to stress is associated with greater stress reactivity in infancy, as well as longer-term difficulties in emotional and cognitive functioning (Oberlander et al., 2008; Sandman et al., 2012).

The biological embedding of maternal stress in fetal development is consistent with a variety of other biological influences on prenatal growth arising from the mother's diet and nutrition, exposure to environmental pollutants, use of controlled substances, and other aspects of maternal care (Almond and Currie, 2011). The importance of prenatal experience to long-term development is sometimes described as "fetal programming" because prenatal conditions appear to calibrate or program a variety of fetal brain systems involved in responses to stress and adversity.

Socioeconomic Status and Early Brain Development

For children, poverty often entails the confluence of multiple sources of chronic stress. For this reason, considerable research on the effects of chronic stress on children's development has focused on children in families living in poverty or with low income. Studies of children in these conditions indicate that the stressors associated with poverty can contribute to problems with coping, self-regulation, health, emotional well-being, and early learning (Blair and Raver, 2012; Evans and Kim, 2013).

Neuroimaging studies show that socioeconomic status is especially associated with brain functioning in areas related to language and self-regulation (Hackman and Farah, 2009; Kishiyama et al., 2009). Luby and colleagues (2013) found that early childhood poverty was associated with smaller volume in a brain structure involved in the formation of new memories from current experience (the hippocampus) and that this association derived from the impact of stressful childhood events and hostile parenting. Hanson and colleagues (2013) found that preschool children growing up in poverty had lower volumes of gray matter—tissue that is important to information processing, especially in areas of the brain relevant to self-regulation and higher-order thinking.

Children growing up in conditions of economic adversity often sustain stress-related perturbations in the development of brain areas associated with important cognitive and self-regulatory functions. Further, these changes may contribute to academic and social-behavioral problems associated with neurocognitive functions, and may also affect the acquisition of learning skills associated with self-regulation and persistence. In other words, in addition to other disadvantages they experience, one reason children in stressful circumstances fall behind academically is that the biological effects of stress impair their capacities for concentrated attention, memory, cognitive self-regulation, language, and focused thinking. One of the reasons these children experience social difficulties, such as peer conflict or poor compliance with teachers, is that the biological effects of stress enhance their emotional reactivity, heighten their threat vigilance, and undermine their emotion regulation and impulse control.

Interaction Between Exposure to Stress and Gene Expression

There is increasing evidence that chronic stress has the biological effects described above because of its consequences for gene expression, and studies of the developmental biology of social adversity contribute to understanding the mechanisms of the combined, interactive influences of genes and experiences (Gilbert, 2002; Gottlieb, 1991; Karmiloff-Smith, 2007; Meaney, 2010; Waddington, 1959, 2012). Stress constitutes one of the most powerful experiential catalysts of epigenetic influences on gene expression in studies of animals and humans, and epigenetic modifications may be the basis for some of the biological and behavioral effects of stress described here. For example, Oberlander and colleagues (2008) described an association between maternal depression during pregnancy and heightened cortisol reactivity when infants were 3 months old. They also found that heightened cortisol was associated with decreases in the expression of the glucocorticoid receptor gene in the infants. Changes in gene expression in the child helped account, in other words, for the enduring influence of prenatal maternal stress.

INDIVIDUAL DIFFERENCES IN SUSCEPTIBILITY TO ENVIRONMENTAL FACTORS

Variability in the effects of context can be seen at the levels of both behavior and biology, and there is an emerging understanding that this is due to differences among individuals in their susceptibility to environmental influence, in which a subset of individuals appears to be more sensitive to the influences of *both* negative and positive environmental factors. The most intensive study in this area has focused on the sometimes dramatic differences in individual variation in the consequences of exposure to early adversity and stress. Among children who face these challenges, many children show immediate and long-term negative effects on health and development, while others thrive and survive with little detrimental effect. Understanding such differences is important as a means to explain stress-related disorders, account for uneven distributions of disorders within populations, shed light on the sources of individual resilience and vulnerability, and provide insights to lead to effective intervention strategies (Boyce and Kobor, 2015).

Early perspectives on such differences in stress response concluded that individuals experienced variable effects of adversity because of either heritable or acquired vulnerabilities to stress and challenge, referred to as the "stress diathesis" model. More recently, a now substantial body of literature suggests that it is not just that some children are more vulnerable to the effects of adversity, but rather that some children are more susceptible, or responsive, to the social environment; these children show either more maladaptive or more positive outcomes, depending on the exposure (e.g., Belsky, 2005; Boyce and Ellis, 2005; Ellis et al., 2011a). Studies have demonstrated this greater susceptibility of neurobiologically responsive children to both positive and negative aspects of their environments in the context of a range of stressors and adversities, including overall family distress (Obradovic et al., 2010), marital conflict (El-Sheikh, 2005; El-Sheikh et al., 2007), paternal depression (Cummings et al., 2007), and parental psychopathology (Shannon et al., 2007). They also have done so in the context of a wide variety of positive environmental features, including parental warmth (Ellis et al., 1999), beneficial experiences and exposures (Pluess and Belsky, 2011), and supportive interventions (Bakermans-Kranenburg et al., 2008a). These studies have examined this variable susceptibility in light of a range of defining biological parameters, including genetic variations (Bakermans-Kranenburg et al., 2008b; Knafo et al., 2011; Manuck et al., 2011), differences in brain circuitry (Whittle et al., 2011), and physiological reactivity (e.g., Alkon et al., 2006; Boyce et al., 1995).

One of the most important findings has been that outcomes for highly susceptible children are affected in both directions in low- and high-stress settings—not just an attenuation of negative effects in low-stress circumstances. Examples of such bidirectional effects have included differential rates of violent injuries among high- and low-reactivity rhesus macaques before and during a prolonged period of confinement stress (Boyce et al., 1998); children's sensitivity to a socioemotional intervention (Bakermans-Kranenburg et al., 2008a); adolescents' susceptibility to parenting influence (Belsky and Beaver, 2011); and trajectories of pubertal development among girls with high- versus low-quality parent relationships (Ellis et al., 2011b). In each case, the "risky phenotype" showed high levels of maladaptive outcomes under stressful conditions but also lower levels of such outcomes than their low-risk counterparts in positive, low-stress conditions.

Together, these findings indicate that while all children exhibit responsiveness to environmental influences, a subset of children show an exaggerated susceptibility to the character of their social environments—heightened risk for morbidity and developmental deviation when reared in harsh, unsupportive conditions but higher levels of health and positive development if reared in environments characterized by nurturance and support. Such children almost certainly contribute substantially to the uneven distribution of ill health, learning difficulties, and troubled development found within childhood populations. However, they may also benefit disproportionately from positive early interventions (Belsky and van Ijzendoorn, 2015).

The mechanisms, consequences, and intervention opportunities related to these kinds of individual differences, including the interplay among environmental exposures and biological and genetic factors, emerge as essential for fully understanding the biology of social adversity.

Conclusion About the Interaction of Biology and the Environment

The capacity for learning is grounded in the development of the brain and brain circuitry. Rather than a structure built from a static "blueprint," the brain architecture that underlies learning is developed through a continuous, dynamic, adaptive interaction between biology and environment that begins at conception and continues throughout life. This accounts for how early experiences (including supports and stressors) affect gene expression and how the brain develops, and it also accounts for how the effects of environmental factors on a child's development may vary depending on underlying individual genetic characteristics. The adaptations that occur as a result of the mutual interactions between "nature" and "nurture" mean that early experiences and early learning environments affect all domains of human development.

REFERENCES

Adolphs, R. 2009. The social brain: Neural basis of social knowledge. *Annual Review of Psychology* 60:693-716.

Alkon, A., S. Lippert, N. Vujan, M. E. Rodriquez, W. T. Boyce, and B. Eskenazi. 2006. The ontogeny of autonomic measures in 6- and 12-month-old infants. *Developmental Psychobiology* 48(3):197-208.

Almond, D., and J. Currie. 2011. Killing me softly: The fetal origins hypothesis. *The Journal of Economic Perspectives* 25(3):153-172.

Bakermans-Kranenburg, M. J., M. H. Van Ijzendoorn, J. Mesman, L. R. Alink, and F. Juffer. 2008a. Effects of an attachment-based intervention on daily cortisol moderated by dopamine receptor D4: A randomized control trial on 1- to 3-year-olds screened for externalizing behavior. *Development and Psychopathology* 20(3):805-820.

Bakermans-Kranenburg, M. J., I. M. H. Van, F. T. Pijlman, J. Mesman, and F. Juffer. 2008b. Experimental evidence for differential susceptibility: Dopamine D4 receptor polymorphism (DRD4 VNTR) moderates intervention effects on toddlers' externalizing behavior in a randomized controlled trial. *Developmental Psychology* 44(1):293-300.

Barr, C. S., T. K. Newman, S. Lindell, C. Shannon, M. Champoux, K. P. Lesch, S. J. Suomi, D. Goldman, and J. D. Higley. 2004. Interaction between serotonin transporter gene variation and rearing condition in alcohol preference and consumption in female primates. *Archives of General Psychiatry* 61(11):1146-1152.

Belsky, J. 2005. Differential susceptibility to rearing influence: An evolutionary hypothesis and some evidence. In *Origins of the social mind: Evolutionary psychology and child development*, edited by B. J. Ellis and D. F. Bjorklund. New York: Guilford Press. Pp. 139-163.

Belsky, J., and K. M. Beaver. 2011. Cumulative-genetic plasticity, parenting and adolescent self-regulation. *Journal of Child Psychology and Psychiatry and Allied Disciplines* 52(5):619-626.

Belsky, J., and M. H. van Ijzendoorn. 2015. What works for whom? Genetic moderation of intervention efficacy. *Development and Psychopathology* 27(Special Issue 01):1-6.

Blair, C., and C. C. Raver. 2012. Child development in the context of adversity: Experiential canalization of brain and behavior. *American Psychologist* 67(4):309-318.

Blair, C., D. A. Granger, K. T. Kivlighan, R. Mills-Koonce, M. Willoughby, M. T. Greenberg, L. C. Hibel, and C. K. Fortunato. 2008. Maternal and child contributions to cortisol response to emotional arousal in young children from low-income, rural communities. *Developmental Psychology* 44(4):1095-1109.

Blair, C., C. C. Raver, D. Granger, R. Mills-Koonce, and L. Hibel. 2011. Allostasis and allostatic load in the context of poverty in early childhood. *Development and Psychopathology* 23(3):845-857.

Blakemore, S. J. 2010. The developing social brain: Implications for education. *Neuron* 65(6):744-747.

———. 2012. Development of the social brain in adolescence. *Journal of the Royal Society of Medicine* 105(3):111-116.

Bloom, F. E., C. A. Nelson, and A. Lazerson. 2001. *Brain, mind, and behavior*. 3rd ed. New York: Worth Publishers.

Borghol, N., M. Suderman, W. McArdle, A. Racine, M. Hallett, M. Pembrey, C. Hertzman, C. Power, and M. Szyf. 2012. Associations with early-life socio-economic position in adult DNA methylation. *International Journal of Epidemiology* 41(1):62-74.

Boyce, W. T., and B. J. Ellis. 2005. Biological sensitivity to context: I. An evolutionary-developmental theory of the origins and functions of stress reactivity. *Development and Psychopathology* 17(2):271-301.

Boyce, W. T., and M. S. Kobor. 2015. Development and the epigenome: The "synapse" of gene-environment interplay. *Developmental Science* 18(1):1-23.

Boyce, W. T., M. Chesney, A. Alkon, J. M. Tschann, S. Adams, B. Chesterman, F. Cohen, P. Kaiser, S. Folkman, and D. Wara. 1995. Psychobiologic reactivity to stress and childhood respiratory illnesses: Results of two prospective studies. *Psychosomatic Medicine* 57(5):411-422.

Boyce, W. T., P. O'Neill-Wagner, C. S. Price, M. Haines, and S. J. Suomi. 1998. Crowding stress and violent injuries among behaviorally inhibited rhesus macaques. *Health Psychology* 17(3):285-289.

Boyce, W. T., M. B. Sokolowski, and G. E. Robinson. 2012. Toward a new biology of social adversity. *Proceedings of the National Academy of Sciences of the United States of America* 109(Suppl. 2):17143-17148.

Bruce, J., M. R. Gunnar, K. C. Pears, and P. A. Fisher. 2013. Early adverse care, stress neurobiology, and prevention science: Lessons learned. *Prevention Science* 14(3):247-256.

Burns, J. G., N. Svetec, L. Rowe, F. Mery, M. J. Dolan, W. T. Boyce, and M. B. Sokolowski. 2012. Gene-environment interplay in *drosophila melanogaster*: Chronic food deprivation in early life affects adult exploratory and fitness traits. *Proceedings of the National Academy of Sciences of the United States of America* 109(Suppl. 2):17239-17244.

Carlson, M., and F. Earls. 1997. Psychological and neuroendocrinological sequelae of early social deprivation in institutionalized children in Romania. *Annals of the New York Academy of Sciences* 807:419-428.

Caspi, A., J. McClay, T. E. Moffitt, J. Mill, J. Martin, I. W. Craig, A. Taylor, and R. Poulton. 2002. Role of genotype in the cycle of violence in maltreated children. *Science* 297(5582):851-854.

Caspi, A., K. Sugden, T. E. Moffitt, A. Taylor, I. W. Craig, H. Harrington, J. McClay, J. Mill, J. Martin, A. Braithwaite, and R. Poulton. 2003. Influence of life stress on depression: Moderation by a polymorphism in the 5-HTT gene. *Science* 301(5631):386-389.

Cicchetti, D., and F. A. Rogosch. 2001. Diverse patterns of neuroendocrine activity in maltreated children. *Development and Psychopathology* 13(3):677-693.

Cole, S. W., G. Conti, J. M. Arevalo, A. M. Ruggiero, J. J. Heckman, and S. J. Suomi. 2012. Transcriptional modulation of the developing immune system by early life social adversity. *Proceedings of the National Academy of Sciences of the United States of America* 109(50):20578-20583.

Cummings, E. M., M. El-Sheikh, C. D. Kouros, and P. S. Keller. 2007. Children's skin conductance reactivity as a mechanism of risk in the context of parental depressive symptoms. *Journal of Child Psychology and Psychiatry and Allied Disciplines* 48(5):436-445.

Danese, A., and B. S. McEwen. 2012. Adverse childhood experiences, allostasis, allostatic load, and age-related disease. *Physiology & Behavior* 106(1):29-39.

De Pisapia, N., M. Serra, P. Rigo, J. Jager, N. Papinutto, G. Esposito, P. Venuti, and M. H. Bornstein. 2014. Interpersonal competence in young adulthood and right laterality in white matter. *Journal of Cognitive Neuroscience* 26(6):1257-1265.

Decety, J., and C. Lamm. 2007. The role of the right temporoparietal junction in social interaction: How low-level computational processes contribute to meta-cognition. *Neuroscientist* 13(6):580-593.

Dozier, M., M. Manni, M. K. Gordon, E. Peloso, M. R. Gunnar, K. C. Stovall-McClough, D. Eldreth, and S. Levine. 2006. Foster children's diurnal production of cortisol: An exploratory study. *Child Maltreatment* 11(2):189-197.

Dunn, E. C., M. Uddin, S. V. Subramanian, J. W. Smoller, S. Galea, and K. C. Koenen. 2011. Research review: Gene-environment interaction research in youth depression—a systematic review with recommendations for future research. *Journal of Child Psychology and Psychiatry and Allied Disciplines* 52(12):1223-1238.

Edwards, V., R. Anda, S. Dube, M. Dong, D. F. Chapman, and I. V. Felitt. 2005. The wide-ranging health consequences of adverse childhood experiences. In *Victimization of children and youth: Patterns of abuse, response strategies*, edited by K. Kendall-Tackett and S. Giacomoni. Kingston, NJ: Civic Research Institute.

Egan, M. F., T. E. Goldberg, B. S. Kolachana, J. H. Callicott, C. M. Mazzanti, R. E. Straub, D. Goldman, and D. R. Weinberger. 2001. Effect of COMT Val108/158 Met genotype on frontal lobe function and risk for schizophrenia. *Proceedings of the National Academy of Sciences of the United States of America* 98(12):6917-6922.

El-Sheikh, M. 2005. The role of emotional responses and physiological reactivity in the marital conflict-child functioning link. *Journal of Child Psychology and Psychiatry and Allied Disciplines* 46(11):1191-1199.

El-Sheikh, M., and S. A. Erath. 2011. Family conflict, autonomic nervous system functioning, and child adaptation: State of the science and future directions. *Development and Psychopathology* 23(2):703-721.

El-Sheikh, M., P. S. Keller, and S. A. Erath. 2007. Marital conflict and risk for child maladjustment over time: Skin conductance level reactivity as a vulnerability factor. *Journal of Abnormal Child Psychology* 35(5):715-727.

Ellis, B. J., S. McFadyen-Ketchum, K. A. Dodge, G. S. Pettit, and J. E. Bates. 1999. Quality of early family relationships and individual differences in the timing of pubertal maturation in girls: A longitudinal test of an evolutionary model. *Journal of Personality and Social Psychology* 77(2):387-401.

Ellis, B. J., W. T. Boyce, J. Belsky, M. J. Bakermans-Kranenburg, and M. H. van Ijzendoorn. 2011a. Differential susceptibility to the environment: An evolutionary—neurodevelopmental theory. *Development and Psychopathology* 23(1):7-28.

Ellis, B. J., E. A. Shirtcliff, W. T. Boyce, J. Deardorff, and M. J. Essex. 2011b. Quality of early family relationships and the timing and tempo of puberty: Effects depend on biological sensitivity to context. *Development and Psychopathology* 23(1):85-99.

Essex, M. J., M. H. Klein, E. Cho, and N. H. Kalin. 2002. Maternal stress beginning in infancy may sensitize children to later stress exposure: Effects on cortisol and behavior. *Biological Psychiatry* 52(8):776-784.

Essex, M. J., E. A. Shirtcliff, L. R. Burk, P. L. Ruttle, M. H. Klein, M. J. Slattery, N. H. Kalin, and J. M. Armstrong. 2011. Influence of early life stress on later hypothalamic-pituitary-adrenal axis functioning and its covariation with mental health symptoms: A study of the allostatic process from childhood into adolescence. *Development and Psychopathology* 23(4):1039-1058.

Essex, M. J., W. T. Boyce, C. Hertzman, L. L. Lam, J. M. Armstrong, S. M. Neumann, and M. S. Kobor. 2013. Epigenetic vestiges of early developmental adversity: Childhood stress exposure and DNA methylation in adolescence. *Child Development* 84(1):58-75.

Evans, G. W., and P. Kim. 2013. Childhood poverty, chronic stress, self-regulation, and coping. *Child Development Perspectives* 7(1):43-48.

Fagiolini, M., C. L. Jensen, and F. A. Champagne. 2009. Epigenetic influences on brain development and plasticity. *Current Opinion in Neurobiology* 19(2):207-212.

Fox, S. E., P. Levitt, and C. A. Nelson, 3rd. 2010. How the timing and quality of early experiences influence the development of brain architecture. *Child Development* 81(1):28-40.

Garner, A. S., and J. P. Shonkoff. 2012. Early childhood adversity, toxic stress, and the role of the pediatrician: Translating developmental science into lifelong health. *Pediatrics* 129(1):e224-e231.

Geronimus, A. T., M. Hicken, D. Keene, and J. Bound. 2006. "Weathering" and age patterns of allostatic load scores among blacks and whites in the United States. *American Journal of Public Health* 96(5):826-833.

Gilbert, S. F. 2002. The genome in its ecological context: Philosophical perspectives on interspecies epigenesis. *Annals of the New York Academy of Sciences* 981:202-218.

Gottlieb, G. 1991. Experiential canalization of behavioral development: Theory. *Developmental Psychology* 27(1):4-13.

Greenough, W. T., and J. E. Black. 1992. Induction of brain structure by experience: Substrates for cognitive development. In *Developmental behavioral neuroscience, Minnesota Symposium on Child Psychology*, edited by M. R. Gunnar and C. A. Nelson. Hillsdale, NJ: Lawrence Erlbaum Associates.

Greenough, W. T., J. E. Black, and C. S. Wallace. 1987. Experience and brain development. *Child Development* 58(3):539-559.

Hackman, D. A., and M. J. Farah. 2009. Socioeconomic status and the developing brain. *Trends in Cognitive Sciences* 13(2):65-73.

Hanson, J. L., N. Hair, D. G. Shen, F. Shi, J. H. Gilmore, B. L. Wolfe, and S. D. Pollak. 2013. Family poverty affects the rate of human infant brain growth. *PLoS ONE* 8(12):e80954.

Hecht, D. 2014. Cerebral lateralization of pro- and anti-social tendencies. *Experimental Neurobiology* 23(1):1-27.

Hertzman, C. 1999. The biological embedding of early experience and its effects on health in adulthood. *Annals of the New York Academy of Sciences* 896:85-95.

———. 2012. Putting the concept of biological embedding in historical perspective. *Proceedings of the National Academy of Sciences of the United States of America* 109(Suppl. 2):17160-17167.

Hertzman, C., and W. T. Boyce. 2010. How experience gets under the skin to create gradients in developmental health. *Annual Review of Public Health* 31:329-347.

IOM (Institute of Medicine) and NRC (National Research Council). 2009. *Preventing mental, emotional, and behavioral disorders among young people: Progress and possibilities.* Washington, DC: The National Academies Press.

Karmiloff-Smith, A. 2007. Atypical epigenesis. *Developmental Science* 10(1):84-88.

Kellett, C. 2015. *Neurons, neural networks and neural pathways.* http://www.achoice2live.com/know-your-addiction/neurons-neural-networks-and-neural-pathways (accessed March 23, 2015).

Kishiyama, M. M., W. T. Boyce, A. M. Jimenez, L. M. Perry, and R. T. Knight. 2009. Socio-economic disparities affect prefrontal function in children. *Journal of Cognitive Neuroscience* 21(6):1106-1115.

Klengel, T., D. Mehta, C. Anacker, M. Rex-Haffner, J. C. Pruessner, C. M. Pariante, T. W. Pace, K. B. Mercer, H. S. Mayberg, B. Bradley, C. B. Nemeroff, F. Holsboer, C. M. Heim, K. J. Ressler, T. Rein, and E. B. Binder. 2013. Allele-specific FKBP5 DNA demethylation mediates gene-childhood trauma interactions. *Nature Neuroscience* 16(1):33-41.

Knafo, A., S. Israel, and R. P. Ebstein. 2011. Heritability of children's prosocial behavior and differential susceptibility to parenting by variation in the dopamine receptor D4 gene. *Development and Psychopathology* 23(1):53-67.

Knickmeyer, R. C., S. Gouttard, C. Kang, D. Evans, K. Wilber, J. K. Smith, R. M. Hamer, W. Lin, G. Gerig, and J. H. Gilmore. 2008. A structural MRI study of human brain development from birth to 2 years. *Journal of Neuroscience* 28(47):12176-12182.

Koch, L. G., and S. L. Britton. 2008. Development of animal models to test the fundamental basis of gene-environment interactions. *Obesity (Silver Spring)* 16(Suppl. 3):S28-S32.

Lam, L. L., E. Emberly, H. B. Fraser, S. M. Neumann, E. Chen, G. E. Miller, and M. S. Kobor. 2012. Factors underlying variable DNA methylation in a human community cohort. *Proceedings of the National Academy of Sciences of the United States of America* 109(Suppl. 2):17253-17260.

Leja, D., and NHGRI (National Human Genome Research Institute). 2010. Chromatin. https://www.genome.gov/dmd/img.cfm?node=Photos/Graphics&id=85280 (accessed March 25, 2015).

Lesch, K. P. 2007. Linking emotion to the social brain. The role of the serotonin transporter in human social behaviour. *EMBO Reports* 8 Spec No:S24-S29.

Luby, J., A. Belden, K. Botteron, N. Marrus, M. P. Harms, C. Babb, T. Nishino, and D. Barch. 2013. The effects of poverty on childhood brain development: The mediating effect of caregiving and stressful life events. *JAMA Pediatrics* 167(12):1135-1142.

Lupien, S. J., B. S. McEwen, M. R. Gunnar, and C. Heim. 2009. Effects of stress throughout the lifespan on the brain, behaviour and cognition. *Nature Reviews Neuroscience* 10(6):434-445.

Manuck, S. B., and J. M. McCaffery. 2014. Gene-environment interaction. *Annual Review of Psychology* 65:41-70.

Manuck, S. B., A. E. Craig, J. D. Flory, I. Halder, and R. E. Ferrell. 2011. Reported early family environment covaries with menarcheal age as a function of polymorphic variation in estrogen receptor-alpha. *Development and Psychopathology* 23(1):69-83.

McEwen, B. S. 2012. Brain on stress: How the social environment gets under the skin. *Proceedings of the National Academy of Sciences of the United States of America* 109(Suppl. 2):17180-17185.

McGowan, P. O., A. Sasaki, A. C. D'Alessio, S. Dymov, B. Labonte, M. Szyf, G. Turecki, and M. J. Meaney. 2009. Epigenetic regulation of the glucocorticoid receptor in human brain associates with childhood abuse. *Nature Neuroscience* 12(3):342-348.

Meaney, M. J. 2010. Epigenetics and the biological definition of gene x environment interactions. *Child Development* 81(1):41-79.

Mehta, D., T. Klengel, K. N. Conneely, A. K. Smith, A. Altmann, T. W. Pace, M. Rex-Haffner, A Loeschner, M. Gonik, K. B. Mercer, B. Bradley, B. Muller-Myhsok, K. J. Ressler, and E. B. Binder. 2013. Childhood maltreatment is associated with distinct genomic and epigenetic profiles in posttraumatic stress disorder. *Proceedings of the National Academy of Sciences of the United States of America* 110(20):8302-8307.

Miller, G. E., E. Chen, and K. J. Parker. 2011. Psychological stress in childhood and susceptibility to the chronic diseases of aging: Moving toward a model of behavioral and
biological mechanisms. *Psychological Bulletin* 137(6):959-997.

Molenaar, D., S. van der Sluis, D. I. Boomsma, C. M. Haworth, J. K. Hewitt, N. G. Martin,
R. Plomin, M. J. Wright, and C. V. Dolan. 2013. Genotype by environment interactions
in cognitive ability: A survey of 14 studies from four countries covering four age groups.
Behavior Genetics 43(3):208-219.

National Scientific Council on the Developing Child. 2004. *Children's emotional development
is built into the architecture of their brains: Working paper #2.* http://www.developing
child.net (accessed April 22, 2014).

Nelson, C. A., N. A. Fox, and C. H. Zeanah. 2014. *Romania's abandoned children: Deprivation, brain development, and the struggle for recovery.* Cambridge, MA: Harvard
University Press.

Norman, G. J., L. C. Hawkley, S. W. Cole, G. G. Berntson, and J. T. Cacioppo. 2012. Social
neuroscience: The social brain, oxytocin, and health. *Social Neuroscience* 7(1):18-29.

NRC (National Research Council) and IOM (Institute of Medicine). 2000. *From neurons to
neighborhoods: The science of early childhood development,* edited by J. P. Shonkoff and
D. A. Phillips. Washington, DC: National Academy Press.

Oberlander, T. F., J. Weinberg, M. Papsdorf, R. Grunau, S. Misri, and A. M. Devlin. 2008.
Prenatal exposure to maternal depression, neonatal methylation of human glucocorticoid
receptor gene (NR3C1) and infant cortisol stress responses. *Epigenetics* 3(2):97-106.

Obradovic, J., N. R. Bush, J. Stamperdahl, N. E. Adler, and W. T. Boyce. 2010. Biological
sensitivity to context: The interactive effects of stress reactivity and family adversity on
socioemotional behavior and school readiness. *Child Development* 81(1):270-289.

Pezawas, L., A. Meyer-Lindenberg, E. M. Drabant, B. A. Verchinski, K. E. Munoz,
B. S. Kolachana, M. F. Egan, V. S. Mattay, A. R. Hariri, and D. R. Weinberger. 2005.
5-HTTLPR polymorphism impacts human cingulate-amygdala interactions: A genetic
susceptibility mechanism for depression. *Nature Neuroscience* 8(6):828-834.

Pluess, M., and J. Belsky. 2011. Prenatal programming of postnatal plasticity? *Development
and Psychopathology* 23(1):29-38.

Provencal, N., M. J. Suderman, C. Guillemin, R. Massart, A. Ruggiero, D. Wang, A. J.
Bennett, P. J. Pierre, D. P. Friedman, S. M. Cote, M. Hallett, R. E. Tremblay, S. J. Suomi,
and M. Szyf. 2012. The signature of maternal rearing in the methylome in rhesus macaque prefrontal cortex and T cells. *Journal of Neuroscience* 32(44):15626-15642.

Robinson, G. E., C. M. Grozinger, and C. W. Whitfield. 2005. Sociogenomics: Social life in
molecular terms. *Nature Reviews: Genetics* 6(4):257-270.

Robinson, G. E., R. D. Fernald, and D. F. Clayton. 2008. Genes and social behavior. *Science*
322(5903):896-900.

Ross, E. D., and M. Monnot. 2008. Neurology of affective prosody and its functional-
anatomic organization in right hemisphere. *Brain and Language* 104(1):51-74.

Rutter, M. 2006. *Genes and behaviour: Nature-nurture interplay explained.* Oxford: Blackwell.

———. 2010. Gene-environment interplay. *Depression and Anxiety* 27(1):1-4.

———. 2012. Achievements and challenges in the biology of environmental effects. *Proceedings of the National Academy of Sciences of the United States of America* 109(Suppl.
2):17149-17153.

Sandman, C. A., E. P. Davis, C. Buss, and L. M. Glynn. 2012. Exposure to prenatal psychobiological stress exerts programming influences on the mother and her fetus. *Neuroendocrinology* 95(1):7-21.

Sasaki, A., W. C. de Vega, and P. O. McGowan. 2013. Biological embedding in mental health:
An epigenomic perspective. *Biochemistry and Cell Biology* 91(1):14-21.

Schore, A. N. 2010. Synopsis, the impact of childhood trauma: Psychobiological sequelae in adults. In *The impact of early life trauma on health and disease: The hidden epidemic*, edited by R. A. Lanius, E. Vermetten, and C. Pain. Cambridge, UK: Cambridge University Press. Pp. 142-148.

———. 2014. The right brain is dominant in psychotherapy. *Psychotherapy (Chicago, Illinois)* 51(3):388-397.

Semrud-Clikeman, M., J. Goldenring Fine, and D. C. Zhu. 2011. The role of the right hemisphere for processing of social interactions in normal adults using functional magnetic resonance imaging. *Neuropsychobiology* 64(1):47-51.

Shannon, K. E., T. P. Beauchaine, S. L. Brenner, E. Neuhaus, and L. Gatzke-Kopp. 2007. Familial and temperamental predictors of resilience in children at risk for conduct disorder and depression. *Development and Psychopathology* 19(3):701-727.

Shonkoff, J. P., and A. S. Garner. 2012. The lifelong effects of early childhood adversity and toxic stress. *Official Journal of the American Academy of Pediatrics* 129(1):e232-e246.

Slavich, G. M., and S. W. Cole. 2013. The emerging field of human social genomics. *Clinical Psychological Science* 1(3):331-348.

Strachan, T., and A. P. Read. 2011. *Human molecular genetics*. New York: Garland Science.

Sturge-Apple, M. L., P. T. Davies, D. Cicchetti, and L. G. Manning. 2012. Interparental violence, maternal emotional unavailability and children's cortisol functioning in family contexts. *Developmental Psychology* 48(1):237-249.

Takesian, A. E., and T. K. Hensch. 2013. Balancing plasticity/stability across brain development. *Progress in Brain Research* 207:3-34.

Thompson, P. M., N. G. Martin, and M. J. Wright. 2010. Imaging genomics. *Current Opinion in Neurology* 23(4):368-373.

Thompson, R. A. 2014. Stress and child development. *The Future of Children* 24(1):41-59.

Tung, J., L. B. Barreiro, Z. P. Johnson, K. D. Hansen, V. Michopoulos, D. Toufexis, K. Michelini, M. E. Wilson, and Y. Gilad. 2012. Social environment is associated with gene regulatory variation in the rhesus macaque immune system. *Proceedings of the National Academy of Sciences of the United States of America* 109(17):6490-6495.

Turner, K. M., and T. H. Burne. 2013. Interaction of genotype and environment: Effect of strain and housing conditions on cognitive behavior in rodent models of schizophrenia. *Frontiers in Behavioral Neuroscience* 7:97.

Ulrich-Lai, Y. M., and J. P. Herman. 2009. Neural regulation of endocrine and autonomic stress responses. *Nature Reviews Neuroscience* 10(6):397-409.

Waddington, C. H. 1959. Canalization of development and genetic assimilation of acquired characters. *Nature* 183(4676):1654-1655.

———. 2012. The epigenotype. 1942. *International Journal of Epidemiology* 41(1):10-13.

Weaver, I. C., J. Diorio, J. R. Seckl, M. Szyf, and M. J. Meaney. 2004. Early environmental regulation of hippocampal glucocorticoid receptor gene expression: Characterization of intracellular mediators and potential genomic target sites. *Annals of the New York Academy of Sciences* 1024:182-212.

Whittle, S., M. B. Yap, L. Sheeber, P. Dudgeon, M. Yucel, C. Pantelis, J. G. Simmons, and N. B. Allen. 2011. Hippocampal volume and sensitivity to maternal aggressive behavior: A prospective study of adolescent depressive symptoms. *Development and Psychopathology* 23(1):115-129.

Zeanah, C. H., M. R. Gunnar, R. B. McCall, J. M. Kreppner, and N. A. Fox. 2011. VI. Sensitive periods. *Monographs of the Society for Research in Child Development* 76(4):147-162.

4

Child Development and Early Learning

The domains of child development and early learning are discussed in different terms and categorized in different ways in the various fields and disciplines that are involved in research, practice, and policy related to children from birth through age 8. To organize the discussion in this report, the committee elected to use the approach and overarching terms depicted in Figure 4-1. The committee does not intend to present this as a single best set of terms or a single best categorical organization. Indeed, it is essential to recognize that the domains shown in Figure 4-1 are not easily separable and that a case can be made for multiple different categorizations. For example, different disciplines and researchers have categorized different general cognitive processes under the categorical term "executive function." General cognitive processes also relate to learning competencies such as persistence and engagement. Similarly, self-regulation has both cognitive and emotional dimensions. It is sometimes categorized as a part of executive function, as a part of socioemotional competence, or as a part of learning competencies. Attention and memory could be considered a part of general cognitive processes, as embedded within executive function, or linked to learning competencies related to persistence. Mental health is closely linked to socioemotional competence, but is also inseparable from health.

The challenge of cleanly separating these concepts highlights a key attribute of all of these domains, which is that they do not develop or operate in isolation. Each enables and mutually supports learning and development in the others. Therefore, the importance of the interactions among the domains is emphasized throughout this chapter. For example, socioemotional

86

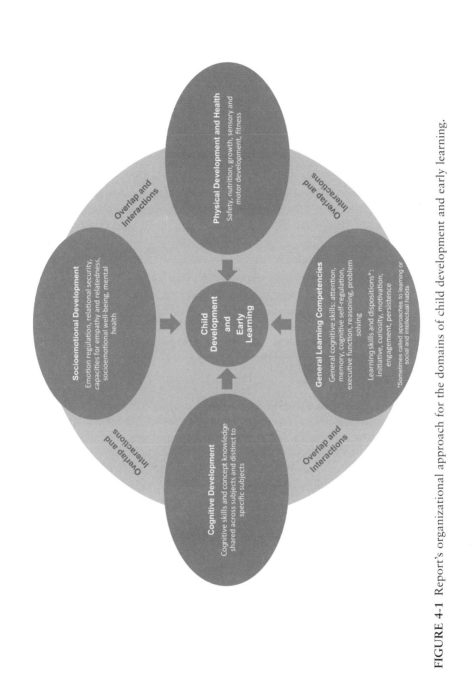

FIGURE 4-1 Report's organizational approach for the domains of child development and early learning.

competence is important for self-regulation, as are certain cognitive skills, and both emotional and cognitive self-regulation are important for children to be able to exercise learning competencies. Similarly, although certain skills and concept knowledge are distinct to developing proficiency in particular subject areas, learning in these subject areas also both requires and supports general cognitive skills such as reasoning and attention, as well as learning competencies and socioemotional competence. In an overarching example of interactions, a child's security both physically and in relationships creates the context in which learning is most achievable across all of the domains.

It is less important that all fields of research, practice, and policy adhere to the exact same categorizations, and more important that all conduct their work in a way that is cognizant and inclusive of all the elements that contribute to child development and early learning, and that all fields recognize that they are interactive and mutually reinforcing rather than hierarchical. This point foreshadows a theme that is addressed more fully in subsequent chapters. Because different fields and sectors may not use the same categorizations and vocabulary for these domains and skills, developing practices and policies that support more consistent and continuous development and early learning across birth through age 8 will require a concerted effort to communicate clearly and come to a mutual understanding of the goals for children. To communicate across fields and between research and practice communities requires being aware of the different categorical frameworks and terms that are used and being able to discuss the various concepts and content—and their implications—with clarity across those different frameworks. Practitioners and policy makers will be aided in achieving greater precision and clarity in their actions and decisions if those conducting and communicating future research keep this challenge in mind across domains, especially in those cases in which the taxonomy is most variable (e.g., self-regulation, executive function, general learning competencies).

With these caveats in mind, the remainder of this chapter addresses in turn the domains of child development and early learning depicted in Figure 4-1: cognitive development, including learning of specific subjects; general learning competencies; socioemotional development; and physical development and health. The final section examines a key overarching issue: the effects on child development and early learning of the stress and adversity that is also an important theme in the discussion of the interaction between biology and environment in Chapter 3.

COGNITIVE DEVELOPMENT

This section highlights what is known about cognitive development in young children. It begins with key concepts from research viewpoints that have contributed to recent advances in understanding of the developing mind, and then presents the implications of this knowledge for early care and education settings. The following section addresses the learning of specific subjects, with a focus on language and mathematics.

Studies of early cognitive development have led researchers to understand the developing mind as astonishingly competent, active, and insightful from a very early age. For example, infants engage in an intuitive analysis of the statistical regularities in the speech sounds they hear en route to constructing language (Saffran, 2003). Infants and toddlers derive implicit theories to explain the actions of objects and the behavior of people; these theories form the foundation for causal learning and more sophisticated understanding of the physical and social worlds. Infants and young children also are keenly responsive to what they can learn from the actions and words directed to them by other people. This capacity for joint attention may be the foundation that enables humans to benefit from culturally transmitted knowledge (Tomasello et al., 2005). Infants respond to cues conveying the communicative intentions of an adult (such as eye contact and infant-directed speech) and tune in to what the adult is referring to and what can be learned about it. This "natural pedagogy" (Csibra, 2010; Csibra and Gergely, 2009) becomes more sophisticated in the sensitivity of preschoolers to implicit pedagogical guides in adult speech directed to them (Butler and Markman, 2012a,b, 2014). Young children rely so much on what they learn from others that they become astute, by the preschool years, in distinguishing adult speakers who are likely to provide them with reliable information from those who are not (Harris, 2012; Jaswal, 2010; Koenig and Doebel, 2013). This connection of relationships and social interactions to cognitive development is consistent with how the brain develops and how the mind grows, and is a theme throughout this chapter.

Much of what current research shows is going on in young children's minds is not transparent in their behavior. Infants and young children may not show what they know because of competing demands on their attention, limitations in what they can do, and immature self-regulation. This is one of the reasons why developmental scientists use carefully designed experiments for elucidating what young children know and understand about the world. By designing research procedures that eliminate competing distractions and rely on simple responses (such as looking time and expressions of surprise), researchers seek to uncover cognitive processes that might otherwise be more difficult to see. Evidence derived in this experimental manner, such as the examples in the sections that follow, can be helpful in explaining young children's rapid growth in language learning, imitation, problem solving, and other skills.

Implicit Theories

One of the most important discoveries about the developing mind is how early and significantly very young children, even starting in infancy, are uniting disparate observations or discrete facts into coherent conceptual systems (Carey, 2009; Gopnik and Wellman, 2012; Spelke and Kinzler, 2007). From very early on, children are not simply passive observers, registering the superficial appearance of things. Rather, they are building explanatory systems—implicit theories—that organize their knowledge. Such implicit theories contain causal principles and causal relations; these theories enable children to predict, explain, and reason about relevant phenomena and, in some cases, intervene to change them. As early as the first year of life, babies are developing incipient theories about how the world of people, other living things, objects, and numbers operates. It is important to point out that these foundational theories are not simply isolated forms of knowledge, but play a profound role in children's everyday lives and subsequent education.

One major example of an implicit theory that is already developing as early as infancy is "theory of mind," which refers to the conceptual framework people use to reason about the mental lives of others as well as themselves. This example is discussed in detail below. Some additional illustrative examples of the development of implicit theories are provided in Box 4-1.

Theory of Mind

People intuitively understand others' actions as motivated by desires, goals, feelings, intentions, thoughts, and other mental states, and we understand how these mental states affect one another (for example, an unfulfilled desire can evoke negative feelings and a motivation to continue trying to achieve the goal). One remarkable discovery of research on young children is that they are developing their own intuitive "map" of mental processes like these from very early in life (Baillargeon et al., 2010; Saxe, 2013; Wellman and Woolley, 1990). Children's developing theory of mind transforms how they respond to people and what they learn from them. Infants and young children are beginning to understand what goes on in people's minds, and how others' feelings and thoughts are similar to and different from their own.

Infants first have a relatively simple theory of mind. They are aware of some basic characteristics: what people are looking at is a sign of what they are paying attention to; people act intentionally and are goal directed; people have positive and negative feelings in response to things around them; and people have different perceptions, goals, and feelings. Children add to this mental map as their awareness grows. From infancy on, developing

BOX 4-1
Examples of the Development of Implicit Theories

Theories of Physical Objects

Even babies hold some fundamental principles about how objects move about in space and time (Baillargeon et al., 2009). For example, babies are surprised (as measured by their increased looking time) if an object in one location pops up in another location when they did not see it traverse the space between.

Theories of Numbers

Even babies seem capable of intuitively understanding something that approximates addition and subtraction, and they are surprised when something counter to these principles occurs (Wynn, 1992a). For example, when babies witness one object that is then screened from view and they see that another object is placed behind the screen, they are surprised when the screen is lowered if there is still only one object there.

There has been a recent explosion of research on quantitative abilities of infants and toddlers. These studies have examined these young children's representations and processing of small exact numbers, as well as their capacities in an approximate number system in which very large numbers can be represented and discriminated from each other (Carey, 2009; Feigenson et al., 2013; Hyde and Spelke, 2011; Pinhas et al., 2014). These very early developing capacities in these two numerical systems lay the foundation for later mathematical abilities that will be taught explicitly to children.

Theories of Living Things

Young children also understand some fundamental characteristics of living things. They distinguish between living and nonliving things; they know living things grow and inanimate objects do not; they know sick or injured people can heal while broken objects do not repair themselves; they attribute life, growth, and biological processes to some sort of vital force or energy, and they know that food is necessary to nourish this vital force (Inagaki and Hatano, 2004).

For example, babies understand observed events in ways that distinguish

theory of mind permeates everyday social interactions—affecting what and how children learn, how they react to and interact with other people, how they assess the fairness of an action, and how they evaluate themselves.

One-year-olds, for example, will look in their mother's direction when faced with someone or something unfamiliar to "read" mother's expression and determine whether this is a dangerous or benign unfamiliarity. Infants also detect when an adult makes eye contact, speaks in an infant-directed between animate and inanimate objects. If 6-month-old babies view a human arm reaching for an object, they interpret this as an intentional agent pursuing a specific goal, and they are surprised if the arm reaches for a different object but not if it changes its trajectory as the object's location changes. In contrast, babies who see an inanimate rod move on the same trajectory toward an object are surprised if the rod changes its trajectory to pursue the object but not if it continues on the old trajectory toward a new object. The emergence of the ability to make this distinction is tied to the baby's own capacity to reach for objects—babies need experience reaching on their own to recognize the intent behind reaching in others (Gerson and Woodward, 2014).

An example of building on intuitive understanding to develop a more elaborate understanding of biology comes from a study on teaching preschool through early elementary school children about nutrition. Children at this age have an understanding that people need food to survive, but their implicit theory provides no causal mechanism for how food accomplishes its vital functions. The approach in this study was to move beyond very simplified, nonexplanatory teaching material and instead to teach children in age-appropriate ways that different foods contain different nutrients that are too small to see, which in turn have different functions that are required to support diverse biological processes. The core concepts and causal principles provided a coherent conceptual framework that explains why it is important to eat a variety of healthy foods. Children became able to explain why it is not healthy to eat only broccoli; they could pick a healthier snack based on the variety of foods included; they understood why people need blood to carry nutrients to all parts of the body. Moreover, when assessed at snack time, the children who received this intuitive theory-based training increased their vegetable consumption (Gripshover and Markman, 2013).

In another example of intentionally contributing to a more elaborate biological theory for children at the older end of the birth-to-8 age range, third- and fourth-grade students during the severe acute respiratory syndrome (SARS) epidemic in Hong Kong increased their hand-washing behaviors after receiving lessons that germs are living things that thrive under some circumstances and die in others, and that reproduce quickly under some conditions and very slowly or not at all in others. These lessons provided children with a conceptual framework that explained the reasons behind the standard instructions provided to the control group, which typically are taught as fact-like, rule-like slogans to wash one's hands and wear a face mask (Au et al., 2008).

manner (such as using higher pitch and melodic intonations), and responds contingently to the infant's behavior. Under these circumstances, infants are especially attentive to what the adult says and does, thus devoting special attention to social situations in which the adult's intentions are likely to represent learning opportunities.

Other examples also illustrate how a developing theory of mind underlies children's emerging understanding of the intentions of others. Take imitation, for example. It is well established that babies and young children imitate the actions of others. Children as young as 14 to 18 months are often imitating not the literal observed action but the action they thought the actor intended—the goal or the rationale behind the action (Gergely et al., 2002; Meltzoff, 1995). Word learning is another example in which babies' reasoning based on theory of mind plays a crucial role. By at least 15 months old, when babies hear an adult label an object, they take the speaker's intent into account by checking the speaker's focus of attention and deciding whether they think the adult indicated the object intentionally. Only when babies have evidence that the speaker intended to refer to a particular object with a label will they learn that word (Baldwin, 1991; Baldwin and Moses, 2001; Baldwin and Tomasello, 1998).

Babies also can perceive the unfulfilled goals of others and intervene to help them; this is called "shared intentionality." Babies as young as 14 months old who witness an adult struggling to reach for an object will interrupt their play to crawl over and hand the object to the adult (Warneken and Tomasello, 2007). By the time they are 18 months old, shared intentionality enables toddlers to act helpfully in a variety of situations; for example, they pick up dropped objects for adults who indicate that they need assistance (but not for adults who dropped the object intentionally) (Warneken and Tomasello, 2006). Developing an understanding of others' goals and preferences and how to facilitate them affects how young children interpret the behavior of people they observe and provides a basis for developing a sense of helpful versus undesirable human activity that is a foundation for later development of moral understanding (cf. Bloom, 2013; Hamlin et al., 2007; Thompson, 2012, 2015).

Developing Implicit Theories: Implications for Adults

The research on the development of implicit theories in children has important implications for how adults work with and educate young children. Failure to recognize the extent to which they are construing information in terms of their lay theories can result in educational strategies that oversimplify material for children. Educational materials guided by the assumption that young children are "concrete" thinkers—that they cannot deal with abstraction or reason hypothetically—leads educators to focus on simple, descriptive activities that can deprive children of opportunities to advance their conceptual frameworks. Designing effective materials in a given domain or subject matter requires knowing what implicit theories children hold, what core causal principles they use, and what misconceptions and gaps in knowledge they have, and then using empirically validated steps to help lead them to a more accurate, more advanced conceptual framework.

Statistical Learning

Statistical learning refers to the range of ways in which children, even babies, are implicitly sensitive to the statistical regularities in their environment, although they are not explicitly learning or applying statistics. Like the development of implicit theories, this concept of statistical learning counters the possible misconception of babies as passive learners and bears on the vital importance of their having opportunities to observe and interact with the environment. Several examples of statistical learning are provided in Box 4-2.

Understanding Causal Inference

Children's intuitive understanding of causal inference has long been recognized as a fundamental component of conceptual development. Young children, although not explicitly or consciously experimenting with causality, can experience observations and learning that allow them to conclude that a particular variable X causes (or prevents) an effect Y. Recent advances in the field have documented the ways young children can implicitly use the statistics of how events covary to infer causal relations, make predictions, generate explanations, guide their exploration, and enable them to intervene in the environment. The understanding of causal inference also provides an example of how different cognitive abilities—such as a sensitivity to statistical regularities and the development of implicit theories based on observation and learning (discussed in the two preceding sections and Box 4-2)—interact with and can mutually support each other. There is now a substantial literature on young children's implicit ability to use what they observe in different conditions to understand the relations between variables. Several examples of young children developing the ability to understand causal inference are provided in Box 4-3.

Sensitivity to Teaching Cues

Csibra and Gergely (2009) argue that humans are equipped with a capacity to realize when someone is communicating something for their benefit and that they construe that information differently than when they merely witness it. As noted previously in the discussion of developing theory of mind, children as early as infancy devote special attention to social situations that are likely to represent learning opportunities because adults communicate that intention. Information learned in such communicative contexts is treated as more generalizable and robust than that learned in a noncommunicative context.

BOX 4-2
Examples of Statistical Learning

Sensitivity to Conditional Probabilities

Infants can use information about the statistics of syllables in the speech they hear to help them parse words. How do we know from hearing *prettybaby* that *baby* is more likely to be a word than *tyba*? One way is that the conditional probability of *by* following *ba* is higher than that of *ba* following *ty*. Babies can use such conditional probabilities of syllables following each other to detect word boundaries, that is, to distinguish between clusters of syllables that form a word and clusters that could be different words strung together. In a pioneering study to test this notion, Saffran and colleagues (1996) exposed 8-month-old babies to recordings of trios of syllables that followed each other more frequently and syllables that were at the junctions between these trios and followed each other less frequently. The latter had a lower conditional probability, representing how words compared with nonwords have syllable combinations that occur more frequently. After a period of exposure to the recording, the time the babies spent looking toward a sound source varied depending on whether they heard a trio of syllables that had appeared together more frequently or one that had appeared together less frequently. This increased attention time served as a measure of their understanding of the difference between what they had been exposed to as "words" versus nonwords. Many subsequent studies have both replicated this finding and extended it to demonstrate that the same sensitivity can be seen in babies' parsing of music (Saffran et al., 1999) and even of how visual displays are organized (Kirkham et al., 2002).

Sensitivity to Sampling Statistics

Babies and young children are sensitive to the statistical likelihood of events, which reveals that they both are attuned to regularities they observe in the world and use such regularities to draw inferences and make predictions based on their observations. In one set of studies, for example, 11-month-old babies were shown a box full of many red balls and only a few white balls. The babies were surprised when balls were poured out of the box and all of them happened to be white or when someone reached into the opaque box and happened to retrieve all white balls. Thus the babies were registering the low proportion of white balls and recognizing the improbability of these events (Xu and Denison, 2009). In an important variation, however, if the experimenter looked into the box as she picked up the balls, the babies were not surprised if all white balls were selected. This finding suggests that babies' implicit knowledge of theory of mind—in this example, understanding that a person can deliberately select objects—will trump their reasoning based on the sampling distribution.

BOX 4-3
Examples of Understanding Causal Inference

Distinguishing Causal Variables

One of the first studies of children's understanding of causal inference showed that children can rule out one variable and isolate another (Gopnik et al., 2001). Preschool children were presented with a machine and told that "blickets" make the machine go. Block A placed on the machine always made it go. Block B was associated with the machine turning on but only when Block A was also on the machine. Children correctly identified Block A as the "blicket" and not Block B. They were also able to intervene correctly to make the machine stop by removing Block A and not Block B.

Using Exploratory Play to Understand Causality

Schulz and Bonawitz (2007) demonstrated that children use exploratory play to help them recognize causal relationships. They presented children (mean age 57 months) with a toy with an ambiguous causal mechanism, being one of two possibilities, or a toy with an unambiguous causal mechanism. In the ambiguous case, children and an adult played with a box that had two levers, one controlled by the child and one by the adult. On the count of three, both the child and the experimenter pressed their levers, and two toys popped out of the box. The child and the experimenter simultaneously released the levers, and both toys disappeared into the box. The ambiguity lay in whether one or both of the levers caused the toys to emerge from the box. In the other case, children had a couple of trials in which they and the experimenter depressed the levers simultaneously on the count of three, but also had trials in which they depressed their levers individually; in the latter cases, the child's lever controlled one toy, while the experimenter's lever controlled the other. After this interaction, a different toy was brought out, and children could play with either of the toys. Children who witnessed ambiguous evidence for the causal mechanism played with the familiar toy more than the novel toy, while children who had seen unambiguous evidence for the mechanism elected to play more with a novel toy. The causal ambiguity of the familiar toy motivated children to continue their exploration. Schulz and Bonawitz (2007, p. 1049) conclude that "the exploratory play of even very young children appears to reflect some of the logic of scientific inquiry."

Using an Understanding of Causality to Solve Problems

Babies also can use the statistical distribution of events to infer the reason for failed actions and then deploy strategies to solve the problem. Suppose babies cannot get a toy to work. Is the failure because the toy is broken or because they do not know how to use it properly? In one series of studies (Gweon and Schulz, 2011), 16-month-old babies witnessed two adults pressing a button on a toy that

continued

BOX 4-3 Continued

then did or did not play music. In one condition, one of the adults succeeded twice in getting the toy to play, while the other adult failed twice. In the other condition, each adult failed once and succeeded once. Babies were then handed a similar toy to play with that failed to produce the music when they pressed the button. Babies who earlier saw one adult succeed and the other fail turned to their mothers for help in getting the toy to work. In contrast, babies who saw each adult succeed and fail once reached for a different toy. Thus, depending on the prior information babies observed, they inferred that there was either some lack of ability on their part or some problem with the toy. When they inferred that the problem was with their ability, they turned to their mother for help; when they inferred that the toy was broken, they reached for another one. Through observing intentional, goal-directed behavior of others, preverbal babies are quickly identifying the goal, registering patterns of others' successes and failures, using those statistical patterns to infer the more likely causes of failure, and subsequently recruiting that information to interpret their own failure and guide their choice of appropriate solutions.

In one study, for example, 9-month-old babies saw an adult either reach for an object (a noncommunicative act) or point to an object (a communicative act). The entire display was then screened from view, and after a brief delay, the curtains were opened, and babies saw either the same object in a new location or a new object in the same location. The short delay imposed a memory requirement, and for babies this young, encoding both the location and the identity of the object taxes their memory. The location of the object will typically be more salient and memorable to babies than the object's properties, but the prediction of this study was that babies who saw the adult point to the object would construe the pointing as a communicative act—"this adult is showing me something"—and would thus be more likely to encode the properties as opposed to the location of the object. Babies' looking times served as a measure of their surprise at or interest in an unexpected event. As predicted, babies appeared to encode different aspects of the event in the different conditions. When they had previously witnessed the adult reaching for the object, they were surprised when the object was in a new location but showed no renewed interest when there was a different object in the old location. In contrast, when babies first saw an adult point to the object, they were surprised when a new object appeared in the old location but not when the old object had changed locations (Yoon et al., 2008).

**Infants' Sensitivity to Teaching Cues:
Implications for Adults**

*Babies have the capacity to realize when someone is communicating
something for their benefit and therefore to construe information differently
than when they merely witness it. When adults use face-to-face contact, call
a baby's name, and point for the baby's benefit, these signals lead babies
to recognize that someone is teaching them something, and this awareness
can affect how and what they learn.*

The significance of eye contact and other communication cues also
is evident in research on whether, how, and when young children learn
from video and other forms of digital media. Experiments conducted with
24-month-olds, for example, revealed that they can learn from a person
on a video screen if that person is communicating with them through a
webcam-like environment, but they showed no evidence of learning from
a prerecorded video of that person. The webcam environment included
social cues, such as back-and-forth conversation and other forms of social
contact that are not possible in prerecorded video. Other studies found
that toddlers learned verbs better during Skype video chats than during
prerecorded video chats that did not allow for authentic eye contact or
back-and-forth interaction (Roseberry et al., 2014; Troseth et al., 2006).
(See also Chapter 6 for more on technology and learning.)

The benefits of communicative pedagogical contexts for the conceptual
development of preschool children also have been investigated. In one set
of studies, 4-year-old children were exposed to a novel object's function
either by seeing an adult deliberately use the object or by seeing the adult
deliberately use the object after maintaining eye contact with the child and
saying "watch this." In both conditions, children noticed the object's property and attempted to elicit it from other similar objects. But when those
objects were doctored to be nonfunctional, the children in the nonpedagogical condition quickly abandoned their attempts to elicit the property and
played with the objects in some other way. Children who saw the same
evidence but with direct communication for their benefit persisted in trying
to elicit the property from other objects (Butler and Markman, 2012a,b).
In other words, children's conviction that other similar objects should have
the same unforeseen property was bolstered by their belief that the adult
was performing the function for their benefit. Moreover the intentional (but
nonpedagogical) condition versus the pedagogical condition produced strik-
ingly different conceptions of the function (Butler and Markman, 2014).
Four- and 5-year-old children witnessed an object's function and were then
given a set of objects to play with. Some objects were identical in appear-

ance to the first object, while some differed in color (in one study) or shape (in another). Half of the objects of each color (or shape) had the unforeseen property, and half did not. Children were told they could play with the objects for a while and then should put them away in their appropriate boxes when done. The goal was to see whether children would sort the objects by the salient perceptual property (color or shape) or by function. Children in the pedagogical condition viewed the function as definitive and classified the objects by systematically testing each to see whether it had the function, while children in the nonpedagogical condition sorted by the salient color or shape. Thus, identical evidence is construed differently when children believe it has been produced for their benefit.

Effects of Adult Language on Cognition

Understanding the power of language is important for people who interact with children. Simple labels can help children unify disparate-looking things into coherent categories; thus labeling is a powerful way to foster conceptual development. Labels also can reify categories or concepts in ways that may or may not be intended. For example, frequently hearing "boys and girls" line up for recess, quiet down, etc. implicitly reinforces gender as an important dimension, compared with saying "children." Box 4-4 presents examples of linguistic distinctions that affect children's construction of conceptual systems.

Effects of Language Used by Adults on Children's Cognitive Development: Implications for Adults

Awareness of the benefits and pitfalls of the language used by adults is important for people who interact with children. The language used by adults affects cognitive growth and learning in children in many subtle ways. Labeling is a powerful way to foster conceptual development. Simple labels can help children unify disparate things into coherent categories, but can also have the unintended consequence of reinforcing categories or concepts that are not desirable.

BOX 4-4
Examples of the Effects of Adult Language on Cognition

Effects of Labeling Objects on Inductive Reasoning

Some kinds of categories—two round balls, for example—are fairly easy to form, such that even babies treat the objects as similar. But many objects that adults view as members of the same category are perceptually dissimilar, and children would not, on their own, categorize them together. Some categories have very diverse members: consider a greyhound and a bichon frise as dogs, or a tie and a raincoat as clothing. Atypical members of categories—thinking of a penguin as a bird, for example—also are difficult for children to categorize on their own. Hearing perceptually diverse objects called by the same label enables children to treat them as members of the same category, which in turn affects the kinds of inductive inferences children draw about them (cf. Gelman, 2003). Even very young children will base their inductive inferences on the category to which objects belong rather than their perceptual features when the objects are labeled. Children who hear, for example, a flamingo called a "bird" and are told that it feeds mashed-up food to its babies whereas a bat feeds milk to its babies will judge that a raven, called a bird, will feed its babies mashed-up food even though it looks more like a bat than a flamingo (Gelman and Markman, 1987). The power of labels to influence children's inductive reasoning has been demonstrated in children as young as 13 months old. Thus, the simple act of providing a label for objects affects children's learning, and what might appear to be merely acquisition of vocabulary, actually has important consequences in shaping a child's conceptual development and knowledge. Providing a common label for perceptually disparate objects also is a way of transmitting cultural knowledge to children. This effect of labeling objects speaks to one of the ways in which ordinary interaction with babies enriches their cognitive development and early learning (Graham et al., 2004). While categorization has many benefits for developing inductive reasoning, it can also ultimately be associated with inferences that exaggerate differences between categories and similarities within categories. This may be linked to some undesirable consequences, such as stereotyping or prejudice based on these inferences (Master et al., 2012).

Effects of Generic Language on Children's Cognition

Generic language—for example, "dogs bark" rather than "this dog is barking"—conveys information about an entire category. It is impossible for any individual to experience first-hand all of the exemplars of a category. The use of generics is thus an indispensable way of learning about the category as a whole. Generics are a powerful way of conveying general facts, properties, or information about a category, and those generalizations often can stand even in the face of counterexamples (Gelman, 2003). The generic statement "dogs bark" is considered true, for example, even though some dogs do not bark and the universal statement "all dogs bark" can be falsified by a counterexample. Therefore, not only

continued

BOX 4-4 Continued

are generic statements an important means of conveying generalizations, but they also lead to a stable form of knowledge that is highly resistant to counterexamples. This stability has many advantages, but as with categorization, it also can be problematic—for example, generic statements about social categories can reify the categories and beliefs about them. When an individual encounters members of a social category that do not share the relevant trait or behavior, those people may then be seen as exceptions, but the generalization will still stand.

Properties conveyed by generics also are construed as central or essential to the category (Cimpian and Markman, 2009). Four- and 5-year-old children given the same information conveyed using generic versus nongeneric phrases interpret the information quite differently. Hearing, for example, that "this snake has holes in its teeth" and then being asked why, preschool children come up with explanations such as it doesn't brush its teeth so it has cavities or it bit into a rock. But hearing that "snakes have holes in their teeth" and then being asked why, children come up with explanations such as they squirt poison out of the holes. Subtle differences in generic versus nongeneric language used to convey information to children can shape the kinds of generalizations they make, the strength of those generaliza-tions, and the extent to which properties are considered central or defining of the category. Here, too, generics can sometimes play an unwanted role (Cimpian and Markman, 2011). Preschoolers who heard that "girls are really good at a game called gorp" would explain this by referring to more central, inherent causes—for example, because girls are smart. Those children who heard "this girl is really good at a game called gorp" would more commonly invoke effort and practice. Dweck and colleagues have shown that children who believe an ability is inherent and fixed are more likely to give up when faced with failure and to lose motivation for and interest in a task, while children who view an ability as malleable are more likely to take on the challenge and work to improve their skill. Therefore, adults' use of generic rather than nongeneric praise for children may undermine their achievement motivation, leading them to believe that their performance is due to an inherent ability (or lack thereof) rather than to effort, practice, and persistence (Cimpian, 2010; Cimpian et al., 2007).

Conclusions About Cognitive Development and Early Learning

Learning begins prenatally, and children are not only "ready to learn" but already actively learning from the time they are born. From birth, children's minds are active and inquisitive, and early thinking is insight-ful and complex. Many of the foundations of sophisticated forms of learning, including those important to academic success, are established in the earliest years of life.

Development and early learning can be supported continuously as a child develops, and early knowledge and skills inform and influence future learning. When adults understand how the mind develops, what progress children make in their cognitive abilities, and how active inquiry and learning are children's natural inclination, they can foster cognitive growth by supporting children's active engagement with new experiences and providing developmentally appropriate stimulation of new learning through responsive, secure, and sustained caregiving relationships.

Implications for Care and Education Settings and Practitioners

The research findings on cognitive development in young children summarized above reflect an evolving understanding of how the mind develops during the early years and should be part of the core knowledge that influences how care and education professionals support young children's learning, as discussed in Chapter 7. Many of these concepts describe cognitive processes that are implicit. By contrast with the *explicit* knowledge that older children and adults can put into words, *implicit* knowledge is tacit or nonconscious understanding that cannot readily be consciously described (see, e.g., Mandler, 2004). Examples of implicit knowledge in very young children include many of the early achievements discussed above, such as their implicit theories of living things and of the human mind and their nonconscious awareness of the statistical frequency of the associations among speech sounds in the language they are hearing. Infants' and young children's "statistical learning" does not mean that they can count, nor are their "implicit theories" consciously worked out. Not all early learning is implicit, of course. Very young children are taking significant strides in their explicit knowledge of language, the functioning of objects, and the characteristics of people and animals in the world around them. Thus early learning occurs on two levels: the growth of knowledge that is visible and apparent, and the growth of implicit understanding that is sometimes more difficult to observe.

This distinction between implicit and explicit learning can be confusing to early childhood practitioners (and parents), who often do not observe or recognize evidence for the sophisticated implicit learning—or even the explicit learning—taking place in the young children in their care. Many of the astonishingly competent, active, and insightful things that research on early cognitive development shows are going on in young children's minds are not transparent in their behavior. Instead, toddlers and young children seem highly distractable, emotional, and not very capable of managing their impulses. All of these observations about young children are true, but at the same time, their astonishing growth in language skills, their very different ways of interacting with objects and living things, and their efforts to share attention (such as through pointing) or goals (such as through helping) with an adult suggest that the cognitive achievements demonstrated in experimental settings have relevance to their everyday behavior.

This point is especially important because the cognitive abilities of young children are so easily underestimated. In the past, for example, the prevalent belief that infants lack conceptual knowledge meant that parents and practitioners missed opportunities to explore with them cause and effect, number, or symbolic play. Similarly, the view that young children are egocentric caused many adults to conclude that there was little benefit to talking about people's feelings until children were older—this despite the fact that most people could see how attentive young children were to others' emotions and how curious about their causes.

In light of these observations, how do early educators contribute to the cognitive growth of children in their first 3 years? One way is by providing appropriate support for the learning that is occurring in these very young children (see, e.g., Copple et al., 2013). Using an abundance of child-directed language during social interaction, playing counting games (e.g., while stacking blocks), putting into words what a classroom pet can do or why somebody looks sad, exploring together what happens when objects collide, engaging in imitative play and categorization (sorting) games—these and other shared activities can be cognitively provocative as long as they remain within the young child's capacities for interest and attention. They also build on understandings that young children are implicitly developing related to language; number; object characteristics; and implicit theories of animate and inanimate objects, physical causality, and people's minds. The purpose of these and other activities is not just to provide young children with cognitive stimulation, but also to embed that stimulation in social interaction that provokes young children's interest, elicits their curiosity, and provides an emotional context that enables them to focus their thinking on new discoveries. The central and consistent feature of all these activities is the young child's shared activity with an adult who thoughtfully capitalizes on his or her interests to provoke cognitive growth. The implications for instructional practices and curricula for educators working with infants and toddlers are discussed further in Chapter 6.

Another way that educators contribute to the cognitive growth of infants and toddlers is through the emotional support they provide (Jamison et al., 2014). Emotional support is afforded by the educator's responsiveness to young children's interests and needs (including each child's individual temperament), the educator's development of warm relationships with children, and the educator's accessibility to help when young children are exploring on their own or interacting with other children (Thompson, 2006). Emotional support of this kind is important not only as a positive accompaniment to the task of learning but also as an essential prerequisite to the cognitive and attentional engagement necessary for young children to benefit from learning opportunities. Because early capacities to self-regulate emotion are so limited, a young child's frustration or distress can easily derail cognitive engagement in new discoveries, and children can lose focus because their attentional self-regulatory skills are comparably limited. An educator's emotional support can help keep young children focused and persistent, and can also increase the likelihood that early learning experiences will yield successful outcomes. Moreover, the secure attachments that young children develop with educators contribute to an expectation of adult support that enables young children to approach learning opportunities more positively and confidently. Emotional support and socioemotional development are discussed further later in this chapter.

The characteristics of early learning call for specific curricular approaches and thoughtful professional learning for educators, but it is also true that less formal opportunities to stimulate early cognitive growth emerge naturally in children's everyday interactions with a responsive adult. Consider, for example, a parent or other caregiver interacting with a 1-year-old over a shape-sorting toy. As they together are choosing shapes of different colors and the child is placing them in the appropriate (or inappropriate) cutout in the bin, the adult can accompany this task with language that describes what they are doing and why, and narrates the child's experiences of puzzlement, experimentation, and accomplishment. The adult may also be using number words to count the blocks as they are deposited. The baby's attention is focused by the constellation of adult behavior—infant-directed language, eye contact, and responsiveness—that signals the adult's teaching, and this "pedagogical orientation" helps focus the young child's attention and involvement. The back-and-forth interaction of child and adult activity provides stimulus for the baby's developing awareness of the adult's thinking (e.g., she looks at each block before commenting on it or acting intentionally on it) and use of language (e.g., colors are identified for each block, and generic language is used to describe blocks in general). In this interaction, moreover, the baby is developing both expectations for what this adult is like—safe, positive, responsive—and skills for social interaction (such as turn taking). Although these qualities and the learning derived from them are natural accompaniments to child-focused responsive social interaction with an adult caregiver, the caregiver's awareness of the child's cognitive growth at this time contributes significantly to the adult's ability to intentionally support new discovery and learning.

As children further develop cognitively as preschoolers, their growth calls for both similar and different behavior by the adults who work with them. While the educator's emotional support and responsiveness remain important, children from age 3 to 5 years become different kinds of thinkers than they were as infants and toddlers (NRC, 2001). First, they are more consciously aware of their knowledge—much more of their understanding is now *explicit*. This means they are more capable of deliberately enlisting what they know into new learning situations, although they are not yet as competent or strategic in doing so as they will be in the primary grades. When faced with a problem or asked a question, they are more capable of offering an answer based on what they know, even when their knowledge is limited. Second, preschoolers are more competent in learning from their deliberate efforts to do so, such as trial-and-error or informal experimentation. While their success in this regard pales by comparison with the more strategic efforts of a grade-schooler, their "let's find out" approach to new challenges reflects their greater behavioral and mental competence in figuring things out. Third, preschoolers also are intuitive and experiential, learning by doing rather than figuring things out "in the head." This makes shared activities with educators and peers potent opportunities for cognitive growth.

Nonetheless, the potential to underestimate the cognitive abilities of young children persists in the preschool and kindergarten years. In one study, for example, children's actual performance was six to eight times what was estimated by their own preschool teachers and other experts in consulting, teacher education, educational research, and educational development (Claessens et al., 2014; Van den Heuvel-Panhuizen, 1996). Such underestimation represents a lost opportunity that can hinder children's progress. A study in kindergarten revealed that teachers spent most of their time in basic content that children already knew, yet the children benefited more from advanced reading and mathematics content (Claessens et al., 2014)—an issue discussed in depth in Chapter 6. Unfortunately, when care and education professionals underestimate children's abilities to understand and learn subject-matter content, the negative impact is greatest on those with the fewest prior learning experiences (Bennett et al., 1984; Clements and Sarama, 2014).

Conversely, when educators practice in a way that is cognizant of the cognitive progress of children at this age, they can more deliberately enlist the preschool child's existing knowledge and skills into new learning situations. One example is interactive storybook reading, in which children describe the pictures and label their elements while the adult and child ask and answer questions of each other about the narrative. Language and literacy skills also are fostered at this age by the adult's use of varied vocabulary in interaction with the child, as well as by extending conversation on a single topic (rather than frequently switching topics), asking open-ended questions of the child, and initiating conversation related to the child's experiences and interests (Dickinson, 2003; Dickinson and Porche, 2011; Dickinson and Tabors, 2001). In each case, dialogic conversation about text or experience draws on while also extending children's prior knowledge and language skills. Language and literacy skills are discussed further in a subsequent section of this chapter, as well as in Chapter 6.

Another implication of these cognitive changes is that educators can engage preschool children's intentional activity in new learning opportunities. Children's interest in learning by doing is naturally suited to experimental inquiry related to science or other kinds of inquiry-based learning involving hypothesis and testing, especially in light of the implicit theories of living things and physical causality that children bring to such inquiry (Samarapungavan et al., 2011). In a similar manner, board games can provide a basis for learning and extending number concepts. In several experimental demonstrations, when preschool children played number board games specifically designed to foster their mental representations of numerical quantities, they showed improvements in number line estimates, count-on skill, numerical identification, and other important quantitative concepts (Laski and Siegler, 2014).

Other research has shown that instructional strategies that promote higher-level thinking, creativity, and even abstract understanding, such as talking about ideas or about future events, is associated with greater cognitive achievement by preschool-age children (e.g., Diamond et al., 2013; Mashburn et al., 2008). For example, when educators point out how cardinal numbers can be used to describe diverse sets of elements (four blocks, four children, 4 o'clock), it helps them generalize an abstract concept ("fourness") that describes a set rather than the characteristics of each element alone. These activities also can be integrated into other instructional practices during a typical day.

Another implication of the changes in young children's thinking during the preschool years concerns the motivational features of early learning. Preschool-age children are developing a sense of themselves and their competencies, including their academic skills (Marsh et al., 1998, 2002). Their beliefs about their abilities in reading, counting, vocabulary, number games, and other academic competencies derive from several sources, including spontaneous social comparison with other children and feedback from teachers (and parents) concerning their achievement and the reasons they have done well or poorly. These beliefs influence, in turn, children's self-confidence, persistence, intrinsic motivation to succeed, and other characteristics that may be described as learning skills (and are discussed more extensively later in this chapter). Consequently, how teachers provide performance feedback to young children and support for their self-confidence in learning situations also is an important predictor of children's academic success (Hamre, 2014).

In the early elementary years, children's cognitive processes develop further, which accordingly influences the strategies for educators in early elementary classrooms. Primary grade children are using more complex vocabulary and grammar. They are growing in their ability to make mental representations, but they still have difficulty grasping abstract concepts without the aid of real-life references and materials (Tomlinson, 2014). This is a critical time for children to develop confidence in all areas of life. Children at this age show more independence from parents and family, while friendship, being liked and accepted by peers, becomes more important. Being in school most of the day means greater contact with a larger world, and children begin to develop a greater understanding of their place in that world (CDC, 2014).

Children's growing ability to self-regulate their emotions also is evident in this period (discussed more extensively later in this chapter). Children understand their own feelings more and more, and learn better ways to describe experiences and express thoughts and feelings. They better understand the consequences of their actions, and their focus on concern for others grows. They are very observant, are willing to play cooperatively and work in teams, and can resolve some conflicts without seeking adult intervention (CDC, 2014). Children also come to understand that they can affect others' perception of their emotions by changing their affective displays (Aloise-Young, 1993). Children who are unable to self-regulate have emotional difficulties that may interfere with their learning. Just as with younger children, significant adults in a child's life can help the child learn to self-regulate (Tomlinson, 2014).

Children's increasing self-regulation means they have a greater ability to follow instructions independently in a manner that would not be true of preschool or younger children. Educators can rely on the growing cognitive abilities in elementary school children in using instructional approaches that depend more independently on children's own discoveries, their use of alternative inquiry strategies, and their greater persistence in problem solving. Educators in these settings are scaffolding the skills that began to develop earlier, so that children are able to gradually apply those skills with less and less external support. This serves as a bridge to succeeding in upper primary grades, so if students lack necessary knowledge and skills in any domain of development and learning, their experience during the early elementary grades is crucial in helping them gain those competencies.

Building on many of the themes that have emerged from this discussion, the following sections continue by looking in more depth at cognitive development with respect to learning specific subjects and then at other major elements of development, including general learning competencies, socioemotional development, and physical development and health.

LEARNING SPECIFIC SUBJECTS

Interrelationships among different kinds of skills and abilities contribute to young children's acquisition of content knowledge and competencies, which form a foundation for later academic success. These skills and abilities include the general cognitive development discussed above, the general learning competencies that allow children to control their own attention and thinking; and the emotion regulation that allows children to control their own emotions and participate in classroom activities in a productive way (the latter two are discussed in sections later in this chapter). Still another important category of skills and abilities, the focus of this section, is subject-matter content knowledge and skills, such as competencies needed specifically for learning language and literacy or mathematics.

Content knowledge and skills are acquired through a developmental process. As children learn about a topic, they progress through increasingly sophisticated levels of thinking with accompanying cognitive components. These developmental learning paths can be used as the core of a learning trajectory through which students can be supported by educators who understand both the content and those levels of thinking. Each learning trajectory has three parts: a goal (to develop a certain competence in a topic), a developmental progression (children constructing each level of thinking in turn), and instructional activities (tasks and teaching practices designed to enable thinking at each higher level). Learning trajectories also promote the learning of skills and concepts together—an effective approach that leads to both mastery and more fluent, flexible use of skills, as well as to superior conceptual understanding (Fuson and Kwon, 1992; National Mathematics Advisory Panel, 2008). See Chapter 6 for additional discussion of using learning trajectories and other instructional practices.

Every subject area requires specific content knowledge and skills that are acquired through developmental learning processes. It is not possible to cover the specifics here for every subject area a young child learns. To maintain a feasible scope, this chapter covers two core subject areas: (1) language and literacy and (2) mathematics. This scope is not meant to imply that learning in other areas, such as science, engineering, social studies, or the arts, is unimportant or less subject specific. Rather, these two were selected because they are foundational for other subject areas and for later academic achievement, and because how they are learned has been well studied in young children compared with many other subject areas.

Language and Literacy

Children's language development and literacy development are central to each other. The development of language and literacy includes knowledge and skills in such areas as vocabulary, syntax, grammar, phonological awareness, writing, reading, comprehension, and discourse skills. The following sections address the development of language and literacy skills, including the relationship between the two; the role of the language-learning environment; socioeconomic disparities in early language environments; and language and literacy development in dual language learners.

Development of Oral Language Skills

Language skills build in a developmental progression over time as children increase their vocabulary, average sentence length, complexity and sophistication of sentence structure and grammar, and ability to express new ideas through words (Kipping et al., 2012). Catts and Kamhi (1999) define five features of language that both work independently and interact as children develop language skills: phonology (speech sounds of language), semantics (meanings of words and phrases), morphology (meaningful parts of words and word tenses), syntax (rules for combining and ordering words in phrases), and pragmatics (appropriate use of language in context). The first three parameters combined (phonology, semantics, and morphology) enable listening and speaking vocabulary to develop, and they also contribute to the ability to read individual words. All five features of language contribute to the ability to understand sentences, whether heard or read (O'Connor, 2014). Thus, while children's development of listening and speaking abilities are important in their own right, oral language development also contributes to reading skills.

Developing oral communication skills are closely linked to the interactions and social bonds between adults and children. As discussed earlier in this chapter, parents' and caregivers' talk with infants stimulates—and affects—language comprehension long before children utter their first words. This comprehension begins with pragmatics—the social aspects of language that include facial and body language as well as words, such that infants recognize positive (and negative) interactions. Semantics (understanding meanings of words and clusters of words that are related) soon follows, in which toddlers link objects and their attributes to words. Between the ages of 2 and 4, most children show dramatic growth in language, particularly in understanding the meanings of words, their interrelationships, and grammatical forms (Scarborough, 2001).

Karmiloff and Karmiloff-Smith (2001) suggest that children build webs among words with similar semantics, which leads to broader generalizations among classes of related words. When adults are responsive to children's questions and new experiences, children expand their knowledge of words and the relationships among them. Then, as new words arise from conversation, storytelling, and book reading, these words are linked to existing webs to further expand the store of words children understand through receptive language and use in their own conversation. The more often adults use particular words in conversation with young children, the sooner children will use those words in their own speech (Karmiloff and Karmiloff-Smith, 2001). Research has linked the size of vocabulary of 2-year-olds to their reading comprehension through fifth grade (Lee, 2011).

One of the best-documented methods for improving children's vocabularies is interactive storybook reading between children and their caregivers (O'Connor, 2014). Conversations as stories are read improve children's vocabulary (Hindman et al., 2008; Weizman and Snow, 2001), especially when children are encouraged to build on the possibilities of storybooks by following their interests (Whitehurst et al., 1988; Zucker et al., 2013). Book reading stimulates conversation outside the immediate context—for example, children ask questions about the illustrations that may or may not be central to the story. This introduces new words, which children attach to the features of the illustrations they point out and incorporate into book-centered conversations. This type of language, removed from the here and now, is decontextualized language. Children exposed to experiences not occurring in their immediate environment are more likely to understand and use decontextualized language (Hindman et al., 2008). Repeated routines also contribute to language development. As books are read repeatedly, children become familiar with the vocabulary of the story and their conversations can be elaborated. Routines help children with developmental delays acquire language and use it more intelligibly (van Kleek, 2004).

Conversation around a story's content and emphasis on specific words in the text (i.e., the phonological and print features of words alongside their meanings) have long-term effects (Zucker et al., 2013). The quality of adult readers' interactions with children appears to be especially important to children's vocabulary growth (see also Coyne et al., 2009; Justice et al., 2005). In a study with preschool children, Zucker and colleagues (2013) found that teachers' intentional talk during reading had a longer-lasting effect on the children's language skills than the frequency of the teachers' reading to the children. Moreover, the effect of the teachers' talk during reading was not moderated by the children's initial vocabulary or literacy abilities. The long-term effect of high-quality teacher–child book-centered interactions in preschool lasted through the end of first grade.

New research shows that the effects of interactive reading also hold when adapted to the use of digital media as a platform for decontextualized language and other forms of language development. A study of videobooks showed that when adults were trained to use dialogic questioning techniques with the videos, 3-year-olds learned new words and recalled the books' storylines (Strouse et al., 2013). However, a few studies of e-books also have shown that the bells and whistles of the devices can get in the way of those back-and-forth conversations if the readers and the e-book designers are not intentional about using the e-books to develop content knowledge and language skills (Parish-Morris et al., 2013). (See also the discussion of effective use of technology in instruction in Chapter 6.)

Alongside developing depth of vocabulary (including the meaning of words and phrases and their appropriate use in context), other important parameters of language development are syntax (rules for combining and ordering words in phrases, as in rules of grammar) and morphology (meaningful parts of words and word tenses). Even before the age of 2, toddlers parse a speech stream into grammatical units (Hawthorne and Gerken, 2014). Long before preschool, most children join words together into sentences and begin to use the rules of grammar (i.e., syntax) to change the forms of words (e.g., adding *s* for plurals or *ed* for past tense). Along with these morphemic changes to words, understanding syntax helps children order the words and phrases in their sentences to convey and to change meaning. Before children learn to read, the rules of syntax help them derive meaning from what they hear and convey meaning through speech. Cunningham and Zibulsky (2014, p. 45) describe syntactic development as "the ability to understand the structure of a sentence, including its tense, subject, and object."

Although syntactic understanding develops for most children through conversation with adults and older children, children also use these rules of syntax to extract meaning from printed words. This becomes an important reading skill after first grade, when text meaning is less likely to be supported with pictures. Construction of sentences with passive voice and other complex, decontextualized word forms are more likely to be found in books and stories than in directive conversations with young children. An experimental study illustrates the role of exposure to syntactic structures in the development of language comprehension (Vasilyeva et al., 2006). Four-year-olds listened to stories in active or passive voice. After listening to ten stories, their understanding of passages containing these syntactic structures was assessed. Although students in both groups understood and could use active voice (similar to routine conversation), those who listened to stories with passive voice scored higher on comprehension of this structure.

Children's understanding of morphology—the meaningful parts of words—begins in preschool for most children, as they recognize and use inflected endings to represent verb tense (e.g., -ing, -ed, -s) and plurals, and continues in the primary grades as children understand and use prefixes and suffixes. By second and third grade, children's use of morphemes predicts their reading comprehension (Nagy et al., 2006; Nunes et al., 2012).

Development of Literacy Skills

Literacy skills follow a developmental trajectory such that early skills and stages lead into more complex and integrated skills and stages (Adams, 1990). For example, phonemic awareness is necessary for decoding printed words (Ball and Blachman, 1991; Bradley and Bryant, 1983; O'Connor et al., 1995), but it is not sufficient. Students need to understand the alphabetic principle (that speech sounds can be represented by letters of the alphabet, which is how speech is captured in print) before they can use their phonemic awareness (the ability to hear and manipulate sounds in spoken words) to independently decode words they have never seen before (Byrne and Fielding-Barnsley, 1989; O'Connor and Jenkins, 1995). Thus, instruction that combines skill development for 4- to 6-year-old children in phonemic awareness, letter knowledge, and conceptual understanding and use of these skills is more effective than teaching the skills in isolation (Byrne and Fielding-Barnsley, 1989; O'Connor and Jenkins, 1995).

Seminal theories and studies of reading describe an inextricable link between language development and reading achievement (e.g., Byrne and Fielding-Barnsley, 1995; Gough and Tunmer, 1986; Hoover and Gough, 1990; Johnston and Kirby, 2006; Joshi and Aaron, 2000; Tunmer and Hoover, 1993; Vellutino et al., 2007). Early oral language competencies predict later literacy (Pearson and Hiebert, 2010). Not only do young children with stronger oral language competencies acquire new language skills faster than students with poorly developed oral language competencies (Dickinson and Porche, 2011), but they also learn key literacy skills faster, such as phonemic awareness and understanding of the alphabetic principle (Cooper et al., 2002). Both of these literacy skills in turn facilitate learning to read in kindergarten and first grade. By preschool and kindergarten listening and speaking abilities have long-term impacts on children's reading and writing abilities in third through fifth grade (Lee, 2011; Nation and Snowling, 1999; Sénéchal et al., 2006).

Vocabulary development (a complex and integrative feature of language that grows continuously) and reading words (a skill that most children master by third or fourth grade) (Ehri, 2005) are reciprocally related, and both reading words accurately and understanding what words mean contribute to reading comprehension (Gough et al., 1996). Because comprehending and learning from text depend largely upon a deep understanding of the language used to communicate the ideas and concepts expressed, oral language skills (i.e., vocabulary, syntax, listening comprehension) are at the core of this relationship between language and reading (NICHD Early Child Care Research Network, 2005; Perfetti, 1985; Perfetti and Hart, 2002). For example, children with larger speaking vocabularies in preschool may have an easier time with phoneme awareness and the alphabetic principle because they can draw on more words to explore the similarities among the sounds they hear in spoken words and the letters that form the words (Metsala and Walley, 1998). Each word a child knows can influence how well she or he understands a sentence that uses that word, which in turn can influence the acquisition of knowledge and the ability to learn new words. A stronger speaking and listening vocabulary provides a deeper and wider field of words students can attempt to match to printed words. Being bogged down by figuring out what a given word means slows the rate of information processing and limits what is learned from a sentence. Thus, differences in early vocabulary can have cascading, cumulative effects (Fernald et al., 2013; Huttenlocher, 1998). The transition from speaking and listening to reading and writing is not a smooth one for many children. Although a well-developed vocabulary can make that transition easier, many children also have difficulty learning the production and meanings of words. Longitudinal studies of reading disability have found that 70 percent of poor readers had a history of language difficulties (Catts et al., 1999).

Conclusion About the Development of Language and Literacy Skills

The oral language and vocabulary children learn through interactions with parents, siblings, and caregivers and through high-quality interactions with educators provide the foundation for later literacy and for learning across all subject areas, as well as for their socioemotional well-being. The language interactions children experience at home and in school influence their developing minds and their understanding of concepts and ideas.

Role of the Language-Learning Environment

Today's science of reading development focuses more broadly than on teaching children to read the actual words on a page. As stressed throughout this report, young children's development entails a back-and-forth process of social interactions with knowledgeable others in their environment (Bruner, 1978; NRC and IOM, 2000; Vygotsky, 1978, 1986), and research has focused on the language of these interactions, examining how children's linguistic experiences influence aspects of their development over time, including their literacy development. The daily talk to which children are exposed and in which they participate is essential for developing their minds—a key ingredient for building their knowledge of the world and their understanding of concepts and ideas. In turn, this conceptual knowledge is a cornerstone of reading success.

The bulk of the research on early linguistic experiences has investigated language input in the home environment, demonstrating the features of caregivers' (usually the mother's) speech that promote language development among young children. The evidence accumulated emphasizes the importance of the quantity of communicative input (i.e., the number of words and sentences spoken) as well as the quality of that input, as measured by the variety of words and syntactic structures used (for relevant reviews, see Rowe, 2012; Vasilyeva and Waterfall, 2011). Because children's language development is sensitive to these inputs, variability in children's language-based interactions in the home environment explains some of the variance in their language development.

A smaller but growing and compelling research base is focused on how children's literacy skills are influenced by language use in early care and education settings and schools—for example, linguistic features of these settings or elementary school teachers' speech and its relationship to children's reading outcomes (Greenwood et al., 2011). This research has particularly relevant implications for educational practices (discussed further in Chapter 6).

The language environment of the classroom can function as a support for developing the kind of language that is characteristic of the school curriculum—for example, giving children opportunities to develop the sophisticated vocabulary and complex syntax found in texts, beginning at a very early age (Schleppegrell, 2003; Snow and Uccelli, 2009). Moreover, advances in cognitive science suggest that it is not enough to be immersed in environments that offer multiple opportunities for exposure to varied and rich language experiences. Rather, the process also needs to be socially mediated through more knowledgeable persons who can impart their knowledge to the learner; again, social interaction is a critical component of cognitive development and learning. Early childhood settings and elementary classrooms thus not only present opportunities for exposure to varied language- and literacy-rich activities (whether written or spoken), but also provide a person who is expert in mediating the learning process—the educator.

Research demonstrates that teachers' use of high-quality language is linked to individual differences in language and literacy skills; this work likewise shows the substantial variation in the quality of teacher talk in early childhood classrooms (e.g., Bowers and Vasilyeva, 2011; Gámez and Levine, 2013; Greenwood et al., 2011; Huttenlocher et al., 2002). For example, Huttenlocher and colleagues (2002) found greater syntactic skills in preschoolers exposed to teachers who used more syntactically complex utterances. Another study found for monolingual English-speaking children that fourth-grade reading comprehension levels were predicted by exposure to sophisticated vocabulary in preschool. These effects were mediated by children's vocabulary and literacy skills in kindergarten (Dickinson and Porche, 2011).

In classroom studies focused on the linguistic environment, the level of analysis has involved broad measures of language use, such as amount of talk (i.e., teacher–student interactions by minute: Connor et al., 2006), amount of instruction (i.e., in teacher-managed versus child-managed instruction: Connor et al., 2007), type of interaction style (i.e., didactic versus cognitively demanding talk or the amount of extended discourse: Dickinson and Smith, 1991; Jacoby and Lesaux, 2014; Smith and Dickinson, 1994), or instructional moves made by the teacher (e.g., modeling: see review in Lawrence and Snow, 2011). A commonly included measurement that has been linked to children's literacy development is *extended discourse,* defined as talk that "requires participants to develop understandings beyond the here and now and that requires the use of several utterances or turns to build a linguistic structure, such as in explanations, narratives, or pretend" (Snow et al., 2001, p. 2). Children are better prepared to comprehend narrative texts they encounter in school if their early language environments provide more exposure to and opportunities to participate in extended discourse. This is because extended discourse and narrative texts share similar patterns for communicating ideas (Uccelli et al., 2006).

Engaging groups of children in effective extended discourse involves asking and discussing open-ended questions and encouraging turn taking, as well as monitoring the group to involve nonparticipating children (Girolametto and Weitzman, 2002). In addition to using interactive storybook and text reading as a platform for back-and-forth conversations (often referred to as interactive or dialogic reading, as described in the preceding section) (Mol et al., 2009; Zucker et al., 2013), engaging children in extended discourse throughout classroom activities (e.g., small-group learning activities, transitions and routines [van Kleek, 2004], dramatic play [Mages, 2008; Morrow and Schickedanz, 2006]) is fundamental to providing a high-quality language-learning environment (Jacoby and Lesaux, 2014).

In an example of the influence of the quantity and quality of teachers' language input in linguistically diverse classrooms, Bowers and Vasilyeva (2011) found that the total number of words produced by teachers and the diversity of their speech (which was entirely in English) were related to vocabulary gains for children from both English-only households and households in which English was not the primary language, respectively. Thus, they found that preschool dual language learners benefited only from increased quantities of language exposure and showed a negative relationship between vocabulary growth and teachers' syntactic complexity. By contrast, the English-only children—who presumably had more developed English language proficiency skills—benefited from the diversity of teachers' vocabulary and syntactic complexity. These findings are consistent with the notion that to promote language learning, different inputs are needed at different developmental stages (Dickinson and Freiberg, 2009; Gámez and Lesaux, 2012). Children benefit from hearing simplified speech during very early word learning (Furrow et al., 1979). With more exposure to language and more advanced vocabulary development, they benefit from speech input that is more complex (i.e., Hoff and Naigles, 2002). Hoff (2006) suggests that if input is too complex, children filter it out without negative consequences—as long as sufficient beneficial input is available to them. On the other hand, "children have no way to make up for input that is too simple" (Hoff, 2006, p. 75).

An important consideration in light of these findings is that recent research in early childhood classrooms serving children from low-income backgrounds suggests that daily high-quality language-building experiences may be rare for these children. For example, in a Head Start organization serving large numbers of Latino children a recent observational study found a preschool environment lacking in the frequent and high-quality teacher–child language interactions that are needed to support language and literacy development (Jacoby and Lesaux, 2014). Literacy instruction was highly routine based and with low-level language structures. Extended discourse was infrequently used; only 22 percent of observed literacy-based lessons included at least one instance of extended discourse between a teacher and a child or group of children. Instead, teachers asked questions that yielded short answers or linked only to the here and now (e.g., *What day is it today? What is the weather today?*). These features of infrequent extended discourse and predominantly routine-based literacy instruction were remarkably stable across teachers and classrooms. Other research investigating teacher talk in Head Start preschool classrooms has produced similar findings (e.g., Dickinson et al., 2008).

This is consistent with findings that there are sizable cultural and socioeconomic differences in high-quality language-promoting experiences in the home and in the classroom environment in early childhood (Dickinson, 2003; Dickinson and Porche, 2011; Dickinson and Tabors, 2001; Raikes et al., 2006), just as such differences have been found in the number of words children hear by the time they enter school (Bradley and Corwyn, 2002; Fernald et al., 2013; Hart and Risley, 1995; Schneidman et al., 2013; Weisleder and Fernald, 2013). At the same time, for children from low-resource backgrounds oral language skills show an even stronger connection to later academic outcomes than for children from high-resource backgrounds. Given these findings, rich linguistic experiences at early ages may therefore be especially important for these children. Even small improvements in the literacy environment can have especially strong effects for children who are raised in low-income households (Dearing et al., 2001; Dickinson and Porche, 2011).

In sum, the language environment has important effects on children's learning, and children benefit from extensive opportunities to listen to and use complex spoken language (National Early Literacy Panel, 2008). Teachers' use of high-quality language is linked to individual differences in language and literacy skills, and there is considerable variation in the quantity and quality of teachers' language use across classrooms. The quality of the classroom language environment is a lever for lasting improvements in children's language and literacy development, and it is important to tailor classroom talk to match the developmental stage of children's language acquisition.

Creating a Rich Language Environment: Implications for Adults

Improving language environments for young children requires daily learning opportunities that focus on the diversity and complexity of language used with young children. Practically speaking, this can be achieved through extended discourse, with multiple exchanges or turns that go beyond the immediate "here and now" using explanations, narratives, or pretend. Extended discourse can take place throughout all activities and in specific interactions, especially using book reading as a platform for back-and-forth conversations.

Further research is needed to advance understanding of language-based classroom processes and how dynamic and ongoing interactions facilitate or impede children's literacy. Such studies could advance existing research in at least two ways. In particular, it could further elucidate how language-based social processes in the classroom affect literacy development for the many students who enter schools and other care and education settings with limited proficiency in English. The majority of published studies focused on language-based interactions are focused on English-only learners, despite the fact that social processes can be experienced differently by different groups, even within the same setting (Rogoff and Angelillo, 2002; Tseng and Seidman, 2007). Gámez and Levine (2013) suggest that future research examine the influence of dual-language input on dual language learners' language development; the nature of teacher talk during different parts of the instructional day, including joint book reading, and how these language experiences predict dual language learners' language skills; and the impact of classroom talk interventions—those that aim to manipulate the frequency and complexity of teachers' language—on both the language environment and dual language learners' language development.

In addition, prior research has measured a two-way process in a largely unidirectional manner—measuring speech only from parent to child or educator to student. It would be more valuable going forward if research were guided by the notion that the language-based interactions between students and educators mediate instruction, and were therefore to explore how communicative feedback loops, both adult–child and child–peer interactions, influence children's learning and development. Taking into account the student's contribution to the classroom language environment is particularly important in light of evidence that teachers modify their speech to conform to their students' limited language proficiency levels, potentially leading to a lower-quality language environment that impedes students' language growth (Ellis, 2008; see Huttenlocher et al., 2010; Justice et al., 2013). More specifically, Justice and colleagues (2013) suggest that future research examine teacher–child language interactions in a multidimensional way to explore how syntactic complexity, cognitive demand, and even linguistic form (e.g., questions, comments) relate to each other; the links between children's use of complex syntax in classroom-based interactions and their future general language ability; and interventions designed to enhance classroom language interactions, focusing on both proximal and distal outcomes for children. Finally, greater understanding is needed of the ways in which the classroom language processes described in this section might act as a foundational mediator of the efficacy of interventions focused on learning outcomes in other domains and subject areas.

Alongside student–educator interactions, studies show that peer-to-peer interactions in the classroom may also have positive impacts on children's vocabulary and expressive language abilities. Children spend a significant amount of time interacting with other children in classroom settings, and a 2009 study examining the language growth and abilities of 4-year-olds in prekindergarten classrooms found that peers who have higher language abilities positively affect other children's language development. This study also found that children with advanced language skills will receive greater benefits from interacting with peers who also have advanced language skills (Mashburn et al., 2009). These findings are similar to another study showing that peer interactions in the classroom, along with the ability level of the peers, have positive effects on the child's cognitive, prereading, expressive language skills (Henry and Rickman, 2007). In order to achieve these benefits, however, the preschool classrooms need to be designed so that peers can interact with one another, and include activities such as reading books and engaging in play together. Children with teachers who organize the day with optimal amounts of time for peer-to-peer interactions may achieve greater language growth (Mashburn et al., 2009).

Language and Literacy Development in Dual Language Learners[1]

For children whose home language is not the predominant language of their school, educators and schools need to ensure the development of English proficiency. Both parents and preschool teachers can be particularly useful in improving these children's depth of vocabulary (Aukrust, 2007; Roberts, 2008). At the same time, children can be helped to both build and maintain their first language while adding language and literacy skills in English (Espinosa, 2005). In support of this as a long-term goal are the potential advantages of being bilingual, including maintaining a cultural and linguistic heritage and conferring an advantage in the ability to communicate with a broader population in future social, educational, and work environments. Additionally, an emerging field of research, albeit with mixed results to date, explores potential advantages of being bilingual that are linked more directly to cognitive development, starting in early childhood and extending to preserving cognitive function and delaying the symptoms of dementia in the elderly (Bialystok, 2011; de Bruin et al., 2015).

Bilingual or multilingual children are faced with more communicative challenges than their monolingual peers. A child who frequently experiences failure to be understood or to understand may be driven to pay more attention to context, paralinguistic cues, and gestures in order to interpret an utterance, and thus become better at reading such cues. The result may be improved development of theory of mind and understanding of pragmatics (Yow and Markman, 2011a,b). In addition, the need to continually suppress one language for another affords ongoing practice in inhibitory or executive control, which could confer advantages on a range of inhibitory control tasks in children and helps preserve this fundamental ability in aging adults (Bialystok, 2011; Bialystok and Craik, 2010; Bialystok et al., 2009).

One challenge in the education of dual language learners is that they sometimes are classified along with children with special needs. One reason for this is the lack of good assessment tools to help distinguish the nature of the difficulties experienced by dual language learners—whether due to a learning disability or to the fact that learning a second language is difficult, takes time, and develops differently in different children (Hamayan et al., 2013).

Mathematics

Children's early knowledge of mathematics is surprisingly important, and it strongly predicts later success in mathematics (Denton and West,

---

[1] An ongoing study and forthcoming report of the Institute of Medicine and the National Research Council focuses on research, practice, and policy for young dual language learners. More information about this study can be found at www.iom.edu/English-DualLanguageLearners.

2002; Koponen et al., 2013; Passolunghi et al., 2007). Mathematics knowledge in preschool predicts mathematics achievement even into high school (National Mathematics Advisory Panel, 2008; NRC, 2009; Stevenson and Newman, 1986). Mathematics ability and language ability also are interrelated as mutually reinforcing skills (Duncan et al., 2007; Farran et al., 2005; Lerkkanen et al., 2005; O'Neill et al., 2004; Praet et al., 2013; Purpura et al., 2011). Indeed, mathematical thinking reaches beyond competence with numbers and shapes to form a foundation for general cognition and learning (Clements and Sarama, 2009; Sarama et al., 2012), and problems with mathematics are the best predictor of failure to graduate high school. Mathematics therefore appears to be a core subject and a core component of thinking and learning (Duncan and Magnuson, 2011; Duncan et al., 2007).

Given its general importance to academic success (Sadler and Tai, 2007), children need a robust foundation in mathematics knowledge in their earliest years. Multiple analyses suggest that mathematics learning should begin early, especially for children at risk for later difficulties in school (Byrnes and Wasik, 2009; Clements and Sarama, 2014). Well before first grade, children can learn the skills and concepts that support more complex mathematics understanding later. Particularly important areas of mathematics for young children to learn include number, which includes whole number, operations, and relations; geometry; spatial thinking; and measurement. Children also need to develop proficiency in processes for both general and specific mathematical reasoning (NRC, 2009).

If given opportunities to learn, young children possess a remarkably broad, complex, and sophisticated—albeit informal—knowledge of mathematics (Baroody, 2004; Clarke et al., 2006; Clements et al., 1999; Fuson, 2004; Geary, 1994; Thomson et al., 2005). In their free play, almost all preschoolers engage in substantial amounts of premathematical activity. They count objects; compare magnitudes; and explore patterns, shapes, and spatial relations. Importantly, this is true regardless of a child's income level or gender (Seo and Ginsburg, 2004). Preschoolers can also, for example, learn to invent solutions to simple arithmetic problems (Sarama and Clements, 2009).

High-quality mathematics education can help children realize their potential in mathematics achievement (Doig et al., 2003; Thomson et al., 2005). However, without such education starting, and continuing throughout, the early years, many children will be on a trajectory in which they will have great difficulty catching up to their peers (Rouse et al., 2005). As discussed further in Chapter 6, early childhood classrooms typically are ill suited to helping children learn mathematics and underestimate their ability to do so. In some cases, children can even experience a regression on some mathematics skills during prekindergarten and kindergarten (Farran et al., 2007; Wright, 1994). Mathematics needs to be conceptualized as more than skills, and its content as more than counting and simple shapes. Without building a robust understanding of mathematics in the early years, children too often come to believe that math is a guessing game and a system of rules without reason (Munn, 2006).

Both education and experience can make a difference, as evidenced by data from the latest international Trends in International Mathematics and Science Study, which added data collection on early mathematics education (Mullis et al., 2012). Students with higher mathematics achievement at fourth and sixth grades had parents who reported that they often engaged their children in early numeracy activities and that their children had attended preprimary education and started school able to do early numeracy tasks (e.g., simple addition and subtraction). Those children who had attended preschool or kindergarten had higher achievement, while the 13 percent who had attended no preprimary school had much lower average mathematics achievement (Mullis et al., 2012).

Developmental Progression of Learning Mathematics

Children move through a developmental progression in specific mathematical domains, which informs learning trajectories as important tools for supporting learning and teaching. Recent work based on empirical research and emphasizing a cognitive science perspective conceptualizes learning trajectories for mathematics as "descriptions of children's thinking and learning in a specific mathematical domain, and a related, conjectured route through a set of instructional tasks designed to engender those mental processes or actions hypothesized to move children through a developmental progression of levels of thinking, created with the intent of supporting children's achievement of specific goals in that mathematical domain" (Clements and Sarama, 2004, p. 83).

Box 4-5 illustrates the concept of a developmental progression through the example of *subitizing*, an oft-neglected mathematical goal for young children. Research shows that subitizing, the rapid and accurate recognition of the number in a small group, is one of the main abilities very young children should develop (Palmer and Baroody, 2011; Reigosa-Crespo et al., 2013). Through subitizing, children can discover critical properties of number, such as conservation and compensation (Clements and Sarama, 2014; Maclellan, 2012) and develop such capabilities as unitizing and arithmetic. Subitizing is not the only way children think and learn about number. *Counting* is the other method of quantification. It is the first and most basic mathematical algorithm and one of the more critical early mathematics competencies (Aunola et al., 2004; National Mathematics Advisory Panel, 2008). Chapter 6 includes examples from a complete learning trajectory— goal, developmental progression, and instructional activities—for counting (Clements and Sarama, 2014).

BOX 4-5
Subitizing: A Developmental Progression

A quantitative, or numerical, "sense" is innate or develops early. For example, very young children possess approximate number systems (ANSs) that allow them to discriminate large and small sets, determining, for example, whether there are more white or gray dots in the figure below. Six-month-olds can discriminate a 1:2 ratio, and by 9 months of age, they can also distinguish sets in a 2:3 ratio (e.g., 12 compared with 18).

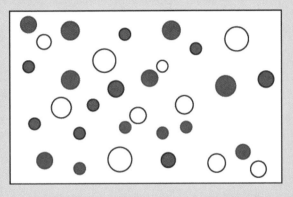

Subitizing involves determining and explicitly identifying the exact number of items in a small set. Subitizing ability develops in a stepwise fashion. In laboratory settings, children can initially differentiate 1 from "more than 1" at about 33 months of age (Wynn, 1992b). Between 35 and 37 months, they differentiate between 1 and 2, but not larger numbers. A few months later, at 38 to 40 months, they can identify 3 as well. After about 42 months, they can identify all numbers that they can count, 4 and higher, at about the same time. However, research in natural, child-initiated settings shows that the development of these abilities can occur much earlier, with children working on 1 and 2 around their second birthday or earlier (Mix et al., 2005). Babies in the first 6 months of life, and even earlier, can discriminate 1 object from 2, and 2 objects from 3 (Antell and Keating, 1983; Wynn et al., 2002). Thus, even infants can discriminate among and match small configurations (1-3) of objects, only for these small numbers. Because children cannot discriminate 4 objects from 5 or 6 until the age of about 3 years, some researchers have suggested that infants use an automatic perceptual process that people, including adults, can apply only to small collections up to around 4 objects (Chi and Klahr, 1975).

A developmental progression moves from foundational but pre-explicit quantification to explicit naming of small quantities. This initially involves only *perceptual subitizing* (Clements, 1999; Kaufman et al., 1949). From their second to third birthdays, most children can name sets of 1 and 2, and then 3 soon thereafter (Mix et al., 2005; Wynn, 1992b). Larger sets are perceived, quantified, and quickly named as the child gains experience. Perceptual subitizing also plays the role of *unit-*

continued

BOX 4-5 Continued

izing, or making single things to count out of the stream of perceptual sensations (Glasersfeld, 1995). Then a qualitative advance is made as *conceptual subitizing* develops. This involves similarly quantifying 2 parts (separately) and then combining them, again, quickly, accurately, and without being explicitly aware of the cognitive processing (Clements, 1999; see empirical evidence for such processes in Trick and Pylyshyn, 1994). That is, one might perceive each side of a domino as composed of 4 individual dots and as "one 4" and phenomenologically experience the domino as "an 8." With appropriate experiences, children can become competent in this type of subitizing with totals from 5 to 10 at ages 4 and 5.

Many theories have been advanced to explain the subitizing process (Baroody et al., 2006; Huttenlocher et al., 1994; Jordan et al., 2003; Mix et al., 2002). A synthesis suggests the following model. The ANS serves as a transition between general, approximate notions of number and one based on an exact, abstract, mental model. Infants quantify collections of rigid objects (not sequences of sounds or materials that are nonrigid and noncohesive such as water) (Huntley-Fenner et al., 2002). These quantifications begin as an undifferentiated, innate notion of amount of objects. Object individuation, which occurs early in preattentive processing (and is a general, not numerical-only, process), helps lay the groundwork for differentiating discrete from continuous quantity. For example, by about 6 months of age, infants may represent very small numbers (1 or 2) as individuated objects. To compare quantities, they process correspondences. Initially, these are inexact estimates, depending on the ratio between the sets (Johnson-Pynn et al., 2005). Once children can represent objects mentally, they also can make exact correspondences between these nonverbal representations and eventually develop a quantitative notion of that comparison (e.g., not just that ••• is more than ••, but also that it contains one more •) (Baroody et al., 2005). Even these correspondences, however, do not imply a cardinal representation of the collection.

To complete the subitizing process, children must make word–word mappings between numbers (e.g., "How many?") and number words, which they do only after they have learned several number words (Sandhofer and Smith, 1999). They then label small number situations with the corresponding number word, mapping the number word to the numerosity property of the collection. They begin this phase even before the age of 2 years, but for some time, this mapping applies mainly to the word "two," a bit less to "one," and with considerable less frequency, "three" and "four" (Fuson, 1992; Wagner and Walters, 1982). Only after many such experiences do children abstract the numerosities from the specific situations and begin to understand that the situations named by "three" correspond. That is, they begin to establish what mathematicians call a numerical equivalence class. Both subitizing- and counting-based verbal systems are then more frequently used and integrated, eventually leading to explicit, verbal mathematical abstractions.

The construction of such schemes probably depends on guiding frameworks and principles developed through interactions with others, such as parents and educators. Part of a learning trajectory is instructional tasks and strategies that promote children's developmental progression. A quasi-experimental study (Hannula, 2005) showed that it is possible to enhance 3-year-old children's spontaneous focusing on numerosity, and thus catalyze their deliberate practice in numerical skills (cf. Ericsson et al., 1993). Research indicates that teachers often do not do sufficient subitizing work, which results in their students' regression in subitizing from the beginning to the end of kindergarten (Wright, 1994). Instead, directing children's attention to patterns through perceptual and especially conceptual subitizing helps children develop abstract number and arithmetic strategies. Activities such as teachers challenging students to name the number of dots in a display shown only for 1-2 seconds have resulted in substantial growth in this ability (Baroody et al., 2008; Clements and Sarama, 2008; Clements et al., 2011, 2013b; Hannula, 2005; Nes, 2009; Van Luit and Van de Rijt, 1998).

Subitizing ability is not merely a low-level, innate process, but develops considerably and combines with other mental processes. Even though they are limited, subitizing capabilities appear to form a foundation for later connection to culturally based cognitive tools such as number words and the number word sequence and the development of exact and extended number concepts and skills. Functional magnetic resonance imaging and other studies have shown that a neural component of numerical cognition present in the early years may be the foundation for later symbolic numerical development (Cantlon et al., 2006; Eimeren et al., 2007; Masataka et al., 2006; Piazza et al., 2004). Subitizing appears to precede and support the development of counting ability and arithmetic skills (Eimeren et al., 2007; Hannula, 2005; Hannula et al., 2007; Le Corre et al., 2006). Children who cannot subitize conceptually are handicapped in learning such arithmetic processes. Those who can subitize may be limited to doing so with small numbers at first, but such actions are useful stepping stones to the construction of more sophisticated procedures with larger numbers. Indeed, lack of this competence may underlie mathematics learning disabilities and difficulties (Ashkenazi et al., 2013; Berch and Mazzocco, 2007; Butterworth, 2010; Chu et al., 2013). Children from low-resource communities and those with special needs often lag in subitizing ability, hindering their mathematical development (Butterworth, 2010; Chu et al., 2013; Clements and Sarama, 2014; Le Corre et al., 2006).

SOURCE: Adapted with permission from Clements and Sarama, 2014, and Sarama and Clements, 2009.

Children with Special Needs

Children with special needs in learning mathematics fall into two categories. Those with mathematical difficulties struggle to learn mathematics for any reason; this category may apply to as many as 35-40 percent of students (Berch and Mazzocco, 2007). Those with specific mathematics learning disabilities are more severe cases; these students have a memory or cognitive deficit that interferes with their ability to learn math (Geary, 2004). This category may apply to about 6-7 percent (Berch and Mazzocco, 2007; Mazzocco and Myers, 2003). In one study, this classification persisted in third grade for 63 percent of those classified as having mathematics learning disabilities in kindergarten (Mazzocco and Myers, 2003).

Mathematics learning disabilities, while assumed to have a genetic basis, currently are defined by students' behaviors—yet with ongoing debate among experts about what those behaviors are. One consistent finding is that students with mathematics learning disabilities have difficulty retrieving basic arithmetic facts quickly. This has been hypothesized to be the result of an inability to store or retrieve facts and impairments in visual-spatial representation. As early as kindergarten, limited working memory and speed of cognitive processing may be problems for these children (Geary et al., 2007). Many young children with learning disabilities in reading show a similar rapid-naming deficit for letters and words (Siegel and Mazabel, 2013; Steacy et al., 2014). Another possibility is that a lack of higher-order, or executive, control of verbal material causes difficulty learning basic arithmetic facts or combinations. For example, students with mathematics learning disabilities may have difficulty inhibiting irrelevant associations. An illustration of this would be hearing "5 + 4" and saying "6" because it follows 5.

One explanation for the difficulty students with mathematics learning disabilities have learning basic arithmetic combinations might be delays in understanding counting. These students may not fully understand counting nor recognize errors in counting as late as second grade. They persist in using immature counting strategies, such as counting "one-by-one" on their fingers, throughout elementary school (Geary et al., 1992; Ostad, 1998). Other experts, however, claim that a lack of specific competencies, such as subitizing, is more important (Berch and Mazzocco, 2007).

Some evidence suggests that it is possible to predict which kindergartners are at risk for mathematics learning disabilities based on skill including reading numerals, number constancy, magnitude judgments of one-digit numbers, or mental addition of one-digit numbers (Mazzocco and Thompson, 2005). However, until more is known, students should be classified as having mathematics learning disabilities only with great caution and after good mathematics instruction has been provided. Such labeling in the earliest years could do more harm than good (Clements and Sarama, 2012).

Interrelationships Between Mathematics and Language

It can appear that language is less of a concern in mathematics compared to other subjects because it is assumed to be based on numbers or symbols, but this is not the case (Clements et al., 2013a). In fact, children learn math mainly from oral language, rather than from mathematical symbolism or textbooks (Janzen, 2008). In addition, "talking math" is more than just using mathematics terms (Clements and Sarama, 2014). Therefore, both oral language and literacy in general, as well as the "language of mathematics," are important for learning (Vukovic and Lesaux, 2013). Vocabulary and knowledge of print are both predictors of later numeracy (Purpura et al., 2011). Similarly, growth in mathematics from kindergarten to third grade is related to both early numerical skills and phonological processing (Vukovic, 2012). In one study of linguistically and ethnically diverse children aged 6-9 years, language ability predicted gains in geometry, probability, and data analysis but not in arithmetic or algebra (controlling for reading ability, visual–spatial working memory, and gender) (Vukovic and Lesaux, 2013). Thus, language may affect how children make meaning of mathematics but not its complex arithmetic procedures.

Moreover, there is an important bidirectional relationship between learning in mathematics and language (Sarama et al., 2012). Each has related developmental milestones. Children learn number words at the same time as other linguistic labels. Most children recognize by the age of 2 which words are for numbers and use them only in appropriate contexts (Fuson, 1988). Each also has related developmental patterns, with learning progressing along similar paths. In both, children recognize the whole before its parts. In learning language, this is word before syllable, syllable before rime-onset, and rime-onset before phoneme (see also Anthony et al., 2003; Ziegler and Goswami, 2005). Similarly in mathematics, numbers are first conceptualized as unbreakable categories and then later as composites (e.g., 5 is composed of 3 and 2) (Butterworth, 2005; Sarama and Clements, 2009). By 6 years old in most cultures, children have been exposed to symbol representations that are both alphabetic and numerical, and they begin to be able to segment words into phonemes and numbers into singletons (e.g., understanding that 3 is 1 and 1 and 1) (Butterworth, 2005; Sarama and Clements, 2009; Wagner et al., 1993). The ability to identify the component nature of words and numbers predicts the ability to read (Adams, 1990; Stanovich and Siegel, 1994) and to compute (Geary, 1990, 1993). In addition to these similarities in typical developmental pathways, many children with learning disabilities experience deficits in competencies related to both language/literacy and numeracy (Geary, 1993; Hecht et al., 2001; NRC, 1998).

Furthermore, there appear to be shared competencies between the two subject areas. For example, preschoolers' narrative abilities (i.e., their abilities to convey all the main events of a story and offer a perspective on its events) have been shown to predict mathematics achievement 2 years later (O'Neill et al., 2004). Beginning mathematics scores have been shown to be highly predictive of subsequent achievement in both reading and mathematics although beginning reading skills (such as letter recognition, word identification, and word sounds) were shown to be highly predictive of later reading (advanced competencies such as evaluation) but not mathematics learning (Duncan et al., 2007).

A causal relationship between rich mathematics learning and developing language and literacy skills is supported by a randomized study of the effects of a math curriculum called *Building Blocks* on prekindergarten children's letter recognition and oral language skills. *Building Blocks* children performed the same as the children in the control group on letter recognition and on three oral language subscales but outperformed them on four subscales: ability to recall key words, use of complex utterances, willingness to reproduce narratives independently, and inference (Sarama et al., 2012). These skills had no explicit relation to the math curriculum. Similarly, a study of 5- to 7-year-olds showed that an early mathematics and logical-mathematical intervention increased later scores in English by 14 percentile points (Shayer and Adhami, 2010).

Time on task (or time on instruction) does affect learning, which naturally leads to consideration of potential conflicts or tradeoffs between time spent on different subjects (e.g., Bodovski and Farkas, 2007). Indeed, a frequent concern is that introducing a mathematics curriculum may decrease the time devoted to language and literacy, impeding children's development in those areas, which are heavily emphasized in early learning goals (see Clements and Sarama, 2009; Farran et al., 2007; Lee and Ginsburg, 2007; Sarama and Clements, 2009). However, this assumes that mathematics activities will not have a positive effect on language and literacy. Yet as described here, evidence from both educational and psychological research suggests the potential for high-quality instruction in each to have mutual benefits for learning in both subjects. Rich mathematical activities, such as discussing multiple solutions and solving narrative story problems, can help lay the groundwork for literacy through language development, while rich literacy activities can help lay the groundwork for mathematics development (Sarama et al., 2012).

Children Who Are Dual Language Learners

For mathematics learning in children who are dual language learners, the language, not just the vocabulary, of mathematics need to be addressed (Clements and Sarama, 2014). Challenges for dual language learners include both technical vocabulary, which can range in how similar or distinct terms are from everyday language, and the use of complex noun phrases. On the other hand, bilingual children often can understand a mathematical idea more readily because, after using different terms for it in different languages, they comprehend that the mathematical idea is abstract, and not tied to a specific term (see Secada, 1992).

There is evidence that the best approach is to teach these young children in their first language (Celedón-Pattichis et al., 2010; Espada, 2012). At a minimum, their teachers need to connect everyday language with the language of math (Janzen, 2008). It is also essential to build on the resources that bilingual children bring to learning mathematics—all cultures have "funds of knowledge" (culturally developed and historically accumulated bodies of knowledge and skills) that can be used to develop mathematical contexts and understandings (Moll et al., 1992). Instructional practices for teaching mathematics with dual language learners are discussed further in Chapter 6.

Conclusions About Learning Specific Subjects

For subject-matter content knowledge and proficiency, children learn best when supported along a trajectory with three components: (1) their understanding of the subject-matter content itself, (2) their progress through predictable developmental levels and patterns of thinking related to their understanding of the content, and (3) instructional tasks and strategies that adults who work with children can employ to promote that learning at each level. For example:

- *Almost all topics in mathematics follow predictable learning trajectories that include number counting and subitizing, number relationships and magnitude comparison, arithmetic operations, geometry and spatial sense, and measurement.*
- *Learning trajectories in literacy include specific developmental sequences in children's learning of phonological awareness and phonics (letter-sound correspondences), which together contribute to children's understanding of how spoken words are captured in reading and writing and thus to their advancement through broader levels of early literacy.*

Some principles of how children learn along a trajectory hold across subject-matter domains, but there are also substantive differences among subjects in the specific skills children need and in the learning trajectories. Both generalizable principles and subject-specific distinctions have implications for the knowledge and competencies needed to work with children.

An important factor in children's learning of subject-matter content is how each of the components of learning trajectories both requires and develops aspects of learning that are not content specific, such as critical reasoning, executive function, self-regulation, learning skills, positive dispositions toward learning, and relationships.

GENERAL LEARNING COMPETENCIES

Educators, developmental scientists, and economists have long known that academic achievement is a result of both the growth of specific knowledge and the development of general learning competencies that regulate how children enlist cognitive resources when they encounter learning challenges, motivate advances in learning, and strengthen children's self-confidence as learners.

These general learning competencies have been labeled and categorized in various ways. Considerable recent research on some of these learning competencies has been conducted using the concept of "executive function," which generally refers to a set of supervisory functions that regulate and control cognitive activity that affects learning (Vitiello et al., 2011) and allow children to persevere with tasks, including learning tasks, even when facing fatigue, distraction, or decreased motivation. In the field of human development "mastery motivation" in infancy typically is indexed by the baby's persistence, focus, and curiosity in exploration and problem solving (Morgan et al., 1990; Wang and Barrett, 2013). In preschool-age children, these skills often are conceptualized as the quality of the child's "approaches to learning," which include motivation, engagement, and interest in learning activities. Heckman (2007) has used the term "noncognitive skills" to refer to many of these learning competencies, including self-control, persistence, self-discipline, motivation, and self-esteem, as well as future orientedness (i.e., the capacity to substitute long-term goals for immediate satisfactions). This label is used in contrast to the "cognitive skills" that are more often measured to predict children's later success, although there is considerable research that the "noncognitive skills" also support learning and achievement (see, e.g., Cunha and Heckman, 2010; Heckman, 2007), and they are highly relevant to cognitive skills in such areas as language, mathematics, science, and other traditional academic fields.

Here the alternative conceptualizations for these important aspects of child development and early learning are grouped as "learning competencies" to reflect their importance for early learning. Individual differences in these competencies are important determinants of learning and academic motivation, and children's experiences at home and in the classroom contribute to some of these differences. This section examines these competencies as well as their interrelationships with the previously discussed subject-matter domains of language and literacy and mathematics.

General Cognitive Skills

Several cognitive control processes are important for planning and executing goal-directed activity, which is needed for successful learning (e.g., Blair, 2002; Lyon and Krasnegor, 1996). These processes include, for example, short-term and working memory, attention control and shifting, cognitive flexibility (changing thinking between different concepts and thinking about multiple concepts simultaneously), inhibitory control (suppressing unproductive responses or strategies), and cognitive self-regulation. These processes also are closely related to emotion regulation, which is discussed later in the section on socioemotional development, and which also contributes to children's classroom success.

As noted previously, many general cognitive processes often are referred to collectively as "executive function," although not everyone defines this construct in the same way (e.g., Miyake et al., 2000; Raver, 2013), and different disciplines and researchers differ as to which cognitive skills it includes. Other theoretical frameworks exist as well. For example, cognitive control and complexity theory postulates that executive function is an outcome, not an explanatory construct, and is the result of children's creation and application of rules (driven perhaps by an increase in reflection afforded by experience-dependent maturation of the prefrontal cortex) (Müller et al., 2008; Zelazo and Carlson, 2012; Zelazo and Lyons, 2012). As with the overall domains of development displayed earlier in Figure 4-1, the committee did not attempt to reconcile those different perspectives.

This variation in perspectives makes it difficult to parse the literature produced by different fields of research and practice. In general, however, executive function appears to improve most rapidly in young children (Best et al., 2011; Blair, 2002; Hughes and Ensor, 2011; Romine and Reynolds, 2005; Schoemaker et al., 2014; Zelazo and Carlson, 2012). Executive function processes appear to be partially dependent on the development of the prefrontal cortex (the site of higher-order cognitive processes), notably through the preschool and kindergarten age range (Bassett et al., 2012; Blair, 2002).

Short-Term and Working Memory

Short-term memory is the ability for short-term recall, such as of a sentence or important details from conversation and reading. *Working memory* allows children to hold in their memory information from multiple sources, whether heard or read, so they can use and link that information. *Updating working memory* is the ability to keep and use relevant information while engaging in another cognitively demanding task (Conway et al., 2003; DeYoung, 2011).

Attention Control and Shifting

Attention control is the ability to focus attention and disregard distracting stimuli (e.g., a continuous performance task that requires a child to identify when some familiar object appears onscreen and ignore other objects that appear, or a task that requires ignoring extraneous information in a mathematics word problem). *Attention shifting* is a related process of switching a "mental set" while simultaneously ignoring distractions (e.g., counting by different units—tens and ones). Attention shifting and *cognitive flexibility* are often grouped.

Cognitive Flexibility

Cognitive flexibility capacities develop gradually throughout early childhood and have significant influences on children's social and academic competence. Cognitive flexibility is important, for example, for reading (Duke and Block, 2012). Children who are better able to consider, at the same time, both letter-sound and semantic (meaning) information about words have better reading comprehension (Cartwright, 2002; Cartwright et al., 2010). Reading comprehension also appears to improve when children are taught about words with multiple meanings (e.g., *spell* or *plane*), and sentences with multiple meanings (e.g., "The woman chased the man on a motorcycle.") (Yuill, 1996; Zipke et al., 2009). In addition, interventions in young children that focus on cognitive flexibility have shown significant benefits for reading comprehension (Cartwright, 2008).

Inhibitory Control

Inhibitory control involves controlling a dominant response (e.g., the first answer that comes to mind) so as to think about better strategies or ideas. The skill of simple response inhibition (withholding an initial, sometimes impulsive, response) develops during infancy through toddlerhood. Infants also develop some control of cognitive conflict in tasks in which an item of interest to them is first hidden in one location and then another, and the child must resist the response of searching in the first location (Diamond, 1991; Müller et al., 2008; Rothbart and Rueda, 2005) (see Marcovitch and Zelazo, 2009, for a model of possible mechanisms). Later in their first year, children can resolve conflict between their line of sight and their line of reaching (Diamond, 1991). By about 30 months, they can successfully complete a spatial conflict task (Rothbart and Rueda, 2005). From 3 to 5 years of age, complex response inhibition and response shifting develop, with attention shifting developing at about age 4 (Bassett et al., 2012). The most rapid increase in inhibitory control is between 5 and 8 years of age, although moderate improvements are seen up to young adulthood (Best et al., 2011).

Inhibitory control supports children's learning across subject-matter areas. As one example of its importance for mathematics, when the initial reading of a problem is not the correct one, children need to *inhibit* their impulse to answer (incorrectly) and carefully examine the problem. Consider the following problem: "There were six birds in a tree. Three birds already flew away. How many birds were there from the start?" Children have to inhibit the immediate desire to subtract prompted by the words "flew away" and perform addition instead.

Cognitive Self-Regulation

Cognitive self-regulation is what helps children plan ahead, focus attention, and remember past experiences. The construct of self-regulation and related concepts have a long history in psychology (e.g., Glaser, 1991; Markman, 1977, 1981; Piaget and Szeminska, 1952; Sternberg, 1985; Vygotsky, 1978; Zelazo et al., 2003) and education (e.g., McGillicuddy-De Lisi, 1982; Steffe and Tzur, 1994). Most recently, researchers and educators have used the broad term *self-regulation* to refer to the processes involved in intentionally controlling attention, thinking, impulses, emotions, and behavior. In this way, self-regulation can be thought of in relation to several aspects of development, including the cognitive processes discussed here and the social and emotional processes discussed later in this chapter. Developmental psychobiological research and neuroimaging indicate that these subclasses are both neurally and behaviorally distinct while also being related and correlated (Bassett et al., 2012; Hofmann et al., 2012; Hongwanishkul et al., 2005; Neuenschwander et al., 2012; Willoughby et al., 2011). Together, these types of self-regulation allow children to persevere with tasks even when facing difficulties in problem solving or learning, fatigue, distraction, or decreased motivation (Blair and Razza, 2007; Neuenschwander et al., 2012). It is thus unsurprising that kindergarten teachers believe self-regulation is as important as academics (Bassok and Rorem, 2014).

Both cognitive self-regulation and emotional self-regulation (discussed later in this chapter) contribute to socioemotional development and also play a role in learning. Although the relationship between various features of cognitive self-regulation and academic achievement has been well documented for older students (e.g., Bielaczyc et al., 1995; Zimmerman, 2002), less was known until recently about how self-regulation developed in the early years contributes to the later development of cognitive and emotional self-regulation and academic achievement (NRC and IOM, 2000).

Children's self-regulation and their ability to successfully function in school settings are related in two ways. First, emotional self-regulation enables children to benefit from learning in various social contexts, including their capacities to manage emotions in interactions with educators as well as peers (e.g., one-on-one, in cooperative pairs, in large and small groups). It also assists them in conforming to classroom rules and routines. Second, cognitive self-regulation enables children to develop and make use of cognitive processes that are necessary for academic learning (Anghel, 2010).

Although most studies have focused on specific effects of either cognitive or emotional self-regulation, evidence suggests that the two are interconnected. This link is probably due to the commonality of the neurological mechanisms governing both emotional and cognitive self-regulation. For example, children lacking emotion regulation are likely also to have problems with regulating cognitive processes, such as attention (Derryberry and Reed, 1996; LeDoux, 1996). Moreover, earlier patterns in the development of emotion control have been shown to be predictive of children's later ability to exercise control over their cognitive functioning (Blair, 2002).

Several studies have shown positive correlations between self-regulation and achievement in young children (e.g., Bierman et al., 2008b; Blair and Razza, 2007; Blair et al., 2010; Bull et al., 1999; Cameron et al., 2012; Neuenschwander et al., 2012; Roebers et al., 2012; Welsh et al., 2010), although there are exceptions (Edens and Potter, 2013). Preschoolers' cognitive self-regulation, including inhibitory control and attention shifting, were found to be related to measures of literacy and mathematics ability in kindergarten (Blair and Razza, 2007). In another study, children with higher self-regulation, including attention, working memory, and inhibitory control, achieved at higher levels in literacy, language, and mathematics (McClelland et al., 2007). Interventions in the area of self-regulation have shown positive effects for reading achievement (Best et al., 2011; Bierman et al., 2008a; Blair and Diamond, 2008; Blair and Razza, 2007; Diamond and Lee, 2011). Among struggling first graders in an effective reading intervention, those who were retained in grade showed significantly weaker self-regulation skills (Dombek and Connor, 2012). Cognitive self-regulation appears to be strongly associated with academic learning (Willoughby et al., 2011), but emotional self-regulation also contributes through children's adjustment to school and attitudes toward learning. In addition, both cognitive and emotional self-regulation contribute to variance in attention, competence motivation, and persistence (Bassett et al., 2012; Willoughby et al., 2011).

In addition, differences in self-regulation competencies raise important issues related to disparities in educational achievement. Children in poverty can have lower self-regulation competencies (e.g., Blair and Razza, 2007; Blair et al., 2010; Bull and Scerif, 2001; Hackman and Farah, 2009; Jenks et al., 2012; Kishiyama et al., 2009; Masten et al., 2012; Mazzocco and Hanich, 2010; McLean and Hitch, 1999; Raver, 2013). One reason is the effect of chronic stress on behavioral and biological capacities for self-control (see discussion of chronic stress and adversity later in this chapter). This risk is exacerbated for children who are also dual language learners (Wanless et al., 2011). Students with special needs are another population who may require focused interventions to develop self-regulation competencies (Harris et al., 2005; Jenks et al., 2012; Lyon and Krasnegor, 1996; Mazzocco and Hanich, 2010; McLean and Hitch, 1999; Raches and Mazzocco, 2012; Toll et al., 2010; Zelazo et al., 2002). Students who are gifted and talented may also have exceptional needs in this domain (e.g., Mooji, 2010).

Adults who work with children have the opportunity to provide environments, experiences, and curricula that can help develop the competencies needed, including for children whose skills were not optimally developed in the earliest years. Importantly, the goal of such interventions is not to "train" children to suppress behaviors and follow rules. Rather, effective educators and programs provide learning activities and environments that increase children's capacity and disposition to set a goal (e.g., join a pretend play activity, complete a puzzle); develop a plan or strategy; and muster their social, emotional, and cognitive faculties to execute that plan. The science of how children develop and learn indicates that integrating academic learning and self-regulation is a sound approach.

Executive Functions and Learning in Specific Subjects

As already noted and shown in several examples, executive function processes are closely related to achievement in both language and literacy and mathematics (Best et al., 2011; Blair and Razza, 2007; Blair et al., 2010; Neuenschwander et al., 2012), and this has also been shown in science (Nayfeld et al., 2013). In some research, executive function has been correlated similarly with both reading and mathematics achievement across a wide age span (5 to 17 years), suggesting its significant role in academic learning (Best et al., 2011; Blair and Razza, 2007; Neuenschwander et al., 2012). In contrast, some studies have found that executive function is more strongly associated with mathematics than with literacy or language (Barata, 2010; Blair et al., 2010; Ponitz et al., 2009; von Suchodoletz and Gunzenhauser, 2013). A strong relationship between executive function and mathematics may reflect that mathematics relies heavily on working memory and attention control, requiring the ability to inhibit an automatic response to a single aspect of a problem, to hold relevant information in mind, and to operate on it while shifting attention appropriately among different elements of a problem (Welsh et al., 2010). This relationship is especially important given that mathematics curricula increasingly require higher-order skills, which executive function competencies provides (Baker et al., 2010).

Some research indicates that most executive function competencies correlate significantly with mathematics achievement (Bull and Scerif, 2001), while other studies suggest a greater role for particular executive function competencies in the learning of mathematics for young children—especially inhibitory control (Blair and Razza, 2007) or working memory (Bull et al., 2008; Geary, 2011; see also, Geary et al., 2012; cf. Neuenschwander et al., 2012; Szűcs et al., 2014; Van der Ven et al., 2012). These latter two competencies have been shown to predict success in mathematics in primary school students (Toll et al., 2010). Working memory tasks have also been shown to predict mathematics learning disabilities, even more so than early mathematical abilities (Toll et al., 2010). Several studies have identified lack of inhibition and working memory as specific deficits for children of lower mathematical ability, resulting in difficulty with switching to and evaluating new strategies for dealing with a particular task (Bull and Scerif [2001] and Lan and colleagues [2011] found similar results). Persistence, another learning skill that is interrelated with cognitive processes, also has been linked to mathematics achievement for both 3- and 4-year-olds (Maier and Greenfield, 2008).

Executive function competencies may be differentially associated with distinct areas of mathematics. For example, executive function was found to be correlated more with solving word problems than with calculation (Best et al., 2011), and appears to play a role in acquiring new mathematics procedures and developing automatic access to arithmetic facts (LeFevre et al., 2013). Different aspects of working memory also may be related to different mathematical areas (Simmons et al., 2012). Parallel observations have been made for executive function and reading, with executive function playing a larger role in reading comprehension than in decoding.

In addition to the role of executive function in learning mathematics, mathematics activities also contribute to developing executive function. Some mathematics activities may require children to suppress prepotent responses, manipulate abstract information, and remain cognitively flexible. Importantly, neuroimaging studies suggest that executive function may be developed through learning mathematics in challenging activities but not in exercising mathematics once learned (Ansari et al., 2005; Butterworth et al., 2011).

Cognitive Skills and Executive Function in Children with Special Needs

Some students with special needs may have a specific lack of certain executive function competencies (Harris et al., 2005; Jenks et al., 2012; Lyon and Krasnegor, 1996; McLean and Hitch, 1999; Raches and Mazzocco, 2012; Schoemaker et al., 2014; Toll et al., 2010; Zelazo et al., 2002). Most of the research on executive function deficits in relation to disabilities that affect young children has focused on specific disorders, particularly attention deficit hyperactivity disorder (ADHD). An early theory posited that ADHD is a lack of the behavioral inhibition required for proficiency with executive functions such as self-regulation of affect, motivation, and arousal; working memory; and synthesis analysis of internally represented information (Barkley, 1997). Research has found that children diagnosed with ADHD are more likely than children without ADHD to have two or more deficits in executive function (Biederman et al., 2004; cf. Shuai et al., 2011). A meta-analysis of studies of one measure of executive function, the Wisconsin Card Sorting Test, suggests that the performance of individuals with ADHD is fairly consistently poorer than that of individuals without clinical diagnoses (Romine et al., 2004). In another study, children with ADHD were found not to have learning problems but rather problems in a measure of inhibitory control, which affected arithmetic calculation (as well as written language) (Semrud-Clikeman, 2012). Other evidence suggests that children diagnosed with ADHD may have deficits not in executive processes themselves but in motivation or response to contingencies, that is, the regulation of effort allocation (Huang-Pollock et al., 2012).

Having ADHD with deficits in executive function, compared to ADHD alone, is associated with an increased risk for grade retention and a decrease in academic achievement (Biederman et al., 2004). The relationship between ADHD and executive functions may also depend on subtype. One study found that children with an inattention ADHD subtype showed deficits in several executive function competencies (Tymms and Merrell, 2011), whereas children with the hyperactive-impulsive ADHD subtype may have fewer executive function deficits (Shuai et al., 2011) and may even have strengths that could be developed in appropriate educational environments.

Deficits in executive function have been studied in other developmental disorders as well, albeit often in less detail. They include autism (Bühler et al., 2011; Hill, 2004; Zelazo et al., 2002); attention and disruptive behavior problems (Fahie and Symons, 2003; Hughes and Ensor, 2011); intellectual disabilities (Nader-Grosbois and Lefèvre, 2011; Neece et al., 2011; Vieillevoye and Nader-Grosbois, 2008); cerebral palsy (Jenks et al., 2012); Turner syndrome (Mazzocco and Hanich, 2010); developmental dyslexia (Brosnan et al., 2002; cf. Romine and Reynolds, 2005); and mathematics learning disabilities (Toll et al., 2010).

Other Learning Skills and Dispositions

Other learning skills that are important to early academic achievement include persistence, curiosity, self-confidence, intrinsic motivation, time perspective (e.g., the willingness to prioritize long-term goals over immediate gratifications), and self-control. The growth of emotional and cognitive self-regulation is also fundamentally related to many of these developing learning skills. In addition, social experiences, discussed later in this chapter, are important for the growth of these learning skills. Note also that although these skills are referred to sometimes as dispositions, they are fostered through early experience and can be supported through intentional caregiving and instructional practices; they are not simply intrinsic traits in the child.

A capacity for focused engagement in learning is apparent from very early in life, although it is also true that these learning competencies develop significantly throughout early childhood as processes of neurobiological development interact with children's social experiences to enable greater persistence, focused attention, delayed gratification, and other components of effective learning and problem solving. As a consequence, very young children are likely to approach new learning situations with enthusiasm and self-confidence but at young ages may not necessarily bring persistence or creativity in confronting and solving challenging problems. Older preschoolers, by contrast, are more self-regulated learners. They approach new learning opportunities with initiative and involvement, and they are more persistent and more likely to solve problems creatively, by proposing their own ideas (NRC, 2001).

Considerable research confirms the importance of these skills to early learning. Individual differences in infants' "mastery motivation" skills—persistence, focus, and curiosity in exploration and problem solving—predict later cognitive abilities and achievement motivation (Busch-Rossnagel, 2005; Morgan et al., 1990; Wang and Barrett, 2013). In preschool-age children, learning skills that include motivation, engagement, and interest in learning activities have been found in longitudinal studies to predict children's cognitive skills at school entry (Duncan et al., 2005, 2007). Similarly, these characteristics continue to be associated with reading and mathematics achievement in the early elementary grades (Alexander et al., 1993).

Differences in these learning skills are especially associated with academic achievement for children in circumstances of economic disadvantage who face various kinds of self-regulatory challenges (Blair and Raver, 2012; Howse et al., 2003a).

Much of school success requires that children prioritize longer-term rewards requiring current effort over immediate satisfactions. The classic demonstration of this skill comes from a series of studies led by Walter Mischel beginning in the 1960s. Young children were offered the option of choosing an immediate, smaller reward or a larger reward if they waited to receive it later. For several years developmental outcomes for these children were tracked, which revealed that children who were better able to delay gratification at age 4 scored higher on measures of language skills, academic achievement, planful behaviors, self-reliance, capacity to cope with stress and frustration, and social competence measured in adolescence and adulthood (Mischel et al., 1988). Other studies have reported consistent findings. Early development in the ability to prioritize future, long-term goals over short-term lesser gains improves children's chances of academic achievement and securing and maintaining employment (Rachlin, 2000). Conversely, the inability to delay gratification is associated with young children's aggressive behavior, conduct problems, poorer peer relationships, and academic difficulty during preschool and the transition to elementary school (Olson and Hoza, 1993) as well as later outcomes, including academic failure, delinquency, and substance abuse in adolescence (Lynam et al., 1993; Wulfert et al., 2002).

The ways that children view themselves as learners are also important. Young children's self-perceived capability to master learning challenges develops early and exerts a continuing influence on their academic success. Early self-evaluations of competence are based on the positive and negative evaluations of children's behavior and competence by parents (Stipek et al., 1992). Parent and educator expectations for children's success remain important. High parent expectations for children's school achievement are associated with children's later academic performance, and this is also true of educator expectations. In one longitudinal study, teacher expectations for children's math achievement in grades 1 and 3 directly predicted children's scores on standardized achievement tests 2 years later, and expectations for reading achievement had indirect associations with later reading scores. There was also evidence in this study that expectations were especially influential for academically at-risk students (Hinnant et al., 2009).

Messages from parents and educators are also important in shaping how children attribute their own success and failure which, in turn, predicts their future effort and expectations of success. Children develop implicit theories in the early years about who they are as a person and what it means to be intelligent. Some children come to view intelligence as a fixed trait (i.e., one is either smart or not), whereas others see it as a more malleable trait that can be changed through effort and persistence. Educators and parents who approach learning goals by promoting and rewarding effort, persistence, and willingness to take on challenging problems increase children's motivation and their endorsement of effort as a path to success. In contrast, children receiving messages that intelligence is stable and cannot be improved through hard work are discouraged from pursuing difficult tasks, particularly if they view their abilities as low (Heyman and Dweck, 1992). These patterns of "helpless" versus "mastery-oriented" motivation are learned in the preschool years and remain stable over time (Smiley and Dweck, 1994).

These perceptions and patterns of motivation can be especially significant as children learn academic subjects, such as mathematics (Clements and Sarama, 2012). People in the United States have many negative beliefs and attitudes about mathematics (Ashcraft, 2006). One deeply embedded cultural belief is that achievement in mathematics depends mainly on native aptitude or ability rather than effort. Research shows that the belief in the primacy of native ability hurts students and, further, it is simply untrue.

Throughout their school careers, students who believe—or are helped to understand—that they can learn if they try working longer on tasks have better achievement than those who believe that either one "has it" (or "gets it") or does not (McLeod and Adams, 1989; Weiner, 1986). Researchers have estimated that students should be successful about 70 percent of the time to maximize motivation (Middleton and Spanias, 1999). If students are directly assured that working hard to figure out problems, including making errors and being frustrated, are part of the learning process it can diminish feelings of embarrassment and other negative emotions at being incorrect. In contrast, students' learning can be impeded if educators define success only as rapid, correct responses and accuracy only as following the educator's example (Middleton and Spanias, 1999). In addition, students will build positive feelings about mathematics if they experience it as a sense-making activity. Most young students are motivated to explore numbers and shapes and have positive feelings about mathematics (Middleton and Spanias, 1999). However, after only a couple of years in typical schools, they begin to believe that only some people have the ability to do math.

A related pattern relating perceptions and emotions to learning is seen with students who experience mathematics anxiety. Primary grade students who have strong math anxiety, even alongside strong working memory, have been found to have lower mathematics achievement because working memory capacity is co-opted by math anxiety (Beilock, 2001; Ramirez et al., 2013). Research has shown that primary grade students who "feel panicky" about math have increased activity in brain regions that are associated with fear, which decreases activity in brain regions associated with problem solving (Young et al., 2012). Early identification and treatment of math anxiety may prevent children with high potential from avoiding mathematics and mathematics courses (Ramirez et al., 2013).

SOCIOEMOTIONAL DEVELOPMENT

The development of social and emotional competence is an important part of child development and early learning. Socioemotional competence has been described as a multidimensional construct that contributes to the ability to understand and manage emotions and behavior; to make decisions and achieve goals; and to establish and maintain positive relationships, including feeling and showing empathy for others. Although their importance is widely recognized, universal agreement is lacking on how to categorize and define these areas of development. The Collaborative for Academic, Social, and Emotional Learning offers a summary construct with five interrelated groups of competencies that together encompass the areas typically considered to be part of socioemotional competence (see Figure 4-2).

Socioemotional competence increasingly is viewed as important for a child's early school adjustment and for academic success at both the preschool and K-12 levels (Bierman et al., 2008a,b; Denham and Brown, 2010; Heckman et al., 2013; La Paro and Pianta, 2000; Leerkes et al., 2008). A growing body of research addresses the relationship between dimensions of socioemotional competence and cognitive and other skills related to early learning and later academic achievement (Bierman et al., 2008a,b; Graziano et al., 2007; Howse et al., 2003b; Miller et al., 2006). Socioemotional development early in life also increasingly is understood to be critically important for later mental well-being, and for contributing to subsequent mental health problems when there are enduring disturbances in socioemotional functions (IOM and NRC, 2009; Leckman and March, 2011).

There are several reasons why socioemotional development is important to early learning and academic success. As discussed in detail later in this section, early learning is a social activity in which these skills are important to the interactions through which learning occurs and is collaboratively shared. Socioemotional competence gives children the capacity to engage in academic tasks by increasing their ability to interact constructively with teachers, work collaboratively with and learn from peers, and dedicate sustained attention to learning (Denham and Brown, 2010). Further, behavioral and emotional problems not only impede early learning but also pose other risks to long-term success. Substantial research has examined the relationship between delays and deficits in children's social skills and challenging behavior, such as serious problems getting along with peers or cooperating with educators (Zins et al., 2007). When challenging behav-

Self-awareness: The ability to accurately recognize one's emotions and thoughts and their influence on behavior. This includes accurately assessing one's strengths and limitations and possessing a well-grounded sense of confidence and optimism.

Self-management: The ability to regulate one's emotions, thoughts, and behaviors effectively in different situations. This includes managing stress, controlling impulses, motivating oneself, and setting and working toward achieving personal and academic goals.

Social awareness: The ability to take the perspective of and empathize with others from diverse backgrounds and cultures, to understand social and ethical norms for behavior, and to recognize family, school, and community resources and supports.

Relationship skills: The ability to establish and maintain healthy and rewarding relationships with diverse individuals and groups. This includes communicating clearly, listening actively, cooperating, resisting inappropriate social pressure, negotiating conflict constructively, and seeking and offering help when needed.

Responsible decision-making: The ability to make constructive and respectful choices about personal behavior and social interactions based on consideration of ethical standards, safety concerns, social norms, the realistic evaluation of consequences of various actions, and the well-being of self and others.

FIGURE 4-2 Elements of socioemotional competence.
SOURCE: Collaborative for Academic, Social, and Emotional Learning (http://www.casel.org/social-and-emotional-learning/core-competencies, accessed March 24, 2015).

ior is not resolved during the early years, children with persistent early socioemotional difficulties experience problems in socialization, school adjustment, school success, and educational and vocational adaptation in adolescence and adulthood (e.g., Dunlap et al., 2006; Lane et al., 2008; Nelson et al., 2004). Thus attention to socioemotional competence also is important from the perspective of addressing early emerging behavior problems before they become more serious.

A variety of evidence-based approaches can be implemented to strengthen socioemotional competence for young children (Domitrovich et al., 2012; IOM and NRC, 2009). These approaches typically entail strategies designed to improve children's emotion identification and understanding combined with the development of social problem-solving skills; practice in simple emotion regulation strategies; and coaching in prosocial behavior through strategies that can involve role playing, modeling, and reinforcement of socially competent behavior. Importantly, as discussed further in Chapter 6, these strategies can be incorporated into daily classroom practice to provide children with everyday socioemotional learning.

Relational Security and Emotional Well-Being

As noted earlier in the discussion of self-regulation, socioemotional competencies contribute to the development of relationships with parents, educators, and peers. The development of positive relationships enables young children to participate constructively in learning experiences that are inherently social. The emotional support and security provided by positive relationships contributes in multifaceted ways to young children's learning success. Research on the security of attachment between young children and their parents illustrates this point, and provides a basis for considering the nature of children's relationships with educators and peers.

A secure parent–child attachment is widely recognized as foundational for healthy development, and the evolving understanding of the importance of attachment encompasses research in developmental psychology and developmental neuroscience (as discussed in Chapter 3) (Schore and Schore, 2008; Thompson, 2013). Research has shown that securely attached children receive more sensitively responsive parental care, and in turn develop greater social skills with adults and peers and greater social and emotional understanding of others, show more advanced moral development, and have a more positive self-concept (see Thompson, 2013, for a review). Securely attached children also have been found to be more advanced in cognitive and language development and to show greater achievement in school (de Ruiter and van IJzendoorn, 1993; van Ijzendoorn et al., 1995; West et al., 2013). This association has been found for infants, preschool-age children, and older children, suggesting that it is fairly robust.

Most researchers believe that the association between attachment security and cognitive competence derives not from a direct link between the two, but from a number of processes mediating a secure attachment and the development of cognitive and language skills (O'Connor and McCartney, 2007). The mediators that have been studied include the following:

- Early confidence and competence at exploration—One of the functions of a secure attachment is to enable infants and young children to better explore the environment, confident in the caregiver's support and responsiveness if things go awry. An extensive research literature, focused primarily on young children, confirms this expectation (van Ijzendoorn et al., 1995). Early in life, exploratory interest is likely to lead to new discoveries and learning.
- Maternal instruction and guidance—Consistent with the sensitivity that initially contributes to a secure attachment, considerable research has shown that the mothers of securely attached children continue to respond supportively in ways that promote the child's social and cognitive achievements (Thompson, in press). In particular, these mothers talk more elaboratively with their children in ways that foster the children's deeper understanding and in so doing help support the children's cognitive growth (Fivush et al., 2006). Furthermore, increased mother–child conversation is likely to foster the child's linguistic skills.
- Children's social competence with adults and peers—Securely attached children develop enhanced social skills and social understanding that enhance their competence in interactions with peers and adults in learning environments. In this light, their greater cognitive and language competencies may derive, at least in part, from more successful interactions with social partners in learning contexts. (See the detailed discussion of social interaction as a forum for cognitive growth later in this section.)
- Self-regulatory competence—Several studies suggest that securely attached children are more skilled in the preschool and early grade school years at self-regulation, especially as it is manifested in greater social competence and emotion regulation. Self-regulatory competence also may extend to children's greater attentional focus, cognitive self-control, and persistence in learning situations. In one recent report, the association of attachment security with measures of school engagement in the early primary grades was mediated by differences in children's social self-control; attentional impulsivity also varied with the security of attachment (Drake et al., 2014; Thompson, 2013).

- Stress management—One of the functions of a secure attachment is that it supports the social buffering of stress by providing children with an adult who regularly assists them in challenging circumstances. The social buffering of stress may be an especially important aspect of how a secure attachment contributes to cognitive competence for children in disadvantaged circumstances when stress is likely to be chronic and potentially overwhelming (see Gunnar and Donzella, 2002, for a review; Nachmias et al., 1996) (see also the discussion of chronic stress and adversity later in this chapter).

In addition to the substantial research on parent–child attachment and the development of cognitive competence, a smaller but significant research literature focuses on the development of attachments between children and educators and how those attachments contribute to children's success in structured learning environments (e.g., Ahnert et al., 2006; Birch and Ladd, 1998; Howes and Hamilton, 1992; Howes et al., 1998; Ladd et al., 1999; Mitchell-Copeland et al., 1997; Pianta and Stuhlman, 2004a,b). In some respects, the processes connecting children's learning achievement with the supportive, secure relationships they develop with educators are similar to those observed with parent–child attachments. As with their parents and other caregivers, children develop attachments to their educators, and the quality of those relationships has a significant and potentially enduring influence on their classroom success (Hamre and Pianta, 2001). Secure, warm relationships with educators facilitate young children's self-confidence when learning and assist in their self-regulatory competence, and there is evidence that children with such relationships in the classroom learn more than those who have more difficult relationships with educators (NICHD Early Child Care Research Network, 2003; Pianta and Stuhlman, 2004b).

In one study, preschoolers identified as academically at risk based on demographic characteristics and reports of problems by their kindergarten teachers were followed to the end of first grade (Hamre and Pianta, 2005). The children with first-grade teachers who provided high amounts of instructional and emotional support had achievement scores comparable to those of their low-risk peers. Support was measured by teacher behaviors such as verbal comments promoting effort, persistence, and mastery; conversations using open-ended questions; encouragement of child responsibility; sensitivity; and a positive classroom climate. O'Connor and McCartney (2007) likewise found that positive educator–child relationships from preschool through third grade were associated with higher third-grade achievement, and that much of this achievement derived from how positive relationships promoted children's classroom engagement.

Positive educator–child relationships are especially important during the transition to school, when children's initial expectations about school and adjustment to its social demands take shape (Ladd et al., 1999; Silver et al., 2005). Children who develop more positive relationships with their teachers in kindergarten are more positive about attending school, more excited about learning, and more self-confident. In the classroom they achieve more compared with children who experience more conflicted or troubled relationships with their teachers (Birch and Ladd, 1997; NICHD Early Child Care Research Network, 2003; Pianta and Stuhlman, 2004b). A positive relationship with educators may be especially important for children who are at risk of academic difficulty because such a relationship can provide support for self-confidence and classroom involvement (Pianta et al., 1995).

A similar association is seen for peer relationships. Children who experience greater friendship and peer acceptance tend to feel more positive about coming to school, participate more in activities in the classroom, and achieve more in kindergarten (Ladd et al., 1996, 1997). Peer rejection is associated with less classroom participation, poorer academic performance, and a desire to avoid school (Buhs and Ladd, 2001).

Taken together, research documenting the association between the security of attachment and the development of cognitive and language competence, as well as the stronger academic performance of securely attached children, highlights the multiple ways in which supportive relationships contribute to early learning. In particular, such relationships with parents, educators, and even peers provide immediate support that helps children focus their energies on learning opportunities, and they also foster the development of social and cognitive skills that children enlist in learning.

Emotion Regulation and Self-Management

Another element of socioemotional competence, touched on earlier in the section on general learning competencies, is self-regulation of emotion, or emotion regulation, which can affect learning behaviors and relationships with adults and peers. As noted in that earlier discussion, emotion regulation is closely intertwined with cognitive self-regulation and executive function. Emotion regulation processes include emotional and motivational responses to situations involving risk and reward (e.g., Kerr and Zelazo, 2004). They are frequently inhibitory; that is, they include the ability to suppress one response (e.g., grabbing a toy from another) so as to respond in a better way (asking for or sharing the toy). The development of emotion regulation and other forms of self-management in the early years is based on slowly maturing regions of the prefrontal cortex that continue to develop throughout adolescence and even early adulthood. Thus, early learners are maturationally challenged to manage their attention, emotions, and behavioral impulses effectively in a care setting or classroom.

Because they have difficulty cooperating or resolving conflicts successfully, children who lack effective self-regulation do not participate in a productive way in classroom activities—including learning activities (Broidy et al., 2003; Ladd et al., 1999; Saarni et al., 1998). Children with poor emotion regulation skills may act disruptively and aggressively; they then receive less support from their peers, which in turn may undermine their learning (Valiente et al., 2011). Poor emotion regulation also diminishes positive educator–child interactions, which, as discussed in the previous section, has been shown to predict poor academic performance and behavior problems (Hamre and Pianta, 2001; Neuenschwander et al., 2012; Raver and Knitzer, 2002).

Coupled with joint attention and delay of gratification, self-regulation skills are linked to social competence and ease the transition to kindergarten (Huffman et al., 2000; McIntyre et al., 2006). Children with difficulty regulating emotion in preschool and kindergarten often display inappropriate behavior, fail to pay attention (affecting whether they recall and process information), and have difficulty following instructions, all of which contribute to learning problems (Eisenberg et al., 2010). Unfortunately, these difficulties tend to be common in preschool and kindergarten. They are an important determinant of whether educators and parents regard young children as "ready for school" (Rimm-Kaufman et al., 2000).

Some researchers also suggest that emotion regulation in preschool and kindergarten serves as an early indicator of later academic success (Graziano et al., 2007; Howse et al., 2003b; Trentacosta and Izard, 2007). In preschool, McClelland and colleagues (2007) found not only that emotion regulation predicted early skills in literacy and mathematics but also that growth in emotion regulation in 4-year-olds over a 1-year period was linked to greater gains in literacy, vocabulary, and math compared with children showing less growth. Reading disability and problem behavior may be a "chicken or egg" problem: students who have behavior problems in first grade are more likely to have reading difficulties in third grade and students who have reading difficulties in first grade are more likely to exhibit behavior problems in third grade (Morgan et al., 2008). Thus a particularly effective learning environment may be one that provides both effective reading instruction and support for behavioral self-regulation (Connor et al., 2014).

Young children are better enabled to exercise self-regulation in the company of educators who have developmentally appropriate expectations for their self-control, provide predictable routines, and offer guidance that scaffolds their developing skills of self-management, especially in the context of carefully designed daily practices in a well-organized setting (Bodrova and Leong, 2012). Indeed, in an intervention for academically at-risk young children, the Chicago School Readiness Project gave Head Start teachers specialized training at the beginning of the year in classroom management strategies to help lower-income preschoolers better regulate their own behavior. At the end of the school year, these children showed less impulsiveness, fewer disruptive behaviors, and better academic performance compared with children in classrooms with teachers who received a different training regimen (Raver et al., 2009, 2011).

Conclusion About the Ability to Self-Regulate

The ability to self-regulate both emotion and cognitive processes is important for learning and academic achievement, affecting children's thinking, motivation, self-control, and social interactions. Children's progress in this ability from birth through age 8 is influenced by the extent to which relationships with adults, learning environments, and learning experiences support this set of skills, and their progress can be impaired by stressful and adverse circumstances.

Social and Emotional Understanding

As described earlier in this chapter, even infants and toddlers have an implicit theory of mind for understanding how certain mental states are associated with people's behavior. From their simple and straightforward awareness that people act intentionally and are goal directed; that people have positive and negative feelings in response to things around them; and that people have different perceptions, goals, and feelings, young children develop increasingly sophisticated understanding of the mental experiences that cause people to act as they do (Wellman, 2011). They realize, for example, that people's beliefs about reality can be accurate or may be mistaken, and this realization leads to their understanding that people can be deceived, that the child's own thoughts and feelings need not be disclosed, and that not everybody can be believed (Lee, 2013; Mills, 2013). They appreciate that people's thinking may be biased by expectations, prior experiences, and desires that cause them to interpret the same situation in very different ways (Lalonde and Chandler, 2002). They also begin to appreciate how personality differences among people can cause different individuals to act in the same situation in very different ways (Heyman and Gelman, 1999).

These remarkable advances in social understanding are important to children's developing socioemotional skills for interacting with educators and peers. These advances also are fostered by children's classroom experiences. Children learn about how people think and feel from directly observing; asking questions; and conversing about people's mental states with trusted informants, such as parents (Bartsch and Wellman, 1995; Dunn, 2002; Thompson et al., 2003). Similarly, interactions with educators and peers provide young children with apt lessons in mutual understanding and perspective taking, cooperation, conflict management, personality differences and similarities, and emotional understanding in an environment where these skills are developing. This is especially so when educators can use children's experiences as forums for developing social and emotional understanding, such as when they explain why peers are feeling the way they do, suggest strategies for resolving conflict over resources or a point of view, or involve children in collective decision making involving different opinions.

Self-Awareness and Early Learning

How young children think of themselves as learners, and in particular their self-perceived efficacy in mastering new understanding, is an early developing and continuously important influence on their academic success. Young children become increasingly sensitive to the positive and negative evaluations of their behavior by parents, which serve as the basis for their self-evaluations (Stipek et al., 1992). In one study, mothers who provided positive evaluations, gentle guidance, and corrective feedback during teaching tasks with their 2-year-olds had children who, 1 year later, were more persistent and less likely to avoid difficult challenges. By contrast, mothers who were intrusively controlling of their toddlers had children who, 1 year later, responded with shame when they had difficulty (Kelley et al., 2000). Gunderson and colleagues (2013) found that 14- to 38-month-old children whose parents praised their efforts during unstructured home observations were more likely, as third graders, to believe that abilities are malleable and can be improved.

An extensive research literature documents the effects of parents' and educators' performance feedback on children's self-concept and motivation to succeed. Most of this research was conducted with older children and adolescents because of their more sophisticated understanding of differences in ability (see Wigfield et al., 2006, for a review); however, preschoolers and early primary grade students are also sensitive to success and failure and to their imputed causes. In a study by Cimpian and colleagues (2007), for example, 4-year-old children were represented by puppets whose performance was praised by a teacher using either generic feedback ("You are a good drawer.") to imply trait-based (ability-centered) success or nongeneric feedback ("You did a good job drawing.") to imply situation-based (effort-centered) success. The children did not differ in their self-evaluations after hearing praise of either kind, but when their puppet subsequently made a mistake and was criticized for it, the 4-year-olds who had heard generic feedback evaluated their performance and the situation more negatively than did children hearing nongeneric feedback, suggesting that they interpreted criticism as reflecting deficits in their ability. Similar results have been reported with kindergarteners by Kamins and Dweck (1999) and by Zentall and Morris (2010), with the latter indicating that task persistence as well as self-evaluation were strengthened by the use of nongeneric performance feedback.

Parent and educator expectations for children's academic success also are important influences. High parental expectations for children's school achievement are associated with children's later academic performance, and this association often is mediated by the greater involvement of parents in the preschool or school program and other practices that support children's school success (Baroody and Dobbs-Oates, 2009; Englund et al., 2004; Mantzicopoulos, 1997). The role of educator expectations in children's success is illustrated by a longitudinal study in which teacher expectations for children's math achievement in grades 1 and 3 directly predicted children's scores on standardized achievement tests 2 years later; teacher expectations for reading achievement had indirect associations with later reading scores. The results of this study also suggest that teacher expectations were especially influential for academically at-risk students (Hinnant et al., 2009).

Social Interaction as a Forum for Cognitive Growth

A wider perspective on the importance of socioemotional skills for academic success is gained by considering the importance of social experiences for early learning. Contemporary research has led developmental scientists to understand the mind's development as deriving jointly from the child's naturally inquisitive activity and the catalysts of social experience. Sometimes these social experiences are in formal teaching and other pedagogical experiences, but often they take the form of adults and children sharing in activities that provide the basis for early learning, in a kind of "guided participation" (e.g., Rogoff, 1991). These activities can be as simple as the one-sided "conversation" parents have with their infant or toddler from which language skills develop, or the shared sorting of laundry into piles of similar color, or labeling of another child's feelings during an episode of peer conflict. In short, considerable early learning occurs in the course of a young child's ordinary interactions with a responsive adult.

Social experiences provide emotional security and support that enables learning and can also contribute to the development of language, number skills, problem solving, and other cognitive and learning skills that are foundational for school readiness and academic achievement. Through their interactions with children, adults provide essential stimulation that provides rapidly developing mental processes with catalysts that provoke further learning. Conversely, the lack of these catalysts contributes to learning disparities by the time that children become preschoolers. These processes are well illustrated by considering the growth of language and literacy skills and of mathematical understanding.

Language and Literacy

It is difficult to think of any child developing language apart from social interactions with others. As discussed earlier in this chapter, variability in these experiences, beginning in infancy, helps account for socioeconomic disparities in language and mathematical skills that are apparent by the time children enter school. In a widely cited study, Hart and Risley (1995) recorded 1 hour of naturally occurring speech in the homes of 42 families at monthly intervals beginning when children were 7-9 months old and continuing until they turned 3 years. They found that by age 3, children living in the most socioeconomically advantaged families had a working vocabulary that was more than twice the size of that of children growing up in the most disadvantaged families. The latter group of children also was adding words more slowly than their advantaged counterparts. The differences in children's vocabulary size were associated, in part, with how many words were spoken to them during the home observations, with a much richer linguistic environment being characteristic of the most advantaged homes. In addition, words were used in functionally different ways, with a much higher ratio of affirmative-to-prohibitive language being used in the most advantaged homes and a much lower ratio (i.e., below 1) being characteristic of the most disadvantaged homes. Differences in the language environment in which children grew up were, in other words, qualitative as well as quantitative in nature. Further research with a subset of 29 families in this sample showed that 3-year-olds' vocabulary size significantly predicted their scores on standardized tests of language skill in third grade (Hart and Risley, 1995).

A later study by Fernald and colleagues (2013) confirms and extends these findings. A sample of 48 English-learning infants from families varying in socioeconomic status was followed from 18 to 24 months. At 18 months, significant differences between infants from higher- and lower-income families were already seen in vocabulary size and in real-time language processing efficiency. By 24 months, a 6-month gap was found between the two groups in processing skills related to language development. A companion study by Weisleder and Fernald (2013) with 29 lower-income Spanish-speaking families found that infants who experienced more child-directed speech at 19 months had larger vocabularies and greater language processing efficiency at 24 months. But adult speech that was simply overheard by infants (i.e., not child directed) at 19 months had no association with later language (Schneidman et al., 2013). These studies indicate that child-directed speech, and perhaps the social interaction that accompanies it, is what strengthens infants' language processing efficiency. As in the Hart and Risley (1995) study, differences in family language environments were both qualitative and quantitative in nature. These findings are important in light of the association between the socioeconomic status of children's families and their language skills (Bradley and Corwyn, 2002).

The findings of these studies are consistent with those of studies of the social experiences in and outside the home that promote language learning in early childhood. (See also the section on language and literacy under "Learning Specific Subjects" earlier in this chapter.) According to one longitudinal study, language and literacy skills in kindergarten were predicted by several aspects of the language environment at home and in classrooms in the preschool years. The characteristics of adult language that stimulated young children's language development included adult use of varied vocabulary during conversations with children; extended discourse on a single topic (rather than frequent topic switching); and diversity of language-related activities, including storybook reading, conversation related to children's experiences and interests, language corrections, and pretend play (Dickinson, 2003; Dickinson and Porche, 2011; Dickinson and Tabors, 2001). These elements of the early childhood social environment predicted both kindergarten language skills and fourth-grade language and reading abilities. Other studies show that extensive use of descriptive language (e.g., labeling and commenting on people's actions) related to the child's current experience contributes to the quality of children's language development. Shared storybook reading also has been found to enhance the language skills of young children in lower-income homes (Raikes et al., 2006). Stated differently, what matters is not just *how much* language young children are exposed to but the *social and emotional contexts* of language shared with an adult.

Language and literacy development is a major focus of instruction in prekindergarten and K-3 classrooms, and the instructional strategies used by teachers are both more formal and more sophisticated than those used in early childhood classrooms. Duke and Block (2012) have noted that in primary grade classrooms, vocabulary, reading comprehension, and conceptual and content knowledge are not adequately emphasized. The practices that would enhance early reading skills are embedded in children's social experiences with educators and peers in the classroom. They involve children interacting with partners throughout reading activity, and teachers explaining and discussing vocabulary terms and encouraging children to make personal connections with the concepts in the text.

Number Concepts and Mathematics

Language and literacy skills are the best-studied area in which early social experiences are influential, but they are not the only skills for which social interactions are important. Social experiences also are important for mathematics, such as for developing an understanding of numbers as well as early number and spatial/geometric language. Infants have an approximate number system that enables them to distinguish different quantities provided that the numerical ratio between them is not small, and this discrimination ability improves with increasing age (see Box 4-5 earlier in this chapter). There is some evidence that early individual differences in this ability are consistent during the first year and predict later mathematical abilities, although the reason for this remains unclear (Libertus and Brannon, 2010; Starr et al., 2013). Toddlers also are beginning to comprehend certain number principles, such as one-to-one correspondence (Slaughter et al., 2011). How adults talk about number is important. In one study, everyday parent–child discourse was recorded for 90 minutes every 4 months when the child was between 14 and 30 months old. The amount of parents' spontaneous "number talk" in these conversations (e.g., counting objects, references to time) was predictive of children's cardinal number knowledge (i.e., the knowledge that "four" refers to sets with four items) at 46 months (Levine et al., 2010). Particularly important was when parents counted or labeled fairly large sets of objects within the child's view, providing concrete referents for parent–child interaction over number (Gunderson and Levine, 2011).

Klibanoff and colleagues (2006) found that in early childhood, teachers' "math language"—that is, the frequency of their verbal references to number and geometric concepts—varied greatly for different teachers, but it significantly predicted progress in preschoolers' mathematical knowledge over the course of the school year. Similarly, another study found that parents' number-related activities at home with their young children were highly variable, but parents who engaged in more of these activities had children with stronger mathematical skill on standardized tests (Blevins-Knabe and Musun-Miller, 1996). These practices in the classroom and at home help explain the significant socioeconomic disparities in number understanding by the time children arrive at school (Klibanoff et al., 2006; Saxe et al., 1987). In addition to spoken references to numerical and geometric concepts, adults stimulate developing mathematical understanding when they incorporate these concepts into everyday activities, including games and other kinds of play; prompt children's explanations for numerical inferences; probe their understanding; and relate mathematical ideas to everyday experience (NRC, 2009). Unfortunately, the quality of mathematical instruction is highly variable in preschool and early primary grades (discussed further in Chapter 6).

Taken together, these studies suggest the diverse ways in which social experiences provide catalysts for children's developing language and number skills that are the focus of later academic work. In these domains, adult practices provide essential cognitive stimulants beginning in infancy. Similar practices—adapted to young children's developing skills—remain important as children proceed through the primary grades.

Relationships and Early Learning: Implications for Adults

The relationship of an adult to a child—the emotional quality of their interaction, the experiences they have shared, the adult's beliefs about the child's capabilities and characteristics—helps motivate young children's learning, inspire their self-confidence, and provide emotional support to engage them in new learning.

Commonplace interactions provide contexts for supporting the development of cognitive and learning skills and the emotional security in which early learning thrives. Applauding a toddler's physical skills or a second-grader's writing skills, counting together the leaves on the sidewalk or the ingredients of a recipe, interactively reading a book, talking about a sibling's temper tantrum or an episode of classroom peer conflict—these and other shared experiences contribute to young children's cognitive development and early learning.

Conclusion About Socioemotional Development

Socioemotional development contributes to the growth of emotional security that enables young children to fully invest themselves in new learning and to the growth of cognitive skills and competencies that are important for learning. These capacities are essential because learning is inherently a social process. Young children's relationships—with parents, teachers, and peers—thus are central to the learning experiences that contribute to their later success.

PHYSICAL DEVELOPMENT AND HEALTH

Child development and early learning are closely intertwined with child health. Indeed, each is a foundation for outcomes in the other: health is a foundation for learning, while education is a determinant of health (Zimmerman and Woolf, 2014). The Center on the Developing Child at Harvard University (2010) has described three foundational areas of child health and development that contribute to physical and mental well-being:

- Stable and responsive relationships—Such relationships provide young children with consistent, nurturing, and protective interactions with adults that enhance their learning and help them develop adaptive capacities that promote well-regulated stress response systems.
- Safe and supportive physical, chemical, and built environments—Such environments provide physical and emotional spaces that are free from toxins and fear, allow active exploration without significant risk of harm, and offer supports for families raising young children.
- Sound and appropriate nutrition—Such nutrition includes health-promoting food intake as well as eating habits, beginning with the future mother's nutritional status even before conception.

This section examines interrelated topics of physical development, child health, nutrition, and physical activity and then touches on partnerships between the health and education sectors (also discussed in Chapter 5).

Physical Development

Physical development goes hand-in-hand with cognitive development in young children, and progress in one domain often relies on progress in the other. Similar to cognitive development, typical physical development follows a common trajectory among children but with individual differences in the rate of development. A child's physical development encompasses healthy physical growth; the development of sensory systems, including vision and hearing; and development of the ability to use the musculoskeletal system for gross motor skills that involve large body movements as well as fine motor skills that require precision and the controlled production of sound for speaking. Sensory and motor development are critical for both everyday and classroom activities that contribute to cognitive development, early learning, and eventually academic achievement.

Young children's growth in gross and fine motor skills develops throughout the birth through age 8 continuum—early on from holding their head up; rolling over; standing, crawling, and walking; to grasping cereal, picking up blocks, using a fork, tying shoelaces, and writing. A number of recent studies have focused on the relationships among the development of fine and gross motor skills in infants and young children, cognitive development, and school readiness. For example, one study found that students showing deficiencies in fine motor skills exhibited lower math and verbal scores (Sandler et al., 1992), and more recent studies have also shown that fine motor skills were strongly linked to later achievement

(Grissmer et al., 2010a; Pagani and Messier, 2012). Some of the same neural infrastructure in the brain that controls the learning process during motor development are also involved in the control of learning in cognitive development (Grissmer et al., 2010a). The evidence of the impact of motor skills on cognitive development and readiness for school calls for a shift in curricula to include activities that focus on fine motor skills, to include the arts, physical education, and play (Grissmer et al., 2010b).

Child Health

Health has an important influence on early learning and academic achievement. Hair and colleagues (2006) found that poor health can be as important in contributing to struggles with academic performance in first grade as language and cognitive skills, along with lack of social skills. Not only are healthy children better prepared to learn, but participation in high-quality early childhood programs leads to improved health in adulthood, setting the stage for intergenerational well-being. Data from Head Start and from the Carolina Abecedarian Project indicate that high-quality, intensive interventions can prevent, or at least delay, the onset of physical and emotional problems from adolescence into adulthood (Campbell et al., 2014; Carneiro and Ginja, 2012). Data from a national longitudinal survey show that involvement in Head Start was associated with fewer behavior problems and serious health problems, such as 29 percent less obesity in males at 12 and 13 years of age. In addition, Head Start participants had less depression and obesity as adolescents and 31 percent less involvement in criminal activity as young adults. Similarly, long-term follow-up of adults who were enrolled in the Carolina Abecedarian Project revealed that males in their mid-30s in the project had lower rates of hypertension, obesity, and metabolic syndrome than controls. None of the males in the project had metabolic syndrome, compared with 25 percent of the control group. Further analysis of growth parameters indicated that those who were obese in their mid-30s were on that trajectory by 5 years of age, indicating the need for emphasis on healthy nutrition and regular physical activity beginning in early childhood. These studies suggest that the impact of early care and education programs on physical and emotional health is long term.

Nutrition

Sufficient, high-quality dietary intake is necessary for children's health, development, and learning. Support for providing healthy nutrition for children and their families, including pregnant and expectant mothers, is vital. Adequate protein, calories, and nutrients are needed for brain development and function. While the rapid brain growth and development that occurs in infants and toddlers may make children in this age group particularly vulnerable to dietary deficiencies, nutrition remains important as certain brain regions continue to develop through childhood into adolescence.

Nutrients, Cognitive Development, and Academic Performance

Deficiencies in protein, energy, and micronutrients such as iron, zinc, selenium, iodine, and omega-3 fatty acids have been linked to adverse effects on cognitive and emotional functioning (Bryan et al., 2004). Research has shown that iron-deficiency anemia (IDA) is associated with lower cognitive and academic performance (Bryan et al., 2004; Nyaradi et al., 2013; Taras, 2005). Children at an early school age who had IDA as an infant were found to have lower test scores than those who did not have IDA. Effects of severe IDA in infancy have been seen in adolescence. These effects include lower scores in motor functioning; written expression; arithmetic achievement; and some specific cognitive processes, such as spatial memory and selective recall (NRC and IOM, 2000). However, it is not clear whether children with iron deficiency but no anemia have similar outcomes (Taras, 2005). A review of daily iron supplementation in children aged 5-12 years studied in randomized and quasi-randomized controlled trials showed improvement in measures of attention and concentration, global cognitive scores, and, for children with anemia, intelligence quotient (IQ) scores (Low et al., 2013).

IDA in infancy also has been associated with impaired inhibitory control and executive functioning. Altered socioemotional behavior and affect have been seen in infants with iron deficiency regardless of whether anemia is present (Lozoff, 2011). One study found an association between iron supplementation in infancy and increased adaptive behavior at age 10 years, especially in the areas of affect and response to reward, which may have beneficial effects on school performance, mental health, and personal relationships (Lozoff et al., 2014).

Folate and iodine also have been shown to be important for brain development and cognitive performance (Bougma et al., 2013; Bryan et al., 2004; Nyaradi et al., 2013), although iodine deficiency is rare in the United States. While there is some evidence that zinc, vitamin B_{12}, and omega-3 polyunsaturated fatty acids also may be important for cognitive development, the research on these associations is inconclusive (Bougma et al., 2013; Bryan et al., 2004; Taras, 2005).

Food Insecurity, Diet Quality, and Healthful Eating

Food insecurity and diet quality in children have both been linked to impaired academic performance and cognitive and socioemotional development. Food insecurity refers to circumstances in which households do not have adequate food to eat, encompassing both inadequate quantity and nutritional quality of food (ERS, 2014). Food insecurity affects development not only by compromising nutrition but also by contributing to a factor in family stress (Cook and Frank, 2008). In 2012, 48 million Americans were food insecure, a fivefold increase from the 1960s and a 57 percent increase from the late 1990s. One in six Americans reported being short of food at least once per year. More than half of affected households were white, and more than half lived outside cities. Indeed, hunger in the suburbs has more than doubled since 2007. Two-thirds of food-insecure households with children have at least one working adult, typically in a full-time job (McMillan, 2014).

A recent review indicates that food insecurity is a "prevalent risk to the growth, health, cognitive, and behavioral potential of low-income children" (Cook and Frank, 2008, p. 202). Studies found that children in food-insufficient families were more likely than those in households with adequate food to have fair/poor health; iron deficiency; and behavioral, emotional, and academic problems. Infants and toddlers are at particular risk from food insecurity even at its least severe levels (Cook and Frank, 2008). Cross-sectional studies of children from developing countries have shown an association among general undernutrition and stunting, IQ scores, and academic performance (Bryan et al., 2004). Alaimo and colleagues (2001) found that food insecurity was linked to poorer academic and psychosocial outcomes in children ages 6 to 11 years. Similarly, Florence and colleagues (2008) observed that students with lower overall diet quality were significantly more likely to fail a literacy assessment. Subsequent research has shown that while food insecurity experienced earlier in childhood was associated with emotional problems that appeared in adolescence, cognitive and behavioral problems could be accounted for by differences in the home environments, such as family income and the household's sensitivity to children's needs (Belsky et al., 2010).

Eating breakfast, which can be related to food insecurity, diet quality, and healthful eating habits, has been associated with improved cognitive function, academic performance, and school attendance (Basch, 2011; Hoyland et al., 2009; Mahoney et al., 2005; Nyaradi et al., 2013; Rampersaud et al., 2005). According to two reviews of the effect of consuming breakfast in children and adolescents, the evidence suggests that children who consume breakfast—particularly those children whose nutritional status is compromised—may have improved cognitive function, test grades, and school attendance. The positive effects of school breakfast programs may be explained in part by their effect of increasing school attendance (Hoyland et al., 2009; Rampersaud et al., 2005). The composition of the breakfast meal may also be important to cognitive performance; a breakfast meal with a low glycemic index, such as oatmeal, has been shown to improve cognitive function (Cooper et al., 2012; Mahoney et al., 2005).

In 2011, the Centers for Disease Control and Prevention (CDC) published a report documenting the relationship between healthy eating and increased life expectancy; improved quality of life; and fewer chronic diseases, including cardiovascular disease, obesity, metabolic syndrome, diabetes, and inadequate bone health (CDC, 2011). The report documents the high rate of iron deficiency among obese children and emphasizes the link between dental caries and unhealthy diet. Children are unlikely to follow recommendations for the number of servings of various food groups and they consume higher-than-recommended amounts of saturated fats, sodium, and foods with added sugar. Children's eating behavior and food choices are influenced not only by taste preferences but also by the home environment and parental influences, including household eating rules, family meal patterns, and parents' lifestyles. The school environment influences children's eating behavior as well. The availability of unhealthy options in schools leads to poor choices by children, whereas research has shown that efforts to reduce the availability of sugar-sweetened beverages in the schools can have a positive impact on children's choices (AAP Committee on School Health, 2004). There are also rising concerns about food insecurity in association with obesity; inexpensive foods tend not to be nutritious, and contribute to increasing rates of obesity (IOM, 2011; McMillan, 2014).

Physical Activity

A recent Institute of Medicine (IOM) study linked increasing physical activity and enhancing physical fitness to improved academic performance, and found that this can be facilitated by physical activity built into children's days through physical education, recess, and physical classroom activity (IOM, 2013). Likewise, the American Academy of Pediatrics recently highlighted the crucial role of recess as a complement to physical education, suggesting that recess offers cognitive, social, emotional, and physical benefits and is a necessary component of a child's development (AAP Council on School Health, 2013). However, fewer than half of youth meet the current recommendation of at least 60 minutes of vigorous- or moderate-intensity physical activity per day, and recent years have seen a significant downward trend in the offering of daily physical education in schools at all levels (CDC, 2012; GAO, 2012). Positive support from friends and family encourages children to engage in physical activity, as do physical environments that are conducive to activity. However, the school environment plays an especially important role. The IOM report recommends that schools provide access to a minimum of 60 minutes of vigorous- or moderate-intensity physical activity per day, including an average of

30 minutes per day in physical education class for students in elementary schools (IOM, 2013).

Partnerships Between Health and Education

Each of the domains of child development and early learning discussed in this chapter can be supported through interventions that involve both the health and education sectors (see also the discussion of continuity among sectors in Chapter 5). Specific activities include coordinating vision, hearing, developmental, and behavioral screening to facilitate early identification of children with special needs; completing daily health checks; making appropriate referrals and collaborating with the child's medical home and dental health services; ensuring that immunizations for the entire family and for the early care and education workforce are up to date; modifying and adapting services to meet the individual needs of the child; and providing support to the early care and education workforce to promote more inclusive practices for children with special needs. In addition, teaching and modeling skills in sanitation and personal hygiene will contribute to preventing illness. Furthermore, pediatric health care professionals can make an important contribution by promoting literacy. Extensive research documents the positive impact on early language and literacy development when a pediatric professional gives advice to parents about reading developmentally appropriate books with children as early as 6 months of age (AAP Council on Early Childhood et al., 2014).

There is evidence that coordinated efforts between educational settings and health care services lead to improved health. Head Start, the Infant Health and Development Program, and the Carolina Abecedarian Project are examples of early care and education programs that have integrated health care services into the intervention design, leading to positive health outcomes. Schools also can partner with pediatric health care professionals in their communities to identify opportunities to enhance physical activity in the school setting (AAP Committee on Sports Medicine and Fitness and AAP Committee on School Health, 2000). CDC (2011) has offered recommendations for promoting healthful eating and physical activity that include the following and, if placed in an appropriate developmental context, can be applied to care and education settings for children aged 0-8:

- Use a coordinated approach to develop, implement, and evaluate healthful eating and physical activity policies and practices.
- Establish school environments that support healthy eating and activity.

- Provide a quality school meal program and ensure that students have only appealing, healthy food and beverage choices offered outside of the school meal program.
- Implement a comprehensive physical activity program with quality physical education as the cornerstone.
- Implement health education that provides students with the knowledge, attitudes, skills, and experiences needed for healthy eating and physical activity.
- Provide students with health, mental health, and social services to address healthy eating, physical activity, and related chronic disease prevention.
- Partner with families and community members in the development and implementation of healthy eating and physical activity policies, practices, and programs.
- Provide a school employee wellness program that includes healthy eating and physical activity services for all school staff members.
- Employ qualified persons and provide them with professional development opportunities in staffing physical education; health education; nutrition services; health, mental health, and social services; and supervision of recess, cafeteria time, and out-of-school-time programs.

School-based health centers are another approach to partnering between health and education. They have been associated with improved immunization rates, better adherence to scheduled preventive examinations, and more treatment for illnesses and injuries, as well as fewer emergency room visits. For example, King and colleagues (2006) found that a school-based vaccination program significantly reduced influenza symptoms in the entire school. School-based mental health services also have been shown to be effective in addressing a wide range of emotional and behavioral issues (Rones and Hoagwood, 2000). School-based health centers have been shown to reduce nonfinancial barriers to health care (Keyl et al., 1996), and families also report more satisfaction with their care than in community or hospital settings (Kaplan et al., 1999).

Conclusion About Health, Nutrition, and Early Learning

Safe physical and built environments, health, and nutrition are essential to early learning and academic achievement. Food security and adequate nutrition are important to support cognitive development and participation in education, and food insecurity and poor nutrition can contribute to early learning difficulties. Care and education settings provide an opportunity to promote healthful eating and physical activity in learning environments. Providing appropriate health and developmental screenings and follow-up care and services also is important in supporting development and early learning.

Health and Early Learning: Implications for Adults

Healthy children supported by healthy adults are better prepared to learn. Child health begins prior to conception and extends through pregnancy and throughout childhood. Therefore, the early care and education workforce must be prepared to work across generations to provide education, support, and community linkages to ensure that children grow up poised for success. Ongoing federal support for evidence-based home visiting programs for high-risk families that begin early in pregnancy and continue through early childhood is essential. Professionals working in family childcare, early childhood education centers, preschools, and early elementary schools need to have working knowledge of the relationship between health and children's learning and development. Guidance related to nutrition, physical activity, oral health, immunizations, and preventive health care is essential across all early care and education settings. These professionals also need to be provided with supports and opportunities for close collaboration with health care services and their potential integration into or strengthened linkages with the early care and education setting.

EFFECTS OF CHRONIC STRESS AND ADVERSITY

As detailed in Chapter 3, one of the most important advances in developmental science in recent years has been the recognition that the brain incorporates experience into its development. Although experience is important at any age, early experiences are especially formative in the development of the brain's structure and function. Human development is the result of the continuous interaction of genetics and experience. This interplay is true not just of brain development but of other aspects of human development as well. Research in this area encourages developmental scientists as well as parents and practitioners to consider how positive early experiences and enrichment, in formal and informal ways, may have a beneficial influence on the developing brain and in turn on the growth of thinking and learning. The brain's openness to experience is, however, a double-edged sword—adverse early experiences can have potentially significant negative consequences for brain development and early learning.

As discussed in Chapter 3, evidence indicates that experiences of stress and adversity are biologically embedded and that individual differences exist in the health and developmental consequences of stress. A substantial body of evidence now shows that adversity and stress in early life are associated with higher rates of childhood mental and physical morbidities, more frequent disturbances in developmental trajectories and educational achievement, and lifelong risks of chronic disorders that compromise health and well-being (Boyce et al., 2012; Hertzman and Boyce, 2010; Shonkoff et al., 2009). Children respond to stress differently. Many exhibit withdrawal, anger and irritability, difficulty paying attention and concentrating, disturbed sleep, repeated and intrusive thoughts, and extreme distress triggered by things that remind them of their traumatic experiences. Some develop psychiatric conditions such as depression, anxiety, posttraumatic stress disorder, and a variety of behavioral disorders (NCTSN, 2005).

What are the circumstances that contribute to chronic adversity and stress for children? All children can experience forms of chronic stress and adversity, but exposures to stress and adversity are socioeconomically layered. Poverty, discussed in more detail below, has been the best studied and is a highly prevalent source of early chronic stress (Blair and Raver, 2012; Evans and Kim, 2013; Jiang et al., 2014). Young children in the United States also suffer high levels of victimization through child abuse and exposure to domestic violence. The U.S. Department of Health and Human Services reported for the year 2012 that of all child abuse victims, approximately 60 percent were age 8 or younger (Children's Bureau, 2013). The highest rates of child abuse and neglect, including fatalities related to child abuse, were reported for children in the first year of life. Comparable biological and behavioral effects of chronic stress have been studied in children in foster care, in those who experience significant or prolonged family conflict, in those who have a depressed parent, and in those who are abused or neglected (see Thompson, 2014, for a review).

It is noteworthy that these circumstances include not only those that most people would regard as sources of extreme stress for children (e.g., child abuse), but also those that an adult might regard as less significant because they may be less severe although persistent (e.g., parents' chronic marital conflict, poverty). This broader range of circumstances that children experience as stressful is consistent with the view that, in addition to situations that are manifestly threatening and dangerous, children are stressed by the denial or withdrawal of supportive care, especially when they are young.

Culture also is closely interrelated with stress and adversity. Culture affects the meaning that a child or a family attributes to specific types of traumatic events as well as the ways in which they respond. Because culture also influences expectations regarding the self, others, and social institutions, it can also influence how children and families experience and express distress, grieve or mourn losses, provide support to each other, seek help, and disclose personal information to others. Historical or multigenerational trauma also can influence cultural differences in responses to trauma and loss (NCTSN Core Curriculum on Childhood Trauma Task Force, 2012).

Building on the discussion in Chapter 3 of the biology of chronic stress and adversity, the following sections describe more broadly some of the contributing circumstances and consequences for young children, including the stressors associated with economic adversity; social buffering of stress; and the relationships among stress, learning, and mental health.

The Stressors of Economic Adversity

Children in any economic circumstances can experience stress and adversity, but considerable research on the effects of chronic stress on children's development has focused on children living in families in poverty or with low incomes. The number of children in these conditions of economic adversity is considerable. In 2012, nearly half the children under age 6 lived in poverty or low-income families (defined as up to 200 percent of the federal poverty level,[2] which remains a meagre subsistence) (Jiang et al., 2014). During that same year, more than half the children living with their families in homeless shelters were under the age of 6 (Child Trends, 2015).

The research is clear that poverty as a form of early chronic adversity is a risk factor to long-term physical and mental health, and that for children it can be a significant threat to their capacities to cope with stress, socialize constructively with others, and benefit from the cognitive stimulating opportunities of an early childhood classroom. Socioeconomic disparities in children's experiences of socioemotional adversity and challenging physical environments are well documented (see, e.g., Evans et al., 2012). Factors other than economic status itself contribute to the challenges and stresses for children living in low-income families (Fernald et al., 2013). Poverty often is accompanied by the confluence of multiple sources of chronic stress, such as food insufficiency, housing instability (and sometimes homelessness), exposure to violence, environmental noise and toxins, dangerous neighborhoods, poor childcare and schools, family chaos, parents with limited capacity (e.g., resources, education, knowledge/information, time, physical or mental energy) to be supportive and nurturing, parents who are anxious or depressed, parents who are harsh or abusive caregivers, impoverished parent–child communication, and home environments lacking cognitively stimulating activities (Evans et al., 2012; Fernald et al., 2013).

As discussed in detail in Chapter 3, the perturbed biological processes that often accompany economic adversity include changes in the structure and function of children's brain circuitry and dysregulation of their central

---

[2] The 2012 federal poverty threshold was $23,364 for a family of four with two children, $18,480 for a family of three with one child, $15,825 for a family of two with one child.

stress response systems. For these children, therefore, the effects of the chronic stresses associated with economic adversity are likely to contribute to academic, social, and behavioral problems. These problems affect not only early learning and the development of cognitive skills (with impacts on the development of language being best documented) but also the development of learning skills associated with self-regulation and persistence, as well as coping ability, health, and emotional well-being (Blair and Raver, 2012; Evans and Kim, 2013).

In addition, developmental consequences related to socioeconomic status are not seen exclusively in children from severely impoverished families. Rather, evidence shows a graded effect of deprivation and adversity across the entire spectrum of socioeconomic status, with even those children from the second-highest social class showing poorer health and development compared with those from families of the very highest socioeconomic status (Adler et al., 1994; Hertzman and Boyce, 2010). Moreover, as discussed in Chapter 3, children are not equally affected by early adverse experiences. Genetic and epigenetic influences may have a role in whether some children are more resilient to early adversity than others (Rutter, 2012).

Detrimental prenatal influences may also be important (Farah et al., 2008; Hackman et al., 2010). Although this report focuses on children beginning at birth, child development and early learning also are affected by what a child is exposed to before birth, including influences of family disadvantage. Box 4-6 highlights major research findings on the relationships among family disadvantage, fetal health, and child development.

Social Buffering of Stress

The neuroscience of stress has yielded greater understanding of how the effects of stress may be buffered through social support. In behavioral and neurobiological studies of humans and animals, researchers have shown how individuals in adversity show diminished behavioral reactivity and better-regulated cortisol response, among other effects, in the company of people who provide them with emotional support. For children, these individuals often are attachment figures in the family or outside the home.

In health psychology, the benefits of social support for the development and maintenance of healthy practices and the control of disease pathology and healing have been studied since the 1970s (e.g., Cassel, 1976; Cobb, 1976). Social support also has been recognized as a contributor to psychological well-being for children and youth in difficult circumstances (Thompson and Goodvin, in press). In recent years, research on the neurobiology of the social buffering of stress has contributed to a better understanding of why social support has these benefits (Hostinar et al., 2014). In human and animal studies, social companionship in the context of adver-

BOX 4-6
Family Disadvantage, Fetal Health, and Child Development

Children from different family backgrounds—affected by systemic inequities and disadvantage—start life with starkly different health endowments. As but one example, having a low-birth-weight child (i.e., less than 2,500 grams) is more than twice as prevalent among African American mothers as white mothers, and the same differential is seen for white mothers with less than a high school degree compared with those with a college degree (Aizer and Currie, 2014). These differences in neonatal health have lasting effects on children's development: studies of twins, sibling pairs, and singleton births indicate that a 10 percent improvement in birth weight is associated with around one-twentieth of a standard deviation increase in children's test scores—a relationship that holds steady from kindergarten readiness through middle school (Bharadwaj et al., 2013; Figlio et al., 2014) and affects educational attainment and labor market success (Oreopoulos et al., 2008; Royer, 2009). Comparing twins and siblings is important because doing so reduces the likelihood of confounding factors (such as environmental exposures or maternal behavior) that affect both fetal health and children's cognitive development. When researchers compare one twin with another, they are explicitly comparing the outcomes of two children who shared the same fetal environment.

Moreover, the existing evidence suggests that postnatal investments are somewhat more effective in improving outcomes for children with better fetal health. For instance, the Infant Health and Development Program, which randomly assigned low-birth-weight infants to preschool programs with varying intensities, had significant effects on child development for relatively high-birth-weight infants but no appreciable effects on the development of relatively low-birth-weight infants (McCormick et al., 2006). In addition, the relationship between fetal health and children's outcomes is stronger for advantaged families (which tend to make greater postnatal investments) than for less advantaged families, suggesting that the efficacy of families' postnatal investments is affected in part by birth weight (Figlio et al., 2014). This suggests that attention needs to be paid to improving birth outcomes rather than assuming that postnatal interventions will be widely and equitably effective.

There are a number of potential mechanisms through which disadvantage can affect children's outcomes both directly and indirectly by way of in utero development and fetal health. For example, mothers exposed to higher levels of pollution tend to bear children who have poorer developmental outcomes compared with the children of equally disadvantaged mothers who have lower degrees of this exposure. This is a research question that is challenging to study because women who are exposed to these types of stressors tend to be particularly disadvantaged and potentially likely to have children with poorer outcomes regardless of the nature of in utero stressors (Almond and Currie, 2011). However, several recent studies have made use of "natural experiments" to obtain causal evidence of the effects of a number of these stressors on children's health and development. For instance, Currie and Walker (2009) made use of the fact that once states moved to electronic toll collection, the rate of engine idling near toll plazas was dramatically reduced, and found substantial improvements in early outcomes for children in families living proximate to toll plazas. Other studies have shown that exposure to air pollution, water pollution, and other environmental toxins contributes to diminished child outcomes (Currie, 2011; Currie et al., 2013; Isen et al., 2014; Sanders, 2012).

Disadvantaged women also face greater degrees of stress in their lives, and maternal exposure to stress is another potential mechanism leading to poorer subsequent developmental outcomes (Sandman et al., 2012; Thayer and Kuzawa, 2014). For example, mothers stressed by exposure to meteorological shocks such as hurricanes and extreme temperatures have children with worse outcomes (Currie and Rossin-Slater, 2013; Deschenes et al., 2009). Children of American women with Arabic names born in the period following the September 2001 terrorist attacks experienced considerably worse outcomes than those born just before the attacks, suggesting an important role of maternal psychological stress in children's development (Lauderdale, 2006). A pronounced stressor for mothers is domestic violence, which is a particular risk for disadvantaged mothers (Vest et al., 2002). The evidence suggests that reducing domestic violence leads to improved outcomes for children in the household (Aizer, 2011).

Another potential mechanism is that women from less advantaged backgrounds have worse health and nutrition during pregnancy than their more advantaged counterparts, and maternal health and nutrition during pregnancy affect children's early outcomes and development. For example, reduced maternal nutrition during pregnancy can result in poorer outcomes for children (Almond and Mazumder, 2011), while there is some evidence to indicate that improved nutrition through supplemental nutrition programs during pregnancy results in better birth outcomes (Colman et al., 2012; Figlio et al., 2014; Hoynes et al., 2011; Rossin-Slater, 2013). Likewise, nutrition supplementation in low-income countries has been shown to improve birth weight and educational outcomes (Abu-Saad and Fraser, 2010; Field et al., 2009).

In addition, disadvantaged expectant mothers are more likely to engage in behaviors detrimental to their health that could disadvantage their children. Disadvantaged expectant mothers have dramatically higher rates of smoking, prepregnancy hypertension, prepregnancy obesity, and prepregnancy diabetes compared with more advantaged mothers (Aizer and Currie, 2014), and at least some of these maternal behaviors are associated with differential outcomes for children. For example, there is causal evidence showing that maternal smoking leads to worse children's outcomes (Bharadwaj et al., 2012; Currie et al., 2009; Lien and Evans, 2005).

sity appears to have effects on the biological regulators of hypothalamic–pituitary–adrenal (HPA) activity, contributing to greater regulation of stress reactivity through cortical and limbic influences. Social support also appears to stimulate the down-regulation of the proinflammatory tendencies induced by chronic stress, as well as processes driven by neurohormones, including oxytocin, that have other positive benefits (Kiecolt-Glaser et al., 2010). Stated differently, social support not only counters the negative effects of chronic stress reactivity but also stimulates constructive influences that contribute independently to greater self-regulation and well-being (Hostinar et al., 2014). This research is still at an early stage, and establishing reliable associations between brain and behavioral functioning in this area is a work in progress, but research findings are providing increasing support for these processes. In one study, for example, greater maternal support measured when children were preschoolers predicted children's larger hippocampus volume at school age (Luby et al., 2012).

The potential benefits of social support as a buffer of chronic stress reactivity underscore the plasticity of developing behavioral and biological systems. Children in adversity need not suffer long-term harms arising from the effects of chronic stress exposure. In a study of families living in rural poverty, for example, toddlers' chronic exposure to domestic violence was associated with elevated cortisol reactivity. However, this effect was buffered when mothers were observed to respond sensitively to their children (Hibel et al., 2011). Experimental interventions designed to change stressful circumstances and promote positive relationships have yielded similar findings. For example a program aimed at easing young children's transition to new foster care placements and promoting warm, responsive, and consistent relationships with new foster parents provided individualized sessions with child therapists, weekly playgroup sessions, and support for foster parents. This program resulted in a normalization of the children's HPA hyporesponsiveness (an effect of stress discussed in Chapter 3) (Fisher et al., 2007, 2011). Another example comes from an intervention based on attachment theory, which trained caregivers to better interpret and respond affectionately to infants and toddlers in foster care and similarly resulted in a normalization of HPA activity and lower cortisol reactivity (Dozier et al., 2006, 2008). There may be limits to these potential ameliorative effects, depending on the severity and duration of the exposure to adversity. Children who lived for an extended period in profoundly depriving Romanian orphanages, for example, did not show recovery of dysregulated cortisol reactivity, even after a prolonged period of supportive adoptive care (Gunnar et al., 2001).

Because interventions that can help children recover from the effects of chronic adversity can be expensive and time-consuming, however, it appears sensible to try to prevent these effects from occurring. This can be accomplished by reducing exposure to influences that cause significant stress for children, and by strengthening supportive relationships that can buffer its effects. The development of warm, secure attachments between parents and children illustrates the latter approach. As discussed earlier in this chapter, attachment theorists argue that the reliable support provided by a secure attachment relationship enables infants and children to explore and learn from their experiences confidently with the assurance that a trusted adult is available to assist if difficulty ensues. In this view, secure attachments buffer stress and significantly reduce the child's need to be vigilant for threat or danger. As noted previously, attachment research documents a range of benefits associated with secure parent–child relationships in childhood, including greater language skill, academic achievement, and social competence (see Thompson, 2008, for a review; West et al., 2013). The view that these accomplishments are explained, at least in part, by how secure attachments buffer stress for children is supported by studies documenting the better-regulated cortisol reactivity of young children with secure attachments in challenging situations (see Gunnar and Donzella, 2002, for a review; Nachmias et al., 1996).

Viewed in this light, it appears that the contributions adults make to children's learning extend significantly beyond their reading, conversing, counting, and providing other direct forms of cognitive stimulation. An essential contribution is the safety and security they provide that not only buffers children against significant stress when this occurs, but also enables children to invest themselves in learning opportunities with confidence that an adult will assist them when needed. Such confidence not only enables children to learn more from the opportunities afforded them in the family and outside the home but also fosters their developing self-confidence, curiosity, and other learning skills that emerge in the context of secure relationships (Thompson, 2008). This is a benefit of secure, warm adult–child relationships for all children, not just those in adverse circumstances. This phenomenon is perhaps analogous to that seen in studies in which rat pups with nurturant mothers show enhanced learning and memory in low-stress contexts, whereas pups with nonnurturant mothers show greater proficiency in fear conditioning (Champagne et al., 2008).

One problem, however, is that children in adverse circumstances usually have parents and other caregivers who are affected by the same conditions of adversity. Thus, their parents may not be able to provide them with the support they need. This realization has led to the growth of two-generation interventions that are designed to assist children by providing support to their parents in difficult circumstances (Chase-Lansdale and Brooks-Gunn, 2014).

Stress, Learning, and Mental Health

Children learn readily in contexts of social support and emotional well-being, which derive from positive relationships with those who care for and educate them in the family and outside the home. In these contexts, adults can support and encourage developing competencies, convey positive values about learning and school, and help instill curiosity and self-confidence in children. By contrast, learning and cognitive achievement are hindered when children are troubled. This is the case for children from infancy through adolescence who are living in homes with significant marital conflict, when mothers are chronically depressed, when parents are hostile and coercive, or in other circumstances of family turmoil (e.g., Bascoe et al., 2009; Brennan et al., 2013; Canadian Paediatric Society, 2004; Davies et al., 2008).

Socioemotional hindrances to learning and cognitive achievement are apparent very early, before children have begun school, and continue to be important as children move into the primary grades. In educational settings, the emotional effects of problems in educator–child relationships can undermine children's performance and their academic success (Hamre and Pianta, 2004; Jeon et al., 2014; Pianta, 1999; Pianta and Stuhlman, 2004b; Skinner and Belmont, 1993). As discussed in Chapter 3, when children are in circumstances of chronic or overwhelming stress, stress hormones affect multiple brain regions, including those relevant to learning, attention, memory, and self-regulation (McEwen, 2012; Ulrich-Lai and Herman, 2009). Over time and with continued exposure to stressful circumstances, these neurocognitive processes become altered as a result of the progressive wear and tear of stress hormones on biological systems as they adapt to this chronic stress. As a consequence, immunologic capacities become weakened (contributing to more frequent acute and chronic illness), self-regulation is impaired (contributing to poorer emotion regulation and impulse control), and cognitive and attentional capabilities are blunted (Danese and McEwen, 2012; Lupien et al., 2009; Miller et al., 2011). For children, these effects can help account for problems in following instructions, paying attention, managing impulsivity, focusing thinking, and controlling emotions in social encounters—each of which can impair classroom performance and academic achievement.

Young children's vulnerability to stress and their reliance on the support of adults are two central considerations in understanding the foundations for childhood mental health (IOM and NRC, 2009). This relationship among stress, early development, and mental health is relevant to understanding the influences that can threaten the socioemotional well-being of younger children—and to understanding why behavior problems can undermine learning and cognitive growth. One illustration of these effects is the high rates of preschool and prekindergarten children being expelled from their classrooms because of disruptive behavior problems—by one report at a rate more than three times the rate of children in the K-12 grades (Gilliam, 2005; see also U.S. Department of Education Office for Civil Rights, 2014). In this study, the likelihood of expulsion decreased significantly when educators were provided access to early childhood mental health consultants who could assist them in managing behavior problems.

Another illustration is reports by kindergarten teachers that social, emotional, and self-regulatory problems are a common impediment to children's readiness to achieve in their classrooms (Lewit and Baker, 1995; Rimm-Kaufman et al., 2000). Other studies have shown that children's conduct problems and internalizing (anxious, depressed) behavior in the classroom can undermine the development of constructive educator–child relationships and foreshadow later social and academic difficulties (Berry and O'Connor, 2010; Koles et al., 2009; Ladd and Burgess, 2001).

Consistent with the research concerning the biological and behavioral effects of chronic stress, there is increasing evidence that even very young children show clear evidence of traumatization and posttraumatic stress, anxious and depressive symptomatology, behavioral and conduct problems, and other serious psychological problems (Egger and Angold, 2006; Lieberman et al., 2011; Luby, 2006; Zeanah, 2009). Sometimes these symptom patterns overlap, such as in the comorbidity in which depressive symptomatology appears along with oppositional behavior in preschoolers (Egger and Angold, 2006). The origins of these problems are multifaceted, but certainly include interaction of environmental stresses with genetic factors that heighten or reduce children's vulnerability to these stresses. Often these environmental stresses undermine the social support that would otherwise buffer the effects of stress on children. Diagnosing these disorders in young children is a challenge because the behaviors associated with early mental health problems in young children can be different from those observed in adults and adolescents (Egger and Emde, 2011). But progress has been made in developing reliable diagnostic criteria for preschoolers (e.g., Egger and Angold, 2006; Keenan et al., 1997; Lavigne et al., 2009) and even infants and toddlers (Zero to Three, 2005). This work provides a foundation for further study of the developmental origins of early mental health challenges and therapeutic interventions that might help these children.

Connecting the Socioemotional Health of Children and Adults

The preceding discussion makes clear that children's socioemotional health is linked to the socioemotional well-being of the adults in their lives. Consistent with the research on the social buffering of stress discussed earlier, when parents and other caregivers are managing well, they can help children cope more competently with the ordinary stresses that inevitably occur. When caregivers are stressed, by contrast, they cannot provide this buffering and are instead more often a source of stress for children. When parents are depressed, for example, they can be unpredictably sad, hostile, critical, and/or disengaged (NRC and IOM, 2009). This constellation of behaviors constitutes a difficult combination of threat and withdrawal of support for children. Young children with a depressed mother are more likely, therefore, to exhibit heightened stress reactivity to moderate challenges; to have an insecure attachment to the parent; to show lower levels of cognitive performance and, later, poorer academic achievement; and to be at greater risk of becoming depressed themselves.

The adult's emotional well-being is important in the classroom as well. Using data from the Fragile Families and Child Wellbeing study, Jeon and colleagues (2014) measured the depressive symptomatology of 761 home- and center-based care providers, as well as overall observed classroom quality, and obtained independent measures of the behavior problems of the 3-year-olds in their classrooms. They found that educator depression was linked to higher levels of behavior problems in children, attributable to the poorer quality of the classroom environment. Notably, this study was conducted with a sample of families in economic stress, with the educators often sharing the same financial difficulties. Nevertheless, the association of educator depression with child behavior problems remained even when family influences, including maternal depression and family poverty status, were controlled for. Similar associations of educator well-being with the quality of the classroom environment and children's learning have been found in studies of children in the early primary grades (e.g., Pianta, 1999; Pianta and Stuhlman, 2004b).

Conclusions About Chronic Stress and Adversity

Chronic stress and adversity constitute fundamental risks to learning and academic success as well as to emotional well-being for many young children. The biological and behavioral effects of stress and adversity can disrupt brain circuitry and stress response systems, affect fundamental cognitive skills, undermine focused thinking and attention, diminish self-regulation, and imperil mental and physical health. Trauma, adversity, and chronic stress can arise from many sources, such as poverty, family conflict, parental depression, abuse, neglect, or exposure to violence in the community. Supportive and stable relationships with adults can help develop children's adaptive capacities and provide them with a significant stress buffer. It is important for adults who work with children to recognize and appreciate the effects of

adversity and to have the capacity to employ strategies for prevent-
ing or mitigating them, as well as for promoting cognitive, social, and
emotional strengths for coping with adverse and stressful experiences.

Given the importance of stable and responsive relationships that pro-
vide consistent and nurturing interactions, the well-being of the adults
who care for young children contributes to their healthy development
and early learning.

The stresses of economic disadvantage are manifested not only in dif-
ferences in children's early experiences in the family and the commu-
nity but also in the quality and stability of the out-of-home care and
education families can access and afford and the quality of the schools
children later attend. Socioeconomic differences in the quality of early
learning opportunities place large numbers of children at a learning
disadvantage and undermine their potential for academic success. These
differences begin early and have a cumulative effect over time. Strength-
ening early learning and developing competencies requires serious and
sustained attention to these socioeconomic disparities in opportunity.

REFERENCES

AAP (American Academy of Pediattics) Committee on School Health. 2004. Soft drinks in schools. *Pediatrics* 113(1 Pt. 1): 152-154.
AAP Committee on Sports Medicine and Fitness and AAP Committee on School Health. 2000. Physical fitness and activity in schools. *Pediatrics* 105(5):1156-1157.
AAP Council on Early Childhood, P. C. High, and P. Klass. 2014. Literacy promotion: An essential component of primary care pediatric practice. *Pediatrics* 134(2):404-409.
AAP Council on School Health. 2013. The crucial role of recess in school. *Pediatrics* 131(1): 183-188.
Abu-Saad, K., and D. Fraser. 2010. Maternal nutrition and birth outcomes. *Epidemiologic Reviews* 32(1):5-25.
Adams, M. J. 1990. *Beginning to read: Thinking and learning about print.* Cambridge, MA: MIT Press.
Adler, N. E., T. Boyce, M. A. Chesney, S. Cohen, S. Folkman, R. L. Kahn, and S. L. Syme. 1994. Socioeconomic status and health. The challenge of the gradient. *American Psychologist* 49(1):15-24.
Ahnert, L., M. Pinquart, and M. E. Lamb. 2006. Security of children's relationships with nonparental care providers: A meta-analysis. *Child Development* 77(3):664-679.
Aizer, A. 2011. Poverty, violence, and health: The impact of domestic violence during pregnancy on newborn health. *Journal of Human Resources* 46(3):518-538.
Aizer, A., and J. Currie. 2014. The intergenerational transmission of inequality: Maternal disadvantage and health at birth. *Science* 344(6186):856-861.
Alaimo, K., C. M. Olson, and E. A. Frongillo, Jr. 2001. Food insufficiency and American school-aged children's cognitive, academic, and psychosocial development. *Pediatrics* 108(1):44-53.

Alexander, K. L., D. R. Entwisle, and S. L. Dauber. 1993. First-grade classroom behavior: Its short- and long-term consequences for school performance. *Child Development* 64(3):801-814.

Almond, D., and J. Currie. 2011. Killing me softly: The fetal origins hypothesis. *Journal of Economic Perspectives* 25(3):153-172.

Almond, D., and B. Mazumder. 2011. Health capital and the prenatal environment: The effect of Ramadan observance during pregnancy. *American Economic Journal: Applied Economics* 3(4):56-85.

Aloise-Young, P. A. 1993. The development of self-presentation: Self-promotion in 6- to 10-year-old children. *Social Cognition* 11(2):201-222.

Anghel, D. 2010. Executive function in preschool children: Working memory as a predictor of mathematical ability at school age. *Revista Romaneasca pentru Educatie Multidimensionala* 2(4):5-16.

Ansari, D., N. Garcia, E. Lucas, K. Hamon, and B. Dhital. 2005. Neural correlates of symbolic number processing in children and adults. *Neuroreport* 16:1769-1775.

Antell, S. E., and D. P. Keating. 1983. Perception of numerical invariance in neonates. *Child Development* 54:695-701.

Anthony, J. L., C. J. Lonigan, K. Driscoll, B. M. Phillips, and S. R. Burgess. 2003. Phonological sensitivity: A quasi-parallel progression of word structure units and cognitive operations. *Reading Research Quarterly* 38(4):470-487.

Ashcraft, M. H. 2006. Math performance, working memory, and math anxiety; some possible directions for neural functioning work. Paper read at The Neural Basis of Mathematical Development, November, Nashville, TN.

Ashkenazi, S., N. Mark-Zigdon, and A. Henik. 2013. Do subitizing deficits in developmental dyscalculia involve pattern recognition weakness? *Developmental Science* 16(1):35-46.

Au, T. K., C. K. Chan, T. K. Chan, M. W. Cheung, J. Y. Ho, and G. W. Ip. 2008. Folkbiology meets microbiology: A study of conceptual and behavioral change. *Cognitive Psychology* 57(1):1-19.

Aukrust, V. G. 2007. Young children acquiring second language vocabulary in preschool group-time: Does amount, diversity, and discourse complexity of teacher talk matter? *Journal of Research in Childhood Education* 22(1):17-37.

Aunola, K., E. Leskinen, M.-K. Lerkkanen, and J.-E. Nurmi. 2004. Developmental dynamics of math performance from pre-school to grade 2. *Journal of Educational Psychology* 96:699-713.

Baillargeon, R., D. Wu, S. Yuan, J. Li, and Y. Luo. 2009. Young infants' expectations about self-propelled objects. In *The origins of object knowledge*, edited by B. M. Hood and L. Santos. Oxford, UK: Oxford University Press.

Baillargeon, R., R. M. Scott, and Z. He. 2010. False-belief understanding in infants. *Trends in Cognitive Sciences* 14(3):110-118.

Baker, D., H. Knipe, J. Collins, J. Leon, E. Cummings, C. Blair, and D. Gramson. 2010. One hundred years of elementary school mathematics in the United States: A content analysis and cognitive assessment of textbooks from 1900 to 2000. *Journal for Research in Mathematics Education* 41(4):383-423.

Baldwin, D. A. 1991. Infants' contribution to the achievement of joint reference. *Child Development* 62(5):875-890.

Baldwin, D. A., and L. J. Moses. 2001. Links between social understanding and early word learning: Challenges to current accounts. *Social Development* 10(3):309-329.

Baldwin, D. A., and M. Tomasello. 1998. Word learning: A window on early pragmatic understanding. In *The Proceedings of the Twenty-ninth Annual Child Language Research Forum*. Vol. 29, edited by E. V. Clark. Chicago, IL: University of Chicago Press. Pp. 3-24.

Ball, E. W., and B. A. Blachman. 1991. Does phoneme awareness training in kindergarten make a difference in early word recognition and developmental spelling? *Reading Research Quarterly* 26(1):49-66.

Barata, M. C. 2010. Executive functions in Chilean preschool children: Investigating the associations of early executive functions with emergent mathematics and literacy skills. PhD diss., Harvard Graduate School of Education.

Barkley, R. A. 1997. Attention-deficit/hyperactivity disorder, self-regulation, and time: Toward a more comprehensive theory. *Journal of Developmental and Behavioral Pediatrics* 18(4):271-279.

Baroody, A. E., and J. Dobbs-Oates. 2009. Child and parent characteristics, parental expectations, and child behaviours related to preschool children's interest in literacy. *Early Child Development and Care* 181(3):345-359.

Baroody, A. J. 2004. The developmental bases for early childhood number and operations standards. In *Engaging young children in mathematics: Standards for early childhood mathematics education*, edited by D. H. Clements, J. Sarama, and A.-M. DiBiase. Mahwah, NJ: Lawrence Erlbaum Associates. Pp. 173-219.

Baroody, A. J., M.-L. Lai, and K. S. Mix. 2005. Changing views of young children's numerical and arithmetic competencies. Paper read at National Association for the Education of Young Children, December, Washington, DC.

———. 2006. The development of young children's number and operation sense and its implications for early childhood education. In *Handbook of research on the education of young children*, edited by B. Spodek and O. N. Saracho. Mahwah, NJ: Lawrence Erlbaum Associates. Pp. 187-221.

Baroody, A. J., X. Li, and M.-l. Lai. 2008. Toddlers' spontaneous attention to number. *Mathematical Thinking and Learning* 10:240-270.

Bartsch, K., and H. M. Wellman. 1995. *Children talk about the mind*. New York: Oxford University Press.

Basch, C. E. 2011. Breakfast and the achievement gap among urban minority youth. *Journal of School Health* 81(10):635-640.

Bascoe, S. M., P. T. Davies, M. L. Sturge-Apple, and E. M. Cummings. 2009. Children's representations of family relationships, peer information processing, and school adjustment. *Developmental Psychology* 45(6):1740-1751.

Bassett, H. H., S. Denham, T. M. Wyatt, and H. K. Warren-Khot. 2012. Refining the preschool self-regulation assessment for use in preschool classrooms. *Infant and Child Development* 21(6):596-616.

Bassok, D., and A. Rorem. 2014. *Is kindergarten the new first grade? The changing nature of kindergarten in the age of accountability.* Charlottesville, VA: University of Virginia.

Beilock, S. L. 2001. Learning and performing math: Self-concept, self-doubt, and self-fulfilling prophesy. *Journal of Experimental Psychology: General* 130:224-237.

Belsky, D. W., T. E. Moffitt, L. Arseneault, M. Melchior, and A. Caspi. 2010. Context and sequelae of food insecurity in children's development. *American Journal of Epidemiology* 172(7):809-818.

Bennett, N., C. Desforges, A. Cockburn, and B. Wilkinson. 1984. *The quality of pupil learning experiences*. Hillsdale, NJ: Lawrence Erlbaum Associates.

Berch, D. B., and M. M. M. Mazzocco, eds. 2007. *Why is math so hard for some children? The nature and origins of mathematical learning difficulties and disabilities*. Baltimore, MD: Paul H. Brookes Publishing Co.

Berry, D., and E. O'Connor. 2010. Behavioral risk, teacher–child relationships, and social skill development across middle childhood: A child-by-environment analysis of change. *Journal of Applied Developmental Psychology* 31(1):1-14.

Best, J. R., P. H. Miller, and J. A. Naglieri. 2011. Relations between executive function and academic achievement from ages 5 to 17 in a large, representative national sample. *Learning and Individual Differences* 21(4):327-336.

Bharadwaj, P., J. V. Johnsen, and K. V. Løken. 2012. Smoking bans, maternal smoking and birth outcomes. IZA Institute for the Study of Labor Discussion Paper No. 7006:72-93.

Bharadwaj, P., J. Eberhard, and C. Neilson. 2013 (unpublished). *Health at birth, parental investments and academic outcomes*. San Diego: University of California, San Diego.

Bialystok, E. 2011. Reshaping the mind: The benefits of bilingualism. *Canadian Journal of Experimental Psychology* 65(4):229-235.

Bialystok, E., and F. I. M. Craik. 2010. Cognitive and linguistic processing in the bilingual mind. *Current Directions in Psychological Science* 19(1):19-23.

Bialystok, E., F. I. M. Craik, D. W. Green, and T. H. Gollan. 2009. Bilingual minds. *Psychological Science in the Public Interest* 10(3):89-129.

Biederman, J., M. C. Monuteaux, A. E. Doyle, L. J. Seidman, T. E. Wilens, F. Ferrero, C. L. Morgan, and S. V. Faraone. 2004. Impact of executive function deficits and attention-deficit/hyperactivity disorder (ADHD) on academic outcomes in children. *Journal of Consulting and Clinical Psychology* 72(5):757-766.

Bielaczyc, K., P. L. Pirolli, and A. L. Brown. 1995. Training in self-explanation and self-regulation strategies: Investigating the effects of knowledge acquisition activities on problem solving. *Cognition and Instruction* 13:221-252.

Bierman, K. L., R. L. Nix, M. T. Greenberg, C. Blair, and C. E. Domitrovich. 2008a. Executive functions and school readiness intervention: Impact, moderation, and mediation in the Head Start REDI program. *Development and Psychopathology* 20(3):821-843.

Bierman, K. L., C. E. Domitrovich, R. L. Nix, S. D. Gest, J. A. Welsh, M. T. Greenberg, C. Blair, K. E. Nelson, and S. Gill. 2008b. Promoting academic and social-emotional school readiness: The Head Start REDI program. *Child Development* 79(6):1802-1817.

Birch, S. H., and G. W. Ladd. 1997. The teacher–child relationship and children's early school adjustment. *Journal of School Psychology* 35(1):61-79.

———. 1998. Children's interpersonal behaviors and the teacher–child relationship. *Developmental Psychology* 34(5):934-946.

Blair, C. 2002. School readiness: Integrating cognition and emotion in a neurobiological conceptualization of children's functioning at school entry. *American Psychologist* 57(2): 111-127.

Blair, C., and A. Diamond. 2008. Biological processes in prevention and intervention: The promotion of self-regulation as a means of preventing school failure. *Development and Psychopathology* 20(3):899-911.

Blair, C., and C. C. Raver. 2012. Child development in the context of adversity: Experiential canalization of brain and behavior. *American Psychologist* 67(4):309-318.

Blair, C., and R. P. Razza. 2007. Relating effortful control, executive function, and false belief understanding to emerging math and literacy ability in kindergarten. *Child Development* 78:647-663.

Blair, C., J. Protzko, and A. Ursache. 2010. Self-regulation and early literacy. In *Handbook of early literacy research*. Vol. 3, edited by S. B. Neuman and D. K. Dickinson. New York: Guilford Press. Pp. 20-35.

Blevins-Knabe, B., and L. Musun-Miller. 1996. Number use at home by children and their parents and its relationship to early mathematical performance. *Early Development and Parenting* 5:35-45.

Bloom, P. 2013. *Just babies: The origins of good and evil*. New York: Crown Publishers.

Bodovski, K., and G. Farkas. 2007. Mathematics growth in early elementary school: The roles of beginning knowledge, student engagement, and instruction. *Elementary School Journal* 108(2):115-130.

Bodrova, E., and D. J. Leong. 2012. Scaffolding self-regulated learning in young children: Lessons from tools of the mind. In *Handbook of early childhood education*, edited by R. C. Pianta, W. S. Barnett, L. M. Justice, and S. M. Sheridan. New York: Guilford Press. Pp. 352-369.

Bougma, K., F. E. Aboud, K. B. Harding, and G. S. Marquis. 2013. Iodine and mental development of children 5 years old and under: A systematic review and meta-analysis. *Nutrients* 5(4):1384-1416.

Bowers, E. P., and M. Vasilyeva. 2011. The relation between teacher input and lexical growth of preschoolers. *Applied Psycholinguistics* 32(1):221-241.

Boyce, W. T., M. B. Sokolowski, and G. E. Robinson. 2012. Toward a new biology of social adversity. *Proceedings of the National Academy of Sciences of the United States of America* 109(Suppl. 2):17143-17148.

Bradley, L., and P. E. Bryant. 1983. Categorizing sounds and learning to read—a causal connection. *Nature* 301(5899):419-421.

Bradley, R. H., and R. F. Corwyn. 2002. Socioeconomic status and child development. *Annual Review of Psychology* 53:371-399.

Brennan, L. M., E. C. Shelleby, D. S. Shaw, F. Gardner, T. J. Dishion, and M. Wilson. 2013. Indirect effects of the family check-up on school-age academic achievement through improvements in parenting in early childhood. *Journal of Educational Psychology* 105(3): 10.1037/a0032096.

Broidy, L. M., D. S. Nagin, R. E. Tremblay, B. Brame, K. A. Dodge, D. Fergusson, J. Horwood, R. Loeber, R. Laird, D. Lyname, T. F. Moffit, J. E. Bates, G. S. Pettit, and F. Vitaro. 2003. Developmental trajectories of childhood disruptive behaviors and adolescent delinquency: A six-site, cross-national study. *Developmental Psychology* 30(2):222-245.

Brosnan, M., J. Demetre, S. Hamill, K. Robson, H. Shepherd, and G. Cody. 2002. Executive functioning in adults and children with developmental dyslexia. *Neuropsychologia* 40(12):2144-2155.

Bruner, J. 1978. The role of dialogue in language acquisition. In *The child's conception of language*, edited by A. Sinclair, R. Jarvella, and W. J. M. Levelt. New York: Springer. Pp. 241-256.

Bryan, J., S. Osendarp, D. Hughes, E. Calvaresi, K. Baghurst, and J. W. van Klinken. 2004. Nutrients for cognitive development in school-aged children. *Nutrition Reviews* 62(8): 295-306.

Bühler, E., C. Bachmann, H. Goyert, M. Heinzel-Gutenbrunner, and I. Kamp-Becker. 2011. Differential diagnosis of autism spectrum disorder and attention deficit hyperactivity disorder by means of inhibitory control and "theory of mind." *Journal of Autism and Developmental Disorders* 41:1718-1726.

Buhs, E. S., and G. W. Ladd. 2001. Peer rejection as an antecedent of young children's school adjustment: An examination of mediating processes. *Developmental Psychology* 37(4):550-560.

Bull, R., and G. Scerif. 2001. Executive functioning as a predictor of children's mathematics ability: Inhibition, switching, and working memory. *Developmental Neuropsychology* 19(3):273-293.

Bull, R., R. S. Johnston, and J. A. Roy. 1999. Exploring the roles of the visual-spatial sketch pad and central executive in children's arithmetical skills: Views from cognition and developmental neuropsychology. *Developmental Neuropsychology* 15(3):421-442.

Bull, R., K. A. Espy, and S. A. Wiebe. 2008. Short-term memory, working memory, and executive functioning in preschoolers: Longitudinal predictors of mathematical achievement at age 7 years. *Developmental Neuropsychology* 33:205-228.

Busch-Rossnagel, N. A. 2005. Mastery motivation, preschool and early childhood. In *Encyclopedia of applied developmental science*, edited by C. Fisher and R. Lerner. Thousand Oaks, CA: Sage Publications, Inc. Pp. 679-681.

Butler, L. P., and E. M. Markman. 2012a. Finding the cause: Verbal framing helps children extract causal evidence embedded in a complex scene. *Journal of Cognition and Development* 13(1):38-66.

———. 2012b. Preschoolers use intentional and pedagogical cues to guide inductive inferences and exploration. *Child Development* 83(4):1416-1428.

———. 2014. Preschoolers use pedagogical cues to guide radical reorganization of category knowledge. *Cognition* 130(1):116-127.

Butterworth, B. 2005. The development of arithmetical abilities. *Journal of Child Psychology and Psychiatry* 46:3-18.

———. 2010. Foundational numerical capacities and the origins of dyscalculia. *Trends in Cognitive Sciences* 14:534-541.

Butterworth, B., S. Varma, and D. Laurillard. 2011. Dyscalculia: From brain to education. *Science* 332:1049-1053.

Byrne, B., and R. Fielding-Barnsley. 1989. Phonemic awareness and letter knowledge in the child's acquisition of the alphabetic principle. *Journal of Educational Psychology* 81(3):313-321.

———. 1995. Evaluation of a program to teach phonemic awareness to young children: A 2- and 3-year follow-up and a new preschool trial. *Journal of Educational Psychology* 87:488-503.

Byrnes, J. P., and B. A. Wasik. 2009. Factors predictive of mathematics achievement in kindergarten, first and third grades: An opportunity–propensity analysis. *Contemporary Educational Psychology* 34:167-183.

Cameron, C. E., L. L. Brock, W. M. Murrah, L. H. Bell, S. L. Worzalla, D. Grissmer, and F. J. Morrison. 2012. Fine motor skills and executive function both contribute to kindergarten achievement. *Child Development* 83(4):1229-1244.

Campbell, F., G. Conti, J. J. Heckman, S. H. Moon, R. Pinto, E. Pungello, and Y. Pan. 2014. Early childhood investments substantially boost adult health. *Science* 343(6178): 1478-1485.

Canadian Paediatric Society. 2004. Maternal depression and child development. *Paediatrics & Child Health* 9(8):575-583.

Cantlon, J. F., E. M. Brannon, E. J. Carter, and K. A. Pelphrey. 2006. Functional imaging of numerical processing in adults and 4-y-old children. *PLoS Biology* 4(5):e125.

Carey, S. 2009. *The origin of concepts*. Oxford and New York: Oxford University Press.

Carneiro, P., and R. Ginja. 2012. *Long term impacts of compensatory preschool on health and behavior: Evidence from Head Start*, IZA Discussion Paper No. 6315. Bonn, Germany: Institute for the Study of Labor.

Cartwright, K. B. 2002. Cognitive development and reading: The relation of reading-specific multiple classification skill to reading comprehension in elementary school children. *Journal of Educational Psychology* 94(1):56-63.

———. 2008. Cognitive flexibility and reading comprehension: Relevance to the future. In *Comprehension instruction: Research-based best practices*, 2nd ed., edited by C. C. Block and S. R. Parris. New York: Guilford Press. Pp. 50-64.

Cartwright, K. B., T. R. Marshall, K. L. Dandy, and M. C. Isaac. 2010. The development of graphophonological-semantic cognitive flexibility and its contribution to reading comprehension in beginning readers. *Journal of Cognition and Development* 11(1):61-85.

Cassel, J. 1976. The contribution of the social environment to host resistance: The fourth Wade Hampton Frost lecture. *American Journal of Epidemiology* 104(2):107-123.

Catts, H. W., and A. G. Kamhi. 1999. *Language and reading disabilities*. Boston, MA: Allyn and Bacon.

Catts, H. W., M. E. Fey, X. Zhang, and J. B. Tomblin. 1999. Language basis of reading and reading disabilities: Evidence from a longitudinal investigation. *Scientific Studies of Reading* 3(4):331-361.

CDC (Centers for Disease Control and Prevention). 2011. School health guidelines to promote healthy eating and physical activity. *Morbidity and Mortality Weekly Report* 60(RR05):1-71.

———. 2012. Youth risk behavior surveillance—United States, 2011. *Morbidity and Mortality Weekly Report: Surveillance Summaries* 61(4):1-162.

———. 2014. *Middle childhood (6-8 years of age): Developmental milestones*. http://www.cdc.gov/ncbddd/childdevelopment/positiveparenting/middle.html (accessed September 15, 2014).

Celedón-Pattichis, S., S. I. Musanti, and M. E. Marshall. 2010. Bilingual elementary teachers' reflections on using students' native language and culture to teach mathematics. In *Mathematics teaching & learning in K-12: Equity and professional development*, edited by M. Q. Foote. New York: Palgrave Macmillan. Pp. 7-24.

Center on the Developing Child at Harvard University. 2010. *The foundations of lifelong health are built in early childhood*. http://www.developingchild.harvard.edu (accessed January 22, 2015).

Champagne, D. L., R. C. Bagot, F. van Hasselt, G. Ramakers, M. J. Meaney, E. R. de Kloet, M. Joels, and H. Krugers. 2008. Maternal care and hippocampal plasticity: Evidence for experience-dependent structural plasticity, altered synaptic functioning, and differential responsiveness to glucocorticoids and stress. *Journal of Neuroscience* 28(23):6037-6045.

Chase-Lansdale, L., and J. Brooks-Gunn. 2014. Two-generation programs in the twenty-first century. *Future of Children* 24(1):13-39.

Chi, M. T. H., and D. Klahr. 1975. Span and rate of apprehension in children and adults. *Journal of Experimental Child Psychology* 19:434-439.

Child Trends. 2015. *Homeless children and youth*. http://www.childtrends.org/?indicators=homeless-children-and-youth (accessed January 27, 2015).

Children's Bureau. 2013. *Child maltreatment 2012*. http://www.acf.hhs.gov/programs/cb/research-data-technology/statistics-research/child-maltreatment (accessed January 27, 2015).

Chu, F. W., K. Vanmarle, and D. C. Geary. 2013. Quantitative deficits of preschool children at risk for mathematical learning disability. *Frontiers in Psychology* 4:195.

Cimpian, A. 2010. The impact of generic language about ability on children's achievement motivation. *Developmental Psychology* 46(5):1333-1340.

Cimpian, A., and E. M. Markman. 2009. Information learned from generic language becomes central to children's biological concepts: Evidence from their open-ended explanations. *Cognition* 113(1):14-25.

———. 2011. The generic/nongeneric distinction influences how children interpret new information about social others. *Child Development* 82(2):471-492.

Cimpian, A., H. C. Arce, E. M. Markman, and C. S. Dweck. 2007. Subtle linguistic cues affect children's motivation. *Psychological Science* 18(4):314-316.

Claessens, A., M. Engel, and F. C. Curran. 2014. Academic content, student learning, and the persistence of preschool effects. *American Educational Research Journal* 51(2):403-434.

Clarke, B. A., D. M. Clarke, and J. Cheeseman. 2006. The mathematical knowledge and understanding young children bring to school. *Mathematics Education Research Journal* 18(1):81-107.

Clements, D. H. 1999. Subitizing: What is it? Why teach it? *Teaching Children Mathematics* 5:400-405.

Clements, D. H., and J. Sarama. 2004. Learning trajectories in mathematics education. *Mathematical Thinking & Learning* 6(2):81-89.

———. 2008. Experimental evaluation of the effects of a research-based preschool mathematics curriculum. *American Educational Research Journal* 45:443-494.

———. 2009. *Learning and teaching early math: The learning trajectories approach.* New York: Routledge.

———. 2012. Learning and teaching early and elementary mathematics. In *Instructional strategies for improving students' learning: Focus on early reading and mathematics*, edited by J. S. Carlson and J. R. Levin. Charlotte, NC: Information Age Publishing.

———. 2014. *Learning and teaching early math: The learning trajectories approach*, 2nd ed. New York: Routledge.

Clements, D. H., S. Swaminathan, M. A. Z. Hannibal, and J. Sarama. 1999. Young children's concepts of shape. *Journal for Research in Mathematics Education* 30:192-212.

Clements, D. H., J. Sarama, M. E. Spitler, A. A. Lange, and C. B. Wolfe. 2011. Mathematics learned by young children in an intervention based on learning trajectories: A large-scale cluster randomized trial. *Journal for Research in Mathematics Education* 42(2):127-166.

Clements, D. H., A. J. Baroody, and J. Sarama. 2013a (unpublished). *Background research on early mathematics*. National Governor's Association (NGA) Center Project on Early Mathematics.

Clements, D. H., J. Sarama, C. B. Wolfe, and M. E. Spitler. 2013b. Longitudinal evaluation of a scale-up model for teaching mathematics with trajectories and technologies: Persistence of effects in the third year. *American Educational Research Journal* 50(4):812-850.

Cobb, S. 1976. Social support as a moderator of life stress. *Psychosomatic Medicine* 38(5): 300-314.

Colman, S., I. P. Nichols-Barrer, J. E. Redline, B. L. Devaney, S. V. Ansell, and T. Joyce. 2012. *Effects of the Special Supplemental Nutrition Program for Women, Infants, and Children (WIC): A review of recent research (summary)*. Alexandria, VA: U.S. Department of Agriculture, Food and Nutrition Service, Office of Research and Analysis.

Connor, C. M., F. J. Morrison, and L. Slominski. 2006. Preschool instruction and children's emergent literacy growth. *Journal of Educational Psychology* 98(4):665-689.

Connor, C. M., F. J. Morrison, and P. S. Underwood. 2007. A second chance in second grade: The independent and cumulative impact of first- and second-grade reading instruction and students' letter-word reading skill growth. *Scientific Studies of Reading* 11(3):199-233.

Connor, C. M., P. A. Alberto, D. L. Compton, and R. E. O'Connor. 2014. *Improving reading outcomes for students with or at risk for reading disabilities: A synthesis of the contributions from the Institute of Education Sciences Research Centers*. NCSER 2014-3000. Washington, DC: National Center for Special Education Research.

Conway, A. R. A., M. J. Kane, and R. W. Engle. 2003. Working memory capacity and its relation to general intelligence. *Trends in Cognitive Sciences* 7(12):547-552.

Cook, J. T., and D. A. Frank. 2008. Food security, poverty, and human development in the United States. *Annals of the New York Academy of Sciences* 1136(1):193-209.

Cooper, D. H., F. P. Roth, D. L. Speece, and C. Schatschneider. 2002. The contribution of oral language skills to the development of phonological awareness. *Applied Psycholinguistics* 23:399-416.

Cooper, S. B., S. Bandelow, M. L. Nute, J. G. Morris, and M. E. Nevill. 2012. Breakfast glycaemic index and cognitive function in adolescent school children. *British Journal of Nutrition* 107(12):1823-1832.

Copple, C., S. Bredekamp, D. G. Koralek, and K. Charner. 2013. *Developmentally appropriate practice. Focus on preschoolers*. Washington, DC: National Association for the Education of Young Children.

Coyne, M. D., D. B. McCoach, S. Loftus, R. Zipoli, Jr., and S. Kapp. 2009. Direct vocabulary instruction in kindergarten: Teaching for breadth versus depth. *Elementary School Journal* 110(1):1-18.

Csibra, G. 2010. Recognizing communicative intentions in infancy. *Mind & Language* 25(2):141-168.

Csibra, G., and G. Gergely. 2009. Natural pedagogy. *Trends in Cognitive Sciences* 13(4):148-153.

Cunha, F., and J. J. Heckman. 2010. *Investing in our young people.* Working paper 1620. Cambridge, MA: National Bureau of Economic Research.

Cunningham, A. E., and J. Zibulsky. 2014. *Book smart: How to develop and support successful, motivated readers.* New York: Oxford University Press.

Currie, J. 2011. Inequality at birth: Some causes and consequences. *American Economic Review* 101(3):1-22.

Currie, J., and M. Rossin-Slater. 2013. Weathering the storm: Hurricanes and birth outcomes. *Journal of Health Economics* 32(3):487-503.

Currie, J., and W. R. Walker. 2009. Traffic congestion and infant health: Evidence from E-ZPass. *National Bureau of Economic Research Working Paper Series* No. 15413.

Currie, J., M. Neidell, and J. F. Schmieder. 2009. Air pollution and infant health: Lessons from New Jersey. *Journal of Health Economics* 28(3):688-703.

Currie, J., J. Graff Zivin, K. Meckel, M. Neidell, and W. Schlenker. 2013. Something in the water: Contaminated drinking water and infant health. *Canadian Journal of Economics* 46(3):791-810.

Danese, A., and B. S. McEwen. 2012. Adverse childhood experiences, allostasis, allostatic load, and age-related disease. *Physiology & Behavior* 106(1):29-39.

Davies, P. T., M. J. Woitach, M. A. Winter, and E. M. Cummings. 2008. Children's insecure representations of the interparental relationship and their school adjustment: The mediating role of attention difficulties. *Child Development* 79(5):1570-1582.

de Bruin, A., B. Treccani, and S. Della Sala. 2015. Cognitive advantage in bilingualism: An example of publication bias? *Psychological Science* 26(1):99-107.

de Ruiter, C., and M. H. van IJzendoorn. 1993. Attachment and cognition: A review of the literature. *International Journal of Educational Research* (19):525-540.

Dearing, E., K. McCartney, and B. A. Taylor. 2001. Change in family income-to-needs matters more for children with less. *Child Development* 72(6):1779-1793.

Denham, S. A., and C. Brown. 2010. "Plays nice with others": Social–emotional learning and academic success. *Early Education and Development* 21(5):652-680.

Denton, K., and J. West. 2002. *Children's reading and mathematics achievement in kindergarten and first grade.* Washington, DC: U.S. Department of Education, National Center for Education Statistics.

Derryberry, D., and M. Reed. 1996. Regulatory processes and the development of cognitive representations. *Development and Psychopathology* 8(1):215-234.

Deschenes, O., M. Greenstone, and J. Guryan. 2009. Climate change and birth weight. *American Economic Review* 99(2):211-217.

DeYoung, C. G. 2011. Intelligence and personality. In *The Cambridge handbook of intelligence,* edited by R. J. Sternberg and S. B. Kaufman. Cambridge, MA, and New York: Cambridge University Press. Pp. 711-737.

Diamond, A. 1991. Neuropsychological insights into the meaning of object concept development. In *The epigenesis of mind: Essays on biology and cognition,* edited by S. E. Carey and R. Gelman. Hillsdale, NJ: Lawrence Erlbaum Associates. Pp. 67-110.

Diamond, A., and K. Lee. 2011. Interventions shown to aid executive function development in children 4 to 12 years old. *Science* 333(6045):959-964.

Diamond, K. E., L. M. Justice, R. S. Siegler, and P. A. Snyder. 2013. *Synthesis of IES research on early intervention and early childhood education.* Washington, DC: National Center for Special Education Research, Institute of Education Sciences, U.S. Department of Education.

Dickinson, D. K. 2003. Why we must improve teacher–child conversations in preschools and the promise of professional development. In *Enhancing caregiver language facilitation in childcare settings*, edited by L. Girolametto and E. Weitzman. Toronto: The Hanen Institute. Pp. 41-48.

Dickinson, D. K., and J. Freiberg. 2009. *Environmental factors affecting language acquisition from birth–five: Implications for literacy development and intervention efforts.* Paper presented at Workshop on the Role of Language in School Learning: Implications for Closing the Achievement Gap, Hewlett Foundation, Menlo Park, CA.

Dickinson, D. K., and M. V. Porche. 2011. Relation between language experiences in preschool classrooms and children's kindergarten and fourth-grade language and reading abilities. *Child Development* 82(3):870-886.

Dickinson, D. K., and M. W. Smith. 1991. Preschool talk: Patterns of teacher–child interaction in early childhood classrooms. *Journal of Research in Childhood Education* 6(1):20-29.

Dickinson, D. K., and P. O. Tabors. 2001. *Beginning literacy with language: Young children learning at home and school.* Baltimore, MD: Paul H. Brookes Publishing Co.

Dickinson, D. K., C. L. Darrow, and T. A. Tinubu. 2008. Patterns of teacher–child conversations in Head Start classrooms: Implications for an empirically grounded approach to professional development. *Early Education and Development* 19(3):396-429.

Doig, B., B. McCrae, and K. Rowe. 2003. *A good start to numeracy: Effective numeracy strategies from research and practice in early childhood.* Canberra ACT, Australia: Australian Council for Educational Research.

Dombek, J. L., and C. M. Connor. 2012. Preventing retention: First grade classroom instruction and student characteristics. *Psychology in the Schools* 49(6):568-588.

Domitrovich, C. E., J. E. Moore, R. A. Thompson, and the CASEL Preschool to Elementary School Social and Emotional Learning Assessment Workgroup. 2012. Interventions that promote social-emotional learning in young children. In *Handbook of early childhood education*, edited by R. C. Pianta, W. S. Barnett, L. M. Justice, and S. M. Sheridan. New York: Guilford Press. Pp. 393-415.

Dozier, M., E. Peloso, O. Lindhiem, M. K. Gordon, M. Manni, S. Sepulveda, J. Ackerman, A. Bernier, and S. Levine. 2006. Developing evidence-based interventions for foster children: An example of a randomized clinical trial with infants and toddlers. *Journal of Social Issues* 62(4):767-785.

Dozier, M., E. Peloso, E. Lewis, J. P. Laurenceau, and S. Levine. 2008. Effects of an attachment-based intervention on the cortisol production of infants and toddlers in foster care. *Development and Psychopathology* 20(3):845-859.

Drake, K., J. Belsky, and R. M. Fearon. 2014. From early attachment to engagement with learning in school: The role of self-regulation and persistence. *Developmental Psychology* 50(5):1350-1361.

Duke, N. K., and M. K. Block. 2012. Improving reading in the primary grades. *The Future of Children* 22(2):55-72.

Duncan, G. J., and K. Magnuson. 2011. The nature and impact of early achievement skills, attention skills, and behavior problems. In *Whither opportunity? Rising inequality and the uncertain life chances of low-income children*, edited by G. J. Duncan and R. Murnane. New York: Russell Sage Press. Pp. 47-70.

Duncan, G. J., A. Claessens, and M. Engel. 2005. *The contributions of hard skills and socio-emotional behavior to school readiness.* http://www.ipr.northwestern.edu/publications/docs/workingpapers/2005/IPR-WP-05-01.pdf (accessed January 20, 2015).

Duncan, G. J., C. J. Dowsett, A. Claessens, K. Magnuson, A. C. Huston, P. Klebanov, L. Pagani, L. Feinstein, M. Engel, J. Brooks-Gunn, H. Sexton, K. Duckworth, and C. Japel. 2007. School readiness and later achievement. *Developmental Psychology* 43(6):1428-1446.

Dunlap, G., P. S. Strain, L. Fox, J. J. Carta, M. Conroy, B. J. Smith, L. Kern, M. L. Hemmeter, M. A. Timm, A. McCart, W. Sailor, U. Markey, D. J. Markey, S. Lardieri, and C. Sowell. 2006. Prevention and intervention with young children's challenging behavior: Perspectives regarding current knowledge. *Behavioral Disorders* 32(1):29-45.

Dunn, J. 2002. Mindreading, emotion understanding, and relationships. In *Growing points in developmental science: An introduction*, edited by W. W. Hartup and R. K. Silbereisen. Hove, NY: Psychology Press. Pp. 167-176.

Edens, K. M., and E. F. Potter. 2013. An exploratory look at the relationships among math skills, motivational factors and activity choice. *Early Childhood Education Journal* 41(3):235-243.

Egger, H. L., and A. Angold. 2006. Common emotional and behavioral disorders in preschool children: Presentation, nosology, and epidemiology. *Journal of Child Psychology and Psychiatry and Allied Disciplines* 47(3-4):313-337.

Egger, H. L., and R. N. Emde. 2011. Developmentally sensitive diagnostic criteria for mental health disorders in early childhood: The Diagnostic and Statistical Manual of Mental Disorders-IV, the research diagnostic criteria-preschool age, and the diagnostic classification of mental health and developmental disorders of infancy and early childhood-revised. *American Psychologist* 66(2):95-106.

Ehri, L. C. 2005. Learning to read words: Theory, findings, and issues. *Scientific Studies of Reading* 9(2):167-188.

Eimeren, L. V., K. D. MacMillan, and D. Ansari. 2007. The role of subitizing in children's development of verbal counting. Paper read at Society for Research in Child Development, April, Boston, MA.

Eisenberg, N., C. Valiente, and N. D. Eggum. 2010. Self-regulation and school readiness. *Early Education and Development* 21(5):681-698.

Ellis, R. 2008. *The study of second language acquisition*. Oxford and New York: Oxford University Press.

Englund, M. M., A. E. Luckner, G. J. L. Whaley, and B. Egeland. 2004. Children's achievement in early elementary school: Longitudinal effects of parental involvement, expectations, and quality of assistance. *Journal of Educational Psychology* 96(4):723-730.

Ericsson, K. A., R. T. Krampe, and C. Tesch-Römer. 1993. The role of deliberate practice in the acquisition of expert performance. *Psychological Review* 100:363-406.

ERS (Economic Research Service). 2014. *Definitions of food security*. http://www.ers.usda.gov/topics/food-nutrition-assistance/food-security-in-the-us/definitions-of-food-security.aspx (accessed March 23, 2015).

Espada, J. P. 2012. The native language in teaching kindergarten mathematics. *Journal of International Education Research* 8(4):359-366.

Espinosa, L. M. 2005. Curriculum and assessment considerations for young children from culturally, linguistically, and economically diverse backgrounds. *Psychology in the Schools* 42(8):837-853.

Evans, G. W., and P. Kim. 2013. Childhood poverty, chronic stress, self-regulation, and coping. *Child Development Perspectives* 7(1):43-48.

Evans, G. W., E. Chen, G. Miller, and T. Seeman. 2012. How poverty gets under the skin: A life-course perspective. In *The Oxford handbook of poverty and child development*, edited by V. Maholmes and R. B. King. New York: Oxford University Press. Pp. 13-36.

Fahie, C. M., and D. K. Symons. 2003. Executive functioning and theory of mind in children clinically referred for attention and behavior problems. *Applied Developmental Psychology* 24:51-73.

Farah, M. J., L. Betancourt, D. M. Shera, J. H. Savage, J. M. Giannetta, N. L. Brodsky, E. K. Malmud, and H. Hurt. 2008. Environmental stimulation, parental nurturance and cognitive development in humans. *Developmental Science* 11(5):793-801.

Farran, D. C., C. Aydogan, S. J. Kang, and M. Lipsey. 2005. Preschool classroom environments and the quantity and quality of children's literacy and language behaviors. In *Handbook of early literacy research*, edited by D. Dickinson and S. Neuman. New York: Guilford Press. Pp. 257-268.

Farran, D. C., M. W. Lipsey, B. Watson, and S. Hurley. 2007. *Balance of content emphasis and child content engagement in an early reading first program.* Paper presented at American Educational Research Association, April, Chicago, IL.

Feigenson, L., M. E. Libertus, and J. Halberda. 2013. Links between the intuitive sense of number and formal mathematics ability. *Child Development Perspectives* 7(2):74-79.

Fernald, A., V. A. Marchman, and A. Weisleder. 2013. SES differences in language processing skill and vocabulary are evident at 18 months. *Developmental Science* 16(2):234-248.

Field, E., O. Robles, and M. Torero. 2009. Iodine deficiency and schooling attainment in Tanzania. *American Economic Journal: Applied Economics* 1(4):140-169.

Figlio, D., J. Guryan, K. Karbownik, and J. Roth. 2014. The effects of poor neonatal health on children's cognitive development? *American Economic Review* 104(12):4205-4230.

Fisher, P. A., M. Stoolmiller, M. R. Gunnar, and B. O. Burraston. 2007. Effects of a therapeutic intervention for foster preschoolers on diurnal cortisol activity. *Psychoneuroendocrinology* 32(8-10):892-905.

Fisher, P. A., M. J. Van Ryzin, and M. R. Gunnar. 2011. Mitigating HPA axis dysregulation associated with placement changes in foster care. *Psychoneuroendocrinology* 36(4):531-539.

Fivush, R., C. A. Haden, and E. Reese. 2006. Elaborating on elaborations: Role of maternal reminiscing style in cognitive and socioemotional development. *Child Development* 77(6):1568-1588.

Florence, M. D., M. Asbridge, and P. J. Veugelers. 2008. Diet quality and academic performance. *Journal of School Health* 78(4):209-215; quiz 239-241.

Furrow, D., K. Nelson, and H. Benedict. 1979. Mothers' speech to children and syntactic development: Some simple relationships. *Journal of Child Language* 6(03):423-442.

Fuson, K. C. 1988. *Children's counting and concepts of number.* New York: Springer-Verlag.

———. 1992. Research on learning and teaching addition and subtraction of whole numbers. In *Handbook of research on mathematics teaching and learning*, edited by G. Leinhardt, R. Putman, and R. A. Hattrup. Mahwah, NJ: Lawrence Erlbaum Associates. Pp. 53-187.

———. 2004. Pre-K to grade 2 goals and standards: Achieving 21st century mastery for all. In *Engaging young children in mathematics: Standards for early childhood mathematics education*, edited by D. H. Clements, J. Sarama, and A.-M. DiBiase. Mahwah, NJ: Lawrence Erlbaum Associates. Pp. 105-148.

Fuson, K. C., and Y. Kwon. 1992. Korean childen's understanding of multidigit addition and subtraction. *Child Development* 63:491-506.

Gámez, P. B., and N. K. Lesaux. 2012. The relation between exposure to sophisticated and complex language and early-adolescent English-only and language minority learners' vocabulary. *Child Development* 83(4):1316-1331.

Gámez, P. B., and S. C. Levine. 2013. Oral language skills of spanish-speaking English language learners: The impact of high-quality native language exposure. *Applied Psycholinguistics* 34(4):673-696.

GAO (U.S. Government Accountability Office). 2012. *K-12 education school-based physical education and sports programs: Report to congressional requesters*. Washington, DC: GAO.

Geary, D. C. 1990. A componential analysis of an early learning deficit in mathematics. *Journal of Experimental Child Psychology* 49:363-383.

———. 1993. Mathematical disabilities: Cognitive, neuropsychological, and genetic components. *Psychological Bulletin* 114:345-362.

———. 1994. *Children's mathematical development: Research and practical applications*. Washington, DC: American Psychological Association.

———. 2004. Mathematics and learning disabilities. *Journal of Learning Disabilities* 37:4-15.

———. 2011. Cognitive addition: A short longitudinal study of strategy choice and speed-of-processing differences in normal and mathematically disabled children. *Developmental Psychology* 47:1539-1552.

Geary, D. C., C. C. Bow-Thomas, and Y. Yao. 1992. Counting knowledge and skill in cognitive addition: A comparison of normal and mathematically disabled children. *Journal of Experimental Child Psychology* 54:372-391.

Geary, D. C., M. K. Hoard, J. Byrd-Craven, L. Nugent, and C. Numtee. 2007. Cognitive mechanisms underlying achievement deficits in children with mathematical learning disability. *Child Development* 78:1343-1359.

Geary, D. C., M. K. Hoard, and L. Nugent. 2012. Independent contributions of the central executive, intelligence, and in-class attentive behavior to developmental change in the strategies used to solve addition problems. *Journal of Experimental Child Psychology* 113(1):49-65.

Gelman, S. A. 2003. *The essential child origins of essentialism in everyday thought*. New York: Oxford University Press.

Gelman, S. A., and E. M. Markman. 1987. Young children's inductions from natural kinds: The role of categories and appearances. *Child Development* 58(6):1532-1541.

Gergely, G., H. Bekkering, and I. Kiraly. 2002. Rational imitation in preverbal infants. *Nature* 415(6873):755.

Gerson, S. A., and A. L. Woodward. 2014. Learning from their own actions: The unique effect of producing actions on infants' action understanding. *Child Development* 85(1): 264-277.

Gilliam, W. S. 2005. *Prekindergarteners left behind: Expulsion rates in state prekindergarten systems*. New York: Foundation for Child Development.

Girolametto, L., and E. Weitzman. 2002. Responsiveness of child care providers in interactions with toddlers and preschoolers. *Language, Speech, and Hearing Services in Schools* 33(4):268-281.

Glaser, R. 1991. The maturing of the relationship between the science of learning of learning and cognition and educational practice. *Learning and Instruction* 1:129-144.

Glasersfeld, E. V. 1995. Sensory experience, abstraction, and teaching. In *Constructivism in education*, edited by L. P. Steffe and J. Gale. Mahwah, NJ: Lawrence Erlbaum Associates. Pp. 369-383.

Gopnik, A., and H. M. Wellman. 2012. Reconstructing constructivism: Causal models, Bayesian learning mechanisms, and the theory theory. *Psychological Bulletin* 138(6):1085-1108.

Gopnik, A., D. M. Sobel, L. E. Schulz, and C. Glymour. 2001. Causal learning mechanisms in very young children: Two-, three-, and four-year-olds infer causal relations from patterns of variation and covariation. *Developmental Psychology* 37(5):620-629.

Gough, P. B., and W. E. Tunmer. 1986. Decoding, reading, and reading disability. *Remedial and Special Education (RASE)* 7(1):6-10.

Gough, P. B., W. A. Hoover, and C. L. Peterson. 1996. Some observations on a simple view of reading. In *Reading comprehension difficulties*, edited by C. Cornoldi and J. Oakhill. Mahwah, NJ: Lawrence Erlbaum Associates. Pp. 1-13.

Graham, S. A., C. S. Kilbreath, and A. N. Welder. 2004. Thirteen-month-olds rely on shared labels and shape similarity for inductive inferences. *Child Development* 75(2):409-427.

Graziano, P. A., R. D. Reavis, S. P. Keane, and S. D. Calkins. 2007. The role of emotion regulation and children's early academic success. *Journal of School Psychology* 45(1):3-19.

Greenwood, C., J. Buzhardt, D. Walker, W. Howard, and R. Anderson. 2011. Program-level influences on the measurement of early communication for infants and toddlers in early Head Start. *Journal of Early Intervention* 33(2):110-134.

Gripshover, S. J., and E. M. Markman. 2013. Teaching young children a theory of nutrition: Conceptual change and the potential for increased vegetable consumption. *Psychological Science* 24(8):1541-1553.

Grissmer, D., K. J. Grimm, S. M. Aiyer, W. M. Murrah, and J. S. Steele. 2010a. Fine motor skills and early comprehension of the world: Two new school readiness indicators. *Developmental Psychology* 46(5):1008-1017.

———. 2010b. *New school readiness indicators*. Research brief. Charlottesville: University of Virginia, Center for Advanced Study of Teaching and Learning.

Gunderson, E. A., and S. C. Levine. 2011. Some types of parent number talk count more than others: Relations between parents' input and children's cardinal-number knowledge. *Developmental Science* 14(5):1021-1032.

Gunderson, E. A., S. J. Gripshover, C. Romero, C. S. Dweck, S. Goldin-Meadow, and S. C. Levine. 2013. Parent praise to 1- to 3-year-olds predicts children's motivational frameworks 5 years later. *Child Development* 84(5):1526-1541.

Gunnar, M. R., and B. Donzella. 2002. Social regulation of the cortisol levels in early human development. *Psychoneuroendocrinology* 27(1-2):199-220.

Gunnar, M. R., S. J. Morison, K. Chisholm, and M. Schuder. 2001. Salivary cortisol levels in children adopted from Romanian orphanages. *Development and Psychopathology* 13(3):611-628.

Gweon, H., and L. Schulz. 2011. 16-month-olds rationally infer causes of failed actions. *Science* 332(6037):1524.

Hackman, D. A., and M. J. Farah. 2009. Socioeconomic status and the developing brain. *Trends in Cognitive Sciences* 13(2):65-73.

Hackman, D. A., M. J. Farah, and M. J. Meaney. 2010. Socioeconomic status and the brain: Mechanistic insights from human and animal research. *Nature Reviews: Neuroscience* 11(9):651-659.

Hair, E., T. Halle, E. Terry-Humen, B. Lavelle, and J. Calkins. 2006. Children's school readiness in the ECLS-K: Predictions to academic, health, and social outcomes in first grade. *Early Childhood Research Quarterly* 21(4):431-454.

Hamayan, E. V., B. Marler, C. Sánchez López, and J. Damico. 2013. *Special education considerations for English language learners: Delivering a continuum of services*, 2nd ed. Philadelphia, PA: Caslon Publishing.

Hamlin, J. K., K. Wynn, and P. Bloom. 2007. Social evaluation by preverbal infants. *Nature* 450(7169):557-559.

Hamre, B. K. 2014. Teachers' daily interactions with children: An essential ingredient in effective early childhood programs. *Child Development Perspectives* 8(4):223-230.

Hamre, B. K., and R. C. Pianta. 2001. Early teacher–child relationships and the trajectory of children's school outcomes through eighth grade. *Child Development* 72:625-638.

———. 2004. Self-reported depression in nonfamilial caregivers: Prevalence and associations with caregiver behavior in child-care settings. *Early Childhood Research Quarterly* 19(2):297-318.

————. 2005. Can instructional and emotional support in the first-grade classroom make a difference for children at risk of school failure? *Child Development* 76(5):949-967.

Hannula, M. M. 2005. *Spontaneous focusing on numerosity in the development of early mathematical skills*. Turku, Finland: University of Turku.

Hannula, M. M., P. Räsänen, and E. Lehtinen. 2007. Development of counting skills: Role of spontaneous focusing on numerosity and subitizing-based enumeration. *Mathematical Thinking and Learning* 9:51-57.

Harris, K. R., B. D. Friedlander, B. Saddler, R. Frizzelle, and S. Graham. 2005. Self-monitoring of attention versus self-monitoring of academic performance: Effects among students with ADHD in the general education classroom. *Journal of Special Education* 39(3):145-156.

Harris, P. L. 2012. *Trusting what you're told: How children learn from others*. Cambridge, MA: Belknap Press of Harvard University Press.

Hart, B., and T. R. Risley. 1995. *Meaningful differences in the everyday experience of young American children*. Baltimore, MD: Paul H. Brookes Publishing Co.

Hawthorne, K., and L. Gerken. 2014. From pauses to clauses: Prosody facilitates learning of syntactic constituency. *Cognition* 133(2):420-428.

Hecht, S. A., J. K. Torgesen, R. K. Wagner, and C. A. Raschotte. 2001. The relations between phonological processing abilities and emerging individual differences in mathematical computation skills: A longitudinal study from second to fifth grades. *Journal of Experimental Child Psychology* 79:192-227.

Heckman, J. J. 2007. The economics, technology, and neuroscience of human capability formation. *Proceedings of the National Academy of Sciences of the United States of America* 104(33):13250-13255.

Heckman, J. J., R. Pinto, and P. Savelyev. 2013. Understanding the mechanisms through which an influential early childhood program boosted adult outcomes. *American Economic Review* 103(6):2052-2086.

Henry, G. T., and D. K. Rickman. 2007. Do peers influence children's skill development in preschool? *Economics of Education Review* 26(1):100-112.

Hertzman, C., and W. T. Boyce. 2010. How experience gets under the skin to create gradients in developmental health. *Annual Review of Public Health* 31:329-347.

Heyman, G. D., and C. S. Dweck. 1992. Achievement goals and intrinsic motivation: Their relation and their role in adaptive motivation. *Motivation and Emotion* 16(3):231-247.

Heyman, G. D., and S. A. Gelman. 1999. The use of trait labels in making psychological inferences. *Child Development* 70(3):604-619.

Hibel, L. C., D. A. Granger, C. Blair, and M. J. Cox. 2011. Maternal sensitivity buffers the adrenocortical implications of intimate partner violence exposure during early childhood. *Development and Psychopathology* 23(2):689-701.

Hill, E. L. 2004. Executive dysfunction in autism. *Trends in Cognitive Sciences* 8(1):26-32.

Hindman, A. H., C. M. Connor, A. M. Jewkes, and F. J. Morrison. 2008. Untangling the effects of shared book reading: Multiple factors and their associations with preschool literacy outcomes. *Early Childhood Research Quarterly* 23(3):330-350.

Hinnant, J. B., M. O'Brien, and S. R. Ghazarian. 2009. The longitudinal relations of teacher expectations to achievement in the early school years. *Journal of Educational Psychology* 101(3):662-670.

Hoff, E. 2006. How social contexts support and shape language development. *Developmental Review* 26(1):55-88.

Hoff, E., and L. Naigles. 2002. How children use input to acquire a lexicon. *Child Development* 73(2):418-433.

Hofmann, W., B. J. Schmeichel, and A. D. Baddeley. 2012. Executive functions and self-regulation. *Trends in Cognitive Sciences* 16(3):174-180.

Hongwanishkul, D., K. R. Happaney, W. S. C. Lee, and P. D. Zelazo. 2005. Assessment of hot and cool executive function in young children: Age-related changes and individual differences. *Developmental Neuropsychology* 28(2):617-644.

Hoover, W. A., and P. B. Gough. 1990. The simple view of reading. *Reading and Writing: An Interdisciplinary Journal* 2(2):127-160.

Hostinar, C. E., R. M. Sullivan, and M. R. Gunnar. 2014. Psychobiological mechanisms underlying the social buffering of the hypothalamic–pituitary–adrenocortical axis: A review of animal models and human studies across development. *Psychological Bulletin* 140(1):256-282.

Howes, C., and C. E. Hamilton. 1992. Children's relationships with child care teachers: Stability and concordance with parental attachments. *Child Development* 63(4):867-878.

Howes, C., C. E. Hamilton, and L. C. Phillipsen. 1998. Stability and continuity of child-caregiver and child-peer relationships. *Child Development* 69(2):418-426.

Howse, R. B., G. Lange, D. C. Farran, and C. D. Boyles. 2003a. Motivation and self-regulation as predictors of achievement in economically disadvantaged young children. *Journal of Experimental Education* 71(2):151-174.

Howse, R. B., S. D. Calkins, A. D. Anastopoulos, S. P. Keane, and T. L. Shelton. 2003b. Regulatory contributors to children's kindergarten achievement. *Early Education and Development* 14(1):101-120.

Hoyland, A., L. Dye, and C. L. Lawton. 2009. A systematic review of the effect of breakfast on the cognitive performance of children and adolescents. *Nutrition Research Reviews* 22(2):220-243.

Hoynes, H., M. Page, and A. H. Stevens. 2011. Can targeted transfers improve birth outcomes?: Evidence from the introduction of the WIC program. *Journal of Public Economics* 95(7-8):813-827.

Huang-Pollock, C. L., S. L. Karalunas, H. Tam, and A. N. Moore. 2012. Evaluating vigilance deficits in ADHD: A meta-analysis of CPT performance. *Journal of Abnormal Psychology* 121(2):360-371.

Huffman, L. C., S. L. Mehlinger, and A. S. Kerivan. 2000. *Risk factors for academic and behavioral problems in the beginning of school.* Chapel Hill: University of North Carolina, Frank Porter Graham Child Development Center.

Hughes, C., and R. Ensor. 2011. Individual differences in growth in executive function across the transition to school predict externalizing and internalizing behaviors and self-perceived academic success at 6 years of age. *Journal of Experimental Child Psychology* 108:663-676.

Huntley-Fenner, G., S. Carey, and A. Solimando. 2002. Objects are individuals but stuff doesn't count: Perceived rigidity and cohesiveness influence infants' representations of small groups of discrete entities. *Cognition* 85:203-221.

Huttenlocher, J. 1998. Language input and language growth. *Preventive Medicine* 27(2):195-199.

Huttenlocher, J., N. C. Jordan, and S. C. Levine. 1994. A mental model for early arithmetic. *Journal of Experimental Psychology: General* 123:284-296.

Huttenlocher, J., M. Vasilyeva, E. Cymerman, and S. Levine. 2002. Language input and child syntax. *Cognitive Psychology* 45(3):337-374.

Huttenlocher, J., H. Waterfall, M. Vasilyeva, J. Vevea, and L. V. Hedges. 2010. Sources of variability in children's language growth. *Cognitive Psychology* 61(4):343-365.

Hyde, D. C., and E. S. Spelke. 2011. Neural signatures of number processing in human infants: Evidence for two core systems underlying numerical cognition. *Developmental Science* 14(2):360-371.

Inagaki, K., and G. Hatano. 2004. Vitalistic causality in young children's naive biology. *Trends in Cognitive Sciences* 8(8):356-362.

IOM (Institute of Medicine). 2011. *Hunger and obesity: Understanding a food insecurity paradigm: Workshop summary*, edited by L. M. Troy, E. A. Miller, and S. Olson. Washington, DC: The National Academies Press.

———. 2013. *Educating the student body: Taking physical activity and physical education to school*, edited by H. W. Kohl III and H. D. Cook. Washington, DC: The National Academies Press.

IOM and NRC (National Research Council). 2009. *Preventing mental, emotional, and behavioral disorders among young people: Progress and possibilities*. Washington, DC: The National Academies Press.

Isen, A., M. Rossin-Slater, and W. R. Walker. 2014. Every breath you take—every dollar you'll make: The long-term consequences of the Clean Air Act of 1970. *National Bureau of Economic Research Working Paper Series* No. 19858.

Jacoby, J. W., and N. K. Lesaux. 2014. Support for extended discourse in teacher talk with linguistically diverse preschoolers. *Early Education and Development* 25(8):1162-1179.

Jamison, K. R., S. Q. Cabell, J. LoCasale-Crouch, B. K. Hamre, and R. C. Pianta. 2014. Class–infant: An observational measure for assessing teacher–infant interactions in center-based child care. *Early Education & Development* 25(4):553-572.

Janzen, J. 2008. Teaching English language learners. *Review of Educational Research* 78:1010-1038.

Jaswal, V. K. 2010. Believing what you're told: Young children's trust in unexpected testimony about the physical world. *Cognitive Psychology* 61(3):248-272.

Jenks, K. M., E. C. van Lieshout, and J. M. de Moor. 2012. Cognitive correlates of mathematical achievement in children with cerebral palsy and typically developing children. *British Journal of Educational Psychology* 82(1):120-135.

Jeon, L., C. K. Buettner, and A. R. Snyder. 2014. Pathways from teacher depression and child-care quality to child behavioral problems. *Journal of Consulting and Clinical Psychology* 82(2):225-235.

Jiang, Y., M. Ekono, and C. Skinner. 2014. *Basic facts about low-income children: Children under 6 years, 2012*. http://nccp.org/publications/pub_1088.html (accessed January 26, 2015).

Johnson-Pynn, J. S., C. Ready, and M. Beran. 2005. Estimation mediates preschoolers: Numerical reasoning: Evidence against precise calculation abilities. Paper read at Biennial Meeting of the Society for Research in Child Development, April, Atlanta, GA.

Johnston, T., and J. Kirby. 2006. The contribution of naming speed to the simple view of reading. *Reading and Writing* 19(4):339-361.

Jordan, N. C., L. B. Hanich, and H. Z. Uberti. 2003. Mathematical thinking and learning difficulties. In *The development of arithmetic concepts and skills: Constructing adaptive expertise*, edited by A. J. Baroody and A. Dowker. Mahwah, NJ: Lawrence Erlbaum Associates. Pp. 359-383.

Joshi, R. M., and P. G. Aaron. 2000. The component model of reading: Simple view of reading made a little more complex. *Reading Psychology* 21(2):85-97.

Justice, L. M., J. Meier, and S. Walpole. 2005. Learning new words from storybooks: An efficacy study with at-risk kindergartners. *Language, Speech, and Hearing Services in Schools* 36(1):17-32.

Justice, L. M., A. S. McGinty, T. Zucker, S. Q. Cabell, and S. B. Piasta. 2013. Bi-directional dynamics underlie the complexity of talk in teacher–child play-based conversations in classrooms serving at-risk pupils. *Early Childhood Research Quarterly* 28(3):496-508.

Kamins, M. L., and C. S. Dweck. 1999. Person versus process praise and criticism: Implications for contingent self-worth and coping. *Developmental Psychology* 35(3):835-847.

Kaplan, D. W., C. D. Brindis, S. L. Phibbs, P. Melinkovich, K. Naylor, and K. Ahlstrand. 1999. A comparison study of an elementary school-based health center: Effects on health care access and use. *Archives of Pediatrics and Adolescent Medicine* 153(3):235-243.

Karmiloff, K., and A. Karmiloff-Smith. 2001. *Pathways to language: From fetus to adolescent.* Cambridge, MA: Harvard University Press.

Kaufman, E. L., M. W. Lord, T. W. Reese, and J. Volkmann. 1949. The discrimination of visual number. *American Journal of Psychology* 62:498-525.

Keenan, K., D. S. Shaw, B. Walsh, E. Delliquadri, and J. Giovannelli. 1997. DSM-III-R disorders in preschool children from low-income families. *Journal of the American Academy of Child and Adolescent Psychiatry* 36(5):620-627.

Kelley, S. A., C. A. Brownell, and S. B. Campbell. 2000. Mastery motivation and self-evaluative affect in toddlers: Longitudinal relations with maternal behavior. *Child Development* 71(4):1061-1071.

Kerr, A., and P. D. Zelazo. 2004. Development of "hot" executive function: The children's gambling task. *Brain and Cognition* 55(1):148-157.

Keyl, P. M., M. P. Hurtado, M. M. Barber, and J. Borton. 1996. School-based health centers. Students' access, knowledge, and use of services. *Archives of Pediatrics and Adolescent Medicine* 150(2):175-180.

Kiecolt-Glaser, J. K., J. P. Gouin, and L. Hantsoo. 2010. Close relationships, inflammation, and health. *Neuroscience and Biobehavioral Reviews* 35(1):33-38.

King, J. C., Jr., J. J. Stoddard, M. J. Gaglani, K. A. Moore, L. Magder, E. McClure, J. D. Rubin, J. A. Englund, and K. Neuzil. 2006. Effectiveness of school-based influenza vaccination. *New England Journal of Medicine* 355(24):2523-2532.

Kipping, P., A. Gard, L. Gilman, and J. Gorman. 2012. *Speech and language development chart*, 3rd ed. Austin, TX: Pro-Ed.

Kirkham, N. Z., J. A. Slemmer, and S. P. Johnson. 2002. Visual statistical learning in infancy: Evidence for a domain general learning mechanism. *Cognition* 83(2):B35-B42.

Kishiyama, M. M., W. T. Boyce, A. M. Jimenez, L. M. Perry, and R. T. Knight. 2009. Socioeconomic disparities affect prefrontal function in children. *Journal of Cognitive Neuroscience* 21(6):1106-1115.

Klibanoff, R. S., S. C. Levine, J. Huttenlocher, M. Vasilyeva, and L. V. Hedges. 2006. Preschool children's mathematical knowledge: The effect of teacher "math talk." *Developmental Psychology* 42:59-69.

Koenig, M. A., and S. Doebel. 2013. Children's understanding of unreliability: Evidence for a negativity bias. In *Navigating the social world*, edited by M. R. Banaji and S. A. Gelman. New York: Oxford University Press. Pp. 235-240.

Koles, B., E. O'Connor, and K. McCartney. 2009. Teacher–child relationships in prekindergarten: The influences of child and teacher characteristics. *Journal of Early Childhood Teacher Education* 30(1):3-21.

Koponen, T., P. Salmi, K. Eklund, and T. Aro. 2013. Counting and ran: Predictors of arithmetic calculation and reading fluency. *Journal of Educational Psychology* 105(1):162-175.

La Paro, K. M., and R. C. Pianta. 2000. Predicting children's competence in the early school years: A meta-analytic review. *Review of Educational Research* 70(4):443-484.

Ladd, G. W., and K. B. Burgess. 2001. Do relational risks and protective factors moderate the linkages between childhood aggression and early psychological and school adjustment? *Child Development* 72(5):1579-1601.

Ladd, G. W., B. J. Kochenderfer, and C. C. Coleman. 1996. Friendship quality as a predictor of young children's early school adjustment. *Child Development* 67(3):1103-1118.

———. 1997. Classroom peer acceptance, friendship, and victimization: Distinct relational systems that contribute uniquely to children's school adjustment? *Child Development* 68(6):1181-1197.

Ladd, G. W., S. Birch, and E. Buhs. 1999. Children's social and scholastic lives in kindergarten: Related spheres of influence? *Child Development* 70:1373-1400.

Lalonde, C. E., and M. J. Chandler. 2002. Children's understanding of interpretation. *New Ideas in Psychology* 20(2-3):163-198.

Lan, X., C. H. Legare, C. C. Ponitz, S. Li, and F. J. Morrison. 2011. Investigating the links between the subcomponents of executive function and academic achievement: A cross-cultural analysis of chinese and American preschoolers. *Journal of Experimental Child Psychology* 108:677-692.

Lane, K., S. Barton-Arwood, J. R. Nelson, and J. Wehby. 2008. Academic performance of students with emotional and behavioral disorders served in a self-contained setting. *Journal of Behavioral Education* 17(1):43-62.

Laski, E. V., and R. S. Siegler. 2014. Learning from number board games: You learn what you encode. *Developmental Psychology* 50(3):853-864.

Lauderdale, D. S. 2006. Birth outcomes for Arabic-named women in California before and after September 11. *Demography* 43(1):185-201.

Lavigne, J. V., S. A. Lebailly, J. Hopkins, K. R. Gouze, and H. J. Binns. 2009. The prevalence of ADHD, odd, depression, and anxiety in a community sample of 4-year-olds. *Journal of Clinical Child and Adolescent Psychology* 38(3):315-328.

Lawrence, J., and C. Snow. 2011. Oral discourse and reading. In *Handbook of reading research*, edited by M. L. Kamil, P. D. Pearson, E. B. Moje, and P. Afflerbach. New York: Routledge.

Le Corre, M., G. A. Van de Walle, E. M. Brannon, and S. Carey. 2006. Re-visiting the competence/performance debate in the acquisition of counting as a representation of the positive integers. *Cognitive Psychology* 52(2):130-169.

Leckman, J. F., and J. S. March. 2011. Editorial: Developmental neuroscience comes of age. *Journal of Child Psychology and Psychiatry* 52(4):333-338.

LeDoux, J. 1996. *The emotional brain: Development and psychopathology*. New York: Simon & Schuster.

Lee, J. S. 2011. Size matters: Early vocabulary as a predictor of language and literacy competence. *Applied Psycholinguistics* 32(1):69-92.

Lee, J. S., and H. P. Ginsburg. 2007. Preschool teachers' beliefs about appropriate early literacy and mathematics education for low- and middle-socioeconomic status children. *Early Education & Development* 18(1):111-143.

Lee, K. 2013. Little liars: Development of verbal deception in children. *Child Development Perspectives* 7(2):91-96.

Leerkes, E. M., M. J. Paradise, M. O'Brien, S. D. Calkins, and G. Lange. 2008. Emotion and cognition processes in preschool children. *Merrill-Palmer Quarterly* 54(1):102-124.

LeFevre, J.-A., L. Berrigan, C. Vendetti, D. Kamawar, J. Bisanz, S.-L. Skwarchuk, and B. L. Smith-Chant. 2013. The role of executive attention in the acquisition of mathematical skills for children in grades 2 through 4. *Journal of Experimental Child Psychology* 114(2):243-261.

Lerkkanen, M.-K., H. Rasku-Puttonen, K. Aunola, and J.-E. Nurmi. 2005. Mathematical performance predicts progress in reading comprehension among 7-year-olds. *European Journal of Psychology of Education* 20(2):121-137.

Levine, S. C., L. W. Suriyakham, M. L. Rowe, J. Huttenlocher, and E. A. Gunderson. 2010. What counts in the development of young children's number knowledge? *Developmental Psychology* 46(5):1309-1319.

Lewit, E. M., and L. S. Baker. 1995. School readiness. *The Future of Children/Center for the Future of Children, the David and Lucile Packard Foundation* 5(2):128-139.

Libertus, M. E., and E. M. Brannon. 2010. Stable individual differences in number discrimination in infancy. *Developmental Science* 13(6):900-906.

Lieberman, A. F., A. Chu, P. Van Horn, and W. W. Harris. 2011. Trauma in early childhood: Empirical evidence and clinical implications. *Development and Psychopathology* 23(2):397-410.

Lien, D. S., and W. N. Evans. 2005. Estimating the impact of large cigarette tax hikes: The case of maternal smoking and infant birth weight. *Journal of Human Resources* 40(2):373-392.

Low, M., A. Farrell, B. A. Biggs, and S. R. Pasricha. 2013. Effects of daily iron supplementation in primary-school-aged children: Systematic review and meta-analysis of randomized controlled trials. *Canadian Medical Association Journal* 185(17):E791-E802.

Lozoff, B. 2011. Early iron deficiency has brain and behavior effects consistent with dopaminergic dysfunction. *Journal of Nutrition* 141(4):740s-746s.

Lozoff, B., M. Castillo, K. M. Clark, J. B. Smith, and J. Sturza. 2014. Iron supplementation in infancy contributes to more adaptive behavior at 10 years of age. *Journal of Nutrition* 144(6):838-845.

Luby, J. L. 2006. *Handbook of preschool mental health: Development, disorders, and treatment*. New York: Guilford Press.

Luby, J. L., D. M. Barch, A. Belden, M. S. Gaffrey, R. Tillman, C. Babb, T. Nishino, H. Suzuki, and K. N. Botteron. 2012. Maternal support in early childhood predicts larger hippocampal volumes at school age. *Proceedings of the National Academy of Sciences of the United States of America* 109(8):2854-2859.

Lupien, S. J., B. S. McEwen, M. R. Gunnar, and C. Heim. 2009. Effects of stress throughout the lifespan on the brain, behaviour and cognition. *Nature Reviews Neuroscience* 10(6):434-445.

Lynam, D., T. Moffitt, and M. Stouthamer-Loeber. 1993. Explaining the relation between IQ and delinquency: Class, race, test motivation, school failure, or self-control? *Journal of Abnormal Psychology* 102(2):187-196.

Lyon, G. R., and N. A. Krasnegor. 1996. *Attention, memory, and executive function*. Baltimore, MD: Paul H. Brookes Publishing Co.

Maclellan, E. 2012. Number sense: The underpinning understanding for early quantitative literacy. *Numeracy* 5(2):1-19.

Mages, W. K. 2008. Does creative drama promote language development in early childhood?: A review of the methods and measures employed in the empirical literature. *Review of Educational Research* 78(1):124-152.

Mahoney, C. R., H. A. Taylor, R. B. Kanarek, and P. Samuel. 2005. Effect of breakfast composition on cognitive processes in elementary school children. *Physiology and Behavior* 85(5):635-645.

Maier, M. F., and D. B. Greenfield. 2008. *The differential role of initiative and persistence in early childhood*. Paper presented at Institute of Education Science 2007 Research Conference, Washington, DC.

Mandler, J. M. 2004. *The foundations of mind origins of conceptual thought*. http://site.ebrary.com/id/10103678 (accessed January 2, 2015).

Mantzicopoulos, P. 1997. The relationship of family variables to Head Start children's preacademic competence. *Early Education and Development* 8(4):357-375.

Marcovitch, S., and P. D. Zelazo. 2009. A hierarchical competing systems model of the emergence and early development of executive function. *Developmental Science* 12(1):1-25.

Markman, E. M. 1977. Realizing that you don't understand: A preliminary investigation. *Child Development* 48:986-999.

———. 1981. Comprehension monitoring. In *Children's oral communication skills*, edited by W. P. Dickson. New York: Academic Press. Pp. 61-84.

Marsh, H. W., R. Craven, and R. Debus. 1998. Structure, stability, and development of young children's self-concepts: A multicohort-multioccasion study. *Child Development* 69(4):1030-1053.

Marsh, H. W., L. A. Ellis, and R. G. Craven. 2002. How do preschool children feel about themselves? Unraveling measurement and multidimensional self-concept structure. *Developmental Psychology* 38(3):376-393.

Masataka, N., T. Ohnishi, E. Imabayashi, M. Hirakata, and H. Matsuda. 2006. Neural correlates for numerical processing in the manual mode. *Journal of Deaf Studies and Deaf Education* 11(2):144-152.

Mashburn, A. J., R. C. Pianta, B. K. Hamre, J. T. Downer, O. A. Barbarin, D. Bryant, M. Burchinal, D. M. Early, and C. Howes. 2008. Measures of classroom quality in prekindergarten and children's development of academic, language, and social skills. *Child Development* 79(3):732-749.

Mashburn, A. J., L. M. Justice, J. T. Downer, and R. C. Pianta. 2009. Peer effects on children's language achievement during pre-kindergarten. *Child Development* 80(3):686-702.

Masten, A. S., J. E. Herbers, C. D. Desjardins, J. J. Cutuli, C. M. McCormick, J. K. Sapienza, J. D. Long, and P. D. Zelazo. 2012. Executive function skills and school success in young children experiencing homelessness. *Educational Researcher* 41(9):375-384.

Master, A., E. M. Markman, and C. S. Dweck. 2012. Thinking in categories or along a continuum: Consequences for children's social judgments. *Child Development* 83(4):1145-1163.

Mazzocco, M. M. M., and L. B. Hanich. 2010. Math achievement, numerical processing, and executive functions in girls with Turner syndrome: Do girls with Turner syndrome have math learning disability? *Learning and Individual Differences* 20:70-81.

Mazzocco, M. M. M., and G. F. Myers. 2003. Complexities in identifying and defining mathematics learning disability in the primary school-age years. *Annuals of Dyslexia* 53:218-253.

Mazzocco, M. M. M., and R. E. Thompson. 2005. Kindergarten predictors of math learning disability. *Learning Disability Quarterly Research and Practice* 20:142-155.

McClelland, M. M., C. E. Cameron, C. M. Connor, C. L. Farris, A. M. Jewkes, and F. J. Morrison. 2007. Links between behavioral regulation and preschoolers' literacy, vocabulary, and math skills. *Developmental Psychology* 43(4):947-959.

McCormick, M. C., J. Brooks-Gunn, S. L. Buka, J. Goldman, J. Yu, M. Salganik, D. T. Scott, F. C. Bennett, L. L. Kay, J. C. Bernbaum, C. R. Bauer, C. Martin, E. R. Woods, A. Martin, and P. H. Casey. 2006. Early intervention in low birth weight premature infants: Results at 18 years of age for the infant health and development program. *Pediatrics* 117(3):771-780.

McEwen, B. S. 2012. Brain on stress: How the social environment gets under the skin. *Proceedings of the National Academy of Sciences of the United States of America* 109(Suppl. 2):17180-17185.

McGillicuddy-De Lisi, A. V. 1982. The relationship between parents' beliefs about development and family constellation, socioeconomic status, and parents' teaching strategies. In *Families as learning environments for children*, edited by L. M. Laosa and I. E. Sigel. New York: Plenum Press. Pp. 261-299.

McIntyre, L. L., J. Blacher, and B. L. Baker. 2006. The transition to school: Adaptation in young children with and without intellectual disability. *Journal of Intellectual Disability Research* 50(Pt. 5):349-361.

McLean, J. F., and G. J. Hitch. 1999. Working memory impairments in children with specific arithmetic learning difficulties. *Journal of Experimental Child Psychology* 74:240-260.

McLeod, D. B., and V. M. Adams, eds. 1989. *Affect and mathematical problem solving*. New York: Springer-Verlag.

McMillan, T. 2014. The new face of hunger. *National Geographic Magazine*, August 2014, 66-68, 70, 72-74, 77-80, 83-89.

Meltzoff, A. N. 1995. Understanding the intentions of others: Re-enactment of intended acts by 18-month-old children. *Developmental Psychology* 31(5):838-850.

Metsala, J. L., and A. C. Walley. 1998. Spoken vocabulary growth and the segmental restructuring of lexical representations: Precursors to phonemic awareness and early reading ability. In *Word recognition in beginning literacy*, edited by J. L. Metsala and L. C. Ehri. Hillsdale, NJ: Lawrence Erlbaum Associates. Pp. 89-120.

Middleton, J. A., and P. Spanias. 1999. Motivation for achievement in mathematics: Findings, generalizations, and criticisms of the research. *Journal for Research in Mathematics Education* 30:65-88.

Miller, A. L., R. Seifer, L. Stroud, S. J. Sheinkopf, and S. Dickstein. 2006. Biobehavioral indices of emotion regulation relate to school attitudes, motivation, and behavior problems in a low-income preschool sample. *Annals of the New York Academy of Sciences* 1094:325-329.

Miller, G. E., E. Chen, and K. J. Parker. 2011. Psychological stress in childhood and susceptibility to the chronic diseases of aging: Moving toward a model of behavioral and biological mechanisms. *Psychological Bulletin* 137(6):959-997.

Mills, C. M. 2013. Knowing when to doubt: Developing a critical stance when learning from others. *Developmental Psychology* 49(3):404-418.

Mischel, W., Y. Shoda, and P. K. Peake. 1988. The nature of adolescent competencies predicted by preschool delay of gratification. *Journal of Personality and Social Psychology* 54(4):687-696.

Mitchell-Copeland, J., S. A. Denham, and E. K. DeMulder. 1997. Q-sort assessment of child–teacher attachment relationships and social competence in the preschool. *Early Education and Development* 8(1):27-39.

Mix, K. S., J. Huttenlocher, and S. C. Levine. 2002. *Quantitative development in infancy and early childhood*. New York: Oxford University Press.

Mix, K. S., C. M. Sandhofer, and A. J. Baroody. 2005. Number words and number concepts: The interplay of verbal and nonverbal processes in early quantitative development. In *Advances in child development and behavior*. Vol. 33, edited by R. Kail. New York: Academic Press. Pp. 305-345.

Miyake, A., N. P. Friedman, M. J. Emerson, A. H. Witzki, A. Howerter, and T. D. Wager. 2000. The unity and diversity of executive functions and their contributions to complex "frontal lobe" tasks: A latent variable analysis. *Cognitive Psychology* 41(1):49-100.

Mol, S. E., A. G. Bus, and M. T. de Jong. 2009. Interactive book reading in early education: A tool to stimulate print knowledge as well as oral language. *Review of Educational Research* 79(2):979-1007.

Moll, L. C., C. Amanti, D. Neff, and N. Gonzalez. 1992. Funds of knowledge for teaching: Using a qualitative approach to connect homes and classrooms. *Theory into Practice* 31(2):132-141.

Mooji, T. 2010. Design and implementation of ICT-supported education for highly able pupils. Paper read at European Conference on Educational Research, Helsinki, Finland.

Morgan, G. A., R. J. Harmon, and C. A. Maslin-Cole. 1990. Mastery motivation: Definition and measurement. *Early Education and Development* 1(5):318-339.

Morgan, P. L., G. Farkas, P. A. Tufis, and R. A. Sperling. 2008. Are reading and behavior problems risk factors for each other? *Journal of Learning Disabilities* 41(5):417-436.

Morrow, L. M., and J. A. Schickedanz. 2006. The relationships between sociodramatic play and literacy development. In *Handbook of early literacy research*. Vol. 2, edited by D. K. Dickinson and S. B. Neuman. New York and London: Guilford Press.

Müller, U., D. Lieberman, D. Frye, and P. D. Zelazo. 2008. Executive function, school readiness, and school achievement. In *Cognitive development in K-3 classroom learning: Research applications*, edited by C. Fiorello and K. Thurman. Mahwah, NJ: Lawrence Erlbaum Associates. Pp. 41-84.

Mullis, I. V. S., M. O. Martin, P. Foy, and A. Arora. 2012. *TIMSS 2011 international results in mathematics.* Chestnut Hill, MA: Boston College, Trends in International Mathematics and Science Study and Progress in International Reading Literacy Study International Study Center.

Munn, P. 2006. Mathematics in early childhood—the early years math curriculum in the UK and children's numerical development. *International Journal of Early Childhood* 38(1):99-112.

Nachmias, M., M. Gunnar, S. Mangelsdorf, R. H. Parritz, and K. Buss. 1996. Behavioral inhibition and stress reactivity: The moderating role of attachment security. *Child Development* 67(2):508-522.

Nader-Grosbois, N., and N. Lefèvre. 2011. Self-regulation and performance in problem-solving using physical materials or computers in children with intellectual disability. *Research in Developmental Disabilities* 32:1492-1505.

Nagy, W., V. W. Berninger, and R. D. Abbott. 2006. Contributions of morphology beyond phonology to literacy outcomes of upper elementary and middle-school students. *Journal of Educational Psychology* 98(1):134-147.

Nation, K., and M. J. Snowling. 1999. Developmental differences in sensitivity to semantic relations among good and poor comprehenders: Evidence from semantic priming. *Cognition* 70(1):1.

National Early Literacy Panel. 2008. *Developing early literacy: A report of the National Early Literacy Panel.* http://purl.access.gpo.gov/GPO/LPS108121 (accessed December 15, 2014).

National Mathematics Advisory Panel. 2008. *Foundations for success: The final report of the National Mathematics Advisory Panel.* Washington, DC: U.S. Department of Education, Office of Planning, Evaluation and Policy Development.

Nayfeld, I., J. Fuccillo, and D. B. Greenfield. 2013. Executive functions in early learning: Extending the relationship between executive functions and school readiness to science. *Learning and Individual Differences* 26:81-88.

NCTSN (National Child Traumatic Stress Network). 2005. *Understanding child traumatic stress.* http://www.nctsnet.org/sites/default/files/assets/pdfs/understanding_child_traumatic_stress_brochure_9-29-05.pdf (accessed March 23, 2015).

NCTSN Core Curriculum on Childhood Trauma Task Force. 2012. *The 12 core concepts: Concepts for understanding traumatic stress responses in children and families. Core curriculum on childhood trauma.* Los Angeles, CA, and Durham, NC: UCLA-Duke University National Center for Child Traumatic Stress.

Neece, C. L., B. L. Baker, J. Blacher, and K. A. Crnic. 2011. Attention-deficit/hyperactivity disorder among children with and without intellectual disability: An examination across time. *Journal of Intellectual Disability Research* 55(7):623-635.

Nelson, J. R., G. J. Benner, K. Lane, and B. W. Smith. 2004. Academic achievement of K-12 students with emotional and behavioral disorders. *Exceptional Children* 71(1):59-73.

Nes, F. T. v. 2009. Young children's spatial structuring ability and emerging number sense. PhD diss., de Universtiteit Utrecht, Utrecht, The Netherlands.

Neuenschwander, R., M. Röthlisberger, P. Cimeli, and C. M. Roebers. 2012. How do different aspects of self-regulation predict successful adaptation to school? *Journal of Experimental Child Psychology* 113(3):353-371.

NICHD (Eunice Kennedy Shriver National Institute of Child Health and Human Development) Early Child Care Research Network. 2003. Social functioning in first grade: Associations with earlier home and child care predictors and with current classroom experiences. *Child Development* 74(6):1639-1662.

———. 2005. A day in third grade: A large-scale study of classroom quality and teacher and student behavior. *Elementary School Journal* 105(3):305-323.

NRC (National Research Council). 1998. *Preventing reading difficulties in young children.* Washington, DC: National Academy Press.

———. 2001. *Eager to learn: Educating our preschoolers,* edited by B. T. Bowman, M. S. Donovan, and M. S. Burns. Washington, DC: National Academy Press.

———. 2009. *Mathematics in early childhood: Learning paths toward excellence and equity,* edited by C. T. Cross, T. A. Woods, and H. Schweingruber. Washington, DC: The National Academies Press.

NRC and IOM. 2000. *From neurons to neighborhoods: The science of early childhood development,* edited by J. P. Shonkoff and D. A. Phillips. Washington, DC: National Academy Press.

———. 2009. *Depression in parents, parenting, and children: Opportunities to improve identification, treatment, and prevention.* Washington, DC: The National Academies Press.

Nunes, T., P. Bryant, and R. Barros. 2012. The development of word recognition and its significance for comprehension and fluency. *Journal of Educational Psychology* 104(4):959-973.

Nyaradi, A., J. Li, S. Hickling, J. Foster, and W. H. Oddy. 2013. The role of nutrition in children's neurocognitive development, from pregnancy through childhood. *Frontiers in Human Neuroscience* 7:97.

O'Connor, E., and K. McCartney. 2007. Examining teacher–child relationships and achievement as part of an ecological model of development. *American Educational Research Journal* 44(2):340-369.

O'Connor, R. E. 2014. *Teaching word recognition effective strategies for students with learning difficulties.* New York: Guilford Press.

O'Connor, R. E., and J. R. Jenkins. 1995. Improving the generalization of sound-symbol knowledge: Teaching spelling to kindergarten children with disabilities. *Journal of Special Education* 29(3):255-275.

O'Connor, R. E., J. R. Jenkins, and T. A. Slocum. 1995. Transfer among phonological tasks in kindergarten: Essential instructional content. *Journal of Educational Psychology* 2:202-217.

Olson, S. L., and B. Hoza. 1993. Preschool developmental antecedents of conduct problems in children beginning school. *Journal of Clinical Child Psychology* 22(1):60.

O'Neill, D. K., M. J. Pearce, and J. L. Pick. 2004. Preschool children's narratives and performance on the peabody individualized achievement test—revised: Evidence of a relation between early narrative and later mathematical ability. *First Language* 24(2):149-183.

Oreopoulos, P., M. Stabile, R. Walld, and L. L. Roos. 2008. Short-, medium-, and long-term consequences of poor infant health: An analysis using siblings and twins. *Journal of Human Resources* 43(1):88-138.

Ostad, S. A. 1998. Subtraction strategies in developmental perspective: A comparison of mathematically normal and mathematically disabled children. In *Proceedings of the 22nd Conference for the International Group for the Psychology of Mathematics Education.* Vol. 3, edited by A. Olivier and K. Newstead. Stellenbosch, South Africa: University of Stellenbosch. Pp. 311-318.

Pagani, L., and S. Messier. 2012. Links between motor skills and indicators of school readiness at kindergarten entry in urban disadvantaged children. *Journal of Educational and Developmental Psychology* 2(1):95.

Palmer, A., and A. J. Baroody. 2011. Blake's development of the number words "one," "two," and "three." *Cognition and Instruction* 29:265-296.

Parish-Morris, J., N. Mahajan, K. Hirsh-Pasek, R. M. Golinkoff, and M. F. Collins. 2013. Once upon a time: Parent–child dialogue and storybook reading in the electronic era. *Mind, Brain, and Education* 7(3):200-211.

Passolunghi, M. C., B. Vercelloni, and H. Schadee. 2007. The precursors of mathematics learning: Working memory, phonological ability and numerical competence. *Cognitive Development* 22(2):165-184.

Pearson, P. D., and E. H. Hiebert. 2010. National reports in literacy: Building a scientific base for policy and practice. *Educational Researcher* 39:286-294.

Perfetti, C. A. 1985. *Reading ability*. New York: Oxford University Press.

Perfetti, C. A., and L. Hart. 2002. The lexical quality hypothesis. In *Precursors of functional literacy*. Vol. 11, edited by L. T. Verhoeven, C. Elbro, and P. Reitsma. Amsterdam and Philadelphia, PA: John Benjamins Publishing Company. Pp. 67-86.

Piaget, J., and A. Szeminska. 1952. *The child's conception of number*. London: Routledge and Kegan Paul.

Pianta, R. C. 1999. *Enhancing relationships between children and teachers*. Washington, DC: American Psychological Association.

Pianta, R. C., and M. W. Stuhlman. 2004a. Conceptualizing risk in relational terms: Associations among the quality of child–adult relationships prior to school entry and children's developmental outcomes in first grade. *Educational and Child Psychology* 21(1):32-45.

———. 2004b. Teacher–child relationships and children's success in the first years of school. *School Psychology Review* 33(3):444-458.

Pianta, R. C., M. S. Steinberg, and K. B. Rollins. 1995. The first two years of school: Teacher–child relationships and deflections in children's classroom adjustment. *Development and Psychopathology* 7(02):295-312.

Piazza, M., V. Izard, P. Pinel, D. Le Bihan, and S. Dehaene. 2004. Tuning curves for approximate numerosity in the human intraparietal sulcus. *Neuron* 44:547-555.

Pinhas, M., S. E. Donohue, M. G. Woldorff, and E. M. Brannon. 2014. Electrophysiological evidence for the involvement of the approximate number system in preschoolers' processing of spoken number words. *Journal of Cognitive Neuroscience* 26(9):1891-1904.

Ponitz, C. C., M. M. McClelland, J. S. Matthews, and F. J. Morrison. 2009. A structured observation of behavioral self-regulation and its contribution to kindergarten outcomes. *Developmental Psychology* 45(3):605-619.

Praet, M., D. Titeca, A. Ceulemans, and A. Desoete. 2013. Language in the prediction of arithmetics in kindergarten and grade 1. *Learning and Individual Differences* 27:90-96.

Purpura, D. J., L. E. Hume, D. M. Sims, and C. J. Lonigan. 2011. Early literacy and early numeracy: The value of including early literacy skills in the prediction of numeracy development. *Journal of Experimental Child Psychology* 110:647-658.

Raches, D., and M. M. M. Mazzocco. 2012. Emergence and nature of mathematical difficulties in young children with Barth syndrome. *Journal of Developmental and Behavioral Pediatrics* 33(4):328-335.

Rachlin, H. 2000. *The science of self-control*. Cambridge, MA: Harvard University Press.

Raikes, H., B. A. Pan, G. Luze, C. S. Tamis-LeMonda, J. Brooks-Gunn, J. Constantine, L. B. Tarullo, H. A. Raikes, and E. T. Rodriguez. 2006. Mother-child bookreading in low-income families: Correlates and outcomes during the first three years of life. *Child Development* 77(4):924-953.

Ramirez, G., E. A. Gunderson, S. C. Levine, and S. L. Beilock. 2013. Math anxiety, working memory, and math achievement in early elementary school. *Journal of Cognition and Development* 14(2):187-202.

Rampersaud, G. C., M. A. Pereira, B. L. Girard, J. Adams, and J. D. Metzl. 2005. Breakfast habits, nutritional status, body weight, and academic performance in children and adolescents. *Journal of the American Dietetic Association* 105(5):743-760; quiz 761-742.

Raver, C. C. 2013. *Targeting self-regulation through intervention: Lessons from RCTS.* Paper presented at Society for Research on Educational Effectiveness (SREE), September 27, Washington, DC.

Raver, C. C., and J. Knitzer. 2002. *Ready to enter: What research tells policymakers about strategies to promote social and emotional school readiness among three- and four-year-old children.* New York: Columbia University, National Center for Children in Poverty, Mailman School of Public Health.

Raver, C. C., S. M. Jones, C. Li-Grining, F. Zhai, M. W. Metzger, and B. Solomon. 2009. Targeting children's behavior problems in preschool classrooms: A cluster-randomized controlled trial. *Journal of Consulting and Clinical Psychology* 77(2):302-316.

Raver, C. C., S. M. Jones, C. Li-Grining, F. Zhai, K. Bub, and E. Pressler. 2011. CSRP's impact on low-income preschoolers' preacademic skills: Self-regulation as a mediating mechanism. *Child Development* 82(1):362-378.

Reigosa-Crespo, V., E. González-Alemañy, T. León, R. Torres, R. Mosquera, and M. Valdés-Sosa. 2013. Numerical capacities as domain-specific predictors beyond early mathematics learning: A longitudinal study. *PLoS ONE* 8(11):e79711.

Rimm-Kaufman, S. E., R. C. Pianta, and M. J. Cox. 2000. Teachers' judgments of problems in the transition to kindergarten. *Early Childhood Research Quarterly* 15(2):147-166.

Roberts, T. A. 2008. Home storybook reading in primary or second language with preschool children: Evidence of equal effectiveness for second-language vocabulary acquisition. *Reading Research Quarterly* 43(2):103-130.

Roebers, C. M., P. Cimeli, M. Röthlisberger, and R. Neuenschwander. 2012. Executive functioning, metacognition, and self-perceived competence in elementary school children: An explorative study on their interrelations and their role for school achievement. *Metacognition Learning* 7(3):151-173.

Rogoff, B. 1991. *Apprenticeship in thinking: Cognitive development in social context.* New York: Oxford University Press.

Rogoff, B., and C. Angelillo. 2002. Investigating the coordinated functioning of multifaceted cultural practices in human development. *Human Development* 45(4):211-225.

Romine, C. B., and C. R. Reynolds. 2005. A model of the development of frontal lobe functioning: Findings from a meta-analysis. *Applied Neuropsychology* 12(4):190-201.

Romine, C. B., D. Lee, M. E. Wolfe, S. Homack, C. George, and C. A. Riccio. 2004. Wisconsin card sorting test with children: A meta-analytic study of sensitivity and specificity. *Archives of Clinical Neuropsychology* 19(8):1027-1041.

Rones, M., and K. Hoagwood. 2000. School-based mental health services: A research review. *Clinical Child and Family Psychology Review* 3(4):223-241.

Roseberry, S., K. Hirsh-Pasek, and R. M. Golinkoff. 2014. Skype me! Socially contingent interactions help toddlers learn language. *Child Development* 85(3):956-970.

Rossin-Slater, M. 2013. WIC in your neighborhood: New evidence on the impacts of geographic access to clinics. *Journal of Public Economics* 102:51-69.

Rothbart, M. K., and M. R. Rueda. 2005. The development of effortful control. In *Developing individuality in the human brain: A tribute to Michael I. Posner,* edited by U. Mayr, E. Awh, and S. Keele. Washington, DC: American Psychological Association. Pp. 167-188.

Rouse, C., J. Brooks-Gunn, and S. McLanahan. 2005. Introducing the issue. *The Future of Children* 15:5-14.

Rowe, M. L. 2012. A longitudinal investigation of the role of quantity and quality of child-directed speech in vocabulary development. *Child Development* 83(5):1762-1774.

Royer, H. 2009. Separated at girth: US twin estimates of the effects of birth weight. *American Economic Journal: Applied Economics* 1(1):49-85.

Rutter, M. 2012. Achievements and challenges in the biology of environmental effects. *Proceedings of the National Academy of Sciences of the United States of America* 109(Suppl. 2):17149-17153.

Saarni, C. D., D. Mumme, and J. J. Campos. 1998. Emotional development: Action, communication, and understanding. In *Handbook of child psychology*, 5th ed., edited by W. Damon. New York: Wiley. Pp. 237-309.

Sadler, P. M., and R. H. Tai. 2007. The two high-school pillars supporting college science. *Science* 317:457-458.

Saffran, J. R. 2003. Statistical language learning: Mechanisms and constraints. *Current Directions in Psychological Science* 12(4):110-114.

Saffran, J. R., R. N. Aslin, and E. L. Newport. 1996. Statistical learning by 8-month-old infants. *Science* 274(5294):1926-1928.

Saffran, J. R., E. K. Johnson, R. N. Aslin, and E. L. Newport. 1999. Statistical learning of tone sequences by human infants and adults. *Cognition* 70(1):27-52.

Samarapungavan, A., H. Patrick, and P. Mantzicopoulos. 2011. What kindergarten students learn in inquiry-based science classrooms. *Cognition and Instruction* 29(4):416-470.

Sanders, N. J. 2012. What doesn't kill you makes you weaker: Prenatal pollution exposure and educational outcomes. *Journal of Human Resources* 47(3):826-850.

Sandhofer, C. M., and L. B. Smith. 1999. Learning color words involves learning a system of mappings. *Developmental Psychology* 35:668-679.

Sandler, A. D., T. E. Watson, M. Footo, M. D. Levine, W. L. Coleman, and S. R. Hooper. 1992. Neurodevelopmental study of writing disorders in middle childhood. *Journal of Developmental and Behavioral Pediatrics* 13(1):17-23.

Sandman, C. A., E. P. Davis, C. Buss, and L. M. Glynn. 2012. Exposure to prenatal psychobiological stress exerts programming influences on the mother and her fetus. *Neuroendocrinology* 95(1):8-21.

Sarama, J., and D. H. Clements. 2009. *Early childhood mathematics education research: Learning trajectories for young children*. New York: Routledge.

Sarama, J., A. Lange, D. H. Clements, and C. B. Wolfe. 2012. The impacts of an early mathematics curriculum on emerging literacy and language. *Early Childhood Research Quarterly* 27:489-502.

Saxe, G. B., S. R. Guberman, and M. Gearhart. 1987. Social processes in early number development. *Monographs of the Society for Research in Child Development* 52(2, Serial #216).

Saxe, R. 2013. The new puzzle of theory of mind development. In *Navigating the social world: What infants, children, and other species can teach us*, edited by M. R. Banaji and S. A. Gelman. New York: Oxford University Press.

Scarborough, H. S. 2001. Connecting early language and literacy to later reading (dis)abilities: Evidence, theory, and practice. In *Handbook of early literacy research*, edited by S. B. Neuman and D. K. Dickinson. New York: Guilford Press. Pp. 97-110.

Schleppegrell, M. J. 2003. *Grammar for writing: Academic language and the ELD Standards*. Santa Barbara, CA: University of California Linguistic Minority Research Institute.

Schneidman, L. A., M. E. Arroyo, S. C. Levine, and S. Goldin-Meadow. 2013. What counts as effective input for word learning? *Journal of Child Language* 40(3):672-686.

Schoemaker, K., T. Bunte, K. A. Espy, M. Dekovic, and W. Matthys. 2014. Executive functions in preschool children with ADHD and DBD: An 18-month longitudinal study. *Developmental Neuropsychology* 39(4):302-315.

Schore, J., and A. Schore. 2008. Modern attachment theory: The central role of affect regulation in development and treatment. *Clinical Social Work Journal* 36(1):9-20.

Schulz, L. E., and E. B. Bonawitz. 2007. Serious fun: Preschoolers engage in more exploratory play when evidence is confounded. *Developmental Psychology* 43(4):1045-1050.

Secada, W. G. 1992. Race, ethnicity, social class, language, and achievement in mathematics. In *Handbook of research on mathematics teaching and learning*, edited by D. A. Grouws. Toronto and New York: Macmillan, Maxwell Macmillan Canada, Maxwell Macmillan International. Pp. 623-660.

Semrud-Clikeman, M. 2012. The role of inattention on academics, fluid reasoning, and visual-spatial functioning in two subtypes of ADHD. *Applied Neuropsychology. Child* 1(1):18-29.

Sénéchal, M., G. Ouellette, and D. Rodney. 2006. The misunderstood giant: On the predictive role of early vocabulary in future reading. In *Handbook of early literacy research*. Vol. 2, edited by D. K. Dickinson and S. B. Neuman. New York: Guilford Press. Pp. 173-184.

Seo, K.-H., and H. P. Ginsburg. 2004. What is developmentally appropriate in early childhood mathematics education? In *Engaging young children in mathematics: Standards for early childhood mathematics education*, edited by D. H. Clements, J. Sarama, and A.-M. DiBiase. Mahwah, NJ: Lawrence Erlbaum Associates. Pp. 91-104.

Shayer, M., and M. Adhami. 2010. Realizing the cognitive potential of children 5-7 with a mathematics focus: Post-test and long-term effects of a 2-year intervention. *British Journal of Educational Psychology* 80(3):363-379.

Shonkoff, J. P., W. T. Boyce, and B. S. McEwen. 2009. Neuroscience, molecular biology, and the childhood roots of health disparities: Building a new framework for health promotion and disease prevention. *Journal of the American Medical Association* 301(21):2252-2259.

Shuai, L., R. C. Chan, and Y. Wang. 2011. Executive function profile of Chinese boys with attention-deficit hyperactivity disorder: Different subtypes and comorbidity. *Archives of Clinical Neuropsychology* 26(2):120-132.

Siegel, I. S., and S. Mazabel. 2013. Basic cognitive processes and reading disabilities. In *Handbook of learning disabilities*, edited by H. L. Swanson, K. R. Harris, and S. Graham. New York: Guilford Press. Pp. 186-213.

Silver, R. B., J. R. Measelle, J. M. Armstrong, and M. J. Essex. 2005. Trajectories of classroom externalizing behavior: Contributions of child characteristics, family characteristics, and the teacher–child relationship during the school transition. *Journal of School Psychology* 43(1):39-60.

Simmons, F. R., C. Willis, and A.-M. Adams. 2012. Different components of working memory have different relationships with different mathematical skills. *Journal of Experimental Child Psychology* 111(2):139-155.

Skinner, E. A., and M. J. Belmont. 1993. Motivation in the classroom: Reciprocal effects of teacher behavior and student engagement across the school year. *Journal of Educational Psychology* 85(4):571-581.

Slaughter, V., S. Itakura, A. Kutsuki, and M. Siegal. 2011. Learning to count begins in infancy: Evidence from 18 month olds' visual preferences. *Proceedings: Biological Sciences* 278(1720):2979-2984.

Smiley, P. A., and C. S. Dweck. 1994. Individual differences in achievement goals among young children. *Child Development* 65(6):1723-1743.

Smith, M. W., and D. K. Dickinson. 1994. Describing oral language opportunities and environments in Head Start and other preschool classrooms. *Early Childhood Research Quarterly* 9(3-4):345-366.

Snow, C. E., and P. Uccelli. 2009. The challenge of academic language. *In Cambridge handbook of literacy*, edited by D. R. Olson and N. Torrance. Cambridge, MA: Cambridge University Press. Pp. 112-133.

Snow, C. E., P. O. Tabors, and D. K. Dickinson. 2001. Language development in the preschool years. In *Beginning literacy with language: Young children learning at home and school*, edited by D. K. Dickinson and P. O. Tabors. Baltimore, MD: Paul H. Brookes Publishing Co. Pp. 1-25.

Spelke, E. S., and K. D. Kinzler. 2007. Core knowledge. *Developmental Science* 10(1):89-96.

Stanovich, K. E., and L. S. Siegel. 1994. Phenotypic performance profile of children with reading disabilities. *Journal of Educational Psychology* 86:24-53.

Starr, A., M. E. Libertus, and E. M. Brannon. 2013. Infants show ratio-dependent number discrimination regardless of set size. *Infancy* 1-15.

Steacy, L. M., J. R. Kirby, R. Parrila, and D. L. Compton. 2014. Classification of double deficit groups across time: An analysis of group stability from kindergarten to second grade. *Scientific Studies of Reading* 18(4):255-273.

Steffe, L. P., and R. Tzur. 1994. Interaction and children's mathematics. *Journal of Research in Childhood Education* 8(2):99-116.

Sternberg, R. 1985. *Beyond IQ*. Cambridge, MA: Cambridge University Press.

Stevenson, H. W., and R. S. Newman. 1986. Long-term prediction of achievement and attitudes in mathematics and reading. *Child Development* 57:646-659.

Stipek, D., S. Recchia, and S. McClintic. 1992. Self-evaluation in young children. *Monographs of the Society for Research in Child Development* 57(1):1-98.

Strouse, G. A., K. O'Doherty, and G. L. Troseth. 2013. Effective coviewing: Preschoolers' learning from video after a dialogic questioning intervention. *Developmental Psychology* 49(12):2368-2382.

Szűcs, D., A. Devine, F. Soltesz, A. Nobes, and F. Gabriel. 2014. Cognitive components of a mathematical processing network in 9-year-old children. *Developmental Science* 17(4):506-524.

Taras, H. 2005. Nutrition and student performance at school. *Journal of School Health* 75(6):199-213.

Thayer, Z. M., and C. W. Kuzawa. 2014. Early origins of health disparities: Material deprivation predicts maternal evening cortisol in pregnancy and offspring cortisol reactivity in the first few weeks of life. *American Journal of Human Biology* 26(6):723-730.

Thompson, R. A. 2006. The development of the person: Social understanding, relationships, self, conscience. In *Handbook of child psychology*, 6th ed., Vol. 3, edited by W. Damon and R. M. Lerner. Hoboken, NJ: John Wiley & Sons. Pp. 24-98.

———. 2008. Early attachment and later development: Familiar questions, new answers. In *Handbook of attachment: Theory, research, and clinical applications*, 2nd ed., edited by J. Cassidy and P. R. Shaver. New York: Guilford Press. Pp. 348-365.

———. 2012. Whither the preconventional child? Toward a life-span moral development theory. *Child Development Perspectives* 6(4):423-429.

———. 2013. Attachment theory and research: Precis and prospect. In *Oxford handbook of developmental psychology*. Vol. 2, edited by P. Zelazo. New York: Oxford University Press. Pp. 191-216.

———. 2014. Stress and child development. *The Future of Children* 24(1):41-59.

———. 2015. The development of virtue: A perspective from developmental psychology. In *Cultivating virtue: Perspectives from philosophy, theology, and psychology*, edited by N. E. Snow. New York: Oxford University Press.

———. in press. Early attachment and later development: Reframing the questions. In *Handbook of attachment*, 3rd ed., edited by J. Cassidy and P. R. Shaver. New York: Guilford Press.

Thompson, R. A., and R. Goodvin. in press. Social support and developmental psychopathology. In *Developmental psychopathology*, 3rd ed., edited by D. Cicchetti. New York: John Wiley & Sons.

Thompson, R. A., D. J. Laible, and L. L. Ontai. 2003. Early understandings of emotion, morality, and self: Developing a working model. *Advances in Child Development and Behavior* 31:137-171.

Thomson, S., K. Rowe, C. Underwood, and R. Peck. 2005. *Numeracy in the early years: Project good start*. Camberwell, Victoria, Australia: Australian Council for Educational Research.

Toll, S. W. M., S. Van der Ven, E. Kroesbergen, and J. E. H. Van Luit. 2010. Executive functions as predictors of math learning disabilities. *Journal of Learning Disabilities* 20(10):1-12.

Tomasello, M., M. Carpenter, J. Call, T. Behne, and H. Moll. 2005. Understanding and sharing intentions: The origins of cultural cognition. *Behavioral and Brain Sciences* 28(5):675-691; discussion 691-735.

Tomlinson, H. B. 2014. An overview of development in the primary grades. In *Developmentally appropriate practice*, edited by C. Copple, S. Bredekamp, D. G. Koralek, and K. Charner. Washington, DC: National Association for the Education of Young Children. Pp. 9-38.

Trentacosta, C. J., and C. E. Izard. 2007. Kindergarten children's emotion competence as a predictor of their academic competence in first grade. *Emotion* 7(1):77-88.

Trick, L. M., and Z. W. Pylyshyn. 1994. Why are small and large numbers enumerated differently?: A limited-capacity preattentive stage in vision. *Psychological Review* 101:80-102.

Troseth, G. L., M. M. Saylor, and A. H. Archer. 2006. Young children's use of video as a source of socially relevant information. *Child Development* 77(3):786-799.

Tseng, V., and E. Seidman. 2007. A systems framework for understanding social settings. *American Journal of Community Psychology* 39(3-4):217-228.

Tunmer, W., and W. Hoover. 1993. Components of variance models of language-related factors in reading disability: A conceptual overview. In *Reading disabilities: Diagnosis and component processes*, edited by R. J. Joshi and C. K. Leong. Dordrecht, The Netherlands: Kluwer. Pp. 135-173.

Tymms, P., and C. Merrell. 2011. ADHD and academic attainment: Is there an advantage in impulsivity? *Learning and Individual Differences* 21(6):753-758.

Uccelli, P., L. Hemphill, B. A. Pan, and C. Snow. 2006. Conversing with toddlers about the nonpresent: Precursors to narrative development in two genres. In *Child psychology: A handbook of contemporary issues*, 2nd ed., edited by L. Balter and C. S. Tamis-LeMonda. New York: Taylor & Francis. Pp. 215-237.

Ulrich-Lai, Y. M., and J. P. Herman. 2009. Neural regulation of endocrine and autonomic stress responses. *Nature Reviews: Neuroscience* 10(6):397-409.

U.S. Department of Education Office for Civil Rights. 2014. *Civil rights data collection: Data snapshot (school discipline)* (Issue brief no. 1). http://www2.ed.gov/about/offices/list/ocr/docs/crdc-discipline-snapshot.pdf (accessed February 9, 2015).

Valiente, C., N. Eisenberg, R. Haugen, T. L. Spinrad, C. Hofer, J. Liew, and A. S. Kupfer. 2011. Children's effortful control and academic achievement: Mediation through social functioning. *Early Education & Development* 22(3):411-433.

Van den Heuvel-Panhuizen, M. 1996. *Assessment and realistic mathematics education*. Utrecht, The Netherlands: Utrecht University, Freudenthal Institute.

Van der Ven, S. H. G., E. H. Kroesbergen, J. Boom, and P. P. M. Leseman. 2012. The development of executive functions and early mathematics: A dynamic relationship. *British Journal of Educational Psychology* 82(1):100-119.

van Ijzendoorn, M. H., J. Dijkstra, and A. G. Bus. 1995. Attachment, intelligence, and language: A meta-analysis. *Social Development* 4(2):115-128.

van Kleek, A. 2004. Fostering preliteracy development via storybook-sharing interactions: The cultural context of mainstream family practices. In *Handbook of language and literacy: Development and disorders*, edited by C. A. Stone, E. R. Silliman, B. Ehren, and K. Apel. New York: Guilford Press. Pp. 175-208.

Van Luit, J. E. H., and B. A. M. Van de Rijt. 1998. Effectiveness of the additional early mathematics program for teaching children early mathematics. *Instructional Science* 26:337-358.

Vasilyeva, M., and H. Waterfall. 2011. Variability in language development: Relation to socio-economic status and environmental input. In *Handbook of early literacy research*, Vol. 3, edited by S. B. Neuman and D. K. Dickinson. New York: Guilford Press. Pp. 36-48.

Vasilyeva, M., J. Huttenlocher, and H. Waterfall. 2006. Effects of language intervention on syntactic skill levels in preschoolers. *Developmental Psychology* 42(1):164-174.

Vellutino, F. R., W. E. Tunmer, J. J. Jaccard, and R. Chen. 2007. Components of reading ability: Multivariate evidence for a convergent skills model of reading development. *Scientific Studies of Reading* 11(1):3-32.

Vest, J. R., T. K. Catlin, J. J. Chen, and R. C. Brownson. 2002. Multistate analysis of factors associated with intimate partner violence. *American Journal of Preventive Medicine* 22(3):156-164.

Vieillevoye, S., and N. Nader-Grosbois. 2008. Self-regulation during pretend play in children with intellectual disability and in normally developing children. *Research in Developmental Disabilities* 29(3):256-272.

Vitiello, V. E., D. B. Greenfield, P. Munis, and J. L. George. 2011. Cognitive flexibility, approaches to learning, and academic school readiness in head start preschool children. *Early Education & Development* 22(3):388-410.

von Suchodoletz, A., and C. Gunzenhauser. 2013. Behavior regulation and early math and vocabulary knowledge in German preschool children. *Early Education & Development* 24(3):310-331.

Vukovic, R. K. 2012. Mathematics difficulty with and without reading difficulty: Findings and implications from a four-year longitudinal study. *Exceptional Children* 78:280-300.

Vukovic, R. K., and N. K. Lesaux. 2013. The language of mathematics: Investigating the ways language counts for children's mathematical development. *Journal of Experimental Child Psychology* 115(2):227-244.

Vygotsky, L. S. 1978. *Mind in society: The development of higher psychological processes*, edited by M. Cole, V. John-Steiner, S. Scribner, and E. Souberman. Cambridge, MA: Harvard University Press.

———. 1986. *Thought and language*. Cambridge, MA: MIT Press.

Wagner, R. K., J. K. Torgesen, P. Laughon, K. Simmons, and C. A. Rashotte. 1993. Development of young readers' phonological processing abilities. *Journal of Educational Psychology* 85:83-103.

Wagner, S. W., and J. Walters. 1982. A longitudinal analysis of early number concepts: From numbers to number. In *Action and thought*, edited by G. E. Forman. New York: Academic Press. Pp. 137-161.

Wang, J., and K. C. Barrett. 2013. Mastery motivation and self-regulation during early childhood. In *Handbook of self-regulatory processes in development new directions and international perspectives*, edited by K. C. Barrett, N. A. Fox, G. A. Morgan, D. J. Fidler, and L. A. Daunhauer. Boca Raton, FL: Taylor & Francis Press. Pp. 337-380.

Wanless, S. B., M. M. McClelland, S. L. Tominey, and A. C. Acock. 2011. The influence of demographic risk factors on children's behavioral regulation in prekindergarten and kindergarten. *Early Education & Development* 22(3):461-488.

Warneken, F., and M. Tomasello. 2006. Altruistic helping in human infants and young chimpanzees. *Science* 311(5765):1301-1303.

———. 2007. Helping and cooperation at 14 months of age. *Infancy* 11(3):271-294.

Weiner, B. 1986. *An attributional theory of motivation and emotion.* New York: Springer-Verlag.

Weisleder, A., and A. Fernald. 2013. Talking to children matters: Early language experience strengthens processing and builds vocabulary. *Psychological Science* 24(11):2143-2152.

Weizman, Z. O., and C. E. Snow. 2001. Lexical input as related to children's vocabulary acquisition: Effects of sophisticated exposure and support for meaning. *Developmental Psychology* 37(2):265-279.

Wellman, H. M. 2011. Developing a theory of mind. In *The handbook of childhood cognitive development*, 2nd ed., edited by U. C. Goswami. Malden, MA: Wiley-Blackwell. Pp. 258-284.

Wellman, H. M., and J. D. Woolley. 1990. From simple desires to ordinary beliefs: The early development of everyday psychology. *Cognition* 35(3):245-275.

Welsh, J. A., R. L. Nix, C. Blair, K. L. Bierman, and K. E. Nelson. 2010. The development of cognitive skills and gains in academic school readiness for children from low-income families. *Journal of Educational Psychology* 102(1):43-53.

West, K. K., M. B. L., and K. K. A. 2013. Mother–child attachment and cognitive performance in middle childhood: An examination of mediating mechanisms. *Early Childhood Research Quarterly* 28(2):259-270.

Whitehurst, G. J., F. L. Falco, C. J. Lonigan, F. J. E., B. D. DeBarshe, M. C. Valdez-Menchaca, and M. Caulfield. 1988. Accelerating language development through picture book reading. *Developmental Psychology* 24(4):552-559.

Wigfield, A., J. S. Eccles, U. Schiefele, R. W. Roeser, and P. Davis-Kean. 2006. Development of achievement motivation. In *Handbook of child psychology*, 6th ed., Vol. 3, edited by W. Damon and R. M. Lerner. New York: Wiley. Pp. 933-1002.

Willoughby, M. T., J. Kupersmidt, M. Voegler-Lee, and D. Bryant. 2011. Contributions of hot and cool self-regulation to preschool disruptive behavior and academic achievement. *Developmental Neuropsychology* 36(2):161-180.

Wright, R. J. 1994. A study of the numerical development of 5-year-olds and 6-year-olds. *Educational Studies in Mathematics* 26:25-44.

Wulfert, E., J. A. Block, E. Santa Ana, M. L. Rodriguez, and M. Colsman. 2002. Delay of gratification: Impulsive choices and problem behaviors in early and late adolescence. *Journal of Personality* 70(4):533-552.

Wynn, K. 1992a. Addition and subtraction by human infants. *Nature* 358(6389):749-750.

———. 1992b. Children's acquisition of the number words and the counting system. *Cognitive Psychology* 24:220-251.

Wynn, K., P. Bloom, and W.-C. Chiang. 2002. Enumeration of collective entities by 5-month-old infants. *Cognition* 83:B55-B62.

Xu, F., and S. Denison. 2009. Statistical inference and sensitivity to sampling in 11-month-old infants. *Cognition* 112(1):97-104.

Yoon, J. M., M. H. Johnson, and G. Csibra. 2008. Communication-induced memory biases in preverbal infants. *Proceedings of the National Academy of Sciences of the United States of America* 105(36):13690-13695.

Young, C. B., S. S. Wu, and V. Menon. 2012. The neuro-developmental basis of math anxiety. *Psychological Science Online First* 23(5):10.1177/0956797611429134.

Yow, W. Q., and E. M. Markman. 2011a. Bilingual children's use of paralinguistic cues to determine emotion in speech. *Bilingualism: Language and Cognition* 14(4):562-569.

———. 2011b. Young bilingual children's heightened sensitivity to referential cues. *Journal of Cognition and Development* 12(1):12-31.

Yuill, N. 1996. A funny thing happened on the way to the classroom: Jokes, riddles, and meta-linguistic awareness in understanding and improving poor comprehension in children. In *Reading comprehension difficulties: Processes and intervention*, edited by C. Cornoldi and J. Oakhill. Mahwah, NJ: Lawrence Erlbaum Associates. Pp. 193-220.

Zeanah, C. H. 2009. *Handbook of infant mental health*. New York and London: Guilford Press.

Zelazo, P. D., and S. M. Carlson. 2012. Hot and cool executive function in childhood and adolescence: Development and plasticity. *Child Development Perspectives* 6(4):354-360.

Zelazo, P. D., and K. E. Lyons. 2012. The potential benefits of mindfulness training in early childhood: A developmental social cognitive neuroscience perspective. *Child Development Perspectives* 6(2):154-160.

Zelazo, P. D., S. Jacques, J. A. Burack, and D. Frye. 2002. The relation between theory of mind and rule use: Evidence from persons with autism-spectrum disorders. *Infant and Child Development* 11:171-195.

Zelazo, P. D., U. Müller, D. Frye, S. Marcovitch, G. Argitis, J. Boseovski, J. K. Chiang, D. Hongwanishkul, B. V. Schuster, A. Sutherland, and S. M. Carlson. 2003. The development of executive function in early childhood. *Monographs of the Society for Research in Child Development* 68(3), Serial No. 274.

Zentall, S. R., and B. J. Morris. 2010. "Good job, you're so smart": The effects of inconsistency of praise type on young children's motivation. *Journal of Experimental Child Psychology* 107(2):155-163.

Zero to Three. 2005. *Diagnostic classification of mental health and developmental disorders of infancy and early childhood*. Washington, DC: Zero to Three Press.

Ziegler, J. C., and U. Goswami. 2005. Reading acquisition, developmental dyslexia, and skilled reading across languages: A psycholinguistic grain size theory. *Psychonomic Bulletin* 131:3-29.

Zimmerman, B. J. 2002. Achieving academic excellence: A self-regulatory perspective. In *The pursuit of excellence through education*, edited by M. Ferrar. Mahwah, NJ: Lawrence Erlbaum Associates. Pp. 85-110.

Zimmerman, E., and S. H. Woolf. 2014. *Understanding the relationship between education and health*. Discussion paper. http://www.iom.edu/understandingtherelationship (accessed March 23, 2015).

Zins, J. E., M. R. Bloodworth, R. P. Weissberg, and H. J. Walberg. 2007. The scientific base linking social and emotional learning to school success. *Journal of Educational and Psychological Consultation* 17(2-3):191-210.

Zipke, M., L. C. Ehri, and H. S. Cairns. 2009. Using semantic ambiguity instruction to improve third graders' metalinguistic awareness and reading comprehension: An experimental study. *Reading Research Quarterly* 44(3):300-321.

Zucker, T. A., S. Q. Cabell, L. M. Justice, J. M. Pentimonti, and J. N. Kaderavek. 2013. The role of frequent, interactive prekindergarten shared reading in the longitudinal development of language and literacy skills. *Developmental Psychology* 49(8):1425-1439.

Part II Summation

From the time they are born, children are not just "ready to learn" but already actively learning. Their minds are active and inquisitive, and early thinking is insightful and complex. From the beginning, children's learning is constituted by interactions among and growth in several key domains: cognitive development, including cognitive skills and the acquisition of specific content knowledge and skills; general learning competencies; socioemotional development; and health and physical well-being. Success in learning across all of these domains relates to and is supported by the security of consistent, stable, nurturing, and protective interactions with adults that enable children to engage fully in learning opportunities. Support for interactions among these domains of learning through high-quality, positive learning environments and sustained positive relationships with adults is foundational for the healthy development of young children.

The capacity for learning is grounded in the development of the brain and brain circuitry. The brain architecture that underlies this capacity is developed not from a static "blueprint," but through continuous, dynamic, adaptive interaction between biology and environment that begins at conception and continues throughout life. This interaction accounts for how early experiences (including both stressors and supports) affect gene expression and how the brain develops, and it also accounts for how the effects of environmental factors on a child's development may vary depending on underlying individual genetic characteristics. The adaptations that occur as a result of the interaction between "nature" and "nurture" mean that early experiences and early learning environments critically shape all domains of human development.

205

Many of the foundations of sophisticated forms of learning, including those important to academic success, are established in the earliest years of life. Development and early learning can be supported continuously as a child ages, and early knowledge and skills inform and influence future learning. Growth is fostered by active engagement with new experiences supported through responsive, secure, and sustained relationships with adults who provide developmentally appropriate stimulation of new learning. Part of developmentally appropriate support for learning is expecting some individual variation in the trajectories of children's progress and development across the various domains of learning. For this reason, it is important for adults to be able to support development and learning in ways that recognize and are responsive to individual progress, not just a child's age. In many cases, differences in children's trajectories reflect one or more of the many underlying factors in a child's environment or learning experiences that can—positively or negatively—affect development. Thus when a child is, for example, not as far along as might be expected, this does not reflect an innate, unchangeable reason to lower expectations for progress in the child's development and learning, and recognizing individual differences calls for responding actively, not passively waiting until a child "catches up."

Intervention in early childhood from birth through age 8 offers opportunities to have a positive effect on children and to build a foundation for later success through policies, services, interventions, and high-quality learning experiences designed to promote and sustain healthy growth, development, and learning; to prevent and mitigate harm; and to remediate lags in early achievement. The effectiveness of such intervention relies in large part on the quality practices of adults who have professional responsibilities for young children. A concerted effort focused on these adults represents one of the most important opportunities available for improving the quality of the care and education received by young children, and ultimately improving their outcomes.

Thus, the science of child development and early learning presented in this part of the report is important not just for what it tells us about children, but also for its implications for the professionals who contribute to the development and early learning of children during this period. In this way, the science discussed here provides the foundation for the rest of this report. Its implications apply to the knowledge and competencies that these professionals need, the infrastructure and systems in which they work, their systems for professional learning, and other supports that contribute to improving the quality of professional practice and developing an excellent, robust, and stable workforce across the many professional roles that relate to children from birth through age 8.

Part III
Implications of the Science for
Early Care and Education

This part of the report examines the implications of the science of child development and early learning for the care and education of children from birth through age 8. The discussion is divided into three chapters.

Chapter 5 draws on the science of child development and early learning reported in Part II, as well as the realities of the landscape described in Chapter 2, to establish the critical need for continuity in care and education across the birth through age 8 continuum. It examines both vertical continuity over time as children move from one care and education setting to another, and horizontal continuity across the services and agencies that affect these young children at any given point in time. In addition, the chapter outlines the elements of professional practice, policies, and systems that need to be aligned to support that continuity: professional learning and workforce development; early learning standards; instructional strategies; learning environments; child assessments; accountability systems and data-driven improvement; family engagement; pathways for vertical continuity for children; and coordination and communication across professional roles, settings, and policies.

Chapter 6 then explores in greater depth the educational practices that, when applied with consistency and high quality over time for children as they age, can continuously support the development and early learning of children from birth through age 8. It examines cross-cutting principles for instructional practices and curricula, and their application to specific subject areas. This chapter also considers several other important topics related to educational practices, such as child assessment, working with special populations, engaging with families, and using technology effectively.

Finally, Chapter 7 considers the shared knowledge and competencies needed to provide consistent, high-quality care and education for children from birth through age 8, based on the science of child development and early learning, the knowledge base about educational practices, and the landscape of care and education and related sectors. In keeping with the scope of this report, the primary focus in Chapter 7 is on those professionals with direct, daily or near-daily responsibilities for the care and education of these young children in childcare settings and in preschools and elementary schools, as well as those in leadership roles in those settings. The chapter also discusses competencies that are important for different professional roles to work in synergy, both across settings within the care and education sector and between the care and education sector and other closely related sectors, especially health and social services.

5

The Importance of Continuity for Children Birth Through Age 8

This chapter considers the implications of the science described in Part II for why it is important to create greater continuity in the systems in which the professionals who are the focus of this report work, in turn creating greater continuity in positive, high-quality experiences and environments for young children over time. The concept of "continuity" has two facets when it comes to children from birth through age 8. First, it denotes the consistency of children's experience across diverse care and education settings as they grow up. Viewed in this way, the vertical continuity of high-quality learning experiences for children over time includes the alignment of learning expectations; curricula; and other instructional strategies, assessments, and learning environments to ensure that they are coherent with each other and grounded in the science of child development and of best practices in instruction and other professional responsibilities. With this continuity, early achievements prepare for and are built upon by later ones. Second, continuity refers to the coordination of services and agencies affecting children at any given point in time. This horizontal continuity includes policies and systems for consultations, referrals, and follow-up. It encompasses the need for communication and collaboration among care providers; early educators; health care providers; community support agencies; and, when the need arises, social services and mental health professionals. It also extends to communication and collaboration with families concerning the needs of the child and the services that are provided so that there is alignment in understanding the child's needs, and the practices of professionals and families are complementary. Shared knowledge among these service sectors and between providers and families enables coordination.

Why is continuity of high-quality experiences so important to supporting children's development? As noted throughout Part II, children's growth across all domains is rapid and cumulative. Development and early learning provide a foundation on which later learning is constructed. Continuity is necessary to ensure that children's experiences in care and education settings contribute consistently to these developmental achievements and that early problems are quickly identified and addressed. When vertical continuity over time results in consistent high-quality learning experiences, it helps ensure that early learning achievements prepare children for later achievements such that children's early competencies build on each other over time instead of stagnating or slipping backward. For example, gains made as an infant and toddler need to be built upon in preschool programs, and additional gains made in preschool need to be built upon and extended when children progress to kindergarten and early elementary classrooms.

This vertical continuity requires communication, planning, and coordination among care and education practitioners across the diverse settings that influence children from birth through age 8, including home visitation, early care and education, preschool programs, and elementary schools. When successful, this continuity means that practitioners working with children of any age are aware of the learning experiences that have preceded and those that will follow. This continuity also requires special attention, including communication with families, to young children's transitions between programs, when changing personnel, expectations, and settings can be disruptive.

Horizontal continuity at each developmental stage helps ensure that the diverse programs and agencies affecting children provide coordinated services. This continuity requires coordination and communication among practitioners in different fields and systems. The need for this can arise among diverse types of practitioners and programs within the care and education sector, for example, if a toddler is enrolled in an early education center and also is receiving early intervention services at home. Young children often are enrolled in multiple programs, which need to be aligned in their expectations of high quality for children's experiences, their learning environments, and the practitioners who work with them. The need for horizontal continuity also arises between care and education and other sectors, most often health care, mental health, and social services. The purpose is not only to coordinate services for individual children and their families, but also to create shared understanding of the interconnected quality of developmental processes that each practitioner may see only in part. One result of such continuity is greater opportunities for successful and effective consultation and referrals across professional sectors.

As discussed in Chapter 2, however, the landscape of systems and settings for young children and their families—from both a horizontal and vertical perspective—is complex, and unfortunately it typically is uncoordinated and segmented and too often fails to deliver consistent high-quality experiences for children.

CREATING A CARE AND EDUCATION CONTINUUM

The ultimate goal of a stronger, more seamless care and education continuum is to initiate and sustain a strong foundation for future success by providing effective learning opportunities across the infant-toddler years, preschool ages, and early grades in all settings, including the home, family childcare homes, childcare centers, preschools, and elementary schools. Bringing multiple systems together to make the high quality of early learning opportunities and supports more coherent and consistent as children grow requires coordination and alignment across the many interconnected components of the care and education of children from birth through age 8 described in Chapter 2: public school and other elementary education systems; center-based or school-based programs and services for children younger than kindergarten age; other non-center-based settings for care and education, such as family childcare providers; and consultative or supportive services for young children administered by different agencies and occurring in various settings, such as home visiting and early intervention services.

Creating a stronger continuum and bridging the gaps among different systems and settings entails significant conceptual and logistical challenges for the stakeholders involved: care and education practitioners; leaders, administrators, and supervisors; those who provide professional learning for the care and education workforce; policy makers; health, mental health, and social services providers; and parents and other adults who spend time with children. These different settings and the different professionals who work within them are characterized by differences in terminology, expectations, approaches to teaching and learning, and relationships with families and the community. This fragmentation is due in part to the disparate histories of these professional roles and in part to differences in accountability policies, funding streams, governance, and system priorities and pressures.

The extent to which individual care and education professionals in these settings can foster greater consistency and continuity for children and families throughout the birth through age 8 continuum depends partly on their knowledge and competencies and how they put these into practice in the settings where they work. However, it also depends largely on whether policies and systems at the local, state, and national levels encourage, require, facilitate, or impede continuity and alignment. Several recent analyses have identified ways of overcoming the conceptual and logistical challenges to greater alignment (see, for example, Annie E. Casey Foundation, 2013; Bornfreund et al., 2014; Kauerz and Coffman, 2013; Tout et al., 2013). Across these analyses, the goals of alignment efforts are to develop

- a shared vision of developmentally based, high-quality learning in early learning and elementary school settings;
- a common foundation of knowledge, competencies, norms, and processes for high-quality professional practice and professional collaboration and communication within and across professional roles, settings, and ages from birth through early elementary school;
- a mutual understanding of policies, circumstances, and attributes across settings, systems, and professional roles; and
- implementation plans within and across settings that build on a shared vision, a common foundation, and mutual understanding in learning environments, leadership, policies, and accountability systems.

The efforts needed to achieve these goals have been articulated in slightly different ways, but many common elements emerge, discussed here in the following categories: professional learning and workforce development; early learning standards; instructional strategies; learning environments; child assessments; accountability systems and data-driven improvement; family engagement; pathways for vertical continuity for children; and coordination and communication across professional roles, settings, and policies. This committee was charged with focusing on one of those categories—professional learning and the development of the workforce—but describing this broader range of elements provides context for how the workforce fits into larger efforts to strengthen the care and education continuum. Doing so is important because the different elements overlap and are interconnected, and are best considered together rather than in isolation. Evidence indicates that the more of these elements are implemented well, the more likely it is that efforts will yield the desired outcomes for children (Kauerz and Coffman, 2013).

Professional Learning and Workforce Development: Effective Educators and Leaders

Educators and leaders across the care and education continuum for children from birth through age 8 must possess the knowledge and competencies required to promote learning and development for all children and to address challenges faced by children and families in vulnerable situations (Sadowski, 2006). Opportunities for professional learning vary widely depending on the settings and sectors in which professionals work, and it is particularly challenging to provide effective professional learning in an integrated way for educators working with children from birth through age 8 (Tout et al., 2013). Doing so will require revisiting core competencies, practice standards, and polices as needed and reenvisioning professional learning for practitioners and leaders, certification systems, and systems for evaluation and accountability, among other steps. For a detailed discussion of professional learning and workforce development, see Part IV.

Early Learning Standards

Alignment of learning standards across the birth through age 8 continuum is critical for providing continuity in learning and program quality and supporting children as they transition between settings and learning environments. Developmentally appropriate standards set expectations for what young children should learn and the concepts they should understand. These early learning standards, also often referred to as early learning guidelines, typically reflect expectations within domains of development and learning, such as socioemotional competence, cognitive development, general learning competencies, and specific content areas, including literacy, mathematics, science, social studies, and arts. These standards provide teachers with guidance for developing activities and lessons that reinforce these expectations. Early learning standards also have other implications for educators and for instructional practice as they can shape expectations for educator competencies and quality standards for programs, services, and schools, as well as the policies needed to support those standards and expectations. Thus, early learning standards are one way to improve multiple dimensions of practices, systems, and policies, and they can be an important lever for supporting quality and building continuity among and within systems—provided that they reinforce a shared vision, are built on a shared foundation, and are aligned for all ages, including K-3 academic standards (Annie E. Casey Foundation, 2013; Bornfreund et al., 2014; Kauerz and Coffman, 2013; Tout et al., 2013) (see Figure 5-1).

Early learning guidelines developed by states describe what children should know and be able to do during specified age ranges—sometimes birth through age 3, sometimes preschool, sometimes birth to age 5 (Scott-Little et al., 2010). The National Education Goals Panel (NEGP) identified five dimensions of learning and development of young children: "(1) children's physical well-being and motor development; (2) social and emotional development; (3) approaches to learning; (4) language development; and (5) cognition and general knowledge" (NEGP, 1995, p. 3). These domains, for the most part, provide the framework for the states' early learning guidelines (Barnett et al., 2012; Kagan et al., 1995; Scott-Little et al.,

CHANGE IN PRACTICE/BEHAVIOR

TEACHERS: ECE and K-3 educators use developmentally-appropriate curricula, practices, and learning environments that promote children's continuous growth in all domains in B-3rd standards. They use comprehensive data about children's learning and development to inform practice.

LEADERS: ECE & K-3 leaders provide better instructional support to help teachers address B-3rd standards and create more systemic opportunities for collaboration (e.g., cross-grade meetings, joint PD, joint delivery of ECE services). They use comprehensive data about children's learning and development to inform practice, policies, and allocation of resources.

FAMILIES: Parents and other family members have access to comprehensive data about their children's learning and development and have the capacity to provide them more enriching environments and opportunities that support their growth in all learning and developmental domains from birth.

CHILDREN: More children are enrolled in ECE programs that provide more intentional and developmentally appropriate instruction aligned to B-3rd grade standards.

All children attain better outcomes by the end of 3rd grade across all critical domains of learning and development; Disparities in students' readiness for college and career training decrease over time.

POLICY ACTIONS

· Require/expand use of curricula for infant/toddlers and PreK-3rd that guide teachers to address B-3rd learning standards.
· Align B-3rd assessments, including KEAs, to B-3rd learning standards.
· Support use of assessment results to inform policy and practice.
· Enhance screening and referral systems to help children with special needs progress toward PreK-3rd standards.
· Develop coordinated, longitudinal ECE data systems that link to K-12 SLDS to track children's development across B-3rd standards.
· Support data use within & between ECE and K-3 sectors.
· Develop materials/training to inform and engage families in support of B-3rd standards.
· Support district and community efforts that build parents' capacity to support children's growth in domains represented by B-3rd standards.
· Align core competencies with B-3rd standards.
· Strengthen preparation and professional development policies and requirements (e.g., credential, cerfication, coursework, practicum) to ensure all providers and teachers can effectively implement B-3rd standards.
· Design, select, and implement evaluation and observation system that's responsive to PreK-3 context.
· Improve access to high-quality ECE that implement learning standards.
· Align QRIS to learning standards; Promote participation; Allocate resources for improvement.

IMPLEMENTATION LEVERS

Curriculum

Assessment

Data System

Family Support

B-3rd Teacher/ Leader Prep, PD & Eval

Early Care and Education

LEARNING AND DEVELOPMENT DOMAINS

Cognitive Development

Subject Knowledge (e.g., language, math, science)

Socio-emotional Development

General Learning Competencies

Physical Development and Health

ALIGNING EARLY LEARNING AND K-3 STANDARDS

Consider (both within each set of learning standards and across them)...

· Breadth: Degree to which the learning and developmental domains included in a standards document represent the full range of learning and developmental areas that are critical for academic and lifelong success.
· Depth: Degree to which the skills included within in a learning and developmental domain fully represent healthy or proficient development for that domain.
· Balance: Degree to which a standards document gives similar attention to each learning and developmental domain (i.e, addresses each domain with similar depth).
· Difficulty: Degree to which the skills included in each learning and developmental domain are appropriate for age group or grade level.
· Clarity: Skills are stated as observable and measurable benchmarks for end-of-age-span/ end-of-grade performance.

Ensure...

· Standards are aligned with Common Core State Standards, Head Start and Office of Special Education Outcomes Frameworks.
· Standards are appropriate for DLLs and children with special needs.
· Process includes experts and stakeholders across the B-3rd grade continuum.

Minimize...

· Duplicating/Overlapping skills between age groups or grade levels.
· Creating skills gaps or "cliffs" between age groups or grade levels.

FIGURE 5-1 A theory of change for the role of learning standards.

NOTE: ECE = early childhood education; DLL = dual language learner; KEA = kindergarten entry assessment; Prep, PD & Eval = preparation, professional development, and evaluation; QRIS = Quality Rating and Improvement System; SLDS = Statewide Longitudinal Data Systems.

SOURCE: Adapted from Wat, 2013.

2008). The development of early learning guidelines resulted in part from the federal 2002 Good Start, Grow Smart early childhood initiative, which encouraged states to create voluntary early learning guidelines on language and early literacy skills for children aged 3-5. These guidelines were to be aligned with state public school standards and adaptable to various child-care settings (U.S. White House, 2002). Early learning guidelines for infants and toddlers are more recent.

Early learning guidelines for preschool-age children have been developed for all 56 states and territories, and almost all have early learning guidelines for infants and toddlers. Sixteen states have combined guidelines for children from birth to age 5. The majority of states have either aligned or are in the process of aligning their guidelines across age groups and with the Common Core State Standards for early grades (Barnett et al., 2012; National Center on Child Care Quality Improvement, 2014).

Early learning guidelines articulate age-related benchmarks for development in early childhood so that professionals will use appropriate educational instruction and practices that support child development. They also may serve as a tool for educating parents and the public about child development and learning. Further, policy makers can reference early learning guidelines to support high-quality programs and, by linking the guidelines to elementary expectations, contribute to continuity in children's education (Gebhard, 2010; NAEYC-NAECS/SDE, 2002; Scott-Little et al., 2007, 2008).

When early learning standards were first being developed, some early childhood advocates worried that they carried risks, and experts have stressed safeguards for their appropriate use. One concern was that the standards might not represent the diversity of development and learning in the early years and might wrongly result in labeling a child as an early educational failure, potentially denying the child access to other educational opportunities. Similarly, programs might be unfairly criticized based on children's performance. In addition, there was concern that curricula and instructional practices might be driven by standards that might not be comprehensive and that the goal of ensuring that children in the aggregate would meet the standards might be met at the expense of supporting children's individual learning and growth according to their progress along developmental trajectories (Kagan and Scott-Little, 2004; NAEYC-NAECS/SDE, 2002).

In a joint position statement, the National Association for the Education of Young Children (NAEYC) and the National Association of Early Childhood Specialists in State Departments of Education (NAECS/SDE) (2002) hold that early learning standards can contribute to a comprehensive, high-quality system of services for young children provided they

- emphasize significant, developmentally appropriate content and outcomes;
- are developed and reviewed through informed, inclusive processes;
- use implementation and assessment strategies that are ethical and appropriate for young children; and
- are accompanied by strong supports for early childhood programs, professionals, and families (NAEYC-NAECS/SDE, 2002).

Instructional Strategies

Coherent instructional strategies provide children with a consistent, connected series of learning experiences. Such coherence is based on research that guides standards, goals, and pedagogical strategies. Specific learning goals and activities for each age should be connected along a developmental progression (or learning trajectory) to ensure that they are developmentally appropriate, meaning that they are "challenging but attainable for most children of a given age range, flexible enough to respond to inevitable individual variation, and, most important, consistent with children's ways of thinking and learning" (Clements, 2002; Clements et al., 2004). (Learning trajectories are discussed in greater detail in Chapters 4 and 6.) Dual language learners and children with disabilities should be supported through the use of appropriate educational models tailored to these populations, for which specific strategies have been developed (Bornfreund et al., 2014; Tout et al., 2013).

Educators promote coherence through a deep understanding of the content to be taught, knowledge of children's thinking and learning of that content that encompasses development across ages, and expertise in how instructional tasks and strategies promote this learning, complemented by a thorough understanding of each individual child's progress. When there is consistency from one learning environment to the next and communication and collaboration among educators, children are able to establish connections between lessons, between ideas and processes within a topic, between topics, and between learning from one year to the next.

A comprehensive set of standards for instructional strategies can assist program directors and educators in developing well-rounded curricula that are intentional, relevant, balanced, and clearly sequenced. Such standards also can help provide continuity in learning experiences across settings from birth through third grade (Bornfreund et al., 2014). State standards should specify that curricula

- be research based,
- support foundational competencies for children,
- guide both the content and process of teaching, and

- be reviewed periodically and refined or replaced as needed (Kauerz and Coffman, 2013).

Instructional strategies are discussed further in Chapter 6.

Learning Environments

Evidence indicates that children benefit when learning environments meet well-defined measures of high-quality care and education (Annie E. Casey Foundation, 2013; Tout et al., 2013). The physical environment and socioemotional climate that contribute to favorable outcomes for children encompass learning environments that are sensitive to all cultures in the community; promote positive relationships for children and adults; and are structured and supplied with resources to support a breadth of developmental levels, abilities, and interests. Adequate and safe indoor and outdoor spaces, as well as dedicated areas for adults to collaborate in planning and decision-making processes, are necessary to support active learning and instruction. Care and education professionals need to create organized environments that support learning and the socioemotional development of children. The availability and use of a variety of resources that encourage different sensory experiences and explorations and subject-matter content (e.g., books, manipulatives, technology) are important to children's learning (Kauerz and Coffman, 2013), as are environments that are easy for young children to navigate autonomously to pursue interests.

Care and education professionals need to create environments that are sensitive to the diversity of cultures and languages that children bring to the classroom and to the importance of educating all children about the diversity they will encounter in the world. Such environments include materials that reflect this diversity, including images and toys that depict people from different countries, of different skin colors, in varying family configurations, of different ages, and of different abilities.

The number of hours spent in early education programs also can influence a child's learning and development. Research has found that children attending full-day preschool and kindergarten programs have better academic outcomes than those attending half-day programs (Tout et al., 2013). It has been suggested that children should attend prekindergarten and kindergarten for the same number of hours per day as first grade (Annie E. Casey Foundation, 2013; Bornfreund et al., 2014; Tout et al., 2013). However, for early learning settings for young children there also is growing evidence that the number of hours associated with full-day attendance can be psychologically and biologically stressful for some young children, especially when starting to attend childcare settings early in life, which may contribute to socioemotional and other developmental difficulties (Dmitrieva et al., 2007; Sajaniemi et al., 2011; Watamura et al., 2003).

Child Assessments

Assessment is used to measure children's developmental progress. Assessments also are used to guide intervention and instruction and evaluate the performance and effectiveness of programs and services (Kauerz and Coffman, 2013; NRC, 2008). A comprehensive system includes diagnostic, formative, and summative assessments. Assessments that are developmentally, culturally, and linguistically appropriate provide accurate data that can inform the instructional paths or interventions needed to support a child. Assessments should be designed for a specific purpose and be aligned across all levels, from early learning programs through preschool to K-3 (Annie E. Casey Foundation, 2013; Bornfreund et al., 2014; Kauerz and Coffman, 2013; Tout et al., 2013).

Screening is another form of assessment for eliciting important information about whether a child is progressing as expected. Screening can indicate whether further diagnostic assessments are needed and which intervention services may be warranted. Follow-up action typically requires coordination among families, early educators, and medical or early intervention specialists (Tout et al., 2013).

If data collected through child assessments are to lead to beneficial change, professionals must be trained not only in how to administer them but also in how to interpret their results and apply that information in altering instructional practices and learning environments (Kauerz and Coffman, 2013; Tout et al., 2013). Data collection, interpretation, and sharing in ongoing practice also need to be supported through structured and facilitated means to ensure the quality of data analysis, interpretation, and use. Leaders in educational settings and systems, as well as oversight policies, must support the time and structures needed if assessment data are to fulfill their potential to inform day-to-day instructional practices, professional learning, and organizational planning. In many settings, a shift may be required to decrease the volume of data collection and reorient from a focus on reporting and compliance to emphasize time, support, and resources for data analysis, interpretation, and use (Lesaux et al., 2014).

Child assessments are discussed further in Chapter 6.

Accountability Systems and Data-Driven Improvement

A National Research Council (2008) report on early childhood assessment cautions that it is inappropriate to use data from child assessments independently. Rather, it is important to

- measure children's progress rather than end-of-year status,
- collect data on direct indicators of program quality,
- collect data on the risk status of families and children,
- collect data on program resources (e.g., funding, administrative support, professional development), and
- have a clear plan for program improvement (Tout et al., 2013; Zaslow and Halle, 2009).

Accountability systems utilizing various data sources can be used to improve instructional practices, the provision of services, schools and early care and education programs, professional development, and Quality Rating and Improvement Systems (QRISs), as well as to inform the efficient allocation of monetary resources (Kauerz and Coffman, 2013; Tout et al., 2013). These systems for accountability can help measure progress toward identified goals with defined benchmarks and outcomes (Tout et al., 2013).

Developing longitudinal data systems that are linked among early childhood providers and programs, K-12 schools, and state agencies and that can be disaggregated by age, gender, race/ethnicity, and socioeconomic status, among other factors, can inform strategies for improving program quality and child outcomes. Appropriate assessment methodologies specific to the individual, program, or system being assessed need to be identified and linked. As with individual child-based assessments, valid data collection that can effect beneficial change requires that administrators, care and education professionals, and families receive instruction on the data collection methodology and interpretation of the data (Kauerz and Coffman, 2013; Tout et al., 2013). The need for responsible data use and interpretation means not only that practitioners must be taught how to interpret results and apply that information to make changes, but also that data sharing be conducted through structured and facilitated means to ensure the quality of the data analysis, interpretation, and use. Data gathered from these systems must be used responsibly to inform instructional practices as well as policy and strategic decisions that will ultimately lead to improved child outcomes (Annie E. Casey Foundation, 2013; Bornfreund et al., 2014; Kauerz and Coffman, 2013; Tout et al., 2013).

Family Engagement

Family engagement focuses on building strong relationships between families and staff along the continuum of care and education settings and community programs (Tout et al., 2013). Educators and administrators need to establish a two-way dialogue with families so as to share responsibilities, data, and decision making in support of children's development and learning (Kauerz and Coffman, 2013; Tout et al., 2013). Parents and families have the strongest influence on the growth and development of their children, and the aim of family engagement is to bring staff and families together around the common cause of supporting children's development and learning. Families have valuable knowledge to share with the people helping to care for and educate their children, from the characteristics of a particular child to more general cultural funds of knowledge. Educators and administrators benefit from taking an approach of respectful inquiry when it comes to understanding families' cultural beliefs and practices around, for example, such issues as eating and sleeping, attachment and separation, and the role of play in learning. It is also important to support parents and families in their understanding of child development in order to engage them in their children's education. Care and education professionals also can promote responsive and culturally appropriate parenting, as well as respect for and understanding of the home language and culture, and encourage or facilitate formal and informal support networks. Moreover, supports can be provided at the policy level; many policies can affect various aspects of life for parents and families, including economic stability, education, and health (Tout et al., 2013).

Federal and state government programs such as home visiting, nutrition assistance, childcare assistance, and abuse and neglect prevention provide such support. Parent education programs offer parents knowledge of what to do to encourage their children's success. Policies also can affect the economic stability of families. For example, encouraging successful employment of the adults in a family through education and training programs promotes economic stability for the family. Other important strategies are designed to enable parents to take advantage of such programs by making navigation of systems more manageable—for example, aligning eligibility requirements, streamlining benefits, or offering different modes of applying for services (Annie E. Casey Foundation, 2013; Bornfreund et al., 2014; Tout et al., 2013).

Family engagement is discussed further in Chapter 6.

Pathways for Vertical Continuity for Children

From birth through age 8, children undergo a tremendous developmental period, including physical, cognitive, and socioemotional development (see Chapter 4). During this period, a continuous pathway of high-quality, evidence-based care and education for all children and integrated support are associated with later academic and social success.

The transition to a new setting (for example, when a child is moving from home to a center, from family childcare to a preschool, or from a preschool to an elementary school) can be a major adjustment for young children—a challenge compounded by disconnects or misalignment among systems. For example, the learning environments children encounter in childcare settings can be very different from those in kindergarten classrooms. Transitions within settings also can be challenging for children as they move from year to year in childcare settings and grade to grade in elementary schools (Tout et al., 2013).

Making explicit connections between learning environments can help ease the adjustment for young children and reduce adverse consequences that may result from stresses encountered in transitioning. Bridging activities designed to ease transitions can support and sustain the growth of children's competencies across developmental domains (Bornfreund et al., 2014; Tout et al., 2013). Bridging activities employed within settings or classrooms include having mixed-age classrooms or having an educator move with a group of students for multiple years—for example, to teach the same class of children from ages 3 to 5 or from kindergarten through second grade before starting again with a new class. The success of these approaches will depend on the availability of educators employing a high quality of professional practice, to avoid a cumulative negative effect of children experiencing consecutive years of a low-quality learning environment rather than the desired continuity of a high-quality learning environment. Across settings, bridging activities might include developing partnerships within a community among early care providers, community-based organizations, preschools and elementary schools. Expanding access to high-quality learning programs, including preschool for all low-income children and after-school or extended learning opportunities, is necessary for this approach to be viable. Parental involvement in planning for transitions also has been shown to be instrumental in children's success (Annie E. Casey Foundation, 2013; Bornfreund et al., 2014; Kauerz and Coffman, 2013; Tout et al., 2013). Policies and practices such as standardized forms and processes across settings and age/grade levels and aligned standards, curricula, teaching practices, and assessments can facilitate transitions as well (Annie E. Casey Foundation, 2013; Kauerz and Coffman, 2013). Additional bridging activities and supports are needed for children who are receiving supplemental support services—for example, children receiving early intervention services at home who are transitioning to special education services in a center or school.

Continuity at Kindergarten Entry

Kindergarten entry in particular is a point of discontinuity for young children that has received increasing attention in recent years. For some children, this is a first transition from the home environment to a care and education setting. Even for children in care and education settings prior to kindergarten, the experience in family childcare settings, center-based childcare, and preschools, and even prekindergarten programs in schools, can be very different from the environment of kindergarten, which is typically in an elementary school embedded in a K-12 system. Similarly, the practice environment and professional learning background is typically very different for educators and leaders in settings before kindergarten and those in elementary schools.

The concept of "readiness" to start school has been recognized as encompassing a variety of components. At the level of an individual child's developmental progress, it includes not only cognitive development, language development, and early knowledge in subject areas but also socioemotional development, physical development and health, and growth in learning competencies. It encompasses a child's ability to undertake the learning of specific content (e.g., vocabulary, conceptual skills, progress on early learning trajectories for core content areas such as literacy and math), as well as a child's physical, emotional, social, and behavioral preparedness to engage in the kindergarten and early elementary learning environment.

However, "readiness" is not just a construct at the level of the individual child. Families and communities also are important in the transition to the kindergarten setting, as is the "readiness" of elementary schools to receive the children they serve (Kagan et al., 1995; Shepard et al., 1998). Thus, "readiness" means as well that professionals and the systems in which they work are equipped to facilitate smooth transitions between home and school, as well as to establish continuity between early care and education settings and elementary schools. According to Pianta and colleagues (1999), transition practices of "ready" schools include (1) developing connections with families and preschools, (2) establishing connections even before the first day of kindergarten, and (3) utilizing proactive strategies such as home visiting to make personal connections with children and families.

Through a review of research on the transition to kindergarten, Tout and colleagues (2013) identified promising strategies schools can use to offer support to children. These include forming partnerships among children, parents, and teachers; ensuring that parents understand their role in their child's education; and encouraging professional learning for educators. Research shows that establishing connections between developmental contexts during critical transitions can help ease the stressfulness of these transitions and support and sustain the acquisition of new skills and abilities. For example, Schulting and colleagues (2005) followed a cohort of children across their kindergarten year to examine how child outcomes are affected by school-based transition policies and practices. Their findings indicate a significant association between transition practices and positive academic outcomes at the end of the school year. This effect was strongest for children of low and middle socioeconomic status and was attributed in part to a positive correlation between the transition practices and parent-initiated involvement during the school year. In addition to family engagement in children's learning experiences, family and community involvement entails supporting high-quality comprehensive services to support families, which are critical in particular for fostering at-risk children's overall development and school success (Daily et al., 2010).

Alignment of early learning standards with K-12 curriculum standards, as well as standards across systems for programs and professional practice standards, is necessary to create continuity across the systems through which children transition (Daily et al., 2010). Further, aligning formative assessments across early childhood and early elementary years can ensure that educators are prepared to support children's continuing development consistently during transition periods (Graves, 2006; Tout et al., 2013). If the alignment and use of such assessments are to be effective, precautions and systems must be in place to define the purpose of the assessments clearly, to train care and education professionals in their use, and to provide tools that facilitate appropriate interpretation and use of the results (Daily et al., 2010).

Several states and localities are institutionalizing this process by adopting kindergarten entry assessment systems. Under the appropriate conditions, these assessment systems represent an opportunity to create continuity and support more consistency in high-quality learning experiences for children, building a foundation in early settings that can be sustained continuously into the early elementary years and beyond. These systems are implemented well when the assessments encompass multiple domains of development; when the results are interpreted and used in a structured and facilitated way to support communication among practitioners and settings and to inform instruction and program improvement; and when they catalyze dialogue, cooperation, and alignment among sectors and systems to build shared expectations, standards, and practices for supporting child development and early learning. In Washington State, for example, the Washington Kindergarten Inventory of Developing Skills includes not only a whole-child assessment component but also components for family connections and for early learning collaboration to align practices among kindergarten teachers and professionals in settings prior to elementary school (Washington State Office of Superintendent of Public Instruction, n.d.).

Continuity from Year to Year in Elementary Schools

Consistency and continuity are important not only when children are entering a new setting but also from year to year and grade to grade within the same setting. An example that has received considerable attention in recent years is the discontinuity that occurs during summer breaks for elementary school students. The calendar year for most elementary schools lasts 10 months, followed by a 2-month break, which interrupts children's continuous participation in a consistent learning environment. Research indicates that students can experience a "summer loss" in achievement during this break, and this loss is greater for students with disabilities or reading difficulties and those from economically disadvantaged circumstances (Alexander et al., 2007; O'Connor et al., 2008, 2013). Year-round schooling, in which the number of school days is spread more evenly and continuously over a 12-month period, is an alternative to the 10-month calendar. Although the currently available evidence is inconclusive on whether it solves the problem of "summer loss," two meta-analyses have found that academic achievement is as good or slightly better for students in year-round schools compared with those in traditional schools and that year-round education may be particularly beneficial for students from low-income families (Cooper et al., 2003; Huebner and Educational Leadership, 2010; Worthen and Zsiray, 1994). Research also indicates that in those schools in which year-round schooling results in higher achievement, rearranging the calendar is accompanied by remediation and enrichment during breaks between sessions to help students reinforce, practice, catch up on, and apply skills or experience nonacademic enrichment (McMillen, 2001).

Coordination and Communication Across
Professional Roles, Settings, and Policies

Benefits of collaboration across multiple early childhood programs and systems include not only the "bridging" function described above, but also the opportunity to provide better services to families and to share and maximize resources and training (Tout et al., 2013). Research shows that programs and services delivered with a comprehensive, coordinated approach for infants, toddlers, and their parents through preschool to primary school lead to better child outcomes (Annie E. Casey Foundation, 2013). To this end, individuals and organizations that oversee childcare and education services and programs can work together to develop a strategic and collaborative approach across the age continuum. For example, formal linkages can be established between local early childhood care and learning programs and the elementary schools the children they serve will attend (Kauerz and Coffman, 2013). Innovative approaches to encourage and support collaborative approaches will be needed, such as the coordination of funding sources (Bornfreund et al., 2014; Tout et al., 2013). Possibilities include reallocating funds, securing philanthropic partners, and blending public and private funds. Federal funds that can be leveraged include Title I, Title II, Special Education, Head Start, and the Child Care Development Block Grant (Kauerz and Coffman, 2013; Tout et al., 2013).

Although the challenge is in the implementation, the federal government does encourage some degree of collaboration among care and education programs and services through authorizing legislation, regulations, and initiatives offering federal grants. The Child Care Development Block Grant, Head Start legislation, and the Individuals with Disabilities Education Improvement Act of 2004 all include requirements for partnerships and collaboration (Tout et al., 2013). In addition, many states and local communities are employing collaborative approaches that bring together care and education professionals, such as early intervention specialists and childcare providers or school districts and community-based providers (Tout et al., 2013). Other examples of overlap and sharing also are under way: for example, special education classrooms for 3- and 4-year-olds often are part of elementary schools, and some prekindergarten programs are run by elementary schools using Title I funds.

Box 5-1 provides some illustrative examples of initiatives or approaches focused specifically on collaboration to create a more continuous system for children from birth through age 8. Note that these examples do not represent a comprehensive review of all such initiatives, nor did the committee draw conclusions about best practices or intend to endorse particular exemplars. They are included to illustrate some of the approaches that have been developed and some of the available opportunities for learning from existing efforts.

Coordination with health care and other services outside of the care and education sector is discussed later in this chapter. The competencies required for these kinds of collaborations among different professional roles, referred to as interprofessional practice, are discussed further in Chapter 7.

Conclusions About the Care and Education Continuum

Consistency of high-quality learning environments and learning experiences across settings and sectors as a child ages is important to supporting development and early learning from birth through age 8. Currently, a diverse and usually uncoordinated "system" of funding streams, agencies, and organizations has responsibility or authority over services and support for young children. This fragmentation can result in inconsistent expectations for children's learning and approaches to instructional practice, lack of coordination among services for children, failure to build on learning gains, and inadequate support for children's achievement. Promoting and sustaining early gains requires better alignment and more continuous follow-through across early learning and early elementary settings, based on a developmental orientation that complements educational achievement.

BOX 5-1
Illustrative Examples of Initiatives for Continuity
Within Early Care and Education

McKnight Foundation Education and Learning Program

The McKnight Foundation's Education and Learning (E&L) Program provides grants to schools around the Twin Cities to increase the percentage of children reading at grade level by the end of third grade. Schools participating in this program focus on literacy development across the prekindergarten–grade 3 continuum.

The McKnight Foundation partners with the University of Chicago's Urban Education Institute (UEI) for professional development at the awardee schools to facilitate the implementation of research-based tools. A key component of this program is the development of literacy assessment systems to better inform instruction. District-level staff work with UEI in selecting these assessments and integrating them into the schools. A 2013 evaluation of the E&L Program indicated that students' literacy scores showed improvement, teachers were better able to identify struggling students, and the implementation process created an avenue for across-grade conversations among teachers as well as better communication with parents (SRI and CAREI, 2013). However, teachers also reported a need for additional trainings, particularly in adapting instructional strategies to address individual student needs.

Alignment is another key component of the E&L Program. To ensure that children move from one grade to the next with the core set of knowledge and skills needed to be successful in the following year, educational standards, instructional strategies, and assessments are carefully laid out. Additionally, the schedules, calendars, and salaries of prekindergarten teachers are commensurate with those of other teachers. The program thus facilitates joint professional development activities and allows teachers to inform one another in grade-level transitions. Although the E&L Program has shown many successes in establishing a prekindergarten–grade 3 program throughout the awardee school districts, challenges continue to exist for teachers, who report not having adequate trainings to co-teach effectively or enough planning time for collaboration (SRI and CAREI, 2013).

Naval Avenue Early Learning Center, Bremerton, Washington

The Naval Avenue Early Learning Center provides a comprehensive early childhood through third grade education for children in Bremerton, Washington. Beginning in 2001 as an effort to increase and sustain student achievement, the prekindergarten–grade 3 system was created to align standards, curriculum, and assessment that connect prekindergarten with full-day kindergarten and grades 1 through 3. Staff at the center receive frequent trainings and professional learning support in how to address the individual needs of students across the developmental continuum. There is also a collocated infant-toddler and preschool care and education center on the campus. Bremerton Play School is hosted monthly at the school to provide stay-at-home parents (and grandparents and guardians) and their children an opportunity to interact in a preschool classroom setting while gaining knowledge needed to prepare for kindergarten. In addition, the wider community in Bremerton has an Early Childhood Care and Education Group that was established to link school district early learning programs with other community programs, preschools, and childcare providers. It provides such services as instructional materials for in-home childcare providers, as well as monthly teacher trainings.

Thrive in 5 Boston

Thrive in 5 is a citywide effort in Boston to increase school readiness for children from birth to age 5. It began in 2008 as a public–private partnership between the city of Boston and United Way of Massachusetts Bay and Merrimack Valley. Additional funding partners include foundations, government agencies, and health care organizations.

Building on research and practice, Thrive in 5 utilizes a multisector strategy to ensure school success for all children. Ready Families provides parent education and community capacity building. Ready Educators focuses on high-quality learning environments in all settings, including center-based and family childcare, informal childcare, Early Head Start and Head Start, and school-based early education. Ready Systems addresses the needs of children with developmental delays to make early detection and intervention available in health care. Finally, Ready City is the commitment of all Boston government agencies to make children's school success a continued priority.

The strategy for Ready Educators is to achieve measurably improved child outcomes by supporting practitioners in their ability to identify children's needs and provide necessary supports and resources. Technical assistance providers work with practitioners to develop the skills needed to improve quality of care. Together, they are able to assess the strengths and weaknesses of a program, develop a customized program improvement plan, facilitate the plan's implementation, and assess the plan biannually and revise and adapt it as necessary. Educators participate in targeted professional development to allow them to participate fully.

The Center for Social Policy at the University of Massachusetts Boston prepares periodic reports on the progress of Thrive by 5's program goals. A recent evaluation brief indicates that improvement has been made in year two's implementation plan for increasing outreach activities and reaching families (Friedman et al., 2013). The next evaluation phase will focus on quality improvements for Ready Educators.

NOTE: Additional examples of local initiatives can be found in Appendix F.

Standards or guidelines for developmental milestones or achievements in early learning are most effective when age-graded expectations are accompanied by understanding of each child's developmental pace and trajectory. Standards can guide developmentally appropriate professional practice and support continuity for children if implemented with the understanding that some variability within an age span is normal as part of a continuous developmental trajectory and that children who are not at the standard milestones can be supported with high-quality and responsive instructional practices and interventions. To implement standards in this way, professionals need to be able to recognize and intervene appropriately when children are not on track and may need special help.

Children do better entering a new setting when they have certain knowledge and competencies that are the foundation of a long-range trajectory for deep and coherent learning and that help them thrive in their adjustment to a new learning environment. Expectations and standards for children at entry points into new settings are developmentally appropriate when used to reflect this understanding rather than as fixed criteria for predicting future learning success or as a threshold for advancement.

For children at entry points into new learning environments, "readiness" is not just about the competencies of the child. It is also about the competencies of educators to recognize where children are along their individual trajectories, to support children who are "ready," to help children catch up as needed in acquiring the capabilities to succeed in their adjustment, and to provide appropriate learning experiences for those children who surpass the "readiness" standard. Readiness also is about the capacity of settings and environments to support both children and educators in this work.

To support a more consistent learning experience for children, educators need to have a mutual understanding of the expectations, contexts, and instructional approaches of the settings that precede and follow their own. This understanding is particularly important when children are transitioning from one setting (such as a childcare program or preschool) to another (such as a kindergarten classroom), when the adjustments for children and risks of inconsistent expectations or instructional approaches are greatest.

CONTINUITY AMONG SECTORS

A critical factor in seamlessly supporting children from birth through age 8 is continuity among the diverse services and agencies affecting children and their families. Therefore, children need a workforce trained in supporting linkages and referrals to different sectors and systems. In addition to collaboration and coordination among professionals within sectors, connections are necessary among professionals across sectors, including information and data sharing, handoffs, referrals, case management, and shared professional learning (see Figure 5-2). Coordination with health care, social services, and other services can help ensure that all children receive comprehensive care that addresses the many factors affecting their well-being, that children's early experiences contribute consistently to developmental achievements, and that all professions who work with young children have a shared understanding of the interconnected quality of developmental processes that each may see only in part.

Some of the important connections include screening, consultation, and referral from care and education to specialized education services, as well as health, mental health, and social services such as

- general well-child health services;
- health screening (e.g., hearing, vision);
- mental health services;
- nutrition support services;
- services for children with disabilities and other special needs;
- screening and services to recognize and address child neglect and abuse; and
- support services that facilitate the ability of families to provide a safe and healthy environment for their children, including policies and programs designed to increase resources for disadvantaged and low-income families (e.g., Medicaid, work support policies, the Supplemental Nutrition Assistance Program, cash transfer programs).

Linkages and connections among sectors can take various forms. One form is coordination at the level of policy alignment, shared planning, and coordination among different systems/sectors. For example, states can improve planning and coordination to ensure that children with special needs receive all needed services across sectors and continuously as they move between settings and service delivery systems (Annie E. Casey Foundation, 2013). Another approach is collocation of various services for children such that physical proximity becomes a means of facilitating interprofessional relationships and collaboration. For example, a model of coordination

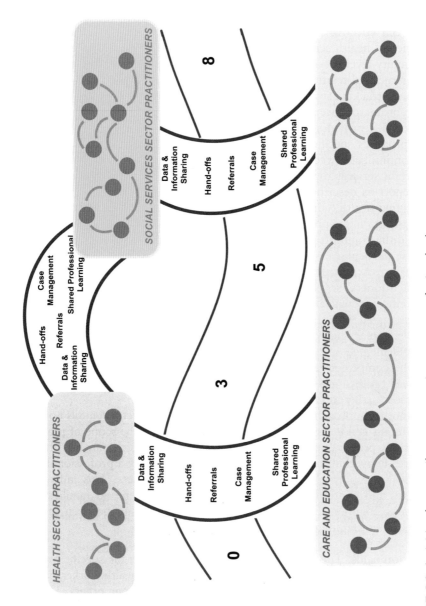

FIGURE 5-2 Activities that contribute to connections among professional roles across sectors.

between health care and Head Start entails providing educational programs and delivering health care services in the same setting. Several states have initiated similar programs that support communities in linking health care and family services through early learning programs; these programs have been effective in reducing nonfinancial barriers to accessing health and mental health services (Tout et al., 2013). Other approaches include community-level service and program collaboration and coordination to build structural relationships among organizations; implementation of referral and tracking systems; and the use of professionals with a specific role as a coordinator/case manager/navigator among services.

Box 5-2 provides some additional illustrative examples of initiatives or approaches specifically focused on improving linkages, collaboration, and continuity between care and education and other sectors that provide important services for children and families. In keeping with the scope of this report as described in Chapter 1, the focus of these examples is on connecting health, education, and social services. As with Box 5-1, these examples do not represent a comprehensive review of all such initiatives, nor did the committee draw conclusions about best practices or intend to endorse particular exemplars. Of particular note, in light of the focus of this report, is that there is little documentation or evaluation of changes to practitioners' scope of work, roles, and responsibilities; specific new required competencies; and training and other professional learning activities associated with the implementation of these approaches. Nonetheless, these examples illustrate some conceptually sound approaches that are being implemented and offer the opportunity to learn from existing efforts.

The competencies required for these kinds of collaborations among different professional roles, referred to as interprofessional practice, are discussed further in Chapter 7.

Another approach for improving linkages across sectors entails not just focusing on making systems changes and expanding the scope of practice of current practitioners to improve coordination, which can be difficult for already overburdened practitioners, but introducing a professional role specifically responsible for coordination among services. This individual manages and coordinates the service needs of children and families and facilitates communication among service providers and between service providers and families.

A wide range of such models have been established in the medical and education fields. The title of the individual varies with the specific model, including patient navigator, case manager, community health worker, home/school coordinator, and family service coordinator, among others. The responsibilities of these individuals include

---

BOX 5-2
Illustrative Examples of Initiatives for Linkage
and Collaboration Among Sectors

Promise Neighborhoods
      The Promise Neighborhoods program creates a "cradle-to-career" continuum by increasing supports within the family, the community, and education systems. Through grants made available from the U.S. Department of Education, programs are implemented within high-needs communities around the country with the goal of increasing the capacity of existing local supports. With schools at the center, these programs focus on building a continuum of care whereby residents can access programs that historically have operated in silos. Once communities have increased resources to a level that allows them to further develop local infrastructure or systems, they are able to expand to surrounding regions, thus creating stronger and more sustainable support systems for residents. Promise Neighborhoods programs currently are being implemented in 20 states and the District of Columbia (U.S. Department of Education, n.d.).

Community Schools
      A community school serves as a place for hosting partnerships aimed at promoting student learning, strengthening families, and promoting healthier communities. The schools remain open throughout the week, including evenings and weekends, to allow residents full access to a wide range of resources and services that include not only academic support for students but also youth development, health and social services, and community engagement and development. This approach builds stronger connections among individuals, families, neighborhoods, schools, and other institutions while allowing programs to develop to meet the unique needs of each community. There are now 39 community schools operating in the United States (Coalition for Community Schools, n.d.).

Magnolia Place Community Initiative, Los Angeles, California
      The Magnolia Place Community Initiative is a prevention model that promotes and strengthens individual, family, and neighborhood protective factors through increased social connectedness, community mobilization, and access to needed services. The Initiative brings together more than 70 county, city, and community efforts around Los Angeles, each committed to improving, aligning, and coordinating efforts to enhance and sustain community health and well-being (Coalition for Community Schools, n.d.).

- facilitating communication between families/patients and professionals in various sectors, including schools;
- removing barriers by assisting with logistical tasks (e.g., transportation issues, making appointments);
- helping to negotiate expectations between families and professionals; and

- using individual case management to establish partnerships with families in the areas of health and social services.

In the education field, Allen and colleagues (1996) describe the role of family service coordinators as helping families navigate services for children in different sectors, including social services, education, health, and nutrition. Acting as advocates for children and families, family service coordinators connect families with these services, which can result in higher levels of family engagement and parents' involvement in their child's education and health. Children may receive direct benefits from navigation services, including regular medical and dental care, as well as follow-up care and healthy snacks in schools. Parents also receive direct benefits, including a parental support network, resources to help them work with their children, and strengthened communication with professionals, which can all empower parents to participate actively in their child's development. Coordinators also work with families to identify individual needs, which helps establish a trusting relationship (Allen et al., 1996).

The state of Kentucky, for example, established a family service coordinator system through the Kentucky Education Reform Act of 1990. This program provides connections between families and social and health services in an effort to ensure that all children have access to care. An 18-month study of this program showed that the system emphasized finding solutions to problems as well as establishing thorough and clear communication of expectations between families and professionals working with children (Smrekar, 1996).

Currently, Part C of the Individuals with Disabilities Education Act includes an Individualized Family Service Plan (Sec. 636) through which a multidisciplinary team collaborates with parents to develop a written individualized plan for infants and toddlers with disabilities and their families. This plan focuses on physical, cognitive, communication, social, emotional, and adaptive development; considers family resources and priorities; and details interventions and expected measurable outcomes. A service coordinator is responsible for implementing the plan, as well as facilitating coordination with other services that are relevant to the needs of the infant or toddler and family members (U.S. Department of Education, 2015).

The approach of introducing a specific role for coordination of services can be informed by similar professional roles that have evolved in the health field to help patients navigate access to care and other services. For example, a "barrier-focused intervention" model includes removing instrumental and relationship barriers. Services of an intervention might include transportation assistance for appointments and other logistical tasks and building and strengthening relationships and communication between patients and providers. Given that the needs of different populations vary, the role of the patient navigator includes assessing the population's needs and adapting the intervention services to meet those needs. For example, navigators work with cancer patients to help remove logistical and communication barriers while facilitating their relationships with physicians. Studies have shown increased screening rates at the population level associated with patient navigation services, with a limited effect on follow-up diagnostic services and treatment. Patients express a strong desire to continue receiving navigation services through the course of their services (Paskett et al., 2011).

Another model is illustrated by Project Access Dallas, which works with community health workers who provide navigation services to those who experience barriers to health care (Gimpel et al., 2010). Community participants in this program indicated that they became comfortable working with their community health worker and asking questions, both medical and nonmedical. Many participants also indicated that through the navigation services, they became independent and acquired the ability to manage their own health care with dignity. This work also helped establish relationships and strengthen social networks within communities (Gimpel et al., 2010). Other examples of navigator models work to manage communication between service providers (formal and informal services and support systems) and individuals with intellectual disabilities (Bigby et al., 2007). Because individuals with disabilities may encounter barriers to accessing services, an effective patient navigator can inform service providers about the needs of individual participants to ensure that services are inclusive of all who need them (Bigby et al., 2007).

Conclusions About Continuity Among Sectors

Child development is highly interactive across different domains, including those supported by professionals not only in care and education but also in other sectors, especially health, mental health, family support, and social services. Yet in the complex landscape of settings and systems for children and families, there are gaps and weaknesses in referral and linkage when children and families need to be connected to services across sectors:

- *Some of these gaps relate to the workforce in the related sectors, including insufficient availability of or access to referred services (such as home visiting, pediatric health services, early intervention services, and mental health consultation and services).*
- *Other gaps relate to the knowledge and competencies of the workforce: lack of skills for screening and assessing a child's sta-*

tus and needs, lack of knowledge about available services, and lack of skills for interprovider communication and collaboration.

- *These gaps highlight the need for the workforce across sectors that serve young children to incorporate interprofessional practice and collaboration as a core competency.*

The responsibility and burden of improving coordination and collaboration cannot rest solely on individual practitioners. Systems barriers need to be removed and facilitative supports put in place to improve communication and interaction among professional roles. In addition, the use of professionals with the primary role of facilitating coordination among services for children, families, and practitioners needs to be enhanced.

REFERENCES

Alexander, K. L., D. R. Entwisle, and L. S. Olson. 2007. Lasting consequences of the summer learning gap. *American Sociological Review* 72(2):167-180.

Allen, S. M., R. Thompson, and J. Drapeaux. 1996. *Providing Head Start-like services from kindergarten through the third grade: The role of family service coordinators.* Paper presented at Head Start National Research Conference, 3rd, June 20-23, Washington, DC.

Annie E. Casey Foundation. 2013. *The first eight years: Giving kids a foundation for lifetime success.* Baltimore, MD: Annie E. Casey Foundation.

Barnett, W. S., M. E. Carolan, J. Fitzgerald, and J. H. Squires. 2012. *The state of preschool 2012: State preschool yearbook.* New Brunswick, NJ: National Institute for Early Education Research.

Bigby, C., C. Fyffe, and E. Ozanne. 2007. *Planning and support for people with intellectual disabilities: Issue for case managers and other professionals.* London: Jessica Kingsley.

Bornfreund, L. A., C. McCann, C. Williams, and L. Guernsey. 2014. *Beyond subprime learning: Accelerating progress in early education.* Washington, DC: New America Foundation.

Clements, D. H. 2002. Computers in early childhood mathematics. *Contemporary Issues in Early Childhood* 3(2):160.

Clements, D. H., A.-M. DiBiase, and J. Sarama. 2004. *Engaging young children in mathematics: Standards for early childhood mathematics education. Studies in mathematical thinking and learning series.* Mahwah, NJ: Lawrence Erlbaum Associates.

Coalition for Community Schools. n.d. *Coalition for community schools.* http://www.communityschools.org (accessed March 6, 2015).

Cooper, H., J. C. Valentine, K. Chalton, and A. Melson. 2003. The effects of modified school calendars on student achievement and on school and community attitudes. *Review of Educational Research* 73(1):1-52.

Daily, S., M. Burkhauser, and T. Halle. 2010. A review of school readiness practices in the states: Early learning guidelines and assessments. *Child Trends Early Childhood Highlights* 1(3):1-12.

Dmitrieva, J., L. Steinberg, and J. Belsky. 2007. Child-care history, classroom composition, and children's functioning in kindergarten. *PSCI Psychological Science* 18(12):1032-1039.

Friedman, D. H., M. Coonan, A. Douglass, O. Gutierrez, and A. Carter. 2013. *Boston children thrive in 5: Connecting families, building community. Year 2 evaluation brief.* http://cdn.umb.edu/images/centers_institutes/center_social_policy/BCT_Year_2_Report_6_10_2013_version_final.pdf (accessed December 19, 2014).

Gebhard, B. 2010. *Putting standards into practice: States' use of early learning guidelines for infants and toddlers.* Washington, DC: Zero to Three.

Gimpel, N., A. Marcee, K. Kennedy, J. Walton, S. Lee, and M. J. DeHaven. 2010. Patient perceptions of a community-based care coordination system. *Health Promotion Practice* 11(2):173-181.

Graves, B. 2006. *PK-3: What is it and how do we know it works?* New York: Foundation for Child Development.

Huebner, T. A., and Educational Leadership. 2010. *What research says about.../year-round schooling.* http://www.ascd.org/publications/educational_leadership/apr10/vol67/num07/Year-Round_Schooling.aspx (accessed March 12, 2015).

Kagan, S. L., and C. Scott-Little. 2004. Early learning standards: Changing the parlance and practice of early childhood education? *Phi Delta Kappan* 85(5):388-396.

Kagan, S. L., E. Moore, and S. Bredekamp. 1995. *Reconsidering children's early development and learning: Toward common views and vocabulary.* Washington, DC: National Education Goals Panel.

Kauerz, K., and J. Coffman. 2013. *Framework for planning, implementing, and evaluating preK-3rd grade approaches.* Seattle: University of Washington, College of Education.

Lesaux, N. K., S. Jones, J. R. Harris, and R. L. Kane. 2014. *Using data for R2 accountability and improvement.* http://isites.harvard.edu/fs/docs/icb.topic1391652.files/R2brief6_Lesaux%20Jones%20Harris%20Kane.pdf (accessed January 23, 2015).

McMillen, B. J. 2001. A statewide evaluation of academic achievement in year-round schools. *Journal of Education Research* 95(2):67-74.

NAEYC-NAECS/SDE (National Association for the Education of Young Children-National Association of Early Childhood Specialists/State Departments of Education). 2002. *Position statement: Early learning guidelines.* http://www.naeyc.org/files/naeyc/file/positions/position_statement.pdf (accessed November 3, 2014).

National Center on Child Care Quality Improvement. 2014. *State/territory early learning guidelines (no. 75).* https://childcareta.acf.hhs.gov/sites/default/files/state_elgs_web_final.pdf (accessed November 6, 2014).

NEGP (National Education Goals Panel). 1995. *Reconsidering children's early development and learning: Toward common views and vocabulary.* Washington, DC: NEGP.

NRC (National Research Council). 2008. *Early childhood assessment: Why, what, and how,* edited by C. E. Snow and S. B. Van Hemel. Washington, DC: The National Academies Press.

O'Connor, R. E., K. M. Bocian, M. Beebe-Frankenberger, and D. L. Linklater. 2008. Responsiveness of students with language difficulties to early intervention in reading. *Journal of Special Education* 43(4):220-235.

O'Connor, R. E., K. M. Bocian, K. D. Beach, V. Sanchez, and L. J. Flynn. 2013. Special education in a 4-year response to intervention (RTI) environment: Characteristics of students with learning disability and grade of identification. *Learning Disabilities Research and Practice* 28(3):98-112.

Paskett, E. D., J. P. Harrop, and K. J. Wells. 2011. Patient navigation: An update on the state of the science. *CA: A Cancer Journal for Clinicians* 61(4):237-249.

Pianta, R. C., M. J. Cox, L. Taylor, and D. Early. 1999. Kindergarten teachers' practices related to the transition to school: Results of a national survey. *Elementary School Journal* 100(1):71-86.

Sadowski, M. 2006. *Core knowledge for PK-3 teaching: Ten components of effective instruction*. New York: Foundation for Child Development.

Sajaniemi, N., E. Suhonen, E. Kontu, P. Rantanen, H. Lindholm, S. Hyttinen, and A. Hirvonen. 2011. Children's cortisol patterns and the quality of the early learning environment. *European Early Childhood Education Research Journal* 19(1):45-62.

Schulting, A. B., P. S. Malone, and K. A. Dodge. 2005. The effect of school-based kindergarten transition policies and practices on child academic outcomes. *Developmental Psychology* 41(6):860-871.

Scott-Little, C., J. Lesko, J. Martella, and P. Milburn. 2007. Early learning standards: Results from a national survey to document trends in state-level policies and practices. *Early Childhood Research and Practice* 9(1).

Scott-Little, C., S. L. Kagan, V. S. Frelow, and J. Reid. 2008. *Inside the content of infant–toddler early learning guidelines: Results from analyses, issues to consider, and recommendations*. Greensboro, NC: University of North Carolina at Greensboro, Department of Human Development and Family Studies.

Scott-Little, C., S. L. Kagan, and V. S. Frelow. 2010. *ELG/ELDs resources: What are ELGs?* http://www.earlylearningguidelines-standards.org/content.php?s=what_are_elgs? (accessed September 24, 2014).

Shepard, L. A., S. L. Kagan, and E. Wurtz. 1998. *Principles and recommendations for early childhood assessments*. Washington, DC: National Education Goals Panel.

Smrekar, C. 1996. The influence of the family services coordinator on family–school interactions in school-linked social service programs. *Elementary School Journal* 96(4):453-467.

SRI (SRI International) and CAREI (Center for Applied Research and Educational Improvement). 2013. *The McKnight Foundation Education and Learning Program: PreK–third grade literacy and alignment formative evaluation findings*. https://www.mcknight.org/system/asset/document/454/ELEvalBriefs_10_14_13.pdf (accessed December 19, 2014).

Tout, K., T. Halle, S. Daily, L. Albertson-Junkans, and S. Moodie. 2013. *The research base for a birth through age eight state policy framework*. Washington, DC: Alliance for Early Success and Child Trends.

U.S. Department of Education. 2015. *IDEA 2004: Building the legacy, part C (birth-2 years old)*. http://idea.ed.gov/part-c/statutes (accessed February 18, 2015).

———. n.d. *Programs: Promise neighborhoods*. http://www2.ed.gov/programs/promise neighborhoods (accessed March 6, 2015).

U.S. White House. 2002. *Good start, grow smart: The Bush administration's early childhood initiative*. http://georgewbush-whitehouse.archives.gov/infocus/earlychildhood/early childhood.html (accessed November 5, 2014).

Washington State Office of Superintendent of Public Instruction. n.d. *Washington Kindergarten Inventory of Developing Skills (WaKIDS)*. http://www.k12.wa.us/wakids (accessed March 6, 2015).

Wat, A. 2013. *Aligning and implementing birth-3rd grade learning standards*. Philadelphia, PA: National Governors Association Policy Forum.

Watamura, S. E., B. Donzella, J. Alwin, and M. R. Gunnar. 2003. Morning-to-afternoon increases in cortisol concentrations for infants and toddlers at child care: Age differences and behavioral correlates. *Child Development* 74(4):1006-1020.

Worthen, B. R., and S. W. Zsiray. 1994. *What twenty years of educational studies reveal about year-round education*. Chapel Hill, NC: North Carolina Educational Policy Research Center.

Zaslow, M., and T. Halle. 2009. Purposeful early childhood assessment. Paper read at Child Care Policy Research Consortium, October 29, Washington, DC.

6

Educational Practices

This chapter provides an in-depth discussion of some of the key educational practices identified in Chapter 5 that, when applied with consistency and high quality over time for children as they age, can continuously support the development and early learning of children from birth through age 8. First is a discussion of cross-cutting principles for instructional practices and curricula, with an overview followed by examples of applications of instructional practices specific to working with infants and toddlers, language and literacy, mathematics, science, and socioemotional development. The sections that follow then cover other important educational practices, including using technology effectively, supporting the early learning of dual language learners, supporting children with and at risk for disabilities, working with families, and conducting child assessments.

CROSS-CUTTING PRINCIPLES FOR INSTRUCTIONAL PRACTICES

This section reviews some of the principles for instructional practices that are generally applicable provided that they are developed and applied in specific ways for different developmental domains and learning needs, including general learning competencies, socioemotional development, cognitive development, and specific subject-matter content (as illustrated in the specific sections that follow). These principles include managing the learning environment, teaching subject-matter content through learning trajectories, using tiered intervention approaches, using a mix of instructional methods, using interdisciplinary approaches to instruction, and ensuring follow-through and continuity. Through the application of these principles, effective educators can challenge and have high expectations for all students to make progress in development and early learning (Askew et al., 1997; Clarke et al., 2002; Clements and Sarama, 2007, 2008; Thomson et al., 2005).

The discussion of several of these principles includes some the context of available validated, research-based curricula and other materials that serve as an important means to support educators in their work, especially given the broad range of content areas and domains they are responsible for in educating young children. These tools help educators by presenting material in sequences aligned with learning trajectories, providing the teacher with instructional activities and questions to ask children, informing the teacher of common misconceptions that children may hold or mistakes commonly made and how to address them, and providing updated information as research becomes available.

Unfortunately, research-based curricula and tools are not equally available across age ranges and subjects. Educators working with infants and toddlers have fewer such resources than other educators, which hinders the quality of their practice and puts the burden entirely on the provider. They lack, for example, developmentally appropriate curricula to help them lay the specific foundations needed for later learning in core subject areas, compared to some tools that have been developed for language and mathematics in preschool and those for educators in the early elementary years, who have greater availability of curricular resources. In addition, some subject areas have had greater research and development invested in curricular tools than others.

Managing the Learning Environment

Managing the learning environment encompasses managing a number of important components of the context in which young children are educated (several of which are also discussed in more depth in subsequent sections of this chapter):

- the physical environment, indoors and outside, to create an environment that is comfortable, safe, and responsive to the needs of young children (e.g., room arrangement, furnishings, use of wall and floor space/lighting/color, storage, use of outdoor space) (LePage et al., 2005; Sutterby and Frost, 2006; Tanner, 2009);
- learning materials (e.g., equipment, toys, technology) (LePage et al., 2005);
- time and structure (e.g., daily schedule, routines, distribution of time to tasks, pacing, transitions) (LePage et al., 2005);

- the materials used in teaching and learning (e.g., forms, assignments, documentation, materials going home and coming in) (Knoche et al., 2012; Wien, 2011);
- instructional strategies (e.g., selecting the instructional strategies best suited to children's needs and the content to be learned, sequencing instruction, diversifying instructional strategies, organizing classroom activities around a validated, research-based curricula) (LePage et al., 2005; Simonsen et al., 2008);
- student behavior (e.g., supporting the development of positive relationships, promoting and teaching responsible behavior, establishing rules and expectations, preventing typical discipline problems, addressing problem behaviors constructively) (LePage et al., 2005; Simonsen et al., 2008);
- communication (e.g., adult–child, child–child, colleagues, classroom teams, families, across settings, across areas of responsibility, and across systems) (Knoche et al., 2012; LePage et al., 2005); and
- classroom climate (e.g., promoting a positive verbal environment, demonstrating respect for culture and diversity among children and families in the program and beyond, practicing democracy, promoting equity and social justice) (LePage et al., 2005).

Teaching Subject-Matter Content Through Learning Trajectories

Although children are ready and eager to learn, many early childhood educators are not prepared to engage children in rich subject-matter experiences that lay the groundwork for success later in school and in the workplace (Brenneman et al., 2009b; Clements and Sarama, 2009; NRC, 2001b, 2007; Sarama and Clements, 2009). In general, teachers historically have not been prepared to teach subject-specific knowledge to young children (Isenberg, 2000), although language and literacy has received more attention for young children relative to other subject-matter areas (Aydogan et al., 2005; Cervetti et al., 2006). Decisions about what subject-matter content is taught are made locally, and such subjects as mathematics and science usually are underemphasized for young children (Barnett et al., 2009).

To teach subject-matter content, educators need three categories of knowledge (Hill et al., 2008; Shulman, 1986; Wilson et al., 2014):

- *General pedagogical knowledge* is knowledge of general teaching strategies that apply to many different subjects.
- *Content knowledge* is knowledge of the subject matter itself, including common content knowledge, specialized content knowledge, and horizon knowledge.
- *Common content knowledge* is that which students are to learn.

- *Specialized content knowledge* includes concepts and skills used in teaching but not taught to students directly.
- *Horizon knowledge* is how the content is developed over years so that teaching and learning are coherent, and teachers are effective with exceptional students. Such knowledge includes how subjects differ. For example, mathematics knowledge relies heavily on logic, and scientific knowledge depends largely on observation and experimentation.
- *Pedagogical content knowledge* is knowing the subject matter for teaching. This involves knowledge of students, including how students understand and learn specific topics; common conceptions or misconceptions; what makes concepts and skills difficult or easy to learn, and what students typically find challenging or motivating. It also involves knowledge of teaching, including how to represent and present concepts from a particular subject such as science or math or reading (through good illustrations, analogies, examples, and explanation), the sequencing of content, and what teaching strategies affect the learning of certain topics.

Children learn in a developmental sequence. Well-designed curricula are therefore based on developmentally sequenced activities, and quality instructional practice requires educators who understand those sequences and can assess progress and remediate accordingly. Learning trajectories can help educators of young children understand and be responsive to children's developmental processes and constraints and their potential for thinking about and understanding content, and apply that understanding in creating more effective environments, instructional activities, and conversations. The learning trajectories construct organizes, connects, and operationalizes the above three types of knowledge—especially content knowledge and pedagogical content knowledge—for teaching specific subject-matter content. It also adds an essential component of knowledge gained from psychological and educational research on how children think and learn about the content. Understanding and applying developmental sequences of learning and teaching requires that educators understand the components of distinct learning trajectories in each subject-matter area. Those components include

- the goal and subject-matter content (understanding the subject itself);
- the developmental progression of children's thinking and understanding as they learn particular content (the levels of thinking through which children develop as they gain competence and the patterns of thinking they display at each level), including the acqui-

sition of new facts and skills and the development of different ways of thinking about the content that are increasingly sophisticated, abstract, and complex; and

- the instructional tasks and strategies that promote learning at each level and how to sequence and individualize those learning activities (knowledge of how to cultivate both content knowledge and learning competencies as part of everyday instructional practices).

Learning trajectories also should be linked to the use of formative assessment—the ongoing monitoring of children's learning to guide and inform instruction (see the section on conducting child assessments later in this chapter).

Conclusion About Learning Trajectories

Learning of subject-matter content for children from birth through age 8 is best promoted through the use of learning trajectories that are specific to subject areas and developed through research as the core of learning standards, instruction, and curricula. To foster comprehensive, high-quality early learning, educators need to understand and employ all three components of learning trajectories: the subject-matter content itself, the developmental progression of how children's thinking and understanding grows as they learn particular content, and the instructional tasks and strategies that promote learning along that progression.

Teaching Subject-Matter Content: Implications for Professional Learning

Professional learning needs to include all three categories of knowledge for teaching subject-matter content: content knowledge, general pedagogical knowledge, and pedagogical content knowledge. Current educational opportunities need to be expanded to help educators develop such knowledge in language and literacy, mathematics, and other core subjects. At the same time, professional learning needs to support professionals in their practice across all domains of development and learning, which will also contribute to children's progress in subject-matter learning.

Using Tiered Intervention Approaches

Tiered intervention approaches, also called response-to-intervention models, have been used to stimulate the learning of children in the areas of reading, mathematics, and socioemotional development. These approaches make use of ongoing formative assessment to determine which children have mastered specific skills or knowledge and which might benefit from additional, more intensive instruction and learning opportunities. These additional learning opportunities, called Tier 2 interventions, are differentiated by being offered in smaller groups with more scaffolded instruction. Often children respond quickly to Tier 2 interventions (e.g., see Fuchs and Fuchs, 2006; Horner, 1990; Lewis et al., 2010; O'Connor et al., 2013; Sugai and Horner, 2009)—some to the extent that they catch up to their peers and begin to learn better in typical preschool and K-3 classroom instruction and experiences.

Conclusion About the Use of Tiered Intervention Approaches

Tiered intervention approaches, in which educators identify which children have learned particular content or skills and which children might benefit from additional instruction and support, are important for early prevention and intervention. Educators need to be able to implement these approaches so that they are continuous, flexible, dynamic, and focused on the range of critical skills and proficiencies children need to develop.

Using a Mix of Instructional Methods

Many seemingly dichotomous approaches to instruction actually serve children best when used in combination. Some of these "dichotomies" include "direct" versus "inquiry" instruction, play-based versus academic instruction, development of content knowledge versus socioemotional learning, and mainstreaming versus special instruction. Even the structure of examining instructional strategies in a dichotomous frame may restrict what can be learned about when, how, and how much to use each. For example, for teaching mathematics a recent review found that different methods are effective for different learning goals, and most dichotomies describing ways of teaching mathematics were not helpful (Hiebert and Grouws, 2007). Similarly, students benefit from a mix of code-based and meaning-based approaches to learning to read compared to instruction that focuses on only one approach (Connor et al., 2009; Graves et al., 2006).

Thus, effective approaches combine multiple complementary instructional strategies, ranging from initial children-centered exploration and invention, to guided lessons on optimal strategies and generalization, to practice for fluency (Clements and Sarama, 2009; Murata and Fuson, 2006; NCTM, 2006; NMP, 2008). The following are examples of such approaches to instruction that are often treated as dichotomous but may in fact be most effective in combination.

Student Centered Versus Educator Directed

One of the 10 pedagogical issues investigated by the National Mathematics Advisory Panel (NMP, 2008) was whether instruction should be student centered or educator directed. Given the tendency of some to promote one approach over the other, the panel's conclusion was important: "all-encompassing recommendations that instruction should be entirely 'student centered' or 'teacher directed' are not supported by research" (NMP, 2008, p. xxii). This same dichotomy has been investigated with respect to instructional practices for reading (Connor et al., 2009).

Another dimension of this discussion is the use of peer-assisted learning. Research has found that cooperative learning strategies lead to more positive academic and social outcomes than competitive or individualistic strategies (see reviews in Johnson and Johnson, 2009; Nastasi and Clements, 1991). For elementary students, for example, such cooperative learning strategies might include constructive group discussions with different views presented, group engagement, solicitation and provision of explanations, and shared leadership (Wilkinson et al., 1994).

Conceptual Versus Practice Based

Substantial practice is required for learning certain knowledge and skills, but this requirement is not incompatible with the establishment of conceptual foundations. The term *repeated experiencing* describes activities that support practice as well as generalization and transfer (Baroody, 1999; Clements and Sarama, 2012; Sarama and Clements, 2009). Also, distributed, spaced practice has been found to be more effective than massed practice (all in one session, repetition of the same item over and over) (Cepeda et al., 2006), although in some cases students learn and retain information longer when they first experience frequent, repetitive practice followed by distributed practice. As an example, in the Swanson and colleagues (1999) meta-analysis of effective interventions for students with learning disabilities (including studies from preschool through grade 3 as well as with older students), focus on practice to achieve mastery of a skill or concept (massed practice) accompanied by distributed practice and review were more effective in promoting reading and mathematics ability than interventions without these components. Distributed practice can be achieved by providing occasional opportunities to use the learned skill after students have demonstrated competence in that skill, or by incorporating newly learned skills into more complex activities that require independent use of the skill, which encourages conceptual knowledge. Because the goal is for the knowledge to be available quickly throughout the student's life, the optimal approach entails short, frequent practice sessions of facts and skills whose conceptual foundations have been well learned and understood.

Findings from a number of studies have found that memorization without understanding does not facilitate student learning. One 2008 study of textbooks that emphasized memorization of math facts found that only 7 percent of students demonstrated adequate progress over the course of 1 year (Henry and Brown, 2008). Another teaching method that showed negative effects was the use of timed tests, which can increase children's math anxiety (Beilock, 2001; Boaler, 2014; Ramirez et al., 2013). Approaches that use thinking strategies are more successful. For instance, in an addition problem students might solve 8 + 7 by thinking, "I need 2 more to make a 10 out of 8. That leaves 5 out of the 7, and 10 and 5 is 15," thus using a strategy to "make 10" of breaking apart numbers (Clements and Sarama, 2012).

Order of Skills Versus Understanding

A related false dichotomy is what should be taught first: skills or conceptual understanding. A better approach appears to be the simultaneous development of conceptual understanding and procedural skill, with the flexible application of multiple strategies (Blote et al., 2001; Clements and Sarama, 2012; Fuson and Briars, 1990).

For young children, shared writing activities in which adults help children to add to a grocery list or generate a thank you note (O'Connor et al., 1996) or write a sentence about a character in a storybook (Aram and Biron, 2004) embody purposes for reading and writing, as well as develop the phonological skills and letter knowledge children will need to read words. Moreover, combining the tasks of identifying a word's first sound and selecting a letter that makes that sound (e.g., "We want bananas; what sound starts 'bananas'? What shall we write?") demonstrates the alphabetic principle (i.e., that any word we say can be broken into sounds, which are represented by letters of the alphabet) in both conceptual and personally meaningful ways. Similarly, educators can emphasize elements of story structures that support reading comprehension (Cain and Oakhill, 1996) alongside phonemic awareness and letter knowledge.

As another example, a 2001 study compared two methods for teaching first-grade math: one focused on ensuring that students mastered step-by-step procedures for solving a math problem, while the other emphasized conceptual understanding and flexible application of multiple strategies and procedures. The students in the flexible group scored higher and showed superior conceptual understanding and were better at recognizing how different concepts were interrelated (Blote et al., 2001). Other research has shown that mechanical instruction is inferior to good conceptual and procedural instruction in helping students achieve mathematical goals (Hiebert and Grouws, 2007). Thus, educators should teach students to help them build skills *and* ideas, using skills adaptively. Effective instruction poses problems and makes connections, leading to solutions that make those connections visible; how active a role the educator takes can vary. Students then have fluent and adaptive expertise rather than mere efficiency (Baroody, 2003). In addition, acquiring skills before developing understanding can lead to learning difficulties (Baroody, 2004a,b; Fuson, 2004; NRC, 2001a; Sophian, 2004; Steffe, 2004).

Research suggests that effective instruction for imparting skills, or promoting instrumental learning, is rapid paced, uses teacher modeling and many teacher-directed product-oriented questions, and smoothly transitions from demonstrations to substantial amounts of error-free practice. Teachers organize, present, and pace information to meet well-defined goals (Hiebert and Grouws, 2007; Kame'enui et al., 2013).

For the purpose of developing conceptual or relational understanding, effective instruction entails attending explicitly to concepts, which means discussing the connections among facts, procedures, concepts, and processes. Several studies have found that this leads to high levels of student achievement, particularly when teaching methods were student centered (Clements and Sarama, 2012; Fuson and Briars, 1990; Hiebert and Wearne, 1993). It is also important that educators allow students to struggle with important concepts or problems (Hiebert and Grouws, 2007) as the process of making connections and working to make sense of a subject can help students achieve conceptual understanding (Clements and Sarama, 2012). This kind of understanding, and teaching to impart it, appears to be as effective in supporting skill development as teaching to impart skills only (Clements and Sarama, 2012; Hiebert and Grouws, 2007).

In summary, concepts and skills develop together and support each other (Carpenter et al., 1998; Fuson and Briars, 1990; Fuson et al., 1997b; Resnick, 1992; Verschaffel et al., 2007). Indeed, instruction and curricula that emphasize conceptual understanding simultaneously with procedural skills and flexible application of multiple strategies lead not only to equivalent skills but also to more fluent, flexible use of those skills, as well as to superior conceptual understanding, compared with approaches that initially emphasize mastery of procedures (Fuson and Kwon, 1992; NMP, 2008). Effective instruction and curricula build on students' thinking, provide opportunities for both invention and practice, and ask students to explain their various strategies (Hiebert, 1999), thereby facilitating higher-order thinking and conceptual growth without sacrificing the learning of skills.

Conclusion About Using a Mix of Instructional Methods

Debates about instruction that treat different approaches as dichotomous or in opposition can dominate discourse about policy and practice when the most effective strategy may be a mix or balance of these approaches, with dichotomies being set aside in favor of more cohesive and coherent practices.

As part of selecting and applying an appropriate mix of established instructional methods, other instructional practices that promote learning of subject-matter content include taking into account such factors as motivation, self-concept, confidence, and engagement; providing opportunities for both creative invention and practice; helping students see connections among various types of knowledge and topics to build well-structured, coherent knowledge; and placing learning in context by using problems that have meaning for students and expecting that students will invent, explain, and critique their own strategies within a social context. Effective educators also consistently integrate real world situations, problem solving, and content into instruction and curricula (Fuson, 2004). For example, making connections to real-life situations enhances students' attitudes about and knowledge of mathematics (Perlmutter et al., 1997), just as explaining words in child-friendly contexts increases children's motivation to learn and their attention to new words they encounter in their environment (Beck and McKeown, 2007).

Using Interdisciplinary Approaches to Instruction

Many argue that curricula should be integrated or combined across domains and subjects because (1) real-world topics and phenomena are inherently interdisciplinary, (2) children's worlds typically are not divided neatly into disciplines, and (3) disciplines can work synergistically. As an example of the latter point, research has shown that exposure to science- and math-oriented curricula helps develop vocabulary and other language and literacy competencies, such as understanding of increasing grammatical complexity, willingness to reproduce narratives independently, and inferential reasoning (French, 2004; Peterson and French, 2008; Raudenbush, 2009; Romance and Vitale, 2001; Sarama et al., 2012). Also, children who engaged in mathematics-related storybook reading, discussed these books, and played with related mathematics materials had a better disposition toward and learning of mathematics than a control group (Hong, 1996; van den Heuvel-Panhuizen and Elia, 2012).

However, little research has explored the question of whether and how multiple subjects can be combined in ways that address time competition in the classroom and do not reduce necessary specificity. For example, those teaching the youngest children argue that they do not have time to include math and science because of other requirements, especially supporting literacy (Greenfield et al., 2009; Sarama and Clements, 2009).

Moreover, reviews of fully integrated curricula (e.g., activities that involve all subject areas) reveal little evidence that they are superior to traditional content-specific curricula and suggest that there are challenges in implementing such curricula (Czerniak et al., 1999). Often these curricula entail thematic units of instruction that connect only surface features (Barton and Smith, 2000). Further, evidence suggests that different areas of knowledge are organized into distinct mental structures rather than into domain-general structures (Gelman and Brenneman, 2004; NRC, 2001b; NRC and IOM, 2000; Sarama and Clements, 2009), which suggests that there may be value to maintaining some subject-specific distinctions in approaches to learning and instruction.

For these reasons, it may be preferable to take an *interdisciplinary* approach to, for example, language and literacy, mathematics, science, and socioemotional competencies, in which rich connections are made among them, but they retain their core conceptual, procedural, and epistemological structures (Gelman and Brenneman, 2004; Mantzicopoulos et al., 2009; Sarama and Clements, 2009). For example, expose children to prerequisite math skills in an appropriate sequence, and design science inquiry (Furtak et al., 2012) to promote a deep understanding of conceptual content and science skills (with language and literacy and socioemotional competencies always at play). Then, when connections are drawn between math and science, they will be genuine and detailed, with their impact undiluted by less productive attempts at integration.

Conclusion About Interdisciplinary Instructional Approaches

Teaching and learning need to be connected across developmental domains and subject areas. Such connections across standards, curricula, and teaching are best made through approaches that are not just "integrated" (which often means making connections that are superficial and do not serve learning goals) but "interdisciplinary"—making rich connections among domains and subject areas, but allowing each to retain its core conceptual, procedural, and epistemological structures.

Interdisciplinary Instructional Approaches: Implications for Professional Learning

Methods courses for educators that emphasize how to connect subjects and domains, such as mathematics, language and literacy, and socioemotional development, could foster early childhood teachers' confidence and attention across developmental domains. However, this approach needs to be adopted without a reduction in disciplinary focus that shortchanges attention to each of the individual domains and subjects.

Ensuring Follow-Through and Continuity

Given how young children develop, it is unrealistic to expect the effects of early interventions to last indefinitely, without continual, progressive support in later schooling of children's nascent learning trajectories (Brooks-Gunn, 2003; O'Connor et al., 2013, 2014). This is especially unrealistic if goals and approaches are not aligned between early childhood and elementary settings or children end up following high-quality early childhood experiences with attendance at poor-quality schools (Brooks-Gunn, 2003; Currie and Thomas, 2000). Early positive effects may be weakened by, for example, later settings that assume low levels of knowledge, focus on lower-level skills, and have low expectations for certain groups (Carpenter and Moser, 1984; Engel et al., 2013; van den Heuvel-Panhuizen, 1996). Similarly, the effects of even high-quality instruction in elementary school can be hampered by children's lack of prior exposure to foundational, high-quality learning experiences. Indeed, there is a cumulative positive effect of students experiencing consecutive years of high-quality teaching and a cumulative negative effect of low-quality teaching (Ballou et al., 2004; Jordan et al., 1997; Sanders and Horn, 1998; Sanders and Rivers, 1996; Wright et al., 1997). Unfortunately, the latter is more probable for high-risk children (Akiba et al., 2007; Darling-Hammond, 2006).

The research on sustaining developmental progress is documented most thoroughly for the preschool and kindergarten years. However, the issues, challenges, and implications apply to all ages, birth through 8 years and beyond. Systems-level approaches to supporting greater continuity and consistency in high-quality learning experiences are discussed in Chapter 5.

Cross-Cutting Conclusions About Instructional Practices

Across the birth through age 8 continuum, children benefit when educators assume both (1) a developmental orientation that engages with the child as an integrated whole, involves a cumulative progression of learning over time, and employs flexible developmental expectations, and (2) an educational orientation that fosters the development of cognitive skills and subject-matter–specific knowledge and skills through guided activity. Early childhood settings typically are viewed as emphasizing a developmental orientation, while early elementary settings typically are viewed as emphasizing an educational orientation. The science of child development and early learning supports professional practice and policies that incorporate both orientations continuously across care and education settings for children.

Proficient learning in each domain of development and early learning is facilitated when standards, curricula, assessments, and teaching practices are coherent, aligned with each other and across ages and grade levels, based on rigorous research and evaluation, and implemented with fidelity.

GENERAL EDUCATIONAL PRACTICES FOR WORKING WITH INFANTS AND TODDLERS

There are some special considerations worth emphasizing for working with infants and toddlers in childcare settings to aid in promoting their optimal development and early learning. Many of these are on a continuum with the principles that apply across age groups, but are manifest in particular ways for professionals working with the youngest children.

Small Groups: Caring for infants and toddlers in small groups is essential, as it reduces noise, distractions, and confusion, and can promote high levels of intimacy between infant and educator. Maximum group sizes and adult–child ratio vary with age.[1] In small and intimate group settings, educators are able to identify and work toward the needs and developmental progress of individual infants. Educators can accommodate to individual eating and sleeping schedules for infants and toddlers, as well as establish potty-training routines when needed. These small settings also make it possible to recognize and meet the needs of children with special needs (Lally et al., n.d.).

Primary Caregiving Assignments and Continuity of Care: In order to build quality and intimate relationships, each child should be assigned to a primary educator who is responsible for establishing a relationship with the child and ensuring their comfort in the childcare setting. The secure attachments that young children develop with educators (discussed in Chapter 4) enable young children to approach learning opportunities more positively and confidently. Emotional support of this kind is important for develop-

---

[1] For group size and caregiver–child ratio, see Lally et al. (n.d).

ment and is a positive accompaniment to the task of learning, and it is also an essential prerequisite to the cognitive and attentional engagement necessary for young children to benefit from learning opportunities.

Continuity of care is also important, yet often lacking, in programs. This can have negative effects on the educator–child relationship. Young children must build relationships and establish trust with their educators, and movement from one to another can create a sense of loss and confusion. Some centers offer a "practicing toddler" group, which dedicates a time for infants to visit their future educators in order to begin establishing trust and building relationships. This process takes place over time and is adjusted to the individual needs of each infant.

Instructional Practices: As discussed in Chapter 4, the cognitive abilities of very young children are easily underestimated. Infants and toddlers are taking significant strides in both their implicit (nonconscious) and explicit knowledge of language, the functioning of objects, and the characteristics of people and animals in the world around them. Early learning occurs rapidly, even when it is sometimes difficult for educators to observe.

Educators can support the growth of these cognitive abilities through their instructional practices in the learning environment. Using an abundance of child-directed language during social interaction, playing sorting and counting games (e.g., while stacking blocks), putting into words what a classroom pet can do or why somebody looks sad, exploring together what happens when objects collide, engaging in imitative play—these and other shared activities build on understandings that young children are implicitly developing related to language; number; object characteristics; and implicit theories of animate and inanimate objects, physical causality, and people's minds. The purpose is to provide young children with cognitive stimulation and to embed that stimulation in social interaction that provokes young children's interest, elicits their curiosity, and provides an emotional context that enables learning.

The central feature of these shared activities is that, rather than being entirely directed by the educator, instruction emerges from the interaction of the educator with the young child and their context. This interaction builds on the child's interests and understanding and the educator's efforts to stimulate early learning by responding to those interests and stimulating them through the learning opportunities afforded by the classroom or other learning context. Instruction thus derives from the educator's observations and immediate efforts to notice young children's interests and questions, extend them, and contribute to further discoveries. The underlying structure relies on the educator's knowledge of the developmental progress for which children of this age are ready, the interests of the particular child, and the effort to create a classroom or other context that has materials to which children can respond (e.g., blocks, storybooks, imaginative play materials). This approach to instruction builds on the cognitive characteristics of young children, particularly the motivation for learning that derives from immediate cognitive engagement, the limitations in cognitive and attentional self-regulation for which adult support can be beneficial, and the importance of the child's affective as well as cognitive response to new learning. This approach to early education has been described in what is known as *emergent curriculum* (Jones and Nimmo, 1994; Stacey, 2009), and other curricular approaches follow similar principles.

It is important to note that such an approach does not mean educators assume a background role. Rather, educators assume an active role both in their structuring of the environment to provide age-appropriate cognitive challenges and in their immediate interaction with the child to stimulate new discovery. In many respects, this approach might be considered a "purposeful play-based" curriculum. It is well suited to very young children who are not yet deliberate, self-regulated learners but whose minds are growing very rapidly based, in part, on the kinds of learning opportunities available to them. This approach advances the standard for quality practice beyond what has often been treated as a dichotomous choice between entirely educator-directed instruction and entirely "play-based" instruction.

Environment, Safety, and Health: The physical environment can affect the educator–child relationship. An inviting and safe environment for infants and toddlers enhances interactions and encourages exploration. Additionally, peer relationships among infants and toddlers can develop through room arrangements and play materials. The environment can also offer parents a space to visit and encourage play, breastfeeding, and the parent–child bond. The environment is also important in ensuring the health and safety of all children in early care and education settings. These settings also offer opportunities to incorporate health and safety education and life skills into everyday activities and for staff to model good health habits (AAP et al., 2011).

Cultural and Familial Continuity: It is important that educators in childcare settings understand the cultural values of the children they serve, which can also facilitate strong relationships with families and help create continuity for children across home and care and education settings. For this reason, it is essential that educators reflect on and explore their own cultural backgrounds in order to understand and be sensitive to culture.

LANGUAGE AND LITERACY

The active ingredient of supporting language development in care and education settings relates to educators' use of high-quality language interactions (such as extending what a child says and using varied and complex language) and social scaffolding of language and literacy skills, a form of instructional guidance by which educators progressively provide less ongoing support as development proceeds to enable students to exercise independent skill (Duke and Block, 2012; Turnbull et al., 2009). Age-appropriate language proficiency can be achieved through systematic instruction in vocabulary, listening comprehension, syntactic skills, and awareness of the components of language (August and Shanahan, 2006; Aukrust, 2007; Bowers and Vasilyeva, 2011; Francis et al., 2006).

As discussed in detail in Chapter 4, there is a reciprocal relationship between vocabulary development (a complex and integrative feature of language that grows continuously) and reading words (a skill that most children master by third or fourth grade), and together these skills support reading comprehension (Ehri, 2005; Gough et al., 1996). In developing language and literacy skills, children benefit from extensive opportunities to listen to and use complex spoken language (National Early Literacy Panel, 2008). A stronger speaking and listening vocabulary provides a deeper and wider field of words with which students can attempt to match a printed with a spoken word and check that the word they select makes sense in a given context. When a child's home language is not the predominant language of the school, parents and preschool educators can be particularly useful in improving depth of vocabulary (Aukrust, 2007; Roberts, 2008).

For children with reading disabilities, longitudinal studies have found that 70 percent of poor readers had a history of language difficulties (Catts et al., 1999), including syntax (rules for combining and ordering words in phrases) (Scarborough, 1991) and morphology (meaningful parts of words and word tenses) (Elbro, 1990). Importantly, understanding and use of syntax and morphology can be taught to young children in preschool through the primary grades. Teaching children to use morphemes in reading and spelling facilitates vocabulary and reading comprehension (Carlo et al., 2004). Reviews of instructional studies beginning as early as kindergarten have found consistent positive effects for teaching children to identify and use morphemes in words (Bowers et al., 2010; Reed, 2008).

Researchers who have developed tiered intervention approaches for children whose reading trajectory suggests risk for reading disabilities and delays have in the last few years incorporated vocabulary and listening comprehension activities along with early reading skills (Case et al., 2014; O'Connor et al., 2013, 2014; Otaiba et al., 2014). Combining these skills in an intervention provides the language stimulation needed by students with poorly developed vocabulary (O'Connor et al., 2010). It also may address the troubling issue of late-emerging learning disabilities (Catts et al., 2012; Kieffer, 2014), whereby reading difficulties emerge in second and third grade and later, primarily in the area of comprehension, despite adequate development of word-level skills. These issues mirror those of children who learn number "facts" on time but continue to struggle with mathematics concepts and problem solving.

High-Quality Practice in Care and Education
Settings Serving Infants and Toddlers

From birth, infants are taking in information from the language environment and using their own voice to communicate their needs and feelings. As they grow into toddlers (~15-33-month-old), children's language acquisition quickly becomes apparent—they are picking up approximately two new word meanings each day, expanding and deepening what they can communicate and understand (Bloom, 2000). But, as discussed in Chapter 4, this language development rests on positive and nurturing language-based interactions with the adults who care for them. Educators serving infants and toddlers can use several key strategies to foster strong early language environments, thereby supporting young children's language development:

- **Use language-based interactions to develop trusting bonds.** Consistently responding to infants' and toddlers' communication with talk and encouragement that is emotionally attuned is crucial for early language development. At this stage of development, it is particularly important that these language interactions be responsive to children's emotional expressions (e.g., laughter, crying) and expressions of need. These relationship-building language practices set in motion reciprocal interactions in which children then respond in turn, with increased attempts at communication.
- **Use talk for learning.** Ongoing exposure to elaborate language, as well as simple requests and questions that draw out children's first words and phrases, all support language development. Therefore, educators of infants and toddlers create high-quality language environments when they intentionally and thoughtfully use their own talk—through explanations, questioning, and descriptions—to build up the knowledge of those in their care. This instructional use of talk includes "narrating" events of the day (e.g., "We're crossing the road to get to the park.") and describing children's actions as they are performing them (e.g., "You're putting your hand in the warm mitten."). In addition, using talk for learning involves extending children's language, repeating their language, and then supplying additional words and more complex sentence structures (e.g., saying, "You want me to pick you up?," when a child says, "up!"). Using talk for learning is most effective when early educators engage in discussions of the here and now that brings young children beyond their immediate surroundings and experiences

(i.e., decontextualized talk). For example, an educator might begin with the here and now (e.g., a child's expression of interest in an object), expand from there (e.g., talking about what one can do with that object, what it feels like, or what it looks like), and then engage in talk that is even more decontextualized (e.g., make a plan for using the object later in the day, remember a prior experience with the object, or discuss other objects and how they are similar or different) (Copple et al., 1984). In this example, the educator is responding to children's interests and real-time experiences, situating language learning in meaningful contexts.

- **Engage in language-rich play.** Play is a means of learning in early childhood, and language learning can be woven throughout the play of young children. Educators can and should use songs and gestures, flannel board stories, puppets, or other materials that prompt the use of talk by children and adults alike. Importantly, at this stage, language-rich play not only includes adult–child interactions and experiences, but beginning as early as toddlerhood, this play for learning can and should take place among groups of children. In this case, the guidance and facilitation of the educator is a key element in making these language-rich experiences. When facilitating play among groups of toddlers, educators should intentionally scaffold the language experience; for example, ask questions, narrate events, model using language to collaborate, and use strategies to encourage peer interactions.

- **Read a variety of books and reread favorites.** Children become "readers" long before they begin to read. Infants and toddlers enjoy listening to, and engaging with, a variety of books: board books with faces, animals, and objects that can be talked about; predictable books that quickly become familiar favorites; and books that include new information and ideas that begin to open up young children's worlds and extend their vocabulary and knowledge. Educators should make shared book reading part of the daily routine, thereby building children's language as well as their interest in print. This is another chance to be emotionally attuned and strengthen bonds with young children.

As described in Chapter 4, interactive book reading between children and their caregivers is one of the best-documented methods for improving the vocabularies of children. Conversations as stories are read improve children's vocabulary (Hindman et al., 2008; Weizman and Snow, 2001), especially when children are encouraged to build on the possibilities of storybooks by following their interests (Whitehurst et al., 1988; Zucker et al., 2013). A book serves as a stimulus for conversation outside the immediate context—the "decontextualized" language described above—and introduces new or less familiar words. As books are read repeatedly, children become familiar with the vocabulary and their conversations can be elaborated. Routines also help children with developmental delays acquire language and use it more intelligibly (van Kleek, 2004).

As digital materials become increasingly available, educators may need to learn how to foster language development through media beyond books (see the discussion of using technology effectively later in this chapter). By drawing attention to items or illustrations on a tablet, smartphone screen, or electronic whiteboard, educators can adapt the skills of interactive reading to ensure that digital media become a platform for decontextualized language and other forms of language development (Strouse et al., 2013). However, a few studies of e-books also have shown that the bells and whistles of the devices can interfere with this interactive process if the readers and the e-book designers are not intentional about the use of e-books to develop content knowledge and language skills (Parish-Morris et al., 2013).

High-Quality Practice in Care and Education Settings Serving Children in Preschool and Early Elementary School

Language and literacy development is a major focus of instruction in prekindergarten and K-3 classrooms. Primary grade educators are strong in certain aspects of effective instruction, such as word-reading skills, but there are also important shortcomings in instructional practices related to language and literacy. In particular, vocabulary, reading comprehension, and conceptual and content knowledge are not emphasized, particularly in the use of informational texts that would enhance early reading skills. Instructional practices in these areas can be intentionally embedded in children's social experiences with educators and peers in the classroom that involve children interacting with partners throughout reading activity, and educators explaining and discussing vocabulary terms and encouraging children to make personal connections with the concepts in text. As noted above, language and literacy skills also benefit from social scaffolding (Duke and Block, 2012).

Research has shown that in high-quality classroom language environments, educators use a variety of abstract words and complex sentences; whether they are providing directions, reviewing information, or posing questions, sophisticated talk permeates classroom instruction and conversation. It is also known that high-quality classroom language environments are interactive spaces where children are part of content-based discussions and purposeful play and above all, have the chance to talk (and talk and talk). The following are three strategies for augmenting the quality of classroom language environments:

- **Organize classroom learning around content-based and multifaceted units of study.** Learning through extensive study of a topic is a hallmark of effective language and literacy instruction in the preschool and early elementary school years. For example, thematic units organized around content-based and multifaceted topics elicit the use of complex vocabulary by teachers and are one approach for fostering this complex language knowledge among children. Each unit should not only revolve around content-rich themes, but also a complementary, small set of target vocabulary words (Neuman et al., 2011). These vocabulary words should be academic in nature (i.e., words that are used much more frequently in the academic content areas than in day-to-day conversation); drawn from texts read during the unit; relevant to the content-based theme, lending themselves to talking and writing throughout the unit; and conceptually abstract—therefore requiring "study" and extended discussion to promote an understanding of the abstract concepts and ideas they represent.

- **Vary instructional groupings such that students have regular, frequent opportunities for extended conversations with their peers and teachers.** Different instructional groupings (i.e., whole group, small group, and pairs) lend themselves to different kinds of language experiences, all of which combine to make for a high-quality classroom language environment. In particular, pairs and small groups often are optimal formats for providing students with the opportunity to participate in strong language experiences. When designing instruction that involves small-group or paired conversations, it is particularly important to (1) plan groupings that strategically support language development (e.g., in heterogeneous groupings, children with stronger language skills around a particular topic can provide a language model for peers with more limited language skills); and (2) integrate strategies for scaffolding peer interactions (e.g., assigning roles, providing language frames, and/or posting visuals that display steps). In all cases, it is important to offer students topics to discuss and/or protocols for conversation. For example, students might participate in literacy-enriched learning centers where they collaboratively investigate and discuss books or artifacts related to the unit's topic. It also is important for students to have regular, frequent opportunities to participate in educator-facilitated small-group discussions. This format lends itself to back-and-forth conversations in which the educator builds on and extends students' language and ideas—a hallmark of a high-quality classroom language environment. The ways in which extended conversations support children's learning is a reminder that the whole day is filled with moments ripe for planned and spontaneous teaching and learning moments. In this sense, every activity is a learning activity because back-and-forth conversations can be incorporated into many aspects of the daily schedule—even during routines such as hand-washing, lining up, and gathering belongings. For example, educators might provide daily questions for students to contemplate as they engage in a transition, lining up to go down the hall for example, and then have students share their responses with a partner when they reach their destination. In addition, "table tents" featuring pictures and/or questions can be placed on the snack or lunch table, providing educators and children with topics for conversation.

- **Use read-alouds as a platform for conversation.** Interactive readings of diverse texts related to the content under study increases the quality of the language environment in at least two ways. First, the language of text, in and of itself, often stands in contrast to conversational, and even instructional, language. It is important to introduce young children to this language of text from their earliest years by listening to and discussing books. Second, classroom read-alouds are foundational for spurring content-rich classroom discussions. The content of high-quality children's literature and informational texts lends itself to discussion of topics rooted in the sciences, social studies, and the arts, all of which spur the use of academic and sophisticated words.

Silverman (2007) compared means of improving the oral language of kindergarten students through storybook read-alouds, and found that teachers who engaged their students in conversations that used new words in contexts outside the storybook generated greater vocabulary gains for both dual language learners and native English speakers. Other preschool and kindergarten studies have similarly shown that the interactive storybook routines and features of educators' talk that support children's use of language during book discussions support vocabulary growth of dual language learners and other children with poorly developed vocabulary in English (Coyne et al., 2007; Loftus et al., 2010; Silverman, 2007). Children who begin school with poorly developed vocabulary can make large language gains when instruction includes interactive book reading and discussion (Beck and McKeown, 2001; Coyne et al., 2012; O'Connor, 2000; O'Connor et al., 1996).

Teaching Language and Literacy:
Implications for Professional Learning

- *Programs that prepare care and education professionals to work with young children should help them understand that children's vocabulary and comprehension improve when they have extended opportunities to discuss stories, use the language of books, and relate new and unusual words to familiar situations. Reading and discussing stories and other texts with children in small groups is consistently more effective than similar approaches in large classes because students in small groups have more opportunities to use words in conversation. These routines can be demonstrated and rehearsed through professional learning.*
- *The notion of scaffolding children's attempts to converse and to answer questions also deserves attention in professional learning. When children have difficulty responding to conversation attempts, educators can expand on children's responses, ask easier questions to facilitate children's use of language, and gradually use more complex questions as children demonstrate understanding of words and their use in speech. Children in scaffolded conditions (e.g., given easier to more difficult prompts and questions depending on their knowledge of words) make greater gains during language interventions regardless of initial vocabulary knowledge.*
- *Educators need to be trained to impart more than simple literacy skills, especially listening and reading comprehension, vocabulary, and conceptual and subject-matter content knowledge (e.g., using informational texts).*

MATHEMATICS

Although learning standards exist and curricular attention to mathematics has increased, this subject is not generally taught well to young children nor is it emphasized in professional learning through educator preparation or in-service programs. Preschool educators tend not to support mathematics learning, and when they do it is often of low quality (Brenneman et al., 2009b; Brown, 2005; Early et al., 2005, 2007; Graham et al., 1997; Rudd et al., 2008; Tudge and Doucet, 2004; Winton et al., 2005). Moreover, achievement gaps in mathematics have origins in the earliest years—for example, low-income children have less extensive math knowledge than middle-income children in preschool, having typically received less support for mathematics learning in their home or childcare environments (Blevins-Knabe and Musun-Miller, 1996; Brenneman et al., 2009a; Griffin et al., 1995; Holloway et al., 1995; Jordan et al., 1992; Saxe et al., 1987; Starkey et al., 1999). The lack of math in the education of young children means that gaps in the foundation for later academic success, especially among underserved populations, are unlikely to improve.

The lack of mathematics learning is illustrated by a study in working- and middle-class preschools, in which 60 percent of 3-year-olds had no mathematical experience of any kind across 180 observations (Tudge and Doucet, 2004). Another study documented dramatic variations in the amount of mathematics-related talk educators provided, which was significantly related to the growth of children's mathematical knowledge over the school year (Klibanoff et al., 2006). Unfortunately, little time is dedicated to mathematics talk in most prekindergarten classrooms. Even when such conversation occurs, it rarely lasts longer than a minute and it is focused on basic concepts such as numeral identification or names of shapes; few or no higher-level mathematical concepts are discussed (Rudd et al., 2008). Preschool educators often believe that when they provide puzzles, blocks, and songs they are "doing mathematics." Even when they teach mathematics, often that content is not the main focus, but is instead "embedded" in a reading or fine-motor activity (Clements and Sarama, 2009; NRC, 2009). Unfortunately, evidence suggests such an approach is ineffective; instead, intentional teaching of mathematics is effective and complements incidental approaches (NRC, 2009).

Even when preschool settings adopt the most commonly used, ostensibly "complete," prekindergarten curricula this often engenders no increase in mathematics instruction (Aydogan et al., 2005; Preschool Curriculum Evaluation Research Consortium, 2008). Not surprisingly, evaluations show little or no learning of mathematics in these preschools (Clements and Sarama, 2007; HHS, 2005). For example, observations of the Opening the World of Learning preschool curriculum, which includes mathematics, revealed that only 58 seconds out of a 360-minute school day was devoted to mathematics. Most children made no gains in math skills over the school year, while some lost mathematics competence (Farran et al., 2007).

Kindergarten classrooms include more mathematics—about 11 percent of the day—than prekindergarten settings. Despite this, many missed opportunities persist, with kindergarten students not being engaged in any instructional mathematics activity in 39 percent of observed intervals (NRC, 2009). Most children entered kindergarten knowing basic verbal counting and simple geometric shapes, but their educators report spending the most mathematics time on just these topics. Further, attention to these low-level competencies is negatively associated with learning, whereas most children benefit from engaging with more advanced content (Engel et al., 2013). Primary grade educators spend yet more time on mathematics than kindergarten teachers, but again, the quality of the mathematics and mathematics instruction often is not high.

Most early childhood educators in the United States receive weak preparation for teaching mathematics, and in particular lack knowledge of mathematical content (Blömeke et al., 2011), probably as a result of a low level of mathematics knowledge prior to any teacher education. This deficiency is exacerbated by a gender gap favoring men in this knowledge category but a preponderance of female educators in the preschool and elementary school years. This may be one reason preschool teachers spend less time engaging children in mathematics than in any other subject (Early et al., 2010). Because content knowledge is a prerequisite for implementing pedagogical knowledge (Baumert et al., 2010), increasing the mathematics knowledge of early childhood educators needs to be a priority.

Educators also need to be familiar with and know how to implement effective, research-based curricula. Such curricula often include a comprehensive set of cognitive concepts and processes; are based on developmentally sequenced instructional activities; and help educators assess and remediate based on those developmental progressions (Clements et al., 2011, 2013; Griffin et al., 1994; Sarama et al., 2012). Many studies of research-based curricula have been directed toward helping children living in poverty and those with special needs. They show statistically and practically significant increases in mathematics achievement (Campbell and Silver, 1999; Fuson et al., 1997a; Griffin, 2004; Griffin et al., 1995; Ramey and Ramey, 1998), which can be sustained into first grade (Clements and Sarama, 2007; Griffin et al., 1994; Magnuson et al., 2004) or even third grade (Gamel-McCormick and Amsden, 2002).

Role of Mathematical Learning Trajectories in the Creation of Research-Based Standards and Curricula

Children generally follow certain developmental paths in learning mathematics, as described in Chapter 4. As they learn about a mathematical topic, they progress through increasingly sophisticated levels of thinking. These form the core of a learning trajectory: to develop a certain mathematical competence (the goal), children construct each level of thinking in turn (the developmental progression), aided by tasks and teaching that are designed to enable thinking at each higher level (instructional activities) (Clements and Sarama, 2014; Sarama and Clements, 2009). Effective educators understand both the mathematics and the progression of levels of thinking along these paths, and are able to sequence and individualize activities accordingly, thereby building effective mathematics learning environments.

Research has suggested that learning trajectories can help early childhood educators recognize children's developmental processes and their potential for thinking about and understanding mathematical ideas (Bobis et al., 2005; Clarke, 2008; Clements and Sarama, 2009, 2014; Dowker, 2007; Franke et al., 2007; Wright, 2003). Learning trajectories have therefore been the basis for several recent efforts to improve mathematics teaching and learning (Bobis et al., 2005; Clarke, 2008; Clarke et al., 2002; Horne and Rowley, 2001; Perry et al., 2008; van Nes, 2009; Wright, 2003). The National Research Council's (2009) report on early mathematics, for example, is subtitled *Learning Paths Toward Excellence and Equity*. Research-based learning trajectories informed the *Common Core State Standards,* which have been adopted by most states to inform instruction (CCSSO and NGA, 2010). The authors used progressions for each major topic to determine the sequence of learning goals, which were then assigned to grade levels, creating the specific standards.

To use learning trajectories, educators need to understand and be able to apply all three components described above. They have to understand the content for which competence is the goal. For example, they must understand how counting involves much more than simple verbal recitation of number words. They also need to understand the levels of thinking in the developmental progression and how to use a variety of assessment strategies to determine where their class—and individual children—are functioning along that developmental progression. Finally, they have to understand what instructional activities are appropriate to support children's development of each level of thinking, why they are appropriate, and how to adapt and implement instructional tasks and activities to support children's learning.

To illustrate, Table 6-1 describes just a few sample levels from a more elaborate learning trajectory for counting (Clements and Sarama, 2014; Sarama and Clements, 2009). The first column names and briefly describes each level of thinking in the counting learning trajectory and provides examples of related behavior. The middle column sketches hypothesized cognitive components for each level of the developmental progression. The column on the right shows instructional tasks matched to each of the levels of thinking in the developmental progression and designed to help children learn the skills and ideas needed to achieve that level.

TABLE 6-1 Sample Levels from a Learning Trajectory for Counting:
The Goal Is to Count Objects with Understanding

Developmental Progression		Instructional Tasks
Level Names and Descriptions	Cognitive Components	
Chanter Chants "sing-song" or sometimes-indistinguishable number words. "one, two-twee, four, seven, ten."	Initial (bootstrap) sensitivity to quantity supports the implicit categorization of words into quantity/number relevant versus irrelevant (Mix et al., 2002). A verbal list composed of a string of paired associates of sounds/syllables is available (and increasingly expanded and differentiated). It can be produced at will.	**Verbal Counting** Repeated experience with the counting sequence in varied context. This can include songs, finger plays such as "This Old Man," counting going up and down stairs, and just verbal counting for the fun of it (how high can you go?).
Reciter Verbally counts with separate words, not necessarily in the correct order after five. "one, two, three, four, five, seven." May put objects, actions, and words in many-to-one or overly rigid one-to-one correspondence. Counts two objects. "two, two, two."	The verbal list is differentiated into distinct number words associated with the term "counting" and the notion of quantifying (Fuson, 1988; Ginsburg, 1977). It is produced reliably from one to five or ten; after ten, increasing amounts, sometimes with omissions or other errors, can be produced (Fuson, 1988). The procedure to produce the list is, with more or less strength, associated with "indicator" acts (frequently pointing), using an initial bootstrap process (probably linked to naming objects and rhythm) to produce a partial correspondence (Sarama and Clements, 2009).	**Count and Move** Have all children count from 1 to 10 or an appropriate number, making motions with each count. For example, say, "one" [touch head], "two" [touch shoulders], "three" [touch head], etc.

TABLE 6-1 Continued

Developmental Progression		Instructional Tasks
Level Names and Descriptions	Cognitive Components	
Corresponder Keeps one-to-one correspondence between counting words and objects (one word for each object), at least for small groups of objects laid in a line, such as: Π Π Π Π "1, 2, 3, 4" May answer "how many?" by recounting the objects, or violate 1-1 or word order to make the last number word be the desired or predicted word.	The counting procedure is further constrained in producing a correspondence, both in the development of the initial bootstrap process (Downs et al., 2009; Gelman and Gallistel, 1978) and by developing conceptual constraints (i.e., the idea to "count each object once and only once") so one-to-one correspondence is maintained in simple contexts (and is strove for in most contexts, until other mental demands, especially fatigue, achieve prominence) (Fuson, 1988). Gesturing helps children maintain both types of correspondences, keeping track and coordinating number words with objects (Alibali and Goldin-Meadow, 1993).	**Kitchen Counter** Students click on objects on a screen one at a time while the numbers from 1 to 10 are counted aloud. For example, they click on pieces of food and a bite is taken out of each as it is counted.
Counter (Small Numbers) Accurately counts objects in a line to 5 and answers "how many" with the last number counted. When objects are visible, especially with small numbers, begins to understand cardinality.	Connection is made between the output of subitizing processes and counting process (Carey, 2009; Eimeren et al., 2007; Sarama and Clements, 2009). During object counting (which can apply to any set of "objects," including events, etc.), a procedure applies to the final counting word makes a count-to-cardinal transition, producing a cardinal value that is associated with the set (Fuson, 1988).	**Game Board Counting Game** Students identify number amounts (from 1 through 5) on a die and move forward a corresponding number of spaces on a game board.

continued

TABLE 6-1 Continued

Developmental Progression		Instructional Tasks
Level Names and Descriptions	Cognitive Components	
Producer (Small Numbers) Counts out objects to 5. Recognizes that counting is relevant to situations in which a certain number must be placed. Produces a group of four objects.	Extended the goal structure (Siegler and Booth, 2004) to a new executive control procedure that monitors the move-and-count procedure to check, at the production of each count word, if that word matches the goal number; if so, stops the move-and-count procedure. This requires the (at least implicit) understanding that a cardinal word sets a goal (cf. Steffe and Cobb, 1988).	**Count Motions** Children count how many times you jump or clap, or some other motion. Then have them do those motions the same number of times. Initially, count the actions with children. Later, do the motions but model and explain how to count silently. Children who understand how many motions will stop, but others will continue doing the motions.

SOURCE: Adapted from Clements and Sarama, 2014.

The Importance of Follow-Through for Mathematics

As noted earlier, the importance of following through on early interventions with continued and cumulative learning support into elementary school and beyond applies across developmental domains and subject areas. For mathematics, research shows that kindergarten curricula and educators fail to build most children's mathematical competencies (Claessens et al., 2014; Engel et al., 2013). As described previously, kindergarten educators spend the majority of classroom time on basic counting and recognition of simple geometric shapes even though most children enter kindergarten with mastery of this content. Such focus is negatively associated with mathematics achievement across kindergarten. Only children with the lowest levels of math skills benefit from exposure to this basic content; all others benefit from exposure to more advanced content, such as adding small numbers and the beginnings of place value. A similar pattern is seen with advanced literacy content. Claessens and colleagues (2014) found that all children, regardless of preschool experience or family socioeconomic status, benefited from additional exposure to advanced mathematics and reading content in kindergarten.

The limited focus on and lack of advanced content in mathematics instruction in kindergarten may be a factor, along with others described previously, in accounting for the lack of longitudinal effects in studies of prekindergarten mathematics, as in the Preschool Curriculum Evaluation Research Consortium (2008) project. One project evaluated the effectiveness of a follow-through intervention, testing a hypothesis that such follow-through is the "missing piece" in many early interventions whose longitudinal evaluations have found less positive effects (MacDonald et al., 2012; Trinick and Stevenson, 2009). An instantiation of the TRIAD (Technology-enhanced, Research-based Instruction, Assessment, and professional Development) scale-up model was designed to teach early mathematics for understanding, emphasizing learning trajectories and technological tools. Schools were randomly assigned to two interventions or control. The interventions were identical at prekindergarten, but only one included TRIAD's follow-through component in students' kindergarten and first-grade years. The effects of the prekindergarten intervention persisted with such follow-through, while without it they were significantly less likely to persist.

The Importance of Fostering Positive Beliefs and Attitudes About Mathematics

Educators help children develop positive beliefs and attitudes about mathematics by providing tasks that make sense to students and relate to their everyday interests and lives. As discussed in Chapter 4, the right degree of challenge and novelty can foster interest and a mastery orientation. Clements and Sarama (2012) have summarized the following characteristics of learning environments that enhance students' attitudes and beliefs about mathematics:

- using problems that have meaning for students (both practical and mathematical);
- expecting that students will invent, explain, and critique their own solution strategies within a social context;
- providing opportunities for both creative invention and practice;
- encouraging and supporting students in progressing toward increasingly sophisticated and abstract mathematical methods and understandings, and in understanding and developing more efficient and elegant solution strategies; and
- helping students see connections among various types of knowledge and topics, with the goal of having each student build a well-structured, coherent knowledge of mathematics.

Teaching Mathematics:
Implications for Professional Learning

- *Given its central role in children's development and in prediction of school success, more emphasis is needed on training educators to teach mathematical concepts, reasoning, problem solving, and communication.*
- *Educators need to understand the mathematics they teach, how children think about and learn that mathematics, and how instructional tasks and strategies can be adapted for children at different levels of thinking. They need to know how to integrate these three components into effective research-based learning trajectories for every topic in mathematics and to use them to conduct effective formative assessment.*
- *Educators need to be able to move beyond false instructional dichotomies and develop sound mathematical concepts, fluent skills, and flexible and adaptive problem-solving abilities in their students.*
- *Educators need to know how to support children in struggling productively with challenging mathematical ideas and problems.*
- *Educators need to know about strategies for developing children's positive attitudes and productive dispositions toward mathematics.*

SCIENCE

Young children are fascinated with and construct many ideas about how the world works. They investigate and refine these ideas by exploring and questioning the world around them. Research shows that preschool children know a great deal about the natural world, including concepts related to physics, biology, psychology, and chemistry (NRC, 2007). As with language and literacy and mathematics, they also possess thinking skills and habits of mind that support later, more sophisticated, scientific reasoning. For example, young children might question why leaves fall from trees or where animal babies come from. They might observe that people's eyes are different colors, and generate possible explanations (Callanan and Oakes, 1992). Older preschoolers interpret simple data patterns and show some understanding of how different patterns support different conclusions (e.g., Klahr and Chen, 2003).

A recent review found that children arrived in kindergarten with lower science readiness scores than in any other subject area or developmental domain (Greenfield et al., 2009). Similarly, international studies have found that knowledge of science, like knowledge of math, is low—at best average internationally—among American students, especially those from low-resource communities (Gonzales et al., 2008). The current frequency and duration of kindergarten teaching of science in the United States was not shown to predict science achievement at the end of kindergarten or the end of third (Saçkes et al., 2011) to eighth grade (Saçkes et al., 2013). However, early instructional experiences appear to be predictive of science achievement in other countries (Tao et al., 2012). Thus, educators need to address both the overall low level and the quality of instruction and curricula in science in the United States, with special attention to more vulnerable populations.

Like mathematics, young children today are not exposed to adequate educational experiences in science, and it also tends not to be emphasized in the professional learning of educators of young children, even though there are learning standards and some increased attention to science curricula (Brenneman et al., 2009b). Evidence suggests that these educators tend not to support science learning through time spent in either planned or spontaneous science-related activities (Brenneman et al., 2009b; Brown, 2005; Early et al., 2007; Gerde et al., 2013; Hanley et al., 2009; Nayfeld et al., 2011; Tu, 2006; Wenner, 1993). Second, educational experiences in science are not of high quality. If science instruction does occur, it tends to consist of simple, isolated activities, giving young children little or no occasion to develop important experiential and skill bases for future science learning. Further, even when teaching science, educators may use general school vocabulary rather than domain-specific vocabulary, especially when they are not secure in their knowledge of the scientific phenomena (Henrichs et al., 2011).

Primary grade educators also devote limited attention to science because of a lack of time, materials, and space, as well as their perceived lack of content knowledge, pedagogical content knowledge, and self-confidence and comfort in the subject (Appleton and Kindt, 1999, 2002; Greenfield et al., 2009; Saçkes et al., 2011). In addition to spending less time on science, they emphasize simple biology over physics and simple hands-on activities over more conceptually rich activities (Akerson, 2004; Appleton and Kindt, 1999; Saçkes et al., 2011). Moreover, educators' expectations for children and strategies for grouping them instructionally can produce inequitable learning opportunities for children from low-resource communities and minority groups (NRC, 2007).

In general, science needs to be reconceptualized as more than teaching facts (NRC, 2007). Giving children opportunities to engage in scientific exploration supports science learning, but it also fosters learning and school readiness in other subject areas and developmental domains, including language and literacy, mathematics, and learning competencies (Gelman et al., 2009). Consistent science experiences are related to children's vocabulary growth (French, 2004) and use of more complex grammatical structures, such as causal connectives (Peterson and French, 2008). Further, the knowledge that children build about the natural world is a critical contributor to later achievement not only in science but also in reading (Grissmer et al., 2010). Moreover, such experiences close a gender gap in motivation and interest (Patrick et al., 2009).

Educators' use of research-based curricula and learning trajectories can help ameliorate problems with early teaching and learning of science (Gelman and Brenneman, 2004; Mantzicopoulos et al., 2009). As with mathematics, research has identified learning trajectories for key content areas in science, such as physics and biology, and has provided evidence for the effectiveness of following these pathways (Gelman and Brenneman, 2004). What is "developmentally appropriate" for children to learn is influenced by maturation but determined mainly by learning along these trajectories (NRC, 2007).

Admittedly, work on identifying learning progressions and core concepts in science is less advanced than in mathematics (Gelman et al., 2009). There is a need to identify a few core ideas and plan standards, curricula, and pedagogy around those ideas (NRC, 2007). Studying successful implementation of research-based curricula (including analyses of video) could be useful to inform instruction strategies. Comprehensive strategies that eschew simple dichotomies such as "play" versus "academic" learning and teaching need to be modeled and researched. An important focus for this work is investigating inquiry approaches and distinguishing them from unguided "discovery" approaches (Clements and Sarama, 2014; Furtak et al., 2012; Sarama and Clements, 2009).

As one example, Preschool Pathways to Science (PrePS) is a science-based curricular planning framework used to plan learning experiences that encourage children to think about and work with a science concept (e.g., change through growth, form and function) for many weeks or months (Gelman et al., 2009). Developed by preschool educators and developmental psychologists, the approach is based on learning research showing that children actively construct knowledge and that this process is facilitated when the information to be learned is connected to what was learned before (NRC, 2000). Moreover, this approach is consistent with recommendations that science curricula and standards identify and support a few core ideas rather than many disconnected topics (NRC, 2007), and that researchers and educators focus on learning trajectories for core concepts instead of trying to teach a little bit of everything. The PrePS approach also incorporates science practices that children use repeatedly across content areas, including observing, predicting, and checking predictions; comparing, contrasting, and experimenting; using the vocabulary and discourse patterns of science; counting, measuring, and using other mathematical skills and reasoning; and recording and documenting science ideas and results (Gelman et al., 2009). In practice, PrePS has good to excellent scores on widely used classroom quality measures, and PrePS researchers recently empirically tested children's learning from specific science units. Successful outcomes were found for units on growth and life cycles of living things (Downs et al., 2009), senses as tools for observation (Brenneman et al., 2009a), and light and shadows (Massey and Roth, 2009).

Teaching Science: Implications for Professional Learning

Content and methods courses in higher education, as well as other professional learning activities, need to enhance the competencies of educators of children from birth through age 8 in all aspects of science learning trajectories: science goals and content, developmental progressions for a variety of science topics, and instructional tasks and strategies.

FOSTERING SOCIOEMOTIONAL DEVELOPMENT

As discussed in Chapter 4, research on socioemotional development illuminates its importance for successful learning. Many young children in early education settings and early elementary classrooms arrive with prior experiences of adversity and chronic stress that can affect their behavior and learning, in part owing to biological effects on brain and behavior (see Chapters 3 and 4). It is important for educators to have the knowledge needed to interpret young children's anxiety, difficulties in paying attention and following instructions, impulsivity, and problems with emotion regulation as arising, in part, from the effects of chronic stress on developing brain systems instead of attributing these characteristics, as adults often do, to uncooperativeness, defiance, or disinterest in learning.

Generally speaking, learning environments that are well structured and predictable, that provide support for children's self-regulatory capacities, and that offer secure and warm relationships with educators will provide the greatest benefits to all children. Children experiencing chronic stress and adversity may have other specific needs for support as well, but such a learning environment can help buffer stress for these children. Providing such an environment not only helps these children, but also helps educators maintain a constructive classroom environment that is not regularly subject to behavioral disruptions.

Instructional Practices and Interventions That Enhance Supportive Relationships and Foster Socioemotional Development

Although the socioemotional development of young children is receiving increased attention, this domain typically is not well supported in the instructional and other practices of educators. National surveys indicate that the field of early education is in need of effective training that can help educators develop skills in promoting socioemotional development. For example, faculty in teacher training institutions reported that, compared with practices across other developmental domains, their graduates were least prepared to address the needs of children with challenging behavior (Hemmeter et al., 2008).

Some curricular resources and other intervention appproaches provide effective approaches for fostering the socioemotional development and learning of children in early childhood and early elementary settings and enhancing supportive relationships (CASEL, 2012; Durlak, 2015; Pianta et al., 2007; Preschool Curriculum Evaluation Research Consortium, 2008). These approaches focus on various aspects of socioemotional competence, including self-regulation and prosocial behaviors toward peers and adults. In most cases, these approaches have both strengths and weaknesses and mixed evidence for success across elements of socioemotional development. However, evaluations have shown that, when implemented at scale with appropriate supports, these approaches can improve some aspects of socio-emotional competence, in some cases especially for children at highest risk or those who begin school with low self-regulation competencies (Morris et al., 2014; Tominey and McClelland, 2011). Box 6-1 lists some examples of these approaches.

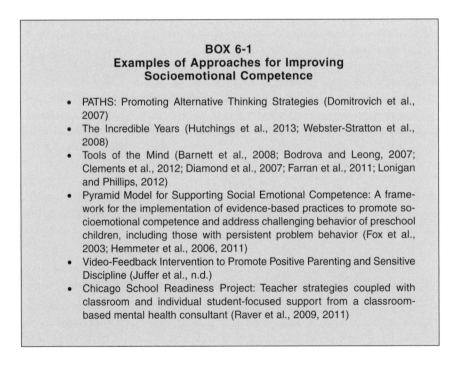

BOX 6-1
Examples of Approaches for Improving
Socioemotional Competence

- PATHS: Promoting Alternative Thinking Strategies (Domitrovich et al., 2007)
- The Incredible Years (Hutchings et al., 2013; Webster-Stratton et al., 2008)
- Tools of the Mind (Barnett et al., 2008; Bodrova and Leong, 2007; Clements et al., 2012; Diamond et al., 2007; Farran et al., 2011; Lonigan and Phillips, 2012)
- Pyramid Model for Supporting Social Emotional Competence: A framework for the implementation of evidence-based practices to promote socioemotional competence and address challenging behavior of preschool children, including those with persistent problem behavior (Fox et al., 2003; Hemmeter et al., 2006, 2011)
- Video-Feedback Intervention to Promote Positive Parenting and Sensitive Discipline (Juffer et al., n.d.)
- Chicago School Readiness Project: Teacher strategies coupled with classroom and individual student-focused support from a classroom-based mental health consultant (Raver et al., 2009, 2011)

Fixsen and colleagues (2005) suggest that it is the combination of effective intervention practices and programs and effective implementation supports that results in positive outcomes for children and families. For educators to implement interventions with fidelity, program-wide implementation supports, including professional learning activities, are needed. Although there is a substantial body of literature on school-wide approaches to implementing tiered behavior support models in elementary, middle, and secondary schools, the literature on implementation of these models in early childhood settings is in its infancy (Fox and Hemmeter, 2009; Frey, 2009; Stormont et al., 2005). The following elements have been explored as important factors for implementation: establishing a leadership team that guides program-wide adoption and engages in data-based decision making, ensuring the buy-in of all staff in the model, creating strategies for promoting family engagement, providing ongoing training and coaching for classroom staff, promoting the use of universal screening and progress monitoring to ensure that children's socioemotional needs are addressed, developing a behavior-support planning process for children whose problem behavior is persistent, and creating an ongoing process for monitoring implementation and outcomes of the approach (Fox and Hemmeter, 2009).

Interventions also have been developed that are aimed at fostering cognitive self-regulation and other cognitive processes, frequently referred to collectively as executive function (see Chapter 4). The rapid development of executive function in the early years makes the use of such interventions optimal during that period, although no age is too late (e.g., Center on the Developing Child, 2015; Zelazo and Carlson, 2012). Some studies have shown enhancement of such capabilities with computer games (e.g., Rothbart and Rueda, 2005; Rueda et al., 2008; Thorell et al., 2009), other executive function tasks (e.g., Espinet et al., 2012), or particular curricula or programs (e.g., Bierman et al., 2008a,b; Diamond, 2012; Diamond and Lee, 2011; Diamond et al., 2007; Klingberg, 2009; Lillard and Else-Quest, 2006; Lyons and Zelazo, 2011; Perels et al., 2009; Raver et al., 2011; Riggs et al., 2006; Weiland and Yoshikawa, 2013; Weiland et al., 2013). The latter often include specific teaching approaches such as guiding impulsive children to self-monitor their behavior by talking to themselves (four different interventions of this sort were effective; see Reid et al., 2005) or teaching 3-year-olds to repeat change-of-criteria categorization tasks (Dowsett and Livesey, 2000).

The Importance of Mental Health Consultation and Cross-Sector Services

As suggested by Gilliam (2005), educators are likely to benefit from consultation with early mental health experts to best understand how to work with children in need of specialized support in their classrooms.

Child mental health consultants can provide educators with guidance on classroom management and instructional practices for all children as well as individualized consultation for particular children based on classroom observations, and offer teachers continuing support as they incorporate these practices (see Amini Virmani et al., 2013; Johnston and Brinamen, 2006). Unfortunately, as noted 15 years ago in the National Research Council and the Institute of Medicine (2000) report *From Neurons to Neighborhoods*, most communities lack expertise in child mental health services and consultation, and no well-developed national infrastructure exists for training developmentally oriented clinicians in providing these services (see also Osofsky and Lieberman, 2011).

More broadly, the importance of socioemotional health to early learning calls for the involvement of multiple service systems that affect young children and their families in meeting the special needs of young children facing mental health challenges (Osofsky and Lieberman, 2011). Thus, beyond incorporating developmental knowledge in this area into educator preparation, it is important to also do so across sectors and settings, for professionals in pediatric practice, the child welfare system, early intervention, special education, childcare and after-school care, and programs for children with special needs. This would help ensure that children experiencing mental health challenges would be identified and provided with appropriate services that would be aligned across different programs with which these children come in contact. Such cross-sector preparation of professionals concerned with young children could even be conducted collaboratively across professional communities. Such a cross-sector approach is especially important given that these different professional sectors have distinctly different professional reference groups and funding streams that tend to make their efforts insular rather than collaborative, even though the same child is the focus of their attention.

An additional benefit of cross-sector collaborative training in the socioemotional needs of young children is that it would enable professionals to coordinate assistance across multiple generations. The connections between the well-being of an adult and the well-being of a child who has an emotional attachment to that adult make it important to coordinate supportive services to parents and children within the family (IOM and NRC, 2009). Thus, for example, a physician treating an adult for depression should have the training to consider the consequences of that depression for children in the adult's care, and any pediatrician identifying characteristics of stress in a young child should seek to understand family processes that may contribute to that stress. Similarly, the benefits demonstrated by intervention programs aimed at supporting the developmental health and learning of young children by providing broader family support should spur efforts to consider how children can be assisted through a two-generational approach

(Chase-Lansdale and Brooks-Gunn, 2014). Similar considerations apply to the associations between the well-being of children and the emotional health of those who care for and educate them outside the home.

Fostering Social and Emotional Development: Implications for Professional Learning

- *Early care and education professionals need training to foster socio-emotional development and create supportive learning environments for all children.*
- *Professionals in education, health, and social services need training to recognize when children need specialized support for their socio-emotional development, to provide that support directly and through linkages to specialized services, and to connect to multigeneration intervention approaches that take into account the mental health and well-being of the adults in children's lives instead of viewing children in isolation.*

USING TECHNOLOGY EFFECTIVELY

The use of technology in educational settings can take two major forms, both of which have implications for the competencies needed by professionals. The first is use of technology as a tool for directly facilitating children's learning. In terms of professional competency, educators must have proficiency in technology as a set of tools that can enhance pedagogy, knowledge of how and when children learn through what kinds of technology and the ability to integrate that knowledge into their pedagogy and lessons, and proficiency in teaching children how to use technology and acquire digital literacy skills. The second entails the use of technology to facilitate other aspects of professional practice, such as assessment of children, creation and management of the learning environment, documentation, information sharing, and communication with families and with other practitioners. This section focuses primarily on the first form of technology use: what knowledge teachers need to have about how children interact with and learn through technology and what skills they need to put that knowledge into practice in the classroom.

Effects of Digital Media on Development and Learning

While there is still much to learn, the science of how children relate to new media has expanded through research over the past decade that offers insights into how, and at what age, young children may develop cognitive skills from using different types of new technology, as well as when professionals and parents should be alert to potential misuse of these technologies. The emergent science on the effects of media is becoming increasingly important for researchers and practitioners who want to meet the needs of today's families. According to a recent national survey of 1,200 American families, more than 8 in 10 children (ages 2-10) use digital media every week and two-thirds have tablets or e-readers.

Questions about video and video screens—sometimes framed in terms of "screen time"—are at the heart of this new science. Developmental scientists long have wondered how babies make sense of the moving image. Some research has shown that until about 18 months of age, infants tend to reach out to touch or grasp an image (whether a picture or a video) instead of pointing to it, as they do after 18 months (DeLoache et al., 1998). Researchers have theorized that the grasping is a sign of babies exploring the image as a physical thing, while their later pointing behavior is a sign that they are starting to gain "symbolic understanding" or "pictorial competence" (DeLoache, 2005). In other words, it appears that infants eventually progress to a stage of cognitive development in which they comprehend that an image is a symbol that represents something instead of being the thing itself. This may be a milestone in children's being developmentally prepared to construct meaning from what they see represented in media of all kinds.

A separate body of research has focused on gleaning evidence that infants and toddlers can learn from what they see on a video screen, and at what age. Research has shown evidence of a "video deficit," a phenomenon whereby children learn less readily from a prerecorded video than from a person talking with them face-to-face, even when the video shows a person speaking as if he/she is face-to-face with the audience (Anderson and Pempek, 2005). This deficit has been seen in children younger than 12 months old and up through age 3. It takes many forms and has been shown in some experiments to be overcome by repetition; that is, if a child sees something on video multiple times, the child can learn from it (Barr and Hayne, 1999; Barr et al., 2007).

Some studies have examined whether children's viewing of these media is replacing important social experiences and "serve and return" interactions that are so strongly associated with cognition and learning (see Chapter 4). A few studies in the mid-2000s showed associations between television viewing in early childhood and poor cognitive outcomes (Christakis et al., 2004), while other studies have shown no impact of television viewing (e.g., Schmidt et al., 2009). In these cases and many others, however, while researchers typically controlled for socioeconomic status of the parents, they did not include information on what types of shows children were watching. More recent studies have rectified this omission by examining the content of the viewing in addition to the quantity. One such study found links between infants regularly watching television shows made for adults (such as dramas and the news) and low scores on tests of executive functioning at age 4 (Barr et al., 2010). Another found associations between attention problems and television viewing for children who watched violent programming, but not educational shows, before age 3 (Zimmerman and Christakis, 2007).

More insight comes from studies on video specifically designed to be educational for children. Studies using randomized controlled trials yielded evidence showing that children learned new vocabulary words and skills such as problem solving and self-regulation after watching videos with an intentional pedagogical approach or curriculum (Singer and Singer, 1998). Longitudinal studies have shown a link between viewing *Sesame Street* before kindergarten and school readiness, as well as positive outcomes in high school (Anderson et al., 2001; Wright et al., 2001).

Effective Use of Technology in Instruction

It is important to emphasize that any benefits of technology will depend on the use of high-quality educational technology implemented well (see, e.g., the negative examples in Plowman and Stephen, 2005). Limited research has examined how different technologies can be used effectively with students at different ages for different subjects, how to incorporate digital content into curricula, and how best to employ technology to enable early skill development. A recent RAND report summarizes how much is still unknown about technology use in early childhood, calling for research on the effects of using different types of technology to determine "whether the intuitive notions of developmentally appropriate use are supported by evidence" (p. 20). Among the factors suggested for consideration are "time, interactions between the student and the software, different approaches to technology use employed by [early childhood education] environments in lower-income versus upper-income areas (perhaps to account for lower parental involvement in the former group), interactions between the student and adult facilitators, interactions between the student and peers, the types of software provided, and the types of devices used" (Daugherty et al., 2014, p. 20). Although these research questions warrant further exploration, available research provides some guidance on how technology can contribute to effective early childhood settings (Clements and Sarama, 2003; Sarama and Clements, 2002).

Appropriate implementation of high-quality educational technology can help teaching and learning be more effective, efficient, and motivating (Bereiter and Scardamalia, 2010; Bus and Kegel, 2013; Clements and Sarama, 2003, 2010; Clements et al., 2014; Fatouros, 1995; Foorman, 2007; Hitchcock, 2008; Lee and Shin, 2012; Neuman, 2013; Penuel, 2012). High-quality educational technology, implemented well in meaningful contexts, can facilitate children's development of knowledge and skills for language and literacy and for mathematics, as well as higher-order thinking skills and creativity (Clements and Sarama, 2007). These benefits extend across diverse populations and may be especially important for children with special needs (e.g., Hutinger and Johanson, 2000).

In some cases, the use of educational technology has been shown to increase social interactions, especially those centered around subject-matter content. Children prefer to work with a peer rather than alone when they use the computer, a context that can promote collaborative work, including helping or instructing each other as well as discussing and building upon each others' ideas. These social interactions in turn generate increased use of language (Clements and Sarama, 2007). Technology-assisted instruction also can help build prereading and reading skills (e.g., Chambers, 2008; Pelletier, 2006), as well as develop writing abilities (Bangert-Drowns, 1993; Gustafsson et al., 1999; Roblyer, 1988; Yost, 1998). Educational technology also can support the teaching and learning of science, technology, engineering, and mathematics (Clements and Sarama, 2008; NMP, 2008; NRC, 2009; Sarama and Clements, 2006). There can also be collateral benefits for digital literacy: the integration of an interactive literacy program into curriculum increases computer skills, computer self-efficacy, and enjoyment of computers (Ross et al., 2001).

Most recently, debates about the value of video in early childhood have centered on whether any positive impact is evident when educational videos are watched before the age of 24 months. Thus far the few studies addressing this question have focused on word learning, and their results are mixed: two showed that children younger than 24 months of age cannot learn words from videos even when the videos are explicitly designed to teach them those words; another two showed that children just a few months shy of 24 months are, in fact, able to learn the words (DeLoache et al., 2010; Krcmar et al., 2007; Richert et al., 2010; Vandewater et al., 2010). With the research still nascent and unsettled, parents and early educators continue to receive mixed messages about the value of so-called baby videos.

Moreover, very little scientific research exists regarding babies' learning from new forms of interactive technology, such as apps for babies on touch-screen tablets. Among the few published studies to delve into toddlers' and preschoolers' use of touch screens, one showed that 3-year-olds can overcome the "video deficit" discussed above when interacting with a video by pressing a button to advance the video's action, but cannot do so when watching video passively (Lauricella et al., 2010). Another study showed that 2-year-olds using touch screens learn more from the on-screen content than those who only watch, as long as they are asked to touch specific areas of the screen that relate to the task they are learning (Choi and

Kirkorian, 2013). A similar study showed that the same caveat applies to word learning as well (Kirkorian et al., 2013).

An only slightly more extensive line of research has emerged on the impact of interactive technologies for children aged 3-8. For example, a study of the Building Blocks Pre-K math curriculum examined, among other questions, whether software integrated into a suite of curricular activities could have a positive impact on student learning. This study, which involved 106 teachers and more than 1,300 students across two states, found a correlation between classrooms using the software and children's performance on assessments of math and expressive language. Students in classrooms using the software scored higher than children in classrooms that employed the curriculum without the software (Sarama and Clements, 2009) (see also, Clements and Sarama, 2007). On the literacy front, a series of e-book studies in Israel with 40 kindergarteners and 50 first-graders showed that digital text with embedded questions and audio dictionaries (definitions spoken aloud when a child clicks on a word) can lead to improvements in phonological awareness, vocabulary knowledge, and word-reading skills (Korat, 2010).

In a 2012 article on literacy software and e-reader research, Biancarosa and Griffiths (2012) review the Israeli e-book study and several others, concluding that while technology appears promising in helping children learn to read, research thus far has been "small-scale in nature, focusing on feasibility and efficacy in tightly controlled contexts rather than on wide-scale use." The authors also stress that teachers get "virtually no empirical guidance" on how to use software and other technology tools to support literacy (Biancarosa and Griffiths, 2012).

Any curricular product's effectiveness will depend on its content and design, as well as how it used by educators, and interactive media and software are no exception. Good results are seen when educators use the products intentionally and are given support in integrating them into their classroom practices. One example comes from research on the television show *The Adventures of SuperWhy*, which is broadcast regularly on PBS and was also designed to be part of a classroom literacy curriculum for children aged 4-5. In an experiment with the curriculum version, children watched episodes twice per week that were linked to teacher-led whole-classroom activities, small-group activities, online games, and individual exploration. Teachers received professional development and training in how to integrate these activities throughout the 10 weeks. With funding from the U.S. Department of Education, researchers conducted a randomized controlled trial of 398 low-income children in 80 preschools to determine the impact of the media-enriched literacy curricula. They found that children outscored the control group on measures of letter recognition, letter sounds, print concepts, and knowing the letters of their names (Penuel et al., 2009). The control group in this case did use digital media in their daily activities, but the media were not focused on improving children's literacy; the study therefore shows the importance of using media that are intentionally integrated with curricula and learning goals.

The most important feature of any high-quality educational environment is a knowledgeable and responsive adult (Darling-Hammond, 1997; Ferguson, 1991; NRC, 2001b; Watson, 1993), and this is no less true for technology as part of the learning environment. As research continues to examine what kinds of tools, media, and curriculum integration may be best for young children at which ages, one area of consensus is already forming: children consistently show greater signs of learning if they watch media with an adult who engages them in the content or helps them connect the ideas on screen to their world. Researchers exploring this concept, known as "joint media engagement," often are building on findings from studies of another type of media—the printed book. Just as they do with books, adults can spark conversations about the subject matter of a video or a game by using dialogic questioning and other ways to prompt deeper engagement. A recent study on video books with 3-year-olds showed that when parents were trained to use questions while watching, their children scored well on later tests about the books' storylines and vocabulary words; children did not show evidence of learning when watching the video books with parents who simply pointed and labeled objects or did not converse with them at all (Strouse et al., 2013). In short, computers and other technology are used well in classrooms where educators use effective instructional strategies. Moreover, there is evidence that if educators receive more support in the use of computers, their students benefit, even more than if the support is targeted at students (Fuller, 2000).

Digital Literacy

As the science of how children are affected by and in what ways they can learn from various forms of media and technology emerges, research is starting to focus on a corollary question: What skills and knowledge do young children need to acquire about how to use technology and media— that is, what does digital literacy or technological fluency look like for young children?

For the latter end of the birth through age 8 spectrum—children in grades K-3—educators regularly face this question even though research on children's development of skills in and knowledge of technology remains sparse. A handful of states have standards for digital literacy or technology use starting in kindergarten, and a majority of states' literacy standards for elementary schools include a reference to children's ability to use online materials.[2] Elementary schools increasingly are employing specialized curricula on such issues as password protection and online etiquette. Many elementary school children are now taught "keyboarding." State standardized tests, which typically are administered to students starting in third grade, increasingly are offered using computers instead of pencil and paper. There are instances of children as young as 5 learning how to produce multimedia projects, and some case studies suggest that such projects could prompt better reading comprehension (Hobbs and Moore, 2013).

For children at the beginning of the birth through age 8 spectrum—toddlers and preschoolers—the issue of digital skill building is emerging from studies of children's learning how video is created. As families snap photos and capture video with mini-cameras, today's young children are witnessing (even participating in) the creation, production, and publication of family videos.

Given the role these tools are already playing in schools and workplaces, more scientific research is needed on how and when young children develop skills in and knowledge about technology and media.

Expectations for Educators

Educators working with older students—5-8 years old—have clearer expectations for the use of technology than their counterparts working with children under age 5. The International Society for Technology in Education (ISTE) has developed comprehensive standards for both educators and students. These standards call for students to be able to demonstrate the following with respect to using technology: research and information fluency; critical thinking, problem solving, and decision making; creativity and innovation; and communication and collaboration (ISTE, 2007a, 2008). At one count, nearly all 50 states had adopted or used part of the ISTE student standards.[3] Neither the ISTE student standards nor the teacher standards are differentiated by grade level, but several states cite them as the base for their K-2 or K-3 technology standards.[4] The Council for Accreditation of Educator Preparation also lists standards for teachers; it calls for teacher

---

[2] For example, the English Language Arts standards in the Common Core State Standards, which have been adopted in 44 states, set expectations for elementary school-age children to, "with guidance and support from adults, explore a variety of digital tools to produce and publish writing, including in collaboration with peers" (CCSSO and NGA, 2010).

[3] In 2007, 49 of 50 states were noted as having adopted or used the ISTE standards in their tech standards development (ISTE, 2007b).

[4] See for example Alabama's technology standards focused on technology operations and concepts, digital citizenship, research and information fluency, communication and collaboration, critical thinking, problem solving and decision making, and creativity and innovation (Morton, 2008).

candidates to "use technology to enhance their teaching" and wants them to "use technology effectively in their job role to support student learning" (CAEP, 2013).

Another indicator of technology expectations for educators comes in the Common Core State Standards. Consider, for example, the kindergarten standard CCSS.ELA-Literacy.W.K.6: "With guidance and support from adults, explore a variety of digital tools to produce and publish writing, including in collaboration with peers" (CCSSO and NGA, 2010). To be able to help children use digital tools for writing, educators themselves need a high level of familiarity with those tools and developmentally appropriate methods for introducing them to young children who are still learning how to write with analog tools such as pens and pencils.

Expectations for the use of technology are very different in settings outside of elementary schools. In prekindergarten and childcare settings, there is no widely adopted set of standards for using technology with these young children, nor are there common standards for what the children should know and be able to do regarding technology. Some states do not mention technology in their early learning guidelines at all (Daugherty et al., 2014).[5] Not surprisingly, technology use varies widely in these settings, as do opinions about what constitutes good teaching with technology. Some preschools proudly advertise the availability of computers and electronic whiteboards for children's use, while some preschools take pains to keep children away from screen media of any kind. Some states' Quality Rating and Improvement System and licensing systems ask childcare centers to limit children's use of screen-based technology to no more than 30 minutes per week (see, for example, National Resource Center for Health and Safety in Child Care, 2012).

In 2012, the joint position statement "Technology and Interactive Media as Tools in Early Childhood Programs Serving Children Birth Through Age 8" was released by the National Association for the Education of Young Children (NAEYC) and the Fred Rogers Center for Early Learning and Children's Media at Saint Vincent College. The intent was to provide guidance to teachers in settings across the birth through 8 age spectrum. The statement says that technology and digital media can be "effective tools in early childhood education when used intentionally and appropriately, taking into consideration each child's age, developmental abilities, and social and cultural life context." It also calls for equitable access for all children; ongoing professional learning for teachers; and careful consideration of public health statements about the importance of avoiding violent content and limiting the use of passive screen media, such as videos, with

---

[5] Six of 23 states' preschool standards surveyed by RAND did not make any mention of technology or computers (Daugherty et al., 2014, p. 12).

infants and toddlers if the use does not promote social interactions. Zero to Three has also developed guidelines specifically for screen use for children under 3 (Lerner and Barr, 2014).

Conclusion About Digital Media and Early Learning

Digital media—whether television, video, or games on interactive tablets—are a regular presence in the lives of young children. How much young children can benefit from various forms of media depends on the content on the screen, the context in which they watch or play, and a child's needs and stages of development.

- *Young children learn more from digital media when they watch or play with adults who talk to them about what they are seeing and playing. This "joint media engagement" benefits children's literacy skills when adults use techniques of discourse to engage with children around themes, concepts, or new vocabulary brought forth by the media, similar to the well-established benefits of interactive book reading.*
- *For passive media without adult mediation, children older than 24 months can learn new vocabulary words and skills such as problem solving and self-regulation from videos developed with an intentional pedagogical approach or curriculum.*
- *For interactive touch screens, some programs integrated with a research-based curriculum have been associated with gains in math and reading skills among children in preschool and above.*

Using Technology Effectively to Foster Early Learning: Implications for Professional Learning

Educators across professional roles and age ranges are expected to have competency in the use of technology for learning. This competency includes knowing how children learn through technology and having the ability to integrate that knowledge into practices that support development and learning. These professionals need better support in the use of technology and more opportunities to learn how to use technology appropriately, effectively, and to its fullest potential to foster early learning for children from birth through age 8.

SUPPORTING THE EARLY LEARNING OF
DUAL LANGUAGE LEARNERS

In addition to what is known about supporting healthy development among children, writ large, the current research base points to a set of essential practices for educators in early care and education settings and elementary schools with respect to the specific language-learning needs of the multilingual population.[6] These features can be categorized into three domains: (1) screening for literacy difficulties; (2) targeted, intensive language-building opportunities; and (3) tailored family partnerships (discussed in the subsequent section on working with families).

Screening for Literacy Difficulties

Comprehensive early screening of the key skills and competencies related to literacy development is essential to prevent risk and vulnerabilities from becoming difficulties, given what is known about the relationships between early language and literacy skills and later academic achievement. The current research base highlights features of effective early assessment practices with multilingual learners, which together make for a comprehensive approach:

- *Screening for word-reading difficulties*—Screening for word-reading difficulties (or risk thereof) among multilingual children should make use of screening practices similar to those established with monolingual English-speaking populations (Francis et al., 2006; Lesaux et al., 2007; Linan-Thompson et al., 2006; Lipka and Siegel, 2007; Otaiba et al., 2009; Samson and Lesaux, 2009). This is because, for both groups of children, word-reading skills are rooted in the development of phonological processing skills (e.g., rhyming and manipulating the sounds in words). In the context of high-quality instruction, on average, young multilingual learners develop phonological processing skills, and subsequently word-reading skills, on par with their English-only-speaking classmates. Therefore, if young multilingual children appear to be struggling with phonological processing skills or with early alphabet knowledge and word reading, they need targeted support. This is the case even when multilingual learners demonstrate underdeveloped English oral language proficiency. A child's phonological processing skills develop similarly across languages, and therefore are not

---

[6] An ongoing study and forthcoming report of the Institute of Medicine and the National Research Council focuses on research, practice, and policy for young dual language learners. More information can be found at www.iom.edu/activities/children/duallanguagelearners.

influenced by exposure to English in the same way as, for example, English vocabulary knowledge. Yet multilingual learners often are overlooked for targeted supports because practitioners think their phonological processing and/or word-reading difficulties will remediate themselves once the children's oral language proficiency develops further.

- *Screening for reading comprehension difficulties*—The multilingual population comprises a diverse, heterogeneous group of learners. Nonetheless, a now robust research base converges on a common source of difficulty among those multilingual learners who experience or are at risk of difficulties with reading comprehension: the language-based competencies central to understanding and making meaning of the words on the page. Therefore, this risk requires timely, ongoing assessment of language-based skills, such as vocabulary knowledge, oral language proficiency, and listening comprehension (Betts et al., 2009; Geva and Yaghoub-Zadeh, 2006; Jean and Geva, 2009; Lesaux et al., 2006, 2010; Mancilla-Martinez and Lesaux, 2011; Proctor et al., 2005). This screening and progress monitoring is particularly important because difficulties in this area often are not readily apparent. Therefore, the role of screening and progress monitoring is to identify these key indicators of later reading comprehension difficulties and provide at-risk learners with targeted supports to boost their development. Many multilingual learners are developing their oral language skills at a fast pace, but still not fast enough to attain age-appropriate levels. When screening and progress monitoring are used to identify underdeveloped language-based skills, and this information is then used to guide targeted language-building opportunities, instruction can capitalize on the rapid learning rates demonstrated by many multilingual learners and further accelerate their language development.
- *Assessments to gauge the quality of the learning environment*—Children's learning environments, and their daily opportunities to learn, are inextricably linked to their development. Yet most available assessment data focus only on the students themselves—not the environments in which they are learning. As setting-level measurement tools become more sophisticated, they can be used to gain a better understanding of the quality of the learning environments provided for children, gauging the appropriateness of instruction in meeting learning needs. This setting-level approach to assessment is particularly important with multilingual children—a group that demonstrates disproportionate risks for academic difficulties and for whom risks are closely linked to inappropriate or inadequate classroom learning opportunities. For many of these learners, for

example, the quality of classroom teaching and curricula is lower than that offered to their English-only-speaking peers. Assessments of the quality of the settings and interactions experienced by multilingual learners can inform agendas for improvement in an ongoing cycle of action to advance the quality of settings and services and, ultimately, children's development.

Providing Targeted, Intensive Language-Building Opportunities

Supporting the development and learning of multilingual children in early care and education settings and schools requires an instructional approach that is organized around language and knowledge building while simultaneously addressing the children's need to acquire early reading skills (e.g., letter knowledge, word reading). Research on effective instructional practices with young multilingual learners highlights the promise and importance of several strategies and approaches that, together, prepare multilingual learners for the oral and written language they will encounter in the later grades:

- A content-rich curriculum is designed around units of study to promote children's content knowledge and features a wide variety of reading materials (e.g., fiction, expository trade books, leveled books, magazines, audio) that are used as platforms for dialogue and learning.
- Scaffolded, back-and-forth conversations, steeped in content, bring learners beyond the here and now and into abstract explanations, narratives, and pretend (Dickinson, 2003). Opportunities for extended conversations, both planned and spontaneous, are embedded in daily routines and occur in various group formats (e.g., whole-group instruction, teacher-led small groups).
- Targeted small-group instruction, using supporting materials that connect to the content of daily instruction, is provided to multilingual learners who demonstrate difficulties (Castro et al., 2011; McMaster et al., 2008; O'Connor et al., 2010, 2013; Vaughn et al., 2006). Combining vocabulary and listening comprehension activities along with early reading skills in an intervention provides the language stimulation needed by students who are dual language learners (O'Connor et al., 2010). In a response-to-intervention approach, small-group instruction focusing on vocabulary and reading skills beginning in kindergarten can improve dual language learners' reading skills and decrease the proportion of students who required assistance in later grades (Connor et al., 2014; O'Connor et al., 2013).

- Instruction builds first-language skills and strategically uses children's first language to support their English-language development (Castro et al., 2006, 2011). However, although considerable research indicates that the use of children's first language in instruction supports development and learning, this research is based on instruction in contexts in which groups of multilingual children's first languages were largely the same (e.g., Spanish speakers), and teachers had relatively high bilingual proficiency. This scenario is not always feasible, and it is important to note that it is the quality and quantity of language-learning opportunities that is most important for multilingual learners' development, not the particular language used (e.g., English versus Spanish). Therefore, educators need to focus first and foremost on fostering cognitively stimulating and interactive classroom language environments.

Supporting Mathematical Learning

In addition to general principles that support all learners (such as small class sizes that allow for tailored individual learning experiences, team teaching with collaborative planning and reflection, and positive relationships between educators and students as well as with their families), Clements and Sarama (2014) have summarized the research on instructional approaches that are beneficial for the mathematics learning of dual language learners:

- bilingual instructional support and consistent access to the home language, including from paraprofessionals (instructional assistants, parent volunteers, and older and more competent students) as well as use of cognates and other means of explaining math concepts with familiar language (Burchinal et al., 2012; Janzen, 2008; Turner and Celedón-Pattichis, 2011);
- discussion between children and educators as well as among children to explain solutions and work toward more formal mathematical language and ideas;
- word problems that are created from students' personal narratives, helping them "mathematize" situations (Janzen, 2008);
- generating mathematical problems through storytelling, giving additional time to problem solving, posing a broad range of problems involving multiple steps (Turner and Celedón-Pattichis, 2011; Turner et al., 2008);
- strong emphasis on language development for mathematics at school and home; encouragement to families to use the home language to talk about mathematics (especially number, arithmetic,

spatial relations, and patterns) with children of all ages and to visit school and share where mathematics is used in the home and community (Kleemans et al., 2013; Levine et al., 2011);

- simple print material in the children's home language in learning centers and labeled objects;
- age-appropriate books and stories in the child's home language (in school and loaned to the home), which might include e-books (Shamir and Lifshitz, 2012); and
- interventions in preschool through the primary grades, preferably with bilingual components (Clements et al., 2011, 2013; Fuchs et al., 2013; Sarama et al., 2012).

SUPPORTING THE EARLY LEARNING OF CHILDREN WITH AND AT RISK FOR DISABILITIES

Researchers have developed specific instructional strategies or components of instructional strategies for the acquisition and generalization of key skills by young children with or at risk for disabilities (Godfrey et al., 2003; Roark et al., 2002; Sewell et al., 1998; Whalen et al., 1996). These approaches vary along several dimensions, including what is taught, when teaching occurs, the spacing of teaching trials, and the type of instructional procedure that is used. An issue with these strategies is how they can be implemented during naturally occurring activities and routines so that the instruction leads not only to the acquisition of new skills but also to higher levels of engagement in ongoing activities and routines for children with disabilities.

A number of studies have evaluated the effects of such strategies on children's learning when the instruction was embedded into ongoing classroom activities and routines (Daugherty et al., 2001; Grisham-Brown et al., 2000; Hemmeter and Grisham-Brown, in press; Hemmeter et al., 1996) and into ongoing routines in the community (Rogers et al., 2010) and home (Hemmeter and Kaiser, 1994; Kaiser and Hemmeter, 1989; Mobayed et al., 2000). These evaluations showed that teachers' implementation of embedded instruction was associated with positive changes in children's target learning behaviors and in some standardized assessment scores.

Although this type of embedded instruction is a recommended practice in early childhood special education (Wolery, 2005) and early childhood education (NAEYC, 2009), evidence indicates that it frequently is not used in early childhood settings. An observational study in primary-grade classrooms found that for some children, across multiple academic and social activities, there were no instructional trials focused on their learning objectives (Schuster et al., 2001).

Another issue of particular concern is how to support children with special needs in mathematics. Until more is known, students should be labeled as "math learning disabled" only with great caution and after good instruction has been provided. For some students math skills may be delayed, but if formally classified as learning disabled they may be miseducated and mislabeled. In the earliest years, such labeling will probably do more harm than good. Instead, high-quality instruction (preventive education) should be provided to all students. This instruction should go beyond that provided regularly to students and should be sustained over months and years to provide dynamic, formative assessments of the students' needs. Foundational abilities in subitizing, counting and counting strategies, simple arithmetic, and magnitude comparison are important. In later years, competencies in arithmetic combinations, place value, and word problem solving should also be ensured (Dowker, 2004). Other students may have a true math learning disability and be in need of specialized instruction.

An example of the value of different kinds of additional instruction comes from a study showing that in the primary years, students with a math learning disability alone or in combination with a reading learning disability performed worse than normally developing students on timed tests but just as well on untimed tests. Students with a math learning disability alone may simply need extra time studying and extra time to complete calculation tasks. Using a calculator and other computational aids can enable these students to concentrate on developing their problem-solving skills. Students with both mathematics and reading learning disabilities may need more systematic remedial intervention that is aimed at problem conceptualization, the development of effective computational strategies, and strategies for efficient fact retrieval (Jordan and Montani, 1997). Further, specific mathematical competencies may have different relationships to reading learning disabilities. In one study, children with dyslexia experienced difficulty with both arithmetic fact fluency and operations. In addition, however, the findings distinguished between these two areas, as arithmetic fact fluency appeared to be affected by domain-general competencies, whereas operations appeared to be related to specific competencies in literacy (Vukovic et al., 2010).

Historically, many have called for Direct Instruction in skills for students with math learning disabilities. This method provides educators with scripts for frequent interactions with students, clear feedback on the accuracy of students' work, and sequencing of problems (Swanson and Hoskyn, 1998). Research also supports other approaches that share characteristics with Direct Instruction—such as explicit, systematic instruction—but include more student problem solving and student-generated talk rather than highly educator-directed lessons with specific instructions and demonstrations of procedures. For example, educators may not only explain and demonstrate specific strategies, but also encourage students to think aloud about their reasoning and to ask and answer questions—thus playing an active role. Further, instruction is not limited to memorization of simple skills but includes computation and solving word problems, including those that apply mathematics to novel situations. Using visual representations may make such explicit instruction even more effective. Further, educators need to ensure that students are acquiring all foundational concepts and skills necessary to learning mathematics at their grade level (NMP, 2008). Such interventions should be used in addition to other mathematics instruction.

Clements and Sarama (2014) have summarized the research on instructional approaches that help students at risk of experiencing problems with learning mathematics:

- Use information about students' performance, share this information with students, and target specific areas of need (supporting formative assessment, including differentiated activities).
- Individualize instruction. Many students with special needs have distinct learning needs (Gervasoni, 2005; Gervasoni et al., 2007).
- Teach with learning trajectories and the use of formative assessment, strategies that are especially helpful for students with special needs.
- Provide clear, specific feedback to parents on their students' mathematics learning.
- Use peers as tutors.
- Encourage students to verbalize their thinking or their strategies, or even the explicit strategies modeled by the teacher.
- Explicitly teach strategies, not just "facts" or practice of "skills." Encourage students to think aloud, and provide feedback from peers and the teacher. Highlight key aspects of each type of problem (not "key words") (Tournaki, 2003).
- Use high-quality, research-based software (Clements and Sarama, 2009).
- Include individualized work, even for brief periods, as a component of focused interventions (Dowker, 2004; Gersten et al., 2008).
- Consider small-group tutorial sessions, including the use of concrete objects, to promote conceptual learning (Fuchs et al., 2005).
- Focus on geometry and spatial sense as well (Clements and Sarama, 2009). It may not be necessary for students to master one domain (e.g., arithmetic) to study another, such as geometry, meaningfully.

There are many gaps in the availability of resources to help students with special needs. For example, there is no widely used measure with which to identify specific learning difficulties or disabilities in mathematics (Geary, 2004). Finally, it may be most important, and have the most potential to prevent most learning difficulties, if high-quality early and elementary childhood mathematics education is provided for all students. Gersten and colleagues (2009) offer specific guidelines to this end.

WORKING WITH FAMILIES

Care and education professionals need skills in communicating, working collaboratively, and developing partnerships with families. They have an important role in preparing families to engage in behaviors and activities that enhance development and early learning, and to maintain continuity and consistency across home and out-of-home settings and learning environments for young children. Even with few resources, there are actions care and education professionals can encourage parents to take to improve their children's school readiness. For example, parents can

- read to children, arrange for other adults and older siblings to do so (Doucet, 2008), and participate in reading and other programs at the public library;
- provide challenging books, games, and puzzles;
- help children learn to count and solve math problems (Sylva et al., 2005); and
- provide warm and consistent parenting (Lara-Cinisomo et al., 2004).

Families are the people most invested in their children's growth and development, they can be the most valuable support they have in their school career—and they are experts on their children. Early educators can and should capitalize on families' commitment to their children's learning by building partnerships that revolve around this shared commitment.

Following are two examples of the role of family partnerships in supporting child development and early learning. The principles illustrated by these examples also can be applied generally across different domains.

Family Partnerships to Support Language Development

Strong partnerships between families and care and education professionals are key to promoting language-rich home environments for the youngest children. With the common goal of supporting children's language and literacy development in mind, educators can take several specific steps to encourage and support families in cultivating strong home language environments:

- **Build relationships with all families.** Before educators can encourage specific language-building activities or have insight into the particular practices that may work best for a family, they need to have an established relationship with the family. Positive and productive relationships are foundational to supporting the home language environment and thus must be formed with all families. Understanding the various concerns that might impede family engagement—from language barriers, to mistrust of institutions, to fears related to documentation status for immigrants—can help providers begin to devise how best to position themselves as trustworthy, respectful, and collaborative partners to families who may be reticent. Strategies for building strong relationships with families include connecting them to the care and education setting's community (e.g., conducting home visits, welcoming families on site, encouraging volunteerism); setting up the center or school as a community resource in which all members of the community can find support; regularly creating forums to enable families to ask questions and interact with educators, and removing barriers to participation in such forums (e.g., providing childcare, food, and transportation; scheduling them in evenings or on weekends); inviting families to weigh in on programmatic or curricular decisions; making interpreters available for non-English-speaking families; and translating newsletters into languages families can readily understand. In sum, a more reciprocal, rather than school-centric, approach to linking "home and school" is key for building relationships with all families.
- **Encourage families to talk, read, and play.** Educators can encourage and support families in talking about what they are doing or thinking, telling stories and recounting memories, and singing or reciting songs and rhymes. Educators also can provide concrete suggestions and tools to help families support their children's learning and development at home and to connect home activities to classroom learning, such as word games, conversation starters, and all types of books—including multilingual and wordless picture books.
- **Share children's progress with families.** Families are best poised to create a developmentally responsive home language environment when they are provided with regular, timely, and accessible updates on their child's progress and learning. Educators should not only provide these updates but also check in with families to ensure that they understand their children's literacy needs and how to help them and connect classroom activities to those being sent home for extended learning. In addition, inviting families to school to share

their knowledge and experiences and to participate in classroom activities can give families additional insight into their children's progress, developmental needs, and learning in the context of the classroom.

- **Foster two-way channels of communication.** Families can provide a wealth of information about their children to educators seeking to promote strong and supportive classroom language environments where all children participate and learn. For example, families can introduce their children to subjects in a way that motivates them and engages them in conversations about topics that interest them, or they can provide the educator with insights regarding the supports their children may need to feel comfortable with participating actively in classroom conversations.

Tailored Family Partnerships for Dual Language Learners

Engaging in practices that promote partnerships with all families also particularly benefits multilingual children's development and learning. Because the cultural constructs for the families of multilingual children are in many cases different from the long-held cultural norms of U.S. schools, practitioners working to cultivate these partnerships must bridge these cultural gaps (Doucet, 2008; Doucet and Tudge, 2007). In all cases, these efforts should affirm and value families' care for and efforts to support their children's development and learning. When building partnerships with linguistically diverse families, it is particularly important for practitioners to provide regular, accessible, accurate updates on their children's progress in learning and development. Also important is to connect families' strong aspirations for their children to the information and ideas provided about how to support children in pursuing those aspirations (Goldenberg et al., 2001). Educators also need to remind families that when they talk and interact with their children, their children learn. Educators should encourage families to talk, read, and play in the language(s) with which they feel the greatest comfort and facility. When caregivers speak using the language that best facilitates sharing ideas, telling stories, and having rich dialogue, they are boosting children's access to vocabulary and their world knowledge, which almost always boosts their ability in *any* language (August and Shanahan, 2006). Families of emerging bilingual (or multilingual) children may have concerns that children will not learn English if they continue to speak in another language (or languages) at home. Care and education professionals are well positioned to share with families the benefits of bilingualism or multilingualism, as well as to celebrate the linguistic diversity in their classrooms with the children themselves (Bialystok, 2001, 2002).

Barriers to Parent–Educator Relationships

The relationship between care and education professionals and families is not always easily negotiated, particularly across ethnic, cultural, linguistic, and socioeconomic differences. Both racism and classism can act as barriers to family and parent engagement in schools. A 2003 study found that parents' perceptions of racism in schools was linked to their involvement in schools and in the home, and found it critical that interventions around family engagement in schools explore perceptions of race and what parents learn from their children about race (McKay et al., 2003). This is also an opportunity for educators to discuss race with their students in order to prepare them for race-related issues they may encounter. However, a 1998 study found that many teachers are unaware of institutional racism and how it affects parents, families, and students (Bernhard et al., 1998).

Similarly, working-class and middle-class families may perceive family engagement and parent involvement in schools differently; working-class families may not recognize the connection between home and school which may lead to less parent involvement (Lareau, 1989; Lareau and Horvat, 1999). A study also found that working-class and low-income parents may be less involved due to feelings of insecurity in their academic skills or because of their own negative experiences they may have had in school (Lareau, 1989; Lawrence-Lightfoot, 2003). The care and education workforce needs to be prepared to recognize and address these barriers to family engagement (Ambe, 2006; Bloch and Swadener, 1992; Strizek et al., 2006).

Power dynamics between parents and educators can also be a barrier to effective family engagement in schools. Some parents may feel intimidated upon entering the classroom, as they may reflect back on their own childhood school experiences, which may have been negative (Lawrence-Lightfoot, 2003). The power structure may also be seen with immigrant parents who may experience language barriers with educators and who also strive to impress their child's teacher (Hanhan, 2003). In order to eliminate the uneven dynamic, the educator has the responsibility to recognize and address any power issues in order to help parents feel comfortable communicating about the child (Doucet and Tudge, 2007; Lawrence-Lightfoot, 2003).

CONDUCTING CHILD ASSESSMENTS

While early learning standards provide a roadmap for what young children should know and be able to do, early care and education professionals, including practitioners and leaders, also need the competencies to understand how individual and groups of children are learning and developing across the birth through age 8 continuum. In the course of their work, early childhood professionals will need answers to a variety of questions about the progress of young children and of early childhood programs: How are an individual child's literacy skills progressing? Are mainstreamed children with special education classifications making the anticipated progress? What competencies do children possess as they enter kindergarten? Are early childhood programs that receive local, state, or federal funds improving in quality and helping young children meet the state's early learning standards? Are children in a program for infants and toddlers developing significantly better than similar children who are not receiving services?

Care and education professionals and policy leaders need information in order to modify instruction, support curriculum reform, fund new and existing programs, and develop regulations that will support student learning. Therefore, child assessments serve a variety of purposes (Chittenden and Jones, 1999). Sometimes "assessments" are used for high-stakes purposes such as obtaining continued program funding or conducting teacher evaluation. Sometimes the term suggests a more diagnostic function, for example, to identify children with special needs. Within the classroom, "assessment" serves to guide instruction and learning. For educators, assessment should enhance their powers of observation and their understanding of children's overall thinking and learning. Across all levels of education systems, assessments can be used to inform continuous quality improvement (Chittenden, 1991; Chittenden and Jones, 1999).

The intended purpose of assessment should determine its content; the methods used to collect information; and the nature of the possible uses—and consequences—for individual students, teachers, schools, or programs. It is confusion of purpose that often leads to misuse of tests and other instruments in early childhood. Instruments designed for one purpose, such as identification, may be totally inappropriate for another, such as measuring the success of a program. Assessments can inform teaching and program improvement and make a crucial contribution to better outcomes for children, but only if they are selected appropriately, matched to their purpose, well designed, implemented effectively in the context of systematic planning, and interpreted and used appropriately. Otherwise, assessment of children and programs can result in negative consequences for both. The potential value of assessments will therefore only be realized if fundamental attention is paid to their purpose (NRC, 2008).

Realizing the potential value of assessment also requires attention to the design of the larger systems in which assessments are used. Although this section focuses on the ability of care and education professionals to conduct child assessments, it is important to emphasize that such child assessment should not occur in isolation but rather as a component of a comprehensive assessment system, as described in Box 6-2 (NRC, 2008).

BOX 6-2
Components of Comprehensive Assessment Systems

Standards: A comprehensive, well-articulated set of standards for both program quality and children's learning that are aligned to one another and that define the constructs of interest as well as child outcomes that demonstrate that the learning described in the standard has occurred.

Assessments: Multiple approaches to documenting child development and learning and reviewing program quality that are of high quality and connect to one another in well-defined ways, from which strategic selection can be made depending on specific purposes.

Reporting: Maintenance of an integrated database of assessment instruments and results (with appropriate safeguards of confidentiality) that is accessible to potential users, that provides information about how the instruments and scores relate to standards, and that can generate reports for varied audiences and purposes.

Professional development: Ongoing opportunities provided to those at all levels (policy makers, program directors, assessment administrators, practitioners) to understand the standards and the assessments and to learn to use the data and data reports with integrity for their appropriate purposes.

Opportunity to learn: Procedures to assess whether the environments in which children are spending time offer high-quality support for development and learning, as well as safety, enjoyment, and affectively positive relationships, and to direct support to those that fall short.

Inclusion: Methods and procedures for ensuring that all children served by the program will be assessed fairly, regardless of their language, culture, or disabilities, and with tools that provide useful information for fostering their development and learning.

Resources: The assurance that the financial resources needed to ensure the development and implementation of the system components will be available.

Monitoring and evaluation: Continuous monitoring of the system itself to ensure that it is operating effectively and that all elements are working together to serve the interests of the children. This entire infrastructure must be in place to create and sustain an assessment subsystem within a larger system of early childhood care and education.

SOURCE: Excerpted from NRC, 2008, pp. 305-306.

Principles for Assessment Literacy

Stiggins (1991, 1999, 2001) coined the term *assessment literacy* to describe the ability of care and education professionals to understand how to select, administer, and interpret a range of assessment instruments (formal and informal) and how to use the information thus gathered both to understand the context and process of young children's learning and development across a broad range of domains and to make decisions about instruction and intervention. The discussion in this section focuses on the principles of assessment and some of the tools and approaches that care and education professionals should be familiar with and able to use as they investigate questions about the progress of children and programs.

The NAEYC has articulated some of the characteristics of appropriate professional practice in the use of child assessments (NAEYC, 2009; NAEYC and NAECS/SDE, 2003). According to the NAEYC, educators should

- support children's learning using a variety of assessment methods, such as observations, checklists, and rating scales;
- use assessment methods and information to plan appropriately challenging curricula and tailor instruction that responds to each child's strengths and needs;
- use assessment methods and information to design goals for individual children and monitor their progress;
- use assessment methods and information to improve teaching strategies;
- use assessment methods that are appropriate for each child's age and level of development and that encompass all domains of development;
- use assessments to help identify children with disabilities and ensure that they receive needed services;
- integrate assessment into their day, rather than making it a large task to be attempted all at once; and
- provide families with information about their children's development and learning on a regular basis to help ensure that assessments occur within the context of reciprocal communications with families and with sensitivity to the cultural contexts in which children develop.

Key to applying these principles using the assessment tools described in the next section is for professionals to be trained not only in how to administer assessments but also in how to interpret their results and apply that information to make changes in instructional practices and learning environments (Kauerz and Coffman, 2013; Tout et al., 2013). In addition, data collection, interpretation, and sharing in ongoing practice need to be supported through structured and facilitated means to ensure the quality of the data analysis, interpretation, and use. Leaders in educational settings as well as systems and oversight policies must support the time and structures needed to realize the potential of assessment data to inform day-to-day instructional practices, professional learning, and organizational planning. In many settings, accountability requirements increasingly demand unprecedented amounts of data gathering. This demand may be having unintended consequences in detracting from meaningful interpretation and use of assessment data. A shift may be required to decrease the volume of data collection and reorient the current focus on reporting and compliance in favor of devoting more time, support, and resources to data analysis, interpretation, and use (Lesaux and Marietta, 2012; Lesaux et al., 2014).

Approaches and Tools for Child Assessments

There exists an array of tools that, when selected wisely and according to the purpose for which they were intended, administered appropriately, and interpreted accurately, can inform practice and policy to help create successful learning environments and achieve strong outcomes for children. The terms used in any assessment discussion (e.g., "assessment," "test," "formative assessment," "summative assessment") have different meanings and connotations for different audiences. This report generally follows the definitions of assessment-related terms from the 2014 Standards for Educational and Psychological Testing Assessment (AERA et al., 2014). Assessment that supports early learning can draw on a range of sources of evidence on children's thinking development, as outlined in Box 6-3. At appropriate ages, all of these sources can be useful.

Screening

Screening is the use of a brief procedure or tool to identify children who may require a more in-depth diagnostic assessment to determine whether they need more in-depth intervention services. When such services are needed, the follow-up typically requires coordination among families, early educators, and medical or early intervention specialists (NRC, 2008). Screening competencies include the knowledge and ability to help ensure that health and developmental screenings are being administered at the right stages and using appropriate, valid screening tools; skills in early identification of the potential need for further assessment and referral for developmental delays, mental health issues, and other such concerns; skills to help families find necessary resources; and skills for follow-up on the outcomes of referrals (HRSA, n.d.; Meisels and Atkins-Burnett, 2005).

BOX 6-3
Sources of Assessment Information

General Observation and Records of Activities
- anecdotal records
- checklists
- projects
- inventories of student activities

Class Discussions and Conversations
- whole-group discussions
- students' comments and questions about their work
- conferences and conversations

Work Samples
- drawings
- writing and journal entries
- constructions

Performance Tasks and Curriculum-Embedded Assessments
- solving a problem, with explanation
- telling a story problem

Interviews and Tests
- teacher-created
- textbook/unit questions
- standardized, norm-referenced

SOURCES: AERA et al., 2014; HighScope Educational Research Foundation, 2003; Meisels et al., 1995; NRC, 2008; Riley-Ayers et al., 2008.

Diagnostic Assessment

Diagnostic assessment is used to better describe an identified problem, to locate a cause, or both. A child identified by a screening assessment as possibly having delayed language development, for example, needs further assessment to determine whether an actual delay exists; whether there are other, related delays (e.g., intellectual functioning, cognitive processing); and whether there are obvious causes (e.g., hearing loss). Individual diagnostic assessments increasingly are being tied to "response to intervention," in other words, to assess what interventions are needed and whether interventions are successful (NRC, 2008).

Formative Assessment

Formative assessment is conducted during instruction to provide information and feedback that can be used to adjust ongoing teaching with the goal of improving students' learning and their achievement on intended outcomes. These assessments are based heavily on educators' observations and documentation of children's learning and development across a range of domains. Research indicates that formative assessment is an effective teaching strategy (Akers et al., 2014; Black and Wiliam, 1998; Clarke, 2008; Clarke et al., 2002; NMP, 2008; Penuel and Shepard, in press; Shepard, 2005). It helps all children learn, but helps lower-achieving children the most. They gain not only subject-matter knowledge but also cognitive competencies often already attained by higher-achieving children. However, the strategy is of little use if educators cannot accurately assess students' progress in learning a topic and determine how to support them in learning the next level of thinking. As described earlier, learning trajectories help define the content educators need to teach, understand it well themselves, and match instructional tasks to children's developmental progression. Formative assessment is an important part of the cycle of understanding the levels of thinking at which students are operating, identifying the next level of thinking they should learn, and matching this to educational activities to support that learning (Clements and Sarama, 2008; Clements et al., 2011, 2013).

The instruments often promoted for formative assessment are "curriculum-embedded assessments," such as small-group record sheets and computer records (Penuel and Shepard, in press; Shepard, 2006). Compared with assessments that are merely curriculum based, curriculum-embedded assessments have the potential to address higher-level thinking and understanding, which has the added advantage of being intrinsically more interesting to students. In addition, although there is reasonable concern that assessments can narrow curriculum and teaching, comprehensive, research-based assessment instruments (often individually administered) (Clements et al., 2011; Ginsburg and Baroody, 2003; Greenfield et al., 2008, 2009) can support and expand learning activities in frequently neglected areas such as science and mathematics (Brenneman et al., 2009a). Along with curriculum-based assessments, they can help educators understand the many concepts and processes young children are capable of learning and, by identifying learning trajectories and children's progress along them, help educators use formative assessment to modify instruction so it is more efficacious.

Summative Assessment

Summative assessments typically are carried out at the completion of a program of learning, such as at the end of an instructional unit, to determine a test taker's knowledge and skills. Summative assessments can be used for multiple purposes. In some cases, they are used for accountability, and sometimes they are administered by educators themselves to be used for that purpose. In such circumstances, a caution is that "performance (classroom-based) assessments of children can be used for accountability, if objectivity is ensured by checking a sample of the assessments for reliability and consistency, if the results are appropriately contextualized in information about the program, and if careful safeguards are in place to prevent misuse of information" (NRC, 2008, p. 11).

REFERENCES

AAP (American Academy of Pediatrics), APHA (American Public Health Association), and National Resource Center for Health and Safety in Child Care and Early Education. 2011. *Caring for our children, national health and safety performance standards: Guidelines for early care and early education programs*. Elk Grove Village, IL: AAP.

AERA (American Educational Research Association), APA (American Psychological Association), and NCME (National Council on Measurement in Education). 2014. *The standards for educational and psychological testing*. Washington, DC: APA.

Akers, L., P. D. Grosso, S. Atkins-Burnett, K. Boller, J. Carta, and B. A. Wasik. 2014. *Tailored teaching: Teachers' use of ongoing child assessment to individualize instruction (Volume II)*. Washington, DC: U.S. Department of Health and Human Service, Administration for Children and Families, Office of Planning, Research, and Evaluation.

Akerson, V. L. 2004. Designing a science methods course for early childhood preservice teachers. *Journal of Elementary Science Education* 126(2):19-32.

Akiba, M., G. K. LeTendre, and J. P. Scribner. 2007. Teacher quality, opportunity gap, and national achievement in 46 countries. *Educational Researcher* 36:369-387.

Alibali, M. W., and S. Goldin-Meadow. 1993. Transitions in learning: What the hands reveal about a child's state of mind. *Cognitive Psychology* 25:468-523.

Ambe, E. B. 2006. Fostering multicultural appreciation in pre-service teachers through multicultural curricular transformation. *Teaching and Teacher Education* 22(6):690-699.

Amini Virmani, E., K. E. Masyn, R. A. Thompson, N. A. Conners-Burrow, and L. Whiteside Mansell. 2013. Early childhood mental health consultation: Promoting change in the quality of teacher–child interactions. *Infant Mental Health Journal* 34(2):156-172.

Anderson, D., and T. Pempek. 2005. Television and very young children. *American Behavioral Scientist* 48(5):505-522.

Anderson, D. R., A. C. Huston, K. L. Schmitt, D. L. Linebarger, J. C. Wright, and R. Larson. 2001. Early childhood television viewing and adolescent behavior: The recontact study. *Monographs of the Society for Research in Child Development* 66(1):i-viii, 1-154.

Appleton, K., and I. Kindt. 1999. Why teach primary science? Influences on beginning teachers' practices. *International Journal of Science Education* 21(2):155-168.

———. 2002. Beginning elementary teachers' development as teachers of science. *Journal of Science Teacher Education* 13(1):43-61.

Aram, D., and S. Biron. 2004. Joint storybook reading and joint writing interventions among low SES preschoolers: Differential contributions to early literacy. *Early Childhood Research Quarterly Early Childhood Research Quarterly* 19(4):588-610.

Askew, M., M. Brown, V. Rhodes, D. Wiliam, and D. Johnson. 1997. Effective teachers of numeracy in UK primary schools: Teachers' beliefs, practices, and children's learning. In *Proceedings of the 21st Conference of the International Group for the Psychology of Mathematics Education*. Vol. 2, edited by E. Pehkonen. Helsinki, Finland: University of Helsinki. Pp. 25-32.

August, D., and T. Shanahan. 2006. *Developing literacy in second-language learners: Report of the National Literacy Panel on Language Minority Children and Youth*. Executive Summary. Mahwah, NJ: Lawrence Erlbaum Associates.

Aukrust, V. G. 2007. Young children acquiring second language vocabulary in preschool group-time: Does amount, diversity, and discourse complexity of teacher talk matter? *Journal of Research in Childhood Education* 22(1):17-37.

Aydogan, C., C. Plummer, S. J. Kang, C. Bilbrey, D. C. Farran, and M. W. Lipsey. 2005. *An investigation of prekindergarten curricula: Influences on classroom characteristics and child engagement*. Paper presented at National Association for the Education of Young Children, April, Washington, DC.

Ballou, D., W. L. Sanders, and P. Wright. 2004. Controlling for student background in value-added assessment of teachers. *Journal of Educational and Behavioral Statistics* 29(1):37-65.

Bangert-Drowns, R. L. 1993. The word processor as an instructional tool: A meta-analysis of word processing in writing instruction. *Review of Educational Research* 63(1):69-93.

Barnett, W. S., K. Jung, D. J. Yarosz, J. Thomas, A. Hornbeck, R. Stechuk, and S. Burns. 2008. Educational effects of the Tools of the Mind curriculum: A randomized trial. *Early Childhood Research Quarterly Early Childhood Research Quarterly* 23(3):299-313.

Barnett, W. S., D. J. Epstein, A. H. Friedman, J. Stevenson-Boyd, and J. T. Hustedt. 2009. *The state of preschool 2008: State preschool yearbook*. New Brunswick, NJ: National Institute for Early Education Research.

Baroody, A. J. 1999. The development of basic counting, number, and arithmetic knowledge among children classified as mentally handicapped. In *International review of research in mental retardation*. Vol. 22, edited by L. M. Glidden. New York: Academic Press. Pp. 51-103.

———. 2003. The development of adaptive expertise and flexibility: The integration of conceptual and procedural knowledge. In *The development of arithmetic concepts and skills constructive adaptive expertise*, edited by A. J. Baroody and A. Dowker. Mahwah, NJ: Lawrence Erlbaum Associates. Pp. 1-34.

———. 2004a. The developmental bases for early childhood number and operations standards. In *Engaging young children in mathematics standards for early childhood mathematics education*, edited by D. H. Clements and J. Sarama. Mahwah, NJ: Lawrence Erlbaum Associates. Pp. 173-219.

———. 2004b. The role of psychological research in the development of early childhood mathematics standards. In *Engaging young children in mathematics standards for early childhood mathematics education*, edited by D. H. Clements and J. Sarama. Mahwah, NJ: Lawrence Erlbaum Associates. Pp. 149-172.

Barr, R., and H. Hayne. 1999. Developmental changes in imitation from television during infancy. *Child Development* 70(5):1067-1081.

Barr, R., P. Muentener, A. Garcia, M. Fujimoto, and V. Chávez. 2007. The effect of repetition on imitation from television during infancy. *Developmental Psychobiology* 49(2):196-207.

Barr, R., A. Lauricella, E. Zach, and S. L. Calvert. 2010. Infant and early childhood exposure to adult-directed and child-directed television programming: Relations with cognitive skills at age four. *Merrill-Palmer Quarterly: Journal of Developmental Psychology* 56(1):21-48.

Barton, K. C., and L. A. Smith. 2000. Themes or motifs? Aiming for coherence through inter-disciplinary outlines. *The Reading Teacher* 54(1):54-63.

Baumert, J., M. Kunter, W. Blum, M. Brunner, T. Voss, A. Jordan, and Y.-M. Tsai. 2010. Teachers' mathematical knowledge, cognitive activation in the classroom, and student progress. *American Educational Research Journal* 47(1):133-180.

Beck, I. L., and M. G. McKeown. 2001. Text talk: Capturing the benefits of read-aloud experiences for young children. *The Reading Teacher* 55(1):10-20.

———. 2007. Increasing young low-income children's oral vocabulary repertoires through rich and focused instruction. *Elementary School Journal* 107(3):251-273.

Beilock, S. L. 2001. Learning and performing math: Self-concept, self-doubt, and self-fulfilling prophesy. *Journal of Experimental Psychology: General* 130:224-237.

Bereiter, C., and M. Scardamalia. 2010. Can children really create knowledge? *Canadian Journal of Learning and Technology* 36(1).

Bernhard, J. K., M. L. Lefebvre, K. Murphy Kilbride, G. Chud, and R. Lange. 1998. Troubled relationships in early childhood education: Parent–teacher interactions in ethnoculturally diverse child care settings. *Early Education and Development* 9(1):5-28.

Betts, J., S. Bolt, D. Decker, P. Muyskens, and D. Marston. 2009. Examining the role of time and language type in reading development for English language learners. *Journal of School Psychology* 47(3):143-166.

Bialystok, E. 2001. *Bilingualism in development: Language, literacy, and cognition.* New York: Cambridge University Press.

———. 2002. Acquisition of literacy in bilingual children: A framework for research. *Language Learning* 52(1):159-199.

Biancarosa, G., and G. G. Griffiths. 2012. Technology tools to support reading in the digital age. *Future of Children* 22(2):139-160.

Bierman, K. L., C. E. Domitrovich, R. L. Nix, S. D. Gest, J. A. Welsh, M. T. Greenberg, C. Blair, K. E. Nelson, and S. Gill. 2008a. Promoting academic and social-emotional school readiness: The Head Start REDI Program. *Child Development* 79(6):1802-1817.

Bierman, K. L., R. L. Nix, M. T. Greenberg, C. Blair, and C. E. Domitrovich. 2008b. Executive functions and school readiness intervention: Impact, moderation, and mediation in the Head Start REDI Program. *Development and Psychopathology* 20(3):821-843.

Black, P., and D. Wiliam. 1998. Assessment and classroom learning. *Assessment in Education: Principles, Policy and Practice* 5(1):7-76.

Blevins-Knabe, B., and L. Musun-Miller. 1996. Number use at home by children and their parents and its relationship to early mathematical performance. *Early Development and Parenting* 5:35-45.

Bloch, M., and B. B. Swadener. 1992. Relationships between home, community and school: Multicultural considerations and research issues in early childhood. In *Research and multicultural education: From the margins to the mainstream*, edited by C. A. Grant. Washington, DC: Falmer Press. Pp. 165-183.

Blömeke, S., U. Suhl, and G. Kaiser. 2011. Teacher education effectiveness: Quality and equity of future primary teachers' mathematics and mathematics pedagogical content knowledge. *Journal of Teacher Education* 62(2):154-171.

Bloom, L. 2000. Pushing the limits on theories of word learning. *Monographs of the Society for Research in Child Development* 65(3):124-135.

Blote, A. W., E. Van der Burg, and A. S. Klein. 2001. Students' flexibility in solving two-digit addition and subtraction problems: Instruction effects. *Journal of Educational Psychology* 93(3):627-638.

Boaler, J. 2014. Research suggests that timed tests cause math anxiety. *Teaching Children Mathematics* 20(8):469-474.

Bobis, J., B. A. Clarke, D. M. Clarke, T. Gill, R. J. Wright, J. M. Young-Loveridge, and P. Gould. 2005. Supporting teachers in the development of young children's mathematical thinking: Three large scale cases. *Mathematics Education Research Journal* 16(3):27-57.

Bodrova, E., and D. J. Leong. 2007. *Tools of the mind: The Vygotskian approach to early childhood education.* 2nd ed. New York: Merrill/Prentice Hall.

Bowers, E. P., and M. Vasilyeva. 2011. The relation between teacher input and lexical growth of preschoolers. *Applied Psycholinguistics* 32(1):221-241.

Bowers, P., J. Kirby, and S. Deacon. 2010. The effects of morphological instruction on literacy skills: A systematic review of the literature. *Review of Educational Research* 80(2):144-179.

Brenneman, K., C. Massey, and K. Metz. 2009a. *Science in the early childhood classroom: Introducing senses as tools for observation.* Paper presented at Biennial Meeting of the Society for Research in Child Development, April, Denver, CO.

Brenneman, K., J. Stevenson-Boyd, and E. C. Frede. 2009b. *Math and science in preschool: Policies and practice.* New Brunswick, NJ: National Institute for Early Education Research.

Brooks-Gunn, J. 2003. Do you believe in magic? What we can expect from early childhood intervention programs. *Social Policy Report* 17(1):1, 3-14.

Brown, E. T. 2005. The influence of teachers' efficacy and beliefs regarding mathematics instruction in the early childhood classroom. *Journal of Early Childhood Teacher Education* 26(26):239-257.

Burchinal, M. R., S. Field, M. L. Lopez, C. Howes, and R. C. Pianta. 2012. Instruction in Spanish in pre-kindergarten classrooms and child outcomes for English language learners. *Early Childhood Research Quarterly* 27(2):188-197.

Bus, A., and C. T. Kegel. 2013. Effects of an adaptive game on early literacy skills in at-risk populations. In *Technology as a support for literacy achievements for children at risk.* Vol. 7, Literacy studies, edited by A. Shamir and O. Korat. Netherlands: Springer. Pp. 11-19.

CAEP (Council for the Accreditation of Educator Preparation). 2013. *CAEP accreditation standards.* https://caepnet.files.wordpress.com/2015/02/final_board_amended_20150213.pdf (accessed March 19, 2015).

Cain, K., and J. Oakhill. 1996. The nature of the relationship between comprehension skill and the ability to tell a story. *British Journal of Developmental Psychology* 14(2):187-201.

Callanan, M. A., and L. A. Oakes. 1992. Preschoolers' questions and parents' explanations: Causal thinking in everyday activity. *Cognitive Development* 7:213-233.

Campbell, P. F., and E. A. Silver. 1999. *Teaching and learning mathematics in poor communities.* Reston, VA: National Council of Teachers of Mathematics.

Carey, S. 2009. *The origin of concepts.* New York: Oxford University Press.

Carlo, M. S., D. August, B. McLaughlin, C. E. Snow, C. Dressler, D. N. Lippman, T. J. Lively, and C. E. White. 2004. Closing the gap: Addressing the vocabulary needs of English-language learners in bilingual and mainstream classrooms. *Reading Research Quarterly* 39(2):188-215.

Carpenter, T. P., and J. M. Moser. 1984. The acquisition of addition and subtraction concepts in grades one through three. *Journal for Research in Mathematics Education* 15:179-202.

Carpenter, T. P., M. L. Franke, V. R. Jacobs, E. Fennema, and S. B. Empson. 1998. A longitudinal study of invention and understanding in children's multidigit addition and subtraction. *Journal for Research in Mathematics Education* 29(1):3-20.

Case, L., D. Speece, R. Silverman, C. Schatschneider, E. Montanaro, and L. Ritchey. 2014. Immediate and long-term effects of tier 2 reading instruction for first-grade students with a high probablity of reading failure. *Journal of Research on Educator Effectiveness* 7:28-53.

CASEL (Collaborative for Academic, Social, and Emotional Learning). 2012. *2013 CASEL guide: Effective social and emotional learning programs. Preschool and elementary school edition.* Chicago, IL: Collaborative for Academic, Social, and Emotional Learning.

Castro, D. C., C. Gillanders, M. Machado-Casas, and V. Buysse. 2006. *Nuestros ninos early language and literacy program.* Chapel Hill: University of North Carolina, Frank Porter Graham Child Development Institute.

Castro, D. C., B. Ayankoya, and C. Kasprzak. 2011. *The new voices, nuevas voces guide to cultural and linguistic diversity in early childhood.* Baltimore, MD: Paul H. Brookes Publishing Co.

Catts, H. W., M. E. Fey, X. Zhang, and J. B. Tomblin. 1999. Language basis of reading and reading disabilities: Evidence from a longitudinal investigation. *Scientific Studies of Reading* 3(4):331-361.

Catts, H. W., D. Compton, J. B. Tomblin, and M. S. Bridges. 2012. Prevalence and nature of late-emerging poor readers. *Journal of Educational Psychology* 104(1):166-181.

CCSSO (Council of Chief State School Officers) and NGA (National Governors Association). 2010. *English language arts standards » writing » kindergarten.* http://www.core standards.org/ELA-Literacy/W/K/#CCSS.ELA-Literacy.W.K.6 (accessed March 19, 2015).

Center on the Developing Child. 2015. *Activities guide: Enhancing and practicing executive function skills with children from infancy to adolescence.* http://developingchild.harvard. edu/resources/tools_and_guides/enhancing_and_practicing_executive_function_skills_ with_children/ (accessed March 23, 2015).

Cepeda, N. J., H. Pashler, E. Vul, J. T. Wixted, and D. Rohrer. 2006. Distributed practice in verbal recall tasks: A review and quantitative synthesis. *Psychological Bulletin* 132(3):354-380.

Cervetti, G., P. D. Pearson, M. A. Bravo, and J. Barber. 2006. Reading and writing in the service of inquiry-based science. In *Linking science and literacy in the K-8 classroom,* edited by R. Douglas, M. P. Klentschy, and K. Worth. Arlington, VA: National Science Teachers Association. Pp. 221-244.

Chambers, C. 2008. Response to intervention (RTI). *Technology and Learning* 29(3):18.

Chase-Lansdale, P. L., and J. Brooks-Gunn. 2014. Two-generation programs in the twenty-first century. *The Future of Children* 24(1):13-39.

Chittenden, E. A. 1991. Authentic assessment, evaluation, and documentation of student performance. In *Expanding student assessment,* edited by V. Perrone. Alexandria, VA: Association for Supervision and Curriculum Development. Pp. 22-31.

Chittenden, E. A., and J. Jones. 1999. Science assessment in early childhood programs. In *Dialogue on early childhood science, mathematics, and technology education,* edited by G. D. Nelson. Washington, DC: American Association for the Advancement of Science. Pp. 106-114.

Choi, K., and H. L. Kirkorian. 2013. *Object retrieval using contingent vs. non-contingent video on touchscreens.* Paper presented at Biennial Meeting of the Society for Research in Child Development, Seattle, WA.

Christakis, D. A., F. J. Zimmerman, D. L. DiGiuseppe, and C. A. McCarty. 2004. Early television exposure and subsequent attentional problems in children. *Pediatrics* 113(4): 708-713.

Claessens, A., M. Engel, and F. C. Curran. 2014. Academic content, student learning, and HTE persistence of preschool effects. *American Educational Research Journal* 51(2):403-434.

Clarke, B. A. 2008. A framework of growth points as a powerful teacher development tool. In *Tools and processes in mathematics teacher education,* edited by D. Tirosh and T. Wood. Rotterdam, The Netherlands: Sense Publishers. Pp. 235-256.

Clarke, D. M., J. Cheeseman, A. Gervasoni, D. Gronn, M. Horne, A. McDonough, P. Montgomery, A. Roche, P. Sullivan, B. A. Clarke, and G. Rowley. 2002. *Early numeracy research project final report*. Melbourne, VIC: Australian Catholic University.

Clements, D. H., and J. Sarama. 2003. Strip mining for gold: Research and policy in educational technology—a response to fools gold. *Educational Technology Review* 11(1):7-69.

———. 2007. Effects of a preschool mathematics curriculum: Summative research on the "building blocks" project. *Journal for Research in Mathematics Education* 38(2):136-163.

———. 2008. Experimental evaluation of the effects of a research-based preschool mathematics curriculum. *American Educational Research Journal* 45(2):443-494.

———. 2009. *Learning and teaching early math: The learning trajectories approach*. 1st ed. New York: Routledge.

———. 2010. Technology. In *Children of 2020: Creating a better tomorrow*, edited by V. Washington and J. Andrews. Washington, DC: Council for Professional Recognition and National Association for the Education of Young Children. Pp. 119-123.

———. 2012. Learning and teaching early and elementary mathematics. In *Instructional strategies for improving students' learning: Focus on early reading and mathematics*, edited by J. S. Carlson and J. R. Levin. Charlotte, NC: Information Age Publishing. Pp. 107-162.

———. 2014. *Learning and teaching early math: The learning trajectories approach*. 2nd ed. New York and Oxford, UK: Routledge.

Clements, D. H., J. Sarama, M. E. Spitler, A. A. Lange, and C. B. Wolfe. 2011. Mathematics learned by young children in an intervention based on learning trajectories: A large-scale cluster randomized trial. *Journal for Research in Mathematics Education* 42(2):127-166.

Clements, D. H., J. Sarama, F. Unlu, and C. Layzer. 2012. *The efficacy of an intervention synthesizing scaffolding designed to promote self-regulation with an early mathematics curriculum: Effects on executive function*: Society for Research on Educational Effectiveness.

Clements, D. H., J. Sarama, C. B. Wolfe, and M. E. Spitler. 2013. Longitudinal evaluation of a scale-up model for teaching mathematics with trajectories and technologies: Persistence of effects in the third year. *American Educational Research Journal* 50(4):812-850.

———. 2014. Sustainability of a scale-up intervention in early mathematics: A longitudinal evaluation of implementation fidelity. *Early Education and Development*.

Connor, C. M., S. B. Piasta, S. Glasney, C. Schatschneider, B. Fishman, and P. Underwood. 2009. Individualizing student instruction precisely: Effects of child × instruction interactions on first graders' literacy development. *Child Development* 80:77-100.

Connor, C. M., P. A. Alberto, D. L. Compton, R. E. O'Connor, and National Center for Special Education Research. 2014. *Improving reading outcomes for students with or at risk for reading disabilities: A synthesis of the contributions from the Institute of Education Sciences Research Centers*. NCSER 2014-3000. Washington, DC: National Center for Special Education Research.

Copple, C., I. E. Sigel, and R. A. Saunders. 1984. *Educating the young thinker: Classroom strategies for cognitive growth*. Hillsdale, NJ: Lawrence Erlbaum Associates.

Coyne, M. D., D. B. McCoach, and S. Kapp. 2007. Vocabulary intervention for kindergarten students: Comparing extended instruction to embedded instruction and incidental exposure. *Learning Disability Quarterly* 30(2):74-88.

Coyne, M. D., A. Capozzoli-Oldham, and D. C. Simmons. 2012. Vocabulary instruction for young children at-risk of experiencing reading difficulties: Teaching word meanings during shared storybook readings. In *Vocabulary instruction: Research to practice*, edited by J. F. Baumann and E. J. Kame'enui. New York: Guilford Press.

Currie, J., and D. Thomas. 2000. School quality and the longer-term effects of Head Start. *Journal of Human Resources* 35(4):755-774.

Czerniak, C. M., W. B. Weber, Jr., A. Sandmann, and J. Ahern. 1999. A literature review of science and mathematics integration. *School Science and Mathematics* 99(8):421-430.

Darling-Hammond, L. 1997. *The right to learn: A blueprint for creating schools that work.* San Francisco, CA: Jossey-Bass.

———. 2006. Securing the right to learn: Policy and practice for powerful teaching and learning. *Educational Researcher* 35(7):13-24.

Daugherty, L., R. Dossani, E.-E. Johnson, and M. Oguz. 2014. *Using early childhood education to bridge the digital divide.* Santa Monica, CA: RAND Corporation.

Daugherty, S., J. Grisham-Brown, and M. L. Hemmeter. 2001. The effects of embedded skill instruction on the acquisition of target and nontarget skills in preschoolers with developmental delays. *Topics in Early Childhood Special Education* 21(4):213-221.

DeLoache, J. S. 2005. Mindful of symbols. *Scientific American* 293(2):72-77.

DeLoache, J. S., S. L. Pierroutsakos, D. H. Uttal, K. S. Rosengren, and A. Gottlieb. 1998. Grasping the nature of pictures. *Psychological Science* 9(3):205-210.

DeLoache, J. S., C. Chiong, K. Sherman, N. Islam, M. Vanderborght, G. L. Troseth, G. A. Strouse, and K. O'Doherty. 2010. Do babies learn from baby media? *Psychological Science* 21(11):1570-1574.

Diamond, A. 2012. Activities and programs that improve children's executive functions. *Current Directions in Psychological Science* 21(5):335-341.

Diamond, A., and K. Lee. 2011. Interventions shown to aid executive function development in children 4 to 12 years old. *Science Science* 333(6045):959-964.

Diamond, A., W. S. Barnett, J. Thomas, and S. Munro. 2007. Preschool program improves cognitive control. *Science* 318(5855):1387-1388.

Dickinson, D. K. 2003. Why we must improve teacher-child conversations in preschools and the promise of professional development. In *Enhancing caregiver language facilitation in childcare settings*, edited by L. Girolametto and E. Weitzman. Toronto: The Hanen Institute. Pp. 41-48.

Domitrovich, C. E., R. C. Cortes, and M. T. Greenberg. 2007. Improving young childrens social and emotional competence: A randomized trial of the preschool paths curriculum. *Journal of Primary Prevention* 28(2):67-91.

Doucet, F. 2008. How African American parents understand their and teachers' roles in children's schooling and what this means for preparing preservice teachers. *Journal of Early Childhood Teacher Education* 29(2):108-139.

Doucet, F., and J. Tudge. 2007. Co-constructing the transition to school: Reframing the "novice" versus "expert" roles of children, parents, and teachers from a cultural perspective. In *School readiness and the transition to kindergarten in the era of accountability*, edited by R. C. Pianta, M. J. Cox, and K. L. Snow. Baltimore, MD: Paul H. Brookes Publishing Co. Pp. 307-328.

Dowker, A. 2004. *What works for children with mathematical difficulties?* (research report no. 554). Nottingham, UK: University of Oxford, Department for Education and Skills.

———. 2007. What can intervention tell us about the development of arithmetic? *Educational and Child Psychology* 24(2):64-82.

Downs, L., K. Brenneman, R. Gelman, C. Massey, I. Nayfeld, and Z. Roth. 2009. *Developing classroom experiences to support preschoolers' knowledge of living things.* Paper presented at Biennial Meeting of the Society for Research in Child Development, April, Denver, CO.

Dowsett, S. M., and D. J. Livesey. 2000. The development of inhibitory control in preschool children: Effects of executive skills training. *Developmental Psychobiology* 36(2):161-174.

Duke, N. K., and M. K. Block. 2012. Improving reading in the primary grades. *The Future of Children* 22(2):55-72.

Durlak, J. A. 2015. *Handbook of social and emotional learning: Research and practice.* New York: The Guilford Press.

Early, D. M., O. Barbarin, D. Bryant, M. R. Burchinal, F. Chang, R. Clifford, G. Crawford, W. Weaver, C. Howes, S. Ritchie, M. Kraft-Sayre, R. Pianta, and W. S. Barnett. 2005. *Pre-kindergarten in eleven states: NCEDL's multi-state study of pre-kindergarten & study of state-wide early education programs (SWEEP).* Chapel Hill, NC: National Center for Early Development & Learning, FPG Child Development Institute.

Early, D. M., K. L. Maxwell, M. Burchinal, S. Alva, R. H. Bender, D. Bryant, K. Cai, R. M. Clifford, C. Ebanks, J. A. Griffin, G. T. Henry, C. Howes, J. Iriondo-Perez, H.-J. Jeon, A. J. Mashburn, E. Peisner-Feinberg, R. C. Pianta, N. Vandergrift, and N. Zill. 2007. Teachers' education, classroom quality, and young children's academic skills: Results from seven studies of preschool programs. *Child Development* 78(2):558-580.

Early, D. M., I. U. Iruka, S. Ritchie, O. A. Barbarin, D.-M. C. Winn, G. M. Crawford, P. M. Frome, R. M. Clifford, M. Burchinal, C. Howes, D. M. Bryant, and R. C. Pianta. 2010. How do pre-kindergarteners spend their time? Gender, ethnicity, and income as predictors of experiences in pre-kindergarten classrooms. *Early Childhood Research Quarterly* 25(2):177-193.

Ehri, L. 2005. Learning to read words: Theory, findings, and issues. *Scientific Studies of Reading* 9:167-188.

Eimeren, L. V., K. D. MacMillan, and D. Ansari. 2007. *The role of subitizing in children's development of verbal counting.* Paper presented at Society for Research in Child Development, Boston, MA.

Elbro, C. 1990. *Differences in dyslexia: A study of reading strategies and deficits in a linguistic perspective.* Copenhagen, Denmark: Munksgaard International Publishers.

Engel, M., A. Claessens, and M. A. Finch. 2013. Teaching students what they already know? The (mis)alignment between mathematics instructional content and student knowledge in kindergarten. *Educational Evaluation and Policy Analysis* 35(2):157-178.

Espinet, S. D., J. E. Anderson, and P. D. Zelazo. 2012. N2 amplitude as a neural marker of executive function in young children: An ERP study of children who switch versus perseverate on the dimensional change card sort. *Developmental Cognitive Neuroscience* 2:49-58.

Farran, D. C., M. W. Lipsey, B. Watson, and S. Hurley. 2007. *Balance of content emphasis and child content engagement in an early reading first program.* Paper presented at American Educational Research Association, Chicago, IL.

Farran, D., M. Lipsey, and S. Wilson. 2011 (unpublished). *Experimental evaluation of the Tools of the Mind pre-k curriculum. Technical report.* Peabody Research Institute, Vanderbilt University.

Fatouros, C. 1995. Young children using computers: Planning appropriate learning experiences. *Australian Journal of Early Childhood* 20(2):1-6.

Ferguson, R. F. 1991. Paying for public education: New evidence on how and why money matters. *Harvard Journal on Legislation* 28:465-498.

Fixsen, D. L., S. F. Naoom, K. A. Blase, R. M. Friedman, and F. Wallace. 2005. *Implementation research: A synthesis of the literature.* Tampa: University of South Florida, Louis de la Parte Florida Mental Health Institute.

Foorman, B. R. 2007. Primary prevention in classroom reading instruction. *Teaching Exceptional Children* 39(5):24-31.

Fox, L., and M. L. Hemmeter. 2009. A programwide model for supporting social emotional development and addressing challenging behavior in early childhood settings. *Handbook of Positive Behavior Support Issues in Clinical Child Psychology* 177-202.

Fox, L., G. Dunlap, M. L. Hemmeter, G. Joseph, and P. Strain. 2003. The teaching pyramid: A model for supporting social emotional competence and preventing challenging behavior in young children. *Young Children* 58:48-52.

Francis, D. J., M. Rivera, N. K. Lesaux, M. J. Kieffer, and H. Rivera. 2006. *Practical guidelines for the education of English language learners: Research-based recommendations for instruction and academic interventions*. Portsmouth, NH: Center on Instruction.

Franke, M. L., E. Kazemi, and D. Battey. 2007. Mathematics teaching and classroom practice. In *Second handbook of research on mathematics teaching and learning*. Vol. 1, edited by F. K. Lester, Jr. New York: Information Age Publishing. Pp. 225-256.

French, L. 2004. Science as the center of a coherent, integrated early childhood curriculum. *Early Childhood Research Quarterly* 19(1):138-149.

Frey, A. 2009. Positive behavior supports and interventions in early childhood education. *NHSA Dialog* 12(2):71-74.

Fuchs, D., and L. S. Fuchs. 2006. Introduction to response to intervention: What, why, and how valid is it? *Reading Research Quarterly* 41(1):93-99.

Fuchs, L. S., D. L. Compton, D. Fuchs, K. Paulson, J. D. Bryant, and C. L. Hamlett. 2005. The prevention, identification, and cognitive determinants of math difficulty. *Journal of Educational Psychology* 97:493-513.

Fuchs, L. S., D. C. Geary, D. L. Compton, D. Fuchs, C. Schatschneider, C. L. Hamlett, J. DeSelms, P. M. Seethaler, J. Wilson, C. F. Craddock, J. D. Bryant, K. Luther, and P. Changas. 2013. Effects of first-grade number knowledge tutoring with contrasting forms of practice. *Journal of Educational Psychology* 105(1):58-77.

Fuller, H. L. 2000. First teach their teachers: Technology support and computer use in academic subjects. *Journal of Research on Computing in Education* 32(4):511-537.

Furtak, E. M., T. Seidel, H. Iverson, and D. C. Briggs. 2012. Experimental and quasi-experimental studies of inquiry-based science teaching: A meta-analysis. *Review of Educational Research* 82(3):300-329.

Fuson, K. C. 1988. *Children's counting and concepts of number*. New York: Springer-Verlag.

———. 2004. Pre-K to grade 2 goals and standards: Achieving 21st century mastery for all. In *Engaging young children in mathematics standards for early childhood mathematics education*, edited by D. H. Clements and J. Sarama. Mahwah, NJ: Lawrence Erlbaum Associates. Pp. 105-148.

Fuson, K. C., and D. J. Briars. 1990. Using a base-ten blocks learning/teaching approach for first- and second-grade place-value and multidigit addition and subtraction. *Journal for Research in Mathematics Education* 21(3):180-206.

Fuson, K. C., and Y. Kwon. 1992. Korean childen's understanding of multidigit addition and subtraction. *Child Development* 63:491-506.

Fuson, K. C., S. T. Smith, and A. Lo Cicero. 1997a. Supporting Latino first graders' ten-structured thinking in urban classrooms. *Journal for Research in Mathematics Education* 28:738-760.

Fuson, K. C., D. Wearne, J. C. Hiebert, H. G. Murray, P. G. Human, A. I. Olivier, T. P. Carpenter, and E. Fennema. 1997b. Children's conceptual structures for multidigit numbers and methods of multidigit addition and subtraction. *Journal for Research in Mathematics Education* 28(2):130-162.

Gamel-McCormick, M., and D. Amsden. 2002. *Investing in better outcomes: The Delaware Early Childhood Longitudinal Study*. Newark, DE: Delaware Interagency Resource Management Committee and the Department of Education.

Geary, D. 2004. Mathematics and learning disabilities. *Journal of Learning Disabilities* 37(1):4-15.

Gelman, R., and K. Brenneman. 2004. Science learning pathways for young children. *Early Childhood Research Quarterly* 19:150-158.

Gelman, R., and C. R. Gallistel. 1978. *The child's understanding of number*. Cambridge, MA: Harvard University Press.

Gelman, R., K. Brenneman, G. Macdonald, and M. Román. 2009. *Preschool pathways to science (PrePS): Facilitating scientific ways of thinking, talking, working, and understanding*. Baltimore, MD: Paul H. Brookes Publishing Co.

Gerde, H. K., R. E. Schachter, and B. A. Wasik. 2013. Using the scientific method to guide learning: An integrated approach to early childhood curriculum. *Early Childhood Education Journal* 41:315-323.

Gersten, R., D. J. Chard, M. Jayanthi, M. S. Baker, S. K. Morpy, and J. R. Flojo. 2008. *Teaching mathematics to students with learning disabilities: A meta-analysis of the intervention research*. Portsmouth, NH: RMC Research Corporation, Center on Instruction.

Gersten, R., S. Beckmann, B. Clarke, A. Foegen, L. Marsh, J. R. Star, and B. Witzel. 2009. *Assisting students struggling with mathematics: Response to intervention (RTI) for elementary and middle schools (NCEE 2009-4060)*. Washington, DC: National Center for Education Evaluation and Regional Assistance, Institute of Education Sciences, U.S. Department of Education.

Gervasoni, A. 2005. The diverse learning needs of children who were selected for an intervention program. In *Proceedings of the 29th Conference of the International Group for the Psychology in Mathematics Education*. Vol. 3, edited by H. L. Chick and J. L. Vincent. Melbourne, Australia: Psychology of Mathematics Education. Pp. 33-40.

Gervasoni, A., T. Hadden, and K. Turkenburg. 2007. Exploring the number knowledge of children to inform the development of a professional learning plan for teachers in the Ballarat Diocese as a means of building community capacity. In *Mathematics: Essential research, essential practice*. Proceedings of the 30th Annual Conference of the Mathematics Education Research Group of Australasia. Vol. 3, edited by J. Watson and K. Beswick. Hobart, Australia: Mathematics Education Research Group of Australasia. Pp. 305-314.

Geva, E., and Z. Yaghoub Zadeh. 2006. Reading efficiency in native English-speaking and English-as-a-second-language children: The role of oral proficiency and underlying cognitive-linguistic processes. *Scientific Studies of Reading* 10(1):31-57.

Gilliam, W. S. 2005. *Prekindergarteners left behind: Expulsion rates in state prekindergarten systems*. New York: Foundation for Child Development.

Ginsburg, H. P. 1977. *Children's arithmetic*. Austin, TX: Pro-ed.

Ginsburg, H. P., and A. J. Baroody. 2003. *Test of early mathematics ability*. 3rd ed. Austin, TX: Pro-ed.

Godfrey, S. W., J. Grisham-Brown, and J. W. Schuster. 2003. The effects of three active responding techniques on student participation and social behavior with preschool children who have special needs. *Education and Treatment of Children* 26:355-373.

Goldenberg, C., R. Gallimore, L. Reese, and H. Garnier. 2001. Cause or effect? A longitudinal study of immigrant Latino parents' aspirations and expectations, and their children's school performance. *American Educational Research Journal* 38(3):547-582.

Gonzales, P., T. Williams, L. Jocelyn, S. Roey, D. Kastberg, and S. Brenwald. 2008. *Highlights from TIMSS 2007: Mathematics and science achievement of U.S. fourth- and eighth-grade students in an international context (NCES 2009-001 revised)*. Washington, DC: U.S. Department of Education, National Center for Education Statistics, Institute of Education Sciences.

Gough, P. B., W. A. Hoover, and C. L. Peterson. 1996. *Reading comprehension difficulties: Processes and intervention*. Mahwah, NJ: Lawrence Erlbaum Associates.

Graham, T. A., C. Nash, and K. Paul. 1997. Young children's exposure to mathematics: The child care context. *Early Childhood Education Journal* 25(1):31-38.

Graves, M. F., R. Calfee, B. B. Graves, and C. Jeuel. 2006. *Teaching reading in the 21st century*. 4th ed. Boston, MA: Allyn & Bacon.

Greenfield, D. B., X. Dominguez, J. M. Fuccillo, M. F. Maier, and A. C. Greenberg. 2008. *The development of an IRT-based direct assessment of preschool science*. Paper presented at Ninth National Head Start Research Conference, June, Washington, DC.

Greenfield, D. B., J. Jirout, X. Dominguez, A. C. Greenberg, M. F. Maier, and J. M. Fuccillo. 2009. Science in the preschool classroom: A programmatic research agenda to improve science readiness. *Early Development and Education* 20(2):238-264.

Griffin, S. 2004. Number worlds: A research-based mathematics program for young children. In *Engaging young children in mathematics: Standards for early childhood mathematics education*, edited by D. H. Clements, J. Sarama, and A.-M. DiBiase. Mahwah, NJ: Lawrence Erlbaum Associates.

Griffin, S., R. Case, and R. S. Siegler. 1994. Rightstart: Providing the central conceptual prerequisites for first formal learning of arithmetic to students at risk for school failure. In *Classroom lessons: Integrating cognitive theory and classroom practice*, edited by K. McGilly. Cambridge, MA: MIT Press.

Griffin, S., R. Case, and A. Capodilupo. 1995. Teaching for understanding: The importance of the central conceptual structures in the elementary mathematics curriculum. In *Teaching for transfer: Fostering generalization in learning*, edited by A. McKeough, J. Lupart, and A. Marini. Mahwah, NJ: Lawrence Erlbaum Associates. Pp. 121-151.

Grisham-Brown, J., J. W. Schuster, M. L. Hemmeter, and B. C. Collins. 2000. Using an embedding strategy to teach preschoolers with significant disabilities. *Journal of Behavioral Education* 10(2/3):139-162.

Grissmer, D., K. J. Grimm, S. M. Aiyer, W. M. Murrah, and J. S. Steele. 2010. Fine motor skills and early comprehension of the world: Two new school readiness indicators. *Developmental Psychology* 46(5):1008-1017.

Gustafsson, K., E. Mellgren, A. Klerfelt, and I. P. Samuelsson. 1999. *Pre-school teachers-children, computers, and IT: An exploratory study*. Paper presented at EARLI 99: The 8th European Conference for Research and Learning, Gothenburg, Sweden.

Hanhan, S. F. 2003. Parent-teacher communication: Who's talking? In *Home-school relations: Working successfully with parents and families*. 2nd ed., edited by G. Olsen and M. L. Fuller. Boston, MA: Allyn & Bacon. Pp. 111-133.

Hanley, G. P., J. H. Tiger, E. T. Ingvarsson, and A. P. Cammilleri. 2009. Influencing preschoolers' free-play activity preferences: An evaluation of satiation and embedded reinforcement. *Journal of Applied Behavior Analysis* 42:33-41.

Hemmeter, M. L., and J. L. Grisham-Brown. In press. The relative effects of child-directed versus didactic instruction on the skill acquisition and generalization for preschoolers with developmental delays.

Hemmeter, M. L., and A. P. Kaiser. 1994. Enhanced milieu teaching: Effects of parent-implemented language intervention. *Journal of Early Intervention* 18(3):269-289.

Hemmeter, M. L., M. J. Ault, B. C. Collins, and S. Meyer. 1996. The effects of teacher-implemented language instruction within free time activities. *Education and Training in Mental Retardation and Developmental Disabilities* 31(3):203-212.

Hemmeter, M. L., M. M. Ostrosky, and L. Fox. 2006. Social emotional foundations for early learning: A conceptual model for intervention. *School Psychology Review* 35:583-601.

Hemmeter, M. L., R. M. Santos, and M. M. Ostrosky. 2008. Preparing early childhood educators to address young children's social-emotional development and challenging behavior: A survey of higher education programs in nine states. *Journal of Early Intervention* 30(4):321-340.

Hemmeter, M. L., P. Snyder, L. Fox, and J. Algina. 2011. *Efficacy of a classroom wide model for promoting social-emotional development and preventing challenging behavior*. Paper presented at the annual meeting of the American Education Research Association, New Orleans, LA.

Henrichs, L. F., P. P. M. Leseman, K. Broekhof, and H. Cohen de Lara. 2011. Kindergarten talk about science and technology. In *Professional development for primary teachers in science and technology: The Dutch VTB-Pro Project in an international perspective*, edited by M. J. de Vries, H. van Keulen, S. Peters, and J. W. van der Molen. Boston, MA: Sense Publishers. Pp. 217-227.

Henry, V. J., and R. S. Brown. 2008. First-grade basic facts: An investigation into teaching and learning of an accelerated, high-demand memorization standard. *Journal for Research in Mathematics Education* 39(2):153-183.

HHS (U.S. Department of Health and Human Services). 2005. *Head Start impact study: First year findings*. Washington, DC: HHS, Administration for Children and Families.

Hiebert, J. C. 1999. Relationships between research and the NCTM standards. *Journal for Research in Mathematics Education* 30(1):3-19.

Hiebert, J. C., and D. A. Grouws. 2007. The effects of classroom mathematics teaching on students' learning. In *Second handbook of research on mathematics teaching and learning*. Vol. 1, edited by F. K. J. Lester. New York: Information Age Publishing. Pp. 371-404.

Hiebert, J. C., and D. Wearne. 1993. Instructional tasks, classroom discourse, and students' learning in second-grade arithmetic. *American Educational Research Journal* 30(2):393-425.

HighScope Educational Research Foundation. 2003. *Preschool child observation record*. Ypsilanti, MI: HighScope Press.

Hill, H. C., D. L. Ball, and S. G. Schilling. 2008. Unpacking pedagogical content knowledge: Conceptualizing and measuring teachers' topic-specific knowledge of students. *Journal for Research in Mathematics Education* 39(4):372-400.

Hindman, A. H., C. M. Connor, A. M. Jewkes, and F. J. Morrison. 2008. Untangling the effects of shared book reading: Multiple factors and their associations with preschool literacy outcomes. *Early Childhood Research Quarterly* 23(3):330-350.

Hitchcock, M. R. 2008. *Making music together: The blending of an on-line learning environment for music artistic practice*. Queensland, Australia: Queensland University of Technology.

Hobbs, R., and D. C. Moore. 2013. *Discovering media literacy: Teaching digital media and popular culture in elementary school*. Thousand Oaks, CA: Corwin.

Holloway, S. D., M. F. Rambaud, B. Fuller, and C. Eggers-Pierola. 1995. What is "appropriate practice" at home and in child care?: Low-income mothers' views on preparing their children for school. *Early Childhood Research Quarterly* 10:451-473.

Hong, H. 1996. Effects of mathematics learning through children's literature on math achievement and dispositional outcomes. *Early Childhood Research Quarterly* 11(4):477-494.

Horne, M., and G. Rowley. 2001. Measuring growth in early numeracy: Creation of interval scales to monitor development. In *Proceedings of the 25th Conference of the International Group for the Psychology in Mathematics Education*. Vol. 3, edited by M. Van den Heuvel-Panhuizen. Utrecht, The Netherlands: Freudenthal Institute. Pp. 161-168.

Horner, R. H. 1990. The role of response efficiency in the reduction of problem behaviors through functional equivalence training: A case study. *Journal of the Association for Persons with Severe Handicaps* 15(2):91-97.

HRSA (Health Resources and Services Administration). n.d. *EPSDT & Title V collaboration to improve child health*. www.mchb.hrsa.gov/epsdt (accessed March 22, 2015).

Hutchings, J., P. Martin-Forbes, D. Daley, and M. E. Williams. 2013. A randomized controlled trial of the impact of a teacher classroom management program on the classroom behavior of children with and without behavior problems. *Journal of School Psychology* 51(5):571-585.

Hutinger, P. L., and J. Johanson. 2000. Implementing and maintaining an effective early childhood comprehensive technology system. *Topics in Early Childhood Special Education* 20(3):159-173.

IOM (Institute of Medicine) and NRC (National Research Council). 2009. *Preventing mental, emotional, and behavioral disorders among young people: Progress and possibilities.* Washington, DC: The National Academies Press.

Isenberg, J. P. 2000. The state of the art in early childhood professional preparation. In *New teachers for a new century: The future of early childhood professional preparation*, edited by D. Horm-Wingerd and M. Hyson. Washington, DC: U.S. Department of Education. Pp. 15-58.

ISTE (International Society for Technology in Education). 2007a. *ISTE standards: Students.* http://www.iste.org/docs/pdfs/20-14_ISTE_Standards-S_PDF.pdf (accessed March 19, 2015).

———. 2007b. *National educational technology standards for students.* 2nd ed. Arlington, VA: ISTE.

———. 2008. *ISTE standards: Teachers.* http://www.iste.org/docs/pdfs/20-14_ISTE_Standards-T_PDF.pdf (accessed March 19, 2015).

Janzen, J. 2008. Teaching English language learners. *Review of Educational Research* 78:1010-1038.

Jean, M., and E. Geva. 2009. The development of vocabulary in English as a second language children and its role in predicting word recognition ability. *Applied Psycholinguistics* 30(1):153-185.

Johnson, D. W., and R. T. Johnson. 2009. An educational ppsychology success story: Social interdependence theory and cooperative learning. *Educational Researcher* 38:365-379.

Johnston, K., and C. Brinamen. 2006. *Mental health consultation in child care: Transforming relationships among directors, staff, and families.* Washington, DC: Zero to Three.

Jones, E., and J. Nimmo. 1994. *Emergent curriculum.* Washington, DC: National Association for the Education of Young Children.

Jordan, H., R. Mendro, and D. Weerasinghe. 1997. *Teacher effects on longitudinal student achievement.* Paper presented at National Evaluation Institute, Indianapolis, IN.

Jordan, N. C., and T. O. Montani. 1997. Cognitive arithmetic and problem solving: A comparison of children with specific and general mathematics difficulties. *Journal of Learning Disabilities* 30:624-634.

Jordan, N. C., J. Huttenlocher, and S. C. Levine. 1992. Differential calculation abilities in young children from middle- and low-income families. *Developmental Psychology* 28:644-653.

Juffer, F., M. J. Bakermans-Kranenburg, and M. H. van Ijzendoorn. n.d. *VIPP-SD: Video-feedback intervention to promote positive parenting and sensitive discipline.* Leiden, The Netherlands: Leiden University.

Kaiser, A. P., and M. L. Hemmeter. 1989. Value-based approaches to family intervention. *Topics in Early Childhood Special Education* 8(4):72-86.

Kame'enui, E. J., H. Fien, and J. Korgesaar. 2013. Direct instruction as eo nomine and contronym: Why the right words and the details matter. In *Handbook of learning disabilities*, edited by H. L. Swanson, K. R. Harris, and S. Graham. New York: Guilford Press.

Kauerz, K., and J. Coffman. 2013. *Framework for planning, implementing, and evaluating preK-3rd grade approaches.* Seattle, WA: University of Washington, College of Education.

Kieffer, M. J. 2014. Morphological awareness and reading difficulties in adolescent Spanish-speaking language minority learners and their classmates. *Journal of Learning Disabilities* 47(1):44-53.

Kirkorian, H. L., K. Choi, and T. A. Pempek. 2013. *Toddlers' word-learning from contingent vs. non-contingent video on touchscreens.* Paper presented at Biennial Meeting of the Society for Research in Child Development, Seattle, WA.

Klahr, D., and Z. Chen. 2003. Overcoming the positive-capture strategy in young children: Learning about indeterminacy. *Child Development* 74(5):1275-1296.

Kleemans, T., E. Segers, and L. Verhoeven. 2013. Relations between home numeracy experiences and basic calculation skills of children with and without specific language impairment. *Early Childhood Research Quarterly* 28(2):415-423.

Klibanoff, R. S., S. C. Levine, J. Huttenlocher, M. Vasilyeva, and L. V. Hedges. 2006. Preschool children's mathematical knowledge: The effect of teacher "math talk." *Developmental Psychology* 42:59-69.

Klingberg, T. 2009. *The overflowing brain information overload and the limits of working memory.* Oxford; New York: Oxford University Press.

Knoche, L. L., D. C. Keely, and C. A. Marvin. 2012. Fostering collaborative partnerships between early childhood professionals and the parents of young children. In *Handbook of early childhood education*, edited by R. C. Pianta, W. S. Barnett, L. M. Justice, and S. M. Sheridan. New York: Guilford Press. Pp. 370-392.

Korat, O. 2010. Reading electronic books as a support for vocabulary, story comprehension and word reading in kindergarten and first grade. *Computers & Education* 55(1):24-31.

Krcmar, M., B. Grela, and K. Lin. 2007. Can toddlers learn vocabulary from television? An experimental approach. *Media Psychology* 10(1):41-63.

Lally, J. R., Y. L. Torres, and P. C. Phelps. n.d. *Caring for infants and toddlers in groups.* http://www.zerotothree.org/early-care-education/child-care/caring-for-infants-and-toddlers-in-groups.html (accessed March 17, 2015).

Lara-Cinisomo, S., E. Maggio, A. R. Pebley, and M. E. Vaiana. 2004. *Are L.A.'s children ready for school?* Santa Monica, CA: RAND.

Lareau, A. 1989. *Home advantage: Social class and parental intervention in elementary education.* New York: Falmer Press.

Lareau, A., and E. M. Horvat. 1999. Moments of social inclusion and exclusion: Race, class, and cultural capital in family-school relationships. *Sociology of Education* 72(1):37-53.

Lauricella, A. R., T. A. Pempek, R. Barr, and S. L. Calvert. 2010. Contingent computer interactions for young children's object retrieval success. *Journal of Applied Developmental Psychology* 31(5):362-369.

Lawrence-Lightfoot, S. 2003. *The essential conversation: What parents and teachers can learn from each other.* New York: Random House.

Lee, D. Y., and D. H. Shin. 2012. An empirical evaluation of multi-media based learning of a procedural task. *Computers in Human Behavior* 28(3):1072-1081.

LePage, P., L. Darling-Hammond, H. Akar, C. Gutierrez, E. Jenkins-Gunn, and K. Rosebrock. 2005. Classroom management. In *Preparing teachers for a changing world: What teachers should learn and be able to do*, edited by L. Darling-Hammond and J. Bransford. San Francisco, CA: Jossey-Bass. Pp. 327-357.

Lerner, C., and R. Barr. 2014. *Screen sense: Setting the record straight. Research-based guidelines for screen use for children under 3 years old.* Washington, DC: Zero to Three.

Lesaux, N. K., and S. H. Marietta. 2012. *Making assessment matter: Using test results to differentiate reading instruction.* New York: Guilford Press.

Lesaux, N. K., K. Koda, L. S. Siegel, and T. Shanahan. 2006. Development of literacy of language minority learners. In *Developing literacy in a second language: Report of the National Literacy Panel*, edited by D. L. August and T. Shanahan. Mahwah, NJ: Lawrence Erlbaum Associates. Pp. 75-122.

Lesaux, N. K., A. A. Rupp, and L. S. Siegel. 2007. Growth in reading skills of children from diverse linguistic backgrounds: Findings from a 5-year longitudinal study. *Journal of Educational Psychology* 99(4):821-834.

Lesaux, N. K., M. J. Kieffer, S. E. Faller, and J. G. Kelley. 2010. The effectiveness and ease of implementation of an academic vocabulary intervention for linguistically diverse students in urban middle schools. *Reading Research Quarterly* 45(2):196-228.

Lesaux, N. K., S. Jones, J. R. Harris, and R. L. Kane. 2014. *Using data for R2 accountability and improvement.* http://isites.harvard.edu/fs/docs/icb.topic1391652.files/R2brief6_Lesaux%20Jones%20Harris%20Kane.pdf (accessed January 23, 2015).

Levine, S. C., E. A. Gunderson, and J. Huttenlocher. 2011. Mathematical development during the preschool years in context: Home and school input variations. In *Developmental science goes to school: Implications for education and public policy research*, edited by N. L. Stein and S. Raudenbush. New York: Taylor & Francis.

Lewis, T. J., S. E. L. Jones, R. H. Horner, and G. Sugai. 2010. School-wide positive behavior support and students with emotional/behavioral disorders: Implications for prevention, identification, and intervention. *Exceptionality* 18(2):82-93.

Lillard, A., and N. Else-Quest. 2006. The early years: Evaluating Montessori education. *Science* 313:1893-1894.

Linan-Thompson, S., S. Vaughn, K. Prater, and P. T. Cirino. 2006. The response to intervention of English language learners at risk for reading problems. *Journal of Learning Disabilities* 39(5):390-398.

Lipka, O., and L. S. Siegel. 2007. The development of reading skills in children with English as a second language. *Scientific Studies of Reading* 11:105-131.

Loftus, S. M., M. D. Coyne, D. B. McCoach, R. Zipoli, and P. C. Pullen. 2010. Effects of a supplemental vocabulary intervention on the word knowledge of kindergarten students at-risk for language and literacy difficulties. *Learning Disabilities Research and Practice* 25(3):124-136.

Lonigan, C. J., and B. M. Phillips. 2012 (March 8). *Comparing skills-focused and self-regulation-focused preschool curricula: Impacts on academic and self-regulatory skills.* Paper presented at the Society for Research on Educational Effectiveness, Washington, DC.

Lyons, K. E., and P. D. Zelazo. 2011. Monitoring, metacognition, and executive function. Elucidating the role of self-reflection in the development of self-regulation. *Advances in Child Development and Behavior* 40:379-380.

MacDonald, A., N. Davies, S. Dockett, and B. Perry. 2012. Early childhood mathematics education. In *Research in mathematics education in Australasia: 2008-2011*, edited by B. Perry, T. Lowrie, T. Logan, A. MacDonald, and J. Greenlees. Rotterdam, The Netherlands: Sense Publishers. Pp. 169-192.

Magnuson, K. A., M. K. Meyers, A. Rathbun, and J. West. 2004. Inequality in preschool education and school readiness. *American Educational Research Journal* 41:115-157.

Mancilla-Martinez, J., and N. K. Lesaux. 2011. The gap between Spanish speakers' word reading and word knowledge: A longitudinal study. *Child Development* 82(5):1544-1560.

Mantzicopoulos, P., A. Samarapungavan, and H. Patrick. 2009. "We learn how to predict and be a scientist": Early science experiences and kindergarten children's social meanings about science. *Cognition and Instruction* 27(4):312-369.

Massey, C., and Z. Roth. 2009. *Conceptual change in preschool science: Understanding light and shadows.* Paper presented at Biennial Meeting of the Society for Research in Child Development, April, Denver, CO.

McKay, M. M., M. S. Atkins, T. Hawkins, C. Brown, and C. J. Lynn. 2003. Inner-city African American parental involvement in children's schooling: Racial socialization and social support from the parent community. *American Journal of Community Psychology* 32(1-2):107-114.

McMaster, K. L., S.-H. Kung, I. Han, and M. Cao. 2008. Peer-assisted learning strategies: A "tier 1" approach to promoting English learners' response to intervention. *Exceptional Children* 74(2):194-214.

Meisels, S. J., and S. Atkins-Burnett. 2005. *Developmental screening in early childhood: A guide (5th edition)*. Washington, DC: National Association for the Education of Young Children.

Meisels, S. J., F. R. Liaw, A. Dorfman, and R. F. Nelson. 1995. The work sampling system: Reliability and validity of a performance assessment for young children. *Early Childhood Research Quarterly* 10:277-296.

Mix, K. S., J. Huttenlocher, and S. C. Levine. 2002. *Quantitative development in infancy and early childhood*. New York: Oxford University Press.

Mobayed, K. L., B. C. Collins, D. E. Strangis, J. W. Schuster, and M. L. Hemmeter. 2000. Teaching parents to employ mand-model procedures to teach their children requesting. *Journal of Early Intervention* 23(3):165-179.

Morris, P., S. K. Mattera, N. Castells, M. Bangser, K. Bierman, and C. Raver. 2014. *Impact findings from the Head Start CARES demonstration: National evaluation of three approaches to improving preschoolers' social and emotional competence*. Washington, DC: Office of Planning, Research and Evaluation, Administration for Children and Families, HHS.

Morton, J. B. 2008. *Alabama course of study: Technology education*. Montgomery: State Superintendent of Education, Alabama Department of Education.

Murata, A., and K. Fuson. 2006. Teaching as assisting individual constructive paths within an interdependent class learning zone: Japanese first graders learning to add using 10. *Journal for Research in Mathematics Education* 37(5):421-456.

NAEYC (National Association for the Education of Young Children). 2009. Developmentally appropriate practice in early childhood programs serving children from birth through age 8. https://www.naeyc.org/files/naeyc/file/positions/position%20statement%20Web.pdf (accessed February 20, 2014).

NAEYC and NAECS/SDE (National Association of Early Childhood Specialists in State Departments of Education). 2003. *Early childhood curriculum, assessment, and program evaluation: Building an effective, accountable system in programs for children birth through age 8. Position statement*. Washington, DC: NAEYC.

Nastasi, B. K., and D. H. Clements. 1991. Research on cooperative learning: Implications for practice. *School Psychology Review* 20(1):110-131.

National Early Literacy Panel. 2008. *Developing early literacy: A report of the National Early Literacy Panel*. Washington, DC: National Institute for Literacy.

National Resource Center for Health and Safety in Child Care. 2012. *User guide for the licensing toolkit action sheets*. http://nrckids.org/default/assets/file/products/toolkits/limit screentimeinchildcare.pdf (accessed March 19, 2015).

Nayfeld, I., K. Brenneman, and R. Gelman. 2011. Science in the classroom: Finding a balance between autonomous exploration and teacher-led instruction in preschool settings. *Early Education and Development* 22(6):970-988.

NCTM (National Council of Teachers of Mathematics). 2006. *Curriculum focal points for prekindergarten through grade 8 mathematics: A quest for coherence*. Reston, VA: NCTM.

Neuman, S. 2013. Giving all children a good start: The effects of an embedded multimedia intervention for narrowing the vocabulary gap before kindergarten. In *Technology as a support for literacy achievements for children at risk*. Vol. 7, Literacy studies, edited by A. Shamir and O. Korat. Netherlands: Springer. Pp. 21-32.

Neuman, S. B., E. H. Newman, and J. Dwyer. 2011. Educational effects of a vocabulary intervention on preschoolers' word knowledge and conceptual development: A cluster-randomized trial. *Reading Research Quarterly* 46(3):249-272.

NMP (National Mathematics Advisory Panel). 2008. *Foundations for success: The final report of the National Mathematics Advisory Panel*. Washington, DC: U.S. Department of Education, Office of Planning, Evaluation and Policy Development.

NRC (National Research Council). 2000. *How people learn: Brain, mind, experience, and school*, edited by J. D. Bransford, A. L. Brown, and R. R. Cocking. Washington, DC: National Academy Press.

———. 2001a. *Adding it up: Helping children learn mathematics*, edited by J. Kilpatrick, J. Swafford, and B. Findell. Washington, DC: National Academy Press.

———. 2001b. *Eager to learn: Educating our preschoolers*, edited by B. T. Bowman, M. S. Donovan, and M. S. Burns. Washington, DC: National Academy Press.

———. 2007. *Taking science to school: Learning and teaching science in grades K-8*, edited by R. A. Duschl, H. A. Schweingruber, and A. W. Shouse. Washington, DC: The National Academies Press.

———. 2008. *Early childhood assessment: Why, what, and how*, edited by C. E. Snow and S. B. van Hemel. Washington, DC: The National Academies Press.

———. 2009. *Mathematics learning in early childhood: Paths toward excellence and equity*, edited by C. T. Cross, T. A. Woods, and H. Schweingruber. Washington, DC: The National Academies Press.

NRC and IOM (Institute of Medicine). 2000. *From neurons to neighborhoods: The science of early childhood development*, edited by J. P. Shonkoff and D. A. Phillips. Washington, DC: National Academy Press.

O'Connor, R. E. 2000. Increasing the intensity of intervention in kindergarten and first grade. *Learning Disabilities Research and Practice* 15(1):43-54.

O'Connor, R. E., A. Notari-Syverson, and P. F. Vadasy. 1996. Ladders to literacy: The effects of teacher-led phonological activities for kindergarten children with and without disabilities. *Exceptional Children* 63(1):117-130.

O'Connor, R. E., K. Bocian, M. Beebe-Frankenberger, and D. L. Linklater. 2010. Responsiveness of students with language difficulties to early intervention in reading. *Journal of Special Education* 43(4):220-235.

O'Connor, R. E., K. M. Bocian, V. Sanchez, K. D. Beach, and L. J. Flynn. 2013. Special education in a four-year response to intervention (RTI) environment: Characteristics of students with learning disability and grade of indentification. *Learning Disabilities Research and Practice* 26:98-112.

O'Connor, R. E., K. M. Bocian, V. Sanchez, and K. D. Beach. 2014. Access to a responsiveness to intervention model: Does beginning intervention in kindergarten matter? *Journal of Learning Disabilities* 47(4):307-328.

Osofsky, J. D., and A. F. Lieberman. 2011. A call for integrating a mental health perspective into systems of care for abused and neglected infants and young children. *The American Psychologist* 66(2).

Otaiba, S. A., C. M. Connor, B. Foorman, L. Greulich, and J. S. Folsom. 2009. Implementing response to intervention: The synergy of beginning reading instruction and early intervening services. *Advances in Learning and Behavioral Disabilities* 22.

Otaiba, S. A., R. K. Wagner, and B. Miller. 2014. Waiting to fail redux: Understanding inadequate response to intervention. *Learning Disability Quarterly* 37(3):129-133.

Parish-Morris, J., N. Mahajan, K. Hirsh-Pasek, R. M. Golinkoff, and M. F. Collins. 2013. Once upon a time: Parent–child dialogue and storybook reading in the electronic era. *Mind, Brain, and Education* 7(3):200-211.

Patrick, H., P. Mantzicopoulos, and A. Samarapungavan. 2009. Motivation for learning science in kindergarten: Is there a gender gap and does integrated inquiry and literacy instruction make a difference. *Journal of Research in Science Teaching* 46(2):166-191.

Pelletier, J. 2006. Relations among theory of mind, metacognitive language, reading skills and story comprehension in l1 and l2 learners. In *Theory of mind and language in developmental contexts*, edited by A. Antonietti, O. Liverta-Sempio, and A. Marchetti. New York: Springer. Pp. 77-92.

Penuel, W. R. 2012. Supplemental literacy instruction with a media-rich intervention: Results of a randomized controlled trial. *Early Childhood Research Quarterly* 27(1):115-127.

Penuel, W. R., and L. A. Shepard. in press. Assessment and teaching. In *Handbook of research on teaching*, edited by D. H. Gitomer and C. A. Bell. Washington, DC: American Educational Research Association.

Penuel, W. R., S. Pasnik, L. Bates, E. Townsend, L. P. Gallagher, C. Llorente, and N. Hupert. 2009. *Summative evaluation of the ready to learn initiative. Preschool teachers can use a media-rich curriculum to prepare low-income children for school success: Results of a randomized controlled trial*. New York: Education Development Center, Inc., and SRI International.

Perels, F., M. Merget-Kullmann, M. Wende, B. Schmitz, and C. Buchbinder. 2009. Improving self-regulated learning of preschool children: Evaluation of training for kindergarten teachers. *The British Journal of Educational Psychology* 79:311-327.

Perlmutter, J., L. Bloom, T. Rose, and A. Rogers. 1997. Who uses math? Primary children's perceptions of the uses of mathematics. *Journal of Research in Childhood Education* 12(1):58-70.

Perry, B., J. M. Young-Loveridge, S. Dockett, and B. Doig. 2008. The development of young children's mathematical understanding. In *Research in mathematics education in Australasia 2004-2007*, edited by H. Forgasz, A. Barkatsas, A. Bishop, B. A. Clarke, S. Keast, W. T. Seah, and P. Sullivan. Rotterdam, The Netherlands, and Taipei, Taiwan: Sense Publishers. Pp. 17-40.

Peterson, S. M., and L. French. 2008. Supporting young children's explanations through inquiry science in preschool. *Early Childhood Research Quarterly* 23:395-408.

Pianta, R. C., J. Belsky, R. Houts, and F. Morrison. 2007. Opportunities to learn in America's elementary classrooms. *Science* 315(5820):1795-1796.

Plowman, L., and C. Stephen. 2005. Children, play and computers in pre-school education. *British Journal of Educational Technology* 36(2):145-158.

Preschool Curriculum Evaluation Research Consortium. 2008. *Effects of preschool curriculum programs on school readiness (NCER 2008-2009)*. Washington, DC: U.S. Government Printing Office.

Proctor, C. P., M. Carlo, D. August, and C. Snow. 2005. Native Spanish-speaking children reading in English: Toward a model of comprehension. *Journal of Educational Psychology* 97(2):246-256.

Ramey, C. T., and S. L. Ramey. 1998. Early intervention and early experience. *American Psychologist* 53:109-120.

Ramirez, G., E. A. Gunderson, S. C. Levine, and S. L. Beilock. 2013. Math anxiety, working memory, and math achievement in early elementary school. *Journal of Cognition and Development* 14(2):187-202.

Raudenbush, S. W. 2009. The Brown legacy and the O'Connor challenge: Transforming schools in the images of children's potential. *Educational Researcher* 38(3):169-180.

Raver, C. C., S. M. Jones, C. Li-Grining, F. Zhai, M. W. Metzger, and B. Solomon. 2009. Targeting children's behavior problems in preschool classrooms: A cluster-randomized controlled trial. *Journal of Consulting and Clinical Psychology* 77(2):302-316.

Raver, C. C., S. M. Jones, C. Li-Grining, F. Zhai, K. Bub, and E. Pressler. 2011. CSRP's impact on low-income preschoolers' preacademic skills: Self-regulation as a mediating mechanism. *Child Development* 82(1):362-378.

Reed, D. K. 2008. A synthesis of morphology interventions and effects on reading outcomes for students in grades k-12. *Learning Disabilities Research & Practice* 23(1):36-49.

Reid, R., A. L. Trout, and M. Schartz. 2005. Self-regulation interventions for children with attention deficit/hyperactivity disorder. *Exceptional Children* 71(4):361.

Resnick, L. B. 1992. From protoquantities to operators: Building mathematical competence on a foundation of everyday knowledge. In *Analysis of arithmetic for mathematics teaching*, edited by G. Leinhardt, R. Putman, and R. A. Hattrup. Hillsdale, NJ: Lawrence Erlbaum Associates. Pp. 373-430.

Richert, R. A., M. B. Robb, J. G. Fender, and E. Wartella. 2010. Word learning from baby videos. *Archives of Pediatrics & Adolescent Medicine* 164(5):432-437.

Riggs, N. R., M. T. Greenberg, C. A. Kusche, and M. A. Pentz. 2006. The mediational role of neurocognition in the behavioral outcomes of a social-emotional prevention program in elementary school students: Effects of the paths curriculum. *Prevention Science* 7:91-102.

Riley-Ayers, S., J. Stevenson-Boyd, and E. C. Frede. 2008. *Improving teaching through systematic assessment: Early learning scale and guidebook*. New Brunswick, NJ: National Institute for Early Education Research.

Roark, T., B. C. Collins, M. L. Hemmeter, and H. Kleinert. 2002. Including manual signing as nontargeted information when using a constant time delay procedure to teach receptive identification of packaged food items. *Journal of Behavior Education* 11:19-38.

Roberts, T. A. 2008. Home storybook reading in primary or second language with preschool children: Evidence of equal effectiveness for second-language vocabulary acquisition. *Reading Research Quarterly* 43(2):103-130.

Roblyer, M. D. 1988. The effectiveness of microcomputers in education: A review of the research from 1980-1987. *Technological Horizons in Education* 16(2):85-89.

Rogers, L., M. Hemmeter, and M. Wolery. 2010. Using a constant time delay procedure to teach foundational swimming skills to children with autism. *Topics in Early Childhood Special Education* 30(2):102-111.

Romance, N. R., and M. R. Vitale. 2001. Implementing an in-depth, expanded science model in elementary schools: Multiyear findings, research issues, and policy implications. *International Journal of Science Education* 23:373-404.

Ross, J. A., A. Hogaboam-Gray, and L. Hannay. 2001. Collateral benefits of an interactive literacy program for grade 1 and 2 students. *Journal of Research on Computing in Education* 33(3):219-234.

Rothbart, M. K., and M. R. Rueda. 2005. The development of effortful control. In *Developing individuality in the human brain: A tribute to Michael I. Posner*, edited by U. Mayr, E. Awh, and S. W. Keele. Washington, DC: American Psychological Association. Pp. 167-188.

Rudd, L. C., M. C. Lambert, M. Satterwhite, and A. Zaier. 2008. Mathematical language in early childhood settings: What really counts? *Early Childhood Education Journal* 36:75-80.

Rueda, M. R., P. Checa, and M. Santonja. 2008. *Training executive attention: Lasting effects and transfer to affective self-regulation*. Paper presented at the annual meeting of the Cognitive Neuroscience Society, San Francisco, CA.

Saçkes, M., K. C. Trundle, R. L. Bell, and A. A. O'Connell. 2011. The influence of early science experience in kindergarten on children's immediate and later science achievement: Evidence from the early childhood longitudinal study. *Journal of Research in Science Teaching* 48(2):217-235.

Saçkes, M., K. C. Trundle, and R. L. Bell. 2013. Science learning experiences in kindergarten and children's growth in science performance in elementary grades. *Education and Science* 38(167):114-127.

Samson, J. F., and N. K. Lesaux. 2009. Language-minority learners in special education: Rate and predictors of indentification for services. *Journal of Learning Disabilities* 42:148-162.

Sanders, W. L., and S. P. Horn. 1998. Research findings from the Tennessee Value-Added Assessment System (TVAAS) database: Implications for educational evaluation and research. *Journal of Personnel Evaluation in Education* 12(3):247-256.

Sanders, W. L., and J. C. Rivers. 1996. *Cumulative and residual effects of teachers on future student academic achievement (research progress report)*. Knoxville: University of Tennessee Value-Added Research and Assessment Center.

Sarama, J., and D. H. Clements. 2002. Learning and teaching with computers in early childhood education. In *Contemporary perspectives on science and technology in early childhood education*, edited by O. N. Saracho and B. Spodek. Greenwich, CT: Information Age Publishing. Pp. 171-219.

———. 2006. Mathematics, young students, and computers: Software, teaching strategies, and professional development. *The Mathematics Educator* 9(2):112-134.

———. 2009. *Early childhood mathematics education research: Learning trajectories for young children*. New York and London: Routledge.

Sarama, J., A. A. Lange, D. H. Clements, and C. B. Wolfe. 2012. The impacts of an early mathematics curriculum on oral language and literacy. *Early Childhood Research Quarterly* 27(3):489-502.

Saxe, G. B., S. R. Guberman, and M. Gearhart. 1987. Social processes in early number development. *Monographs of the Society for Research in Child Development* 52(2):Serial No. 216.

Scarborough, H. S. 1991. Early syntactic development of dyslexic children. *Annals of Dyslexia* 41(1):207-220.

Schmidt, M. E., M. Rich, S. L. Rifas-Shiman, E. Oken, and E. M. Taveras. 2009. Television viewing in infancy and child cognition at 3 years of age in a US cohort. *Pediatrics* 123(3):370-375.

Schuster, J. W., M. L. Hemmeter, and M. J. Ault. 2001. Instruction of students with moderate and severe disabilities in elementary classrooms. *Early Childhood Research Quarterly* 16(3):329-341.

Sewell, T. J., B. C. Collins, M. L. Hemmeter, and J. W. Schuster. 1998. Using simultaneous prompting within an activity-based format to teach dressing skills to preschoolers with developmental delays. *Journal of Early Intervention* 21(2):132-145.

Shamir, A., and I. Lifshitz. 2012. E-books for supporting the emergent literacy and emergent math of children at risk for learning disabilities: Can metacognitive guidance make a difference? *European Journal of Special Needs Education* 28(1):33-48.

Shepard, L. A. 2005. Assessment. In *Preparing teachers for a changing world*, edited by L. Darling-Hammond and J. Bransford. San Francisco, CA: Jossey-Bass. Pp. 275-326.

———. 2006. Classroom assessment. In *Educational measurement*. Vol. 4, edited by R. L. Brennan. Washington, DC: National Council on Measurement in Education and American Council on Education/Praeger. Pp. 623-646.

Shulman, L. S. 1986. Those who understand: Knowledge growth in teaching. *Educational Researcher* 15(2):4-14.

Siegler, R. S., and J. L. Booth. 2004. Development of numerical estimation in young children. *Child Development* 75:428-444.

Silverman, R. 2007. A comparison of three methods of vocabulary instruction during readalouds in kindergarten. *Elementary School Journal* 108(2):97-113.

Simonsen, B., S. Fairbanks, A. Briesch, D. Myers, and G. Sugai. 2008. Evidence-based practices in classroom management: Considerations for research to practice. *Education and Treatment of Children* 31(3):351-380.

Singer, J. L., and D. G. Singer. 1998. Barney & friends as entertainment and education: Evaluating the quality and effectiveness of a television series for preschool children. In *Research paradigms, television, and social behavior*, edited by J. Asamen and G. Berry. Thousand Oaks, CA: Sage Publications. Pp. 305-369.

Sophian, C. 2004. A prospective developmental perspective on early mathematics instruction. In *Engaging young children in mathematics standards for early childhood mathematics education*, edited by D. H. Clements and J. Sarama. Mahwah, NJ: Lawrence Erlbaum Associates. Pp. 253-266.

Stacey, S. 2009. *Emergent curriculum in early childhood settings: From theory to practice.* St. Paul, MN: Redleaf Press.

Starkey, P., A. Klein, I. Chang, D. Qi, P. Lijuan, and Z. Yang. 1999. Environmental supports for young children's mathematical development in China and the United States. Paper read at Society for Research in Child Development, April, Albuquerque, NM.

Steffe, L. P. 2004. PSSM from a constructivist perspective. In *Engaging young children in mathematics standards for early childhood mathematics education*, edited by D. H. Clements and J. Sarama. Mahwah, NJ: Lawrence Erlbaum Associates. Pp. 221-251.

Steffe, L. P., and P. Cobb. 1988. *Construction of arithmetical meanings and strategies.* New York: Springer-Verlag.

Stiggins, R. J. 1991. Assessment literacy. *Phi Delta Kappan* 72(7):534-539.

———. 1999. Evaluating classroom assessment training in teacher education programs. *Educational Measurement: Issues and Practice* 18(1):23-27.

———. 2001. The unfulfilled promise of classroom assessment. *Educational Measurement: Issues and Practice* 20(3):5-15.

Stormont, M., T. J. Lewis, and R. Beckner. 2005. Positive behavior support systems: Applying key features in preschool settings. *Teaching Exceptional Children* 37(July/August):42-49.

Strizek, G. A., J. L. Pittsonberger, K. E. Riordan, D. M. Lyter, and G. F. Orlofsk. 2006. *Characteristics of schools, districts, teachers, principals, and school libraries in the United States, 2003-04, schools and staffing survey.* Washington, DC: U.S. Department of Education, National Center for Education Statistics.

Strouse, G. A., K. O'Doherty, and G. L. Troseth. 2013. Effective coviewing: Preschoolers' learning from video after a dialogic questioning intervention. *Developmental Psychology* 49(12):2368-2382.

Sugai, G., and R. H. Horner. 2009. Responsiveness-to-intervention and school-wide positive behavior supports: Integration of multi-tiered system approaches. *Exceptionality* 17(4):223-237.

Sutterby, J., and J. Frost. 2006. Creating play environments for early childhood: Indoors and out. In *Handbook of research on the education of young children*, edited by B. Spodek and O. N. Saracho. Mahwah, NJ: Lawrence Erlbaum Associates. Pp. 305-322.

Swanson, H. L., and M. Hoskyn. 1998. Experimental intervention research on students with learning disabilities: A meta-analysis of treatment outcomes. *Review of Educational Research* 68(3):277-321.

Swanson, H. L., M. Hoskyn, and C. Lee. 1999. *Interventions for students with learning disabilities: A meta-analysis of treatment outcomes.* New York: Guilford Press.

Sylva, K., E. Melhuish, P. Sammons, I. Siraj-Blatchford, and B. Taggart. 2005. *The Effective Provision of Pre-school Education (EPPE) Project: Final report: A longitudinal study funded by the DfES 1997-2004.* London: University of London, Institute of Education.

Tanner, C. K. 2009. Effects of school design on student outcomes. *Journal of Educational Administration* 47(3):381-399.

Tao, Y., M. Oliver, and G. Venville. 2012. Long-term outcomes of early childhood science education: Insights from a cross-national comparative case study on conceptual understanding of science. *International Journal of Science and Mathematics Education* 10(6):1269-1302.

Thomson, S., K. Rowe, C. Underwood, and R. Peck. 2005. *Numeracy in the early years: Project Good Start*. Camberwell, Victoria, Australia: Australian Council for Educational Research.

Thorell, L. B., S. Lindqvist, S. Bergman Nutley, G. Bohlin, and T. Klingberg. 2009. Training and transfer effects of executive functions in preschool children. *Developmental Science* 12(1):106-113.

Tominey, S., and M. McClelland. 2011. Red light, purple light: Findings from a randomized trial using circle time games to improve behavioral self-regulation in preschool. *Early Education and Development* 22(3):489-519.

Tournaki, N. 2003. The differential effects of teaching addition through strategy instruction versus drill and practice to students with and without learning disabilities. *Journal of Learning Disabilities* 36(5):449-458.

Tout, K., T. Halle, S. Daily, L. Albertson-Junkans, and S. Moodie. 2013. *The research base for a birth through age eight state policy framework*. Washington, DC: Alliance for Early Success and Child Trends.

Trinick, T., and B. Stevenson. 2009. Longitudinal patterns of performance: Te Poutama Tau. In *Findings from the New Zealand numeracy development projects 2008*, edited by Ministry of Education. Wellington, New Zealand: Learning Media. Pp. 27-38.

Tu, T. 2006. Preschool science environment: What is available in a preschool classroom? *Early Childhood Education Journal* 33(4):245-251.

Tudge, J. R. H., and F. Doucet. 2004. Early mathematical experiences: Observing young black and white childrens everyday activities. *Early Childhood Research Quarterly* 19(1):21-39.

Turnbull, K. P., A. B. Anthony, L. Justice, and R. Bowles. 2009. Preschoolers' exposure to language stimulation in classrooms serving at-risk children: The contribution of group size and activity context. *Early Education and Development* 20(1):53-79.

Turner, E. E., and S. Celedón-Pattichis. 2011. Problem solving and mathematical discourse among Latino/a kindergarten students: An analysis of opportunities to learn. *Journal of Latinos and Education* 10(2):146-169.

Turner, E. E., S. Celedón-Pattichis, and M. E. Marshall. 2008. Cultural and linguistic resources to promote problem solving and mathematical discourse amoung Hispanic kindergarten students. In *Promoting high participation and success in mathematics by Hispanic students: Examining opportunities and probing promising practices*. Vol. 1, edited by R. S. Kitchen and E. A. Silver. Tempe, AZ: TODOS: Mathematics for ALL. Pp. 19-42.

van den Heuvel-Panhuizen, M. 1996. *Assessment and realistic mathematics education*. Utrecht, The Netherlands: Utrecht University, Freudenthal Institute.

van den Heuvel-Panhuizen, M., and I. Elia. 2012. Developing a framework for the evaluation of picturebooks that support kindergartners' learning of mathematics. *Research in Mathematics Education* 14:17-47.

van Kleek, A. 2004. Fostering preliteracy development via storybook-sharing interactions: The cultural context of mainstream family practices. In *Handbook of language and literacy: Development and disorders*, edited by C. A. Stone, E. R. Silliman, B. Ehren, and K. Apel. New York: Guilford Press. Pp. 175-208.

van Nes, F. T. 2009. Young children's spatial structuring ability and emerging number sense. Doctoral dissertation. de Universtiteit Utrecht. Utrecht, The Netherlands.

Vandewater, E. A., R. F. Barr, S. E. Park, and S.-J. Lee. 2010. A US study of transfer of learning from video to books in toddlers. *Journal of Children and Media* 4(4):451-467.

Vaughn, S., P. Mathes, S. Linan-Thompson, P. Cirino, C. Carlson, S. Pollard-Durodola, and D. Francis. 2006. Effectiveness of an English intervention for first-grade English language learners at risk for reading problems. *Elementary School Journal* 107(2):153-180.

Verschaffel, L., B. Greer, and E. De Corte. 2007. Whole number concepts and operations. In *Second handbook of research on mathematics teaching and learning: A project of the National Council of Teachers of Mathematics*, edited by F. K. Lester. New York: Information Age Publishing. Pp. 557-628.

Vukovic, R. K., N. K. Lesaux, and L. S. Siegel. 2010. The mathematics skills of children with reading difficulties. *Learning and Individual Differences* 20(6):639-643.

Watson, D. 1993. *The ImpacT Report: An evaluation of the impact of information technology on children's achievements in primary and secondary schools*. London, UK: King's College London.

Webster-Stratton, C., M. J. Reid, and M. Stoolmiller. 2008. Preventing conduct problems and improving school readiness: Evaluation of the incredible years teacher and child training programs in high-risk schools. *Journal of Child Psychology and Psychiatry* 49(5):471-488.

Weiland, C., and H. Yoshikawa. 2013. Impacts of a prekindergarten program on children's mathematics, language, literacy, executive function, and emotional skills. *Child Development* 84(6):2112-2130.

Weiland, C., K. Ulvestad, J. Sachs, and H. Yoshikawa. 2013. Associations between classroom quality and children's vocabulary and executive function skills in an urban public prekindergarten program. *Early Childhood Research Quarterly* 28(2):199-209.

Weizman, Z. O., and C. E. Snow. 2001. Lexical input as related to children's vocabulary acquisition: Effects of sophisticated exposure and support for meaning. *Developmental Psychology* 37(2):265-279.

Wenner, G. 1993. Relationship between science knowledge levels and beliefs towards science instruction held by preservice elementary teachers. *Journal of Science Education and Technology* 2:461-468.

Whalen, C. K., D. A. Granger, B. Henker, and C. Cantwell. 1996. ADHD boys' behavior during structured classroom social activities: Effects of social demands, teacher proximity, and methylphenidate. *Journal of Attention Disorders* 1(1):16-30.

Whitehurst, G. J., F. L. Falco, C. J. Lonigan, J. E. Fischel, B. D. DeBarshe, M. C. Valdex-Menchaca, and M. Caulfield. 1988. Accelerating language development through picture book reading. *Developmental Psychology* 24(4):552-559.

Wien, C. A. 2011. Learning to document in Reggio-inspired education. *Early Childhood Research & Practice* 13(2).

Wilkinson, L. C., L. Martina, and G. Cammili. 1994. Groups that work: Social factors in elementary students' mathematics problem solving. In *Research on learning and instruction of mathematics in kindergarten and primary school*, edited by J. E. H. van Luit. Doetinchem, The Netherlands: Graviant Publishing Co.

Wilson, P. H., P. Sztajn, C. Edgington, and J. Confrey. 2014. Teachers use of their mathematical knowledge for teaching in learning a mathematics learning trajectory. *Journal of Mathematics Teacher Education* 17(2):149-175.

Winton, P., V. Buysse, D. Bryant, D. Clifford, D. Early, and L. Little. 2005. NCEDL prekindergarten study. *Early Developments* 9(1):1-31.

Wolery, M. 2005. DEC recommended practices: Child-focused practices. In *DEC recommended practices: A comprehensive guide for practical application in early intervention/ early childhood special education*, edited by S. Sandall, M. L. Hemmeter, B. Smith, and M. McLean. Missoula, MT: Division for Early Childhood.

Wright, J. C., A. C. Auston, K. C. Murphy, M. St. Peters, R. S. Pinon, and J. Kotler. 2001. The relations of early television viewing to school readiness and vocabulary of children from low-income families: The early window project. *Child Development* 72(5):1347-1366.

Wright, R. J. 2003. A mathematics recovery: Program of intervention in early number learning. *Australian Journal of Learning Disabilities* 8(4):6-11.

Wright, S. P., S. P. Horn, and W. L. Sanders. 1997. Teacher and classroom context effects on student achievement: Implications for teacher evaluation. *Journal of Personnel Evaluation in Education* 11:57-67.

Yost, N. J. M. 1998. Computers, kids, and crayons: A comparative study of one kindergarten's emergent literacy behaviors. Ph.D. dissertation, Pennsylvania State University, State College, Pennsylvania.

Zelazo, P. D., and S. M. Carlson. 2012. Hot and cool executive function in childhood and adolescence: Development and plasticity. *Child Development Perspectives* 6(4):354-360.

Zimmerman, F. J., and D. A. Christakis. 2007. Associations between content types of early media exposure and subsequent attentional problems. *Pediatrics* 120(5):986-992.

Zucker, T. A., S. Q. Cabell, L. M. Justice, J. M. Pentimonti, and J. N. Kaderavek. 2013. The role of frequent, interactive prekindergarten shared reading in the longitudinal development of language and literacy skills. *Developmental Psychology* 49(8):1425-1439.

7

Knowledge and Competencies

This chapter considers the knowledge and competencies needed by adults to more seamlessly support the health, learning, development, and school success of children from birth through age 8 by providing consistent, high-quality care and education. For its articulation of these competencies, the committee draws on the science of child development and early learning, the knowledge base about educational practices, and the landscape of care and education and related sectors. The chapter first summarizes foundational knowledge, skills, and abilities, or competencies, needed by adults who have professional responsibilities for young children. This is followed by a discussion of specialized competencies needed for quality practice for the care and education workforce, including the extent to which current statements of professional standards encompass these competencies. The final two sections examine knowledge and competencies for leaders and administrators, and for collaborative and coordinated practice among professionals within and across the closely related sectors of care and education, health, and social services.

FOUNDATIONAL KNOWLEDGE AND COMPETENCIES

The committee identifies the general knowledge and competencies in Box 7-1 as an important foundation for all adults with professional responsibilities for young children, across settings and sectors.

BOX 7-1
Foundational Knowledge and Competencies for All Adults with Professional Responsibilities for Young Children

All adults with professional responsibilities for young children need to know about

- How a child develops and learns, including cognitive development, specific content knowledge and skills, general learning competencies, socioemotional development, and physical development and health.
- The importance of consistent, stable, nurturing, and protective relationships that support development and learning across domains and enable children to fully engage in learning opportunities.
- Biological and environmental factors that can contribute positively to or interfere with development, behavior, and learning (for example, positive and ameliorative effects of nurturing and responsive relationships, negative effects of chronic stress and exposure to trauma and adverse events, positive adaptations to environmental exposures).

All adults with professional responsibilities for young children need to use this knowledge and develop the skills to

- Engage effectively in quality interactions with children that foster healthy child development and learning in routine everyday interactions, in specific learning activities, and in educational and other professional settings in a manner appropriate to the child's developmental level.
- Promote positive social development and behaviors and mitigate challenging behaviors.
- Recognize signs that children may need to be assessed and referred for specialized services (for example, for developmental delays, mental health concerns, social support needs, or abuse and neglect); and be aware of how to access the information, resources, and support for such specialized help when needed.
- Make informed decisions about whether and how to use different kinds of technologies as tools to promote children's learning.

SPECIALIZED KNOWLEDGE AND COMPETENCIES FOR EDUCATORS

This section considers what educators and education leaders who work with children from birth through age 8 need to know and be able to do to support important domains of development and learning and to support greater continuity for children along the birth through age 8 continuum. The discussion begins with a summary of what the committee has identified as the shared core knowledge and competencies needed by educators, or those professionals who provide direct, regular care and education for young children from birth through age 8, who may work with these children in home- or center-based childcare settings, early childhood education centers and preschools, and elementary schools. This is followed by an overview of the extent to which current statements of core competencies at the national and state levels encompass the identified knowledge and competencies. Knowledge and competencies for leadership in care and education are discussed later in the chapter, as well as competencies for collaboration and communication among different professional roles, referred to in this report as interprofessional practice.

As described in Chapter 1, the committee's focus was identifying the competencies that, to support greater consistency in high-quality learning experiences for children, need to be shared in common for educators across the birth through age 8 continuum and across professional roles and practice settings, as stated in the statement of task. This includes areas in which these care and education professionals will benefit from understanding the scope of learning—and the scope of educational practices—for the settings and ages that precede or follow them within the birth through 8 age range. Further specialized competencies and professional learning differentiated by age, setting, and/or role are important, but this study avoids duplicating or supplanting existing infrastructure or processes for articulating, reviewing, and guiding them. Rather, this committee's charge was to bridge those efforts and assist each of them in refining their efforts to collectively and more effectively contribute to greater consistency and continuity for children.

Finally, while this section and this chapter cover knowledge and competencies at the individual level, it is important to note that a focus on the individual is not sufficient, and professionals cannot be expected to bear the responsibility for quality practice alone. Part IV covers professional learning systems with responsibility for supporting and continuously updating the acquisition and application of these knowledge and competencies. Even beyond professional learning systems, however, adults who have mastery of the necessary knowledge and competencies may still be constrained in putting them into practice by the circumstances and work environments of the settings and systems in which they practice and by the policies that support those settings and systems, as previously described in Chapter 2. Therefore, Part IV also examines characteristics of settings and systems that are needed to ensure quality and to support individual practitioners.

Core Competencies for Educators

In addition to the foundational knowledge and competencies described in the preceding section, the committee identifies in Box 7-2 the knowledge

BOX 7-2
Knowledge and Competencies for Care and Education Practitioners

Core Knowledge Base
- Knowledge of the developmental science that underlies important domains of early learning and child development, including cognitive development, specific content knowledge and skills, general learning competencies, socioemotional development, and physical development and health.
- Knowledge of how these domains interact to facilitate learning and development.
- Knowledge of content and concepts that are important in early learning of major subject-matter areas, including language and literacy, mathematics, science, technology, engineering, arts, and social studies.
- Knowledge of the learning trajectories (goals, developmental progressions, and instructional tasks and strategies) of how children learn and become proficient in each of the domains and specific subject-matter areas.
- Knowledge of the science that elucidates the interactions among biological and environmental factors that influence children's development and learning, including the positive effects of consistent, nurturing interactions that facilitate development and learning, as well as the negative effects of chronic stress and exposure to trauma and adversity that can impede development and learning.
- Knowledge of principles for assessing children that are developmentally appropriate; culturally sensitive; and relevant, reliable, and valid across a variety of populations, domains, and assessment purposes.

Practices to Help Children Learn
- Ability to establish relationships and interactions with children that are nurturing and use positive language.
- Ability to create and manage effective learning environments (physical space, materials, activities, classroom management).
- Ability to consistently deploy productive routines, maintain a schedule, and make transitions brief and productive, all to increase predictability and learning opportunities and to maintain a sense of emotional calm in the learning environment.
- Ability to use a repertory of instructional and caregiving practices and strategies, including implementing validated curricula, that engage children through nurturing, responsive interactions and facilitate learning and development in all domains in ways that are appropriate for their stage of development.
- Ability to set appropriate individualized goals and objectives to advance young children's development and learning.
- Ability to use learning trajectories: a deep understanding of the content; knowledge of the way children think and learn about the content; and the ability to design and employ instructional tasks, curricula, and activities that effectively promote learning and development within and across domains and subject-matter areas.

- Ability to select, employ, and interpret a portfolio of both informal and formal assessment tools and strategies; to use the results to understand individual children's developmental progression and determine whether needs are being met; and to use this information to individualize, adapt, and improve instructional practices.
- Ability to integrate and leverage different kinds of technologies in curricula and instructional practice to promote children's learning.
- Ability to promote positive social development and self-regulation while mitigating challenging behaviors in ways that reflect an understanding of the multiple biological and environmental factors that affect behavior.
- Ability to recognize the effects of factors from outside the practice setting (e.g., poverty, trauma, parental depression, experience of violence in the home or community) that affect children's learning and development, and to adjust practice to help children experiencing those effects.

Working with Diverse Populations of Children
- Ability to advance the learning and development of children from backgrounds that are diverse in family structure, socioeconomic status, race, ethnicity, culture, and language.
- Ability to advance the learning and development of children who are dual language learners.
- Ability to advance the development and learning of children who have specialized developmental or learning needs, such as children with disabilities or learning delays, children experiencing chronic stress/adversity, and children who are gifted and talented. All early care and education professionals—not just those in specialized roles—need knowledge and basic competencies for working with these children.

Developing and Using Partnerships
- Ability to communicate and connect with families in a mutually respectful, reciprocal way, and to set goals with families and prepare them to engage in complementary behaviors and activities that enhance development and early learning.
- Ability to recognize when behaviors and academic challenges may be a sign of an underlying need for referral for more comprehensive assessment, diagnosis, and support (e.g., mental health consultation, social services, family support services).
- Knowledge of professional roles and available services within care and education and in closely related sectors such as health and social services.
- Ability to access and effectively use available referral and resource systems.
- Ability to collaborate and communicate with professionals in other roles, disciplines, and sectors to facilitate mutual understanding and collective contributions to improving outcomes for children.

Continuously Improving the Quality of Practice
- Ability and motivation to access and engage in available professional learning resources to keep current with the science of development and early learning and with research on instructional and other practices.
- Knowledge and abilities for self-care to manage their own physical and mental health, including the effects of their own exposure to adversity and stress.

and competencies that are important for all professionals who provide direct, regular care and education for young children to support development, foster early learning, and contribute to greater consistency along the birth through age 8 continuum.

Current Statements of Professional Standards and Core Competencies for Educators

One of the factors that contributes to continuity in high-quality learning experiences is continuity in the stated expectations for the care and education professionals who work with children throughout the age 0-8 continuum. This section describes the extent to which the knowledge and competencies identified in the preceding sections are reflected in current statements of professional standards and core competencies, focusing on the role of educators. This is followed by a discussion of how stated core competencies could be improved to better reflect both the science of child development and the science of instruction, as well as to reflect more aligned expectations for care and education professionals across roles and settings.

Comparison of National Statements

A scan of the stated professional standards or core competencies from four national organizations provides a sense of the expectations that have been articulated for care and education professionals who work with children through age 8:

- The National Association for the Education of Young Children (NAEYC) has developed "Standards for Early Childhood Professional Preparation" (NAEYC, 2009).
- The National Board for Professional Teaching Standards (NBPTS) has a set of "Early Childhood Generalist Standards" that apply to teachers of children from ages 3 to 8 (NBPTS, 2012).
- The Interstate Teacher Assessment and Support Consortium (InTASC) of the Council of Chief State School Officers (CCSSO) offers "Model Core Teaching Standards" for K-12 teachers (CCSSO, 2011).
- The Division for Early Childhood (DEC) of the Council for Exceptional Children has issued "Recommended Practices in in Early Intervention/Early Childhood Special Education" (DEC, 2014).

These statements from national organizations are consistent in saying that effective educators need to possess the following knowledge and competencies, which also are consistent with those identified by this committee:

- working effectively and equitably with children from diverse backgrounds—cultural, socioeconomic, and linguistic—and of different ability levels;
- creating and using supportive learning environments, including physical space, materials, and activities;
- having the capacity (knowledge and skills) to support children's learning and development across multiple domains, including cognition, language and literacy, socioemotional skills, learning competencies, executive function, physical health, and moral and ethical development;
- understanding core concepts of major content areas and having the ability to use that knowledge to design curricula and activities that help children understand and apply these concepts;[1]
- knowing how to assess children appropriately and using assessment results to inform practice;
- setting appropriate goals and objectives for learners based on understanding of the children's development across domains and content knowledge, and planning, designing, and selecting instructional activities and approaches accordingly;
- using a repertoire of strategies that engage children across content areas and domains in developmentally appropriate ways while making ongoing adjustments based on children's progress to foster further growth;
- engaging in professional learning opportunities to improve practice and in leadership opportunities to advance the field;
- collaborating with other early care and education professionals and those from related fields to support children holistically; and
- partnering with family members to support children's learning and development.

Given the commonly cited differences in philosophies, policies, and approaches between the early childhood (birth to age 5) and elementary education communities, some of the above similarities are worth highlighting. First, there is an assumption that elementary education systems neglect children's development in areas other than the academic, and that "standards-based" reform is "pushing" expectations and teaching strategies down the age continuum from the older grades and encouraging practices that are inappropriate for children in prekindergarten through third grade. Setting aside whether that is indeed the case, it is interesting that all of the above national statements expect professionals—whether they are working with the youngest children or third graders—to know how to support

---

[1] The InTASC standards do not name specific content areas.

children's development across domains, in general cognitive skills, specific academic skills, learning competencies, socioemotional development, and health and physical well-being. All four statements of competencies also expect professionals to work with children in developmentally appropriate ways and to collaborate with colleagues in early care and education and in other related fields if necessary to support children's learning and development comprehensively.

Similarly, a common perception about early childhood professionals (those who work with children under the age of 5) is that they lack adequate understanding of early learning in content areas or focus more on how children are developing in the socioemotional domain and in general learning competencies than on the foundations of learning discrete subjects. Yet both the NAEYC and the NBPTS standards express explicit expectations that these professionals understand content knowledge in specific subject areas and have the ability to use that understanding to develop curricula, learning environments, and learning activities.

While these four statements suggest significant agreement as to what early care and education providers for children under age 5 and early elementary grade educators should know and be able to do, some nuances and variations exist in a number of areas:

- *Assessment*—The NAEYC and DEC standards place more emphasis on professionals' proficiency in using observational assessments, systematic and everyday documentation of children's progress, and screening tools. The InTASC standards emphasize using multiple assessment strategies and distinguishing between formative and summative assessments—concepts that are not mentioned in the NAEYC statement. The NBPTS standards address the need to differentiate between formative and summative assessments, but also the value of observations and performance-based assessment that yield anecdotal evidence and work samples that can be meaningful. Both InTASC and the NBPTS, however, are largely silent on knowledge of and the ability to use screening tools. The InTASC standards also do not focus on professionals' ability to communicate assessment results to family members and other colleagues—skills that are included in the NAEYC, DEC, and the NBPTS standards.
- *Family engagement*—While all four sets of standards speak to skills related to engaging families, the InTASC standards tend to emphasize these skills as means to support children's learning and development. The NAEYC, DEC, and the NBPTS also discuss this purpose of partnering with families, but they also expect professionals to have competencies related to helping families access other services that support their children's well-being.

- *Technology*—The NAEYC's position statement on technology provides guidance on developmentally appropriate practices for educators with respect to interactive media and technology, though it does not identify required competencies. Technology is identified as an important influence on children's learning and development, and while there are no NAEYC standards specific to technology, it is integrated as a component of the NAEYC standards. The recognition of technology is limited to its use as a method of communication between educators and families, as well as a source of tools for child assessment and professional learning (NAEYC, 2009). Conversely, the NBPTS standards include technology as a subject matter and state that educators should support young children in using technology as a tool. The NBPTS further articulates that accomplished educators are knowledgeable about technology and aware of new technological advances, and understand how children use technology to nurture their curiosity and learning (NBPTS, 2012). Similarly, InTASC identifies technology as a theme that cuts across many standards related to learning environment, content, application, and assessment; planning; instructional strategies; professional learning; and leadership (CCSSO, 2011). InTASC's definition of learning environment includes the use of technology, which can allow children to work and engage with collaborators outside the classroom, as well as personalize their own learning. Standards require educators to teach and promote responsible and safe use of technology in order to achieve specific learning goals, help build children's capacity for working productively and collaboratively, and understand the demands and challenges of using technology (CCSSO, 2011).

Comparison of National and State Statements

Many states also have developed formal core competencies for early care and education professionals.[2] Most of them focus on professionals who work with children below the age of 5, although many also include those who work with K-3 and in a few cases even older students as well. Some states have different sets of competencies for more specialized roles, such as home visitors or early interventionists, and for different settings, such as home-based or center-based care. This discussion focuses on competency statements for educators.

---

[2] A scan was conducted of a sample of states to compare examples of core competencies statements for care and education professionals in the birth through age 8 continuum across states and between state and national statements.

In general, states' expectations for early care and education profession-als align with those articulated in national statements, especially that of the NAEYC. Importantly, state and national statements of core competencies reflect the notion that "education" goes beyond academic success to encom-pass other domains, such as socioemotional development and physical and mental health, that also contribute in important ways to students' success in school and in life. Thus, statements for both educators who work with young children and those who work with early elementary students uphold the importance of addressing all of the domains of development and learn-ing, not just academic skills. These statements also expect professionals to learn how to collaborate with each other and colleagues from other fields so that if necessary, children have access to other services that contribute to their well-being and academic success.

For states that have articulated core competencies specifically for those who work with infants and toddlers;[3] these statements tend to elevate the importance of being effective in partnering with and supporting family members and include more specialized skills for this, such as "family-centered practices" that include joint decision making between family mem-bers and practitioners (Ohio Child Care Resource & Referral Association, 2008); skills related to applying theories of attachment and separation in practice and integrating families into the process of identifying and address-ing children's special needs through early intervention (New York State Association for the Education of Young Children, 2009); and understand-ing the family's beliefs and values related to child-rearing, communicating with the family about children's growth and development, collaborating with parents throughout the assessment process, and integrating families' goals and culture into curricula and learning environments (New Hamp-shire Department for Health and Human Services and Child Development Bureau, 2013).

Despite this broad agreement between the core competencies identified by states and national organizations, some significant differences exist. First, the core competencies of states tend to place more emphasis on skills

---

[3] Only three states have separate documents outlining specific competencies for profes-sionals who work with infants and toddlers. Those states are Maine (http://muskie.usm. maine.edu/maineroads/pdfs/ITC1_Cred_Guide_Manual.pdf, accessed March 25, 2015), New Hampshire (http://www.dhhs.state.nh.us/dcyf/cdb/documents/infant-toddler-competencies.pdf, accessed March 25, 2015), and New York (http://nysaeyc.org/wp-content/uploads/ITCEC-Competencies.pdf, accessed March 25, 2015). Two states have published documents for these professionals that are used to augment generalized early childhood competencies: Minnesota (Companion document) (http://www.cehd.umn.edu/ceed/projects/ittcguide/default.html, ac-cessed March 25, 2015) and Ohio (standards including infant and toddler caregiver compe-tencies) (http://occrra.org/it/documents/ITStandards.pdf, accessed March 25, 2015). Personal communication, B. Gebherd, ZERO TO THREE, 2014.

related to promoting health, safety, and nutrition, often calling them out as separate competency areas. Second, states also tend to include competencies related to the business of operating or managing an early learning program, such as relevant legal issues, financial planning, and human resources. Third, instead of calling out content knowledge as a competency area, as the national statements do, early care and education competencies from states embed it in other competencies, such as "teaching practices" or "learning environment and curriculum." Most of these statements do differentiate professionals' competencies in instruction, building a curriculum, and creating a learning environment for different content areas, which often include mathematics, language and literacy, science, social studies, art, and sometimes technology. In some cases, though, the concept of content knowledge appears to be broadly defined as language and literacy and part of cognitive development.

Opportunities for Statements of Educator Core Competencies to Better Reflect the Science

The above scan of both national and state statements of core competencies suggests that there is broad agreement on what educators who work with children from infancy through age 8 need to know and be able to do. The existence of core competencies for professionals in early childhood settings represents an effort to bring coherence to a workforce with highly diverse expectations and backgrounds, and the general agreement among the competencies is an indication of some emerging alignment. Despite this broad agreement, however, there are also some variations in emphasis in a few areas. As described previously, the early childhood and elementary education fields vary somewhat in their statements of what educators' competencies should be in the areas of assessment and family engagement, and reconciling these differences could be constructive for educators, children, and families.

At the same time, the science of how children develop and learn (as described in Part II) and the important role of high-quality educational practice in fostering developmental progress for children (as described in Chapter 6) point to a number of areas in which both national and state statements of core competencies could be improved. These areas are also emphasized in the competencies identified by this committee (see Box 7-2).

Teaching subject-matter–specific content Just having knowledge about various content areas and the major stages or milestones experienced by children is inadequate. As discussed in Chapter 6, effective instruction in subject areas (such as reading and math) results from a combination of knowledge of the subject; of the learning trajectories necessary for children to gain proficiency in the subject's major concepts, themes, and topics; and of developmentally appropriate pedagogy and content knowledge for teaching, that is, how to represent and convey specific content and how to design learning experiences to support children's progression along the learning trajectories in the subject. Each subject area calls for a distinctive body of knowledge and set of competencies. In short, having content knowledge and knowing the major developmental milestones in any given subject area does no good if the educator does not know how to link that knowledge to instructional practices and engineer the learning environment to support children's growth in that subject.

Among states' statements of core competencies for early childhood educators, New Mexico's comes close to this concept. It calls for early learning professionals to be able to "use their child development knowledge, their knowledge of developmentally appropriate practices, and their content knowledge to design, implement, and evaluate experiences that promote optimal development and learning" for all children from birth through age 8. For example, to support the development of emergent literacy skills in young children, educators should be able to describe and implement developmentally appropriate strategies based on the stages of reading and writing across the developmental continuum, and identify ways to effectively implement these strategies (New Mexico Early Childhood Higher Education Task Force, 2011). Among the national statements, the NBPTS's standards for early childhood generalists go into greater detail than others about the concepts for each subject area—language and literacy, mathematics, science, social studies, visual arts, music and drama, health education, physical education, and technology—and the skills professionals need to support children's development in each.

Seen in this light, discussions of content knowledge in most existing statements of core competencies—whether at the state or national level—lack specificity (e.g., major concepts and themes in a content area are rarely included), or differentiation (e.g., embedding math and science under "cognitive development"), or both. Most existing core competencies for educators of young children are lacking in the area of describing developmentally appropriate practice for teaching specific content areas.

Addressing stress and adversity Educators of young children need to understand recent research on the interplay among chronic adverse experiences (e.g., poverty, trauma, stress); brain development; and children's capacity to learn, exert self-control, and develop positive relationships (as discussed in Chapter 4). For example, Vermont's core competencies for early childhood professionals expect beginning practitioners to understand that stress from adverse childhood experiences (e.g., trauma, abuse, neglect, poverty) affects child development and behavior and to be able to identify strategies that can help recognize this stress. More experienced professionals are expected to consider the origins and effects of stress when working with children as well as the available ways to address their needs (Vermont Northern Lights Career Development Center, 2013).

Most existing statements of core competencies do emphasize the importance of working effectively with children with different learning needs and from diverse cultural, socioeconomic, and linguistic backgrounds, but nonetheless may not adequately address the competencies needed for early care and education professionals to work with children experiencing chronic stress and adversity. Competency statements could be improved by articulating what knowledge and skills early care and education professionals need to recognize learning challenges that result from stress and adversity, to adapt instructional practices that take these issues into account, and to implement what are sometimes referred to as "trauma-informed" practices that help children manage their emotions and behaviors while engaged in learning activities. The National Child Traumatic Stress Network has developed 12 core concepts that provide a rationale for trauma-informed assessment and intervention (NCTSN Core Curriculum on Childhood Trauma Task Force, 2012), covering considerations for how to assess, understand, and assist children, families, and communities who have experienced trauma.

Fostering socioemotional development and general learning competencies
According to national and state statements of core competencies, educators are expected to understand socioemotional development as well as how children develop general learning competencies, and to be able to create learning environments and experiences that support development in both of these major areas. However, most of the existing competencies related to these two domains tend to treat them monolithically or define them through a list of examples of skills that differ somewhat from document to document. In other words, most statements of competencies related to these domains do not appear to be grounded in a strong conceptual framework that identifies and differentiates major areas of development that care and education professionals should understand in addition to understanding relationships among the domains.

As discussed in Chapter 4, a growing body of research is focused on the important role of the development of executive function and self-regulation not just during the early childhood and early elementary years but throughout a student's academic career and indeed, into adulthood. National organizations and states may also need to catch up with this research and articulate what educators of young children need to know about how generalized self-regulatory capacities regarding emotion, behavior, attention, and focus are linked to each other and to academic achievement and how to design learning environments and engage specific teaching strategies to create experiences that cultivate these skills in children in developmentally appropriate ways.

Statements of core competencies tend not to specify what educators should know about how children's socioemotional development and acquisition of learning competencies progresses as they grow from infants to toddlers to preschoolers to older students. As a result, most competency statements, especially those of states, only articulate generally what educators need to know to promote development in these areas; they do not address practices and strategies that they can design in these areas that are appropriate and specific for different age groups or for the distinct domains of socioemotional development and the growth of learning competencies. These domains of development are included in most national and state early learning standards for children, revealing a gap between what is expected for children and the specific competencies needed for educators to foster those learning outcomes.

Working with dual language learners Research on young dual language learners suggests that working effectively with these children requires both fundamental understanding of child development and learning and more specialized knowledge about how these children develop in various domains, how they respond to instruction, and what evidence-based practices have demonstrated success with this population. Yet while many statements of core competencies speak to the general need to respect cultural and linguistic diversity, they do not discuss in depth the knowledge professionals need of how these children learn, including the distinctive knowledge and capabilities required to support English acquisition and children's home language development. Given that dual language learners are one of the fastest-growing populations in the nation, better articulation of these competencies is needed. California's core competencies statement, for example, includes one of the most comprehensive discussions of this topic (California Department of Education and First 5 California, 2011). In addition, the Alliance for a Better Community (2012) recently developed "Dual Language Learner Teacher Competencies" that articulate what early childhood teachers should know and be able to do to support language and literacy development as well as socioemotional skills for dual language learners. The California competencies also are differentiated by the teachers' linguistic skills (monolingual, bilingual, or biliterate), cultural background (monocultural or bicultural), and levels of experience.

Integrated technology into curricula Technology is everywhere: students in elementary schools are increasingly expected to develop digital literacy skills; technology and media have become nearly ubiquitous in the lives of most families with young children; and professional information, curriculum materials, and children's books already are being delivered digitally to schools and early childhood centers. Competency statements on technology may need to be two-pronged: (1) expressing expectations around the use of new tools by educators for professional communication, information sharing, and assessment; and (2) articulating more specifically what educators should know when using technology to teach young children, including the teaching of emergent digital literacy skills and the teaching of particular content or subject matter (see Chapter 6). The second prong should involve knowing how to be selective in adopting technology and interactive media products, and knowing how and under what conditions to use various technologies with young children effectively. In addition to the technology skills outlined by the NBPTS and InTASC, a joint position statement from the National Association for the Education of Young Children and the Fred Rogers Center for Early Learning and Children's Media at Saint Vincent College provides guidance to educators in settings across the birth through age 8 spectrum (NAEYC and Fred Rogers Center for Early Learning and Children's Media at Saint Vincent College, 2012). ZERO TO THREE has also developed guidelines specifically for children under 3 (Lerner et al., 2014).

Conclusion About Competencies for Educators

Having a role in the early learning of a child is a complex responsibility that requires a sophisticated understanding of the child's cognitive and socioemotional development; knowledge of a broad range of subject-matter content areas; and skills for developing high-quality interactions and relationships with children, their families, and other professionals. The importance and value of these skills is often underestimated.

Conclusion About Core Competency Statements for Educators

A scan across national and state statements of core competencies for educators suggests that there is broad agreement on what educators who work with children from infancy through age 8 need to know and be able to do. However, there are variations in emphasis and gaps. Organizations and states that issue statements of core competencies for these educators would benefit from a review aimed at improving consistency in family engagement and assessment and enhancing their statements to reflect recent research on how children learn and develop and the role of educators in the process. Areas likely in need of enhancement in many existing statements include teaching subject-matter–specific content, addressing stress and adversity, fostering so-

cioemotional development, promoting general learning competencies, working with dual language learners, and integrating technology into curricula.

KNOWLEDGE AND COMPETENCIES FOR LEADERS AND ADMINISTRATORS

Elementary school principals, early learning center directors or program directors, family childcare owners, and other supervisors and administrators play an instrumental role in helping care and education professionals who work with young children strengthen their core competencies and in creating a work environment in which these professionals can fully use their knowledge and skills (see Figure 7-1 for a summary of levels of effective

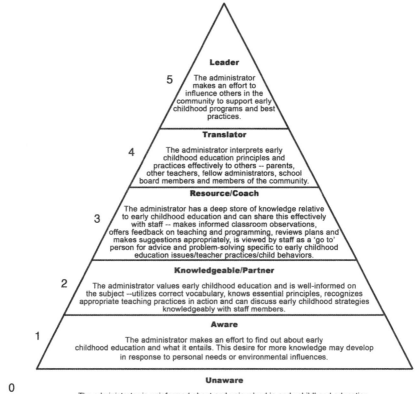

FIGURE 7-1 Administrator's contribution to care and education for young children.
SOURCE: Kostelnik and Grady, 2009, p. 26.

contributions from leadership).[4] These leaders are an important factor in the quality of early learning experiences for the children in the settings they oversee. Principals and directors often take a lead role in selecting instructional content and activities for professional learning within their school, center, or program (Matsumura et al., 2010; Snyder et al., 2011).

In addition, leaders, including not only principals and directors but also superintendents and other administrators, have a major influence because they are responsible for workforce hiring practices. They need to be able to seek and hire educators with the appropriate and necessary knowledge and competencies to work with children in the settings they lead. While licensure/credentialing systems for educators are one tool to assess whether prospective candidates are qualified, leaders also need to know and be able to assess a wide range of characteristics that contribute to quality practice.

Leaders also serve as a point of linkage among different stakeholders, professionals, and settings (see Figure 7-2). By sharing information, planning together, and introducing shared professional learning for their staff, a cross-sector cohort of leaders can play an important role in facilitating the communication and collaboration necessary to improve both vertical continuity within the care and education sector and horizontal continuity with other sectors, such as health and social services (continuity is discussed further in Chapter 5).

The quality of leadership is connected to the quality of early learning for children. For example, the levels of education and specialized training for directors in center-based early learning programs are linked to program quality, as indicated by observations of the learning environment, instructional leadership practices, and program accreditation (McCormick Center for Early Childhood Leadership, 2010, 2014). One meta-analysis of studies of K-12 schools showed a correlation between principals' leadership behaviors and student achievement (Marzano et al., 2005), and a recent study found that effective principals can boost student achievement by an equivalence of 2-7 months in a school year (Branch et al., 2013).

While the importance of school and program leadership is unequivocal, the capacity of these leaders to support high-quality instruction and services in the early years is questionable. Early childhood center and program directors suffer from a lack of specialized training as early learning instructional leaders. Elementary school principals, because of the way they are prepared or recruited, often lack understanding of early childhood development research and best practices in instruction in preschool and the primary grades. The National Association of Elementary School Principals

---

[4] Murphy (2003) also provides a useful outline of the role of an effective leader in promoting children's academic success, although the focus is not specifically early childhood.

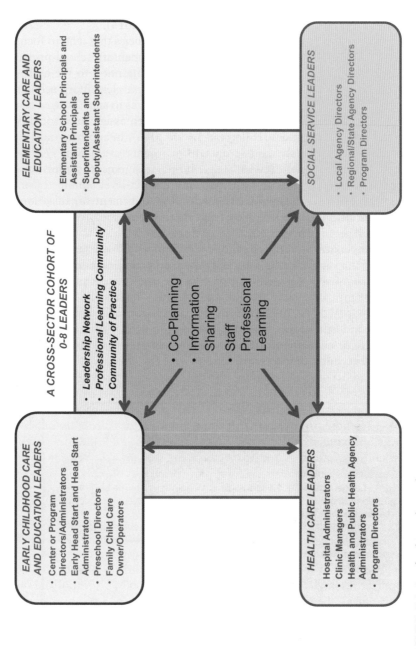

FIGURE 7-2 Leadership roles and connections.

has reported that more than half of practicing elementary school principals work in schools with prekindergarten programs serving children ages 3-4, and much of their knowledge about child development is self-taught (National Association of Elementary School Principals, 2014).

As a result of federal and state accountability policies that tend to focus on the academic performance of older students, elementary school principals have less immediate pressure to devote more attention to the earlier grades (Mead, 2011). One study of North Carolina elementary schools suggests that over time, tying high-stakes consequences to standardized test scores in grades 3 through 8 has caused principals to assign lower-quality teachers to the earlier grades (Fuller and Ladd, 2013). In another study on the extent to which principals use data from teacher evaluation systems to inform their personnel decisions (e.g., hiring, assignment, professional development), interviews with principals and district-level administrators in six urban districts and two charter school management organizations found that principals were assigning teachers they perceived to be poor to the early grades (Goldring et al., 2014).

The complexity of early childhood development discussed in earlier chapters and the sophisticated knowledge and competencies needed by early care and education professionals to be effective raise significant questions about the extent to which (1) school and program leaders are expected to have the capacity to support high-quality instruction and interactions in early childhood and early elementary settings, and (2) state and federal policies motivate and support these leaders in acquiring the knowledge and skills needed to fulfill that responsibility.

Perspectives from the Field

A leader's job is multifaceted, and requires instructional and operational capabilities.

Leaders have an important role in incentivizing staff to seek professional learning supports and encouraging them to seek supports tailored to their individual needs.

The specific role of leaders as a "hub" between systems is particularly important, but requires that they learn competencies that they often currently do not have and that they receive support and are incentivized to make connections among leaders in early childhood education, early elementary, and other sectors, such as health.

See Appendix C for additional highlights from interviews.

BOX 7-3
Knowledge and Competencies for Leadership in
Settings with Children Birth Through Age 8

Practices to Help Children Learn
- Understanding the implications of child development and early learning for interactions between care and education professionals and children, instructional and other practices, and learning environments.
- Ability to keep current with how advances in the research on child development and early learning and on instructional and other practices inform changes in professional practices and learning environments.

Assessment of Children
- Knowledge of assessment principles and methods to monitor children's progress and ability to adjust practice accordingly.
- Ability to select assessment tools for use by the professionals in their setting.

Fostering a Professional Workforce
- Knowledge and understanding of the competencies needed to work with children in the professional setting they lead.
- Ability to use knowledge of these competencies to make informed decisions about hiring and placement of practitioners.
- Ability to formulate and implement policies that create an environment that enhances and supports quality practice and children's development and early learning.
- Ability to formulate and implement supportive and rigorous ongoing professional learning opportunities and quality improvement programs that

---

Core Competencies for Leadership

In addition to the foundational knowledge and competencies described for all adults who work with children (see Box 7-1), center directors, principals, and other leaders who oversee care and education settings for young children from birth through age 8 need both specific competencies and general competencies that overlap with those of the professionals they supervise. In Box 7-3, the committee identifies the competencies needed by these leaders.

Existing Statements of Leadership Competencies

A review of examples of statements of core leadership competencies from two early childhood organizations and two elementary education reflect current knowledge of child development and of effective, high-quality instructional and other practices.

- Ability to foster the health and well-being of their staff and to seek out and provide resources that can help staff manage stress.

Assessment of Educators

- Ability to assess the quality of instruction and interactions, to recognize high quality, and to identify and address poor quality through evaluation systems, observations, coaching, and other professional learning opportunities.
- Ability to use data from assessments of care and education professionals appropriately and effectively to make adjustments to improve outcomes for children and to inform professional learning and other decisions and policies.

Developing and Fostering Partnerships

- Ability to support collaboration among the different kinds of providers under their leadership.
- Ability to enable interprofessional opportunities for themselves and their staff to facilitate linkages among health, education, social services, and other disciplines not under their direct leadership.
- Ability to work with families and support their staff to work with families.

Organizational Development and Management

- Knowledge and ability in administrative and fiscal management, compliance with laws and regulations, and the development and maintenance of infrastructure and an appropriate work environment.

leadership organizations suggests that there is a distinction between the stated expectations for these two categories of leaders whose professional roles fall within the birth through age 8 range.

- McCormick Center for Early Childhood Leadership Program Administration Competencies (Bloom, 2007)
- Head Start Director Core Competencies (Office of Head Start, 2008)
- National Association of Elementary School Principal Competencies for Leading pre-K-3 Learning Communities (National Association of Elementary School Principals, 2014)
- Council of Chief State School Officers Draft Standards for School Leaders (CCSSO, 2014)

Compared with competencies for educators, which show considerable agreement in the stated expectations, there is a more pronounced disconnect in expectations for leaders between elementary school settings and early childhood settings outside of elementary schools. Competency statements for leaders from organizations representing elementary school principals and chief state school officers are much more focused than those representing early childhood professions on knowledge and skills required for instructional leadership. Most of the NAESP and CCSSO competencies are related to leaders' ability to create working environments and supports for educators that help them improve their instructional practice. In contrast, most of the competencies specified by the McCormick Center for Early Childhood Leadership and Head Start have to do with how well a leader can develop and manage a well-functioning organization. In fact, the "Technical Competencies" described as part of the "core" for Head Start directors recommend only that directors have "general knowledge" of the content areas of the Head Start program performance standards and not necessarily of how they need to use that knowledge to support Head Start educators' practice. The other skills described under "Technical Competencies" could be considered related more to organizational development and management than to instructional leadership.

This emphasis on organizational management for early childhood program leaders relates to an important aspect of their work. Many early childhood providers are essentially small businesses with minimal to no support infrastructure (compared with a school district). Therefore, it is important for leaders to get the business side of their job right. Yet, given the science of child development and early learning reviewed in Part II, the complex and sophisticated professional competencies needed by the practitioners in these settings, and the importance of the work environment in supporting quality professional practice, adequate attention also needs to be paid to the ability of leadership to support high-quality instruction.

CCSSO's standards include some of the most specific mentions of child development and other principles that may be associated with early childhood research and best practices. For example, the standards state that leaders are expected to

- ensure that instruction is anchored in the best understandings of child development;
- emphasize assessment systems congruent with understandings of child development and standards of measurement;
- ensure that each student is known, valued, and respected;
- ensure that students are enmeshed in a safe, secure, emotionally protective, and healthy environment; and

- ensure that each student has an abundance of academic and social support.

Based on what is needed to foster the early learning of children, effective educational leadership in all settings needs to be driven by a common impetus, one that is articulated in the CCSSO standards as the expectation that leaders focus first and foremost on supporting student and adult learning.

Conclusion About Competencies for Leadership

The complexity of childhood development and early learning and the sophisticated knowledge and competencies needed by care and education professionals have important implications for the knowledge and competencies of leadership in settings for children from birth through age 8. These leaders and administrators need to understand developmental science and instructional practices for educators of young children, as well as the ability to use this knowledge to guide their decisions on hiring, supervision, and selection of tools for assessment of children and evaluation of teacher performance, and to inform their development of portfolios of professional learning supports for their settings.

Conclusion About Core Competency Statements for Leaders

To create a more consistent culture of leadership expectations better aligned with children's need for continuous learning experiences, states' and organizations' statements of core competencies for leadership in elementary education would benefit from a review of those statements to ensure that the scope of competencies for instructional leadership encompasses the early elementary years, including pre-K as it increasingly becomes included in public school systems. States and organizations that issue statements of core competencies for leadership in centers, programs, family childcare, and other settings for early childhood education would benefit from a review of those statements to ensure that competencies related to instructional leadership are emphasized alongside administrative and management competencies.

KNOWLEDGE AND COMPETENCIES FOR INTERPROFESSIONAL PRACTICE

A critical competency for all professionals with roles in seamlessly supporting children from birth through age 8 is the ability to work in synergy, both across settings within the care and education sector and between the care and education sector and other closely related sectors, especially health, mental health, and social services. The concept of interprofessional practice has been an increasing focus in the health sector, and many of the principles that have been developed in that sector apply as well to the care and education sector. The health sector also has recognized the interdependency between interprofessional practice and interprofessional education in creating a workforce prepared for collaborative practice as one way to improve the quality of health care services and ameliorate fragmentation in health systems (D'Amour and Oandasan, 2005; Frenk et al., 2010; WHO, 2010). This principle applies well to the challenges and professional learning needs that arise from the diffuse systems that make up the care and education sector (as described in Chapter 2).

An increasing focus on interprofessional competencies in the health sectors provides useful groundwork for strengthening these competencies in the care and education sector. Barr (1998) distinguishes among "complementary" competencies that are specific to a professional role but enhance the qualities of other professionals in providing care; "common" or overlapping competencies expected of multiple professional roles in a sector (like those for educators in Box 7-2); and "collaborative" competencies that professionals use to work with one another within and across specialties and sectors, as well as with families and communities (Barr, 1998) (see Figure 7-3).

Core interprofessional collaborative competencies have been articulated for the health sector in four main areas: (1) values and ethics for interprofessional practice, (2) roles and responsibilities for collaborative practice, (3) interprofessional communication practices, and (4) interprofessional teamwork and team-based practices (Interprofessional Education Collaborative Expert Panel, 2011).[5] Competencies related to values and ethics for interprofessional and collaborative practice identify the importance of showing respect for patients and families, as well as a mutual trust and respect for team members, health professionals, and individual experts. Interprofessional ethics, an emerging component of interprofessional competencies, can help health professionals understand one another and facilitate working relationships among professions to provide collaborative care for patients.

The ability to communicate one's own role and responsibilities and understand the roles and responsibilities of team members and other professionals is a key competency to facilitate cooperation, coordination, and col-

---

[5] The Interprofessional Education Collaborative Expert Panel (2011) articulated interprofessional competencies that converge across those identified previously by professional health organizations and educational institution in the United States, as well as national and international literature. The full statement of competencies can be found at http://www.aacn.nche.edu/education-resources/ipecreport.pdf (accessed March 22, 2015).

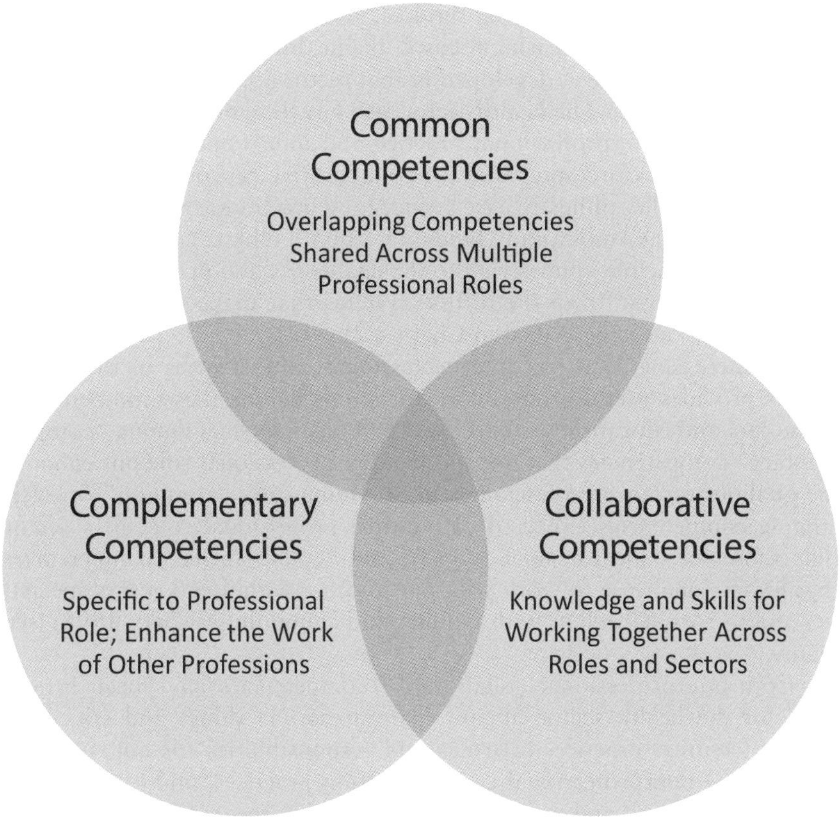

FIGURE 7-3 Three types of interprofessional competencies.
SOURCE: Adapted from Interprofessional Education Collaborative Expert Panel, 2011.

laboration among the team and to address the needs of patients. Moreover, effective teamwork requires ongoing communication and learning which can aid in further defining the roles of each health professional. Thus, interprofessional communication is a competency domain that involves respectful communication with patients, families, and other health professionals. This competency involves communicating information using a common language that is understandable for patients and health professionals in other disciplines. Effective communication also requires listening and providing instructive and respectful feedback to help facilitate collaborative teamwork as well as considering how one's levels of experience and expertise, culture, and power can impact working relationships.

The final interprofessional competency domain emphasizes components of teamwork and team building, and ways in which health professionals can effectively collaborate on behalf of shared goals. Specific competencies include engaging other professionals and integrating their knowledge and expertise in a patient-centered effort. Professionals should also understand team development processes and recognize areas of improvement through individual and team reflection. Furthermore, professionals need to recognize that shared accountability and decision making requires "relinquishing some professional autonomy to work closely with others, including patients and communities, to achieve better outcomes" (Interprofessional Education Collaborative Expert Panel, 2011, p. 24).

These core competencies embody a number of principles that also apply to what care and education professionals need to know and be able to do to work well both across roles and settings within the care and education sector and with professional colleagues in other sectors. Indeed, an analysis of competencies for school mental health professionals included several similarly applicable competencies for communication, collaboration, and data sharing across multiple systems (see Box 7-4) (Ball et al., 2010). For the health sector, these competencies were articulated to inform interprofessional practice as well as behavioral learning objectives for interprofessional education, with the intent that they would be used in parallel with specific and differentiated competencies within professions in the health sector (Interprofessional Education Collaborative Expert Panel, 2011). A similar approach could be used to improve the acquisition and application of these skills in the training and practice of care and education professionals.

**BOX 7-4
Competencies for Communication and
Collaboration Across Systems**

Communication and Building Relationships
- Demonstrates effective communication skills with school personnel, families, and community and other stakeholders.
- Collaborates with others in ways that demonstrate a valuing of and respect for the input and perspectives of multiple professionals and disciplines.
- Builds positive relationships with other school personnel, families, and the community.
- Participates effectively in teams and structures.
- Provides effective consultation services to teachers, administrators, and other school staff.
- Facilitates effective group processes (e.g., confljict resolution, problem solving).
- Demonstrates knowledge of variances in communication styles.
- Identifies, describes, and explains the differing roles and responsibilities of other helping professionals working in and with schools.

Engagement in Multiple Systems and Cross-Systems Collaboration
- Collaborates with families in support of healthy student development.
- Collaborates effectively within and across systems.
- Values the input and perspectives of multiple stakeholders.
- Identifies and knows the protocols for accessing various school- and community-based resources available to support overall school success and promote healthy student development.
- Effectively navigates school-based services through appropriate preferral and referral processes.
- Participates effectively in planning, needs assessment, and resource mapping with families and school and community stakeholders.
- Coordinates and tracks the comprehensive services available within the community to support healthy student and family development.

Data Use
- Uses clear and effective protocols to assist in sharing and using data for decision making.

SOURCE: Adapted from Ball et al., 2010.

REFERENCES

Alliance for a Better Community. 2012. *Dual language learner teacher competencies (DLLTC) report*. Los Angeles, CA: Alliance for a Better Community.

Ball, A., D. Anderson-Butcher, E. A. Mellin, and J. H. Green. 2010. A cross-walk of professional competencies involved in expanded school mental health: An exploratory study. *School Mental Health* 2(3):114-124.

Barr, H. 1998. Competent to collaborate: Towards a competency-based model for interprofessional education. *Journal of Interprofessional Care* 12(2):181-187.

Bloom, P. J. 2007. *From the inside out: The power of reflection and self-awareness, Director's toolbox*. Lake Forest, IL: New Horizons.

Branch, G. F., E. A. Hanushek, and S. G. Rivkin. 2013. School leaders matter: Measuring the impact of effective principals. *Education Next* 13(1):62-69.

California Department of Education and First 5 California. 2011. *California early childhood educator competencies*. Sacramento: California Department of Education.

CCSSO (Council of Chief State School Officers). 2011. *Interstate Teacher Assessment and Support Consortium (INTASC): Model core teaching standards: A resource for state dialogue*. Washington, DC: CCSSO.

———. 2014. *2014 Interstate School Leaders Licensure Consortium (ISLLC) draft standards*. Washington, DC: CCSSO.

D'Amour, D., and I. Oandasan. 2005. Interprofessionality as the field of interprofessional practice and interprofessional education: An emerging concept. *Journal of Interprofessional Care* 19:8-20.

DEC (Division for Early Childhood). 2014. *DEC recommended practices in early intervention/early childhood special education 2014*. Arlington, VA: Council for Exceptional Children.

Frenk, J., L. Chen, Z. A. Bhutta, J. Cohen, N. Crisp, T. Evans, H. Fineberg, P. Garcia, Y. Ke, P. Kelley, B. Kistnasamy, A. Meleis, D. Naylor, A. Pablos-Mendez, S. Reddy, S. Scrimshaw, J. Sepulveda, D. Serwadda, and H. Zurayk. 2010. Health professionals for a new century: Transforming education to strengthen health systems in an interdependent world. *Lancet* 376(9756):1923-1958.

Fuller, S. C., and H. F. Ladd. 2013. *School based accountability and the distribution of teacher quality across grades in elementary school, working paper 75*. Washington, DC: National Center for Analysis of Longitudinal Data in Education Research.

Goldring, E. B., C. M. Neumerski, M. Cannata, T. A. Drake, J. A. Grissom, M. Rubin, and P. Schuermann. 2014. *Summary report: Principals' use of teacher effectiveness data for talent management decisions*. Nashville, TN: Vanderbilt University Peabody College.

Interprofessional Education Collaborative Expert Panel. 2011. *Core competencies for interprofessional collaborative practice: Report of an expert panel*. Washington, DC: Interprofessional Education Collaborative.

Kostelnik, M. J., and M. L. Grady. 2009. *Getting it right from the start: The principal's guide to early childhood education*. Thousand Oaks, CA: Corwin.

Lerner, C., and R. Barr. 2014. *Screen sense: Setting the record straight. Research-based guidelines for screen use for children under 3 years old*. Washington, DC: Zero to Three.

Marzano, R. J., T. Waters, and B. A. McNulty. 2005. *School leadership that works from research to results*. Alexandria, VA: Association for Supervision and Curriculum Development.

Matsumura, L., H. Garnier, and L. Resnick. 2010. Implementing literacy coaching: The role of school social resources. *Educational Evaluation and Policy Analysis* 32(2):249-272.

McCormick Center for Early Childhood Leadership. 2010. *Research notes. Connecting the dots: Director qualifications, instructional leadership practices, and learning environments in early childhood programs.* Wheeling, IL: National Louis University, McCormick Center for Early Childhood Leadership.

———. 2014. *Leadership matters.* Wheeling, IL: National Louis University, McCormick Center for Early Childhood Leadership.

Mead, S. 2011. *PreK-3rd: Principals as crucial instructional leaders.* New York: Foundation for Child Development.

Murphy, J. 2003. *Leadership for literacy: Research-based practice, preK-3.* Thousand Oaks, CA: Corwin Press.

NAEYC (National Association for the Education of Young Children). 2009. *NAEYC standards for early childhood professional preparation.* Washington, DC: NAEYC.

NAEYC and Fred Rogers Center for Early Learning and Children's Media at Saint Vincent College. 2012. *Technology and interactive media as tools in early childhood programs serving children from birth through age 8.* Washington, DC: NAEYC.

National Association of Elementary School Principals. 2014. *Leading pre-K-3 learning communities: Competencies for effective principal practice, executive summary.* Alexandria, VA: National Association of Elementary School Principals.

NBPTS (National Board for Professional Teaching Standards). 2012. *Early childhood generalist standards*, 3rd ed. Arlington, VA: NBPTS.

NCTSN (National Child Traumatic Stress Network) Core Curriculum on Childhood Trauma Task Force. 2012. *The 12 core concepts: Concepts for understanding traumatic stress responses in children and families.* Los Angeles, CA, and Durham, NC: UCLA-Duke University National Center for Child Traumatic Stress.

New Hampshire Department for Health and Human Services and Child Development Bureau. 2013. *New Hampshire's infant and toddler workforce specialized competencies.* http://www.dhhs.state.nh.us/dcyf/cdb/documents/infant-toddler-competencies.pdf (accessed March 17, 2015).

New Mexico Early Childhood Higher Education Task Force. 2011. *Common core content and competencies for personnel in early care, education and family support in New Mexico: Entry level through bachelor's level.* Santa Fe, NM: New Mexico Children, Youth and Families Department.

New York State Association for the Education of Young Children. 2009. *New York state infant toddler care and education credential competencies.* http://nysaeyc.org/wp-content/uploads/ITCEC-Competencies.pdf (accessed March 17, 2015).

Office of Head Start. 2008. *Head Start director core competencies.* http://eclkc.ohs.acf.hhs.gov/hslc/tta-system/operations/leadership/HeadStartDirect.htm (accessed March 6, 2016).

Ohio Child Care Resource & Referral Association. 2008. *Standards of care & teaching for Ohio's infants & toddlers.* http://occrra.org/it/documents/ITStandards.pdf (accessed March 17, 2015).

Snyder, P. A., M. K. Denney, C. Pasia, S. Rakap, and C. Crowe. 2011. Professional development in early childhood intervention: Emerging issues and promising approaches. In *Early childhood intervention: Shaping the future for children with special needs and their families (Vols. 1-3),* edited by C. Groark and L. A. Kaczmarek. Santa Barbara, CA: Praeger/ABC-CLIO. Pp. 169-204.

Vermont Northern Lights Career Development Center. 2013. *Core knowledge areas and competencies for early childhood professionals: The foundation for Vermont's unified professional development system.* Montpelier: Vermont Northern Lights Career Development Center.

WHO (World Health Organization). 2010. *Framework for action on interprofessional education and collaborative practice.* Geneva: WHO.

Part IV

Developing the Care and Education Workforce for Children Birth Through Age 8

This part of the report focuses on the development of the care and education workforce that supports children from birth through age 8. The goal is to review the available mechanisms that can contribute to developing a workforce with the appropriate knowledge, competencies, and supports for quality professional practice.

As described in previous chapters, children from birth through age 8 interact with a large number of professional roles in many different settings and sectors. As discussed in this part of the report, different roles have variations in pathways for training, professional learning systems, licensure and credentialing systems, and other policies for oversight and accountability. In keeping with the scope of this study (described in Chapter 1), this part of the report focuses on educators who have regular (daily or near-daily), direct responsibilities for the care and education of young children in home- and center-based childcare settings that span birth through age 8, as well as preschools and elementary schools. In some cases, as with the knowledge and competencies addressed in Chapter 7, the discussion is inclusive of closely related professions such as home visitors, early intervention specialists, and mental health consultants, who may not have the same frequency of direct interaction with a child as educators but are closely linked to the professional practice of the educators who do and share some of the same professional learning systems. Those in leadership roles are also included as an important part of the care and education workforce.

This part of the report consists of four chapters. It begins with Chapter 8, which presents a framework for considering the key factors that contribute to workforce development and quality professional practice for care and education professionals who work with children aged 0-8. This framework extends beyond the systems and processes that contribute directly to the development of knowledge and competencies to encompass such elements as the practice environment, policies affecting professional requirements, evaluation systems, and the status and well-being of these professionals.

Chapter 9 focuses on higher education programs and on professional learning during ongoing practice. Chapter 10 turns to several other key factors in the comprehensive framework presented in Chapter 8. It begins by reviewing current qualification requirements for educators who work with children from birth through age 8, and considers the extent to which these existing requirements accomplish the goal of standardizing the quality of professional practice across this workforce. This chapter also examines systems and processes for evaluating educators of children from birth through age 8, as well as program accreditation and quality improvement systems.

Finally, Chapter 11 turns to factors in the committee's framework for quality practice that are not always thought of as aspects of professional learning, but are nonetheless essential to developing a workforce capable of providing high-quality care and education for children from birth through age 8. These include institutional and other factors that contribute to the work environment and the status and well-being of these educators, such as compensation and benefits, staffing structures and career advancement pathways, retention, and health and well-being.

Part V/Chapter 12 of the report then builds on these and the preceding chapters to present the committee's recommendations for how stakeholders at the local, state, and national levels can work together to improve systems for professional learning and workforce development.

8

Overview of Factors That Contribute to Quality Professional Practice

Anumber of factors contribute to workforce development and quality professional practice for any professional role. Preparation programs, training, mentoring and coaching, and in-service professional development are all critical direct mechanisms for developing and sustaining the knowledge and competencies of professionals. Various other mechanisms can also contribute to ensuring that the early care and education workforce has what it needs to deliver quality practice that will foster continuous progress in the development and early learning of children from birth through age 8. This report uses the term "professional learning" to describe all opportunities to gain and reinforce necessary knowledge and competencies for quality professional practice.

In addition, other systemic or contextual factors are important to support quality practice, and in many cases are influenced or controlled by stakeholders other than the professionals themselves or the systems that provide them with education and training. These factors include the practice environment, such as working conditions, staffing structures, staff-to-child ratios; the availability of resources such as curricular materials and instructional tools, resources for conducting child assessments, and supplies; policies that affect professional requirements; opportunities for professional advancement; systems for evaluation and ongoing quality improvement; and the status and well-being of the professionals, encompassing, for example, incentives that attract and retain teachers, perceptions of the profession, compensation, and stressors and the availability of supportive services to help manage them.

It is important that these factors work collectively toward the ultimate aim of ensuring sustained, positive outcomes for children, illustrated in Figure 8-1. Part of these factors working collectively as professional learning and workforce development is that they be mutually driven by the science of child development, and be supported through coherent systems of evaluation and assessment that contribute to continuous quality improvement.

There are several challenges to a comprehensive discussion of professional learning for care and education professionals who work with young children. As will be discussed in the chapters that follow, these challenges highlight some of the fundamental barriers to and opportunities for improving professional learning in this field. Educators who work with children from birth through age 8 encompass a variety of professional roles, there are a variety of entry points to the field, and individuals may follow a variety of pathways to an ultimate professional role in caring for and educating young children. These entry points and pathways vary both by professional role and by the state and local contexts in which individuals work. Professional learning also can occur in a number of different types of settings—for example, in higher education institutions (community colleges, 4-year colleges and universities, graduate schools), in community-based organizations that provide training, and during ongoing practice in the workplace. Support for professional learning also can occur through many different systems, including ones not designed primarily to serve as pathways to education or professional development—for example, program accreditation standards and quality assurance programs. Some of these professional learning opportunities are centered on the practitioner, while others are centered on the program or setting but have components that affect the practitioner or the quality of practice. Professional learning opportunities also vary in their duration: some are time-limited (one-time or periodic), while others are ongoing. For some opportunities, access is practitioner-driven (the practitioner chooses to pursue the activity), while others are dependent on other systems/settings (e.g., what the workplace requires or makes available).

There are large variations in the quantity, quality, and types of professional learning experiences across professional roles working with children from birth through age 8. Furthermore, professional learning currently occurs in fragmented systems that have differing infrastructure and use differing tools and approaches. Professional learning lacks consistency and coordination across types of professional learning supports and across educators who work in different roles and age ranges within the birth through age 8 continuum—this despite the strong rationale for providing children with consistency and continuity in learning experiences as described in Chapter 5. This report puts forth a concept of "professional learning" that is both broader and more cohesive than the siloed ways in which these activities often are implemented in the care and education sector. This concept

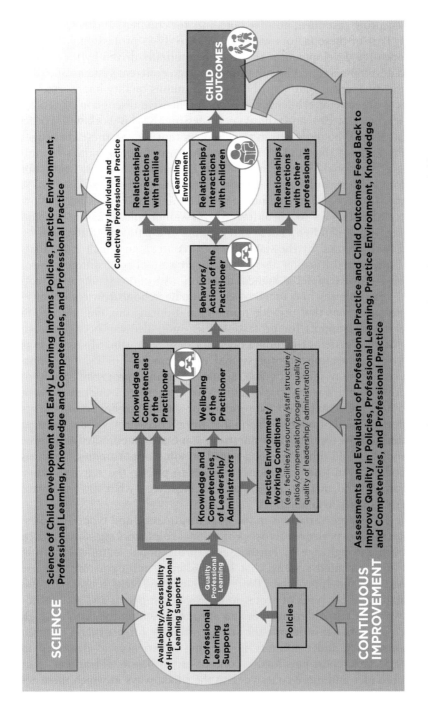

FIGURE 8-1 Factors that contribute to quality professional practice and ultimately to improving child outcomes.

encompasses all of the activities that contribute to developing and sustaining quality professional practice and draws attention to common features of high-quality professional learning that contribute to quality practice. These features include

- clarity of purpose;
- content based in the foundations of the science of child development and early learning;
- approaches based on the science of adult learning;
- emphasis on applying theory to practice, including field- and practice-based professional learning experiences;
- alignment with professional standards and guidelines;
- accountability for the quality of professional learning; and
- affordability and equitable access to professional learning, including adequate funding and financing.

Some aspects of professional learning and practice need to be tailored to specific professional roles—for example, educators of infants and toddlers will need to develop certain competencies more fully than educators of older children, who likewise will need to master their own specific instructional strategies. Early intervention specialists or other professionals providing consulting services will need to develop in depth different competencies from those needed by their colleagues who are classroom educators. Yet specialization need not inherently produce or reinforce fragmentation. In fact, such specificity needs to be developed in the context of the shared foundation of child development and early learning. For example, all professionals need to know the basics of how to foster language and literacy development over time even as they learn to apply different instructional practices that are specific to their professional roles and the age range with which they work.

Based on the shared foundation of child development and early learning, all educators need to develop core competencies to move children along a continuous trajectory of learning and developmental goals. Greater consistency and commonality can result from aligning around a shared knowledge base, establishing shared expectations, using common tools where appropriate, building greater mutual understanding of language and terminology across professional roles and professional learning systems, and participating together in some aspects of professional learning. As discussed further in Part V of this report, embracing a broader and more unified concept of professional learning will facilitate a process of coming together across types of professional learning support and across settings and professional roles to arrive at improved consistency and commonality in care and education for children from birth through age 8.

In Figure 8-2, the four grey boxes categorize types of professional learning supports. Although they are depicted in separate boxes, it is important to note that the elements within these boxes interact or overlap with one another. For example, formal coursework can be designed to lead to qualification for a license or credential. Continuing education requirements often are fulfilled through coursework and trainings. For simplicity's sake, this figure does not depict the various ways in which the elements interact.

The arrows linking "Professional Learning Processes" and the categories of professional learning supports indicate that various processes (e.g., supportive supervision, mentoring, reflective practice) can occur through many of the professional learning supports. The interaction between these processes and learning supports influences quality practice. This graphic makes no judgment on which supports or processes improve practice more than others.

Some of these elements typically are thought of as part of professional learning, often with a framing of "preparation" as learning that takes place before entering practice and "professional development" as learning that takes place for practicing professionals. Other elements, such as program quality assurance systems and peer networks, may not be considered in an integrated way as part of the system of supports for professional learning. These elements are included here because they can contribute directly to the quality of professional practice, and therefore represent an opportunity to expand the concept of professional learning to a comprehensive and more coordinated system.

Figure 8-2 intentionally does not categorize these supports by the settings in which they are delivered or the entities that provide them. These are essential factors that influence how changes in the professional learning system are implemented, but a setting-based schematic also can reinforce barriers or silos based on the current systems infrastructure. Therefore, these factors were set aside for the purpose of starting with a neutral conceptualization of all the potential professional learning mechanisms.

Also absent from Figure 8-2 is a sequencing of these supports. Intentionally designed sequencing is important to quality within some professional learning components that are designed to build a knowledge base and set of competencies in a sequenced manner. More broadly, however, many professionals pursue different professional learning supports in a nonlinear fashion, and it may not be necessary or feasible to represent or prescribe a single best sequence. For example, many teachers at a childcare center may pursue coursework toward a degree concurrently with active practice, often after many years of experience during which they participated in in-service professional learning supports. On the other hand, many elementary school teachers may take a more linear path of pursuing degree-related coursework

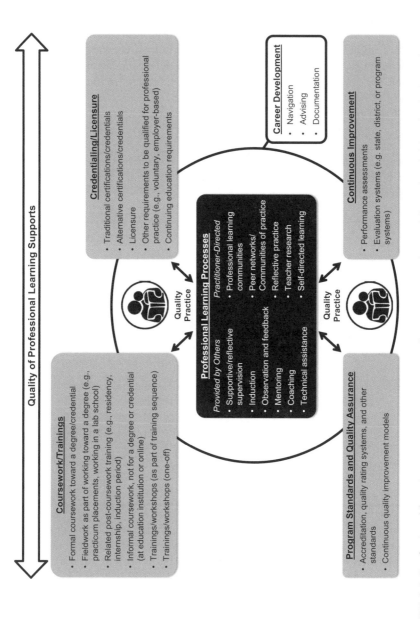

Quality of Professional Learning Supports

Coursework/Trainings
- Formal coursework toward a degree/credential
- Fieldwork as part of working toward a degree (e.g., practicum placements, working in a lab school)
- Related post-coursework training (e.g., residency, internship, induction period)
- Informal coursework, not for a degree or credential (at education institution or online)
- Trainings/workshops (as part of training sequence)
- Trainings/workshops (one-off)

Credentialing/Licensure
- Traditional certifications/credentials
- Alternative certifications/credentials
- Licensure
- Other requirements to be qualified for professional practice (e.g., voluntary, employer-based)
- Continuing education requirements

Professional Learning Processes

Provided by Others
- Supportive/reflective supervision
- Induction
- Observation and feedback
- Mentoring
- Coaching
- Technical assistance

Practitioner-Directed
- Professional learning communities
- Peer networks/ Communities of practice
- Reflective practice
- Teacher research
- Self-directed learning

Quality Practice

Career Development
- Navigation
- Advising
- Documentation

Program Standards and Quality Assurance
- Accreditation, quality rating systems, and other standards
- Continuous quality improvement models

Continuous Improvement
- Performance assessments
- Evaluation systems (e.g. state, district, or program systems)

FIGURE 8-2 Professional learning supports to ensure quality practice in the workforce for children birth through age 8.

before starting practice, while others may complete degrees in other fields and transition into preparing for a teaching license at a later stage.

The arrow across the top of Figure 8-2 emphasizes that the availability of these supports alone is not sufficient to contribute to quality practice; the supports also need to be of high quality themselves, both well designed and implemented well. Elements of high quality include, for example, that supports develop both knowledge (e.g., child development, subject-matter content, pedagogical content knowledge—see Chapter 6) and the requisite professional competencies (see Chapter 7); that they incorporate instructional best practices for adult learning; and that they acknowledge the need for shared knowledge and competencies across professional roles and across the birth through age 8 age spectrum, thus promoting cross-age, cross-role, and cross-sector learning opportunities. In reality, there is wide variability in the content and quality of these professional learning supports.

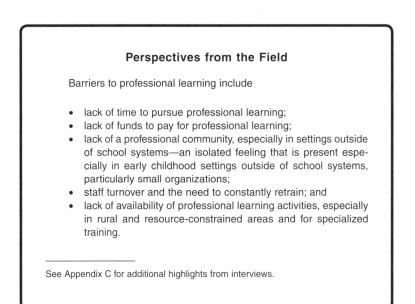

Perspectives from the Field

Barriers to professional learning include

- lack of time to pursue professional learning;
- lack of funds to pay for professional learning;
- lack of a professional community, especially in settings outside of school systems—an isolated feeling that is present especially in early childhood settings outside of school systems, particularly small organizations;
- staff turnover and the need to constantly retrain; and
- lack of availability of professional learning activities, especially in rural and resource-constrained areas and for specialized training.

See Appendix C for additional highlights from interviews.

The availability of professional learning supports and the degree to which they are accessed vary greatly across professional roles (e.g., a family childcare provider receives different types and amounts of support than a kindergarten teacher) and across programs or settings (e.g., the experience of professionals in a Head Start program differs from that of professionals in an elementary school). The availability of and access to these supports also vary greatly from place to place. Thus, the supports in Figure 8-2 depict a combination of the current state for some professional roles in some places and the "universe" of what could be available for other professional roles.

Conclusions About Factors That Affect Quality Practice

A range of factors affect quality practice, including the quality of the care and education environment; working conditions; the knowledge and competencies of the practicing professionals (and the professional learning supports that contribute to their acquisition); the well-being of the workforce; workplace policies; and local, state, and federal policies.

Currently, professional learning for educators of children from birth through age 8 typically takes place in a fragmented, nonsystematic way, with different quantities and types of activities in different settings and systems. Greater consistency and commonality can result from aligning around a shared knowledge base, establishing shared expectations, using common tools where appropriate, building greater mutual understanding of language and terminology across professional roles and professional learning systems, and participating together in some aspects of professional learning. Despite the challenges of doing so, all of the components that contribute to professional learning need to be consolidated in a more comprehensive system of learning supports that are designed, implemented, and provided or accessed in intentional sequences over time to contribute collectively to improving the quality of professional practice.

9

Higher Education and Ongoing
Professional Learning

This chapter considers higher education and ongoing professional learning for educators who provide care and education for children from birth through age 8. It begins by reviewing higher education programs that prepare these professionals for practice, and then turns to opportunities for professional learning during ongoing practice.

HIGHER EDUCATION PROGRAMS

This section examines formal education and coursework for educators of children birth through age 8 that takes place in institutions of higher education and is designed to lead to a degree (associate's, bachelor's, or graduate) or certificate. Although this is often referred to as "preparation" or "preservice" education, it is sometimes undertaken during ongoing practice, especially by professionals practicing in early care and education settings outside of elementary schools or for those pursuing advanced degrees.

Teaching is one of the most common occupations in the United States (Bureau of Labor Statistics and U.S. Department of Labor, 2014; Peterson et al., 2009), yet as a nation the United States lacks a common vision for or standardization of how to prepare educators. This lack of standardization has influenced perceptions of the occupation, as well as policies and practices for teacher preparation. The lack of standardization and its effects become even more striking when viewed in light of the broad variations in the preparation of educators across professional roles and settings for children birth through age 8. Compared with educators teaching in childcare centers, early childhood programs, and preschools outside of public school systems, early elementary educators teaching in public elementary schools engage in a comparatively structured, established, and regulated system. Yet neither "system" is producing sufficient numbers of educators who are well qualified to support the early learning of children from birth through age 8, and the diffuse and variable nature of the preparation of educators of young children presents a challenge to the development and implementation of policy approaches that will lead to meaningful change.

This section first gives an overview of the current landscape of education pathways and expectations for care and education professionals across roles and settings, and then places this current state in the context of the historical development of expectations for these roles. Subsequent subsections then consider factors that contribute to the availability and quality of professional learning in higher education settings for these care and education professionals.

Overview of Current Education Pathways for Educators of Children from Birth Through Age 8

Preparation pathways for educators vary, as do governance, oversight, standards, and funding structures (NRC, 2010). Different standards and requirements for qualification to practice as an educator are one of the major drivers of differences in the educational pathways among different professional roles, especially between those who teach in elementary school settings (which can be prekindergarten through third grade or kindergarten through third grade, depending on the school system) and those who teach in settings outside of elementary school systems, such as early education programs or preschools, childcare centers, and family childcare (Whitebook, 2014).

For educators in kindergarten through third grade (and for prekindergarten teachers in some school systems), "teacher preparation" refers to preservice education in a degree-granting program and subsequent licensure that are typically required before employment. Teacher preparation programs often include coursework requirements and student teaching experiences, required by policy in most states (Loeb et al., 2009). Attainment of a degree often is followed by induction or mentoring programs for new teachers (Whitebook, 2014). Candidates for teaching in the elementary grades must have a bachelor's degree and state certification, but there remains a lack of standardization and consistent quality in preparation programs, including those offered by traditional institutes of higher education, community colleges, and alternative-route programs such as Teach For America (Whitebook et al., 2009).

Standards for training of educators in early childhood programs and childcare are even more variable than those for elementary teachers, being set by each state with the exception of Head Start and Military Child Care, which establish uniform national requirements for teachers and other personnel (Whitebook, 2014). Unlike educators in elementary schools, many of these educators do not participate in preservice education; their participation in formal education or training for their profession may not commence until after they have become employed in the field. As a result, for many of these educators, their first job serves as their opportunity for "practice teaching," but rarely with a formal induction period or structure of close supervision with an educational aim (Whitebook et al., 2012). However, as educational requirements are increasing in programs such as Head Start, in publicly funded prekindergarten, and in state quality rating and improvement systems, educators in professional roles outside of the elementary grades are increasingly attending college or university programs to complete required credits or to earn degrees, either before working or while employed (Whitebook, 2014).

Historical Perspective on Educator Preparation in the United States

As described in Chapter 1, education for children from birth through age 8 in the United States has its roots in five distinct traditions: (1) childcare; (2) nursery schools; (3) kindergartens; (4) compensatory education (to compensate for unfavorable developmental or environmental circumstances experienced by children, particularly those from low-income families); and (5) compulsory education at the primary level or early elementary school. For many years, these initiatives proceeded along relatively separate paths, and each has had its own historical evolution in pathways to professional learning.

As efforts emerge to help these traditions converge, the different philosophies and historical perspectives associated with each sometimes complement one another and sometimes clash. As context for understanding the current status of preparation and training for these professional roles, Appendix D provides timelines briefly describing these different histories. The following subsections summarize some key themes in the evolution of expectations for training and professional learning over time.

Professional Silos

Preparation for roles in early childhood and for roles in elementary grades have existed in silos from the beginning, with some minor efforts at integration over time. One transition that occurred is that kindergarten shifted from being treated primarily as similar to other early childhood settings to becoming recognized as part of the country's public school system. Kindergarten became integrated into public education, and with it, training for kindergarten teachers. A similar shift may be starting to occur as prekindergarten becomes incorporated into public education in some states and municipalities.

Aims of Professional Practice

Training for professional roles in early childhood, including kindergarten teachers, has historically taken a broad perspective on the goals of child learning and development and therefore on the skills and knowledge educators need. Preparation for these professionals has commonly focused on supporting children's emerging development by providing experiences related to physical, social, emotional, behavioral, language, and cognitive processes and skills. Although the distinction is not absolute, preparation programs for public school teachers from early on focused on preparing them to teach academics and "knowledge."

Educational Expectations and Perceived Status or Prestige

Educational expectations and perceived status or prestige have fluctuated by professional role over time. Nursery school teachers initially were expected to have 4-year degrees and to operate as equals among other professionals, and childcare providers also were required historically to have higher education. However, a shift occurred over time to lower expectations for early childhood educators. On the other hand, elementary school teachers were initially expected to obtain less training and education than secondary school teachers, although as they were integrated into public school systems, those expectations gradually increased. These divergent expectations and perceptions of prestige between early childhood and elementary and between elementary and secondary educators remain today. Society (the general public, policy makers, and even care and education professionals themselves) has tended to perceive working with younger children as less demanding and prestigious work, a perception that runs counter to the science of child development and early learning presented in Part II.

Conclusion About Divergence Between Early Childhood and Elementary School Educators

Significant differences exist in the settings, professional identity, expected knowledge and competencies, licensure and credentialing, organizational supports, and professional learning resources for professionals who work in roles and settings such as family childcare and childcare centers compared with those who work in elementary school settings. This divergence is dissonant with what the science of early

*learning reveals about the enormously formative growth in early learn-
ing that is already occurring from birth and about the core competencies that all care and education professionals should possess. Reducing
this dissonance will require major changes to policies and practices that
have evolved through historical trends and are entrenched in current
systems.*

Characteristics of Programs in Higher Education

Because of the lack of uniformity in and comprehensive data on teacher
preparation, it is difficult to clearly delineate different pathways for educators and provide precise characteristics of each. Paralleling variability in
expectations for and participation in higher education across professional
roles is a great deal of variability across institutions and programs. Policies
that set qualification requirements for practice (such as licensure or credentialing and hiring policies) do not always distinguish which of those pathways yield the knowledge and competencies needed by care and education
professionals to do their jobs well. Several general characteristics contribute
to how these programs—whether in 2- or 4-year institutions—prepare educators. The following subsections address several of these key characteristics, including the current institutional fragmentation of educator training
in higher education, the content of coursework, field-based learning experiences, admission requirements, faculty characteristics, diversity of faculty
and students, access to higher education, and relationships between 2- and
4-year institutions.

Institutional Fragmentation

Wide variation exists both among and within institutions that educate
students for careers in care and education. This lack of consistency creates
a highly fragmented approach to preparing educators for practice. First, a
number of different kinds of institutions offer programs for professional
roles in care and education, including institutions of higher education at
the 2-year, 4-year, and graduate levels, as well as other institutions that
administer alternative certification pathways for educators. These various
institutions have evolved in their purposes over time (see Table 9-1).

Within this array of institutions exist a multitude of degree and certificate programs intended to prepare professionals for various job titles and
roles in working with children from birth through age 8. These programs
are called by various names and are organized in various ways, for example,

- by role (e.g., teachers, administrators, program directors, coordinators, principals, superintendents, paraprofessionals, aides, assistant

teachers, after-school care providers, early intervention specialists, special education teachers, school therapists/counselors);

- by age range or grade level (e.g., birth-3, 3-5, prekindergarten to third grade, kindergarten to fifth grade, kindergarten to eighth grade);
- by setting (e.g., Head Start, childcare, public school); and
- by academic discipline, school, and department (e.g., education, health and human services, social and/or behavioral sciences such as developmental psychology, professional studies, liberal arts, agricultural sciences, and technology) (Saluja et al., 2002).

Approaches used in preparation programs for elementary school educators vary, although these approaches are more consistent than those of programs for care and education professionals outside of elementary school settings. For educators preparing to teach at the elementary level in public schools or other school systems,

- all states have schools of education, located in 4-year universities and colleges, that are charged with preparing teachers (Levine, 2013);
- all states offer alternative pathways for teacher preparation (Levine, 2013); and
- all teacher preparation programs include some clinical or student teaching experience (Levine, 2013).

For educators preparing to practice in early childhood settings outside of elementary schools or public school systems, early childhood–related higher education degree programs are found in both 2- and 4-year colleges, but the majority of departments designated explicitly as early childhood are found in 2-year institutions (Whitebook et al., 2012).

In addition to the variability across institutions and across professional roles, fragmentation results from organizational variability within institutions. It is common to have multiple programs focused on professions related to early childhood that are operating on the same campus but are scattered across the same institution, housed in separate departments with different expectations and requirements (Whitebook and Ryan, 2011).

Content of Coursework

Ultimately, the aim of coursework for prospective care and education professionals is to help them both acquire knowledge and be capable of integrating that knowledge into competencies that translate into their practices and behaviors with children in learning environments. One of

TABLE 9-1 Historical Institutional Traditions for Teacher Education

Institution	Form	Elements/Themes	Primary Clientele
State normal schools (1839-1940s) and state teachers colleges (1920s-1940s)	2-year course of study: pedagogy and review of subjects learned in elementary and high school and pedagogy	• Institutional autonomy • Professional esprit de corps • Art and science of teaching • Professional treatment of subject matter: "method of the subject" versus "academic" knowledge • Practical pedagogy • Close tie between theory and practice • Technical theory and methods: "rules of teaching the subject" • Explicit attention to supervising practice and even "campus schools" • Clear sense of purpose (educating teacher)	Elementary teachers
Liberal arts colleges (1800s-present)	Embedded in 4-year baccalaureate program	• Liberal arts as preparation for teaching: humane values, critical thinking, historical perspective, broad knowledge • Education as a liberal art • Intellectual values, knowledge, and skills • Common learning and cultural knowledge	Secondary teachers
University schools of education (1900s-present)	Graduate programs	• Scientific research ideal • Education as applied social science: "science of education" • Specialized knowledge • Professionalization through graduate study • Devaluing of experience • Multiple missions beyond educating teachers	Education leaders

SOURCE: Adapted from Feiman-Nemser, 2012.

the greatest challenges in the field is a lack of widespread implementation of agreed-upon standards for what constitutes a high-quality educator preparation program. The current high variability in program content and requirements cannot be expected to produce consistently effective results.

The content of a course of study in a higher education program for prospective educators can be informed by multiple sources, including institutional leadership and faculty, state learning goals and standards, state teaching standards, criteria in state laws and policies for licensure or certification (discussed in more detail later in this chapter), state rules that govern higher education institutions, and voluntary accrediting bodies often organized by profession (also discussed in more detail later in this chapter). Degree programs vary in the content of required coursework and in the age ranges included for pedagogical strategies and student teaching. Elementary school educators typically are required to complete a course of study that aligns with state certification or licensure requirements, providing some benchmarks for consistency, yet programs continue to vary widely in content and in the extent to which they adequately address the teaching of children in the early elementary years. Early childhood higher education programs have historically been even less consistent, with courses of study within one of several disciplines being considered acceptable, although efforts to expand accreditation of these programs are under way, described later in this chapter (Maxwell et al., 2006; Whitebook et al., 2012). As many care and education professionals enter the field from a wide array of educational backgrounds, another challenge the field faces is identifying ways for all professionals to receive the content of this coursework, especially those who do not enter the field through traditional programs in institutions of higher education (Whitebook et al., 2009).

Formal coursework topics commonly, but not consistently or comprehensively, required in educator preparation programs at the associate's, bachelor's, and master's levels, as well as for the Child Development Associate credential, can include the following: education and care of children across the age continuum, including dual language learners and young children with disabilities; interactions with children and families from ethnically and culturally diverse backgrounds; assessment/observation of young children; literacy, language, and numeracy instructional strategies; social and emotional development; physical health and motor development; and classroom and behavioral management (Maxwell et al., 2006).

Formal coursework content in programs that prepare educators fall into three categories: foundational theories of development and learning, subject-matter content, and methods of teaching and pedagogy (both general and specific to subject matter) (Whitebook et al., 2009). Despite the wide array of courses, curricula often do not delve deeply enough into the material to give students a profound understanding of it (Bornfreund,

2011). Child development is important core knowledge for care and education professionals, yet in many programs, courses focused on the science of child development are either not offered or offered only at the introductory level (Bornfreund, 2011). A further challenge faced by programs is how to link child development to pedagogy to help prospective educators learn how to apply developmentally appropriate practices in the classroom. Research has found that many educators are unable to identify what factors impact the quality of their teaching (Whitebook et al., 2009). Efforts of preparation programs to train educators to teach culturally, ethnically, and socioeconomically diverse students also are limited, and many teachers do not learn to set aside their own biases in practice (Whitebook et al., 2009). Furthermore, while courses focused on interacting with families are common in early childhood teacher preparation programs, they are less common in K-5 programs (Bornfreund, 2011). A review of course content across 1,179 teacher preparation programs in the United States revealed several gaps in formal coursework. For example, only a small number of programs required any coursework focused on bilingual children, program administration, and adult learning, even at the master's level (Maxwell et al., 2006).

Field-Based Learning Experience

Field experience, such as student teaching and practicums or field placements, is required in 38 states for public elementary school teaching candidates (Maxwell et al., 2006; Whitebook et al., 2009). In a 2006 survey of early education preparation programs, approximately 96 percent of associate's and bachelor's degree programs required field placements (Maxwell et al., 2006). Yet states have not implemented specific standards for this experience regarding setting, length of placement, and supervision nor is there a standard for what content should be covered in such experience (Maxwell et al., 2006; Whitebook and Ryan, 2011; Whitebook et al., 2009). This leaves room for the focus by default to be finding a placement and completing the required hours rather than the quality of the field-based learning experience. In the same 2006 survey of early education preparation programs, the content of field placements ranged to include care and education of infants and toddlers and preschool-aged children, care and education of young children with disabilities, family engagement, and working with bilingual children. The fewest number of programs required a practicum involving working with bilingual children (Maxwell et al., 2006). For the many teachers of children in settings outside of public school systems who enter the workplace without prior coursework or formal educational background, field experience is acquired on the job. These early care and education professionals often work without the guidance associated with a field placement as part of a training program, such as formal observations, reflective practice, and reflective supervision (Whitebook et al., 2009).

The ideal practicum experience should be completed alongside formal coursework so prospective educators can apply what they are learning to their practice (Whitebook et al., 2009). Given that fieldwork often is conducted after the completion of formal coursework, during a candidate's final term in school, there are few opportunities to make this connection consistently over the course of their degree program (Bornfreund, 2011). Although field placements are considered one of the most important elements of educator preparation, the experience varies, and many prospective educators acquire no real practice in the classroom with effective teachers (Bornfreund, 2011).

There are also opportunities to provide prospective educators with supplemental experiences that include working with individual students and small groups or observing ongoing classroom instruction (Bornfreund, 2011; Whitebook et al., 2009). In addition, given the importance of family engagement as a professional competency, it may be worth considering expanding field experiences to include participating in home visits and other engagement with families (Whitebook et al., 2009).

Finding high-quality field placements can be a challenge for educator preparation programs, although some believe there are opportunities for reflection and learning even when practicums are completed in poor-quality settings (Whitebook et al., 2009). Another challenge is that arranging for supervised practicums and completing student teaching requirements frequently pose scheduling and compensation challenges for those students who are completing degree programs while also working full time (Whitebook et al., 2011).

Perspectives from the Field

A critical skill for educators in all settings is the ability to apply what is learned in formal coursework to real-world practice settings. This necessary skill highlights the importance of integrating field experiences throughout formal education or certification programs.

Field placements in diverse settings are also one opportunity to train educators in areas such as working with diverse populations of students, cultural sensitivity, and family engagement.

See Appendix C for additional highlights from interviews.

Admission Requirements

Admission requirements for higher education programs that prepare educators are often minimal, often involving a minimum grade point average and selected course prerequisites. These limited requirements may lead to a lack of selectivity among applicants, as most who apply are offered admission. This is in contrast with other fields, such as business or medicine, which have highly selective admission standards (Bornfreund, 2011).

Researchers recognize that qualities and dispositions that make individuals strong educators may not be reflected in grades and test scores. A 2008 review identified such traits as exhibiting fairness, empathy, enthusiasm, thoughtfulness, and respectfulness (Rike and Sharp, 2008). Incorporating interviews, writing samples, and recommendations as part of the application process can be a step toward strengthening the selection of applicants and recognizing a wider range of important traits that reflect the potential for quality professional practice (Bornfreund, 2011).

A 2003 study, for example, assessed the effectiveness of group-assessment interviews as a component of admissions criteria for teacher education programs. The group-assessment procedure consisted of a 90-minute interview with eight teacher candidates and two trained evaluators. During the session, candidates engaged in a group discussion, participated in problem-solving activities, and completed a self-assessment. This process was used to evaluate candidates' communication, interpersonal, and leadership skills. The study found that the group-assessment interview procedure could more strongly predict performance in student teaching than academic criteria (grades and standardized tests) (Byrnes et al., 2003).

Faculty Characteristics

The faculty in a training program for educators are an important factor in the program's quality. Concerns over the composition of faculty have been raised in multiple reports in the past decade, particularly for programs that train educators for practice in early childhood settings outside of elementary school systems (Bornfreund, 2011). Professionals preparing the early childhood workforce ideally are trained academically, having received a graduate degree, and have the practical experience needed to prepare prospective educators to meet standards for professional competency (NAEYC, 2011b).

One challenge is insufficient faculty members in small programs or institutions, such that the breadth and depth needed for a high-quality preparation program are lacking. For example, a shortage of faculty has been linked to a shortage of qualified and effective special education teachers (Smith et al., 2001). The Special Education Faculty Needs Assessment project found that nearly half of advertised positions were vacant because of retirement. The turnover rate for educators in special education programs is 21 percent, and the turnover rate for faculty in institutions of higher education is double this number (Smith et al., 2011).

Another challenge is the use of part-time faculty. A 2006 study found that more than half of the faculty in early childhood programs across 2- and 4-year institutions of higher education were employed part time. The number and percentage of part-time faculty was higher at 2-year institutions (69 percent) than at 4-year institutions (42 percent) (Early and Winton, 2001; Maxwell et al., 2006). In another study, 42 early childhood teacher preparation programs had an average of 3.5 full-time faculty members, supported by adjuncts who, because of their status, were ineligible for tenure (Johnson et al., 2010). Early childhood programs also tend to make greater use of part-time faculty than their institutions as a whole (Early and Winton, 2001). The reliance on adjuncts and part-time faculty to support early childhood educator preparation programs can lead to inconsistent teaching practices, as well as long work hours, more administrative tasks, low salaries, and few benefits for faculty, all of which can negatively affect student learning (Early and Winton, 2001; Johnson et al., 2010). In addition, part-time status limits the time during which faculty are available to meet the needs of students seeking additional guidance and mentorship outside the classroom (Early and Winton, 2001).

The preparedness of faculty is a concern as well; variability in their expected qualifications and inconsistencies in their expertise and experience may lead to variations in program quality. Qualifications for faculty in early childhood educator preparation programs vary by program and position title. Job requirements for these types of positions commonly include experience teaching courses related to education in such areas as curriculum development, student guidance, and teacher education (O*Net Online, 2011). Programs find that faculty members may lack expertise in specific content areas, including early childhood education (Bornfreund, 2011). In addition, faculty with prior experience working directly with children in early childhood settings are found less often in 4-year than in 2-year institutions (Maxwell et al., 2006). Table 9-2 provides some recent examples of faculty qualification requirements. It shows that faculty may be required to hold a bachelor's or graduate degree in a related field, and often are required to have experience teaching adults and/or direct experience working with children in early childhood settings, as either an educator or an administrator. Faculty members often are required to have experience working with diverse populations and diverse learners. Some position descriptions include an interest in research and scholarly activities; commitment to social justice; and knowledge of program approval, state licensure, and accreditation standards.

TABLE 9-2 Illustrative Examples of Requirements for Faculty Positions

Position Title	Requirements
Adjunct Instructor, Early Childhood Education-Administrator Credential (HigherEdJobs, 2014a)	**Required** • Bachelor's degree or higher in Early Childhood or Elementary Education; or bachelor's degree or higher in an unrelated field plus 36 related credits in early childhood education. • Minimum of 5 years (10,000 hours) working as an administrator or director of a preschool or early childhood education program. **Desired** • Experience teaching adults.
Part-Time Child Development Instructor (HigherEdJobs, 2014c)	**Required** • Education—Possess any one of the following: – Master's degree in child development, early childhood education, human development, home economics/family and consumer studies with a specialization in child development/early childhood education, or educational psychology with a specialization in child development/early childhood education; OR – Bachelor's degree in any of the above AND master's degree in social work, educational supervision, elementary education, special education, psychology, bilingual/bicultural education, life management/home economics, family life studies, or family and consumer studies; OR – A valid California Community College Instructors Credential in the discipline; OR – The equivalent of the above. • Demonstrated ability to effectively work with persons of diverse socioeconomic, cultural, disability, and ethnic backgrounds.

continued

TABLE 9-2 Continued

Position Title	Requirements
Urban Early Childhood/ Elementary Education Faculty (full time) (HigherEdJobs, 2014d)	**Required** • Master's degree in early childhood, elementary education or related field and be enrolled in a doctoral program. A doctoral degree must be completed before the tenure review. • Experience in early childhood/elementary education (birth to grade 6) with urban and/or ethnically diverse learners. • Ability to teach introductory and advanced courses to urban teacher candidates. • Excellent cross-cultural skills, including evidence of working effectively within culturally, linguistically, and socioeconomically diverse urban settings, such as classrooms. **Desired** • Three years licensed teaching experience, birth to grade 6. • Ph.D. or Ed.D. in Early Childhood Education, Elementary Education, Urban Education, Math Education, Science Education, Special Education, ESL/Bilingual Education, Curriculum & Instruction, or related field. • College teaching experience in a teacher education program. • Advanced training in the teaching of science and/ or math curriculum and methods courses for early childhood and elementary teacher candidates. • Experience as a department chair and/or interest in serving the department in such capacity. • Knowledge of teaching licensure standards and state program approval/accreditation requirements. • Excellent communication skills (written and verbal) to communicate with a variety of persons and groups.

TABLE 9-2 Continued

Position Title	Requirements
Department of Elementary and Early Childhood Education, Assistant Professor-generalist (full time) (HigherEdJobs, 2014b)	**Required** • Earned Ph.D. or Ed.D. • Two years of full-time public school teaching at the elementary or early childhood levels. • Experience teaching academically diverse students and significant expertise in the use of differentiating instruction and Universal Design. **Desired** • Possess both a public school license in either Elementary Education (grades 1-6) or Early Childhood Education (PK-2) and in Special Education (PK-8). • A minimum of 4 years of public school teaching experience; an M.Ed. in either a Content area or an M.Ed. in Special Education. • Content expertise in at least one curriculum area (i.e., Mathematics, Science, Social Studies, Literacy). • College teaching experience. • Experience teaching in an urban and/or economically diverse setting. • Experience teaching online and/or demonstrated competency using new technologies (such as iPads, Interactive Whiteboards, Web-based teaching). • Demonstrated an ability to work collaboratively with colleagues. • Interest in scholarly activities. • A demonstrated commitment to social justice.

A promising practice for ameliorating some faculty-related issues is the appointment of full-time faculty, although often nontenured, who focus on instruction, working closely with students, and supervision of field experiences rather than on research activities (Ernst et al., 2005). Professors of practice are part of the faculty in the University of California's Schools of Education, for example, and it is their responsibility to provide prospective educators with a full understanding of skills needed to practice in the field, as well as the opportunity to interact with knowledgeable and experienced professionals (University of California, San Diego, 2013). Although the number of professors of practice appointed as full-time faculty often is low compared with the numbers of academic and research faculty, their contribution can be highly valuable because of the competencies they have developed through their practical experience and expertise in the field (Ernst et al., 2005).

Diversity of Faculty and Students

Another challenge for programs that prepare educators is the lack of diversity among faculty members, whose composition does not tend to reflect the teacher candidates in preparation programs or young children in early childhood programs. A 2006 report on faculty and student characteristics reflected a lack of diversity among faculty, and a 2010 report likewise found that more than one-third of institutes of higher education surveyed had no faculty members of color or minority ethnicity. Specifically in early childhood educator preparation programs, most faculty were white non-Hispanic (Bornfreund, 2011; Johnson et al., 2010; Maxwell et al., 2006). This lack of diversity can be a limitation for creating a diverse workforce, particularly in leadership and director positions (Early and Winton, 2001). Many program chairs and directors acknowledge that without racial and ethnic diversity among faculty, students in preparation programs and those seeking advanced degrees may have few role models in this field (Early and Winton, 2001).

The composition of children and families served by elementary schools and early childhood settings has shifted dramatically over the last two decades, with significant growth in immigrant and non-English-speaking families. Projections are that by 2050, about half of all children and adolescents under 17 in the United States will be Hispanic (36 percent), Asian (6 percent), or multiracial (7 percent) (Federal Interagency Forum on Child and Family Statistics, 2013; National Partnership for Teaching in At-Risk Schools, 2005). Whitebook (2014, p. 8) describes the issue thus:

> The increasing diversity of the child population requires changes in teacher preparation and professional development at all levels of education to ensure that teachers are knowledgeable and skilled in meeting the needs of children from a range of cultural and linguistic backgrounds. It also requires greater attention to the issues surrounding the racial/ethnic and linguistic backgrounds of the teacher workforce in both ECE [early care and education] and K-12 sectors. Teachers representing minority groups are invaluable in providing positive role models for all children and responding to the needs of minority children. For example, minority teachers typically hold higher expectations for minority children, and are less likely to misdiagnose them as special education students. Minority teachers often are more attuned to the challenges related to poverty, racism and immigration status that many children of color face in their communities (Learning Point Associates, 2005). For children younger than five, teachers who speak the home language of the young children are a critical asset in promoting their school readiness, engaging with families, and communicating with children who are learning English as a second language. (García, 2005)

Different care and education settings face somewhat different challenges with respect to diversity. The early care and education workforce is more racially, ethnically, and linguistically diverse than the elementary school workforce (see Table 9-3). In one survey, 84 percent of K-12 teachers were white (Feistritzer, 2011), while studies have found that one-third to one-half of early care and education teachers are people of color (Child Care Services Association, 2013; NSECE, 2011; Whitebook et al., 2006).[1] However, there is stratification by position along the dimensions of race, ethnicity, and language, with lead teachers and directors more likely to be monolingual English speakers and white (Whitebook et al., 2008a). Thus, for elementary schools, recruiting and retaining minority educators is the primary challenge (Ingersoll and May, 2011). For early childhood settings, the challenges are maintaining a culturally and linguistically diverse workforce even with increasing qualification requirements and reducing stratification among lead educators and program leaders (Whitebook, 2014).

Recruiting diverse faculty and prospective educators now will help create a diverse body of teachers that resembles the population of young children they teach (Maxwell et al., 2006). The NAEYC and the Society for Research in Child Development have made recommendations to work toward creating a diverse group of professionals who prepare educators (NAEYC, 2011b). There are examples of initiatives aimed at helping to increase racial, ethnic, and linguistic diversity among early care and education teachers by supporting their access to higher education and success in attaining degrees (Whitebook et al., 2008b, 2013).

Access to Higher Education

The demographics of levels of higher education among care and education professionals reflect both expectations for and access to higher education (see Table 9-3). The trends closely follow the differing educational expectations for the different categories of professional roles. Elementary school teachers are all college educated, with nearly half having earned an advanced degree (Feistritzer, 2011). By contrast, the education levels of educators working with children aged 3-5 in center-based settings may have a bachelor's degree or higher, an associate's degree, some college, or a high school education or less. Those working with infants and toddlers cover a similar range, but with a greater percentage of them with less education

---

[1] For example, a statewide study of California's early care and education (ECE) workforce found that 58 percent of family childcare providers, 47 percent of center teachers, and 63 percent of center assistant teachers were people of color, compared with 26 percent of K-12 teachers (Whitebook et al., 2006). In 2012 in North Carolina, for example, just under half of center-based ECE teaching staff (49 percent) were people of color. Slightly fewer center directors (44 percent) were people of color (Child Care Services Association, 2013).

TABLE 9-3 Demographic Characteristics for Educators in Early Elementary and Early Childhood Care and Education Settings

K-12 Schools	Early Childhood Settings
Teachers are typically female, represent a range of age groups, and are predominantly white.	Teachers are almost exclusively female, represent a range of age groups, and are ethnically diverse.
As of 2010, • 16 percent of public school teachers were male • 23 percent were aged 29 or younger; 26 percent were aged 30-39; 21 percent were aged 40-49; and 30 percent were aged 50 or older • 84 percent were white; 7 percent were black; 6 percent were Hispanic; and 4 percent were of other ethnicities[a] (Feistritzer, 2011)	As of 2007, for educators working in Head Start,[b] • 98 percent were female • More than half were aged 30-49 • 20 percent were identified as Hispanic/Latino; data for other ethnicities were not available (Aikens et al., 2010; NSECE, 2011) In a statewide study of California's early care and education workforce, people of color made up 58 percent of family childcare providers, 47 percent of center teachers, and 63 percent of center assistant teachers (Whitebook et al., 2006). In 2012 in North Carolina, 49 percent of center-based teaching staff and 44 percent of center directors were people of color. Almost all were women (Child Care Services Association, 2013).

In 2011,

- All were college-educated
- Nearly half had earned an advanced degree

(Feistritzer, 2011)

In 2012, for educators working with children aged 3-5 in center-based settings,

- 45 percent held a bachelor's degree or higher
- 17 percent held an associate's degree
- 24 percent had completed some college
- 13 percent had completed high school or less

For educators working with infants and toddlers aged 0-3,

- 19 percent held a bachelor's degree or higher
- More than 15 percent held an associate's degree
- 36 percent had completed some college experience
- Nearly 30 percent had a high school diploma or less

(NSECE, 2013)[c]

---

[a] The National Center for Education Information surveyed 2,500 randomly selected K-12 public school teachers from Market Data Retrieval's database of teachers (Feistritzer, 2011).

[b] No comparable national data are available for educators in state-funded prekindergarten or other early childhood center-based settings. The forthcoming National Survey of Early Care and Education (NSECE) (Aikens et al., 2010; NSECE, 2011) will provide information on gender, age, ethnicity, and language.

[c] The NSECE is based on more than 10,000 questionnaires completed in 2012.

SOURCE: Adapted from *Building a Skilled Workforce* (prepared for The Bill & Melinda Gates Foundation) (Whitebook, 2014).

(NSECE, 2013). As a result of the emergence of statutory requirements for educators in Head Start and prekindergarten to have a college degree, those working on those settings have become better represented among the more highly educated.

Variables that influence access to higher education programs include, for example, geographic access, affordability, program flexibility, program focus/content, and program length. The availability of financial support (such as tuition reimbursement, scholarships, Pell grants, Teacher Education and Compensation Helps [T.E.A.C.H.] scholarships, and Office of Special Education Programs) is one way to increase access. Another is to address the challenges of succeeding in higher education programs through such support as counseling, tutoring, and cohort models.

Perspectives from the Field

Grants, scholarships, and tuition and loan forgiveness programs are key to making formal coursework in a higher education setting more accessible to larger portions of the workforce for children birth through age 8. In addition to cost, time and geographic accessibility are also barriers.

For a family childcare educator, for example, long days, the responsibilities of owning and operating a business, and the need to arrange for a substitute are all challenges to pursuing higher education.

See Appendix C for additional highlights from interviews.

Relationships Between 2- and 4-Year Institutions

Community colleges play a key role in preparing educators for degrees and certifications. In some cases, associate's degree or certificate programs are completed entirely within a community college's system. In addition, students often take general education courses, which may include teacher education, at community colleges before transferring to 4-year institutions. Students also may earn their teacher license by pursuing postbaccalaureate courses through a community college, usually on a noncredit basis. Another option available through some community colleges is a baccalaureate program. These programs maintain flexibility to meet the needs of students (Coulter and Vandal, 2007).

The ability to transfer credits from a community college to a 4-year institution can be hampered or facilitated by the structure of articulation agreements between these two types of institutions. Articulation agreements link community colleges to 4-year institutions and provide continuity for the role of community colleges in educator preparation. The agreements may include such features as a common course numbering system or a joint admission program allowing for easy transitions between institutions. However, they are often limited by a top-down system in which articulation effort is controlled by the 4-year university. Strengthened collaboration between the two types of institutions is one way to establish educator preparation as a process that includes the community college system (Coulter and Vandal, 2007).

Alternative Pathways for Educating Educators

Alternative programs provide individuals who have previously received a bachelor's degree outside of the field of education with formal coursework in education, job training, and support and mentoring in the classroom (U.S. Department of Education and Office of Postsecondary Education, 2013). These programs have become more common over the past 30 years. In 1985, fewer than 300 individuals became certified teachers through alternative programs; by 2006, this number had increased to just over 50,000 (Feistritzer and Haar, 2008). Although the majority of teaching candidates participate in traditional teaching programs, approximately 87,000 students were enrolled in alternative programs in 2009-2010 (U.S. Department of Education and Office of Postsecondary Education, 2013). The push for alternative pathways to teacher certification began as a solution to an increasing number of students enrolling in schools and a shortage due to teachers' retiring and otherwise leaving the profession, leaving a need for more than 2 million new teachers in 10 years (Feistritzer and Haar, 2008; Johnson et al., 2005). These programs also help meet the increasing demand for diversity of educators as well as the need for educators with certain subject-matter knowledge (Alhamisi, 2008).

The Teach For America program is an example of an alternative pathway to teacher certification that recruits and trains new college graduates to teach in schools in vulnerable and high-risk communities. Teach For America launched an Early Childhood Education initiative in 2006, recognizing the need to ensure that all children have access to high-quality prekindergarten education. Prospective educators are provided with summer preservice training, regional induction, and regional orientation, as well as in-service virtual and in-person coaching. Since its launch, Teach For America has placed more than 1,000 new teachers in prekindergarten programs throughout the nation (Teach For America Inc., 2015).

The U.S. Department of Education identified several elements of effectiveness for these programs, including quality recruitment processes and selection criteria and screening of applicants. Applicant screening, often a multistep process, includes a minimum grade point average and submission of writing samples, interviews with a selection committee, and sample lessons. Effective alternative programs also provide flexibility to meet the needs of their students, such as a shortened or fast-track program and evening or weekend classes to minimize any loss of income, as well as assistance with job placement. They also provide support to their students, including supervision on the job, mentoring, and opportunities for support from their cohort (U.S. Department of Education Office of Innovation and Improvement, 2004).

Conclusions About Higher Education Programs for Educators

The education that is available and expected for educators of children from birth through age 8 varies widely for different professionals based on role, ages of children served, and practice setting even though these candidates will have similar responsibilities for young children. Each of the different "worlds" that result from this variability has different values and priorities, different communities, different pathways for entering higher education, and different research bases. As a result, programs lack a consistent orientation and are extremely variable and fragmented across and within institutions. This lack of consistency has important implications for how educators are trained to work with children:

- *There is a lack of widespread implementation of agreed-upon standards that guide program design, such as curriculum content, pedagogy, intensity of field-based learning experiences, and duration of study.*
- *There is a lack of strategies for ensuring that care and education professionals across settings and roles have access to high-quality higher education programs that leads them to acquire and apply in practice the core body of knowledge and competencies they need.*

For higher-quality programs that are better matched to the competencies required for professional practice in both early childhood settings and early elementary settings, the following improvements are needed to content, curriculum, and pedagogy:

- *Educators of children from birth through age 8 need to be taught instructional and assessment strategies that are informed by research on child development and early learning.*
- *These educators need to be taught learning trajectories specific to particular content areas, including the content, children's learning*

of and thinking about this content, and how to provide experiences integrating this content into curricula and teaching practices.

- *These educators need high-quality field placements that build instructional competencies and also allow them to gain experience working with diverse populations of children and families.*

The lack of valid and reliable data collection and measurement strategies has resulted in limited information about the content knowledge and pedagogical approaches that lead to effective higher education programs for educators.

Illustrative Examples of Higher Education Programs with a Birth Through Age 8 Orientation

The issue of quality in higher education extends to how well care and education professionals are equipped with the knowledge and competencies needed across professional roles and settings to support continuity in high-quality learning experiences for children from birth through age 8. Therefore, it is worth including here some examples of higher education programs developed with the specific intent of achieving a more continuous birth through age 8 orientation (see Box 9-1). These examples are not derived from a comprehensive research effort, nor do they reflect any conclusions the committee drew about best practices or exemplars. They are provided to illustrate some of the approaches that are being used with the aim of improving the quality and consistency of higher education programs for care and education professionals.

Governance and Oversight of Institutions of Higher Education

The governance and oversight of institutions of higher education play a key role in shaping programs for care and education professionals, with implications for program quality, efforts to improve or update program content, and policy development. State agencies, state licensure for teachers, funding sources for institutions of higher education, and accreditation standards are four elements that influence the content and quality of educator preparation programs.

State agencies are responsible for administering and overseeing higher education programs, and they create policies on teacher education and certification, funding, and program approval (Perry, 2011). Many states work toward connecting their policies on teacher certification and licensure with standards set by the National Council for Accreditation of Teacher Education (NCATE) and other organizations (Perry, 2011; Pianta et al., 2010) and establish criteria for specific program requirements, includ-

BOX 9-1
Examples of Higher Education Programs with
a Birth Through Age 8 Orientation

New Mexico State University Early Childhood Education Program
The Early Childhood Education program at New Mexico State University (NMSU) is a 2- or 4-year program that grants an associate's or bachelor's degree in early childhood education to prospective educators who successfully meet all the program requirements. These requirements include coursework and practicum experience in such areas as family engagement, intersectoral collaboration, and diversity.

Prospective educators at NMSU must complete a field placement requirement. They have the option of completing their practicum at Myrna's Children Village Laboratory School, which, as part of NMSU, provides services to children, ages 6 weeks to 5 years, of students, faculty, staff, and community members. The program also has field placements in local public elementary schools so that students can experience working with children through third grade.

Courses cover family and community engagement, through which the role of the educator in establishing and maintaining relationships with families is emphasized. Advanced courses also are available, focused on the diversity of families and the influence of culture, socioeconomic status, and language on the development of children and families. Coursework touches as well on working with children and families from culturally and linguistically diverse backgrounds and with children with developmental delays or disabilities.

Prospective educators must also acquire the skills to access community resources that have positive impacts on families and children's development. These include health, mental health, and adult education services.

University of Oklahoma–Tulsa Early Childhood Education Bachelor's Completion Program
The University of Oklahoma–Tulsa Early Childhood Education program is a five-semester program that has an articulation agreement with the 2-year associate's program at Tulsa Community College. Successful candidates earn a bachelor of science degree in education upon completion of the program.

Coursework has a child-development focus and includes classwork on infant-toddler development, early childhood development, and language and literacy development for children from birth through third grade. Prospective educators also must complete a field experience requirement with the following age groups: infants/toddlers, preschool-aged children, and primary grade-level children (kindergarten through third grade).

Family engagement is emphasized in both the coursework and practicum requirements. In the infant/toddler course, family engagement is discussed particularly in terms of collaborating with families, maintaining cultural continuity, and understanding cultural contexts children experience outside the classroom. Prospective educators must work with one child and conduct home visits during the semester as a requirement for the Family and Community Connections course. In addition, they must observe conferences between educators and families.

In an effort to establish connections with practitioners in other sectors, candidates are required to interview early intervention specialists from such programs as Oklahoma Parents as Teachers, Family and Children's Services, and Sooner Start. They also may collaborate with pediatricians and community activities for their service learning project.

University of Pittsburgh CASE (Combined Accelerated Studies in Education) Program

The CASE program at the University of Pittsburgh is a 5-year program that offers both undergraduate and graduate coursework. Students in the early childhood education program begin their coursework in the Applied Developmental Psychology department. Upon graduation, they receive a bachelor of science degree in applied developmental psychology and a master of education degree in early childhood education.

The required coursework for this program emphasizes child development. It includes a course on development from conception through early childhood and the psychology of learning and development for education, among others. Several courses focus on diversity, including working with dual language learners and understanding race and racism in education. Prospective educators also are required to have knowledge of diverse learners as a field experience competency.

To meet the field experience requirements, candidates must complete passive observations in early childhood classrooms during their sophomore and junior years. During their senior year, they must complete 200-hour field experiences in prekindergarten classrooms and in early intervention or life skills settings. At the graduate level, students are required to serve as full-time student teachers in a primary grade-level classroom and in a special education classroom. Each student teaching experience lasts 14 weeks.

Family engagement is a component of both coursework and training at the University of Pittsburgh. It is discussed extensively in the Child Development course, the Developmental Curriculum course, a number of methods courses, a course on working with dual language learners, and a special education course called Partnership with Families. In practice, prospective educators apply their knowledge of family engagement by volunteering through the Child Development Association student group and other work within the community.

SOURCES: Personal communication, A. Arlotta-Guerrero, University of Pittsburgh, 2014; personal communication, E. Cahill, New Mexico State University, 2014; personal communication, D. M. Horm, University of Oklahoma–Tulsa, 2014; New Mexico State University, 2014; University of Oklahoma, n.d.; University of Pittsburgh School of Education, 2015.

ing recruitment and admission of students, field experience, training, and coursework hours and content (Perry, 2011). NCATE has recommended that states establish policies on incorporating the science of child development into teacher preparation programs, as teacher evaluation systems are moving toward recognizing a teacher's knowledge of child development and how it is applied in the classroom (Pianta et al., 2010). States also are strengthening policies on teacher effectiveness, having identified teacher assessments as an opportunity to raise standards for teacher preparation programs (NCTQ, 2012).

Teacher licensure and certification (discussed in more detail in Chapter 10) also affect the content and emphasis of higher education programs designed to prepare students to practice. Licenses often cover a broad range of grades, such as prekindergarten to grade 3, kindergarten to grade 5, and kindergarten to grade 12. The overlapping structure of these licenses can lead to overlapping preparation programs that can limit opportunities for learning at either end of the grade spectrum. Additionally, many states do not require that educators of children in kindergarten have any preparation in early childhood development (Bornfreund, 2011). The National Association for the Education of Young Children's (NAEYC's) report on early childhood teacher certification raises the concern that preparation programs for prekindergarten to grade 6 focus on teaching methods suited to older children, and that those graduating from such programs may not have the skills necessary for teaching children in kindergarten classrooms (NAEYC, n.d.). Furthermore, states require exams (Praxis) that measure the knowledge and teaching abilities of prospective educators as a condition for obtaining a teaching license. According to the New America Foundation, however, these tests are not an effective tool for evaluating whether one is an effective teacher as the minimum passing scores "can be so low that they are meaningless" (Bornfreund, 2011).

Sources of funding that are subject to conditions or requirements (such as state funds, grants, scholarships, and financial aid) also can influence the quality and content of educator preparation programs. For example, the Teacher Quality Partnership grant program under Title II of the Higher Education Act is intended to increase student achievement in high-need schools by improving the quality of current and prospective educators. This program holds institutions of higher education accountable for preparing qualified and effective teachers (Cohen-Vogel, 2005; U.S. Department of Education, 1998). Funds from this grant can be used for prebaccalaureate programs that prepare prospective educators, as well as for teacher residency and leadership programs. Specifically, funds can be used to evaluate and improve curriculum, develop field experience criteria, and create induction programs for new teachers (U.S. Department of Education, 1998). Additionally, the T.E.A.C.H. grant is available to prospective teachers entering teacher preparation programs who agree to teach in a high-need or low-resourced school upon completing their program. Under this agreement, students receive up to $4,000 per year to cover tuition costs. The preparation programs are required to produce highly qualified teachers with the competencies needed to work in low-resourced settings (U.S. Department of Education, n.d.).

Voluntary accreditation standards are another mechanism for influencing higher education programs for care and education professionals. Accrediting agencies are private associations that document whether educational institutions and programs meet a certain level of quality. Although educational institutions are not accredited through the U.S. Department of Education, the government provides the public with a list of accrediting agencies that are recognized for quality based on specified standards (U.S. Department of Education, 2014). The Council for Higher Education Accreditation (CHEA) also recognizes accrediting agencies based on its own standards (CHEA, 2010). As of 2007, the U.S. Department of Education recognized 58 accreditors, and CHEA recognized 60 accreditors. At this time, more than 7,000 institutions and fewer than 20,000 programs had been accredited (CHEA, 2008). According to CHEA, accreditation is important for several reasons. First, educational institutions and programs must meet the expectations of the accrediting agencies, which promotes quality. Additionally, students attending accredited institutions and programs have greater access to financial aid, tuition assistance, federal grants, and other funds, and they can more easily transfer credits to other institutions (CHEA, 2015).

Examples of accreditation standards that apply to institutions of higher education with programs for care and education professionals working with children from birth through age 8 include the Council for the Accreditation of Educator Preparation (CAEP) (2013) Interim Standards and the NAEYC Early Childhood Associate Degree Accreditation (ECADA) standards (NAEYC, 2011a). These standards emphasize several themes that influence educator preparation programs, including program content and faculty requirements.

Both ECADA and CAEP emphasize program resources and content in their standards for educator preparation programs. ECADA notes that programs should arrange courses in a logical developmental sequence, and should offer a combination of coursework and practicum requirements relevant to the course content. The required field experiences should allow candidates to apply their coursework knowledge in practice while reflecting the standards of the NAEYC. During the field experiences, faculty should be available to work with the candidates to evaluate and reflect on their experiences. Similarly, the CAEP interim standards require candidates to demonstrate knowledge and skills for working effectively with students in the classroom, as well as their positive effect on student learning in pre-kindergarten through grade 12. Prospective educators also must foster the development of all students, assess student learning, and communicate with families. The educator preparation provider must ensure that candidates can demonstrate their skills and knowledge through assessments, and establish program policies and practices that support prospective educators.

High-quality and effective faculty are essential to educator preparation programs, as identified in five of the ECADA standards. Faculty must teach strategies that foster candidates' learning and application of knowledge, and their coursework must derive from current research. Both the CAEP and ECADA standards identify requirements for quality and effective faculty, including the ability to demonstrate knowledge needed for academic and clinical training in the area in which they are teaching, as well as experience and a degree in early childhood education. Faculty also must be part of the system that supports and advises candidates, along with others who provide career counseling and financial aid information and advisors who ensure that candidates are on the track to complete their program. Additionally, professional learning opportunities for faculty need to be available to keep them engaged in the field and aware of current research and practices.

The ECADA standards focus on many areas related to a preparation program's mission and overarching goals. To meet the ECADA standards, preparation programs must create a conceptual framework that is connected to the program's mission, encompasses collaboration with stakeholders, and sets goals and objectives for the program. The framework also should include methods for supporting and preparing prospective educators to teach in diverse, equitable, and inclusive settings. These standards help educator preparation programs align required coursework and field placements with their mission and achieve integration within their communities. Additionally, the ECADA standards reinforce the impact of faculty throughout the preparation program, particularly in the areas of advising and supporting students and fulfilling their responsibilities in the classroom, within the institution, and in the community—an area that is explored less in the CAEP standards.

Conclusion About Accreditation for Higher Education Programs

Carefully considered voluntary standards for quality have been developed for programs offering degrees and certifications for educators of children from birth through age 8, yet these standards have been not been translated consistently into the preparation students receive in higher education programs. Standards, incentives, and resources for accrediting institutions of higher education need to be strengthened, and regulatory systems need to be aligned with these standards so the standards will be adopted and implemented more consistently and rigorously.

PROFESSIONAL LEARNING DURING ONGOING PRACTICE

This section covers those activities that provide professional learning during ongoing practice, also commonly known as "professional development" or "in-service training." It is worth noting that some of these learning activities also occur during degree- or certificate-granting programs. Conversely, it is worth noting as well that for many practitioners who do not participate in formal preparation programs, such as those in early childhood settings, these activities during ongoing professional practice often overlap as default preparation for practice.

Professional learning during ongoing practice may include such activities as workshops/trainings/courses, coaching and mentoring, reflective practice, learning networks, and communities of practice. These activities can be delivered through a variety of mechanisms—as part of regular practice, as a training activity embedded in the workplace setting, as an offsite activity in a higher education or other setting (such as nonmetric courses or continuing education units), or through technology-based delivery methods. These activities can be part of a sequenced series of activities or ad hoc activities for specific one-time purposes.

Professional learning during ongoing professional practice can have many purposes, including supporting core competencies; introducing skills, concepts, and instructional strategies that were not mastered or introduced in educator preparation programs; and training educators in new science related to child development and early learning and new instructional tools and strategies. All professional learning has the shared purpose of improving or sustaining the quality of professional practice (Howes et al., 2012), and ultimately improving child outcomes (Blank and de las Alas, 2009; Yoon et al., 2007). The effectiveness of professional learning can therefore be viewed in terms of how well it achieves those two aims.

Professional learning during ongoing practice also is one avenue for promoting more consistent and continuous high-quality learning experiences for children if it is provided with intentional consistency and collaboration among professional learning systems across settings and professional roles. Content and curriculum materials that are developed consistently around the science of child development as well as early learning and professional learning activities that are interconnected provide shared language and goals for educators that facilitate working with each other and other groups, as well as peer communication and collaboration (Brendefur et al., 2013; Bryk et al., 2010; Garet et al., 2001).

The subsections that follow offer an overview of access to and expectations for ongoing professional learning for different professional roles and practice settings, an overview of general standards for professional learning, and then more in-depth discussion of the major types of professional learning and principles for quality that apply to each.

Access to and Expectations for Professional Learning During Ongoing Practice

Expectations and resources for professional learning during ongoing practice vary by professional role and practice setting (see Table 9-4). Educators in elementary school systems typically have requirements for and access to professional learning activities. For educators in other settings and systems, expectations and resources vary by program type and funding stream. Many states have no well-defined, comprehensive system to ensure ongoing professional learning, nor do they have agreed-upon standards or approval systems to ensure the quality of those who provide professional learning activities. Educators in better-funded, school-sponsored public prekindergarten and Head Start programs are more likely to participate in learning opportunities that occur during their paid working hours than are their counterparts in privately operated and funded nonprofit or for-profit centers and programs. These latter educators are more often expected to complete professional learning activities during unpaid evening or weekend hours (Whitebook, 2014).

Perspectives from the Field

Family childcare educators face significant barriers in accessing trainings and workshops and other professional learning supports even when they are made available. These educators often work long hours, usually by themselves, and do not have someone to substitute for them. On top of that, family childcare educators are often owners of their own business, playing the dual-function of administrator and practitioner, leaving little time and space for professional learning.

———————

See Appendix C for additional highlights from interviews.

TABLE 9-4 Overview of Differences in Infrastructure, Requirements, Expectations, and Common Practices for Ongoing Professional Learning

K-12 Schools	Early Childhood Settings		
Induction programs that support teachers in the first years on the job, as well as systems of ongoing professional development throughout their careers, are widespread, and public funding is routinely earmarked for them.	"Professional development" is a catchall phrase that covers nearly the entire spectrum of training and education available in the field—from introductory training, to informal workshops, to continuing education courses for credit, to college-level work for credit or a degree (Whitebook et al., 2009).		
School districts, unions, institutions of higher education, and other organizations provide professional development (Whitebook et al., 2009).	Induction and mentoring programs are not routinely available, and many settings do not have a continuing education requirement for teachers (Whitebook et al., 2009).		
	Approximately 30 states have developed training and trainer approval systems to reach all practitioners who work in licensed facilities (Kipnis et al., 2013).		
	State-Funded Prekindergarten	Head Start	All Other Early Childhood Center-Based Programs
• 27 states require some form of induction or mentoring support for new teachers (Goldrick et al., 2012). • 22 states require completion of or participation in an induction program for advanced teaching certification (Goldrick et al., 2012, p. 6). • 17 states provide some dedicated funding for teacher induction (Goldrick et al., 2012, p. 6). • Most states require teachers to complete a specific amount of professional development every 5 years (Loeb et al., 2009).	• Teacher in-service requirements vary by state and by program within states, representing a range of clock and credit hours. Two programs have no requirements (Barnett et al., 2012, p. 195).	• Many Head Start teachers participate in mentoring and coaching programs. • Head Start provides resources for ongoing professional development of teaching staff (U.S. Department of Health and Human Services and Administration for Children and Families, n.d.).	• 23 states require less than 15 hours of annual training for teachers in licensed centers. • More than one-fifth of states do not require teaching staff to be trained in fire safety and other health and safety skills or any pedagogical content (Child Care Aware of America, 2014).

SOURCE: Adapted from *Building a Skilled Workforce* (prepared for The Bill & Melinda Gates Foundation) (Whitebook, 2014).

Existing Standards for Professional Learning Supports

Learning Forward (2014b) has established a set of standards for professional learning, shown in Figure 9-1. It also has suggested several prerequisites for effective, professional learning. One is that the foundation of effective professional learning is participating educators who are committed to engaging in continuous improvement that will foster knowledge and skills to meet the learning needs of all students. Without such continuous learning, knowledge, skills, and practices degrade over time and educators become less adaptable, self-confident, and effective in their work. Part of this commitment is being receptive to professional learning experiences, which is enhanced when the systems providing the professional learning ensure that it is relevant and useful. Another prerequisite is that professional learning needs meet the individual needs of educators, because all learners learn at different rates and in different ways. Different educators may benefit from different types of learning experiences, and may need more or less support in translating new knowledge and skills into practice. Finally, professional learning should have the potential to foster collaborative learning among the participating educators, who may come from different settings or teaching environments and may have disparate levels of experience (Learning Forward, 2014b).

Professional Learning for Instructional Strategies and Tools

Research indicates that effective in-service professional learning is ongoing, intentional, reflective, goal-oriented, based on specific curricula and materials, focused on content knowledge and children's thinking, and situated in the classroom (Bodilly, 1998; Borman et al., 2003; Bryk et al., 2010; Cohen, 1996; Elmore, 1996; Guskey, 2000; Hall and Hord, 2001; Kaser et al., 1999; Klingner et al., 2003; Pellegrino, 2007; Schoen et al., 2003; Showers et al., 1987; Sowder, 2007; Zaslow et al., 2010). These studies also illustrate the need for professional learning activities to focus on content, including accurate and adequate subject-matter knowledge. Professional learning with the goal of preparing educators to teach subject-matter material is more effective if it is grounded in specific curricula and develops teachers' knowledge and belief that the curriculum they are learning to use is appropriate, and its goals are valued and attainable. Ideally, the curricula used are research-based materials specifically designed to be educative (Drake et al., 2014). In addition, such training works best when it promotes risk taking, sharing, and learning from and with peers and when it situates work in the classroom. This allows for formative evaluation of fidelity of implementation, with feedback and support from coaches in real time. The

STANDARDS FOR PROFESSIONAL LEARNING			
Professional learning that increases educator effectiveness and results for all students ...	**LEARNING COMMUNITIES:** Professional learning that increases educator effectiveness and results for all students occurs within learning communities committed to continuous improvement, collective responsibility, and goal alignment.	**LEADERSHIP:** Professional learning that increases educator effectiveness and results for all students requires skillful leaders who develop capacity, advocate, and create support systems for professional learning.	**RESOURCES:** Professional learning that increases educator effectiveness and results for all students requires prioritizing, monitoring, and coordinating resources for educator learning.
DATA: Professional learning that increases educator effectiveness and results for all students uses a variety of sources and types of student, educator, and system data to plan, assess, and evaluate professional learning.	**LEARNING DESIGNS:** Professional learning that increases educator effectiveness and results for all students integrates theories, research, and models of human learning to achieve its intended outcomes.	**IMPLEMENTATION:** Professional learning that increases educator effectiveness and results for all students applies research on change and sustains support for implementation of professional learning for long-term change.	**OUTCOMES:** Professional learning that increases educator effectiveness and results for all students aligns its outcomes with educator performance and student curriculum standards.

Relationship between professional learning and student results

1. When professional learning is standards-based, it has greater potential to change what educators know, are able to do, and believe.
2. When educators' knowledge, skills, and dispositions change, they have a broader repertoire of effective strategies to use to adapt their practices to meet performance expectations and student learning needs.
3. When educator practice improves, students have a greater likelihood of achieving results.
4. When student results improve, the cycle repeats for continuous improvement.

This cycle works two ways: If educators are not achieving the results they want, they determine what changes in practice are needed and then what knowledge, skills, and dispositions are needed to make the desired changes. They then consider how to apply the standards so that they can engage in the learning needed to strengthen their practice.

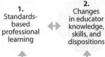

FIGURE 9-1 Standards for professional learning.

notion that professional learning should be situated in the classroom does not imply that all training occurs in classroom settings. However, offsite intensive training should remain focused on and connected to classroom practice and be complemented by classroom-based enactment (Bodilly, 1998; Borman et al., 2003; Bryk et al., 2010; Carlisle and Berebitsky, 2010; Clarke, 1994; Cohen, 1996; Elmore, 1996; Garet et al., 2001; Guskey, 2000; Hall and Hord, 2001; Kaser et al., 1999; Klingner et al., 2003; Pellegrino, 2007; Schoen et al., 2003; Showers et al., 1987; Sowder, 2007; Zaslow et al., 2010).

Research findings also have implications for the nature and structure of professional development. Combinations of layers of professional development that include workshops, coaching, and professional development communities can improve teachers' understanding and use of more effective instructional practices, which in turn result in greater learning for children in their care (Biancarosa et al., 2010; Buysse et al., 2010; Carlisle et al., 2011).

Research suggests that effective professional learning for instructional practices has several key features:

- Develops knowledge of the specific content to be taught, including deep conceptual knowledge of the subject and its processes (Blömeke et al., 2011; Brendefur et al., 2013; Garet et al., 2001).
- Gives corresponding attention to specific pedagogical content knowledge, including all three aspects of learning trajectories: the goal, the developmental progression of levels of thinking, and the instructional activities corresponding to each level—and especially their connections. This feature of professional learning also helps build a common language for educators in working with each other and other groups (Brendefur et al., 2013; Bryk et al., 2010).
- Includes active learning involving the details of setting up, conducting, and formatively evaluating subject-specific experiences and activities for children, including a focus on reviewing student work and small-group instructional activities (Brendefur et al., 2013; Garet et al., 2001).
- Focuses on common actions and problems of practice, which, to the extent possible, should be situated in the classroom.
- Grounds experiences in particular curriculum materials and allows educators to learn and reflect on that curriculum, implement it, and discuss their implementation.
- Includes in-classroom coaching. The knowledge and skill of coaches are of critical importance. Coaches also must have knowledge of the content, general pedagogical knowledge, and pedagogical con-

tent knowledge, as well as knowledge of and competencies in effective coaching.

- Employs peer study groups or networks for collective participation by educators who work together (Garet et al., 2001).
- Incorporates sustained and intensive professional learning experiences and networks rather than stand-alone professional learning activities (Garet et al., 2001).
- Ensures that all professional learning activities (e.g., trainings, adoption of new curricula, implementation of new standards) are interconnected and consistent in content and approach (Brendefur et al., 2013; Garet et al., 2001). This consistency also involves a shared language and goal structure that promote peer communication and collaboration.
- Ties professional learning to the science of adult learning. There is now increasing recognition of the importance of multiple, comprehensive domains of knowledge and learning for adults (NRC, 2012).
- Addresses equity and diversity concerns in access to and participation in professional learning.
- Addresses economic, institutional, and regulatory barriers to implementing professional learning.

The following subsections provide examples of the features of high-quality professional learning applied for different subject-matter content, namely literacy and mathematics, as well as for the use of technology for instruction. Although this section focuses on instructional strategies and tools, it is important to note that care and education professionals also need to learn both to develop high-quality environments and to have high-quality interactions with children within those environments. For example, research suggests that in addition to stronger gains in language, reading, and math skills due to the quality of instruction in higher-quality preschool classrooms, the quality of teacher–child interactions was linked to higher social competence and lower levels of behavior problems (Burchinal et al., 2010). This finding reaffirms the importance of supporting early childhood professionals in both instructional strategies and in establishing positive educator–child relationships with the aim of helping students make greater academic and social gains. As discussed in Chapter 4, positive educator–child interactions have a strong influence on multiple outcomes of development and early learning.

Literacy

Findings of studies of professional development aimed at helping educators improve instruction for young children in language and reading skills have been promising (Brady et al., 2009; Carlisle et al., 2011; O'Connor et al., 1996; Piasta et al., 2009). When educators improve their knowledge of language and reading instruction, their students' skills also improve. Various studies suggest that to increase student achievement in literacy, stand-alone professional learning is not optimally effective. More effective is training, especially around specific curriculum materials or approaches, complemented by strong in-class coaching or mentoring (Biancarosa and Bryk, 2011; Garet et al., 2008; Gersten et al., 2010). Coaching is crucial, but does not guarantee gains (Garet et al., 2008; Hsieh et al., 2009); it must be intensive, ongoing, and conducted by knowledgeable coaches (Biancarosa and Bryk, 2011; Carlisle and Berebitsky, 2010; Powell et al., 2010). Comprehensive approaches have shown the most success. In one study, for example, a combination of these features and detailed, instructionally linked feedback resulted in the greatest improvements in both teaching practices and preschoolers' competencies in literacy and language (Landry et al., 2009).

Mathematics

There are indications that certification alone is not a reliable predictor of high-quality teaching (NMP, 2008), probably because of the wide variety of certification programs and the low quality of many. However, direct measures that focus on teachers' content knowledge of mathematics as well as what they know about teaching and learning of mathematics are linked to teacher quality and student achievement gains (Hill et al., 2005; NMP, 2008). Research-based approaches to support teacher quality through professional learning have been successful for educators working in both preschool (Sarama and Clements, 2013; Sarama and DiBiase, 2004) and primary grades (Abdulhamid and Venkat, 2014). Providing professional learning experiences in mathematics increases children's mathematical competencies across a wide range of topics (Brendefur et al., 2013; Clements et al., 2011, 2013). The research on professional learning for teaching mathematics is not complete but does provide some guidance.

What is not effective High-quality professional learning designed to advance competencies and knowledge of math content and learning trajectories is limited for many teachers. One study found that teachers receive, on average, fewer than 9 hours of math-related professional learning, and just over 5 hours of "in-depth study" over a 1-year period (Birman et al., 2007).

Early childhood teachers receive even fewer opportunities for professional learning in math, or none at all. Despite it being a common practice, ignoring math in professional learning opportunities is not effective (Clements and Sarama, 2012).

Furthermore, as Sarama and DiBiase (2004) argue, what is available to educators is ineffective. For example, 1-day workshops are ineffective because the amount of time is insufficient to engage in the material. In addition, workshop topics often do not address educators' needs and concerns, as they are selected by others rather than by those receiving the instruction. In one study the majority of teachers reported having no say in what or how they learned (Darling-Hammond, 1998). Additionally, professional learning strategies that do not convene teachers from the same site can limit collaboration and social support in applying the knowledge gained in the workplace (Clements and Sarama, 2012; Fullan, 1982).

What appears to be effective For professional learning strategies for teaching mathematics to have the greatest effect, they need to be research-based and emphasize how to implement theory into practice, as well as focus on teachers' knowledge of content, curriculum, and how students learn math (Carpenter et al., 1988; Kennedy, 1998; Peterson et al., 1989; Sarama, 2002). Most successful programs identify ways in which students learn and stress how this can be meaningful for educators in their everyday practice (Sarama, 2002). Another component of successful professional learning is collaboration and interactions with mentors or university professors. One study found positive effects in students' content knowledge of mathematics due to intensive (more than 50 hours), content-based, and sustained professional learning opportunities (Birman et al., 2007; Clements and Sarama, 2012).

Success with professional learning models such as the Internet software application Building Blocks Learning Trajectories (BBLT) and TRIAD (Technology-enhanced, Research-based, Instruction, Assessment, and professional Development) model of scale-up (see Box 9-2) is arguably attributable largely to their focus on learning trajectories (Clements and Sarama, 2008). In the TRIAD model, teachers were provided with video segments illustrating the levels of children's learning and instructional tasks to use in the classroom to promote children's progress, which they viewed, discussed, and analyzed (Sarama and Clements, 2013). The BBLT tool, which connects the three trajectory components—goals, learning levels, and instructional tasks—includes a self-evaluation feature. This feature is an essential component of this tool, as it provides opportunities for teachers to assess their ability to determine learning levels of children. This tool also includes access to research-based instructional strategies to advance children's learning (Sarama et al., 2012a).

BOX 9-2
Example of a Professional Learning Model
Focused on Learning Trajectories

The TRIAD (Technology-enhanced, Research-based, Instruction, Assessment, and professional Development) model of scale-up has learning trajectories at the core to ensure it addresses the triad of essential components of educators' knowledge of the subject, how students think about and learn the subject, and how to teach students at each level of thinking (see Chapters 2 and 4). The model consists of 10 research-based guidelines.

1. *Involve, and promote communication among key groups around a shared vision of the innovation* (Hall and Hord, 2001). Emphasize connections between the project's goals, national and state standards, and greater societal need. Promote clarity of these goals and of all participants' responsibilities. School and project staff must share goals and a vision of the intervention (Bryk et al., 2010; Cobb et al., 2003). This institutionalizes the intervention, for example, in the case of ongoing socialization and training of new teachers (Elmore, 1996; Fullan, 2000; Huberman, 1992; Kaser et al., 1999; Klingner et al., 2003; Sarama et al., 1998).

2. *Promote equity* through equitable recruitment and selection of participants, allocation of resources, and use of curriculum and instructional strategies that have demonstrated success with underrepresented populations (Kaser et al., 1999). The TRIAD instantiations to date have used two research-based curricula that fit these criteria (Clements et al., 2013; Sarama and Clements, 2013; Sarama et al., 2008).

3. *Plan for the long term.* Recognizing that scale-up is not just an increase in number, but also of complexity, provide continuous, adaptive support over an extended period of time. Plan an incremental implementation and use dynamic, multilevel, feedback, and self-correction strategies (Bryk et al., 2010; Coburn, 2003; Fullan, 1992; Guskey, 2000). Implementations of TRIAD have involved two continuous years of working with school districts.

4. *Focus on instructional change that promotes depth of children's thinking, placing learning trajectories at the core* of the teacher/child/curriculum triad to ensure that curriculum, materials, instructional strategies, and assessments are aligned with (a) national and state standards and a vision of high-quality education, (b) each other, and (c) "best practice" as determined by research, including formative assessment (Ball and Cohen, 1999; Bodilly, 1998; Bryk et al., 2010; Fullan, 2000; Kaser et al., 1999; NMP, 2008; Sowder, 2007). This guideline is important for implementation with fidelity at any scale, although alignment is increasingly important at larger scales.

5. *Provide professional development that is ongoing, intentional, reflective, goal-oriented, focused on content knowledge and children's thinking, grounded in particular curriculum materials, situated in the classroom and the school.* A focus on content includes accurate and adequate subject-matter knowledge both for teachers and for children. A focus on children's thinking emphasizes the learning trajectories' developmental progressions and their pedagogical application in formative assess-

ment. Grounding in particular curriculum materials should include all three aspects of learning trajectories, especially their connections. This also provides a common language for teachers in working with each other and other groups (Bryk et al., 2010). Situated in the classroom does not imply that all training occurs within classrooms. However, off-site intensive training remains focused on and connected to classroom practice and is completed by classroom-based enactment with coaching. Implementations of TRIAD involved 2 years of work with teachers, including 12 full-day professional development sessions and twice-per-month visits from coaches.

6. *Build expectations and camaraderie to support a consensus around adaptation.* Promote "buy-in" in multiple ways, such as dealing with all participants as partners and distributing resources to support the project. Establish and maintain cohort groups. Facilitate teachers visiting successful implementation sites. Build local leadership by involving principals and encouraging teachers to become teacher leaders (Berends et al., 2001; Borman et al., 2003; Elmore, 1996; Fullan, 2000; Glennan et al., 2004; Hall and Hord, 2001).

7. *Ensure school leaders are a central force supporting the innovation and provide teachers continuous feedback that children are learning what they are taught and that these learnings are valued.* Leaders, especially principals, must show that the innovation is a high priority, through statements, resources, and continued commitment to permanency of the effort. An innovation champion leads the effort within each organization (Bodilly, 1998; Bryk et al., 2010; Glennan et al., 2004; Hall and Hord, 2001; Rogers, 2003; Sarama et al., 1998).

8. *Give latitude for adaptation to teachers and schools, but maintain integrity.* Emphasize the similarities of the curriculum with sound practice and what teachers already are doing. Help teachers distinguish productive adaptations from lethal mutation (Brown and Campione, 1996). Also, do not allow dilution due to uncoordinated innovations (Fullan, 2000; Huberman, 1992; Sarama et al., 1998; Snipes et al., 2002).

9. *Provide incentives for all participants, including intrinsic and extrinsic motivators linked to project work,* such as external expectations—from standards to validation from administrators. Show how the innovation is advantageous to and compatible with teachers' experiences and needs (Berends et al., 2001; Borman et al., 2003; Cohen, 1996; Darling-Hammond, 1996; Elmore, 1996; Rogers, 2003).

10. *Maintain frequent, repeated communication, assessment ("checking up"), and follow-through efforts at all levels within each school district, emphasizing the purpose, expectations, and visions of the project, and involve key groups in continual improvement through cycles of data collection and problem solving* (Fullan, 1992; Hall and Hord, 2001; Huberman, 1992; Kaser et al., 1999; Snipes et al., 2002). Throughout, connections with parents and community groups is especially important, to meet immediate and long-range (sustainability) goals.

SOURCE: Adapted from Sarama and Clements, 2009, pp. 355-357.

This and several other successful mathematics-related professional learning models share several key features, including a research-based framework and the use of developmental progressions of learning trajectories. They also require educators to have subject-matter knowledge and an understanding of how young children learn the content as well as the best strategies to teach it. Additionally, successful models require intensive professional learning that lasts up to 2 weeks, is conducted school-wide, and is followed by ongoing and reflective school-based support, rather than a single-day workshop (Bobis et al., 2005; Bright et al., 1997; Clements and Sarama, 2008, 2012; Clements et al., 2011; Sarama et al., 2008; Wright et al., 2002).

Studies also emphasize the combination of workshops, in-school support, and modeling for effective professional learning (Thomas and Tagg, 2004; Young-Loveridge, 2004). It is also essential that educators commit time for and actively participate in professional learning. The TRIAD/BBLT tools, for example, emphasize the importance of ongoing coaching and mentoring, which helps sustain certain classroom innovations (coaching and mentoring is discussed further later in this chapter) (Certo, 2005; Clarke, 1994; Clements and Sarama, 2008, 2012; Copley, 2004; Costa and Garmston, 1994; Nettles, 1993).

Use of Technology for Instruction

Surveys show that educators across grade levels want more opportunities to learn how to use technology effectively. In a survey of the NAEYC members in 2012, for example, 39 percent of respondents reported insufficient or no technical support in using technology, and 57 percent reported they receive professional development in technology once per year or less (Wartella et al., 2013). The vast majority of the respondents in the NAEYC survey worked in settings with 3- and 4-year-olds, but there are also needs among K-12 teachers. A 2012 poll by the LEAD Commission, an organization created to support the U.S. Department of Education and the Federal Communications Commission, showed that 82 percent of K-12 teachers believe they are not receiving the necessary training to use technology to its fullest potential in the classroom (Lead Commission, 2012).

A few institutions are trying to fill this void by providing webinars and online materials, including the TEC Center at Erikson Institute, the Fred Rogers Center, and the *Young Children* magazine published by the NAEYC. The NAEYC has also published two books on the topic recently: *Beyond Remote-Controlled Childhood* and *Technology and Digital Media in the Early Years*. In addition, a few members of the Association of Children's Library Services (a part of the American Library Association) have offered workshops on digital media to early childhood professionals, such as family-based childcare providers.

Although there is a relative lack of research on how to train educators to use technology, let alone how to use different technologies effectively with students at different ages for different subjects, there has been some work in this area. In addition to general characteristics of effective professional learning described earlier in this chapter, professional learning on the use of technology needs to take place with access to high-quality software; be embedded in curricula; combine learning formats; and include information about its benefits as well as collaboration with learning partners and opportunities for practice, feedback, and sustained assistance (Clements and Sarama, 2002; Fullan, 1992; Prieto et al., 2011).

In the TRIAD example described previously (see Box 9-2), the model is enhanced by the use of technology (Clements et al., 2011; Sarama et al., 2012b). The interventions included nontechnological and technological components, but classroom observations indicated that use of the computer software was one of the highest correlates with gains in mathematics achievement (Sarama et al., 2008). Technology support in the classroom was essential, and teachers were more likely to adopt and sustain new practices with technology when they had opportunities to see others using the innovation and when they observed positive child outcomes (Clements and Sarama, 2014). Similar findings were reported for the Early Childhood Comprehensive Technology System, which implemented and maintained a comprehensive technology system based on combining four components of nationally recognized demonstration models and peer-reviewed outreach models. In addition to resulting in positive outcomes for families and children in multiple development domains, there were increased technology skills among teachers. The technology components incorporated in the program included technology integration into the classroom curriculum; team-based technology assessments for children with moderate to severe disabilities; and ongoing training for teachers, with an emphasis on hands-on work with computers, software, and adaptive devices, as well as an on-site technology support team. These components were effective in establishing, maintaining, and institutionalizing computer technology in a large preschool program (Clements and Sarama, 2002; Hutinger and Johanson, 2000; Hutinger et al., 1998).

Coaching and Mentoring

Coaching and mentoring involve a collaborative partnership in which adult learning strategies are used to impart the knowledge and skills of the coach/mentor to the teacher or practitioner. Coaching and mentoring are seen as strategies for providing support for practitioners and improving the quality of instruction in early care and education (Isner et al., 2011; Powell et al., 2012; Whitebook and Bellm, 2013). These strategies offer a practical way for practitioners to grow on the job. The terms "coaching" and "mentoring" are often used interchangeably. However, mentors may focus more on working with individual educators with mutual agreed-upon goals for the process, whereas coaches may work with individuals or groups of classroom instructors and may have a planned program. A relationship is built between the coach/mentor and educator to enable the effort to take place with mutual respect (Whitebook and Bellm, 2013). Most coaches/ mentors of early childhood educators have education credentials and extensive work experience in an early childhood care and education setting. Coaching/mentoring may include assessment of the practitioner's learning style, observation, demonstrations, reflective practice, and evaluation (Sheridan et al., 2009; Whitebook and Bellm, 2013). The process varies in length from a few months to 1 year or more (Isner et al., 2011; Whitebook and Bellm, 2013).

Coaching/mentoring is aimed at improving the overall quality of instruction or providing assistance with practices specific to content areas, such as language and literacy or socioemotional development (Isner et al., 2011; Whitebook and Bellm, 2013). A review of the research on coaching examined the outcomes for early childhood practitioners and children including effects on practices and observed quality (Isner et al., 2011). The studies included in the review were conducted in a range of settings that encompassed childcare centers, Head Start programs, family childcare programs, prekindergarten/preschool programs, and early elementary grades. The authors concluded that there was "limited evidence . . . that coaching significantly impacts practitioners' knowledge, attitudes, and beliefs" (p. 14). Although there was evidence that coaching contributed to improved quality and practices, the authors were unable to attribute the improvement to specific features of the coaching. On the other hand, the review found evidence that "coaching had a positive effect on children's language and literacy outcomes" (p. 14), especially when the coaching model focused on language and literacy teaching methods (Isner et al., 2011).

Another review of the early childhood coaching literature found improvement in teacher behaviors and practices with a combination of coaching and professional development, although the authors were unable to identify specific interventions used by coaches to improve teacher practices (Gupta and Daniels, 2012). Similarly, in an article examining professional development in early childhood programs, Sheridan and colleagues (2009) summarize meta-analysis results indicating that the combination of specific training with on-the-job coaching promotes the use of new skills by teachers. Studies also have shown promise for online coaching in early childhood settings (Hemmeter et al., 2011; Powell and Diamond, 2011).

Several challenges and opportunities for improvement were identified in a study of the coaching approach used by Los Angeles Universal Preschool. One challenge was limited time to meet, particularly outside of the classroom and away from children. Possible solutions included meeting during nap times, coordinating times for special trainings, and communicating via phone or email. Additionally, coaches reported that some teachers were hesitant to engage, which may have been due to high staff turnover rates and a lack of trust between coach and teacher. The study also found that some coaches did not discuss high-level goals for the teacher; rather, the focus of the coaching was on what had been observed on a particular day. While there are many areas in which coaching can improve, all teachers in this study reported having positive experiences with their coach and valued the feedback and guidance they received (Winston et al., 2012).

Perspectives from the Field

Many educators, especially in center-based childcare settings and family childcare, lack formal mentoring and coaching support that allows them to apply what they may have learned in formal coursework, trainings, or workshops to their own practice.

"Mentoring and coaching [are] happening more, but most programs don't have sufficient resources set aside in terms of subs and scheduling staffing to really make that as meaningful as it could be."

For family childcare educators, who are often the only adults in their setting, opportunities for mentoring and coaching are often informal and depend on the individual educator's professional peer network.

See Appendix C for additional highlights from interviews.

Supervision

Although supervisors and coaches/mentors may use similar principles and strategies to communicate pedagogical knowledge to an educator, the two do not have the same roles. Mentors must establish a trusting relationship with practitioners. This relationship allows practitioners to be comfortable in sharing any challenges they may be experiencing and to be willing to risk making errors in the process of learning. Supervisors have duties that can be inconsistent with a true mentoring relationship— primarily the authority to make decisions that can affect the practitioner's employment status. If practitioners are being evaluated in relation to their employment, they are unlikely to be open and sharing with their mentor (Lloyd and Modlin, 2012; Whitebook and Bellm, 2013). In today's early childhood environment, however, the same person may be asked to act as both a supervisor and a mentor. If this is the case, it is imperative that the mentor/supervisor be explicit about what function she or he is performing at a specific time (Chu, 2014).

Reflective Practice

Reflective practice is considered a key tool for professional learning. Rodgers and Rodgers (2007) define reflection as "a careful self-analysis of one's own work" (p. 60), and identify necessary components of reflective practice:

- questioning assumptions,
- identifying alternatives,
- weighing options,
- deliberating on how to proceed,
- choosing courses of action,
- planning how to proceed, and
- implementing one's plan.

By reflecting on the relationship between their own knowledge, skills, personal experiences, attitudes, and beliefs and their current teaching practices, educators become open to new ideas, willing to try new approaches, and motivated to refine their methods (Chu, 2014; Im et al., 2007).

According to Peterson and colleagues (Peterson et al., 2009, p. 501) "coaching for self-reflection is a collaborative model in which the coach and the teacher work in partnership to make more effective decisions about classroom instruction." A study of the coaching conversation model implemented in the Minnesota Reading First Professional Development Program identified the use of concrete information about the teacher's instruction as an essential component to self-reflection that leads to reviewing their practice and identifying ways of changing or altering their practice (Peterson et al., 2009).

Although reflection is considered by many to be a powerful tool, both external and internal factors may limit its effectiveness. The culture of the school may be such that it poses barriers to the changes the educator would like to make. The teacher's willingness or ability to take action to modify his or her teaching practices also may limit the benefit of reflection (Rodgers and Rodgers, 2007).

Perspectives from the Field

To improve professional learning and help translate theory into practice, the working environment needs to be adjusted to allow space and dedicated time for more ongoing practice supports like reflective practice, mentoring, coaching, and reflective supervision to take place in a meaningful way.

―――――――――――

See Appendix C for additional highlights from interviews.

Professional Learning Communities

Professional learning communities are collaborative learning groups participating together in inquiry, reflective dialogue, use of data to determine student and educator learning needs, and shared professional learning, with the shared goal of improving the effectiveness of educators and student outcomes (Bolam et al., 2005; Learning Forward, 2014a; Saunders et al., 2009). Learning Forward (2014a) has described learning communities this way:

> [L]earning within communities requires continuous improvement, promotes collective responsibility, and supports alignment of individual, team, school, and school system goals. Learning communities convene regularly and frequently during the workday to engage in collaborative professional learning to strengthen their practice and increase student results. Learning community members are accountable to one another to achieve the shared goals of the school and school system and work in transparent, authentic settings that support their improvement. Communities of learners may be various sizes, include members with similar or different roles or responsibilities, and meet frequently face-to-face, virtually, or through a combination.

In their examination of effective professional learning communities, Bolam and colleagues (2005, p. i) found that such a community "fully exhibits eight key characteristics: shared values and vision; collective responsibility for pupils' learning; collaboration focused on learning; individual and collective professional learning; reflective professional enquiry; openness, networks and partnerships; inclusive membership; mutual trust, respect and support." The authors link these characteristics to benefits for both students (improved attendance, interest in learning, and extent of learning) and teachers (greater professional learning and improvements in practice and morale). For example, in a quasi-experimental study Saunders and colleagues (2009) found that school-based training for principals and teacher leaders on how to stabilize team settings and use explicit protocols for grade-level meetings was associated with greater achievement growth over 3 years on state-mandated tests and an achievement index. Zaslow and colleagues (2010) identify additional important features of professional learning communities: including teachers from the same classrooms or schools, which aids in sustaining the techniques and skills that are imparted; including administrators, which helps maintain consistency in the messages teachers receive; and including teachers of different age groups or grades, which can support continuity in children's educational experiences over time.

Perspectives from the Field

"It's more motivating to folks to be in a cohort of teammates or other professionals."

Educators in family childcare can be isolated without access to the professional supports derived from working with other teachers in a center-based setting. Some family childcare providers have access to ad hoc community-based associations or networks from which they obtain support, receive training, or reflect together with peers.

See Appendix C for additional highlights from interviews.

Conclusion About Professional Learning During Ongoing Practice

The general characteristics of effective professional learning during ongoing practice have been identified, yet there is variability in the availability of and access to high-quality learning activities across professional roles and practice settings for professionals who work with children from birth through age 8. Expectations for ongoing professional learning need to be more consistent across professional roles, and systems and incentives need to be strengthened so that standards and best practices will be adopted and implemented more consistently and rigorously in available professional learning activities. Factors that affect the availability of and access to high-quality professional learning during ongoing professional practice include leadership; funding; regu-

latory and incentive systems; coordination among professional learning systems and activities; and the ability of educators to engage in these activities, which includes consideration of time and financial resources.

REFERENCES

Abdulhamid, L., and H. Venkat. 2014. Research-led development of primary school teachers' mathematical knowledge for teaching: A case study. *Education as Change* 18:S137-S150.

Aikens, N., L. Tarullo, L. Hulsey, C. Ross, J. West, and Y. Xue. 2010. *A year in Head Start: Children, families and programs*. Washington, DC: U.S. Department of Health and Human Services, Administration for Children and Families.

Alhamisi, J. C. 2008. Comparison of alternative and traditional teacher preparation programs for first year special education teachers in northwest Ohio. Doctoral dissertation, University of Toledo, Toledo, OH.

Ball, D. L., and D. K. Cohen. 1999. *Instruction, capacity, and improvement*. Philadelphia: University of Pennsylvania, Graduate School of Education, Consortium for Policy Research in Education Publications.

Barnett, W. S., M. E. Carolan, J. Fitzgerald, and J. H. Squires. 2012. *The state of preschool 2012: State preschool yearbook*. Rutgers, NJ: National Institute for Early Education Research.

Berends, M., S. N. Kirby, S. Naftel, and C. McKelvey. 2001. *Implementation and performance in new American schools: Three years into scale-up*. Santa Monica, CA: RAND Corporation.

Biancarosa, G., and A. S. Bryk. 2011. Effect of literacy collaborative professional development: A summary of findings. *Journal of Reading Recovery* 10:25-32.

Biancarosa, G., A. S. Bryk, and E. R. Dexter. 2010. Assessing the value-added effects of literacy collaborative professional development on student learning. *Elementary School Journal* 111(1):7-34.

Birman, B. F., K. C. LeFloch, A. Klekotka, M. Ludwig, J. Taylor, K. Walters, A. Wayne, and K. S. Yoon. 2007. *State and local implementation of the No Child Left Behind Act, Volume II—teacher quality under NCLB: Interim report*. Washington, DC: U.S. Department of Education, Office of Planning, Evaluation and Policy Development, Policy and Program Studies Service.

Blank, R. K., and N. de las Alas. 2009. *The effects of teacher professional development on gains in student achievement: How meta analysis provides scientific evidence useful to education leaders*. Washington, DC: Council of Chief State School Officers.

Blömeke, S., U. Suhl, and G. Kaiser. 2011. Teacher education effectiveness: Quality and equity of future primary teachers' mathematics and mathematics pedagogical content knowledge. *Journal of Teacher Education* 62(2):154-171.

Bobis, J., B. A. Clarke, D. M. Clarke, T. Gill, R. J. Wright, J. M. Young-Loveridge, and P. Gould. 2005. Supporting teachers in the development of young children's mathematical thinking: Three large scale cases. *Mathematics Education Research Journal* 16(3):27-57.

Bodilly, S. J. 1998. *Lessons from new American schools' scale-up phase*. Santa Monica, CA: RAND Education.

Bolam, R., A. McMahon, L. Stoll, S. Thomas, M. Wallace, A. Greenwood, K. Hawkey, M. Ingram, and A. S. Atkinson. 2005. *Creating and sustaining effective professional learning communities*. Nottingham, UK: Department for Education and Skills.

Borman, G. D., G. M. Hewes, L. T. Overman, and S. Brown. 2003. Comprehensive school reform and achievement: A meta-analysis. *Review of Educational Research* 73:125-230.

Bornfreund, L. A. 2011. *Getting in sync: Revamping licensing and preparation for teachers in pre-K, kindergarten and the early grades.* Washington, DC: New America Foundation.

Brady, S., T. Smith, M. Gillis, M. Lavalette, L. Liss-Bronstein, E. Lowe, W. North, E. Russo, and T. D. Wilder. 2009. First grade teachers' knowledge of phonological awareness and code concepts: Examining gains from an intensive form of professional development and corresponding teacher attitudes. *Reading and Writing* 22(4):425-455.

Brendefur, J., S. Strother, K. Thiede, C. Lane, and M. Surges-Prokop. 2013. A professional development program to improve math skills among preschool children in Head Start. *Early Childhood Education Journal* 41(3):187-195.

Bright, G. W., A. H. Bowman, and N. N. Vacc. 1997. Teachers' frameworks for understanding children's mathematical thinking. In *Proceedings of the 21st Conference of the International Group for the Psychology of Mathematics Education.* Vol. 2, edited by E. Pehkonen. Lahti, Finland: University of Helsinki. Pp. 105-112.

Brown, A. L., and J. C. Campione. 1996. Psychological theory and the design of innovative learning environments: On procedures, principles, and systems. In *Innovations in learning: New environments for education,* edited by L. Schauble and R. Glaser. Mahwah, NJ: Erlbaum. Pp. 289-325.

Bryk, A. S., P. B. Sebring, E. Allensworth, S. Suppescu, and J. Q. Easton. 2010. *Organizing schools for improvement: Lessons from Chicago.* Chicago, IL: University of Chicago Press.

Burchinal, M. R., N. Vandergrift, R. C. Pianta, and A. J. Mashburn. 2010. Threshold analysis of association between child care quality and child outcomes for low-income children in pre-kindergarten programs. *Early Childhood Research Quarterly* 25(2):166-176.

Bureau of Labor Statistics and U.S. Department of Labor. 2014. *News release: Occupational employment and wages—May 2013.* Washington, DC: Bureau of Labor Statistics.

Buysse, V., D. C. Castro, and E. Peisner-Feinberg. 2010. Effects of a professional development program on classroom practices and outcomes for Latino dual language learners. *Early Childhood Research Quarterly* 25(2):194-206.

Byrnes, D. A., G. Kiger, and Z. Shechtman. 2003. Evaluating the use of group interviews to select students into teacher-education programs. *Journal of Teacher Education* 54(2): 163-172.

CAEP (Council for the Accreditation of Educator Preparation). 2013. *CAEP interim standards for accreditation of educator preparation.* http://caepnet.org/standards/interim-standards (accessed March 15, 2015).

Carlisle, J. F., and D. Berebitsky. 2010. Literacy coaching as a component of professional development. *Reading and Writing* 24(7):773-800.

Carlisle, J. F., B. Kelcey, B. Rowan, and G. Phelps. 2011. Teachers' knowledge about early reading: Effects on students' gains in reading achievement. *Journal of Research on Educational Effectiveness* 4(4):289-321.

Carpenter, T. P., E. H. Fennema, P. L. Peterson, and D. A. Carey. 1988. Teacher's pedagogical content knowledge of students' problem solving in elementary arithmetic. *Journal for Research in Mathematics Education* 19:385-401.

Certo, J. L. 2005. Support, challenge, and the two-way street: Perceptions of a beginning second-grade teacher and her quality mentor. *Journal of Early Childhood Teacher Education* 26:3-21.

CHEA (Council for Higher Education Accreditation). 2008. *Council for Higher Education Accreditation: Fact sheet #1.* Washington, DC: CHEA.

———. 2010. *Recognition of accrediting organizations: Policy and procedures.* Washington, DC: CHEA.

———. 2015. *Information about accreditation.* http://www.chea.org/pdf/fact_sheet_1_profile.pdf (accessed January 8, 2015).

Child Care Aware of America. 2014. *Training requirements*. http://www.naccrra.org/about-child-care/state-child-care-licensing/training-requirements (accessed January 8, 2015).

Child Care Services Association. 2013. *Working in early care and education in North Carolina: 2012 workforce study*. Chapel Hill, NC: Child Care Services Association.

Chu, M. 2014. *Developing mentoring and coaching relationships in early care and education: A reflective approach*. Boston, MA: Pearson.

Clarke, D. 1994. Ten key principles from research for the professional development of mathematics teachers. In *Professional development for teachers of mathematics*, edited by D. B. Aichele and A. F. Coxford. Reston, VA: National Council of Teachers of Mathematics. Pp. 37-48.

Clements, D. H., and J. Sarama. 2002. Teaching with computers in early childhood education: Strategies and professional development. *Journal of Early Childhood Teacher Education* 23:215-226.

———. 2008. Experimental evaluation of the effects of a research-based preschool mathematics curriculum. *American Educational Research Journal* 45(2):443-494.

———. 2012. Learning and teaching early and elementary mathematics. In *Instructional strategies for improving students' learning: Focus on early reading and mathematics*, edited by J. S. Carlson and J. R. Levin. Charlotte, NC: Information Age Publishing. Pp. 107-162.

———. 2014. Learning and teaching early math: The learning trajectories approach. New York: Routledge, Taylor & Francis Group.

Clements, D. H., J. Sarama, M. E. Spitler, A. A. Lange, and C. B. Wolfe. 2011. Mathematics learned by young children in an intervention based on learning trajectories: A large-scale cluster randomized trial. *Journal for Research in Mathematics Education* 42(2):127-166.

Clements, D. H., J. Sarama, C. B. Wolfe, and M. E. Spitler. 2013. Longitudinal evaluation of a scale-up model for teaching mathematics with trajectories and technologies: Persistence of effects in the third year. *American Educational Research Journal* 50(4):812-850.

Cobb, P., K. McClain, T. d. S. Lamberg, and C. Dean. 2003. Situating teachers' instructional practices in the institutional setting of the school and district. *Educational Researcher* 32(6):13-24.

Coburn, C. E. 2003. Rethinking scale: Moving beyond numbers to deep and lastsing change. *Educational Researcher* 32:3-12.

Cohen, D. K. 1996. Rewarding teachers for student performance. In *Rewards and reforms: Creating educational incentives that work*, edited by S. H. Fuhrman and J. A. O'Day. San Francisco, CA: Jossey Bass. Pp. 61-112.

Cohen-Vogel, L. 2005. Federal role in teacher quality: "Redefinition" or policy alignment? *Educational Policy* 19(1):18-43.

Copley, J. V. 2004. The early childhood collaborative: A professional development model to communicate and implement the standards. In *Engaging young children in mathematics: Standards for early childhood mathematics education*, edited by D. H. Clements, J. Sarama, and A.-M. DiBiase. Mahwah, NJ: Lawrence Erlbaum Associates. Pp. 401-414.

Costa, A., and R. Garmston. 1994. *The art of cognitive coaching: Supervision for intelligent teaching. Training syllabus, equity and choice*. Sacramento, CA: Institute for Intelligent Behavior.

Coulter, T., and B. Vandal. 2007. *Community colleges and teacher preparation: Roles, issues and opportunities*. Issue paper. Denver, CO: Education Commission of the States.

Darling-Hammond, L. 1996. Restructuring schools for high performance. In *Rewards and reform: Creating educational incentives that work*, edited by S. H. Fuhrman and J. A. O'Day. San Francisco, CA: Jossey-Bass. Pp. 144-192.

———. 1998. Teachers and teaching: Testing policy hypotheses from a national commission report. *Educational Researcher* 27:5-15.

Drake, C., T. J. Land, and A. M. Tyminski. 2014. Using educative curriculum materials to support the development of prospective teachers' knowledge. *Educational Researcher* 43(3):154-162.

Early, D., and P. Winton. 2001. Preparing the workforce: Early childhood teacher preparation at 2- and 4-year institutes of higher education. *Early Childhood Research Quarterly* 16:285-306.

Elmore, R. F. 1996. Getting to scale with good educational practices. *Harvard Educational Review* 66:1-25.

Ernst, B., D. A. Hollinger, and J. Knight. 2005. Professors of practice. *Academe* 91(1):60-61.

Federal Interagency Forum on Child and Family Statistics. 2013. *America's children: Key national indicators of well-being, 2013*. Washington, DC: Federal Interagency Forum on Child and Family Statistics.

Feiman-Nemser, S. 2012. *Teachers as learners*. Cambridge, MA: Harvard Education Press.

Feistritzer, C. E. 2011. *Profile of teachers in the U.S., 2011*. Washington, DC: National Center for Education Information.

Feistritzer, C. E., and C. K. Haar. 2008. *Alternate routes to teaching*. Upper Saddle River, NJ: Pearson/Merrill/Prentice Hall.

Fullan, M. 1982. *The meaning of educational change*. New York: Teachers College Press.

———. 1992. *Successful school improvement: The implementation perspective and beyond*. Buckingham, England, and Philadelphia, PA: Open University Press.

———. 2000. The return of large-scale reform. *Journal of Educational Change* 1(1):5-28.

García, E. E. 2005. *Teaching and learning in two languages: Bilingualism and schooling in the United States*. New York: Teachers College Press.

Garet, M. S., A. C. Porter, L. Desimone, B. F. Birman, and K. S. Yoon. 2001. What makes professional development effective? Results from a national sample of teachers. *American Educational Research Journal* 38:915-945.

Garet, M. S., S. Cronen, M. Eaton, A. Kurki, M. Ludwig, W. Jones, K. Uekawa, A. Falk, H. S. Bloom, F. Doolittle, P. Zhu, and L. Sztejnberg. 2008. *The impact of two professional development interventions on early reading instruction and achievement (NCEE 2008-4030)*. Washington, DC: National Center for Education Evaluation and Regional Assistance, Institute of Education Sciences, U.S. Department of Education.

Gersten, R., J. Dimino, M. Jayanthi, J. S. Kim, and L. E. Santoro. 2010. Teacher study group: Impact of the professional development model on reading instruction and student outcomes in first grade classrooms. *American Educational Research Journal* 47(3):694-739.

Glennan, T. K., S. J. Bodilly, J. Galegher, and K. A. Kerr. 2004. *Expanding the reach of education reforms: Perspectives from leaders in the scale-up of educational interventions*. Santa Monica, CA: RAND Corporation.

Goldrick, L., D. Barlin, D. Osta, and J. Burn. 2012. *Review of state policies on teacher induction*. Santa Cruz, CA: New Teacher Center.

Gupta, S. S., and J. Daniels. 2012. Coaching and professional development in early childhood classrooms: Current practices and recommendations for the future. *NHSA Dialog* 15(2):206-220.

Guskey, T. R., ed. 2000. *Evaluating professional development*. Thousand Oaks, CA: Corwin Press.

Hall, G. E., and S. M. Hord. 2001. *Implementing change: Patterns, principles, and potholes*. Boston, MA: Allyn & Bacon.

Hemmeter, M. L., P. Snyder, K. Kinder, and K. Artman. 2011. Impact of performance feedback delivered via electronic mail on preschool teachers' use of descriptive praise. *Early Childhood Research Quarterly* 26(1):96-109.

HigherEdJobs. 2014a. *Adjunct instructor, early childhood education-administrator creden-tial*. http://www.higheredjobs.com/faculty/details.cfm?JobCode=175987473&Title=Adjunct%20Instructor%2C%20Early%20Childhood%20Education-Administrator%20Credential (accessed November 26, 2014).

———. 2014b. *Dept. of elementary and early childhood education, assistant professor*. http://www.higheredjobs.com/faculty/details.cfm?JobCode=175970389&Title=Dept%2E%20of%20Elementary%20and%20Early%20Childhood%20Education%2C%20Assistant%20Professor%20%28Generalist%29 (accessed November 26, 2014).

———. 2014c. *Part-time child development instructor (pool)*. http://www.higheredjobs.com/faculty/details.cfm?JobCode=175987713&Title=Part-Time%20Child%20Development%20Instructor%20%28Pool%29 (accessed November 26, 2014).

———. 2014d. *Urban early childhood/elementary education faculty*. http://www.higheredjobs.com/faculty/details.cfm?JobCode=175976841&Title=Urban%20Early%20Childhood%2FElementary%20Education%20Faculty%20%282%20positions%29 (accessed November 26, 2014).

Hill, H. C., B. Rowan, and D. L. Ball. 2005. Effects of teachers' mathematical knowledge for teaching on student achievement. *American Educational Research Journal* 42:371-406.

Howes, C., B. K. Hamre, and R. C. Pianta. 2012. *Effective early childhood professional development: Improving teacher practice and child outcomes*. Baltimore, MD: Paul H. Brookes Publishing Co.

Hsieh, W.-Y., M. L. Hemmeter, J. A. McCollum, and M. M. Ostrosky. 2009. Using coaching to increase preschool teachers' use of emergent literacy teaching strategies. *Early Childhood Research Quarterly* 24:229-247.

Huberman, M. 1992. Critical introduction. In *Successful school improvement*, edited by M. G. Fullan. Philadelphia, PA: Open University Press. Pp. 1-20.

Hutinger, P. L., and J. Johanson. 2000. Implementing and maintaining an effective early child-hood comprehensive technology system. *Topics in Early Childhood Special Education* 20(3):159-173.

Hutinger, P. L., C. Bell, M. Beard, J. Bond, J. Johanson, and C. Terry. 1998. *The early child-hood emergent literacy technology research study. Final report*. Washington, DC: Office of Special Education and Rehabilitative Services.

Im, J. H., C. A. Osborn, S. Y. Sanchez, and E. K. Thorp. 2007. *Cradling literacy, building teachers' skill to nurture early language and literacy from birth to five: A ZERO TO THREE training curriculum*. Washington, DC: Zero to Three.

Ingersoll, R. M., and H. May. 2011. The minority teacher shortage: Fact or fable? *Education Week*. http://www.edweek.org/ew/articles/2011/09/01/kappan_ingersoll.html (accessed January 7, 2015).

Isner, T., K. Tout, M. Zaslow, M. Soli, K. Quinn, L. Rothenberg, and M. Burkhauser. 2011. *Coaching in early care and education programs and Quality Rating and Improvement Systems (QRIS): Identifying promising features*. Washington, DC: Child Trends, Inc.

Johnson, J. E., R. Fiene, K. McKinnon, and S. Babu. 2010. *Policy brief: Penn State study of early childhood teacher education*. University Park, PA: Pennsylvania State University.

Johnson, S. M., S. E. Birkeland, and H. G. Peske. 2005. Life in the fast track: How states seek to balance incentives and quality in alternative teacher certification programs. *Educational Policy* 19(1):63-89.

Kaser, J. S., P. S. Bourexis, S. Loucks-Horsley, and S. A. Raizen. 1999. *Enhancing program quality in science and mathematics*. Thousand Oaks, CA: Corwin Press.

Kennedy, M. 1998. *Form and substance of inservice teacher education (research monograph no. 13)*. Madison: University of Wisconsin-Madison, National Institute for Science Education.

Kipnis, F., M. Whitebook, L. Austin, and L. Sakai. 2013. *Assessing the quality of New Jersey's professional preparation and professional development system for the early learning workforce.* Berkeley: University of California, Berkeley, Center for the Study of Child Care Employment.

Klingner, J. K., S. Ahwee, P. Pilonieta, and R. Menendez. 2003. Barriers and facilitators in scaling up research-based practices. *Exceptional Children* 69:411-429.

Landry, S. H., J. L. Anthony, P. R. Swank, and P. Monseque-Bailey. 2009. Effectiveness of comprehensive professional development for teachers of at-risk preschoolers. *Journal of Educational Psychology* 101(2):448-465.

Lead Commission. 2012. *Poll finds support for use of technology.* http://www.leadcommission. org/poll-finds-overwhelming-support-for-greater-use-of-technology-in-k-12-education-among-teachers-and-parents-a-diverse-sampling-of-u-s-teachers-and-parents-strongly-believe-schools-should-increase-ado (accessed January 9, 2015).

Learning Forward. 2014a. *Learning communities.* http://learningforward.org/standards/learning-communities#.U_PHUbxdX6I (accessed August 22, 2014).

———. 2014b. *Standards for professional learning: Quick reference guide.* Oxford, OH: Learning Forward: Professional Learning Association.

Learning Point Associates. 2005. *Quality teaching in at-risk schools: Key issues.* Washington, DC: Learning Point Associates.

Levine, A. 2013. *Fixing how we train U.S. teachers.* http://hechingerreport.org/content/fixing-how-we-train-u-s-teachers_12449 (accessed November 24, 2014).

Lloyd, C. M., and E. L. Modlin. 2012. *Coaching as a key component in teachers' professional development: Improving classroom practices in Head Start settings.* Washington, DC: Office of Planning, Research and Evaluation; Administration for Children and Families; U.S. Department of Health and Human Services.

Loeb, S., L. C. Miller, and K. O. Strunk. 2009. *The state role in teacher professional development and education throughout teachers' careers.* Stanford, CA: Stanford University, Institute for Research on Education Policy & Practice.

Maxwell, K. L., C. I. Lim, and D. M. Early. 2006. *Early childhood teacher preparation programs in the United States: National report.* Chapel Hill: University of North Carolina, Frank Porter Graham Child Development Institute.

NAEYC (National Association for the Education of Young Children). 2011a. *Early childhood associate degree accreditation: Accreditation handbook.* Washington, DC: NAEYC.

———. 2011b. *National Association for the Education of Young Children early childhood associate degree accreditation: Accreditation handbook.* http://www.naeyc.org/ecada/files/ecada/AccreditationHandbook.pdf (accessed March 4, 2015).

———. n.d. *Early childhood teacher certification: The current state policies landscape and opportunities.* Washington, DC: NAEYC.

National Partnership for Teaching in At-Risk Schools. 2005. *Qualified teachers for at-risk schools: A national imperative.* Washington, DC: National Partnership for Teaching in At-Risk Schools.

NCTQ (National Council on Teacher Quality). 2012. *State of the states 2012: Teacher effectiveness policies.* Washington, DC: NCTQ.

Nettles, S. M. 1993. Coaching in community settings. *Equity and Choice* 9(2):35-37.

New Mexico State University. 2014. *Early childhood education.* http://college.education.nmsu. edu/advising/ugradmajors/early-childhood (accessed March 4, 2015).

NMP (National Mathematics Advisory Panel). 2008. *Foundations for success: The final report of the National Mathematics Advisory Panel.* Washington DC: U.S. Department of Education, Office of Planning, Evaluation and Policy Development.

NRC (National Research Council). 2010. *Preparing teachers: Building evidence for sound policy.* Washington, DC: The National Academies Press.

————. 2012. *Education for life and work: Developing transferable knowledge and skills in the 21st century*, edited by J. W. Pellegrino and M. L. Hilton. Washington, DC: The National Academies Press.

NSECE (National Survey of Early Care and Education). 2011. *Center-based provider questionnaire*. Washington, DC: Office of Planning, Research, and Evaluation; Administration for Children and Families; U.S. Department of Health and Human Services.

————. 2013. *Number and characteristics of Early Care and Education (ECE) teachers and caregivers: Initial findings from the National Survey of Early Care and Education (NSECE)*. Washington, DC: Office of Planning, Research, and Evaluation; Administration for Children and Families; U.S. Department of Health and Human Services.

O'Connor, R. E., A. Notari-Syverson, and P. F. Vadasy. 1996. Ladders to literacy: The effects of teacher-led phonological activities for kindergarten children with and without disabilities. *Exceptional Children* 63(1):117-130.

O*Net Online. 2011. *Education teachers, postsecondary*. http://www.onetonline.org/link/summary/25-1081.00 (accessed December 15, 2014).

Pellegrino, J. W. 2007. From early reading to high school mathematics: Matching case studies of four educational innovations against principles for effective scale up. In *Scale up in practice*, edited by B. Schneider and S.-K. McDonald. Lanham, MD: Rowman and Littlefield. Pp. 131-139.

Perry, A. 2011. *Revision: Teacher preparation programs: A critical vehicle to drive student achievement*. Durham, NC: James B. Hunt, Jr. Institute for Educational Leadership Policy.

Peterson, D. S., B. M. Taylor, B. Burnham, and R. Schock. 2009. Reflective coaching conversations: A missing piece. *The Reading Teacher* 62(6):500-509.

Peterson, P. L., T. P. Carpenter, and E. H. Fennema. 1989. Teachers' knowledge of students' knowledge in mathematics problem solving: Correlational and case analyses. *Journal of Educational Psychology* 81:558-569.

Pianta, R. C., R. Hitz, and B. West. 2010. *Increasing the application of developmental sciences knowledge in educator preparation: Policy and practice issues*. Washington, DC: National Council for Accreditation of Teacher Education.

Piasta, S. B., C. M. Connor, B. J. Fishman, and F. J. Morrison. 2009. Teachers' knowledge of literacy concepts, classroom practices, and student reading growth. *Journal of Poverty* 13(3):224-248.

Powell, D. R., and K. E. Diamond. 2011. Improving the outcomes of coaching-based professional development interventions. In *Handbook of early literacy research*. Vol. 3, edited by S. B. Neuman and D. K. Dickinson. New York: Guilford Press. Pp. 295-307.

Powell, D. R., K. E. Diamond, M. R. Burchinal, and M. J. Koehler. 2010. Effects of an early literacy professional development intervention on Head Start teachers and children. *Journal of Educational Psychology* 102(2):299-312.

Powell, D. R., K. E. Diamond, and M. R. Burchinal. 2012. Using coaching-based professional development to improve Head Start teachers' support of children's oral language skills. In *Effective professional development in early childhood education: Improving teacher practice and child outcomes*, edited by C. Howes, B. K. Hamre, and R. C. Pianta. Baltimore, MD: Paul H. Brookes Publishing Co. Pp. 13-29.

Prieto, L. P., S. Villagrá-Sobrino, I. M. Jorrin-Abellán, A. Martinez-Monés, and Y. Dimitriadis. 2011. Recurrent routines: Analyzing and supporting orchestration in technology-enhanced primary classrooms. *Computers and Education* 57(1):1214-1227.

Rike, C. J., and L. K. Sharp. 2008. Assessing preservice teachers' dispositions: A critical dimension of professional preparation. *Childhood Education* 84(3):150-153.

Rodgers, A., and E. M. Rodgers. 2007. Scaffolding reflection. In *The effective literacy coach: Using inquiry to support teaching and learning*. New York: Teachers College, Columbia University.

Rogers, E. M. 2003. *Diffusion of innovations*. New York: Free Press.

Saluja, G., D. M. Early, and R. M. Clifford. 2002. Demographic characteristics of early childhood teachers and structural elements of early care and education in the United States. *Early Childhood Research & Practice* 4(1).

Sarama, J. 2002. Listening to teachers: Planning for professional development. *Teaching Children Mathematics* 9:36-39.

Sarama, J., and D. H. Clements. 2009. *Early childhood mathematics education research: Learning trajectories for young children*. New York and London: Routledge.

———. 2013. Lessons learned in the implementation of the triad scale-up model: Teaching early mathematics with trajectories and technologies. In *Applying implementation science in early childhood programs and systems*, edited by T. G. Halle, A. J. Metz, and I. Martinez-Beck. Baltimore, MD: Paul H. Brookes Publishing Co. Pp. 173-191.

Sarama, J., and A.-M. DiBiase. 2004. The professional development challenge in preschool mathematics. In *Engaging young children in mathematics: Standards for early childhood mathematics education*, edited by D. H. Clements, J. Sarama, and A.-M. DiBiase. Mahwah, NJ: Lawrence Erlbaum Associates. Pp. 415-446.

Sarama, J., D. H. Clements, and J. J. Henry. 1998. Network of influences in an implementation of a mathematics curriculum innovation. *International Journal of Computers for Mathematical Learning* 3(2):113-148.

Sarama, J., D. H. Clements, P. Starkey, A. Klein, and A. Wakeley. 2008. Scaling up the implementation of a pre-kindergarten mathematics curriculum: Teaching for understanding with trajectories and technologies. *Journal of Research on Educational Effectiveness* 1:89-119.

Sarama, J., D. H. Clements, C. B. Wolfe, and M. E. Spitler. 2012a. Longitudinal evaluation of a scale-up model for teaching mathematics with trajectories and technologies. *Journal of Research on Educational Effectiveness* 5(2):105-135.

Sarama, J., A. A. Lange, D. H. Clements, and C. B. Wolfe. 2012b. The impacts of an early mathematics curriculum on oral language and literacy. *Early Childhood Research Quarterly* 27(3):489-502.

Saunders, W. M., C. N. Goldenberg, and R. Gallimore. 2009. Increasing achievement by focusing grade-level teams on improving classroom learning: A prospective, quasi-experimental study of Title I schools. *American Educational Research Journal* 46(4):1006-1033.

Schoen, H. L., K. J. Cebulla, K. F. Finn, and C. Fi. 2003. Teacher variables that relate to student achievement when using a standards-based curriculum. *Journal for Research in Mathematics Education* 34(3):228-259.

Sheridan, S. M., C. P. Edwards, C. A. Marvin, and L. L. Knoche. 2009. Professional development in early childhood programs: Process issues and research needs. *Early Education & Development* 20(3):377-401.

Showers, B., B. Joyce, and B. Bennett. 1987. Synthesis of research on staff development: A framework for future study and a state-of-the-art analysis. *Educational Leadership* 45(3):77-87.

Smith, D. D., G. Pion, N. C. Tyler, P. Sindelar, and M. Rosenberg. 2001. *The shortage of special education faculty: Why it is happening, why it matters, and what we can do about it*. Washington, DC: U.S. Department of Education, Office of Special Education Programs.

Smith, D. D., B. E. Montrosse, S. M. Robb, N. C. Tyler, and C. Young. 2011. *Assessing trends in leadership: Special education's capacity to produce a highly qualified workforce*. 2011 final report: Narrative. Claremont, CA: Claremont Graduate University, School of Educational Studies.

Snipes, J. C., F. C. Doolittle, and C. Herlihy. 2002. *Foundations for success: Case studies of how urban school systems improve student achievement.* Washington, DC: Council of the Great City Schools.

Sowder, J. T. 2007. The mathematical education and development of teachers. In *Second handbook of research on mathematics teaching and learning.* Vol. 1, edited by F. K. Lester, Jr. New York: Information Age Publishing. Pp. 157-223.

Teach For America Inc. 2015. *Early childhood education initiative.* https://www.teachforamerica.org/our-organization/special-initiatives/early-childhood-education (accessed February 4, 2015).

Thomas, G., and A. Tagg. 2004. *An evaluation of the early numeracy project 2003.* Wellington, NZ: Ministry of Education.

University of California, San Diego. 2013. *Professor of practice implementation guidelines.* http://academicaffairs.ucsd.edu/_files/aps/docs/Prof-of-Practice-Implem-Guidelines.pdf (accessed December 15, 2014).

University of Oklahoma. n.d. *Requirements for the bachelor of science in education and certification in field of study.* http://checksheets.ou.edu/14checksheets/earlychd-2014.pdf (accessed March 4, 2015).

University of Pittsburgh School of Education. 2015. *Master of education in early childhood education.* http://www.education.pitt.edu/AcademicDepartments/InstructionLearning/Programs/EarlyChildhoodEducation/MasterofEducationinEarlyChildhoodEducation.aspx (accessed March 4, 2015).

U.S. Department of Education. 1998. *1998 amendments to Higher Education Act of 1965.* http://www2.ed.gov/policy/highered/leg/hea98/sec201.html (accessed January 8, 2015).

———. 2014. *Accreditation in the United States.* http://www2.ed.gov/admins/finaid/accred/accreditation_pg13.html (accessed January 8, 2015).

———. n.d. *Teach grant.* https://studentaid.ed.gov/types/grants-scholarships/teach#eligible-programs (accessed January 8, 2015).

U.S. Department of Education and Office of Postsecondary Education. 2013. *Preparing and credentialing the nation's teachers: The secretary's ninth report on teacher quality.* Washington, DC: U.S. Department of Education.

U.S. Department of Education Office of Innovation and Improvement. 2004. *Innovations in education: Alternative routes to teacher certification.* http://purl.access.gpo.gov/GPO/LPS61260 (accessed March 4, 2015).

U.S. Department of Health and Human Services and Administration for Children and Families. n.d. *Early Head Start National Resource Center.* http://eclkc.ohs.acf.hhs.gov/hslc/tta-system (accessed January 8, 2015).

Wartella, E., C. K. Blackwell, A. R. Lauricella, and M. B. Robb. 2013. *Technology in the lives of educators and early childhood programs: 2012 survey of early childhood educators.* Latrobe, PA: Saint Vincent College, Fred Rogers Center for Early Learning and Children's Media.

Whitebook, M. 2014. *Building a skilled teacher workforce: Shared and divergent challenges in early care and education and in grades K-12.* Berkeley: University of California, Berkeley, Institute for Reseach on Labor and Employment.

Whitebook, M., and D. Bellm. 2013. *Supporting teachers as learners: A guide for mentors and coaches in early care and education.* Washington, DC: American Federation of Teachers.

Whitebook, M., and S. Ryan. 2011. *Degrees in context: Asking the right questions about preparing skilled and effective teachers of young children: Preschool policy brief.* New Brunswick, NJ: Rutgers University, National Institute for Early Education Research.

Whitebook, M., L. Sakai, F. Kipnis, Y. Lee, D. Bellm, M. Almaraz, and P. Tran. 2006. *California early care and education workforce study: Licensed child care centeres: Statewide 2006*. Berkeley, CA: University of California, Berkeley, Center for the Study of Child Care Employment and California Child Care Resource and Referral Network.

Whitebook, M., F. Kipnis, and D. Bellm. 2008a. *Diversity and stratification in California's early care and education workforce*. Berkeley: University of California, Berkeley, Center for the Study of Child Care Employment.

Whitebook, M., F. Kipnis, L. Sakai, M. Almaraz, and D. Bellm. 2008b. *Learning together: A study of six B.A. completion cohort programs in early care and education: Year 1 report*. Berkely: University of California, Berkeley, Center for the Study of Child Care Employment, Institute of Industrial Relations.

Whitebook, M., D. Gomby, D. Bellm, L. Sakai, and F. Kipnis. 2009. *Preparing teachers of young children: The current state of knowledge, and a blueprint for the future*. Executive Summary. Berkeley: University of California, Berkeley, Center for the Study of Child Care Employment, Institute for Research on Labor and Employment.

Whitebook, M., F. Kipnis, L. Sakai, and M. Almaraz. 2011. *Learning together: A study of six B.A. completion cohort programs in early care and education: Year 3*. Berkeley: University of California, Berkeley, Center for the Study of Child Care Employment, Institute of Industrial Relations.

Whitebook, M., L. J. E. Austin, S. Ryan, F. Kipnis, M. Almaraz, and L. Sakai. 2012. *By default or by design? Variations in higher education programs for early care and education teachers and their implications for research methodology, policy, and practice*. Executive Summary. Berkely: University of California, Berkeley, Center for the Study of Child Care Employment, Institute of Industrial Relations.

Whitebook, M., D. Schaack, F. Kipnis, L. J. E. Austin, and L. Sakai. 2013. *From aspiration to attainment: Practices that support educational success, Los Angeles universal preschool's child development workforce initiative*. Berkeley: University of California, Berkeley, Center for the Study of Child Care Employment.

Winston, P., S. Atkins-Burnett, Y. Xue, E. Moidduddin, E. Smith, N. Aikens, J. Lyskawa, R. Mason, and S. Sprachman. 2012. *Quality support coaching in LAUP: Findings from the 2011-2012 program year, final report*. Washington, DC: Mathematica Policy Research, First 5 LA.

Wright, R. J., J. Martland, A. K. Stafford, and G. Stanger. 2002. *Teaching number: Advancing children's skills and strategies*. London, UK: Paul Chapman/Sage.

Yoon, K. S., T. Duncan, S. Wen-Yu Lee, B. Scarloss, and K. L. Shapley. 2007. *Reviewing the evidence on how teacher professional development affects student achievement*. Washington, DC: National Center for Educational Evaluation and Regional Assistance, Institute of Education Sciences, U.S. Department of Education.

Young-Loveridge, J. M. 2004. *Patterns of performance and progress on the numeracy projects 2001-2003: Further analysis of the numeracy project data*. Wellington, NZ: Ministry of Education.

Zaslow, M., K. Tout, T. Halle, J. V. Whittaker, and B. Lavelle. 2010. *Toward the identification of features of effective professional development for early childhood educators: Literature review*. Washington, DC: U.S. Department of Education, Office of Planning, Evaluation and Policy Development, Policy and Program Studies Service.

10

Qualification Requirements, Evaluation Systems, and Quality Assurance Systems

This chapter examines three important factors that contribute to workforce development and quality professional practice for educators who work with children from birth through age 8: requirements to qualify for professional practice, evaluation of practice quality, and program accreditation and quality improvement systems. Each of these factors is examined in turn in the sections that follow.

STANDARDIZING QUALITY: REQUIREMENTS TO QUALIFY FOR PROFESSIONAL PRACTICE

Standards for requirements to be qualified to practice are one tool for contributing to the quality of professional practice among those responsible for the care and education of young children. These standards typically are set through systems that establish and administer either legal licenses to practice or credentials, certificates, or endorsements that may be a legal requirement, a condition for funding, or voluntarily adopted by an employer as a condition of employment or augmentation of baseline qualifications. In addition to these systems for individual practitioners, standards for requirements may be set through systems that establish licensing or funding criteria for a program or center.

Current systems vary widely in what is required, depending on what agency or institution has jurisdiction or authority to set qualification requirements; who administers both required and voluntary qualifications; and the professional role, the practice setting, and the age ranges of children served.[1] The following section describes this variety of requirements and examines its implications in light of findings from the science of child development that every setting is a learning environment for young children, and every professional who works with these children has a similarly complex and important role in fostering child development and early learning. The subsequent section then delves in more depth into the issue of variability in degree requirements across professional roles.

Current Qualification Requirements for the Care and Education Workforce

Each of the 50 states (as well as U.S. territories) sets its own qualifications for public school teachers, as well as for teachers, assistant teachers, and directors in licensed early childhood programs and for regulated family childcare centers and home-based childcare providers. Table 10-1 provides an overview of the typical differences in qualification expectations across professional roles and settings. In public school systems, educators are required to be individually licensed or certified. By contrast, in settings outside of elementary schools, with the exception of some prekindergarten programs, it is much rarer for educators to be required to be individually licensed or certified (Kleiner, 2013). In most of these settings, state licensing standards for the program or center set the basic level of health and safety requirements for facilities and the education qualifications for teaching and administrative staff. Most of these programs also are supported by federal, state, and/or private funds that prescribe widely varying expectations for preservice and ongoing training, as well as certification. The exceptions are Head Start and Military Child Care, which set uniform national requirements for teachers and other personnel. Varying qualifications across different types of settings reflect the varying historical purposes of early care and education programs: programs originally conceived primarily as childcare support services for working parents generally set lower teacher standards than those originally designed to provide early education (such as preschools and public prekindergarten programs) (Whitebook, 2014).

---

[1] Terminology indicating that an educator has obtained the required knowledge and experience to be qualified for teaching varies within and across settings and sectors. In school systems, states use one or more terms—"certification," "license," and "credential"—to indicate that a teacher is qualified. In early care and education, a "license" generally indicates that a program, center, or school meets standards rather than referring to educator qualifications, which are more commonly described by the terms "certification" and "credential." Such documentation of qualifications is not required for most early childhood educators, and the education and experience required to qualify for various certificates and credentials vary depending on setting, funding source, and regulatory agency (Whitebook, 2014).

TABLE 10-1 Overview of Differences in Qualification Expectations for Early Childhood Settings and Early Elementary Settings

	K-12 Schools	Early Childhood Settings
Licensure/ Certification	All public school teachers must be licensed or certified through traditional or alternative programs recognized by the state (Exstrom, 2012). Only 23 states require all charter school teachers to be licensed or certified through traditional or alternative programs; 14 states require only a certain percentage of teachers in a charter school to be licensed or certified; 4 states and the District of Columbia leave decisions about licensure or certification to the individual charter school (Exstrom, 2012). Private school teachers typically are not required to be certified or licensed.	Individual teacher certification is uncommon for most lead teachers, although it is more common for those who work in public prekindergarten programs (Kleiner, 2013).[a] Almost all state-funded prekindergarten programs require certification, licensure, or endorsement; some require the same licensure for prekindergarten teachers as for early elementary teachers (Exstrom, 2012).[b] Certification is not routinely linked to successful completion of a degree in many states.
Qualifications	Education requirements are relatively uniform across districts and states. All public school teachers are required to have at least a bachelor's degree and provisional or actual certification before they begin teaching. Typically, successful completion of approved degree or credential programs aligns directly with certification requirements.	Teacher qualifications vary widely based on program types and funding requirements—from little or no education to a bachelor's or higher degree. Each state sets its own teacher qualifications for early care and education (ECE) programs, with the exception of Head Start and Military Child Care, for which teacher qualifications are set by the federal government. In 2012, of the 568,000 center-based teachers and caregivers serving children 3-5 years old, 45.1 percent held a bachelor's degree or higher, 17.4 percent held an associate's degree, 24.3 percent had completed some college, and 13.2 percent had completed high school or less (NSECE, 2013).

continued

TABLE 10-1 Continued

	K-12 Schools	Early Childhood Settings		
		State-Funded Prekindergarten[d]	Head Start	All Other Center-Based Programs[e]
Qualifications (continued)	The vast majority (93 percent) of elementary and middle school teachers held at least a bachelor's degree in 2012 (Department for Professional Employees and AFL-CIO, 2013).[c] Among those, nearly 48 percent held a master's degree or greater (Department for Professional Employees and AFL-CIO, 2013).	• 58 percent of programs require a bachelor's degree for all lead teachers (Barnett et al., 2012, p. 11). • 85 percent of programs require specialized prekindergarten training for lead teachers (Barnett et al., 2012, p. 11). • 29 percent of programs require assistant teachers to have a competency-based certification (Barnett et al., 2012, p. 11), such as the Child Development Associate (CDA) credential (CPR, 2013d).[f]	• At least 50 percent of Head Start teachers nationwide must have a bachelor's or advanced degree in early childhood education, OR a bachelor's or advanced degree in any subject and coursework equivalent to a major relating to ECE, along with experience teaching preschool-age children (Office of Head Start, 2012). • 66 percent of Head Start teachers working with preschoolers held at least a bachelor's degree in 2013 (Office of Head Start, 2013a).[g]	• 17 states require less than a high school diploma or General Educational Development (GED) credential. • 14 states require a high school diploma or GED. • 10 states require clock hours in ECE, credits, or a credential less than a CDA. • 7 states require a CDA credential. • 1 state requires an associate's degree in ECE or a related field. • 1 state requires a bachelor's degree in ECE or a related field (Child Care Aware of America, 2013).

No experience is required for teachers with an associate's, bachelor's, or higher degree in ECE. Degrees in other fields require experience, as determined by the grantee.

In 41 states, no prior experience is required to be employed as a teacher in licensed childcare programs (Barnett et al., 2011).

---

[a] About one-quarter of teachers in public and private preschools are required to meet individual licensing requirements.

[b] Only charter preschools in one state and in Washington, DC, do not require some type of certification for prekindergarten teachers. Certifications in some states are different for prekindergarten teachers who work in school-sponsored and not-school-sponsored settings.

[c] There were 1,981,280 elementary and middle school teachers employed in the United States in 2012.

[d] Aggregated data reported throughout this table are based on 52 state-funded preschool programs (Barnett et al., 2012).

[e] The category "all other center-based programs" includes privately operated childcare and preschools funded by parent fees and/or Child Care Development Fund subsidies. These programs represent a diversity of qualifications for teaching staff.

[f] The CDA credential is a competency-based national certification earned by early childhood educators, often those who work as assistant teachers.

[g] Twenty-seven percent of Early Head Start teachers working with infants and toddlers held at least a bachelor's degree in 2013 (Whitebook, 2014).

SOURCE: Adapted from *Building a Skilled Workforce* (prepared for The Bill & Melinda Gates Foundation) (Whitebook, 2014).

State Public School Licensure for Educators of Children from Birth Through Age 8

State public school licensure systems encompass professional roles that entail working with young children. These systems use a number of different age ranges and combinations of grade levels: some extend from birth through age 5 or up to age 8, while others cover ages in public school settings, extending from prekindergarten or kindergarten to as high as sixth grade or higher in the same license. Many states also have multiple licenses that include some segment of the birth through age 8 range; for example, some states have both a birth through age 8 license and a kindergarten through sixth grade license or a prekindergarten through third grade license and one for kindergarten through fifth or sixth grade (Bornfreund, 2011; Crandall et al., 2014).

As of summer 2014, 27 states and the District of Columbia offered public school teachers' licenses beginning at birth, with some states offering more than one such license. Table 10-2 shows the earliest-age license available across states.

TABLE 10-2 Earliest Points of Available Public School Licensure Across States in 2014

B-Age 4	B-K/Age 5	B-2nd Grade	B-3rd Grade/ Age 8	B-5th Grade	B-6th Grade
Florida	Connecticut	Delaware	Alabama	Georgia	New York
	Kansas	Nevada	Arizona		Wisconsin
	Kentucky	New York	Colorado		
	Maine	Rhode Island	Idaho		
	North Carolina		Illinois		
	Wyoming		Iowa		
			Minnesota		
			Missouri		
			New Hampshire		
			New Jersey		
			New Mexico		
			North Dakota		
			South Dakota		
			Vermont		
			Wisconsin		
			Wyoming		

NOTE: B = birth; K = kindergarten; Pre-K = prekindergarten.
SOURCE: Crandall et al., 2014. The University of Arkansas conducted a study through a contract with the National Academy of Sciences that examined the early childhood public school teacher licenses available in the 50 states and the District of Columbia. Data were collected in summer 2014 through Internet searches and telephone interviews for each of

Of the configurations of licenses available, a birth to age 8/third grade license is the most prevalent (16 states). The next most prevalent is birth through kindergarten/age 5 (6 states). The remainder of the configurations include birth through second grade (4 states), birth through fifth grade (Georgia), birth through age 4 (Florida), and birth through sixth grade (2 states).

Compared with a prior scan conducted in 2009 (Jones et al., 2009), some changes have occurred over time in the available licenses that apply to the birth through age 8 range. Two states (Alabama and New Jersey) have added licensure beginning at birth since 2009, and a third state (Arkansas) is planning to do so in 2015. In the 2009 scan, Alabama was listed as offering an early childhood certificate covering prekindergarten to grade 3; today the state offers an early childhood education license that covers birth through age 8. New Jersey now offers an early childhood education license that covers birth through third grade, while in 2009 it offered a prekindergarten through third grade certificate. In addition, the Arkansas Board of Education, which currently has a K-6 license, is slated to roll out its birth through kindergarten licensure in fall 2015.

Pre-K-3rd Grade/ Age 8	Pre-K	Pre-K-K	Pre-K- 2nd Grade	Pre-K- 6th Grade
Alaska	Mississippi	Michigan	Massachusetts	Oregon
California	Pennsylvania	West Virginia		Texas
Hawaii	West Virginia			
Indiana				
Louisiana				
Maryland				
Montana				
Nebraska				
New Jersey				
Ohio				
Oklahoma				
South Carolina				
Tennessee				
Virginia				
Washington, DC				

the licensing entities. In all cases, telephone interviews were held to confirm the information. However, such data are fluid because they are based on policy decisions that can change as a result of several possible factors.

Conversely, some states that previously had a license from birth have since dropped it. Five states—Indiana, Massachusetts, Nebraska, Oregon, and West Virginia—were identified in 2009 as offering licensure for public school beginning at birth; as of 2014, each offered licensure only beginning at the prekindergarten level. Three of these five states have not abandoned regulation for those involved professionally with infants and toddlers; rather, they now offer different certification programs. The Oregon Department of Education, for example, now offers birth through age 3 early intervention and age 3 through school entry early childhood special education certification for those involved in early intervention work. Massachusetts now offers certificates for professionals working in various roles within the childcare sector. Nebraska's early childhood certificate for those working with children under age 3 can be used for childcare settings and is available for those trained at a minimum of the Child Development Associate credential or bachelor's degree level. Two of the states, however, no longer cover the age span from birth to preschool. The West Virginia Board of Education does not have purview over birth certifications, so it no longer issues licenses covering that age span. Additionally, Indiana now offers a "generalist" early childhood license covering preschool through grade 3 and an early and middle childhood license for teachers of kindergarten through grade 6 (Crandall et al., 2014).

Implications and Consequences of Overlapping State Qualification Standards

In addition to variations in licensure across states, one clear trend is that overlap in state licensure is common. This means that prospective educators can, for example, choose to qualify for a birth to third grade license or a K-8 license (Bornfreund, 2011; Crandall et al., 2014). One of the consequences of this overlap in qualification systems is the possibility that none of the available standards captures the full range of competencies needed for teaching children from birth through age 8. Few states have systems set up in such a way that prospective educators wishing to teach in prekindergarten through third grade only have the option of acquiring a license that is inclusive of early childhood. Because the earliest age span covered in some states ends at or before kindergarten, kindergarten teachers typically obtain a license that extends to the upper elementary grades instead of one focused specifically on the early grades. They are therefore unlikely to have any specific training in early childhood. Florida, like many other states, has overlapping licenses for the early grades and offers an example of the consequences. According to Bornfreund (2011, p. 11):

Teachers seeking a pre-k-third license are expected to identify the sequence of development for typical children as well as to identify atypical development. But teachers seeking a K-6 license are not. Instead, K-6 teacher candidates appear to be expected to exhibit a deeper knowledge and understanding of content areas including math, science, and social studies than pre-k-third candidates (Florida Department of Education, 2011). Ideally, states should set standards that encompass the best of both worlds, requiring teachers in pre-k, kindergarten and the early grades to gain both a strong grasp of math and science content plus developmental knowledge and pedagogical skills.

The structure of licenses also influences how education schools prepare prospective educators. According to Bornfreund (2011), states with overlapping licenses tend also to have overlapping teacher preparation programs. In New Jersey, for example, prospective educators can pursue a prekindergarten through third grade early childhood degree or an elementary degree covering kindergarten through fifth grade. In many states, licenses for these two grade-level spans can be obtained simultaneously in the same program. As a result, these programs may focus on the grades in the middle of this span and neglect the earlier and later grades (Bornfreund, 2011). Take the example of Rider University, whose dual track entails taking the elementary track plus three early childhood courses. Although the course descriptions convey appropriate content, they do not entail field experience in prekindergarten through third grade settings. A student teaching experience is included, but this need not take place in the early grades (Bornfreund, 2011).

Another potential consequence is that licensure structures, in combination with hiring practices, may incentivize educators to obtain the broadest possible degree and license, thereby foregoing more specialized training to prepare them for specific settings and professional roles. Bornfreund (2011, pp. 10-11) illustrates this point by citing the case of Georgia:

> Georgia offers another example of the problems that can come with overlap. The state's birth-kindergarten (B-K) license was created about five years ago to strengthen the early childhood profession. However, prospective teachers who are considering teaching pre-kindergarten or kindergarten can also attain Georgia's P-5 license, which allows them to teach from pre-k through fifth grade. The P-5 license makes teachers more marketable to elementary school principals seeking versatile candidates who can be re-located to multiple grade levels. It also would be more likely to lead to the higher salary and benefits that come with a public school job. With a B-K license, the odds are long that teachers could find jobs with a professional salary unless they were hired by a principal specifically looking for a pre-k or kindergarten teacher who valued their B-K experience over versatility. Teachers in infant and toddler centers, as well as many in preschools, are paid far less than public school teachers.

Prospective educators are likely to pursue the license that makes them less likely to be subject to disparities in compensation and as employable as possible. Hiring decisions can be driven by the grade-level divisions in public school buildings, and the need for flexibility in being able to place educators in different grade levels over time. This may match the groupings of some licenses better than others. In an elementary school that has kindergarten through fifth grade, for example, an individual with a K-5 license may be a more appealing candidate than one with a birth through age 8 license who is not qualified to teach in fourth and fifth grade. Further, elementary school principals hiring teachers may not fully grasp the differences between preparation for early childhood and elementary educators. Moreover, they may move weaker teachers from an upper elementary grade to an earlier grade so that stronger teachers will be in those grades that are subject to state tests and school accountability (Bornfreund, 2011; Fuller and Ladd, 2013; Goldring et al., 2014).

Unfortunately, little evidence is available on which licensure standards ensure the most effective educators and produce better outcomes for young children. As a result, there are a number of considerations to be weighed in determining state licenses. Some believe that a birth through third grade, or at least prekindergarten through third grade, license is best aligned with how the science of child development and early learning supports the need for consistency and continuity in instructional practices for educators working with young children in this age range. However, this approach does not align well with practice settings. For example, understanding the foundations of development across the age span is key for any care and education professional regardless of setting. However, when it comes to more specialized competencies, educators planning to work in most public school systems will not be working with infants and toddlers, while those interested in working with infants and toddlers will not be working with children in the early elementary grades. Thus there is a rationale for a license that matches age span to setting, with reform not so much in the age span as in the content of the requirement to ensure that expectations for knowledge and competencies are more consistent across roles and settings and align more fully with research on child development and instruction for young children.

Another, similar consideration is flexibility in employment options, from the perspective of both the educator and the principals and administrators who hire and distribute staff. One potential option is a base license that would ensure common competencies across a broader age and grade span but would be accompanied by a required endorsement or certification ensuring specific competencies for subset ranges within that span. An educator might start a career with one endorsement, but could acquire another midcareer if asked to shift between earlier and upper grades.

Nongovernmental Credentialing Systems

Child Development Associate (CDA) credential   The CDA credential, administered by the Council for Professional Recognition, is a national accreditation system that provides credentialing for the early childhood workforce. The credential is available for professionals in a number of settings and across the age range from birth to age 5: infant/toddler (birth to age 3) and preschool (3-5) endorsements for center-based programs; birth to age 5 endorsement for family childcare programs; and families with children from birth to age 5 endorsements for home visiting programs. Professionals working in bilingual settings also can earn a bilingual specialization to promote the development of children in a dual language environment (CPR, 2013c).

This credentialing system is intended to ensure that early childhood professionals have the competencies needed to work with children from birth through age 5. The six competencies goals of the CDA credential described by the Council for Professional Recognition (CPR, 2013a) are to

- establish and maintain a safe, healthy learning environment;
- advance physical and intellectual competence;
- support social and emotional development and provide positive guidance;
- establish positive and productive relationships with families;
- ensure a well-run, purposeful program responsive to participant needs; and
- maintain a commitment to professionalism.

The CDA credential may contribute to some aspects of quality and may be beneficial for child outcomes. Specifically, professionals with the credential and with limited formal education may act more positively with children and make more opportunities to engage in play with language than those without knowledge and previous coursework in early childhood education. A 2006 study found that children with CDA-credentialed teachers achieved greater gains in nonstandardized measures than children without a CDA-credentialed teacher, particularly in rhyming and naming letters, numbers, and colors. On standardized measures for language and math, however, there was no evidence that the CDA credential had any impact. The authors suggested that the Council for Professional Recognition review the CDA credentialing process and make the changes needed to improve outcomes, which could mean focusing more strongly on language and math (Early et al., 2006). Other authors recommended that the CDA credential's contributions to quality be further examined (Tout et al., 2006).

In June 2013, the Council for Professional Recognition launched a revised CDA credentialing process, developed after feedback was received from professionals and practitioners in early childhood education as well as CDA instructors. The updated system is intended to simplify the credentialing process for candidates. While some components, including competency goals, remain unchanged, certain aspects are new. The updated system includes a CDA professional development specialist who provides the candidate with coaching and facilitates reflection. The professional development specialist also conducts a verification visit with candidates that entails reviewing the required professional portfolio, observing the candidate with children, and reflecting on areas of strength with the candidate.

Those holding a high school diploma (or equivalent) and high school students enrolled in an early childhood education technical program are eligible to apply for the CDA credential. Candidates must complete 120 hours of child development courses at any time prior to submitting the application, as well as 480 hours of direct experience working with children. Candidates can take the CDA exam at any time (CPR, 2013b).

National Board for Professional Teaching Standards   The National Board for Professional Teaching Standards (NBPTS), founded in 1987, describes the knowledge and competencies of educators across 25 subject areas and developmental stages (NBPTS, 2014a). Competencies for generalists working in early and middle childhood are included (NBPTS, n.d.). The NBPTS report *What Teachers Should Know and Be Able to Do* details five core propositions (NBPTS, 1989):

- Teachers are committed to students and their learning.
- Teachers know the subjects they teach and how to teach those subjects to students.
- Teachers are responsible for managing and monitoring student learning.
- Teachers think systematically about their practice and learn from experience.
- Teachers are members of learning communities.

The NBPTS offers a voluntary certification for education professionals, and licensed teachers with a bachelor's degree and a minimum of 3 years of teaching experience in an accredited early childhood, elementary, middle, or secondary school are eligible to apply. The application process includes a computer-based assessment through which the candidate must demonstrate content knowledge of developmentally appropriate practices. Candidates also must submit a portfolio including work on differentiation in the classroom, video recordings of teaching practices, and evidence of effective and reflective practices. Support and financial assistance are available to candidates, varying by state (NBPTS, 2014b).

As of 2014, more than 110,000 teachers across the nation had earned the NBPTS certification; 4,000 earned it in 2013-2014 alone. This number, however, is a small fraction of the number of professionals working in classrooms (NBPTS, 2014c). A 2004 study found that education professionals in affluent and advantaged districts are more likely than those in other districts to apply for the NBPTS credential because of incentives such as the district's covering the application fee and offering salary increases for those who become certified. It also is not evident that low-quality teachers are being encouraged to apply for the credential (Goldhaber et al., 2004).

According to a report of the National Research Council (NRC) (2008a) the NPBTS certification has varying impacts on student achievement. Some studies show achievement gains on standardized exams for students with NBPTS-certified teachers, whereas others show no impact at all. The report identified only one study that looked at impact on student outcomes beyond achievement on state standardized tests, such as attitudes and motivation in the classroom, which may reflect quality and effectiveness of teachers (NRC, 2008a).

Conclusions About Qualification Requirements for Educators

The requirements and expectations for educators of children from birth through age 8 vary widely for different professionals based on their role, the ages of the children with whom they work, and the practice setting. Requirements also vary depending on what agency or institution has jurisdiction or authority for setting qualification criteria. The result is a varied mix of licenses and certifications that represent legally required qualifications for the workforce and voluntary certificates, endorsements, and credentials that funders or employers may adopt as requirements or that professionals may pursue to augment and document their qualifications.

Differing qualification requirements drive differences among professional roles in terms of education, training, hiring prospects, career pathways, and infrastructure for professional learning during ongoing practice. As a result, different qualification requirements also drive differences and inequities in the quality of professional practice in different settings. This landscape is dissonant with what the science of child development and early learning reveals about the core competencies that all care and education professionals need and the importance of consistency in learning experiences for children in this age range. Greater coherence in the content of and processes for meeting qualifica-

tion requirements would improve the quality of professional practice within settings and the consistency and continuity of quality learning experiences for children as they grow from birth through age 8.

Little evidence is available on which systems of qualification requirements lead to the best outcomes, or on whether national credentials produce more effective teachers and better outcomes for children. As a result, policy makers and others who determine qualification requirements need to make choices that include consideration of practice setting and employment flexibility in designing qualification systems. Any of the available choices can be implemented with adherence to the principle of ensuring that requirements reflect consistent expectations for the core knowledge and competencies needed by all care and education professionals who work with children from birth through age 8.

Degree Requirement

While there is wide consensus across states and types of schools that early elementary educators should obtain at least a bachelor's degree, a similar "educational floor" is not consistently in place for educators working with younger children (Whitebook, 2014). Almost all rigorous studies of early childhood programs that have shown large effects have come from programs with licensed teachers who have bachelor's degrees (Barnett, 2008). However, as with many areas of education research, existing research on the relationship between the education level of educators and the quality of instruction or children's learning and development is inconclusive.

Early and colleagues (2007) analyzed data from seven previous studies of prekindergarten programs and found null or contradictory associations between the bachelor's degree or other features of teachers' education attainment and classroom quality or child outcomes. Some studies found positive associations, while others found no association or negative associations. They conducted 27 analyses across studies to examine the relationship between the degree attainment of the lead teacher and classroom quality and children's academic outcomes. They report that only eight of those analyses showed any evidence of association: six in the direction of a positive association and two in the direction of a negative association. In an unpublished working paper, Kelley and Camilli (2007) present a review of 32 studies, with a separate analysis for 18 comparative studies. They found that a college education had a modest, but positive, relationship with classroom quality and children's learning and development.

Two studies published more recently than those included in these multi-study analyses have also examined this question. When Mashburn and colleagues (2008) compared the relative significance of "structural" quality in preschool programs (e.g., teacher's education level, class size, adult–child ratio) to "process" quality (e.g., quality of instruction, teacher–child interactions, classroom climate), they found that only the latter was significantly related to children's learning and development. Vu and colleagues (2008) conducted an analysis of California's state-funded preschool programs to examine the relationship between teachers' education and classroom quality in the context of other variables, such as program setting (i.e., childcare centers, Head Start, public schools) and program leaders' qualifications. They found that a bachelor's degree was associated with higher quality instruction for teachers who worked in childcare and Head Start programs, but not for those in public schools. The authors theorized that public school systems may have the capacity to offset lower education by providing more supports, such as supervision and classroom materials.

In New Jersey, a natural experiment arose when high-quality preschool education, with a requirement for educators with a bachelor's degree and early childhood certification, was mandated in 31 districts. Prior to implementation, overall observed quality, including factors such as classroom interactions supporting development and learning, was low in private preschool programs. Yet after educators in these programs had the time and financial support to meet the educational and certification requirements (and their compensation was raised to match the qualification standards), observed quality increased, with most private programs rating good or excellent and no difference in quality levels found between private programs and public schools (Barnett, 2011; Frede et al., 2007, 2009). The Abbot preschool program in New Jersey is a well-documented example of successful implementation of a requirement for all lead prekindergarten teachers to have a minimum bachelor's degree (Barnett et al., 2012).

While these findings from existing studies offer a range of results, the authors' conclusions are not entirely inconsistent. Even in analyses that found weak or no relationships between educators with a bachelor's degree and classroom quality and child outcomes, none of the researchers conclude that higher education does not matter, and in fact have stated that their findings should not be construed as indicating that teacher education is not important for quality. Early and colleagues (2007, p. 575) themselves caution that their findings "should not be interpreted as an indictment of the role of education in high-quality programs." Similarly, the interpretation of Mashburn and colleagues (2008, p. 744) was that structural quality characteristics like teacher's education may have indirect impacts on children's learning and development by creating a classroom environment in which quality instruction is more likely. They offer that "teachers with higher credentials may indeed influence children's outcomes, to the extent that these qualifications lead to higher quality emotional and instructional interactions that children experience in classrooms."

There are several reasons why the evidence is difficult to interpret clearly. The design, scale, and original purpose of the studies used in the existing analyses vary greatly, and were typically not designed explicitly to determine the level of education required to ensure high-quality and effective early learning; rather, teacher education is one among several variables studied (Barnett, 2011; Burchinal et al., 2008; Whitebook and Ryan, 2011). As a consequence, it is difficult to determine whether teacher education alone or other variables affect quality and outcomes, and in reporting the analyses described above each of the author groups acknowledges variables they were not able to take into account, often because data were either unavailable or inconsistently reported in the original studies. Similar challenges, and similar inconsistency of findings, are seen in the research literature on teacher qualifications in K-12 education, a system in which all teachers nonetheless are required to have bachelor's degrees (Barnett, 2011; Early et al., 2006, 2007).

In addition, as noted by the researchers themselves and others, the available studies were not able to take into account factors that affect teacher education and teaching environments, such as the quality and content of the college degree or early childhood major; working conditions that the educators experience, such as access to ongoing professional learning, adequate instructional materials and facilities, effective leadership, and commensurate compensation; the educator's years of experience; and state and local policies that could promote or hinder effective practice (Early et al., 2007; Hyson et al., 2009; NRC and IOM, 2012; Whitebook and Ryan, 2011). These other variables in question are not insignificant. For example, degree programs vary widely, which means they do not all consistently lead to the same desired quality of practice. In addition, degree requirements set by state or program policies may or may not specify an early childhood focus with a basis in developmental science that includes subject-matter content and pedagogical strategies (Whitebook et al., 2012).

Indeed, one area of agreement emerges across these study authors and perspectives from other researchers in this field. While not ruling out the importance of education levels, the authors of these studies conclude that college education or a specialization in early childhood education *alone* is not a guarantee of better instruction and improved child outcomes. This assessment is echoed by many who have interpreted the available evidence across studies (Hyson et al., 2009; NRC and IOM, 2012; Whitebook and Ryan, 2011; Zigler et al., 2011). As noted above, many other factors that affect quality practice cannot be ensured solely through the acquisition of a degree. The quality of teachers' prior learning experiences in higher education *and* the quality of their ongoing professional learning and working environments all play important roles in enabling effective teaching and learning. These factors are discussed in more detail elsewhere in this report—in particular, in the preceding chapter on higher education and ongoing professional learning and in the chapter that follows on workforce status and well-being.

The confluence of factors that affects practice quality indicates that policy reforms to address levels of education are unlikely to be as effective as desired unless they also address other interrelated factors. In addition, changes to degree requirements may have effects for those working in early learning settings beyond simply increasing their level of education. It has been suggested that benefits of raising education standards for early care and education professionals could extend beyond improved quality of professional practice to include support for higher compensation; easier recruitment of well-qualified candidates to a wider range of professional roles; and reduced staff turnover, resulting in a more stable workforce (Bueno et al., 2010).

Furthermore, there are consequences of the current disparities in expectations for educators. Lower educational expectations for early childhood educators than for elementary school teachers perpetuates the perception—and policies that reflect the perception—that educating children before kindergarten requires less expertise than educating K-3 students, which makes it difficult to maximize the potential of young children through the early learning programs that serve them. Furthermore, there is also now considerable variation among professional roles working with younger children because a degree is increasingly being required in some early childhood settings as a result of requirements in Head Start and other settings and because more states and municipalities now have publicly funded prekindergarten programs that require educators to obtain preschool through early elementary certification.

These disparate policies create a bifurcated job market in which educators who are more able to seek higher education that qualifies them for better-compensated positions leave programs that serve young children to work in schools with older children, or leave less well-resourced preschool and childcare settings for better resourced ones. This not only introduces disparities for the workforce, it also means inequities for children across and within states and local communities, potentially perpetuating a cycle of disparity in the quality of the learning experiences of young children. Children in early care and education settings that should be equivalent may be experiencing a learning environment with an educator whose background ranges from a master's degree to no or very little college education (Barnett et al., 2013).

Finally, the implications of more widely requiring a bachelor's degree for educators need to be carefully considered. There would be an inevitable and considerable resource need in order to train and employ more college-educated professionals in these roles (Barnett, 2011). The ability to meet such a requirement would also in large part depend on the capacity of the higher education community to provide quality programs for prospective and current early childhood care and education professionals. As discussed in Chapter 9, improvements needed in the higher education system include, among others, sufficient numbers of full-time early childhood–trained faculty who are knowledgeable about the current research and evidence-based practices, appropriate course offerings, application of appropriate accreditation criteria for higher education programs, and articulation programs between 2- and 4-year colleges (Bueno et al., 2010; Hyson et al., 2009). Another factor to consider regarding the ability to meet the requirement of a bachelor's degree for those typically employed in early childhood settings is the tuition and other costs for a degree, especially when compared with their income, as well as the time required to complete the training while employed full time (Bueno et al., 2010). It is also important to recognize that many higher education and credentialing systems are undergoing significant changes with the advent of online courses and other technology-driven changes, a trend that could have implications for mitigating the challenges facing educators seeking additional qualifications.

Conclusions About Degree Requirements

Challenges to interpreting the existing research about the relationship between the education level of educators and the quality of instruction and children's learning and development arise from variability in their design and purpose and the extent to which other variables—such as the quality of the degree-granting program; state and local policies; and features of the practice setting, such as the work environment, curriculum, educator supports, ongoing professional learning opportunities, collaboration among educators, and compensation—can be taken into account in interpreting the findings. The available studies alone are insufficient to enable conclusions as to whether a bachelor's degree improves the quality and effectiveness of educators, whether for early childhood settings or for K-12 schools.

The consistency in education expectations that would result from requiring educators who work with children from birth through age 8 to have a minimum of a bachelor's or equivalent degree, with qualifications based on core competencies, could contribute to improving the quality of professional practice, stabilizing the workforce, and achieving greater consistency in learning experiences and optimal outcomes for children. However, a policy requirement for a degree implemented

*in isolation, without addressing other workforce development consid-
erations, would be insufficient to yield these improvements.*

Qualification Requirements for Leadership

Given the complexity of early childhood development, the sophisticated
knowledge and competencies needed by care and education professionals to
be effective, and the important role of the work environment in supporting
quality practice, leadership in birth through age 8 settings (administrators,
program directors, family childcare owners, coordinators, principals, superintendents) needs to have an understanding of developmental science;
of instructional practices for educators of young children; and for how this
knowledge should guide decision making on hiring, supervision, evaluation
of educator performance, and the development of portfolios of available
professional learning supports. Yet there is currently wide variation in the
expectation for these leaders (see Table 10-3).

Leadership in Early Childhood Settings

The current standards and expectations for directors in early childhood
settings are insufficient for the knowledge and competencies needed to lead
in learning environments for young children. Education and certification
requirements for directors are inconsistent across states. Twenty-eight states
recognize the administrative competency of center directors by issuing a
director or administrator credential. In almost all of these states, the credential is voluntary (Bloom et al., 2013). In fact, only four states require
a center director to have a degree at any level (Bloom et al., 2013). In 10
states, an individual with a high school diploma or lower educational attainment, with no coursework in early childhood education, can become
a center director (Child Care Aware of America, 2013). Only five states
(California, Colorado, Florida, New Hampshire, and Texas) require even
one college course related to administration or business before the position of director of a licensed childcare center is assumed (Bloom et al.,
2013). While the majority of directors hold a bachelor's degree or higher,
that percentage decreased from 72 percent in 2001 to 66 percent in 2008
(McCormick Center for Early Childhood Leadership, 2013).

The Illinois director credential has served as a model for qualification
requirements. As of 2013, 520 early childhood professionals held this
credential. The core knowledge and skill areas of the credential have been
adapted by the National Association for the Education of Young Children
(NAEYC) to define the competencies needed for effective program administration (Bloom et al., 2013; McCormick Center for Early Childhood
Leadership, 2012). As of 2016, the Illinois director credential will be em-

TABLE 10-3 Overview of Differences in Qualification Expectations for Leadership in Early Childhood and Early Elementary Settings

K-12 Schools	Early Childhood Settings
K-12 school principals are required to have an administrative credential and/or a master's degree and some teaching experience (Whitebook et al., 2009). Often no distinction is made between qualifications for an elementary school and a high school principal. Only one state, Illinois, requires principals of K-12 schools that operate prekindergarten programs to obtain certification across the span of prekindergarten through grade 12 that includes content and field experiences integrating early childhood education (Brown et al., 2014; Leadership to Integrate the Learning Continuum, 2015; Rice and Costanza, 2011).[a]	Qualifications for directors or administrators vary by state, ranging from no set requirements to a bachelor's degree (Barnett et al., 2012. • 11 states have no requirements for directors. • 13 states require a Child Development Associate (CDA) credential. • 5 states require a CDA credential plus credits. • 9 states require clock hours, with an average of 92 hours and a range of 30-135 hours. • 2 states require credits, with a range of 9-12 credits. • 7 states require other credentials: 5 states require a director credential, 1 state requires a vocational certificate, and 1 state requires a national director credential. • 2 states require an associate's degree. • 1 state requires a bachelor's degree. A Quality Rating and Improvement System (QRIS) is one strategy for increasing the qualifications of directors (McCormick Center for Early Childhood Leadership, 2012). • Nine states require directors to hold an administrator credential to achieve one or more star levels in their QRIS. • Seven states have embedded the Program Administration Scale in the quality standards of their QRIS or as a tool to measure whether standards have been met.

[a] The prekindergarten through grade 12 principal certification also covers special education and English language learners. Nonmandatory training for principals and other early care and education administrators is encouraged in New Jersey and other states.

SOURCE: Adapted from *Building a Skilled Workforce* (prepared for The Bill & Melinda Gates Foundation) (Whitebook, 2014).

bedded in the state's Quality Rating and Improvement System (QRIS). At the national level, 24 states have a director credential or enhanced director qualifications embedded in QRIS.[2]

---

[2] A regularly updated summary of state director credential initiatives and quality rating requirements for early childhood administrators can be found on the McCormick Center's website (http://McCormickCenter.nl.edu/category/research-resources-library/director-qualifications [accessed November 9, 2014]).

Leadership in Elementary Schools

Current policies for training or certifying elementary school principals also are not well aligned with the interests of early elementary educators and students. Even though most principals work in elementary schools and the science clearly indicates the importance of the early years for future academic success, public education policies tend not to emphasize early childhood development for elementary school principals. The use of broad K-12 principal licensure allows flexibility across schools and grades in hiring principals, but is not beneficial for the potential contribution of principals to leadership in education for young children. The science of child development and of developmentally appropriate practices becomes just one of an extremely broad range of competencies and expectations. This broad licensure also reduces the specificity of practicum or internship experiences such that they include limited time in early elementary settings and little or no time in prekindergarten settings, even as an increasing number of school systems are implementing prekindergarten programs. Some policies even ascribe a lower status to elementary school principals relative to those in middle and high schools. For example, the average salary for elementary school principals is more than 5 percent lower than that for middle school principals and almost 12 percent lower than that for high school principals (Herbert, 2011). Elementary school principal positions are often seen as "entry level." Another challenge to principals' contributing to continuity in learning experiences is the reliance in some cases on community education programs to administer preschool programs. Removing this responsibility from elementary school principals because of their overly broad position description is counter to supporting greater continuity in high-quality learning experiences for children.

Conclusions About Leadership Qualifications

The importance of leadership is unequivocal, yet the expectations for leaders in settings for children from birth through age 8 do not accord with the responsibilities of these leaders for fostering early learning and development. Current expectations and policies for education and certification of elementary school principals are not well aligned with the interests of early elementary educators and students and the need to understand childhood development research and best practices in instruction in preschool and the primary grades. Current education and certification requirements and expectations for directors in early childhood settings outside of school systems are inconsistent across states, credentialing is largely voluntary, and the current standards do not adequately reflect the knowledge and competencies needed to lead in learning environments for young children.

It is important that policies on qualification requirements and the available and expected professional learning for leadership in birth through age 8 settings (administrators, program directors, family childcare owners, coordinators, principals, and superintendents) be structured to ensure that they have an understanding of developmental science; of instructional practices for educators of young children; of how to integrate this knowledge into their instructional leadership; and of how to use this knowledge to guide decision making on hiring, supervision, evaluation of educator performance, and the development of portfolios of professional learning supports for their settings.

EVALUATION OF PRACTICE QUALITY

Current Systems for Evaluating Educators of Children from Birth Through Age 8

As with other aspects of professional learning, evaluation systems used to support continuous quality improvement vary greatly across professional roles and settings for children from birth through age 8 (see Table 10-4 for an overview).

Outside of federally funded Head Start programs or school-based programs, structured systems for evaluation are nearly absent in early childhood settings, with evaluation policies being set program by program. Structured systems for evaluating programs and centers have historically focused on program quality assurance, with educator performance as a component (program quality systems are discussed in a subsequent section).

In public school systems, the past few years have seen a sea change in state and district policies for evaluating the effectiveness of educators and other professionals who work with children. These reforms have been prompted in part by federal initiatives such as Race to the Top and requests for waivers to No Child Left Behind requirements, and in part by states' own legislators and governors. At both levels, the general intent is to develop more meaningful evaluation methods that improve professional practice and child outcomes by differentiating effective from ineffective instruction, creating a stronger link to student performance, and informing professional development. The most significant changes include the following:

- The inclusion of some measure of student achievement or growth as part of the professional evaluation rating—Forty states and the District of Columbia now require such measures in teacher ratings (NCTQ, 2013).

- The inclusion of some measure of instruction quality as part of the teacher evaluation rating—Forty-four states and the District of Columbia now require classroom observations as part of an evaluation for all teachers (NCTQ, 2013).
- The use of teacher evaluation ratings to make high-stakes decisions about compensation (15 states), tenure (19 states), and dismissal (23 states) (NCTQ, 2013).

In states that have implemented these policies, these reforms apply to all K-3 teachers who work in public school systems. They typically apply also to educators who work with children who have not yet entered kindergarten, especially prekindergarten teachers in state-funded programs or those who teach in other early learning settings that require a public school teaching license (e.g., teachers in state-funded prekindergarten programs or early childhood special education programs) (Connors-Tadros and Horowitz, 2014). Those who work in programs not formally connected to the public education system, such as childcare and home visiting, usually are not subject to these evaluation policies. Nor do the policies apply to Head Start programs unless those programs are administered by school districts that consider their Head Start teachers to be public school employees. In other words, these policies, where applied, affect all educators of children who are aged 5-8 and some educators of children who are aged 3-4 and in some cases, even younger.

The discussion that follows examines the extent to which educator evaluation reforms reflect research on how children learn and develop and on the professional knowledge and competencies needed to support them effectively. Even though current policies typically do not apply to professionals who work with young children but are not licensed by the state's public education system, the questions raised in this discussion can be applied to their evaluation as well.

Challenges and Reforms in Evaluating Educators of Young Children

Children within the birth through age 8 age range learn in different ways from those of their older peers. As described in Chapters 4 and 6, younger children tend to thrive with environments and learning experiences that are designed intentionally by educators to encourage students to explore their interests, initiate their own inquiries, and at the same time progress along specific learning and developmental trajectories. In such environments, children's competencies and skills can be taught directly, but young children may acquire them more successfully if they are also taught in an interdisciplinary way, so that, for example, an art activity is also connected to language, math, and socioemotional learning. Younger

TABLE 10-4 Overview of Differences in Evaluation Systems for Early Childhood and Early Elementary Settings

K-12 Schools	Early Childhood Settings
States are adopting more rigorous systems, with increased reliance on student performance as a significant measure (NCTQ, 2013).	Evaluation historically has focused on program quality, with observed teacher interactions being an important component.
States may mandate a particular system, provide a model, or allow districts discretion in evaluation policies.	Evaluation policies are set by program guidelines rather than by states. All states and territories have early learning guidelines for children aged 3-5, and 45 states and 4 territories have such guidelines for those aged birth to 3; 49 of the 56 states and territories have developed core knowledge and competencies for early educators working with children from birth to 5 (National Center on Child Care, 2014; Whitebook, 2014); 38 states and the District of Columbia have established Quality Rating and Improvement Systems (QRISs); and 11 states and territories are developing a QRIS (QRIS National Learning Network, 2014; Schmit et al., 2013).
States vary in how they use teacher evaluation results, but the results increasingly are tied to compensation, firing, layoff, and tenure decisions (Thomsen, 2014a,b).	Increasing emphasis on educator performance related to child outcomes in prekindergarten and Head Start is complicated by issues of assessing young children, the collaborative nature of early childhood teaching, and recruitment and retention challenges (LeMoine, 2009; Meisels, 2006; Regenstein and Romero-Jurado, 2014).

	State-Funded Prekindergarten	Head Start	All Other Center-Based Programs
• 27 states require an annual evaluation of all teachers (NCTQ, 2013). • 40 states and the District of Columbia use student achievement on standardized tests as a factor in teacher evaluation (NCTQ, 2013). • 15 states use unannounced observations of teachers (NCTQ, 2013).	• School-sponsored: most prekindergarten teachers are evaluated similarly to K-3 teachers according to district policy, but criteria for evaluation related to student performance in "untested" grades have yet to be determined in many states. • Not school sponsored: varies by the design of the public preschool program.	• Head Start, not school sponsored: the CLASS™ Teacher-Child Observation Instrument is used periodically in a sample of classrooms in all Head Start programs. Results are calculated for the grantee, not by classroom, and used to determine whether the grantee must recompete for funding (Office of Head Start, 2013b).[a]	• Varies by state and program; typically, there are no teacher evaluations (NSECE, 2011).[b]

[a] Section 641A(c)(2)(F) of the Head Start Act (the Act) requires that the Office of Head Start's monitoring review process include the use of "a valid and reliable research based observational instrument, implemented by qualified individuals with demonstrated reliability, that assesses classroom quality, including assessing multiple dimensions of teacher-child interactions that are linked to positive child development and later achievement." The Act also states, in Section 641(c)(1)(D), that such an instrument should be used as part of the system for designation renewal. Grantees with average CLASS™ scores below the established minimum on any of the three CLASS™ domains or receiving scores in the lowest 10 percent of the grantee pool assessed in a given year are required to recompete for funding.

[b] Forthcoming data from the National Survey of Early Care and Education will include information about whether teachers receive formal review and feedback on performance at least annually.

SOURCE: Adapted from *Building a Skilled Workforce* (prepared for The Bill & Melinda Gates Foundation) (Whitebook, 2014).

students also demonstrate their knowledge, skills, and understanding of concepts in different ways from those of their older peers. Their skills are more likely to be evidenced in their everyday behaviors than in verbal or written explanations, given that children at these ages are still learning basic verbal and writing skills. Not surprisingly, then, instructional strategies and interactions that work well for children in this age span look different from those that are effective for older students.

Thus, applying the current paradigm for evaluation reforms to those who work with children within the birth through age 8 age span requires addressing a number of challenges that are unique to this group of professionals. More specifically, tying their evaluation results primarily to student performance and observations of instructional practice requires different strategies from doing so with educators of older children. Because of the variable nature of learning and development during these years, triangulating assessment data with other sources of evidence from multiple methods and at multiple times may help educator evaluation systems derive a more reliable and valid measure of student achievement or growth during this age span (Epstein et al., 2004; Goe et al., 2011; Snow, 2011).[3] Nonetheless, most states that have implemented these reforms have not developed research-based policies or guidance for evaluating this population of professionals. Only 18 states and the District of Columbia have explicit policies on how to incorporate measures of student performance into evaluations of teachers in *any* untested grades and subjects, much less for prekindergarten through third grade in particular (NCTQ, 2013). Finally, it is important to examine the extent to which current reform efforts reflect the research—both established and emerging—on how children learn and develop during this period and on what professionals need to know and be able to do to help them be successful in the short and long terms.

Using Student Achievement to Evaluate Educator Performance

Measuring student achievement or growth in prekindergarten programs and in primary grades presents challenges distinct from those of measuring students' achievement in older grades (see the discussion of child assessment in Chapters 5 and 6) (Marsico Institute for Early Learning and Literacy, 2010; NEGP, 1998; NRC, 2008b). States that have incorporated measures of student performance into their evaluation policies typically rely on statewide standardized test results to evaluate educators from third through

---

[3] For guiding questions for designing various components of teacher evaluation systems, see http://www.lauragoe.com/LauraGoe/practicalGuideEvalSystems.pdf (accessed March 24, 2015).

eighth grade.[4] However, standardized tests typically are not administered statewide for children before third grade, nor is it advisable to use them for this age group for high-stakes purposes, such as decisions about educators' rating, compensation, or tenure (NEGP, 1998).[5] These tests assume an ability to focus and be sedentary for an extended period of time and a certain level of manual dexterity and literacy skills that younger students have not yet developed. Moreover, young children's performance on a task on a particular day (or at a particular moment) is variable and highly susceptible to environmental factors, which makes obtaining an accurate and reliable assessment of their ability challenging (Marsico Institute for Early Learning and Literacy, 2010; NEGP, 1998; NRC, 2008b). The typical rate of learning and development during the preschool years also is highly variable (National Early Childhood Accountability Task Force, 2007). Young children who may appear to be "behind" by a certain standard may be well within the normal range of development and catch up with or exceed their peers later. Finally, many students at this age may not be familiar with "tests" and their purpose, and may lack the skills and motivation to perform that older children have (Epstein et al., 2004).

For these reasons, the National Education Goals Panel has stated that "the younger the child, the more difficult it is to obtain reliable and valid assessment data. It is particularly difficult to assess children's cognitive abilities accurately before age 6." The panel also recommended that child assessments not be used for high-stakes accountability purposes for students, schools, or educators until the end of third or fourth grade (NEGP, 1998). These cautions against high-stakes uses of assessment results for young children remain relevant. Indeed, the lack of consensus in state and local education systems on the appropriate assessments and outcome data to use as part of the evaluation of preschool and K-3 educators suggests that implementers of evaluation reforms continue to struggle with the issues raised by the National Education Goals Panel and need more research on which guidance can be based.

Because of these challenges, children at these ages commonly are assessed through everyday observation and documentation of their behaviors and performance against clear performance benchmarks or indicators or through one-on-one assessments of specific skills, both of which require the educator to interact with students in small groups or individually (National Early Childhood Accountability Task Force, 2007; NEGP, 1998; Snow,

---

[4] Some states or districts measure student growth by comparing their end-of-year performance on state tests with the previous year's results. With this approach, third-grade test scores may not be used to evaluate third-grade teachers, since states typically do not require statewide standardized testing for second grade.

[5] In fact, using standardized tests to measure student achievement or growth is feasible with only about one-third of the K-12 teaching profession. See Prince et al. (2009).

2011). When this approach is used to evaluate an educator's performance, however, it creates an inherent conflict of interest for the educator. Because of the challenges described above, combining educator-engaged approaches with assessments that children can complete independently is less feasible for younger than for older children.

In addition, young children's socioemotional development and their growth as effective learners (e.g., ability to focus, self-regulate, persist) are as critical for success as their proficiency in academic content areas such as literacy and math, a balance that continues to be important into the later elementary grades, high school, college, and beyond (Educational Policy Improvement Center, 2013; Farrington et al., 2012; Hein et al., 2013; NAEYC-NAECS/SDE, 2003; NRC, 2008b, 2012). Yet measures of student achievement used in educator evaluation systems tend not to take these skills into account for children of any age, potentially missing a significant aspect of educators' competencies as professionals.

To be sure, valid and reliable standardized tests of children's learning and development during the prekindergarten through grade 3 continuum do exist—for certain purposes. Screening tools have been validated, for example, that produce reliable data suggesting that a child may have a developmental delay or disability. Similarly, valid diagnostic tools exist with which to identify specific delays or problems a child may have in different domains of learning and development. There are also validated assessments for this age group that measure growth and achievement in certain domains of learning and development and can be used to evaluate the effectiveness of instruction or interventions. However, policy leaders making decisions about the selection of assessments for educator evaluation purposes should keep in mind that assessments are valid and reliable only for the purposes for which they were designed. Professional associations and expert panels alike have warned against using assessments for purposes for which they have not been validated. Most recently, the Gordon Commission on the Future of Assessment in Education stated, "In all cases, assessment instruments and procedures should not be used for purposes other than those for which they have been designed and for which appropriate validation evidence has been obtained" (Gordon Commission on the Future of Assessment in Education, 2013). This conclusion has been echoed by the NAEYC, the National Education Goals Panel, and the NRC (NEGP, 1998; NRC, 2008b; Snow, 2011).

In addition, when the use of child assessments leads to high-stakes consequences for educators (of any age group), it is of paramount importance that what is attributed to the educator and his or her instruction be as precise as possible. Learning and development are a product of many factors inside and outside the classroom and the school, so using multiple measures of children and the environment in which they live and learn is critical. For example, an NRC report concluded that any high-stakes use of student assessments in K-12 systems needs to be contextualized with data on the learning environment, the children themselves, and the supports to which the school and educators have access. According to the group, teacher evaluations should not be based on student assessments "without also knowing about access to resources, to professional development, to mental health consultation, to supervision, and so on" (NRC, 2008b, p. 356).

Given the above challenges and limitations, states and districts are adapting their approaches. To derive a measure of students' achievement or growth in prekindergarten through grade 3 in the absence of standardized test data, states and districts have relied largely on the following strategies (Bornfreund, 2013; Gill et al., 2013; Goe, 2011; Marion and Buckley, 2011; Prince et al., 2009):

- Student learning objectives (SLOs)—SLOs are goals that educators set for their students—either as a class or as subgroups—based on understanding of the students' competency levels in various learning and developmental areas. SLOs often are developed in collaboration with principals and sometimes with other educators of the same grade. Once SLOs have been identified, educators work with principals and other colleagues to develop an assessment strategy. Assessment can use a commercially available or locally created instrument that relies on assessing children through standardized tasks (i.e., direct assessment), or an authentic assessment process that collects evidence of students' competency through everyday observations and documentation of students' work and performance.
- Curriculum-based assessments, other commercial measures, or locally developed assessments—Some states and districts have chosen to adopt a common assessment for each grade within the prekindergarten to grade 3 continuum and use the data to represent the student performance or growth portion of the educator's evaluation. As with SLOs, these products can rely on direct assessment methods or authentic assessment approaches. Typically, existing assessments for these grade levels are designed for screening, diagnostic, and formative purposes, not for high-stakes educator evaluation.
- Shared attribution—In some districts and states, the student performance measure is derived from a school-wide indicator of achievement or growth, such as growth in reading or math proficiency at the end of third grade. The assumption is that prekindergarten

through grade 3 educators contributed collectively to the third graders' progress or lack thereof.

Observing Professional Practice

Evaluating prekindergarten and early elementary educators' practice through observation requires a body of knowledge about teaching, learning, and child development different from that needed for observing educators of older students. Yet the most common observation instruments currently used by states and districts for educator evaluation purposes were developed and validated with educators of older students. Many use the same instruments for all educators, including those in prekindergarten through grade 3. The extent to which these instruments can identify effective practices and distinguish them from poor instruction in K-3 classrooms is mainly assumed rather than based on rigorous research (Kane and Staiger, 2012).

For this reason, some states, such as Illinois, New Jersey, Ohio, and Pennsylvania, are adapting existing instruments or providing guidance for observers to help them identify effective or ineffective strategies, interactions, and instruction for prekindergarten through grade 3 students. Effective observations of prekindergarten through grade 3 educators require instruments and observers (e.g., principals) that are sensitive to research-based interactions and instructional strategies that are appropriate for this age group, such as those highlighted by statements of core competencies from the NAEYC, the NBPTS, and the Council of Chief State School Officers (Prince et al., 2009).[6] Observation instruments may be inappropriate for prekindergarten and early elementary educators if they do not include evidence or examples of practice that reflect effective instructional strategies and other core competencies critical in early elementary classrooms (Pianta, 2012).[7]

A number of observational tools have been developed for use in younger children and have been adopted in many early care and education settings. These tools support the collection of observational data on child–educator interactions, environmental settings, and quality of instruction (Guernsey and Ochshorn, 2011). A few states allow districts and schools to use such observation tools that were designed and validated for early-childhood classrooms for evaluating prekindergarten through grade 3 edu-

---

[6] For broader discussions of the need to train and support principals to conduct teacher evaluations effectively, see Grossman (2011) and Jerald (2012).

[7] See http://www.americanprogress.org/issues/education/report/2012/05/15/11650/implementing-observation-protocols (accessed March 24, 2015) for guiding principles on choosing or designing observation instruments.

cators (Connors-Tadros and Horowitz, 2014). However, doing so requires that principals and other administrators learn how to use multiple tools, and to conduct observations in K-3 classrooms they may need specialized training in best practices and research on early learning to evaluate these educators' practices effectively, provide appropriate feedback, and offer ongoing support (Szekely, 2013).

Conclusions About Evaluation/Assessment of Educators

Many states and districts are recognizing the need to adapt methods for measuring the performance of educators. Based on the science of child development and early learning and its implications for professional competencies, however, the current accommodations are not sufficient, and indeed may produce unreliable data about children's learning and development and the quality of instruction for those who work with children in the preschool and early elementary years. Current reforms focus on student outcomes in one or two content areas instead of capturing the full range of competencies and skills that are important to the developmental nature of early learning. In addition, evaluation systems do not consistently capture important educator competencies such as assessment, trauma-informed practice, family engagement, and interprofessional practice. As a result, current evaluation policies and systems may reinforce and reward a narrow view of "effectiveness" while missing best practices that should be fostered and recognized in the early learning profession.

Developing and implementing more appropriate educator evaluation systems will require a shift from the current reform paradigm. It may not be feasible to incorporate every element of a fully comprehensive approach. But to make informed decisions about priorities in the reform of evaluation systems, district and state leaders would benefit from taking stock of which outcomes and practices their current evaluation policies value, which they omit, and how these decisions affect educators' professional growth and students' learning and development.

More research and development is needed to inform the design of student assessment strategies and professional evaluation for professionals working with young children. Assessment and evaluation methods need to be capable of effectively distinguishing high-quality from poor practice, providing data to inform improvement efforts, and being integrated with professional learning strategies.

PROGRAM ACCREDITATION AND QUALITY
IMPROVEMENT SYSTEMS

Accreditation and quality improvement systems with a focus on the quality of the center or program are increasingly being employed in early childhood settings. Given the importance of the professionals working in a setting to the quality of the learning environment, these systems can drive standards for their education requirements and other qualifications, as well as include assessments of and in some cases feedback for these professionals. When designed and implemented well, these quality assurance efforts have the potential to bridge early learning standards, program quality standards, and core competency standards for professionals. They can serve to foster both a quality learning environment for children and an appropriate workplace environment that supports quality practice among care and education professionals. Therefore, quality assurance efforts can serve as a lever to affect individual practitioners' knowledge, skills, and behaviors even though these efforts are not always thought of in conjunction with or strategically coordinated with professional learning systems. Examples of these systems include national voluntary accreditation systems for family childcare and childcare centers, as well as state and local QRISs (see Box 10-1).

Professional learning can be incorporated in the context of quality assurance systems such as QRISs if their scope and intent are extended to include rating standards that are linked more comprehensively and closely to instructional practices and child outcomes and coordinated with efforts to improve the quality of professional practice. A 2014 report calls for a review and expansion of the conceptual framework for QRISs to include not only the child outcomes that are central to those systems but also outcomes related to increasing family engagement and the professionalization of the early care and education workforce and improving early care and education systems (Zaslow and Tout, 2014).

Coaching in the context of a QRIS is another opportunity to align with broader professional learning aims. The intent of this coaching can be related to the rating process by either preparing providers for the rating, facilitating the rating process, or improving the rating. Often the coaching is focused on overall quality improvement rather than enhancement of specific content areas, skills, or curriculum. Coaching in the QRIS context frequently lasts longer than non-QRIS coaching. Data are not currently available on the impact of coaching on program-level or child outcomes (Isner et al., 2011).

BOX 10-1
Examples of Accreditation and Quality Assurance Systems

National Accreditation for Childcare Centers, Preschools, and Kindergartens

Childcare centers, preschools, and kindergartens must complete a rigorous four-step review process to earn accreditation from the National Association for the Education of Young Children (NAEYC), including an on-site visit by a trained NAEYC assessor. Programs use more than 400 criteria to demonstrate that they are meeting the 10 NAEYC Early Childhood Program Standards (NAEYC, 2006). The NAEYC accreditation lasts for 5 years, during which programs must submit annual reports and are subject to unannounced visits by assessors to ensure that they remain in compliance. The National Association of Child Care Resource and Referral Agencies offers support to programs seeking the NAEYC accreditation (National Early Childhood Program Accreditation, 2013).

Accreditation for Family Childcare

To receive accreditation from the National Association for Family Child Care (NAFCC), family childcare providers must first undergo an in-depth review process. This process includes proof of licensing, observation by an NAFCC representative, review of family childcare records, a written self-evaluation by the provider, a parent review of the provider's self-evaluation, and interviews with the provider (NAFCC, 2014).

Quality Rating Improvement Systems (QRISs)

QRISs for early care and education have been developed and implemented at the state and local levels for more than a decade. The goal is to improve outcomes with respect to children's social, emotional, cognitive, and physical development and to make quality programs more transparent to parents, funders in the public and private sectors, and other interested parties. The approach in general is to assess multiple indicators of program quality and combine them into a single summary rating, although there is considerable variation in the structure of QRISs across jurisdictions (Karoly, 2014).

Perspectives from the Field

Quality Rating Improvement Systems can be levers for change if they offer more than a "checklist." If paired with resources to improve quality, they could serve as an opportunity for reflection and continuous improvement and as more of an opportunity to ensure that best practices are actually seeing wider use.

See Appendix C for additional highlights from interviews.

REFERENCES

Barnett, W. S. 2008. *Preschool education and its lasting effects: Research and policy implications*. East Lansing, MI: Great Lakes Center for Education Research and Practice.

———. 2011. Minimum requirements for preschool teacher educational qualifications. In *The preK debates: Current controversies and issues*, edited by E. F. Zigler, W. S. Gilliam and W. S. Barnett. Baltimore, MD: Paul H. Brookes Publishing Co. Pp. 48-54.

Barnett, W. S., M. E. Carolan, J. Fitzgerald, and J. H. Squires. 2011. *The state of preschool 2011: State preschool yearbook*. New Brunswick, NJ: Rutgers University, National Institute for Early Education Research.

———. 2012. *The state of preschool 2012: State preschool yearbook*. New Brunswick, NJ: Rutgers University, National Institute for Early Education Research.

———. 2013. *The state of preschool 2013: State preschool yearbook*. Executive summary. New Brunswick, NJ: Rutgers University, National Institute for Early Education Research.

Bloom, P. J., S. Jackson, T. N. Talan, and R. Kelton. 2013. *Taking charge of change: A 20-year review of empowering early childhood administrators through leadership training*. Wheeling, IL: McCormick Center for Early Childhood Leadership.

Bornfreund, L. A. 2011. *Getting in sync: Revamping licensing and preparation for teachers in pre-K, kindergarten and the early grades*. Washington, DC: New America Foundation.

———. 2013. *An ocean of unknowns: Risks and opportunities in using student achievement data to evaluate preK-3rd grade teachers*. Washington, DC: New America Foundation.

Brown, K. C., J. Squires, L. Connors-Tadros, and M. Horowitz. 2014. *What do we know about principal preparation, licensure requirements, and professional development for school leaders?* New Brunswick, NJ: Rutgers University, Center on Enhancing Early Learning Outcomes.

Bueno, M., L. Darling-Hammond, and D. M. Gonzales. 2010. *A matter of degrees: Preparing teachers for the pre-K classroom*. Washington, DC: PEW Center on the States.

Burchinal, M., M. Hyson, and M. Zaslow. 2008. *Competencies and credentials for early childhood educators: What do we know and what do we need to know?* NHSA dialog briefs. Alexandria, VA: National Head Start Association.

Child Care Aware of America. 2013. *We can do better: Child Care Aware of America's ranking of state child care center regulations and oversight*. Arlington, VA: Child Care Aware of America.

Connors-Tadros, L., and M. Horowitz. 2014. *How are early childhood teachers faring in state teacher evaluation systems?* CEELO policy report. New Brunswick, NJ: Center on Enhancing Early Learning Outcomes.

CPR (Council for Professional Recognition). 2013a. *CDA competency standards*. http://www.cdacouncil.org/the-cda-credential/about-the-cda/cda-competency-standards (accessed December 17, 2014).

———. 2013b. *CDA questions and answers*. http://www.cdacouncil.org/the-cda-credential/230-cda-20-qaa#VV (accessed February 4, 2015).

———. 2013c. *CDA settings*. http://www.cdacouncil.org/the-cda-credential/about-the-cda/cda-settings (accessed February 4, 2015).

———. 2013d. *Council for Professional Recognition*. http://www.cdacouncil.org (accessed January 9, 2015).

Crandall, M., J. Henk, and Z. Conley. 2014 (unpublished). *An investigation of available public school teaching licenses beginning at birth in the United States in 2014*. Paper commissioned by the Committee on the Science of Children Birth to Age 8: Deepening and Broadening the Foundation for Success, IOM/NRC, Washington, DC.

Department for Professional Employees and AFL-CIO (American Federation of Labor-Congress of Industrial Organizations). 2013. *Teachers: Preschool through postsecondary*. http://dpeaflcio.org/professionals/professionals-in-the-workplace/teachers-and-college-professors (accessed January 9, 2015).

Early, D. M., D. M. Bryant, R. C. Pianta, R. M. Clifford, M. R. Burchinal, S. Ritchie, C. Howes, and O. A. Barbarin. 2006. Are teachers' education, major, and credentials related to classroom quality and children's academic gains in pre-kindergarten? *Early Childhood Research Quarterly* 21:174-195.

Early, D. M., K. L. Maxwell, M. R. Burchinal, S. Alva, R. H. Bender, D. Bryant, K. Cai, R. M. Clifford, C. Ebanks, J. A. Griffin, G. T. Henry, C. Howes, J. Iriondo-Perez, H.-J. Jeon, A. J. Mashburn, E. Peisner-Feinberg, R. C. Pianta, N. Vandergrift, and N. Zill. 2007. Teachers' education, classroom quality, and young children's academic skills: Results from seven studies of preschool programs. *Child Development* 78:558-580.

Educational Policy Improvement Center. 2013. *College and career readiness: Preparing students for success beyond high school*. http://www.epiconline.org/readiness (accessed October 23, 2014).

Epstein, A. S., L. J. Schweinhart, A. DeBruin-Parecki, and K. B. Robin. 2004. *Preschool assessment: A guide to developing a balanced approach*. New Brunswick, NJ, and Ypsilanti, MI: National Institute for Early Education Research.

Exstrom, M. 2012. *Teaching in charter schools*. Washington, DC: National Conference of State Legislatures.

Farrington, C. A., M. Roderick, E. Allensworth, J. Nagaoka, T. S. Keyes, D. W. Johnson, and N. O. Beechum. 2012. *Teaching adolescents to become learners: The role of noncognitive factors in shaping school performance: A critical literature review*. http://ccsr.uchicago.edu/sites/default/files/publications/Noncognitive%20Report.pdf (accessed February 4, 2015).

Florida Department of Education. 2011. *Competencies and skills required for teacher certification in Florida*, 15th ed. http://www.fldoe.org/accountability/assessments/postsecondary-assessment/ftce/tdi/comps-and-skills.stml#Fifteenth (accessed February 2, 2015).

Frede, E., K. Jung, W. S. Barnett, C. E. Lamy, and A. Figueras. 2007. *The Abbott Preschool Program Longitudinal Effects Study (APPLES): Interim report*. New Brunswick, NJ: Rutgers University, National Institute for Early Education Research.

Frede, E. C., K. Jung, W. S. Barnett, and A. Figueras. 2009. *The APPLES Blossom Abbott Preschool Program Longitudinal Effects Study (APPLES): Preliminary results through 2nd grade*. Interim report. http://nieer.org/pdf/apples_second_grade_results.pdf (accessed February 4, 2015).

Fuller, S. C., and H. F. Ladd. 2013. *School based accountability and the distribution of teacher quality across grades in elementary school*. Washington, DC: National Center for Analysis of Longitudinal Data in Education Research.

Gill, B., J. Bruch, and K. Booker. 2013. *Using alternative student growth measures for evaluating teacher performance: What the literature says*. Washington, DC: U.S. Department of Education, Institute of Education Sciences, National Center for Education Evaluation and Regional Assistance, Regional Educational Laboratory Mid-Atlantic.

Goe, L. 2011. *Measuring teachers' contributions to student learning growth for nontested grades and subjects*. Washington, DC: National Comprehensive Center for Teacher Quality.

Goe, L., L. Holdheide, and T. Miller. 2011. *A practical guide to designing comprehensive teacher evaluation systems: A tool to assist in the development of teacher evaluation systems*. Washington, DC: National Comprehensive Center for Teacher Quality.

Goldhaber, D., D. Perry, and E. Anthony. 2004. The National Board for Professional Teaching Standards (NBPTS) process: Who applies and what factors are associated with NBPTS certification? *Educational Evaluation and Policy Analysis* 26(4):259-280.

Goldring, E. B., C. M. Neumerski, M. Cannata, T. A. Drake, J. A. Grissom, M. Rubin, and P. Schuermann. 2014. *Principals' use of teacher effectiveness data for talent.* Nashville, TN: Vanderbilt Peabody College.

Gordon Commission on the Future of Assessment in Education. 2013. *A public policy statement.* Princeton, NJ: Gordon Commission on the Future of Assessment in Education.

Grossman, T. 2011. *Preparing principals to evaluate teachers.* Washington, DC: National Governors Association Center for Best Practices.

Guernsey, L., and S. Ochshorn. 2011. *Watching teachers work: Using observation tools to promote effective teaching in the early years and early grades.* Washington, DC: New America Foundation.

Hein, V., B. Smerdon, and M. Sambolt. 2013. *Predictors of postsecondary success.* Washington, DC: American Institutes for Research.

Herbert, M. 2011. The 11th annual salary survey: They work hard for the money. *District Administration.* http://www.districtadministration.com/article/11th-annual-salary-survey-they-work-hard-money (accessed January 13, 2015).

Hyson, M., H. Tomlinson, M. Biggar, and A. S. Carol. 2009. Quality improvement in early childhood teacher education: Faculty perspectives and recommendations for the future. *Early Childhood Research & Practice* 11(1).

Isner, T., K. Tout, M. Zaslow, M. Soli, K. Quinn, L. Rothenberg, and M. Burkhauser. 2011. *Coaching in early care and education programs and Quality Rating and Improvement Systems (QRIS): Identifying promising features.* Washington, DC: Child Trends, Inc.

Jerald, C. 2012. *Ensuring accurate feedback from observations.* Seattle, WA: The Bill & Melinda Gates Foundation.

Jones, R. C., S. Martin, and M. Crandall. 2009. *Early childhood public school teacher licensure for the fifty states and Washington, D.C.: An inquiry to ascertain student age ranges for public school licensure.* http://arkansasagnews.uark.edu/986.pdf (accessed February 4, 2015).

Kane, T. J., and D. O. Staiger. 2012. *Gathering feedback for teaching: Combining high-quality observations with student surveys and achievement gains.* Research paper. MET Project. Seattle, WA: The Bill & Melinda Gates Foundation.

Karoly, L. A. 2014. *Validation studies for early learning and care quality rating and improvement systems: A review of the literature.* Santa Monica, CA: RAND Corporation.

Kelley, P., and G. Camilli. 2007. *The impact of teacher education on outcomes in center-based early childhood education programs: A meta-analysis.* New Brunswick, NJ: National Institute for Early Education Research.

Kleiner, M. M. 2013. Licensing occupations: How time and regulatory attainment matter. *Employment Research* 20(4):4-6.

Leadership to Integrate the Learning Continuum. 2015. *LINC principal preparation program redesign.* http://leadershiplinc.illinoisstate.edu/LINC-principal (accessed January 13, 2015).

LeMoine, S. 2009. *Professional development system policy overview.* Washington, DC: National Association for the Education of Young Children.

Marion, S., and K. Buckley. 2011. *Approaches and considerations for incorporating student performance results from "non-tested" grades and subjects into educator effectiveness determinations.* Denver, CO: National Center for the Improvement of Educational Assessment.

Marsico Institute for Early Learning and Literacy. 2010. *The case against testing young children to evaluate teacher effectiveness: A position statement from the Marsico Institute for Early Learning and Literacy.* Denver, CO: University of Denver, Morgridge College of Education.

Mashburn, A. J., R. C. Pianta, B. K. Hamre, J. T. Downer, O. A. Barbarin, D. Bryant, M. Burchinal, D. M. Early, and C. Howes. 2008. Measures of classroom quality in pre-kindergarten and childrens development of academic, language, and social skills. *Child Development* 79(3):732-749.

McCormick Center for Early Childhood Leadership. 2012. *Director qualifications in state professional development and quality rating and improvement systems.* Wheeling, IL: National Louis University.

———. 2013. *Leadership Matters.* http://mccormickcenter.nl.edu/wp-content/uploads/2012/08/Leadership-Matters-11-14-13exp.pdf (accessed November 9, 2014).

Meisels, S. J. 2006. *Accountability in early childhood: No easy answers.* Chicago, IL: Herr Research Center for Children and Social Policy, Erikson Institute.

NAEYC (National Association for the Education of Young Children). 2006. *Press Releases—2006.* http://www.naeyc.org/newsroom/pressreleases/archive2006/20060801 (accessed March 14, 2015).

NAEYC-NAECS/SDE (NAEYC-National Association of Early Childhood Specialists/State Departments of Education). 2003. *Early childhood curriculum, assessment, and program evaluation: Building an effective, accountable system in programs for children birth through age 8. Position statement.* Washington, DC: NAEYC.

NAFCC (National Association for Family Child Care). 2014. *National Association for Family Child Care accreditation.* http://nafcc.org/index.php?option=com_content&view=article&id=70&Itemid=765 (accessed January 12, 2015).

National Center on Child Care. 2014. *Professional development systems and workforce initiatives.* https://childcareta.acf.hhs.gov/stateterritory-professional-development-system-overviews-0 (accessed January 9, 2015).

National Early Childhood Accountability Task Force. 2007. *Taking stock: Assessing and improving early childhood learning and program quality: The report of the National Early Childhood Accountability Task Force.* Philadelphia, PA: Pew Charitable Trusts.

National Early Childhood Program Accreditation. 2013. *NECPA standards.* http://necpa.net/necpastandards.php (accessed January 12, 2015).

NBPTS (National Board for Professional Teaching Standards). 1989. *What teachers should know and be able to do.* Detroit, MI: NBPTS.

———. 2014a. *About us.* http://www.nbpts.org/national-board-certification (accessed December 17, 2014).

———. 2014b. *Guide to national board certification for candidates beginning the national board certification process in 2014-2015: Version 1.5.* Detroit, MI: NBPTS.

———. 2014c. *National board certification.* http://www.nbpts.org/national-board-certification (accessed December 17, 2014).

———. n.d. *Certificates, standards, and instructions for first-time candidates.* http://boardcertifiedteachers.org/certificate-areas (accessed December 17, 2014).

NCTQ (National Council on Teacher Quality). 2013. *State of the states 2013. Connect the dots: Using evaluations of teacher effectiveness to inform policy and practice.* Washington, DC: NCTQ.

NEGP (National Education Goals Panel). 1998. *Principles and recommendations for early childhood assessments*, edited by A. Falk. Washington, DC: NEGP.

NRC (National Research Council). 2008a. *Assessing accomplished teaching advanced-level certification programs: Committee on evaluation of teacher certification by the National Board for Professional Teaching Standards.* Washington, DC: The National Academies Press.

———. 2008b. *Early childhood assessment: Why, what, and how.* Washington, DC: The National Academies Press.

———. 2012. *Education for life and work: Developing transferable knowledge and skills in the 21st century,* edited by J. W. Pellegrino and M. L. Hilton. Washington, DC: The National Academies Press.

NRC and IOM (Institute of Medicine). 2012. *The early childhood care and education workforce: Challenges and opportunities: A workshop report.* Washington, DC: The National Academies Press.

NSECE (National Survey of Early Care and Education). 2011. *Workforce [classroom staff] questionnaire.* Washington, DC: Office of Planning, Research, and Evaluation; Administration for Children and Families; U.S. Department of Health and Human Services.

———. 2013. *Number and characteristics of early care education (ECE) teachers and caregivers: Initial findings from the National Survey of Early Care and Education (NSECE).* Washington, DC: Office of Planning, Research, and Evaluation; Administration for Children and Families; U.S. Department of Health and Human Services.

Office of Head Start. 2012. *Statutory degree and credentialing requirements for Head Start teaching staff.* http://eclkc.ohs.acf.hhs.gov/hslc/standards/im/2008/resour_ime_012_0081908.html (accessed January 9, 2015).

———. 2013a. *Head Start program facts, fiscal year 2013.* http://eclkc.ohs.acf.hhs.gov/hslc/mr/factsheets/docs/hs-program-fact-sheet-2013.pdf (accessed January 9, 2015).

———. 2013b. *Use of Classroom Assessment Scoring System (CLASS) in Head Start.* Washington, DC: Office of Planning, Research, and Evaluation; Administration for Children and Families; U.S. Department of Health and Human Services.

Pianta, R. 2012. *Implementing observation protocols: Lessons for K-12 education from the field of early childhood.* Washington, DC: Center for American Progress.

Prince, C. D., P. J. Schuermann, J. W. Guthrie, P. J. Witham, A. T. Milanowski, and C. A. Thorn. 2009. *The other 69 percent: Fairly rewarding the performance of teachers of nontested subjects and grades: Guide to implementation: resources for applied practice.* Nashville, TN: Vanderbilt Peabody College, Center for Educator Compensation Reform.

QRIS (Quality Rating and Improvement System) National Learning Network. 2014. *Current status of QRIS in states.* www.qrisnetwork.org (accessed January 9, 2015).

Regenstein, E., and R. Romero-Jurado. 2014. *Ounce policy conversations: A framework for rethinking state education accountability and support from birth through high school.* Chicago, IL: The Ounce.

Rice, C., and V. Costanza. 2011. *Building early learning leaders: New Jersey's preK-3rd leadership training. A case study.* Newark: Advocates for Children of New Jersey.

Schmit, S., H. Matthews, S. Smith, and T. Robbins. 2013. *Investing in young children: A fact sheet on early care and education participation, access, and quality.* New York and Washington, DC: National Center for Children in Poverty, Center for Law and Social Policy.

Snow, K. 2011. *Developing kindergarten readiness and other large-scale assessment systems: Necessary considerations in the assessment of young children.* Washington, DC: National Association for the Education of Young Children.

Szekely, A. 2013. *Leading for early success: Building school principals' capacity to lead high-quality early education.* Washington, DC: National Governors Association.

Thomsen, J. 2014a. *A closer look: Teacher evaluations and reduction-in-force policies.* Denver, CO: Education Commission of the States.

———. 2014b. *A closer look: Teacher evaluations and tenure decisions.* Denver, CO: Education Commission of the States.

Tout, K., M. Zaslow, and D. Berry. 2006. Quality and qualifications: Links between professional development and quality in care and education settings. In *Critical issues in early childhood professional development*, edited by M. Zaslow and I. Martinez-Beck. Baltimore, MD: Paul H. Brookes Publishing Co.

Vu, J. A., H.-J. Jeon, and C. Howes. 2008. Formal education, credential, or both: Early childhood program classroom practices. *Early Education and Development* 19(3):479-504.

Whitebook, M. 2014. *Building a skilled teacher workforce: Shared and divergent challenges in early care and education and in grades K-12.* Berkeley: University of California, Berkeley, Institute for Reseach on Labor and Employment.

Whitebook, M., and S. Ryan. 2011. *Degrees in context: Asking the right questions about preparing skilled and effective teachers of young children: Preschool policy brief.* New Brunswick, NJ: Rutgers University, National Institute for Early Education Research.

Whitebook, M., D. Gomby, D. Bellm, L. Sakai, and F. Kipnis. 2009. *Preparing teachers of young children: The current state of knowledge, and a blueprint for the future.* Executive summary. Berkeley: University of California, Berkeley, Center for the Study of Child Care Employment, Institute for Research on Labor and Employment.

Whitebook, M., L. J. E. Austin, S. Ryan, F. Kipnis, M. Almaraz, and L. Sakai. 2012. *By default or by design? Variations in higher education programs for early care and education teachers and their implications for research methodology, policy, and practice. Executive Summary.* Berkeley: University of California, Berkeley, Center for the Study of Child Care Employment, Institute of Industrial Relations.

Zaslow, M., and K. Tout. 2014. *Reviewing and clarifying goals, outcomes, and levels of implementation: Toward the next generation of Quality Rating and Improvement Systems (QRIS).* Washington, DC: Office of Planning, Research and Evaluation; Administration for Children and Families; U.S. Department of Health and Human Services.

Zigler, E. F., W. S. Gilliam, and W. S. Barnett, eds. 2011. *The pre-K debates: Current controversies and issues.* Baltimore, MD: Paul H. Brookes Publishing Co.

11

Status and Well-Being of the Workforce

This chapter examines a variety of factors that contribute to the work environment, status, and well-being of the professionals who provide care and education for children from birth through age 8, including discussion in the key areas of compensation and benefits, staffing structures and career advancement, retention, and health and well-being. As described in Chapter 8, these factors—many of which are at the institutional or systems level—play important roles in the capacity of these educators for quality professional practice.

COMPENSATION AND BENEFITS

The current status of compensation, benefits, and related factors about the work environment for educators are summarized in Table 11-1. The Society for Research in Child Development reported that adequate compensation for teachers as well as opportunities for professional learning, mentoring, and supervision can lead to the development of an effective and strong early childhood workforce (Rhodes and Huston, 2012). However, the recent follow-up report to the 1989 National Child Care Staffing Study found that little progress has been made over the past 25 years in addressing the need for increased supports and compensation for early childhood professionals. Despite advances in the science of child development and knowledge of the impact of care and education professionals on the development of young children, many of these professionals still are receiving low wages. The result is high turnover rates in the field and increased economic instability among staff. Since 1997, compensation for childcare educators has

TABLE 11-1a Overview of Factors That Affect the Status and Well-Being of the Care and Education Workforce

	K-12 Schools	Early Childhood Settings			
		State-Funded Prekindergarten	Head Start	All Other Center-Based Programs	Home-Based/Family Childcare
Compensation and Benefits	Uniform pay scales are established by local public school districts.	Teaching staff typically are paid by the hour. Pay varies dramatically within and across sectors, and formal pay scales are uncommon.[a]			
	Employer-offered health and retirement benefits are included in pay packages provided to the vast majority of public school teachers.	One-quarter of teachers are estimated to have no health care coverage; those covered may receive insurance through a spouse, public agency, or employer.[b]			
	Payment for vacation, holidays, sick leave, planning, and professional sharing time, is standard.	Payment for vacation, holidays, sick leave, planning, and professional sharing time is not standard (Whitebook et al., 2009).			
	K-12 teachers typically work a 10-month year.	Teachers are predominantly full-time workers. Teachers in state-funded prekindergarten and Head Start programs typically work a 10-month year, while teachers in most other center-based programs and childcare work a 12-month year.[c]			
	2012 mean annual salary[d]: • Kindergarten teachers: $53,030 (mean hourly wage approximately $30.83, based on 40 hours per week for 10 months) • Elementary teachers: $56,130 (mean hourly wage approximately $32.63, based on 40 hours per week for 10 months) • Two-thirds of charter schools offer pay similar to public schools; some pay higher salaries for teaching in difficult-to-staff schools and subjects (Exstrom, 2012)	2012 mean hourly wages: • School sponsored: $19.40[e] • Not school sponsored: $14.40 • Teachers with a bachelor's degree: school sponsored—$22.90; not school sponsored—$19.00 (NSECE, 2013)[f]	2012 mean hourly wages: • Not school sponsored: $15.50 • Teachers with a bachelor's degree; not school sponsored—$18.20 (NSECE, 2013)	2012 mean hourly wages: • All private, for-profit, and nonprofit, although some programs may receive public subsidies (vouchers) for qualifying low-income children: $13.70	Median wage for "childcare workers": $9.38 per hour/$19,510 per year (Bureau of Labor Statistics and U.S. Department of Labor, 2014d)[g]

- On average, private school teacher pay is approximately 75 percent of public school teachers' pay (NCES, 2008)

- Teachers with a bachelor's degree: $17.10 (NSECE, 2013)

[a] Only 4 states and 1 territory have a salary or wage scale for various professional roles; 37 states and 1 territory provide financial rewards for participation in professional development (e.g., a one-time salary bonus for completing training); 12 states provide sustained financial support on a periodic, predictable basis (e.g., annual wage supplement, based on the highest level of training and education achieved) (NSECE, 2013; Whitebook, 2014).

[b] Six states and 1 territory offer or facilitate benefits (e.g., health insurance coverage, retirement) for the workforce (NSECE, 2013; Whitebook, 2014).

[c] In 2012, 74 percent of center-based teachers were full-time workers; the median hours worked per week by early care and education teachers was 39.2 (NSECE, 2013).

[d] The averages are based on 157,370 kindergarten teachers and 1,360,380 elementary teachers. Comparable annual salary data for early childhood educators by public prekindergarten, Head Start, and childcare are not available from the Bureau of Labor Statistics. However, comparable data are available for the more inclusive categories of childcare worker ($21,230) and preschool teacher in public or private programs ($30,750). The Bureau of Labor Statistics is considering new occupational definitions to capture more accurate information about early childhood industries. (Bureau of Labor Statistics and U.S. Department of Labor, 2014b).

[e] While pay is higher for teachers in school-sponsored public prekindergarten, it is important to note that only 6 percent of preschool teachers work in such programs nationally (NSECE, 2013).

[f] The NSECE is based on more than 10,000 questionnaires.

[g] Data are for "childcare workers" which include those employed in childcare centers, preschools, public schools, and private homes.

SOURCE: Adapted from *Building a Skilled Workforce* (prepared for The Bill & Melinda Gates Foundation) (Whitebook, 2014).

TABLE 11-1b Overview of Factors That Affect the Status and Well-Being of the Care and Education Workforce

| | K-12 Schools | Early Childhood Settings | |
		School- or Center-Based	Home-Based/Family Childcare
Work Environment	The staffing structure typically is a teacher working primarily alone in the classroom; an assistant teacher or paraprofessional may be present in the early grades or to assist children with special needs. Staff cohesion, collaboration, the availability of teacher leadership opportunities, and the quality of school leadership are identified by teachers as factors influencing the quality of the work environment (Tooley, 2013).	The staffing structure typically is a teacher working with other teachers or assistants in the classroom because of the greater need of young children for individual attention. Assistant teachers are included in the required ratio of adults to children set by licensing laws determined by each state. Working conditions vary by sector and funding stream, with publicly funded programs typically offering better support (Whitebook et al., 2009). Staff stability and training, staff cohesion, collaboration, the availability of teacher leadership opportunities, and the quality of school/program leadership are identified by teachers as factors influencing the quality of the work environment (Whitebook and Ryan, 2011; Whitebook and Sakai, 2004).	Depending on program size, a typical teacher may work individually or in teams with other teachers or assistant teachers. The age range of the children may include infants and toddlers and preschool-age children, as well as school-age children before and after school. Family childcare workers typically work in their own home (Bureau of Labor Statistics and U.S. Department of Labor, 2014d). Practitioners may work part time and/or be self-employed. Practitioners also often perform tasks related to running their business (Bureau of Labor Statistics and U.S. Department of Labor, 2014d). For example, a 2003 survey of family childcare providers in Massachusetts found that providers spent 52 hours per week working directly with children and an additional 10 hours per week on tasks related to their business (Marshall et al., 2003).

SOURCE: Adapted from *Building a Skilled Workforce* (prepared for The Bill & Melinda Gates Foundation) (Whitebook, 2014).

TABLE 11-1c Overview of Factors That Affect the Status and Well-Being of the Care and Education Workforce

	K-12 Schools	Early Childhood Settings			
		State-Funded Prekindergarten	Head Start	All Other Center-Based Programs	Home-Based/Family Childcare
Unionization	Thirty-five states and the District of Columbia have laws guaranteeing collective bargaining rights for K-12 teachers. Teacher unions exist in all 50 states (Whitebook et al., 2009). Working conditions, including benefits, are established through collective bargaining agreements. • Union density in 2012: 48 percent of 1.9 million elementary and middle school teachers.[c] • Twenty states exempt charter schools from collective bargaining agreements; others allow some negotiation for individual charter schools (Exstrom, 2012).	Union presence is limited and varies by sector. Teachers in school-sponsored preschools and Head Start are the most likely to be members of unions.[a] Teacher membership in professional organizations is low.[b] Union density: 16.7 percent of 1.5 million preschool and kindergarten teachers[d]	No current data available	No current data available	Fourteen states allow unions to represent home-based providers (Blank et al., 2010)

[a] Forthcoming data from the National Survey of Early Care and Education (NSECE) will include information on union density across early care and education sectors (NSECE, 2011).

[b] The National Association for the Education of Young Children (NAEYC), the largest ECE professional organization, has approximately 80,010 members. However, many of its members do not teach children directly but hold such roles as teacher educator or director. Membership has declined in recent years (NAEYC, n.d.-b).

[c] Union density figures cannot be disaggregated for elementary and middle school teachers (Department for Professional Employees and AFL-CIO, 2013).

[d] Union density figures cannot be disaggregated for preschool and kindergarten teachers. Because more kindergarten than preschool teachers are employed by public schools, union density among preschool teachers is likely to be much lower than 16.7 percent. Preschool and kindergarten teachers who were union members earned more than twice as much as those who were not. Several unions represent early childhood practitioners, most notably the Service Employees International Union; the American Federation of State, County and Municipal Employees; the American Federation of Teachers; and the National Education Association (NEA). The NEA allows private preschool workers to seek union membership (Department for Professional Employees and AFL-CIO, 2013).

SOURCE: Adapted from *Building a Skilled Workforce* (prepared for The Bill & Melinda Gates Foundation) (Whitebook, 2014).

seen a 1 percent increase, whereas salaries for preschool educators have increased by 15 percent. Childcare educators earn an average of $10.33 per hour, preschool educators earn $15.11, and kindergarten educators earn $25.40, although these numbers vary by setting (Whitebook et al., 2014).

Wages also do not reflect the education and qualifications of the professionals in the field; the mean annual salary for early care and education professionals holding bachelor's degrees is considerably lower than the salaries earned by professionals with a bachelor's degree in other fields. For example, the average hourly wages of center-based educators vary with education level, ranging from $9.60 for those with a high school diploma or less to $17.30 for those holding a bachelor's degree or higher (NSECE, 2013) (see Table 11-2).

Professionals working with children from birth through age 5 earn on average approximately 50 percent of what women in the civilian labor force earn and nearly 32 percent of what men in the civilian labor force earn. Those in school-sponsored prekindergarten are closer to the mean, while kindergarten and elementary school teachers earn salaries nearly equal to the mean for women (see Figure 11-1) (Whitebook et al., 2014).

Additionally, benefits for the early care and education workforce outside school settings are limited for some and unavailable for others. A 2012 study reviewing compensation and benefits for employees in North Carolina early care and education programs found that nearly half of the centers provided either full or partial financial assistance for health care services, and nearly 70 percent of programs provided full or partial assistance for childcare costs. While many programs offered paid holiday and vacation time, only two-thirds provided paid sick leave. In family childcare programs, however, it is less common for early childhood professionals to receive any paid benefits, as programs often are small and run by a single individual (Child Care Services Association, 2013). Home-based providers in Massachusetts, for example, indicated closing their homes for holidays or vacation for a minimum of 5 days per year. The majority of providers took

TABLE 11-2 Mean Hourly Wage of Center-Based Educators

Highest Degree Received	Mean Hourly Wage of Center-Based Educators
High school or less	$9.60
Some college, no degree	$10.50
Associate's degree	$12.90
Bachelor's degree or higher	$17.30
Total	$13.10

SOURCE: Adapted from *Building a Skilled Workforce* (prepared for The Bill & Melinda Gates Foundation) (Whitebook, 2014).

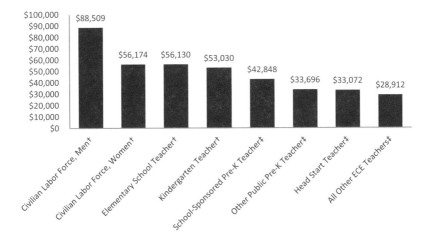

Labor Force Participants	Mean Annual Salary for BA Degree or Higher, 2012	Percent of Mean Earnings of Women in the Civilian Labor Force with BA or Higher Degree	Percent of Mean Earnings of Men in the Civilian Labor Force with BA or Higher Degree
Civilian Labor Force, Men†	$88,509		
Civilian Labor Force, Women†	$56,174		
Elementary School Teacher†	$56,130	99%	63%
Kindergarten Teacher†	$53,030	94%	59%
School-Sponsored Pre-K Teacher‡	$42,848	76%	48%
Other Public Pre-K Teacher‡	$33,696	59%	38%
Head Start Teacher‡	$33,072	58%	37%
All Other Early Care and Education Teachers‡	$28,912	51%	32%

FIGURE 11-1 Compensation for the care and education workforce.
NOTES:
† The wages are based on 1,360,380 elementary school teachers and 157,370 kindergarten teachers (Bureau of Labor Statistics and U.S. Department of Labor, 2014b).
‡ National Survey of Early Care and Education Project Team (2013). Number and characteristics of early care and education teachers and caregivers: Initial findings, Table 17 and Appendix Table 11, p. 27.
ECE = early care and education.
SOURCE: Adapted from *Building a Skilled Workforce* (prepared for The Bill & Melinda Gates Foundation) (Whitebook, 2014).

no sick leave, and 11 percent had no type of health insurance (Marshall et al., 2003).

Early care and education professionals outside of school settings often have no workplace standards such as paid planning time and a dependable schedule, nor do they have many opportunities for increased compensation based on education and training (Whitebook et al., 2014). Moreover, many of these professionals experience economic insecurity and express concern over having money to cover food, transportation, health care, and housing costs; having their work hours or benefits reduced; having their classes canceled because of low enrollment; or being laid off. Because of their low wages and concern over financial issues, it is common for professionals working in early care and education to participate in public support programs regardless of their educational background (Whitebook et al., 2014). Some also need to pursue a second job to make ends meet (Child Care Services Association, 2013). Program directors have difficulty attracting quality and effective professionals to the field because of the low compensation, minimal benefits, and lack of job security (Child Care Services Association, 2013).

In 2012, the Society for Research in Child Development offered policy recommendations for supporting the financial status of early care and education professionals, including increases in wages and benefits and opportunities for training and professional learning. Other suggestions included pay parity, better working conditions, and trainings to support the mental and emotional well-being of professionals working with young children (Society for Research in Child Development, 2012).

Currently, a number of financial supports are available to those in the care and education workforce. To raise the education levels of those working with young children, the Teacher Education and Compensation Helps (T.E.A.C.H.) scholarship offers early childhood teachers and assistant teachers the opportunity for continued education. More than 80 percent of those who participate do so to ease the financial burden of education costs (Child Care Services Association, 2013). The Child Care WAGE$ program is another opportunity for financial support available to low-paid childcare educators and directors who work with children from birth through age 5 in Florida, Kansas, and North Carolina (NAEYC, n.d.-a). This program provides salary supplements with the aim of lowering turnover rates in childcare programs, as well as creating opportunities for educational growth among early care and education professionals. Benefits of the WAGE$ program include financial stability, increased staff morale in the workplace, and decreased turnover rates. Additional supports that can help alleviate financial stress among early care and education professionals include paid time for training, breaks, and planning (Child Care Services Association, 2013).

Along with financial supports and salary supplements, several states are implementing policies that call for reducing pay discrepancies between professionals working with children in prekindergarten classrooms and public school teachers. Opportunities for pay parity can reduce the financial stress experienced by professionals in the field and attract qualified and effective educators. New Jersey and Oklahoma both have implemented policies on pay parity, and the Alliance for Early Childhood Finance has established a set of policy recommendations for narrowing the wage gap in Louisiana (Bornfreund, 2013; Stoney, 2013; WestEd E3 Institute, 2013).

STAFFING STRUCTURES AND CAREER ADVANCEMENT PATHWAYS

Two key institutional factors that affect quality practice—staffing structures and career options and opportunities for advancement—are closely interrelated. Staffing structures encompass how settings are staffed with tiered professional roles (such as lead educators, assistant educators or aides, master educators, mentors/coaches, and supervisors). Career advancement pathways encompass what professional roles and opportunities for career advancement are available to an individual professional, which include advancing in experience level within a role, such as novice to expert, as well as advancement and promotion to higher-level professional roles. Professional learning systems need to be equipped to prepare care and education professionals to assume the roles that are needed.

Policies on staffing of classrooms and centers determine the types of professional roles needed and the responsibilities of each role, as well as how many positions within those roles are needed in the system. These numbers in turn determine the opportunities for employment and advancement available to individuals. These decisions are sometimes based on a child development perspective, but more often are based on an organizational or financial perspective.

Staffing Structures

Evidence is lacking with which to definitively recommend ideal staffing structures and staffing supports across different settings and age groups. No comparative research has examined how different staffing structures contribute to the learning and development of young children. Staffing also depends on such contextual factors as resources in the setting and the labor market in a given geographic area. Even in the absence of a best-case staffing structure, however, it is important that any process designed to improve professional learning and the quality of professional practice include careful consideration be given to such issues as

- limiting teacher–child ratios and class sizes;
- using a tiered professional structure, for example,
  - director or principal (plus assistant director/principal depending on size),
  - lead educator in each classroom who is responsible for the learning environment and for curriculum implementation, including individualized instructional strategies,
  - assistant educators,
  - availability of some kind of coach or mentor (either a more experienced colleague, a designated coach role, or from an external source), and
  - support staff that either provide services from other sectors (e.g., health and mental health, family support services) or help with referrals or navigating other systems with which care and education teachers may not be familiar;
- supervisory support that provides both oversight/accountability and supportive/reflective supervision;
- everyday practical support (e.g., supplies, learning environment); and
- consultant and referral supports (designated staff, as well as resources and tools) for screening/identification and linking to additional services.

Career Advancement Pathways

Many states or localities are describing pathways for career development to help with retention and recruitment of good educators. A common challenge in both cases is how to make these pathways reflective of increasing competency, as opposed to increasing education. This is happening for both early childhood and elementary school settings, although for somewhat different reasons. Elementary school efforts are more about identifying educators who have demonstrated greater competency among their peers and/or have taken leadership roles within their schools or districts. Early childhood efforts are focused mainly on professionalizing the field and pointing a path toward more knowledge and skills, starting from a relatively low level. A recent scan of statewide "career lattices"[1] found that 37 states have some form of documentation describing how an early childhood professional might acquire more training, education, and competencies to support career advancement (Missouri Coordinating Board for Early Childhood, 2014). In many cases, the term "career" was used broadly

---

[1] The terms used vary greatly, including "lattice," "ladder," "steps," "tiers," "spectrum," and "pathway."

to mean training/education/etc. that one might obtain to advance in one's career, rather than to refer to a direct link to job eligibility. These pathways shared a number of common features, such as formal education, college credits, training hours, membership in a professional organization, meeting licensure requirements or obtaining a certificate or credential.

RETENTION

The current status of recruitment and retention for educators is summarized in Table 11-3. Just as early care and education professionals have seen no significant changes in wages over the past 25 years, there has been very little change in turnover rates, which have remained at 14 to 15 percent since 2002. Nearly one-third of professionals who have left the field have done so because of inadequate compensation (Whitebook et al., 2014). A 2003 study on job turnover (leaving the job) and occupational turnover (leaving the field) among childcare center educators and directors found that childcare centers had the highest turnover rate in the care and education field. Data show that the average turnover rate in childcare settings is more than four times higher than that in elementary schools. High turnover rates can lower the quality of childcare and education programs, as frequent staff changes can have negative effects on children's development—particularly for infants and toddlers, whose attachments and relationships with educators are disrupted (Rhodes and Huston, 2012). Indeed, continual changes and instability in caregivers can cause a child to demonstrate aggressive behaviors and become socially withdrawn.

Educators and directors report leaving their jobs or the field because of concerns and pressures involving low pay, job instability, and changes in staff or leadership. Highly qualified staff are drawn to and tend to continue their employment in centers that exhibit stability among their teaching and leadership staff and offer salaries that exceed the median wage. High-quality centers are often those that offer higher salaries (Whitebook and Sakai, 2003). However, it is difficult for childcare centers to retain highly trained educators with bachelor's degrees as they may also be qualified to teach in elementary schools or other settings that, as mentioned earlier, offer better salaries and benefits and greater stability (Whitebook and Sakai, 2003). Approaches to minimizing job turnover rates in this field include increasing wages and benefits for educators, directors, and administrative staff, as well as implementing quality policies regarding hiring practices and the work environment (Whitebook and Sakai, 2003). Conversely, it is worth noting that job turnover can be perceived as positive when ineffective educators leave the field (NRC and IOM, 2012).

TABLE 11-3a Overview of Factors That Affect the Status and Well-Being of the Care and Education Workforce

	K-12 Schools	Early Childhood Settings		
		State-Funded Prekindergarten	Head Start	All Other Center-Based Programs
Recruitment	Estimated replacement rates (2012-2022) for elementary school teachers are 22 percent.[a] Employment of elementary school teachers is projected to grow by 12 percent from 2012 to 2022.[b]	Estimated replacement rates (2012-2022) are 28.1 percent for preschool teachers and 29.4 percent for childcare workers.[c] Employment is projected to grow by 17 percent for preschool teachers and 14 percent for childcare workers from 2012 to 2022 (Bureau of Labor Statistics and U.S. Department of Labor, 2014b,c).		
	Estimated replacement rates (2012-2022) for elementary and secondary principals is 26.6 percent (Bureau of Labor Statistics and U.S. Department of Labor, 2014a). Employment of elementary and secondary principals are projected to grow by 6 percent from 2012 to 2022 (Bureau of Labor Statistics and U.S. Department of Labor, 2014c).	Estimated replacement rates (2010-2022) for preschool and childcare administrators is 26.6 percent (Bureau of Labor Statistics and U.S. Department of Labor, 2014a). Employment of preschool and childcare administrators is projected to grow by 17 percent from 2012 to 2022 (Bureau of Labor Statistics and U.S. Department of Labor, 2014b,c).		
	Recruitment pressures are higher among schools considered difficult to staff (typically those in low-income, high-poverty communities, and often staffed by novice teachers).	• Approximately 100,000 new teachers with bachelor's degrees will be needed for proposed expansion of publicly funded prekindergarten (Whitebook, 2014). • Recruitment pressures are greater in programs that do not pay salaries comparable to those for K-12 teachers.	• Recruitment pressures are high because teachers with bachelor's degrees leave to work in school-sponsored prekindergarten settings, which pay higher salaries (Whitebook, 2013a).	• Higher salaries in other early care and education sectors (such as school-sponsored prekindergarten) increase recruitment challenges for programs seeking teachers with associate's or higher degrees (Whitebook, 2013b).

[a] "Replacement rates" refers to the estimated job openings resulting from the flow of workers out of an occupation. This includes separations due to retirements as well as other reasons for departure. Estimates reflect decreases in job demand in an occupation, but not potential expansion (Bureau of Labor Statistics and U.S. Department of Labor, 2014a).

[b] Projected growth refers to the projected increase in demand for workers during a specified period. The growth rate for overall employment in the United States is estimated at 10.8 percent for 2012 to 2022 (Bureau of Labor Statistics and U.S. Department of Labor, 2014c).

[c] In most occupations, separations occur mainly among workers over 40; occupations with relatively low entrance requirements and compensation (as is typical of many early care and education jobs) typically have large net separations among young workers (Bureau of Labor Statistics and U.S. Department of Labor, 2014a).

SOURCE: Adapted from *Building a Skilled Workforce* (prepared for The Bill & Melinda Gates Foundation) (Whitebook, 2014).

TABLE 11-3b Overview of Factors That Affect the Status and Well-Being of the Care and Education Workforce

	K-12 Schools	Early Childhood Settings
Turnover/ Retention/ Dismissal	Teachers in unions typically have job protection once they have achieved tenure; dismissal follows collective bargaining protocol. Increasingly, states are mandating consideration of more stringent measures of teacher performance in awarding tenure and determining layoffs.[a]	Job turnover is high primarily because of low wages (Ryan and Whitebook, 2012).
		Dismissal is at the discretion of the program administrator in accordance with state and federal employment law, unless collective bargaining protocol is in place.
	Teachers leave their jobs for a variety of reasons: 24.9 percent seek a different occupation; 13.7 identify pregnancy or family issues; 22.4 percent retire; 25.1 percent identify dissatisfaction with administration or lack of support on the job; and 13.9 percent list other reasons.[b]	High rates of job turnover are associated with low program quality, inability of programs to improve and sustain improvements, and negative outcomes for children. Frequent staff changes create challenges in building essential cohesive classroom teaching teams (Whitebook and Sakai, 2003).
	Compensation influences turnover, but work environment plays a significant role (Glazerman et al., 2013).	Many teachers who leave their jobs remain in the occupation but move to other early care and education sectors that pay higher salaries.[c]
	In 2008-2009, 14.6 percent of elementary school teachers left teaching; 6.4 percent changed schools. 22.9 percent of all teachers (K-12) with 1-3 years' experience left teaching; 6.5 percent changed schools (Institute of Education Sciences and National Center for Education Statistics, 2008-2009b).	A study in Massachusetts found that 25 percent of family childcare providers intended to quit within the next 3 years, and another 25 percent intended to quit within the next 9 years; another quarter expected to stay in their positions for the next 15 years. One-quarter of family care providers noted that upon leaving their positions, they would pursue work or school in another field (Marshall et al., 2003).
		No current national data are available for turnover for educators in early childhood settings.[d]

[a] In 2014, for example, 16 states required the results of teacher performance evaluations for tenure decisions, compared with 10 states in 2011 (Fensterwald, 2014; Thomsen, 2014).

[b] In 2007-2008, there was a total of 347,000 leavers (Institute of Education Sciences and National Center for Education Statistics, 2008-2009a).

[c] Movement from one job to another in the field explains the relatively long occupational tenure for early care and education teachers (NSECE, 2013). In a 2011 study of early childhood teachers in North Carolina, 81 percent of teachers identified higher pay as the most important motivator for their remaining in the field (Child Care Services Association, 2012).

[d] Forthcoming data from the NSECE will provide information on turnover; Center-based Provider Questionnaire (published November 28, 2011) (NSECE, 2011).

SOURCE: Adapted from *Building a Skilled Workforce* (prepared for The Bill & Melinda Gates Foundation) (Whitebook, 2014).

HEALTH AND WELL-BEING

The health and well-being of care and education professionals play a critical role in their effectiveness as educators and thus in the development of children. The socioemotional competence of educators can influence student behavior and the classroom environment (Klassen et al., 2012). At the same time that socioemotional well-being is so important for the quality of their professional practice, however, care and education professionals experience higher rates of stress than those in many other fields, and this is a primary reason why many people leave the field (Friedman-Krauss et al., 2013). Teachers experience a number of sources of stress in their daily routine (Montgomery and Rupp, 2005). This stress can lead to emotional exhaustion, physical illness, burnout, and loss of interest in the teaching field (Klassen et al., 2012; Richards, 2012). Depression and other mental health conditions also are not uncommon among early childhood professionals. Sixteen percent of family care providers and approximately 30 percent of center-based staff and directors have depressive symptoms, and this rate is highest for professionals working with children in low-income households (Whitebook and Sakai, 2004). These effects of the stressors they experience can restrict the ability of educators to create positive, high-quality learning environments for their students (Friedman-Krauss et al., 2013).

Professionals who are socially and emotionally competent are self-aware and can identify how to engage and motivate their students (Jennings and Greenberg, 2009). Those who have a feeling of connectedness or relatedness with their students often find greater enjoyment in their daily work, which leads to a strong commitment to their job. They also experience less anxiety, anger, and burnout (Klassen et al., 2012). Executive function abilities such as working memory, inhibition of immediate reactions or impulses, and rapid shift in focus may help educators maintain control in the classroom and appropriately handle students' behavioral issues by moderating their response to these stressors. Establishing a positive classroom environment, moreover, helps educators achieve their teaching goals (Friedman-Krauss et al., 2013).

For some educators the effort to support individual children with specific behavioral issues exceeds their available emotional resources, which can increase their stress levels. The bidirectional relationship between children's behavioral problems and educators' experience of job stress can lead to a cycle of heightened negative interactions between students and educators (Friedman-Krauss et al., 2013).

An additional source of stress is uncertainty in the education profession. Care and education professionals react differently to this uncertainty: some become anxious and frustrated and feel that that they are falling short of the standards they are expected to meet, while others feel that the evolving expectations of what defines good teaching can help them improve upon their teaching practice (Helsing, 2003). Helsing (2003) describes how uncertainty in teaching can lead to routinized lessons, predictability, and boredom, and suggests that leaders can work toward minimizing uncertainty by identifying key elements of good teaching and reinforcing the need for collaboration and reflective practice.

A survey of Head Start programs in Pennsylvania offers a glimpse into how working conditions affect the physical and mental health of Head Start professionals. Head Start employs nearly 200,000 staff, including teachers, managers, and home visitors, in stressful working conditions, primarily with children who exhibit poor self-regulation. This survey looked at the mental and physical health of 2,200 staff in 66 Head Start and Early Head Start programs. The staff surveyed had a high rate of physical issues, including back pain, headaches, obesity, asthma, hypertension, and diabetes. The primary mental health issue was depression, with depressive symptoms being experienced by 25 percent of those surveyed. Additionally, a large percentage of staff frequently felt ill or missed work, which has been shown to disrupt healthy development of children in these programs (Whitaker et al., 2013).

There are several approaches to promoting educators' mental and emotional wellness. These approaches include trainings that promote emotional awareness, socioemotional competence, stress reduction, and reflective practices (Jennings and Greenberg, 2009). Some programs also offer retreats that support healthy personal development by focusing on establishing relationships with colleagues and students, as well as workshops that promote stress reduction techniques (Jennings and Greenberg, 2009). While educators are unable to change the contexts in which they teach and the levels of stress they experience, they can improve their management of stress by improving their coping strategies. These strategies include maintaining a positive attitude and sense of humor; turning to family and social supports; finding time for relaxation, reflection, hobbies, and exercise; and getting adequate sleep (Richards, 2012). Additionally, some schools provide mindfulness training for educators, which has been reported to reduce stress levels and depression, as well as increase awareness and self-regulation (Flook et al., 2013; Gold et al., 2010). Mindfulness in educators also is linked to better health and functioning in the classroom, which can affect student outcomes (Flook et al., 2013; Gold et al., 2010; NAEYC, n.d.-a; Stoney, 2013; WestEd E3 Institute, 2013; Whitaker et al., 2014).

Perspectives from the Field

"I don't think we have the right supports in place to increase quality practice. People aren't getting paid enough. The professionals carry the brunt of the underfunding of the system and are trying to do their best without sufficient resources."

See Appendix C for additional highlights from interviews.

Conclusions About the Status and Well-Being of the Workforce

The early care and education workforce is at risk financially, emotionally, and physically, subject to a vicious cycle of inadequate resources, low qualification expectations, low education levels, and low wages that is difficult to break. Appropriate income, resources, support, and opportunities for career development are essential for bringing excellent candidates into the workforce, retaining them as they further develop their knowledge and skills, and ensuring that they advance their knowledge and skills through professional learning opportunities.

The early childhood workforce in settings outside of elementary schools is particularly affected by a quality/cost mismatch in the care and education market. Childcare costs are highly driven by personnel and worker turnover is high. Federal subsidies often are inadequate to pay for the high quality of care they are intended to promote, and most families are unable to pay for the quality of care they desire.

REFERENCES

Blank, H., N. D. Campbell, and J. Entmacher. 2010. *Getting organized: Unionizing home-based child care providers, 2010 update.* Washington, DC: National Women's Law Center.

Bornfreund, L. A. 2013. *An ocean of unknowns: Risks and opportunities in using student achievement data to evaluate preK-3rd grade teachers.* Washington, DC: New America Foundation.

Bureau of Labor Statistics and U.S. Department of Labor. 2014a. *Employment projections: Replacement needs.* http://www.bls.gov/emp/ep_table_110.htm (accessed January 12, 2015).

———. 2014b. *Occupational employment and wages news release.* http://www.bls.gov/news.release/ocwage.htm (accessed January 12, 2015).

———. 2014c. *Occupational outlook handbook.* http://www.bls.gov/ooh (accessed January 12, 2015).

———. 2014d. *Occupational outlook handbook: Childcare workers.* http://www.bls.gov/ooh/personal-care-and-service/childcare-workers.htm (accessed July 7, 2014).

Child Care Services Association. 2012. *Working in early care and education in North Carolina: 2011 workforce study.* Chapel Hill, NC: Child Care Services Association.

———. 2013. *Working in early care and education in North Carolina: 2012 workforce study.* Chapel Hill, NC: Child Care Services Association.

Department for Professional Employees and AFL-CIO (American Federation of Labor and Congress of Industrial Organizations). 2013. *Teachers: Preschool through postsecondary.* http://dpeaflcio.org/professionals/professionals-in-the-workplace/teachers-and-college-professors (accessed January 9, 2015).

Exstrom, M. 2012. *Teaching in charter schools.* Washington, DC: National Conference of State Legislatures.

Fensterwald, J. 2014. Judge strikes down all 5 teacher protection laws in Vergara lawsuit. *EdSource.* http://edsource.org/2014/judge-strikes-down-all-5-teacher-protection-laws-in-vergara-lawsuit/63023#.VLVUEivF-Sp (accessed January 13, 2015).

Flook, L., S. B. Goldberg, L. Pinger, K. Bonus, and R. J. Davidson. 2013. Mindfulness for teachers: A pilot study to assess effects on stress, burnout, and teaching efficacy. *Mind, Brain, and Education* 7(3):182-195.

Friedman-Krauss, A. H., C. C. Raver, J. M. Neuspiel, and J. Kinsel. 2013. Child behavior problems, teacher executive functions, and teacher stress in Head Start classrooms. *Early Education and Development* 1-22.

Glazerman, S., A. Protik, B. Teh, J. Bruch, and J. Max. 2013. *Transfer incentives for high performing teachers: Final results from a multisite experiment.* Washington, DC: National Center for Education Evaluation and Regional Assistance, Institute of Education Sciences, U.S. Department of Education.

Gold, E., A. Smith, I. Hopper, D. Herne, G. Tansey, and C. Hulland. 2010. Mindfulness-Based Stress Reduction (MBSR) for primary school teachers. *Journal of Child and Family Studies* 19(2):184-189.

Helsing, D. 2003. *Regarding uncertainty in teachers and teaching: Learning to love the questions.* Cambridge, MA: Harvard University, Graduate School of Education.

Institute of Education Sciences and National Center for Education Statistics. 2008-2009a. *Schools and Staffing Survey (SASS): Number and percentage of public and private school teacher leavers who rated various factors as very important or extremely important in their decision to leave their 2007-08 base year school, by selected teacher and school characteristics in the base year: 2008-09.* http://nces.ed.gov/surveys/sass/tables/tfs0809_027_f12n.asp (accessed January 13, 2015).

———. 2008-2009b. *Schools and Staffing Survey (SASS): Percentage distribution of private school teachers by stayer, mover, and leaver status for selected teacher and school characteristics in the base year: 1994-95, 2000-01, 2004-05, and 2008-09.* http://nces.ed.gov/surveys/sass/tables/tfs0809_022_cf2n.asp (accessed January 13, 2015).

Jennings, P. A., and M. T. Greenberg. 2009. The prosocial classroom: Teacher social and emotional competence in relation to student and classroom outcomes. *Review of Educational Research* 79(1):491-525.

Klassen, R. M., N. E. Perry, and A. C. Frenzel. 2012. Teachers' relatedness with students: An underemphasized component of teachers' basic psychological needs. *Journal of Educational Psychology* 104(1):150-165.

Marshall, N. L., C. L. Creps, N. R. Burstein, K. E. Cahill, W. W. Robeson, S. Y. Wang, J. Schimmenti, and F. B. Glantz. 2003. *Family child care today: A report of the findings of the Massachusetts Cost/Quality Study: Family child care homes.* Wellesley, MA: Wellesley Centers for Women and Abt Associates, Inc.

Missouri Coordinating Board for Early Childhood. 2014. *"Career lattice" paper: Early childhood state charts describing steps for advancement.* Jefferson City: Missouri Coordinating Board for Early Childhood.

Montgomery, C., and A. A. Rupp. 2005. A meta-analysis for exploring the diverse causes and effects of stress in teachers. *Canadian Journal of Education* 28:458-486.

NAEYC (National Association for the Education of Young Children). n.d.-a. *Critical facts about the early childhood workforce.* http://www.naeyc.org/policy/advocacy/ECWorkforceFacts#WAGE (accessed March 22, 2015).

———. n.d.-b. *Membership.* http://www.naeyc.org/membership (accessed January 12, 2015).

NCES (National Center for Education Statistics). 2008. *Average salaries for full-time teachers in public and private elementary and secondary schools, by selected characteristics.* http://nces.ed.gov/programs/digest/d09/tables/dt09_075.asp (accessed January 12, 2015).

NRC (National Research Council) and IOM (Institute of Medicine). 2012. *The early childhood care and education workforce: Challenges and opportunities: A workshop report.* Washington, DC: The National Academies Press.

NSECE (National Survey of Early Care and Education). 2011. *Workforce [classroom staff] questionnaire.* Washington, DC: Office of Planning, Research, and Evaluation; Administration for Children and Families; U.S. Department of Health and Human Services.

———. 2013. *Number and characteristics of early care education (ECE) teachers and caregivers: Initial findings from the National Survey of Early Care and Education (NSECE).* Washington, DC: Office of Planning, Research, and Evaluation; Administration for Children and Families; U.S. Department of Health and Human Services.

Rhodes, H. H., and A. C. Huston. 2012. *Building the workforce our youngest children deserve. Social policy report.* Ann Arbor, MI: Society for Research in Child Development.

Richards, J. 2012. Teacher stress and coping strategies: A national snapshot. *The Educational Forum* 76(3):299-316.

Ryan, S., and M. Whitebook. 2012. More than teachers: The early care and education workforce. In *Handbook of early childhood education,* edited by R. C. Pianta. New York: Guilford Press. p. 98.

Society for Research in Child Development. 2012. *Strengthening the early childhood care and education workforce would benefit young children.* Ann Arbor, MI: Society for Research in Child Development.

Stoney, L. 2013. *Early care education compensation: Policy options for Louisiana.* West Palm Beach, FL: Alliance for Early Childhood Finance.

Thomsen, J. 2014. *Teacher performance plays growing role in employment decisions.* Denver, CO: Education Commission of the States.

Tooley, M. 2013. *Is money enough to keep more high-quality teachers in high-need schools?* http://www.edcentral.org/is-money-enough-to-keep-more-high-quality-teachers-in-high-need-schools/#sthash.hTWyRIVF.dpuf (accessed January 12, 2015).

WestEd E3 Institute. 2013. *Early childhood credentials and systems for professional preparation: Comparative data from 5 states (Illinois, Massachusetts, New Jersey, New York, Oklahoma).* http://www.ctc.ca.gov/educator-prep/early-care-files/2014-01-ECE-summary.pdf (accessed January 5, 2015).

Whitaker, R. C., B. D. Becker, A. N. Herman, and R. A. Gooze. 2013. The physical and mental health of Head Start staff: The Pennsylvania Head Start Staff Wellness Survey, 2012. *Preventing Chronic Disease* 10:E181.

Whitaker, R. C., T. Dearth-Wesley, R. A. Gooze, B. D. Becker, K. C. Gallagher, and B. S. McEwen. 2014. Adverse childhood experiences, dispositional mindfulness, and adult health. *Preventive Medicine* 67:147-153.

Whitebook, M. 2013a. *Preschool teaching at a crossroads.* Kalamazoo, MI: W.E. Upjohn Institute for Employment Research.

———. 2013b. Staffing a universal preschool program will be no small task. *EdSource,* http://edsource.org/2013/staffing-a-universal-preschool-program-will-be-no-small-task/30091#.VLVDUivF-Sp (accessed January 13, 2015).

———. 2014. *Building a skilled teacher workforce: Shared and divergent challenges in early care and education and in grades K-12.* Berkeley, CA: University of California, Berkeley, Institute for Reseach on Labor and Employment.

Whitebook, M., and S. Ryan. 2011. *Degrees in context: Asking the right questions about preparing skilled and effective teachers of young children: Preschool policy brief.* New Brunswick, NJ: Rutgers University, National Institute for Early Education Research.

Whitebook, M., and L. Sakai. 2003. Turnover begets turnover: An examination of jobs and occupational instability among child care center staff. *Early Childhood Research Quarterly* 18(3):273-293.

———. 2004. *By a thread: How child care centers hold on to teachers, how teachers build lasting careers.* Kalamazoo, MI: W.E. Upjohn Institute for Employment Research.

Whitebook, M., D. Gomby, D. Bellm, L. Sakai, and F. Kipnis. 2009. *Preparing teachers of young children: The current state of knowledge, and a blueprint for the future.* Executive summary. Berkeley, CA: University of California, Berkeley, Center for the Study of Child Care Employment, Institute for Research on Labor and Employment.

Whitebook, M., C. Howes, and D. Phillips. 2014. *Worthy work, still unlivable wages: The early childhood workforce 25 years after the national child care staffing study.* Berkeley, CA: University of California, Berkeley, Center for the Study of Child Care Employment.

Part IV

Summation

As adults with responsibility for young children, all professionals in the early care and education workforce have a similarly complex and challenging scope of work and make a highly valuable contribution to healthy child development and early learning. However, the sophistication and complexity of these professional roles are not consistently recognized and reflected in practices and policies regarding education requirements, professional learning expectations and supports, and compensation and other working conditions.

Science has converged on the importance of early childhood, but that understanding is not yet reflected in recognition of the critical role of the professionals who work with young children from infancy through the early elementary years. There is a growing base of knowledge about how children learn and develop, what children need from their interactions and relationships with adults, and what adults should be doing to support children from the beginning of their lives. Yet that knowledge is not consistently channeled to adults who are responsible for supporting the development and early learning of children, and those adults are not consistently implementing that knowledge in their professional practice and interactions with young children. This gap exists in large part because current policies and systems fall far short of placing enough value on the knowledge and competencies required of high-quality professionals in the care and education workforce for children birth through age 8, and the expectations and conditions of their employment do not adequately and consistently reflect their significant contribution to children's long-term success.

Much is known not only about what professionals who provide care and education for young children should know and be able to do, but also about what professional learning and other supports are needed for prospective and practicing educators. Although this knowledge and understanding has informed standards and other statements and frameworks articulating what should be, those standards are not fully reflected in the current capacities, practices, and policies of the workforce and their leadership; the settings and systems in which they work; the infrastructure and systems that set qualifications and provide professional learning in higher education and during ongoing practice; and the government and other funders that support and oversee those systems.

The breakdowns that have led to this gap include the lingering influence of historical differences in how different professional roles have evolved with different expectations and status; limited mutual understanding, communication, and strategic coordination across decentralized and diverse communities of practice and policy; and a lack of a concerted effort to review and improve professional learning systems that support educators before and during practice. These barriers impede both improving how the current workforce is supported and transforming how the future workforce is cultivated. Changes within and across multiple systems are needed to strengthen the early care and education workforce through supports that include informed leadership; access to high-quality degree-granting programs; ongoing professional learning opportunities; practice environments that enable and reinforce the quality of their work; and attention to their working conditions, well-being, compensation, and perceived status or prestige. These changes would help lead to a convergent rather than a divergent approach to caring for and teaching young children, one that would allow for continuity from birth through elementary school settings.

Perspectives from the Field

"We'll never move things forward unless we create disruption."

See Appendix C for additional highlights from interviews.

Part V

Blueprint for Action

12

A Blueprint for Action

Children's development from birth through age 8 is rapid and cumulative, and the environments, supports, and relationships they experience have profound effects. Their health, development, and early learning provide a foundation on which later learning—and lifelong progress—is constructed. Young children thrive and learn best when they have secure, positive relationships with adults who are knowledgeable about how to support their individual progress, and consistency in high-quality care and education experiences as children grow supports their continuous developmental achievements. Thus, the adults who provide for the care and education of young children bear a great responsibility. Indeed, the science of child development and early learning makes clear the importance and complexity of working with children from birth through age 8.

Although they share the same objective—to nurture young children and secure their future success—the various professionals who contribute to the care and education of these children are not perceived as a cohesive workforce, unified by their contributions to the development and early learning of young children and by the shared knowledge base and competencies needed to do their jobs well. An increasing public understanding of the importance of early childhood is reflected by greater emphasis on this age group in policy and investments. Yet the sophistication of the professional roles of those who work with children from infancy through the early elementary years is not consistently recognized and reflected in practices and policies that have not kept pace with what the science of child development and early learning indicates children need.

A growing base of knowledge describes what adults should be doing to support children from the beginning of their lives. Much is known about how children learn and develop, what professionals who provide care and education for children need to know and be able to do, and what professional learning supports are needed for prospective and practicing care and education professionals. Although that knowledge increasingly informs standards and other statements and frameworks articulating what *should be*, it is not fully reflected in what *is*—the current capacities, practices, and policies of the workforce, the settings and systems in which they work, the infrastructure and systems that set qualifications and provide professional learning, and the governmental and other funders that support and oversee those systems. As a result, knowledge is not consistently channeled to adults who are responsible for supporting the development and early learning of children, and those adults do not consistently implement that knowledge in their professional practice and interactions with children. This gap exists in part because current policies and systems do not place enough value on the knowledge and competencies required of professionals in the workforce for children from birth through age 8, and the expectations and conditions of their employment do not adequately reflect their significant contribution to children's long-term success.

The breakdowns that have led to this gap include the lingering influence of the historical evolution of the expectations and status of various professional roles that entail working with young children; limited mutual understanding, communication, and strategic coordination across decentralized and diverse communities of practice and policy; and limited resources for concerted efforts to review and improve professional learning systems. These disconnects and limitations serve as barriers to both improving how the current workforce is supported and transforming how the workforce needed for the future is prepared.

Better support for care and education professionals will require mobilizing local, state, and national leadership; building a culture in higher education and ongoing professional learning that reflects the importance of establishing a cohesive workforce for children from birth through age 8; ensuring practice environments that enable and reinforce the quality of their work; making substantial improvements in working conditions, well-being, compensation, and perceived status or prestige; and creating consistency across local, state, and national systems, policies, and infrastructure. As with multiple sets of complex gears, many interconnected elements need to move together to support a convergent approach to caring for and teaching young children—one that allows for continuity across settings from birth through elementary school, driven by the shared core of the science of child development and early learning (see Figure 12-1).

Yet strengthening the workforce is challenging because the systems, services, and professional roles that contribute to supporting the health,

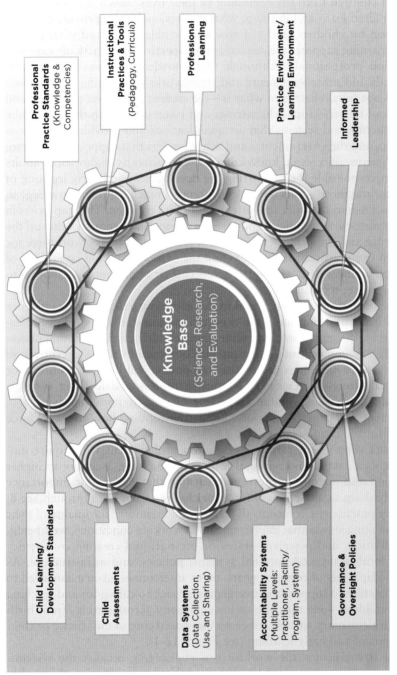

FIGURE 12-1 Interacting elements of supporting quality professional practice for the care and education of children from birth through age 8.

development, and early learning of children from birth through age 8 are diverse and often decentralized. Those who care for and educate young children work in disparate settings such as homes, childcare centers, preschools, educational programs, and elementary schools. Their work relates directly to those who provide such services as home visiting, early intervention, and special education, and is also closely connected to the work of pediatric health professionals and social services professionals who work with children and families. Oversight and influence are complicated, and achieving coherence is challenging, because the care and education of young children take place in so many different contexts with different practitioner traditions and cultures; funded through multiple governmental and nongovernmental sources; and operating under the management or regulatory oversight of diverse agencies with varying policies, incentives, and constraints.

At the same time, this means that there are many diverse ways to drive changes to strengthen the workforce at the community, state, and national levels. Some opportunities are centralized, such as federally funded programs for early childhood care and education or federal programs that support elementary education. Others are predominantly local, such as public education. Still others are in the private sector, although often subject to state-level regulation, such as childcare centers and family childcare, as well as private elementary schools. Education professionals, the organizations that support and train them, and administrators and leaders can identify and create opportunities for improvement in numerous ways. State and federal policy makers can help by eliminating barriers to a well-qualified professional workforce and to a streamlined and aligned system of services for children from birth through age 8. National organizations outside of government can inform changes by providing guidance and support.

Synchronous changes at all of these levels, and carried out within and across different systems, will require coordinated, strategic systems change in which stakeholders work more collectively and with better, mutually beneficial alignment among policies, resource allocation, infrastructure, professional learning, leadership, and professional practice.

This chapter presents the committee's recommendations, together with considerations for their implementation, as a blueprint for action that can be taken by stakeholders at the local, state, and national levels to help achieve this systems change and close the gap between what is known and what is done. These recommendations are based on the findings and conclusions, presented in depth in the preceding chapters of this report, that resulted from the committee's review of evidence, analysis and interpretation, and deliberations.

This blueprint for action is based on a unifying foundation that encompasses essential features of child development and early learning, shared knowledge and competencies for care and education professionals, and principles for effective professional learning. This foundation is meant to help provide coherence in informing the coordinated change that is needed across systems. Because this will require a collective approach among multiple sectors and a range of stakeholders, the blueprint also offers a framework for collaborative change of this kind.

As the core of the blueprint, the committee offers recommendations for specific actions to improve professional learning systems and policies and practices related to the development of the early care and education workforce. Figure 12-2 illustrates how changes in the committee's major areas of recommendations are interconnected and unified by a shared foundation. The two leftmost circular arrows show how local, state, and national changes need to work in synchronicity, while the central circular arrows show how changes in different aspects of professional learning and workforce development need to work together to lead to quality professional practice, including qualification requirements, higher education, profes-

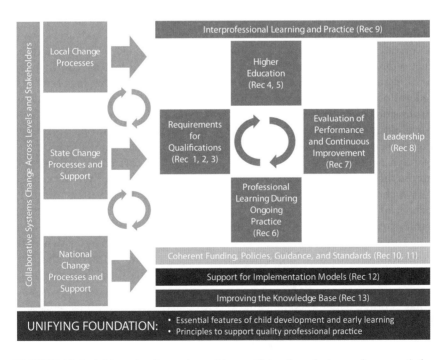

FIGURE 12-2 A blueprint for action with a unifying foundation, a framework for collaborative systems change, and interrelated recommendations.

sional learning during ongoing practice, and evaluation and assessment of professional practice. Several important elements—including interprofessional practice; well-informed and capable leadership; coherent policies, guidance, and standards; support for implementation; and a connection to the evolving knowledge base—make up a frame for workforce development and professional learning and provide the coherence needed to align specific actions.

The committee recognizes the challenges of the complex, long-term systems change that will be required to implement its recommendations. Full implementation in some cases could take years or even decades; at the same time, the need to improve the quality, continuity, and consistency of professional practice for children from birth through age 8 is urgent. Balancing this reality and this urgent need will require strategic prioritization of immediate actions as well as long-term goals with clearly articulated intermediate steps as part of pathways over time. The pace of progress will depend on the baseline status, existing infrastructure, and political will in different localities. Significant mobilization of resources will be required, and therefore assessments of resource needs, investments from government at all levels and from nongovernmental sources, and financing innovations will all be important.[1]

A UNIFYING FOUNDATION

The foundation for a workforce that can truly meet the needs of children from birth through age 8 is based on essential features of child development and early learning and on principles that guide support for high-quality professional practice with respect to individual practitioners, leadership, systems, policies, and resource allocation.

---

[1] While acknowledging that the availability of resources is an important reality that would affect the feasibility of the committee's recommendations, the sponsors specified in clarifying the study charge that this committee not conduct analyses addressing funding and financing. The sponsors did not want the committee to be swayed by foregone conclusions about the availability of resources in interpreting the evidence and the current state of the field and in carrying out deliberations about its recommendations. The sponsors also recognized that the breadth of expertise required to fulfill this committee's broad and comprehensive charge precluded assembling a committee with sufficient additional breadth and depth of expertise in economics, costing and resource needs assessment, financing, labor markets, and other relevant areas to address funding and financing issues (public information-gathering session, December 2013).

Essential Features of Child Development and Early Learning

Several essential features of child development and early learning inform not only what children need but also how adults can meet those needs, with support from the systems and policies that define and support their work:

- Children are already learning actively at birth, and the early foundations of learning inform and influence future development and learning continuously as they age.
- A continuous, dynamic interaction among experiences (whether nurturing or adverse), gene expression, and brain development underlies the capacity for learning, beginning before birth and continuing throughout life.
- Young children's development and early learning encompass cognitive development; the acquisition of subject-matter knowledge and skills; the development of general learning competencies; socioemotional development; and health and physical well-being. Each of these domains is crucial to early learning, and each has specific developmental paths. They also are overlapping and mutually influential: building a child's competency in one domain supports competency-building in the others.
- Stress and adversity experienced by children can undermine learning and impair socioemotional and physical well-being.
- Secure and responsive relationships with adults (and with other children), coupled with high-quality, positive learning interactions and environments, are foundational for the healthy development of young children. Conversely, adults who are underinformed, underprepared, or subject to chronic stress themselves may contribute to children's experiences of adversity and stress and undermine their development and learning.

Principles to Support Quality Professional Practice

The following principles are based on what the science of child development and early learning reveals about the necessary competencies and responsibilities of practitioners in meeting the needs of young children. They encompass the high-quality professional learning and supports needed for practitioners to acquire, sustain, and update those competencies. Yet adults who master competencies can still be constrained in applying them by the circumstances of their settings and by the systems and policies of governance, accountability, and oversight that affect their practice. Thus, the following principles also apply to the characteristics of practice environments, settings, systems, and policies that are needed to ensure quality practice and to support individual practitioners in exercising their competencies.

For the diverse agencies, institutions, funders, and professionals involved in the care and education of young children, coming together to adopt these principles across sectors, systems, settings, and professional roles will create a shared identity. This identity will be based not on historical traditions or practice settings, but on integrally related and mutually supportive contributions to sustained positive outcomes for the development and early learning of young children. The emergence of this shared identity and unified purpose has the potential to be transformative if accompanied by a willingness to develop shared strategies for investment and to share both responsibility and credit for long-term outcomes.

- **Professionals need foundational and specific competencies.** Care and education professionals are best able to help young children from birth through age 8 develop and learn when they have a shared foundation of knowledge and competencies related to development and early learning across this age span (see Box 12-1). This foundation needs to be augmented by shared specialized knowledge and competencies within a type of profession (see Box 12-2 for educators and Box 12-3 for education leadership), as well as further differentiated competencies that depend on specialty or discipline and age group.
- **Professionals need to be able to support diverse populations.** Care and education professionals, with the support of the systems in which they practice, need to be able to respectfully, effectively, and equitably serve children from backgrounds that are diverse with respect to family structure, socioeconomic status, race, ethnicity, culture, language, and ability.
- **Professional learning systems need to develop and sustain professional competencies.** To foster high-quality practice, care and education professionals need access to high-quality professional learning that supports them in the acquisition and application of the competencies they need, both in degree- and certificate-granting programs and during ongoing practice throughout their career. High-quality professional learning systems encompass a coherent series of activities that prepare professionals for practice, assess and ensure their competency to practice, and enhance the quality of their ongoing professional practice. High-quality professional learning activities are intentional, ongoing, coherent, collaborative and interdisciplinary, tied to practice experience, and responsive (see Box 12-4).

- **Practice environments need to enable high-quality practice.** Care and education professionals are best able to engage in high-quality professional practice when the settings in which they work are safe and well maintained, provide a high-quality learning environment for children, maintain a reasonable class size and ratio of adults to children for substantial and consistent group and individualized interactions to support learning, are well resourced with materials and supplies, and are guided by informed and competent leadership.

- **Practice supports need to facilitate and sustain high-quality practice.** Care and education professionals are best able to engage in high-quality professional practice when they experience the support of supervisors, mentors, and a community of peers; regularly assess and reflect on the effectiveness of their practices in order to improve them; are guided by thoughtfully designed workplace and oversight policies that support their practices; are compensated in a manner that recognizes their important role with young children; and have access to and time and resources for ongoing professional learning and career development.

- **Systems and policies need to align with the aims of high-quality practice.** Children benefit from consistency and continuity in high-quality learning experiences over time. This results when policies are aligned in accord with principles for high quality across the professional roles and settings that provide care and education for different age groups/grade levels, as well as across the sectors that provide closely related services for young children, especially health and social services.

- **Professional practice, systems, and polices need to be adaptive.** Research will continue to provide new information about how children learn and develop; how adults can best support them; and how adults can best be supported in their professional learning, practice environments, and practice supports. Accordingly, the systems that support children, the professionals who work within them, and their professional learning systems all need to adapt iteratively, with evaluative components that are embedded in continuous improvement processes.

BOX 12-1
Foundational Knowledge and Competencies for All Adults
with Professional Responsibilities for Young Children

The committee identifies the following general knowledge and competencies as an important foundation for all adults with professional responsibilities for young children.

All adults with professional responsibilities for young children need to know about

- How a child develops and learns, including cognitive development, specific content knowledge and skills, general learning competencies, socioemotional development, and physical development and health.
- The importance of consistent, stable, nurturing, and protective relationships that support development and learning across domains and enable children to fully engage in learning opportunities.
- Biological and environmental factors that can contribute positively to or interfere with development, behavior, and learning (for example, positive and ameliorative effects of nurturing and responsive relationships, negative effects of chronic stress and exposure to trauma and adverse events; positive adaptations to environmental exposures).

All adults with professional responsibilities for young children need to use this knowledge and develop the skills to

- Engage effectively in quality interactions with children that foster healthy child development and learning in routine everyday interactions, in specific learning activities, and in educational and other professional settings in a manner appropriate to the child's developmental level.
- Promote positive social development and behaviors and mitigate challenging behaviors.
- Recognize signs that children may need to be assessed and referred for specialized services (for example, for developmental delays, mental health concerns, social support needs, or abuse and neglect); and be aware of how to access the information, resources, and support for such specialized help when needed.
- Make informed decisions about whether and how to use different kinds of technologies as tools to promote children's learning.

BOX 12-2
Knowledge and Competencies for Educators
of Children Birth Through Age 8

In addition to the foundational knowledge and competencies in Box 12-1, the committee identifies the following as important shared competencies that all professionals who provide direct, regular care and education for young children need to support development and foster early learning with consistency for children on the birth through age 8 continuum.

Core Knowledge Base
- Knowledge of the developmental science that underlies important domains of early learning and child development, including cognitive development, specific content knowledge and skills, general learning competencies, socioemotional development, and physical development and health.
- Knowledge of how these domains interact to facilitate learning and development.
- Knowledge of content and concepts that are important in early learning of major subject-matter areas, including language and literacy, mathematics, science, technology, engineering, arts, and social studies.
- Knowledge of the learning trajectories (goals, developmental progressions, and instructional tasks and strategies) of how children learn and become proficient in each of the domains and specific subject-matter areas.
- Knowledge of the science that elucidates the interactions among biological and environmental factors that influence children's development and learning, including the positive effects of consistent, nurturing interactions that facilitate development and learning as well as the negative effects of chronic stress and exposure to trauma and adversity that can impede development and learning.
- Knowledge of the principles for assessing children that are developmentally appropriate; culturally sensitive; and relevant, reliable, and valid across a variety of populations, domains, and assessment purposes.

Practices to Help Children Learn
- Ability to establish relationships and interactions with children that are nurturing and use positive language.
- Ability to create and manage effective learning environments (physical space, materials, activities, classroom management).
- Ability to consistently deploy productive routines, maintain a schedule, and make transitions brief and productive, all to increase predictability and learning opportunities and to maintain a sense of emotional calm in the learning environment.
- Ability to use a repertory of instructional and caregiving practices and strategies, including implementing validated curricula, that engage children through nurturing, responsive interactions and facilitate learning and

continued

BOX 12-2 Continued

development in all domains in ways that are appropriate for their stage of development.

- Ability to set appropriate individualized goals and objectives to advance young children's development and learning.
- Ability to use learning trajectories: A deep understanding of the subject, knowledge of the way children think and learn about the subject, and the ability to design and employ instructional tasks, curricula, and activities that effectively promote learning and development within and across domains and subject-matter areas.
- Ability to select, employ, and interpret a portfolio of both informal and formal assessment tools and strategies; to use the results to understand individual children's developmental progression and determine whether needs are being met; and to use this information to individualize, adapt, and improve instructional practices.
- Ability to integrate and leverage different kinds of technologies in curricula and instructional practice to promote children's learning.
- Ability to promote positive social development and self-regulation while mitigating challenging behaviors in ways that reflect an understanding of the multiple biological and environmental factors that affect behavior.
- Ability to recognize the effects of factors from outside the practice setting (e.g., poverty, trauma, parental depression, experience of violence in the home or community) that affect children's learning and development, and to adjust practice to help children experiencing those effects.

Working with Diverse Populations of Children

- Ability to advance the learning and development of children from backgrounds that are diverse in family structure, socioeconomic status, race, ethnicity, culture, and language.
- Ability to advance the learning and development of children who are dual language learners.
- Ability to advance the development and learning of children who have specialized developmental or learning needs, such as children with disabilities or learning delays, children experiencing chronic stress/adversity, and children who are gifted and talented. All early care and education professionals—not just those in specialized roles—need knowledge and basic competencies for working with these children.

Developing and Using Partnerships

- Ability to communicate and connect with families in a mutually respectful, reciprocal way, and to set goals with families and prepare them to engage in complementary behaviors and activities that enhance development and early learning.

- Ability to recognize when behaviors and academic challenges may be a sign of an underlying need for referral for more comprehensive assessment, diagnosis, and support (e.g., mental health consultation, social services, family support services).
- Knowledge of professional roles and available services within care and education and in closely related sectors such as health and social services.
- Ability to access and effectively use available referral and resource systems.
- Ability to collaborate and communicate with professionals in other roles, disciplines, and sectors to facilitate mutual understanding and collective contribution to improving outcomes for children.

Continuously Improving Quality of Practice

- Ability and motivation to access and engage in available professional learning resources to keep current with the science of development and early learning and with research on instructional and other practices.
- Knowledge and abilities for self-care to manage their own physical and mental health, including the effects of their own exposure to adversity and stress.

Comparison to National and State Statements of Core Competencies

A scan across national and state statements of core competencies for educators suggests that there is broad agreement on what educators who work with children from infancy through age 8 need to know and be able to do.[a] However, there are variations in emphasis and gaps. Organizations and states that issue statements of core competencies for these educators would benefit from a review aimed at improving consistency in family engagement and assessment and enhancing their statements to reflect recent research on how children learn and develop and the role of educators in the process. Areas likely in need of enhancement in many existing statements include teaching subject matter–specific content, addressing stress and adversity, fostering socioemotional development, promoting general learning competencies, working with dual language learners, and integrating technology into curricula.

---

[a] See Chapter 7 for an in-depth discussion of the example competency statements.

BOX 12-3
Knowledge and Competencies for Leadership in
Settings with Children Birth Through Age 8

In addition to the foundational knowledge and competencies in Box 12-1, center directors, childcare owners, principals, and other leaders and administrators who oversee care and education settings for young children birth through age 8 need both specific competencies and overlapping general competencies with the roles of the specific professionals they supervise. The committee identifies the following important competencies that are needed by these leaders across settings:

Practices to Help Children Learn
- Understanding the implications of child development and early learning for interactions of care and education professionals with children, instructional and other practices, and learning environments.
- Ability to keep current with how advances in the research on child development and early learning and on instructional and other practices inform changes in professional practices and learning environments.

Assessment of Children
- Knowledge of assessment principles and methods to monitor children's progress and ability to adjust practice accordingly.
- Ability to select assessment tools for use by the professionals in their setting.

Fostering a Professional Workforce
- Knowledge and understanding of the competencies needed to work with children in the professional setting they lead.
- Ability to use knowledge of these competencies to make informed decisions about hiring and placement of practitioners.
- Ability to formulate and implement policies that create an environment that enhances and supports quality practice and children's development and early learning.
- Ability to formulate and implement supportive and rigorous ongoing professional learning opportunities and quality improvement programs that reflect current knowledge of child development and of effective, high-quality instructional and other practices.
- Ability to foster the health and well-being of their staff and seek out and provide resources for staff to manage stress.

Assessment of Educators
- Ability to assess quality of instruction and interactions, to recognize high quality, and to identify and address poor quality through evalua-

tion systems, observations, coaching, and other professional learning opportunities.

- Ability to use data from assessments of care and education professionals appropriately and effectively to make adjustments to improve outcomes for children and to inform professional learning and other decisions and policies.

Developing and Fostering Partnerships

- Ability to support collaboration among the different kinds of providers under their leadership.
- Ability to enable interprofessional opportunities for themselves and their staff to facilitate linkages among health, education, social services, and other disciplines not under their direct leadership.
- Ability to work with families and support their staff to work with families.

Organizational Development and Management

- Knowledge and ability in administrative and fiscal management, compliance with laws and regulations, and the development and maintenance of infrastructure and an appropriate work environment.

Comparison to Statements of Leadership Competencies

A review of examples of statements of core competencies from early childhood organizations and elementary education leadership organizations suggests that there is a distinction in the stated expectations for these two categories of leaders whose professional roles fall within the birth through age 8 range.[a] Those for principals include competencies for organizational management but are mainly focused on knowledge and competencies needed for instructional leadership to create working environments and supports for educators that help them improve their instructional practice. Those representing leaders in early childhood settings focus on how well a leader can develop and manage a well-functioning organization.

To create a more consistent culture of leadership expectations better aligned with children's need for continuous learning experiences, states' and organizations' statements of core competencies for leadership in elementary education would benefit from a review of those statements to ensure that the scope of competencies for instructional leadership encompasses the early elementary years, including prekindergarten as it increasingly becomes included in public school systems. States and organizations that issue statements of core competencies for leadership in centers, programs, family childcare, and other settings for early childhood education would benefit from a review of those statements to ensure that competencies related to instructional leadership are emphasized alongside administrative and management competencies.

---

[a] See Chapter 7 for an in-depth discussion of the example competency statements.

BOX 12-4
Principles for Professional Learning Systems

A high-quality professional learning system provides practitioners with coherent, interrelated, and continuous professional learning activities and mechanisms that are aligned with each other and with the science of child development. These activities and mechanisms need to be sequenced to prepare practitioners for practice, assess and ensure their competency to practice, continuously enhance the quality of their ongoing professional practice throughout their career, and provide opportunities for career development and advancement. High-quality professional learning activities and mechanisms have the following characteristics:

Intentional
- Guided by the available science on child development and early learning, instructional and other practices, and adult learning.
- Guided by alignment between the developmental needs of children and professional learning needs for acquiring and sustaining core competencies and professional practice standards.
- Guided by the context of the diverse settings in which professionals might practice and the diverse populations of children and families with whom they might work.

Ongoing
- Designed to support cumulative and continuous learning over time, with preparation experience that leads to a period of supervised practice, followed by independent practice with ongoing, individualized supports from supervisors, coaches, mentors, and/or peers.

Coherent
- Coherent in the types and sequence of professional learning to which individual practitioners have access and in which they engage to support a continuum of growth, as opposed to discrete, potentially disjointed learning experiences.
- Coherent and aligned with a shared foundation of knowledge of child development across professional roles.

A FRAMEWORK FOR COLLABORATIVE SYSTEMS CHANGE

The collective insight, expertise, and action of multiple stakeholders are needed to guide the implementation of changes to policies and systems that affect workforce development across settings and roles involved in the care and education of children from birth through age 8. Important work related to the principles and recommendations in this report is currently being carried out by many strong organizations. However, much of this work is being done in relative isolation or as part of collaborations that are not comprehensive in encompassing all that is needed to support de-

- Coherent and comprehensive in what professional learning is available in a given local system.
- Coherent and aligned in content and aims across the full breadth of supports and mechanisms that contribute to improving professional practice, including higher education, ongoing professional learning, the practice environment, opportunities for professional advancement, systems for evaluation and support for ongoing quality improvement, and supports for the status and well-being of the workforce.
- Coherent and coordinated with respect to professional learning activities for professional roles across practice settings and age ranges within the birth through age 8 span.

Collaborative and Interdisciplinary
- Based on an ethic of shared responsibility and collective practice for promoting child development and early learning.
- Providing shared professional learning opportunities for professional roles across practice settings and age ranges within the birth through age 8 span (e.g., cross-disciplinary courses and professional learning communities).
- Leveraging collaborative learning models (e.g., peer-to-peer learning and cohort models).

Tied to Practice
- Designed to provide field experiences and/or to tie didactic learning to applied practice experience with ongoing, individualized feedback and support.

Responsive
- Designed to take into account variations in entry points and sequencing for accessing professional learning.
- Designed to take into account career stage, from novice to experienced.
- Designed to take into account challenges faced by practitioners with respect to accessibility, affordability, scheduling/time/logistics constraints, baseline skills, and perceptions about professional learning activities and systems.

velopment and early learning for these young children. This existing work can be leveraged to accomplish more effective, widespread, and lasting change if knowledge and expertise are shared and efforts are coordinated through a more comprehensive framework. The persistently diffuse nature of the many systems and organizations that serve these children calls for approaches that are more collaborative and inclusive, and many of the committee's recommendations rely on a collective approach of this kind.

Drawing on the unifying foundation presented in the preceding section and best practices for collaborative approaches to systems change,

BOX 12-5
Features of Collaborative Systems Change
for the Birth Through Age 8 Workforce

All systems change efforts are grounded in professional competencies for child development and early learning.

Collective efforts need to be guided by the science of child development and early learning and aligned with the core competencies for care and education professionals outlined in Boxes 12-2 and 12-3 and with the principles for professional learning listed in Box 12-4. Therefore, an important part of the formative work for agencies and organizations involved in supporting children from birth through age 8 at the national, state, and local levels is to assess and revise as needed any current statements of professional competencies for both practitioners and leaders, and to review the extent to which all professional learning and workforce development opportunities, policies, and supports are informed by and aligned with those competencies.

A comprehensive view of the workforce is taken across professional roles, settings, and age ranges.

Attention to the workforce for early childhood education often centers on the preschool years, and discussion of improving continuity often focuses on children entering kindergarten. This focus is due in part to the relative strength of central oversight for publicly funded or subsidized preschools through Head Start and the emergence of preschool as part of public elementary school systems. Attention to these settings and age ranges continues to be important, but to be successful, collective efforts need to place similar emphasis along the full birth through age 8 range and across professional roles and settings.

In particular, concerted attention is needed to incorporate into these efforts the workforce development needs of those who provide care and education for infants and toddlers. These professionals have historically had the weakest, least explicit and coherent, and least resourced infrastructure for professional learning and workforce supports. Practitioners in settings outside of centers and schools, such as family childcare, have historically had even less infrastructure for professional learning and workforce supports. A critical role of these collective efforts, then, is to create this much-needed infrastructure for these professionals.

At the other end of the age spectrum, concerted attention is also needed to incorporate educators and other professional roles in early elementary schools. For them, professional learning is already supported through a more explicit and robust infrastructure. However, the practices entailed in educating the youngest elementary students can be insufficiently emphasized in the context of the broader K-12 professional learning systems that incline toward the education of older children. The collective efforts envisioned by the committee therefore need to inform and improve this existing infrastructure.

A comprehensive view is taken of professional learning and factors that affect professional practice.

A number of factors contribute to workforce development and to quality professional practice for both practitioners and leaders. Higher education programs, mentoring and coaching, and in-service professional development are all important mechanisms for developing and sustaining the knowledge and competencies of professionals. Other elements not always treated as an integrated part of professional learning, such as agencies that regulate licensure and credentialing systems and program quality assurance systems, also can contribute directly to the quality of professional practice. All of these elements need to be represented in collaborative efforts to develop a comprehensive and more coordinated system of professional learning so that goals are aligned across the elements, and each contributes to systems that are better coordinated and less disparate. Other factors also are important and are influenced or controlled by stakeholders other than the professionals themselves or the systems that provide their education and training. These include the practice environment, such as staffing structures, working conditions, and staff-to-child ratios; the availability of supplies, instructional materials, and other resources; the policies that affect professional requirements, opportunities for professional advancement, and assessment systems; and the status and well-being of the workforce, such as incentives that attract and retain these professionals, perceptions of care and education professions, compensation, and stressors and the availability of supportive services to help manage them. To achieve the ultimate aim of ensuring sustained systems change, it is important to see these factors as working collectively and to engage stakeholders with influence across these various elements.

Diverse stakeholders are engaged in collaborative efforts.

In addition to comprehensive representation of practice communities across professional roles, settings, and age ranges as described above, engaging diverse stakeholders means representing the multiple relevant disciplines in the research community, policy research and analysis, policy makers and government leadership, higher education, agencies that oversee licensure and credentialing as well as accreditation, and organizations that provide ongoing professional learning. For some areas of action, it may also be important to collaborate or consult with organizations whose mission relates to the professionals who work with children and families in the closely related sectors of health and social services, as well as with organizations that represent family perspectives.

In addition, the workforce itself and the children and families it serves represent a racially, ethnically, linguistically, and socioeconomically diverse population. The entities that assume responsibility and leadership for changes that will affect them need to ensure that this diversity is considered and reflected in their decision making and actions and to include perspectives from individuals that reflect a similar diversity. Similarly, circumstances vary widely in different localities, which makes geographic diversity another important dimension to consider, especially

continued

BOX 12-5 Continued

for national coordination efforts or for state efforts in states with a wide range of local contexts.

Context matters.

The steps needed for change will depend on factors that are specific to the context of different state and local environments, and different strategies and timelines will be needed accordingly. Different localities will have different strengths and different gaps in their professional learning infrastructure at the outset, and the amount and sources of their financial and other resources will vary. Education levels in the population and the labor market also will vary, which affects the supply and demand characteristics of both the current workforce and the pipeline for the potential future workforce. Solutions may vary as well according to population density and the availability and accessibility of services and institutions.

A backbone infrastructure is established.

A key factor in the success and sustainability of collaborative efforts is having some form of backbone infrastructure. The role of a backbone organization is to convene the various stakeholders; to maintain and refine the collaborative strategy; and to facilitate, coordinate, and monitor the progress of collaborative efforts. There currently exists no such backbone organization to represent workforce development comprehensively across professional roles, settings, and age ranges entailed in care and education for children from birth through age 8.

One approach would be to create a new backbone organization to facilitate collective efforts, such as a new coalition at the national, state, or local level. Such a backbone organization could provide sustainable leadership for the change process—a challenge for diverse stakeholders that each are understandably driven by their own priorities based on the oversight mechanisms and incentive structures that inform their routine responsibilities and functioning. However, forming a new organization would require significant financial resources. Another approach would be for an existing organization to assume the leadership role in facilitating the collaborative change process. This approach would not eliminate the resource requirement, but would limit the need for investment in new organizational infrastructure. With this approach, however, the direction of collective efforts could be drawn toward the core priorities of the lead organization, which also could lack credibility or have difficulty gaining the confidence of other sectors or disciplinary perspectives. Therefore, the lead organization would need to commit to inclusivity and neutrality. For example, a lead organization whose primary or historical focus was early childhood education would need to commit to being inclusive of early elementary perspectives and stakeholders. Similarly, a lead organization typically focused on higher education would need to commit to being inclusive of other components that contribute to ongoing professional learning.

A smaller-scale alternative to a full-scale collaborative initiative would be to establish periodic convenings and other mechanisms for communication among stakeholders doing related work. This approach would require fewer resources, but might also be less likely to lead to concrete collaborative actions and might be difficult to sustain.

One way individual organizations could enhance their commitment to ongoing collaboration and inclusivity would be to broaden their internal guidance and oversight mechanisms, such as their boards of directors or advisory committees, to include expertise and representation across the birth through age 8 continuum, even if their core mission is related to a subset of roles, age ranges, or settings. Doing so would reinforce the importance of aligning across professional roles and settings, facilitate communication with collaborative partners, and hold the organization accountable for a commitment to an inclusive and collaborative approach.

Another important aspect of coordinated systems change is that not every action taken to improve professional learning and workforce development will require the collective action of all stakeholders. Some actions will be specific to a subset of professional roles, such as infant-toddler specialists, early elementary teachers, Head Start center directors, or mental health consultants. Some actions can be taken at the level of smaller collaborations or at the level of institutions or even individuals. But through the facilitation of a backbone infrastructure, these cascading levels of implementation can be linked to contribute to the ultimate common agenda so that each aspect of professional practice strengthens and is improved by advances in other aspects.

Duplication of effort is avoided.

Collaborative systems change will be most effective when it draws on available resources, frameworks, and guidance and builds on any collaborative efforts already under way—engaging established organizations and leveraging current efforts to avoid creating entirely new infrastructure and solutions. In some cases, existing national-, state-, or community-level efforts already cover some elements of the comprehensive systems change that is needed. For example, many states and communities already have early learning councils or coalitions or similar organizations. Implementation of this report's recommendations can serve to inform and reinforce the importance of those efforts, to strengthen their infrastructure and resources, and to catalyze a more comprehensive approach. Where coalitions have not yet been formed, local communities can learn from the experiences of other communities that share similar characteristics.

To avoid unnecessary duplication while also more effectively supporting consistency and continuity for children from birth through age 8, existing coalitions could benefit from reviewing their efforts in light of the principles put forth in this report, the specific actions laid out in the recommendations and implementation considerations that follow in this chapter, and the scope of their current coalition partners. For example, are current early learning coalitions focused on workforce development and professional learning? Are they adequately inclusive of both early childhood and early elementary settings? Are current collaborative efforts that focus primarily on services for children inclusive of what is needed to support the adults who work with children? Are these collaborative efforts reaching out to collaborate and coordinate with the health and social services sectors?

Box 12-5 provides a framework for collaborative systems change consisting of features that are key to improving workforce development for care and education professionals who work with children from birth through age 8. In brief, for collaborative change to achieve lasting success it is important to be inclusive in recruiting stakeholders who need to be involved; to establish a backbone infrastructure; to conduct an assessment of baseline capacities, activities, and needs; and to develop a common agenda, mutually reinforcing activities, continuous communication, and a shared measurement approach that can be applied to track progress and course correct as needed.

Appendix F provides examples of references, tools, and resources for best practices in implementing collaborative systems change as a process in general and in particular for early care and education. Examples are also provided of existing initiatives using collaborative approaches; additional examples can be found in the discussion of continuity in Chapter 5 (see Boxes 5-1 and 5-2). The tools and resources described do not represent a comprehensive review, and the committee did not draw conclusions to endorse particular exemplars. Rather, these examples are provided as a prompt to explore available options and resources that can assist in collaborative systems change efforts.

RECOMMENDATIONS

The committee's recommendations to improve professional learning and policies and practices related to the development of the workforce that provide care and education for children from birth through age 8 address the following key areas: qualification requirements for professional practice (Recommendations 1-3), higher education (Recommendations 4 and 5), professional learning during ongoing practice (Recommendation 6), evaluation and assessment of professional practice (Recommendation 7), the critical role of leadership (Recommendation 8), interprofessional practice (Recommendation 9), support for implementation (Recommendations 10-12), and improving the knowledge base to inform professional learning and workforce development (Recommendation 13). Considerations for implementing these recommendations are highlighted throughout.

Qualification Requirements for Professional Practice

All care and education professionals have a similarly complex and challenging scope of work. However, this fact is not consistently reflected in practices and policies regarding requirements for qualification to practice. Instead the requirements and expectations for educators of children from birth through age 8 vary widely for different professionals based on their role, the ages of the children with whom they work, their practice setting, and what agency or institution has jurisdiction or authority for setting qualification criteria. The result is a mix of legally required licensure qualifications and voluntary certificates, endorsements, and credentials that employers may adopt as requirements or professionals may pursue to augment and document their qualifications.

These different standards for qualification, which often are based more on historical professional traditions or what systems can afford than on what children need, drive differences among professional roles in terms of professional learning, hiring prospects, and career pathways—and ultimately can lead to significant variations in knowledge and competencies and in the quality of professional practice in different settings. This lack of consistency is dissonant with what the science of early learning reveals about the foundational core competencies that all care and education professionals need and the importance of consistency in learning experiences for children in this age range. Greater coherence in qualification requirements across professional roles would improve the consistency and continuity of high-quality learning experiences for children from birth through age 8.

The analogy of a tree is a useful way to characterize the currently diffuse landscape of professional roles in a more coherent way, with both shared and specialized standards for knowledge and competencies (see Figure 12-3). The tree has *roots* that represent how individuals enter into a role working with young children in different ways with different preexisting qualifications, yet all need access to learning supports to achieve a shared foundation of knowledge and competencies. The *trunk* represents that shared foundation, from which *branches* extend to represent the specialized knowledge and competencies needed as individuals pursue differentiated professional roles. As the branches extend, they reflect further differentiation into specialized roles, as well as progression from novice to experienced, including potential advanced education and certification. Even as these roles differentiate, they also need to maintain connections to and alignment with each other to support continuity of care and education and linkages to professionals in other sectors.

A tiered trunk represents first the child development fundamentals that everyone working with children should have (tier 1 in Figure 12-3; see also Box 12-1 earlier in this chapter). From this lower tier as a foundation, professionals in health and social services branch off to their own specific professional qualifications, which both encompass and extend beyond the birth through age 8 range. The middle tier of the trunk represents a core of qualifications related to fostering development and learning that are shared across all professional roles within the care and education sector (tier 2 in Figure 12-3). From this tier extend branches for specialist and consultant professionals who see children for periodic or referral services, such as home visitors, early intervention specialists, and mental health consultants, and who in addition have existing qualification systems specific to their

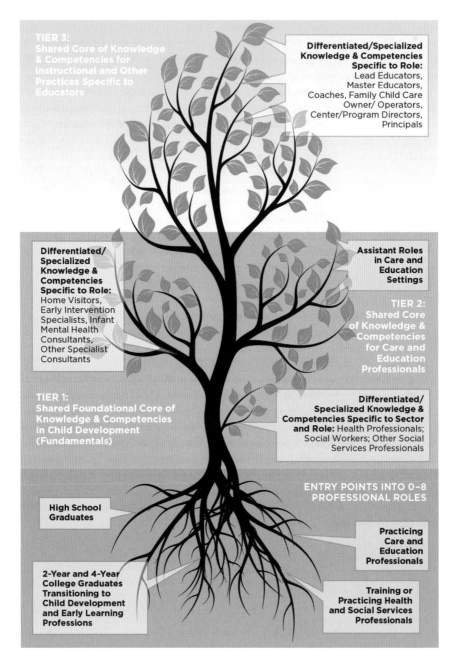

TIER 3:
Shared Core of Knowledge
& Competencies for
Instructional and Other
Practices Specific to
Educators

Differentiated/Specialized
Knowledge & Competencies
Specific to Role:
Lead Educators,
Master Educators,
Coaches, Family Child Care
Owner/ Operators,
Center/Program Directors,
Principals

Differentiated/
Specialized
Knowledge &
Competencies
Specific to Role:
Home Visitors,
Early Intervention
Specialists, Infant
Mental Health
Consultants,
Other Specialist
Consultants

Assistant Roles
in Care and
Education
Settings

TIER 2:
Shared Core
of Knowledge &
Competencies
for Care and
Education
Professionals

TIER 1:
Shared Foundational Core of
Knowledge & Competencies
in Child Development
(Fundamentals)

Differentiated/
Specialized Knowledge &
Competencies Specific to Sector
and Role: Health Professionals;
Social Workers; Other Social
Services Professionals

ENTRY POINTS INTO 0–8
PROFESSIONAL ROLES

High School
Graduates

Practicing
Care and
Education
Professionals

2-Year and 4-Year
College Graduates
Transitioning to
Child Development
and Early Learning
Professions

Training or
Practicing Health
and Social Services
Professionals

FIGURE 12-3 Tiered representation of shared and specialized standards for knowledge and competencies of professionals who work with young children.

roles. This core is shared with those professionals who are responsible for regular, daily care and education of children from birth through age 8. Branches also extend from this core for closely supervised assistant roles in care education settings, such as aides and assistant teachers. For other roles, the trunk first extends to another tier with a more specialized set of shared knowledge and competencies related to instructional and other practices that foster development and early learning (tier 3 in Figure 12-3; see also Boxes 12-2 and 12-3 earlier in this chapter). This tier represents those responsible for planning and implementing activities and instruction or those in a leadership position overseeing the professionals who plan and implement instruction, such as the lead educator in classroom settings, the owner/operator in family childcare, the center director/program director, and the principal and assistant principal in schools that include early elementary students. The branches that extend from this trunk represent differentiated competencies and practice experience relevant and specific to subsets within the birth through age 8 continuum of settings; age ranges; roles; and content, subject matter, or other specialization.

Recommendation 1: Strengthen competency-based qualification requirements for all care and education professionals working with children from birth through age 8.

Government agencies[2] and nongovernmental resource organizations[3] at the national, state, and local levels should review their standards and policies for workforce qualification requirements and revise them as needed to ensure they are competency based for all care and education professionals. These requirements should be consistently aligned with the principles delineated in this report to reflect foundational knowledge and competencies shared across professional roles working with children from birth through age 8, as well as specific and differentiated knowledge and competencies matched to the practice needs and expectations for specific roles.

---

[2] Government agencies when referred to in this report, whether national (federal), state, and/or local, include those with responsibilities for education (early childhood, elementary, higher education), health and human services, social welfare, and labor, as well as elected officials in executive offices and legislatures.

[3] Nongovernmental resource organizations when referred to in this report include those that provide funding, technical assistance, voluntary oversight mechanisms, and research and policy guidance, such as philanthropic and corporate funders, national professional associations for practitioners and leadership, unions, research institutions, policy and advocacy organizations, associations that represent institutions of higher education, and associations that represent providers of professional learning outside of higher education.

The current requirements and expectations for educators of children from birth through age 8 vary widely not only for different professional roles but also by what agency or institution has jurisdiction or authority for setting qualification criteria. Differing standards for qualification drive differences among professional roles in terms of education, training, and infrastructure for professional learning during ongoing practice, and hence differences in knowledge and competencies in different settings.

A review process guided by mutual alignment with the principles set forth in this report across agencies and organizations and across the national, state, and local levels would lay the groundwork for greater coherence in the content of and processes for qualification requirements, such as those for credentialing and licensure. As a result, even when different systems or localities have policies that are organized differently by age ranges and roles, those policies could still work in concert to foster quality practice across professional roles and settings that support more consistent high-quality learning experiences for children from birth through age 8. The scan of example competency statements in Chapter 7, summarized previously in Boxes 12-2 and 12-3, highlights areas likely to be most in need of review in policies for licensure and credentialing.

At the national level, for example, multiple federal programs provide funding, technical assistance, and other support for young children. Examples include the Maternal and Child Health Services Block Grant Program; the Child Care and Development Fund; Head Start/Early Head Start; Maternal, Infant, and Early Childhood Home Visiting Programs; Preschool Development Grants; Race to the Top funds; and grants through the Individuals with Disabilities Education Act and the Elementary and Secondary Education Act. An effort among the agencies responsible for these programs to use the principles of this report to review and revise expectations for the qualifications of the workforce hired using federal funds would contribute to greater consistency and quality in the experiences that affect the development and early learning of young children. A similar review by national nongovernmental credentialing systems, such as the Child Development Associate (CDA) and National Board for Professional Teaching Standards (NBPTS), would likewise yield opportunities for revisions to optimize continuity for children without disrupting existing specialized and differentiated credentialing systems.

At the state level, there is wide variation in licensure, and licensure commonly has overlap within the birth through age 8 continuum. Review processes within states—driven by mutual alignment with the principles laid out in this report—would ensure that professional practice expectations are more widely in keeping with the science of child development and early learning and more consistent across professional roles and from state to state.

Recommendation 2: Develop and implement comprehensive pathways and multiyear timelines at the individual, institutional, and policy levels for transitioning to a minimum bachelor's degree qualification requirement, with specialized knowledge and competencies, for all lead educators[4] working with children from birth through age 8.

Currently, most lead educators in care and education settings prior to elementary school are not expected to have the same level of education— a bachelor's degree—as teachers leading elementary school classrooms. A transition to a minimum bachelor's degree requirement for all lead educators—if implemented through a comprehensive approach alongside other related changes—is likely to contribute to improving the quality of professional practice, creating coherence in qualification systems such as credentialing and licensure, stabilizing the workforce, and improving consistency in high-quality learning experiences and optimal outcomes for children from birth through age 8.

Recommendation 2a: State leadership and licensure and accreditation agencies, state and local stakeholders in care and education, and institutions of higher education should collaboratively develop a multiyear, phased, multicomponent, coordinated strategy to set the expectation that lead educators who support the development and early learning of children from birth through age 8 should have at a minimum a bachelor's degree and specialization in the knowledge and competencies needed to serve as a care and education professional. This strategy should include an implementation plan tailored to local circumstances with coordinated pathways and timelines for changes at the individual, institutional, and policy levels.

Recommendation 2b: Federal government agencies and nongovernmental resource organizations should align their policies with a multiyear, phased strategy for instituting a minimum bachelor's degree requirement. They should develop incentives and dedicate resources from existing and new funding streams and technical assistance programs to support individual, institutional, systems, and policy pathways for meeting this requirement in states and local communities.

---

[4] Lead educators are those who bear primary responsibility for children and are responsible for planning and implementing activities and instruction and overseeing the work of assistant teachers and paraprofessionals. They include the lead educator in classroom and center-based settings, center directors/administrators, and owner/operators and lead practitioners in home-based or family childcare settings (tier 3 in Figure 12-3).

Policy decisions about qualification requirements are complex, as is the relationship among level of education, high-quality professional practice, and outcomes for children. Given that empirical evidence about the effects of a bachelor's degree is inconclusive, a decision to maintain the status quo and a decision to transition to a higher level of education as a minimum requirement entail similar uncertainty and as great a potential consequence for outcomes for children. In the absence of conclusive empirical evidence, the committee draws on its collective expert judgment to make this recommendation on the following grounds:

- Existing research on this question has important limitations and has produced mixed findings, and as a result it does not provide conclusive guidance. The research does not discount the potential that a high-quality college education can better equip educators with the sophisticated knowledge and competencies needed to deliver high-quality educational practices that are associated with better child outcomes at all ages.
- Holding lower educational expectations for early childhood educators than for elementary school educators perpetuates the perception that educating children before kindergarten requires less expertise than educating K-3 students, which helps to justify policies that make it difficult to maximize the potential of young children and the early learning programs that serve them.
- Disparate degree requirement policies create a bifurcated job market, both between elementary schools and early care and education as well as within early care and education as a result of degree requirements in Head Start and other settings as well as publicly funded prekindergarten programs. Educators who are more able to seek higher education, continue their professional growth, and acquire credentials that qualify them for better-compensated positions leave programs that serve young children and work in schools with older children, or leave less well-resourced preschool and childcare settings for young children for better resourced ones. This situation potentially perpetuates a cycle of disparity in the quality of the learning experiences of young children.
- The current differences in expectations across professional roles are largely an artifact of the historical traditions and perceived value of these jobs, as well as the limited resources available to the care and education sector, rather than being based on the needs of children. These expectations lag behind the science of child development and early learning, which shows clearly that the experiences of children in the earliest years—including their interactions with care

and education professionals—have profound effects, building the foundation for lifelong development and learning.

- The high level of complex knowledge and competencies that the science of child development and early learning indicates is necessary for educators working with young children of all ages is a strong rationale for equal footing among those who share similar lead educator roles and responsibilities for children. Few would argue, for example, that current expectations for early elementary school teachers should be lowered, and if the work of lead educators for younger children is based on the same science of child development and early learning and the same foundational competencies, it follows that they should be expected to have the same level of education.

- Greater consistency in the minimum educational expectations for similar professional roles regardless of the age of the child will bring the care and education sector in line with other sectors, which do not vary in minimum expectations based on the age of the child. For example, neonatologists and physicians who work with older children have the same minimum education requirement, and the minimum education requirement is the same for social workers who work with young children and their families and those who work with elementary-age children and their families.

The committee is cognizant of the complex issues that accompany a minimum degree requirement. Most important for this recommendation is that simply instituting policies requiring a minimum bachelor's degree is not sufficient, and this recommendation is closely interconnected with those that follow. A more consistent bachelor's degree requirement will be feasible and its potential benefits will be realized only if it is implemented carefully over time in the context of efforts to address other interrelated factors and with supportive federal, state, and local policies and informed, supportive leadership. These multiple factors, to return to the metaphor used earlier, are like interconnected gears that will not function if moved in isolation (see Figure 12-4). Therefore, strategies and implementation plans should include

- Pathways and timelines for lead educators, differentiated by individual needs, to acquire the necessary education in child development and early learning. Considerations should include
  - differentiation between pathways for current professionals with practice experience and those for the pipeline of prospective future professionals entering the field;

516

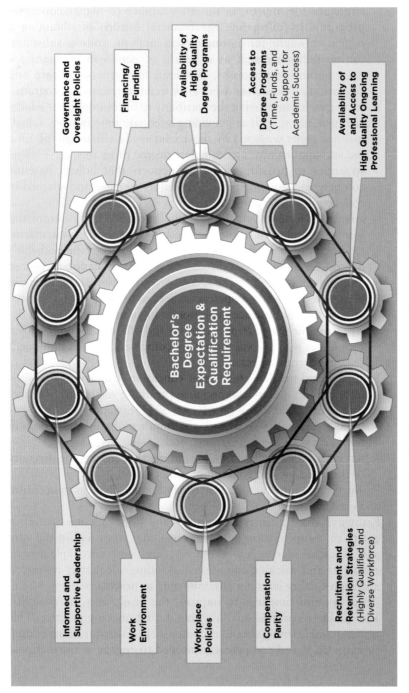

FIGURE 12-4 Interrelated components involved in implementing a minimum bachelor's degree requirement.

- strategies for improving the affordability of higher education programs by mitigating the financial burden of obtaining a degree through, for example, scholarships, tuition subsidies, tuition reimbursement as a benefit of employment, loans for degree-granting programs, and loan forgiveness for care and education professionals who work in underresourced programs;
- strategies for improving the feasibility of accessing higher education programs, such as providing adequate time in work schedules and other ways to give those who need to maintain full-time income opportunities to complete degree programs;
- strategies to provide academic supports that bolster baseline competencies for prospective educators to enter and succeed in college programs; and
- adaptive considerations for potential evolution in the nature and format of higher education degree and credentialing systems, including potential future alternative equivalents to the bachelor's degree—as long as the same general level of education is ensured and is accompanied by the specialized education and training in the knowledge and competencies needed to serve as an educator of young children. Such evolution in higher education might derive from the use of remote courses and other technology-driven changes as well as explorations of competency-based fulfillment of degree requirements.

- Pathways and timelines for higher education institutions to
  - improve the quality of specialized training related to practices that foster child development and early learning;
  - build the capacity to absorb the number of students who will need access to those programs; and
  - recruit a pool of educators-in-training that reflects the diversity of the children and communities they serve.
- Pathways and timelines for systems and policy changes to licensure and credentialing.
- Pathways and timelines for systems and policy changes to effect parity in compensation across professional roles within the care and education sector; in workplace policies; and in workplace environments and working conditions, including adequately resourced and high-quality learning environments in practice settings.
- Pathways and timelines to improve the availability, accessibility, and quality of professional learning during ongoing practice. This professional learning should encompass specialized training related to knowledge and competencies needed to engage in instructional

and other practices that foster childhood development and early learning, following the principles laid out earlier.

- Assessments of resource needs, followed by resource mobilization plans and innovative financing strategies such as scholarships and stipends for individuals, subsidies for higher education programs, and adjustments to the increased labor costs that will result from parity in compensation and benefits in the care and education sector.[5]
- Assessments to examine and plans to monitor and mitigate possible negative consequences, such as workforce shortages, reduced diversity in the professions, increased disparities among current and future professionals, upward pressure on out-of-pocket costs to families for care and education (creating a financial burden and potentially driving more families into the unregulated informal sector), and disruptions to the sustainability of operating in the for-profit and not-for-profit care and education market.
- Recruitment plans to engage a new, diverse generation of care and education professionals, highlighting the prospect of a challenging and rewarding career.
- Assessment plans to monitor progress and adapt implementation strategies as needed.

Successful strategies will require cooperative efforts that involve sectors beyond those involved directly in early childhood and elementary education, such as those focused on economic development and postsecondary education. At the federal level, for example, current interagency efforts organized around early learning programs should consult and coordinate with the Office of Postsecondary Education and the U.S. Department of Labor. A similar diversity of sectors will need to be represented in efforts at state and local levels. The range and complexity of factors that need to be coordinated also means that changes to degree requirement policies will need to be implemented over time with careful planning, and as a result, concurrent steps need to be taken to ensure that specialized training related to early childhood development and the core competencies that are critical for quality practice can be achieved through a range of professional learning mechanisms.

If implemented successfully, the shift that will result from this recommendation has the transformative potential to develop a more coherent

---

[5] As noted earlier, while acknowledging that the availability of resources and the implications of increased costs are an important reality that would affect the feasibility of the committee's recommendations, in clarifying the study charge the sponsors specified that the committee should exclude from its task conducting analyses about funding and financing.

workforce across all professional roles that support children from birth through age 8, with easier recruitment and better retention of well-qualified individuals for all of these professional roles as well as less competition among settings for the best-prepared employees. In addition, when professionals who work with children prior to elementary school and those working in elementary school settings are expected to have the same credentials and receive comparable rewards, these professionals will be better able to see themselves as part of a continuum with mutual respect and expectations that enable better connections, communication, and collaboration.

Implementation Considerations for Recommendation 2

Phased Approach

This recommendation will need to be implemented through a phased approach. Pathways should be developed as long-term strategies with immediate steps and short-term actions matched to the most critical needs. Phases of implementation should be planned with specific ambitious yet feasible timeline benchmarks for percentages of care and education professionals with a bachelor's degree. Specific timeline benchmarks for quality improvements and the capacity to absorb more students in degree-granting programs in institutions of higher education will also need to be set and aligned with the timeline for degree requirements. Similarly, timeline benchmarks for changes to related policies will need to be set and aligned. These timelines will also need to be aligned with resource mobilization and financing strategies.

The Importance of Context

Context will be of utmost importance in implementing this recommendation. This is why the committee recommends that pathways and benchmarks be developed at the local level with support, guidance, and incentives from national organizations and from government at the federal and state levels, as well as consequences that can be tied to funding and other oversight mechanisms. Setting overall state and national goals will be important, but it is critical to tailor specific timeline benchmarks to the local context (at the district/municipality/county level). The actions needed and the pace that is feasible will vary based on such community characteristics as population density, baseline requirements and trends in the number of educators with a bachelor's degree, the general education level of the population, local socioeconomic conditions and labor markets, the availability of higher education, and local resources for financing options. In addition, local targets will help counter the possibility that progress toward an overall benchmark will mask inequitable distribution across the state/nation when some geographic locations accelerate beyond the benchmark and those lagging significantly behind are not supported sufficiently because the overall average is on target.

Considerations for the Content and Quality of Degree Programs That Meet the Qualification Requirement

It is important for the degree requirement to acknowledge and be responsive to the many different pathways through which individuals enter this field, as well as to those already practicing in the field who will enter degree-granting programs as a result of this requirement. For this reason, the important criterion is not that the degree itself be in a specified major but that to be qualified to practice as a care and education professional, a candidate both have a bachelor's degree and complete a formally defined, accredited course of study in child development, early learning, and instruction. Such a course of study cannot just be related to child development in some way but should be appropriately designed to provide the knowledge and competencies associated with being a care and education professional and to meet the standards for components of a high-quality higher education program. Thus, the program should include, for example, coursework in development, subject-matter content, and instructional and relationship-building and other practices that foster development and early learning; field experiences; and documented demonstration of mastery of practice. Additional considerations for an appropriate course of study are outlined in the implementation considerations for Recommendation 5 later in this chapter.

In some cases, this defined, accredited course of study could be a specified degree or major, but it could also be a program or concentration or certificate in child development, early learning, and instruction that a student would complete along with another major or as a postbaccalaureate certificate program. Different options will best suit different types of degree candidates. For example, a currently practicing care and education professional might be best suited to pursuing a higher education program with a very targeted major in order to complete the new requirement to have a degree. On the other hand, a prospective candidate entering the field might pursue a broader undergraduate education with a different major while also completing the specific program or concentration in order to be qualified to practice upon graduation. And someone entering the field who became interested in working in the care and education of young children after already having completed a bachelor's degree might be best suited to a program or concentration that could be completed as a postbaccalaureate option instead of completing a second bachelor's degree. The criteria for a quality program would be the same for each of these scenarios, so that all programs would lead to assurances and documentation that the candidate has the necessary knowledge and competencies for quality professional practice.

Supply and Demand

The pathways to completing this transition will not succeed unless supply and demand move together. Higher education will need to absorb a larger number of degree candidates, creating the "supply," and at the same time policies need to have an aligned trajectory for requiring the hiring of lead educators with a bachelor's degree to create the "demand," and to support that requirement with the necessary incentives and financing. To ensure that qualified individuals remain in the professional roles that need to be filled, lead educators will need to be compensated at a level expected for those having a college degree and with parity across roles and settings. Federal and state policies need to support a shift in compensation standards that is tied to funding, resource mobilization, and financing strategies to garner the financial support, subsidies, or revenue necessary for governmental and nongovernmental centers, programs, and schools to be able to increase compensation levels.

Attention to Other Professional Learning Supports

As changes to degree requirements are being implemented over time with careful planning, efforts to improve the quality of other current professional learning mechanisms cannot be abandoned. In parallel, the quality and accessibility of all professional learning needs to be improved so that better-quality practice for today's children is not dependent on long-term change. Concurrent steps such as those outlined in the recommendations that follow need to be taken to ensure that specialized training in child development and early learning, including the knowledge and competencies necessary for quality practice, can also be achieved through a range of professional learning mechanisms, as long as they are of sufficient quality and are accessible to the workforce.

> **Recommendation 3: Strengthen practice-based qualification requirements, including a supervised induction period, for all lead educators working with children from birth through age 8.**
>
> Agencies and organizations at the national, state, and local levels should develop standards and implementation guidance for expanding qualification requirements for all lead educators to incorporate an

induction period with closely supervised practice before final qualification for autonomous practice is acquired.

The opportunity for supervised practice is important to ensure that practitioners have mastered the competencies necessary to work with children from birth through age 8, yet many professional roles in care and education currently are not required to have a supervised induction period as a transition to autonomous practice.

In introducing this requirement, it will be necessary in parallel to consider and develop strategies for addressing such implications as the need to develop a greater number and diversity of field placements capable of providing this kind of professional learning with appropriately qualified supervisors and mentors. It will also be necessary to consider how to differentiate and apply this requirement for experienced practitioners who are acquiring this qualification while already practicing.

Higher Education

Recommendation 4: Build an interdisciplinary foundation in higher education for child development.

The goal of this recommendation is for higher education to foster a fundamental shared knowledge base and competencies around child development for professionals in all sectors who work with young children, based on requirements for core coursework, other learning activities, and field-based learning experiences. Guided by the science of child development, this could serve as a baseline prerequisite for further study or as a child specialization enhancement. This would support preparation for various professional roles working with children from birth through age 8 in care and education, social services, and health/allied health professions. Additional coursework, learning, and practicum requirements would be differentiated according to the specific professional pathway students follow. The conceptual basis for this structure closely follows that for the core and differentiated professional qualifications previously visualized in Figure 12-3.

Recommendation 4a: To improve the consistency of the knowledge base for professionals working with young children, institutions of higher education, including leadership, administrators, and faculty, should review and revise their programs, policies, and infrastructure so they support child development as a cross-departmental, cross-disciplinary foundation that feeds into specialized degree and certificate programs for multiple specific professional roles.

Recommendation 4b: Federal and state government agencies and non-governmental resource organizations that fund initiatives in higher education should incentivize an interdisciplinary approach in programs that award degrees or certificates in fields related to young children.

Recommendation 4c: Voluntary accrediting agencies and governmental oversight mechanisms for educational and research institutions should include in their review criteria the extent to which an interdisciplinary approach is used in programs that award degrees or certificates in fields related to young children.

Implementation Considerations for Recommendation 4

Considerations for the Goals and Content of the Foundational Baseline

This foundational baseline across professional roles and sectors should

- orient students to the field through an interdisciplinary introduction that incorporates content and context from multiple fields associated with the science of childhood, team taught across disciplines;
- include requirements for core coursework that are designed to establish a more continuous and comprehensive understanding of child development;
- inform students about the broad range of professional roles from which to choose a future career;
- provide advising for students to learn about and select pathways starting from the core prerequisites to their chosen professional role;
- lay the foundation for competencies in interprofessional practice to support communication and collaboration across professional roles, settings, and sectors;
- provide opportunities for students to build relationships with individuals preparing for multiple professional roles and to understand the implications of the science across those roles;
- provide cross-disciplinary field experiences so that students pursuing professions in health, mental health, and social work can experience the realities of health and social service needs in childcare, kindergarten, and early elementary settings, and educators can experience the health settings and social service agencies where children they support are referred for services; and
- provide incentives and reduced administrative barriers for faculty and student participation in degree-granting pathways that cross departments and majors.

Considerations for Leadership and Administration in Institutions of Higher Education

The active participation of administrative and departmental leadership will be needed to address barriers resulting from the silos that commonly exist today among disciplines in institutions of higher education. These leaders should take steps to create infrastructure that will support cross-disciplinary work. For example, they should create opportunities for teams of faculty and students to come together based on common interests, opportunities for faculty from different disciplines to interact, seeded projects that cross disciplinary lines, agreements between administrators that underscore the value of group and cross-disciplinary efforts, faculty rewards and incentives for cross-departmental and cross-disciplinary work, and benchmarks for promotion and tenure documentation that account for and value excellence in group work. Mechanisms to support interdisciplinary faculty might include

- enabling faculty to readily cross departments, campuses, and schools in their teaching and research by
  - developing "professional learning communities" throughout campuses with joint appointments across departments,
  - incentivizing cross-departmental participation, and
  - using learning institutes that address teaching, research, and community engagement;
- using team teaching to provide students with both breadth and depth of expertise in a course and to model cross-disciplinary collaboration for students;
- facilitating knowledge sharing among faculty by supporting them in working in teams within and across programs; and
- educating people at the graduate school level who are rooted in the sciences of child development and pedagogy but are interdisciplinary in their training and approach.

Considerations for Incentives from Funders

To be feasible, implementing an interdisciplinary approach in higher education programs will require resources and incentives tied to funding. Government agencies and other organizations that fund initiatives in higher education should include

- funding mechanisms for institutions and faculty that are linked to participation in cross-department institutes, which should be formed with a core focus on developmental science and with a mis-

sion to foster interaction among faculty from different departments
and among students interested in a wide range of professional roles
that entail working with young children;

- funding mechanisms for institutions that are linked to building
  strong relationships with practice settings in their communities
  to create opportunities for field experiences for students and for
  practice-based research projects; and
- multidisciplinary training grants that bring developmental psychologists and other developmental scientists, health care professionals,
  educators, and social workers into a common training arena.

**Recommendation 5: Develop and enhance programs in higher educa-
tion for care and education professionals.**

Building on the cross-disciplinary foundation described in Recommendation 4, high-quality programs in higher education are needed that further
ensure and document the acquisition of the knowledge and competencies
needed for quality professional practice in care and education for children
from birth through age 8. As described previously, these programs need to
provide a formally defined, accredited course of study in child development,
early learning, and instruction. Such a course of study needs to provide students with coursework in development, subject-matter content, and instructional and other practices to foster development and early learning; field
experiences; and methods to document demonstrated mastery of practice.
In some cases this defined, accredited course of study could be a specified
degree or major, but it could also be a concentration or certificate in child
development, early learning, and instruction that a student would complete
alongside another major or as a postbaccalaureate program. Programs that
are differentiated for specific age ranges, subject-matter specialization, or
responsibilities should also ensure adequate knowledge of the development
and learning of children across the birth through age 8 continuum so that
care and education professionals will be prepared to support consistent
learning experiences for children.

> **Recommendation 5a: Institutions of higher education, including leader-
> ship, administrators, and faculty, should review and revise the require-
> ments and content of programs for students pursuing qualification to
> practice as care and education professionals working with children
> from birth through age 8.**
>
> **Recommendation 5b: Institutions of higher education should work with
> local practice communities to contribute a practice-based perspective to**

the design of higher education programs; to facilitate cross-institutional relationships that bolster the quality, availability, and accessibility of programs; and to facilitate the identification of appropriate and diverse field placements capable of contributing to the training of students.

Implementation Considerations for Recommendation 5

Considerations for Improving Content, Curriculum, and Pedagogy for Students Pursuing Care and Education Professions

The following considerations should guide efforts to improve higher education programs for those pursuing professions entailing the care and education of children from birth through age 8:

- Align content, curriculum, and pedagogy with the core knowledge and competencies identified in this report.
- Provide training that integrates knowledge with behaviors and practices.
- Enable students to develop the following in parallel rather than sequentially:
  - knowledge of the fundamentals of the science of early childhood development and learning;
  - general pedagogical knowledge;
  - subject-matter knowledge; and
  - pedagogical content knowledge, including all three aspects of learning trajectories—the goal (the subject-matter knowledge), the developmental progression of levels of thinking, the instructional activities corresponding to each level, and especially their connections.
- Enable students to develop competencies in child assessment (including formative assessment) and in the use of information from child assessments to modify and improve their instructional practice.
- Enable students to develop competencies to communicate and collaborate appropriately and productively with other practitioners working with a child, as well as with the child's parents or primary caretaker/guardian. To this end, students will need to develop
  - knowledge of the different nomenclature and terminology used in different care and education systems, as well as in the health and social services sector, to enable mutual understanding in interprofessional communications;
  - knowledge and skill in the use of discussion protocols and other tools for structured, facilitated information sharing that will

support appropriate analysis and interpretation of child data and avoid misuse and misinterpretation of data with potential negative consequences, such as assigning diagnoses to children incorrectly or prematurely and introducing biased expectations for children; and

- skills to recognize and work to mitigate, to the extent possible as an individual practitioner, systemic barriers to communication so that the sharing of knowledge and information among professionals will benefit students, parents, and educators.

• Provide high-quality practice-based and field-based learning experiences that enable students to

- access practice experience in the field to apply and build instructional and other competencies;
- experience supportive supervision, mentoring, coaching, and reflective practice;
- gain experience working with populations of children and families that are diverse in family structure, socioeconomic status, race, ethnicity, culture, language, and ability;
- gain experience engaging with families in practice settings and through home and community visits; and
- gain exposure to a range of different settings and systems across the age continuum from birth through age 8 (not limited to the practice settings they will enter in their professional role) so they can gain the understanding needed to support continuity for children across settings and professional roles in care and education.

Pathways for Transitioning Professionals

Institutions of higher education should develop tailored pathways for transitioning professionals, including differentiated pathways for practicing professionals in care and education seeking additional levels of qualification and for those in other sectors who decide late in their training or while in practice to focus on care and education for children from birth through age 8.

Considerations for Faculty (Full Time, Part Time, and Adjunct)

Implementing this recommendation will require faculty development. There is a need not only for faculty who are rooted in the sciences of child development and pedagogy but also for faculty whose primary valued competencies are in teaching students how to practice. Institutions of higher education therefore need to make a commitment to treating science and research related to practice, as well as faculty competencies in teaching students how to practice, with the same deference as that accorded theory and developmental research. Options to this end might include

- valuing and developing these skills equally in individual faculty hires and ensuring a balance; and
- establishing two separate but equally valued tracks for faculty (research faculty and applied/practice/instructional faculty)—tensions in which practice faculty are traditionally seen as less prestigious or less rigorous than research faculty will need to be addressed.

Considerations Across Institutions

As described above, a quality program relies on having sufficient depth and breadth of faculty to cover the range and diversity of expertise required to impart to students the scope of knowledge and competencies they need to acquire. Meeting this need is particularly challenging for smaller institutions and departments. Collaborations and connections across institutions are one way to meet this challenge by allowing students in smaller institutions to access courses and learning experiences with the necessary depth and specificity at institutions with greater faculty capacity. Such coordination is crucial both to ensure higher and more consistent quality in higher education and to provide higher education programs at the scale necessary to accommodate increasing enrollment in bachelor's degree programs when Recommendation 2 is implemented. Mechanisms for collaborations across institutions include

- establishing agreements between and among 2- and 4-year colleges in the same locality to develop consistent pathways and efficient transitions between institutions and into specialized programs—for example:
  - articulation agreements regarding credit transfers,
  - agreements about cross-enrollment of students in courses,
  - collaborative program development,
  - convening of faculty across institutions to share information about programs and to participate in joint planning and implementation of cross-institutional agreements; and
- building professional communities for faculty across institutions in the same locality through such mechanisms as
  - sharing of faculty through cross-appointments or teaching of courses across institutions,
  - joint faculty development activities,
  - coordinated identification and vetting of field experiences, and

– coordination to identify efficiencies and reduce duplication during the scale-up that will be necessary to accommodate increasing enrollment in bachelor's degree programs.

Professional Learning During Ongoing Practice

Recommendation 6: Support the consistent quality and coherence of professional learning supports during ongoing practice for professionals working with children from birth through age 8.

The goal of this recommendation is to incentivize greater quality, consistency, and parity in learning opportunities across settings and roles for care and education professionals who work with children from birth though age 8 through technical assistance; funding mechanisms such as interagency pooling of resources; and support for clearinghouses, quality assurance systems, and other means of better coordinating professional learning systems.

Recommendation 6a: State and local governmental and nongovernmental stakeholders should collaboratively develop a clearinghouse and quality assurance system for locally available services and providers that can offer opportunities for professional learning during ongoing practice. These tools should serve to promote access to consistent quality and content in professional learning and to promote joint participation in professional learning activities across settings and professional roles for care and education professionals who work with children birth though age 8.

This clearinghouse and quality assurance system should

- define local gaps and needs in the availability and accessibility of professional learning activities;
- draw on the related efforts of existing organizations and initiatives and on resources already developed;
- provide guidance for individuals and employers or institutions on how to set professional learning objectives, select and prioritize professional learning activities, map out a sequence of professional learning activities, and access financial and other supports;
- coordinate with state accreditation or regulatory mechanisms for professional learning providers to create a quality assurance, accreditation, or endorsement infrastructure;
- coordinate with state quality rating and improvement systems or other quality improvement systems that apply to programs and

services provided to children to ensure that standards and opportunities for professional learning and support for quality practice
are aligned and strategically coordinated;

• promote joint professional learning opportunities among care and
education professionals across roles, age groups, and settings, and
provide a forum to facilitate collaborations; and

• develop assessment plans to monitor and continuously improve the
availability and quality of professional learning activities, as well
as the availability of services adequate to meeting the needs of the
workforce.

**Recommendation 6b: Federal and state government agencies and non-
governmental resource organizations that fund or provide technical
assistance for professional learning during ongoing practice should
incentivize greater consistency and parity in learning opportunities
across settings and roles for care and education professionals who work
with children from birth though age 8. These efforts should include
interagency pooling of resources to support clearinghouses, quality assurance systems, and other means of better coordinating professional
learning systems.**

Implementation Considerations for Recommendation 6

*Taking into Account the Current Status of Professional Learning Across
Professional Roles, Settings, and Age Ranges*

To be successful, collective efforts to improve systems for professional
learning during ongoing practice must place equal emphasis along the
birth through age 8 continuum and across professional roles and settings.
Particular attention is needed to those who provide care and education for
infants and toddlers and to practitioners in settings outside of centers and
schools, such as family childcare. These care and education professionals
have historically had the weakest, least explicit and coherent, and least
resourced infrastructure for professional learning. The collective efforts
proposed in this recommendation should serve to create much-needed infrastructure for these professionals.

For educators of children in the middle and upper range of the birth
through age 8 continuum, professional learning is currently supported
through a more explicit and robust infrastructure—this is most true for
early elementary school educators in school systems, and also to a lesser
extent for preschool educators, especially those supported through, for
example, federal programs or in elementary schools. For these educators,

the goals may be twofold. The first is to promote professional learning that is specialized for birth through age 8 and may need to occur outside of those existing professional learning systems. The second is to identify more clearly what professional learning activities are available within existing systems; to broaden that availability to other professionals who could benefit; and to improve the content of what is available so it is more relevant for educating younger children, such as content for the early elementary grades in the broader K-12 professional learning systems, which sometimes incline toward practices for the education of older children.

Elements of Quality Assurance, Guidelines, and Criteria

Quality assurance, guidelines, and criteria for professional learning should include the following elements. These elements should inform the actions of both those who provide professional learning activities and leaders in care and education settings, who need to understand how to select and structure effective professional learning activities for the practitioners and settings they oversee:

- Standards for quality that are based on best practices and evidence-based strategies to support the acquisition and maintenance of core competencies and accord with the principles for professional learning outlined earlier in Box 12-4.
  - Effective professional learning during ongoing practice should encompass active learning involving the details of setting up, conducting, and formatively evaluating experiences and activities for children, including a focus on review of children's progress and small-group instructional activities.
  - Professional learning related to instructional strategies for specific subject areas should develop knowledge of the content to be taught, including deep conceptual knowledge of the subject and its processes. It should give corresponding attention to specific pedagogical content knowledge, including all three aspects of learning trajectories: the goal, the developmental progression of levels of thinking, and the instructional activities corresponding to each level. This also helps build common understanding for care and education professionals to employ in working with each other and professionals in other sectors.
  - Professional learning also should focus on common actions and problems of practice, which, to the extent possible, should be situated in the classroom and allow for care and education professionals to actively implement what they are learning and discuss their experiences in doing so.

- Professional learning should include coaching embedded in the practice setting. The knowledge and skill of coaches are of critical importance. Coaches must have knowledge of instructional and other practices to foster development and learning, as well as knowledge and competencies in effective coaching.
- Approaches used should include peer study groups or networks and collective participation by care and education professionals who work together.
- Sustained and intensive professional learning experiences are preferable to stand-alone professional learning activities.
- Professional learning activities (e.g., trainings, adoption of new curricula, implementation of new standards) should be interconnected and consistent in content and approach, with a shared language and goal structure that promote peer communication and collaboration.
- Professional learning should be tied to the science of adult learning and recognize the importance of multiple, comprehensive domains of knowledge and learning for adults.
- Economic, institutional, and regulatory barriers to the availability of and access to professional learning, including equity and diversity concerns, should be addressed.

- Guidance on how to design professional learning portfolios that build on the entire range of learning activities and training mechanisms available, cover the full scope of knowledge and competencies that need to be supported, and are linked to incentives and career advancement.
- Guidance on balancing professional learning activities that provide deep specificity for particular roles and specializations and those that are comprehensive and relevant across professional roles, settings, and ages.
- Guidance on when to implement joint professional learning and when to focus on professional learning for specific roles.
- Guidance on effective joint professional learning that
  - promotes professional practice with greater continuity across age ranges and settings;
  - promotes participation of professionals from different roles and settings in the same professional learning activities;
  - offers activities specifically designed to bring together professionals who work with different age ranges within the birth through age 8 span and in different settings and to provide training in better supporting children as they move from infant/toddler services to preschool to kindergarten to grades 1-3, such

as by developing more continuous and aligned curricula and learning environments;
- supports professional learning communities and other partnerships and convenings across roles, settings, and age ranges; and
- provides incentives for professionals across roles, settings, and age ranges to participate in the same activities and systems for ongoing professional learning.
- Guidance on the effective the use of technology and remote learning as a way to deliver professional learning services.

The Need to Improve Systemic Supports for Access to Professional Learning

High-quality professional learning during ongoing practice needs to be not only available but also accessible. Therefore, access needs to be a fundamental aspect of quality assurance systems. Factors that affect access for diverse professional roles and diverse populations of practitioners include affordability and financial support, geographic location and convenience, and time available to participate. Although barriers in these areas affect care and education professionals across settings and roles, they are particularly challenging for those in smaller organizations or family childcare, as well as those in rural areas or in urban areas with limited transportation.

A comprehensive systems change approach therefore needs to include such actions as cataloging (and developing if needed) sources for scholarships and subsidies or tuition and fee reimbursement incentive programs, and encouraging supervisors to allow employees time to participate without jeopardizing their income or placing an undue burden on their time outside of work. Employers, especially those in small organizations with low revenue margins, also need supports to help them facilitate participation in professional learning, such as subsidies to cover paid employee time away from work to participate and assistance in accessing and paying qualified substitutes.

Evaluation and Assessment of Professional Practice

Based on the science of child development and early learning and its implications for professional competencies, current systems for measuring the performance of educators—and even current reforms to those systems—are not sufficient for those who work with children in the early elementary years and younger; indeed, they may produce unreliable data about children's learning and development and the quality of instruction. Current reforms focus on student outcomes and instructional practices in one or two areas, instead of capturing the developmental nature of early learning and the full range of domains that are important. In addition, evaluation and assessment systems fail to capture important competencies such as trauma-informed practice, family engagement, and collaboration and communication with other professionals. As a result, current evaluation and assessment policies and systems may reinforce and reward a narrow view of effectiveness while missing best practices that should be fostered and recognized in professionals working with children from birth through age 8.

> Recommendation 7: Develop a new paradigm for evaluation and assessment of professional practice for those who work with children from birth through age 8.

> Recommendation 7a: Federal and state policy makers, school district leadership, and school, center, and program leadership, in partnership with representatives of professionals and of families whose children are served in their settings, should review and improve their current policies and systems for evaluation and assessment of care and education professionals.[6] The goal should be to improve the extent to which current evaluation and assessment procedures, including portfolios of assessment and observation tools, achieve the following: (1) assess children's progress in all domains of development and early learning, (2) assess a broad range of professional knowledge and competencies, (3) account for setting-level and community-level factors, and (4) are incorporated in a continuous system of supports to inform and improve professional practice and professional learning systems.

Developing and implementing more appropriate systems for evaluating and assessing the performance of care and education professionals will require a shift from the current paradigm. Because of the variable nature of learning and development from birth through age 8, considering multiple sources of evidence derived with multiple methods and at multiple times is important when evaluating and assessing educator performance. A continuous improvement system of evaluation and assessment should align with research on the science of how young children develop and learn, be comprehensive in its scope of early developmental and learning objectives, reflect day-to-day practice competencies and not just single-point assessments that may be subject to misrepresentation or manipulation, reflect what

---

[6] Federal and state policy makers include those in elected office as well as those in education and health agencies that administer early childhood care and education and early elementary education. School district leadership includes such roles as school superintendents and school boards. School, center, and program leadership includes such roles as principals and center directors. Representatives of professionals include professional associations, unions, and practitioner groups. Representatives of families include advocacy organizations and parent groups.

professionals do in their practice settings and also how they work with professional colleagues and with families, be tied to access to professional learning, and account for setting-level and community-level factors beyond the control of practitioners that affect their capacity to practice effectively.

It may not be feasible for education systems and settings to incorporate every element of a fully comprehensive evaluation and assessment approach. Nonetheless, to make more informed decisions about priorities in reforming evaluation and assessment systems, district and state leaders would benefit from taking stock of which outcomes and practices their current evaluation and assessment policies favor, which they omit, and how these decisions affect the professional growth of care and education professionals and children's progress in learning and development. This review should be informed by whether evaluation and assessment systems are able to answer the following questions:

- How effective are professionals at knowing and implementing practices that support the development of general cognitive skills, academic skills and content knowledge in specific subject areas, socioemotional skills, learning competencies and dispositions, executive function, and mental and physical health in developmentally appropriate ways for the age group and population with which they work?
- How effective are professionals at conducting ongoing formative assessment in each of these domains for the age group and population with which they work? How effective are professionals at using the data from these assessments to inform their interactions with children and their caregiving, instructional, and other practices?
- How are the children with whom professionals are working developing in each of these domains?
- Do professionals demonstrate knowledge and capacity for trauma-informed practice when working with young children who have experienced or are experiencing significant stress or chronically adverse environments?
- Do professionals demonstrate knowledge and capacity for best practices in working with dual language learners to support their growth across all learning and developmental domains?
- Do professionals demonstrate knowledge and capacity for best practices in working with children with disabilities to support their growth across all learning and developmental domains?
- How skilled are professionals at collaborating with their colleagues both within and beyond their fields (e.g., health, social work) to

support the success and well-being of the children with whom they work?

- How skilled are professionals at engaging family members from diverse cultural and socioeconomic backgrounds as partners in supporting students' learning and development, and at connecting family members with services and resources that support their own well-being?

In addition, more research and development is needed to inform the design of evaluation and assessment systems for practitioners working with young children that distinguish high-quality from poor practice, provide data to inform improvement efforts, and are integrated with professional learning strategies.

> Recommendation 7b: Federal and state policy makers in education and health, along with nongovernmental resource organizations, should invest in research and development to improve or create new tools for evaluating and assessing the practice of professionals who provide care and education for children from birth through age 8. The priority focus areas for this research and development should include (1) improving assessment of children across all domains of development and early learning, (2) improving assessment of instructional and other practices that foster childhood development and early learning in care and education settings, (3) developing tools with which to assess family engagement and collaboration with other professionals, and (4) assessing what portfolios of evaluation and assessment tools contribute to comprehensive effective evaluation systems.

Research is needed to yield a better understanding of what combinations of sources and tools can help evaluation systems produce more reliable and valid assessments of both educator performance and student achievement or growth during this age span, while also being feasible within the time and other constraints faced by educators and leaders. A few areas of research are particularly needed. One such area is efforts to develop more valid and reliable assessments for content knowledge development, for socioemotional development, and for learning competencies and dispositions that are appropriate for children from birth through age 8. Domains of development and learning for these ages have received less attention from assessment researchers and developers than is warranted. Research also is needed to better understand the appropriateness of these assessments as measures of the performance of adult practitioners. In addition, such tools may need to leverage technology and other approaches to minimize the practitioner's role in the assessment process and prevent significant conflicts of interest when child assessments are used as a metric in determining rewards or punitive measures.

More research also is needed on effective methods for assessing instructional and other practices that foster child development and early learning in care and education settings, especially the extent to which commonly used observation instruments are validated for educators in prekindergarten through third grade and for educators of younger children in settings outside of school systems. Findings of this research would inform specific adaptations of these instruments to make them effective at distinguishing good and poor practice in such settings. These findings also would help identify other instruments or inform the development of new tools that might be a better fit for these settings. Importantly, observation tools should be able to identify practices that are effective for children with specific learning needs, such as dual language learners, children who have experienced trauma, and children with disabilities.

In addition, what care and education professionals do outside their immediate practice setting can be critical to student success. Research and innovation are needed for ways to assess how effectively these professionals collaborate with their peers and with professionals in other sectors and engage with and support family members, as well as how these activities are related to children's learning and development.

Implementation Considerations for Recommendation 7

Practitioner-Level Considerations

As part of their professional learning, practitioners need to be taught about assessment tools that can be used to capture how children are doing and how that information can be used to improve their practice. Evaluation and assessment systems should be designed and implemented to encourage a comprehensive approach to practice across all domains of child development and early learning that affect child outcomes.

Setting-Level and Community-Level Considerations

Evaluation and assessment systems need to take into account that setting-level factors outside of the practitioner's control can affect both the outcomes of the children with whom they are working and their own performance and quality of practice. Examples of such factors include overcrowded classrooms, poorly resourced settings, lack of access to professional learning supports, quality and quantity of supportive community factors, and quality of home environments. There is a risk that evaluation and assessment systems will hold individual practitioners accountable for effects on children due to such factors, and thereby contribute to challenges with equitable recruitment and retention of quality professionals across diverse practice settings.

Leadership-Level Considerations

As part of their professional learning, center/program directors, principals, and administrators need training and support to understand appropriate expectations for the knowledge and competencies needed by professionals who work with children from birth through age 8 so they know how to assess them. These leaders also need to understand what constitutes appropriate assessment tools and multicomponent evaluation systems and how to use the information thus gained to improve the practice of the workforce they supervise.

Policy- and Systems-Level Considerations

Program and reporting, oversight, and quality improvement requirements need to be aligned with each other and with what is feasible and valid through multicomponent measurement and accountability systems that reflect comprehensively what is needed to have a quality practice environment and high-performing practitioners. Therefore, evaluation systems should be developed, evaluated, and improved with meaningful involvement of early learning practitioners and experts. In addition, even if evaluation policies and systems successfully capture the needed information, they will serve their purpose—to improve professional practice and ultimately to improve outcomes for children—only if the information they produce is used to shape local-, district-, and state-level professional learning activities, investments, and policies.

Finally, those engaged in the review and redesign of evaluation and assessment policies and systems should be mindful of the potential to inform and be informed by, and to coordinate with when possible, ongoing efforts throughout the systems of care and education for young children so as to improve alignment with what is known about child development and early learning, effective instruction in the early grades, and best practices in early childhood assessments.

The Critical Role of Leadership

Elementary school principals, early care and education center directors or program directors, and other administrators are an important factor in the quality of early learning experiences for the children in the settings they oversee. These leaders play an instrumental role in helping care and education professionals strengthen their core competencies and in creating a work environment in which they can fully use their knowledge and skills. Principals and directors often take a lead role in selecting content and activities for professional learning. In addition, leaders—including not only principals and directors but also superintendents and other administrators—have a major influence because they are responsible for workforce hiring practices and for the systems used for evaluating the performance of the professionals they oversee. They need to have the knowledge and competencies to hire and supervise educators who are capable of working with children in the settings they lead. In addition, leaders play an important role in facilitating the necessary communication and collaboration among different kinds of professionals to improve both continuity within the care and education sector for children as they transition among settings and continuity with other sectors, such as health and social services.

While the importance of school and program leadership is unequivocal, current policies for training or certifying elementary school principals are not well aligned with the interests of children. Even though most principals work in elementary schools and the science clearly indicates the importance of the early years for future academic success, public education policies tend not to emphasize early childhood development for elementary school principals. Because of the way they are prepared, recruited, and licensed, principals often lack understanding of research on early childhood development and best practices in instruction in preschool and the primary grades. For early childhood center and program directors, education and certification requirements are inconsistent across states, credentialing is largely voluntary, and the current standards and expectations are insufficient for the knowledge and competencies needed for instructional leadership in learning environments for young children.

Recommendation 8: Ensure that policies and standards that shape the professional learning of care and education leaders encompass the foundational knowledge and competencies needed to support high-quality practices for child development and early learning in their organizations.

States and organizations that issue statements of core competencies and other policies related to professional learning and qualifications for leadership in public education would benefit from a review to ensure that the scope of instructional leadership is inclusive of the early elementary years, including prekindergarten as it increasingly becomes included in public school systems. States and organizations that issue statements of core competencies and other policies related to professional learning and qualifications for leadership in centers, programs, family childcare, and other settings for early childhood education would benefit from a review to ensure that competencies related to instructional leadership are emphasized alongside administrative and management competencies.

> Recommendation 8a: The nation's major early childhood policy and research organizations and major governmental and nongovernmental funders should review existing statements of core competencies and qualification requirements for early care and education leaders and establish updated and comprehensive standards that reflect what these leaders need to know and be able to do, especially in the area of instructional leadership. These standards should be accompanied by guidance on the implications for qualifications and professional learning for leaders.

> Recommendation 8b: Federal, state, and local departments of education, voluntary accrediting and certification entities, and institutions of higher education should integrate early learning principles and best practices throughout the principal development pipeline, including policies and accreditation standards for certification programs for school administrators; coursework, practicum, and evaluation requirements for principal candidates; and ongoing professional learning support systems and recertification requirements.

Implementation Considerations for Recommendation 8

Both elementary school principals and early childhood program leaders support staff whose work should be informed by the science of early childhood development. Thus, statements about what these two types of professionals should know and be able to do should be aligned in terms of both specific competencies and the general principles on which they are based. In addition, both types of leaders need specific competencies for collaboration and communication because of their important role in bridging systems to support greater continuity in early learning experiences before and after young children enter school systems.

Considerations for Leaders in Early Childhood Settings

The effort to develop a consensus statement of core competencies for early childhood leaders should be undertaken in collaboration with organizations that have developed similar statements for principals, such as the Council of Chief State School Officers and the National Association of Elementary School Principals. Better statements of core competencies are only the beginning; realizing those competencies in practice is where the contribution to improving early learning for children will occur. Federal programs and state policy leaders should use these national standards to align their competency standards and qualification requirements, and states should develop criteria for licensing or credentialing early childhood leaders so as to acknowledge the specialized knowledge and competencies needed to be both leaders in instruction and experts in organizational development and management. Thus, it will be necessary to rethink requirements for such leaders related to education, credentials, coursework, and professional experience. In turn, any reform in this system will require building the capacity of institutions of higher education to provide the needed preparation.

Any benefits of retooling these policies will be difficult to realize without also addressing more systemic issues discussed elsewhere in this report, including how early childhood education is funded, low levels of compensation for educators and leaders who work with young children, and the supports needed for the existing workforce to meet higher expectations. For these reasons, the considerations for this recommendation are parallel to those articulated for Recommendation 2 on implementing a minimum bachelor's degree requirement for lead educators.

Considerations for Early Elementary Principals

To better connect the foundational knowledge and core competencies elementary school principals need to policies that govern their training and ongoing professional learning, state policy leaders can look to states such as Illinois that have made progress in improving the expectations and supports for integrating instructional leadership for early learning into the principal development pipeline. Existing avenues for developing instructional leadership competencies could be expanded to integrate considerations and best practices for principals with leadership responsibilities in the early elementary years, which now includes prekindergarten in many school systems. The U.S. Department of Education, in collaboration with relevant national organizations and professional associations, could support state efforts to reflect differentiated instructional leadership competency by developing a definition of a "highly qualified principal" for elementary, middle, and high schools. Such a definition could be integrated into existing federal and state accountability and school improvement policies (e.g., the Elementary and Secondary Education Act). The definition of a "highly qualified principal" would include both core competencies and past teaching and leadership experiences specific to the age range the principal has been responsible for and has knowledge of working with. In this way, the recruitment, hiring, and placement of these principals could better reflect a match between the candidate and the job, with equal value being placed across grades and settings instead of elementary schools being placed at the bottom of a hierarchy of positions. As a result, recruitment and placement decisions for elementary school principals would be made in a more intentional and evidence-based fashion.

Any effort to revise policies for principal development also needs to reflect the increasing array of responsibilities, regulations, and pressures to which principals must respond, such as more rigorous teacher evaluation protocols, the implementation of new learning standards and assessments, and new accountability measures at both the state and federal levels. To the extent possible, policies and programs that help elementary school principals become more effective early education leaders need to be aligned with and contribute to these existing responsibilities.

Interprofessional Practice

A critical factor in providing consistent support for children from birth through age 8 is the ability of care and education professionals to work in synergy with other professionals both across settings within the care and education sector and in other closely related sectors, especially health and social services.

Recommendation 9: Improve consistency and continuity for children from birth through age 8 by strengthening collaboration and communication among professionals and systems within the care and education sector with closely related sectors, especially health and social services.

Continuity across care and education settings and among diverse services and agencies is important not only to provide more consistent and better-coordinated services for individual children and their families but also to create shared understanding of the interconnected quality of developmental processes that each practitioner, focused on a specialized scope of practice, may see only in part.

Recommendation 9a: To improve continuity within the care and education sector, practitioners, leaders, and policy makers at the state and local levels should develop strategies and mechanisms for strengthening collaboration and communication among professionals and systems across care and education professional roles and practice settings.

Strategies and mechanisms to support interprofessional practice should include the following:

- Create structures and provide training for facilitated sharing and interpretation of data and other information on children's status and progress among practitioners, especially as children are moving from one setting or learning environment to another. These structures should include the use of discussion protocols and other tools for structured, facilitated information sharing that will support appropriate analysis and interpretation of child data and avoid misuse and misinterpretation of data with potential negative consequences, such as assigning diagnoses to children incorrectly or prematurely and introducing biased expectations for children.

- Encourage professional associations of educators and leaders to create partnerships and conduct meetings that allow for sharing information and activities across settings and age groups.
- Support a specific professional role for facilitating connections for children and families (such as navigators or case managers) so that the entire burden of collaboration does not fall on practitioners.
- Assess and develop plans to address policy and systems barriers to coordination and collaboration, such as conflicting eligibility criteria and time periods, redundant paperwork for accessing services, and limitations and variability in policies on reimbursable services.
- Create mechanisms for interaction and collaboration at the level of agencies and institutions, not just individual practitioners.

One particularly important area of collaboration is in infant and child mental health. Educators benefit from consultation with mental health experts to best understand how to work with children in need of specialized support in their classrooms. Child mental health consultants can provide teachers with guidance and ongoing support for classroom management and instructional practices for all children as well as individualized consultation and referral services for particular children. Unfortunately, most communities lack sufficient capacity in child mental health services and consultation, and national infrastructure is insufficient for training developmentally oriented clinicians in providing these services.

Recommendation 9b: To improve linkages that support children's mental health and socioemotional development, leaders in care and education settings should facilitate greater availability of child mental health professionals to assist care and education professionals with consultation and referrals for comprehensive services.

Recommendation 9c: To address shortcomings in the availability of mental health consultants to assist care and education professionals, the National Institute of Mental Health and the Substance Abuse and Mental Health Services Administration, in coordination with other agencies in the U.S. Department of Health and Human Services, the

U.S. Department of Education, and professional organizations concerned with both mental health and education, should establish as a priority the funding of integrated training programs focused on both early learning and early childhood mental health.

Although the conclusions and recommendations in this report were not developed to be specific to the professional learning systems for the health and social services sectors, many of the core principles that inform the committee's recommendations for developing the care and education workforce would also inform a review of professional learning for these other sectors.

Recommendation 9d: Given their critical connections to child development and early learning and to the early childhood care and education sector, decision makers and leaders in health, mental health, and social services should review their standards, practices, and systems for professional learning to better incorporate expectations for fundamental knowledge in child development, as well as the competencies needed to work with young children and to collaborate with care and education professionals.

The foundational competencies (see Box 12-1) and principles presented earlier offer guidance that could be generalized to incorporate into existing processes for workforce development, education, and training specific to these professions. The relevant leaders and stakeholders in these sectors are encouraged to consider using this report as a basis and a catalyst for reviewing their current workforce development, with the aim of better supporting the appropriate knowledge, competencies, and professional practice of those professionals in their sectors who work with children from birth through age 8.

Support for Implementation

Implementing the preceding recommendations will require better, more inclusive coordination and alignment among the major funders, oversight agencies, and other stakeholders that influence children from birth through age 8.

Recommendation 10: Support workforce development with coherent funding, oversight, and policies.

To support efforts to transform the professional workforce for children from birth through age 8, national, state, and local government agencies and nongovernmental resource organizations should review and revise their policies, guidelines, programmatic portfolios, oversight provisions, and incentives for professional learning and quality professional practice to ensure that they are oriented to the primary aim of optimal support for child development and early learning (aligned with the unifying foundational principles in this report). These efforts should include revision of categorical policies and funding streams to identify and remove barriers to continuity across practice settings, professional roles, and age ranges for the birth through 8 age span. The review and alignment process within each agency or organization should be achieved in part through collaborative efforts, such as interagency working groups, technical consultations across governmental and nongovernmental organizations, and support from elected officials to facilitate these collaborations.

Recommendation 11: Collaboratively develop and periodically update coherent guidance that is foundational across roles and settings for care and education professionals working with children from birth through age 8.

Recommendation 11a: To provide guidance and support for efforts at the local, state, and national levels, national nongovernmental organizations that offer resources and support for the care and education workforce should collaborate to provide and periodically update shared, coherent foundational guidance for care and education professionals working with children from birth through age 8. This collaborative effort should represent professional roles across settings and age ranges to improve the consistency and continuity of high-quality developmental support and learning experiences for children as they age.

Recommendation 11b: Local, state, and national governmental and nongovernmental organizations, institutions of higher education, and those who provide professional learning should use this guidance to align and augment their own standards for care and education professionals who work with children from birth through age 8.

Clarity and agreement are needed among stakeholders on standards for qualification requirements, higher education, ongoing professional learning, and evaluation of quality practice. To achieve this, ongoing, credible, practical, evidence-based guidance is needed on how diverse stakeholders can align and implement their standards and policies. The aim of this recommendation is to promote consistency among the various entities with oversight and influence over the many professional roles that entail working with children from birth through age 8. Providing comprehensive guidelines drawing on collective expertise in the field will improve the availability of high-quality, continuous developmental support and learning experiences for children as they age. Guided by the science of child development and early learning, research on instructional and other professional practices, the principles laid out in this report, and the framework for collaborative systems change, this effort should include the following actions:

- Garner, coordinate, build on, and mutually inform and support the work of organizations across professional roles, settings, and age ranges, and avoid duplicating or competing against existing efforts and organizations.
- Periodically review the science of child development and early learning and translate its findings into updated guidance to serve as a foundation for quality professional practice across professional roles, practice settings, and age ranges. The products of these efforts should inform competency standards, qualification requirements, standards for higher education programs and other professional learning activities, and standards for evaluation of quality practice.
- Support funders or regulatory and oversight agencies in offering incentives for adherence to the national guidance.
- Disseminate the guidance and provide technical assistance for its use.
- Provide coherent expert assistance for the review and revision of existing national, state, and local systems of credentialing and licensing to align them with the national foundational guidelines.
- Periodically review research and implementation science and translate it into guidance for establishing and maintaining professional learning systems.
- Develop and implement national supports for professional learning to fill gaps in currently available institutions and agencies.
- Develop and administer an "early development fundamentals" endorsement to augment existing qualification requirements for professional roles that currently have no mechanism for documenting competencies in child development yet whose responsibilities require core knowledge and competencies for working with children from birth through age 8.
- Assess national progress on this effort, and regularly produce a public report.

Recommendation 11c: The U.S. Department of Education and the U.S. Department of Health and Human Services, in partnership with national philanthropic and other private-sector funders, should support

the establishment of the above collaborative effort to provide national guidance by jointly convening an initial meeting among relevant national nongovernmental organizations. The aim of this meeting should be to catalog current related activities, develop a plan for a more permanent organizational infrastructure, identify the needed participants, develop a common agenda and initial priorities, and solicit funding commitments for ongoing support.

Implementation Considerations for Recommendation 11

Considerations for Participating Organizations

As described in the framework for collaborative systems change, the success of collective efforts depends on having balanced representation among the professional roles and settings involved in care and education across the birth through age 8 continuum from infancy through early elementary school. The representation in such efforts also should reflect practice communities, the research community, policy research and analysis, policy makers and government leadership, higher education, agencies that oversee licensure and credentialing as well as accreditation, and organizations that provide ongoing professional learning. For guidance in some areas, it will also be important to collaborate or consult with organizations whose mission relates to the professionals who work with these children and their families in the closely related sectors of health and social services. These collaborators might include, for example, professional associations for pediatricians, family physicians, school nurses, and social workers. Finally, as discussed previously, another key consideration for representation both within and across participating organizations is to reflect the racial, ethnic, and linguistic diversity of the workforce itself and the children and families served, as well as geographic diversity that captures the varied circumstances in different local contexts.

Considerations for Collaborative Infrastructure

As described in the framework for collaborative systems change, a collaborative effort of this kind will require some form of backbone infrastructure. One option would be to create a new organization to facilitate the collective effort as an independent national coalition. Another option would be for an existing organization to assume the leadership role in facilitating the collaborative process, committing to an inclusive and neutral approach. For either option, a key criterion is that the organizational lead must have trust and credibility across the professional roles, settings, disciplinary perspectives, and sectors/systems engaged in the development and early learning of children from birth through age 8.

Avoidance of Duplication of Effort

This collaborative effort will be most effective if it draws and builds on the existing resources of participating organizations instead of creating new solutions and infrastructure. The aim is to build both a more robust and coherent platform for what is common across professional roles and a shared foundation that consistently informs the work of collaborating organizations in their specialized areas of workforce development.

Considerations for Use of the National Collaborative Guidelines

The aim of the proposed national collaborative guidelines is to promote consistency among the various entities with oversight and influence over the many professional roles that entail working with children from birth through age 8. Providing comprehensive guidelines based in evidence and drawing on collective expertise in the field will improve the consistency and continuity of high-quality developmental support and learning experiences for children as they age. Considerations for use of these guidelines include the following:

- Work closely with state agencies with oversight over higher education and existing accrediting organizations such as the National Association for the Education of Young Children and the Council for the Accreditation of Educator Preparation to develop or review and revise as needed national standards for high-quality programs in higher education that prepare students to work with children from birth through age 8.
- Disseminate knowledge of the latest research and development in professional learning activities.
- Develop and regularly update (1) guidelines for quality professional learning across settings and roles for care and education professionals who work with children from birth though age 8 and (2) criteria for assessing and endorsing providers of professional learning.
- Provide guidance and technical assistance for the development and implementation of the recommended individual, institutional, systems, and policy pathways and timelines for transitioning to a requirement for a minimum bachelor's degree for lead educators.

Not only should agencies and organizations either align with or adopt the national guidelines, but regulators and funders should also use them to create new incentives that promote a more continuous approach to care and education across the birth through age 8 continuum. For example, states could require that care and education professionals can qualify for licensure only if they have graduated from programs that adhere to the national guidelines. Similarly, grants and other funding mechanisms could be contingent on adherence to the national guidelines for professional qualifications.

Documentation of Adherence to the National Guidelines

High standards will be required for the documentation demonstrating alignment with or successful voluntary adoption of the national guidelines. The standards for documentation will have to be aligned with the full breadth of expected competencies and draw on best practices in the types of evidence used to document those competencies, including observed performance.

Considerations for the "Early Development Fundamentals" Endorsement

The proposed "early development fundamentals" endorsement is not intended to replace or duplicate existing credentialing systems—such as state licensure systems or the national CDA or the NBPTS credentials—as they already apply to professionals working with children from birth through age 8. Rather, the purpose of the endorsement is to create a new credential for those professional roles that currently have no mechanism for documenting competencies in child development yet whose responsibilities require core knowledge and competencies for working with children from birth through age 8. These roles include those professions whose current licensure systems cover their field broadly but lack a specific specialization in these young children—for example, some health and social services professions. The endorsement also could be used to augment the credentialing for those care and education professional roles not already covered by the CDA or by state licensure for birth through age 8. Examples include elementary school teachers or principals who live in states that do not offer licenses for prekindergarten through third grade or birth through age 8 and may be transitioning to early elementary settings. Instead of creating a new license, states or districts could require these professionals to obtain this national endorsement to augment their existing broader licenses.

This endorsement should be developed collaboratively, drawing on the collective expertise and experience of existing organizations that credential and certify care and education professionals (e.g., Council for Professional

Recognition and the NBPTS), as well as professional associations that represent the types of practitioners to whom the endorsement would be applicable. To that end, close collaboration will be warranted with the professional associations and licensing institutions for professionals working in health and social services for children and families so that the endorsement will be comprehensive in covering all facets of child development without duplicating existing credentialing and licensure requirements.

Another consideration in administering this endorsement will be the costs and additional training entailed in obtaining it, and whether those costs will be the burden of practitioners or their employers. Government policies and public–private partnerships will need to be mobilized to offer subsidies and scholarships. Paying out of pocket for these costs might be more acceptable to practitioners if their employers offered incentives related to career advancement or salary bonuses; to this end, employers would need incentives for recognizing the endorsement.

> **Recommendation 12: Support comprehensive state- and local-level efforts to transform the professional workforce for children birth through age 8.**
>
> **Federal and state government agencies and national nongovernmental resource organizations should support collective efforts at the state and local levels to transform the professional workforce for children from birth through age 8. To this end, they should collaborate to provide technical support and cross-sector financial resources, including public–private partnerships, that can be combined with local resources. To model this approach, the U.S. Department of Education and the U.S. Department of Health and Human Services, in partnership with national philanthropic and other private-sector funders, should jointly fund at least 10 local or state coalitions[7] to undertake 10-year initiatives for a collective effort to review, assess, and improve professional learning and workforce development for the care and education workforce for children from birth through age 8.**

---

[7] The coalitions should comprise relevant leaders and stakeholders at the level of the district, municipality, county, region within a state, or state. Coalition representatives might include government agencies in health, human services, and education (early childhood, elementary, and higher education); governmental and nongovernmental workforce and economic development agencies and organizations; elected officials in executive offices and legislatures, local councils, or school boards; philanthropic and private-sector funders; representatives of practitioners and leaders across practice settings and age groups within the birth through age 8 range (direct representation and professional associations and unions); institutions of higher education; representatives of providers of professional learning services outside of higher education; and local research, policy, and advocacy organizations that focus on young children.

The pilot initiatives should

- Be selected through a competitive federal funding initiative that leverages existing federal funding streams for workforce development in the education sector, including for example those available through the Child Care Development Block Grant, Head Start, Race to the Top, and programs authorized under the Elementary and Secondary Education Act. Given the cross-sectoral nature of care and education and the major current challenges with diverse funding streams, this recommended funding initiative may be a natural candidate for funding mechanisms that allow states and localities to pool discretionary funds received through multiple federal streams, for example through expansion of the federal Performance Partnership to apply to care and education for children birth through age 8.
- Be collaboratively funded as a public–private partnership with national philanthropic and private-sector funders.
- Include a matching funding requirement drawing on state or local governmental and nongovernmental resources.
- Include at least four localities with existing early childhood or other related collaborative bodies that can be built on and at least four localities with no existing collaborative mechanism, so as to provide models and lessons learned for a range of baseline levels of infrastructure for collaborative systems change.
- Represent diverse regions of the country.
- Include resources and mechanisms for process and outcome evaluations with interim reporting.
- Facilitate regular knowledge exchange so that other localities implementing such initiatives can learn from the pilots iteratively and in real time.

Guided by the science of child development and early learning, these initiatives should implement a collective effort to build a more coherent infrastructure of professional learning supports; improve the quality, availability, and accessibility of professional learning activities; and revise and align policies, incentives, and financial and technical support. To that end, these state or local coalitions should be supported in carrying out the following efforts:

- Ascertain the current status and landscape of the local care and education workforce for children from birth through age 8 across professional roles, settings, and age ranges (including demographics, practice settings, practice requirements and qualifications, salaries, and participation in current professional learning systems).

- Map the local landscape of stakeholders with a role in professional learning and workforce development, including the activities they are undertaking and/or the policies and practices for which they have oversight.
- Identify the strengths, gaps, unmet needs, and fragilities in current systems.
- Establish and clearly articulate an organizational and decision-making structure, priorities, goals, planned activities and policy changes, timelines, and benchmarks for progress.
- Estimate resource needs, and develop a plan for financing and resource mobilization to increase, diversify, and strategically allocate funding that takes into account public investments at the federal, state, and local levels; investments from private philanthropic and corporate sources; and out-of-pocket spending by families.
- Facilitate ongoing stakeholder coordination and sharing of information related to funding, activities, and data collection and use.
- Document and share actions undertaken and lessons learned.

Improvement of the Knowledge Base

Recommendation 13: Build a better knowledge base to inform workforce development and professional learning services and systems.

Several of the preceding recommendations for workforce development hinge on the ability of local, state, and national stakeholders and policy makers to understand the current status, characteristics, and needs of the workforce across professional roles and settings that serve children from birth through age 8, and to monitor the progress over time that results from change efforts. This information also is essential for mobilizing resources and galvanizing public support for new initiatives. However, the sources for this information are dispersed, inconsistent, and often simply unavailable. There is a need for a more systematic approach to gathering and using information of this kind.

> **Recommendation 13a: State and municipal governments, in collaboration with nongovernmental resource organizations and with the financial and technical support of federal agencies, should establish data systems for systematically gathering information on the workforce across professional roles and settings that serve children from birth through age 8. This information should include demographics, education, qualifications, experience, income, and participation in pro-**

fessional learning. These data systems should be developed in coordination with data systems that gather information on children.

An important component of the knowledge base for workforce development and professional learning is the dynamic cycle of continuously learning about child development and best practices and translating that knowledge into widespread professional practice. If emerging science is not reflected in instructional practice and in professional learning activities and systems, familiar but possibly inappropriate instructional practices and learning environments will be reinforced and maintained.

This is a shared responsibility: support is required to advance the research itself, and mechanisms are also needed to connect that research to the practice community. The latter might include involving the practice community in research, as well as making research findings and their implications more timely, accessible, and available to practicing professionals. Professionals in turn need to understand the importance of continuously updating their knowledge and competencies and to have the motivation and incentives to do so.

> Recommendation 13b: Federal, state, and nongovernmental research funders should expand and develop grantmaking portfolios to improve the knowledge base for supporting quality professional practice and improving professional learning for those who work with children from birth through age 8. Research grant funding mechanisms should be structured so that a greater proportion of requests for proposals and awarded grants incentivize and encourage interdisciplinary teams, as well as research and evaluation that bridges disciplines and research and practice partnerships and environments.

> Recommendation 13c: Funders should accompany research investments with funding for dissemination and knowledge exchange efforts designed to facilitate connections between the research and practice communities. Examples of such efforts include regional meetings, publications, registries of practice-based evidence, and technical assistance for incorporating research-driven changes into professional learning systems.

Throughout this study, the committee identified areas in which continued expansion of the knowledge base is needed. Although not a comprehensive research agenda, Box 12-6 provides examples of some of the ongoing major areas of inquiry that warrant new or enhanced investments in evaluation and research as part of the funding portfolios of governmental and nongovernmental research funding sources. Given the complexity of child development and of the systems of professional practice, evaluation and research approaches also will need to keep pace with the state of the art in research designs that are suited to understanding effects in complex systems. Such designs include multidisciplinary and mixed-methods approaches, as well as long-term studies that reflect the realities of practice environments. As evidenced by the examples in Box 12-6, improving the knowledge base will also require expertise not only in disciplines traditionally involved in child development, health, and education, but also in other disciplines related to workforce development, such as labor economics, systems financing, and law.

BOX 12-6
Examples of Ongoing Evaluation and Research Needs

Basic and Applied Developmental Science
- Better understanding of the manner in which early social experience contributes to the development of very early implicit understanding and explicit knowledge in infants and toddlers
- Better understanding of the processes that can help mitigate the effects of chronic stress on child development and early learning
- Better understanding of how executive function and cognitive and emotional self-regulation can be strengthened in young children, especially those growing up in adversity
- Better understanding of the connections between the mental health of young children and the mental health of those who teach and care for them in settings outside the home
- Better understanding of the use of digital media in concert with direct teaching practices to foster early learning, including studies of various types of content (e.g., characters, concepts, storylines, imagery, animations, game mechanics, functionality), various types of contexts (joint engagement with adults versus solo use, the type of settings in which media are used), and various groups of children (differentiating by age and stage of development, social demographics, native language, etc.)
- Better understanding of the development of digital and media literacy to determine the age at which children should gain exposure to various technologies and learn to interpret content from various types of media
- Better understanding of the impact of "digital divides" that reflect disparities in access to technology among young children

Improving Professional Practice and Practice Environments
- What are the general and age- or setting-specific components of high-quality care and education for infants and toddlers, for children in preschool settings, and for children in early elementary classrooms? How

BOX 12-6 Continued

can this knowledge be used to improve professional practice, develop curricular materials and other instructional tools, and inform the content of professional learning supports? How can those components of quality be measured in ways relevant to improving how the quality of early care and education programs is assessed and systems for continuous quality improvement are instituted?

- How do different staffing structures in different practice settings compare in supporting the learning and development of young children across age groups?
- How should technology be integrated into curricula at various ages to augment instruction in subject matter and provide children with foundations for technological fluency?

Understanding the Effectiveness of Qualification Requirements

- How do different models for components included and methods of documentation for qualification requirements compare in leading to a qualified and sustainable workforce?

Understanding the Effectiveness of Professional Learning

- What characteristics of educational pathways and programs of study—such as coursework content and field-based learning experiences, the pedagogy used for adult learning, and the dosage and sequencing of different aspects of a program—are most likely to lead to care and education professionals whose practice will support children's development and improve child outcomes and academic achievement in the short and long terms?
- What are the best approaches to training prospective and current care and education professionals to integrate knowledge and competencies across the developmental continuum from birth through age 8?
- What are the best approaches for training prospective and current care and education professionals and improving settings to best support children with special needs?
- How can technology be used effectively to enable professional learning?
- How do changes to institutional infrastructure (e.g., to reduce fragmentation and promote interdisciplinary approaches) and faculty hiring practices, supports, and incentives affect the quality of higher education programs for care and education professionals?
- What institutional and policy changes (e.g., financial assistance, technology for remote education, academic supports, cohort/network models) are most effective for addressing geographic, socioeconomic, racial, ethnic, and cultural disparities in access to higher education?
- What are the best methods and approaches for evaluating the effectiveness of professional learning activities in higher education and during ongoing practice for their alignment with the science of child development,

continued

BOX 12-6 Continued

their effects on the quality of professional practice, and their effects on child outcomes?

Evaluating Assessment and Accountability Systems (see also Recommendation 7b)

- How effective are current accountability measures and systems for assessing the ability of professionals to facilitate a child's development and early learning in all domains?
- How can measures of children's outcomes and achievement from birth through age 8 be used appropriately to contribute to assessments as measures of the performance of adult practitioners?
- How can evaluation systems and tools for assessing the practice of professionals who provide care and education for children from birth through age 8 be improved?
- What combination of tools and measures is needed for appropriate and feasible assessment and continuous quality improvement of the performance of care and education professionals and the systems in which they work?

Evaluating Systems and Systems Change

- How can the link between what care and education professionals learn (knowledge and skills) and what they do (competencies in practice) be strengthened?
- How effective are approaches and initiatives for improving coordination and collaboration both within the care and education sector and between it and other sectors, especially health and social services? What new professional roles and responsibilities, competencies, and professional learning supports are needed to implement these approaches successfully?
- What are successful models and best practices for financing sustainable workforce development efforts and for financing care and education programs in ways that better support workforce needs?
- What strategies can affect the intersections among labor markets, market costs for high-quality care and education, and other factors to adequately support compensation parity while sustaining publicly funded and private enterprises in the early care and education market?
- How are systems changes affecting the quality of practice, the status of the workforce, and outcomes for children?

THE REALITY OF RESOURCES

Significant resources will be needed for the comprehensive changes in workforce development the committee believes are required to achieve the quality of professional practice that is needed to better support children from birth through age 8. Although there has been growing attention to and investment in the care and education of young children, it falls far short of the need. The shortfall is not just in the resources expended but also in how those resources are allocated and used to ensure the desired outcomes for children. Strategic, coordinated investments are needed across all components of the system, and critical among these are investments in the workforce.

This committee was not charged with making recommendations about specific funding sources or financing mechanisms for its recommended actions.[8] Nonetheless, as demonstrated in many of the considerations for implementation described previously, the committee recognizes that implementing its recommendations will require the allocation of new or reallocation of existing resources and therefore some discussion of this issue is warranted.

To transform workforce development and professional learning for those who provide care and education for children from birth through age 8, all of the relevant stakeholders will have to come to terms with the true costs of high-quality professional practice that accord with the importance of these professional roles. These costs include, for example, making investments in scholarships, subsidies, and other financial support to make professional learning available and accessible, and building a compensation structure that attracts and retains talented individuals and makes upgrading the expectations and education of those entering and already in the workforce feasible. These costs need to be reviewed relative to the budgets and revenue of education programs and services for children from birth through age 8. Currently, the market for care and education services in early childhood is inadequate to support the costs of high-quality professional practice, and supporting those costs out of pocket would be prohibitive for many families—a fact that contributes to socioeconomic disparities in access to high-quality supports for child development and early learning. Similarly, adequate resources commonly are not allocated for high-quality professional practice in early elementary grades, where investments in professional learning and compensation may be higher than in settings outside of schools but still do not adequately reflect the value and importance of these educators.

Evolving strategies for financing services for children that support their development and early learning must adequately account for the higher costs of quality professional practice while still making quality services

---

[8] As noted earlier, while acknowledging that the availability of resources is an important reality that would affect the feasibility of the committee's recommendations, in clarifying the study charge the sponsors specified that the committee should exclude from its task conducting analyses about funding and financing.

available to all children and addressing current geographic and socioeconomic disparities in access to such services. Although the quality of services that children can access may inevitably vary, financing strategies are needed to ensure equitable access to a minimum standard of quality that is much higher than the current system supports so that no young children are in substandard learning environments as a result of their family's geographic location and/or economic resources.

One strategy for increasing funding is to simply increase allocations for the existing programs and funding streams described in Chapter 2. However, this approach is unlikely to yield the level of new investment that is necessary or to fully eliminate current barriers to collaborative approaches. Therefore, it is worthwhile to explore multiple complementary funding approaches that strategically combine federal, state, and local government funding sources with philanthropic and corporate funding and revenue from out-of-pocket spending by families on care and education.

Appendix G provides some examples of innovative approaches and promising strategies for generating resources to improve the quality of care and education for children from birth through age 8, illustrated in brief in Box 12-7. The committee did not conduct a comprehensive review

---

BOX 12-7
Innovative Funding Strategies

The reality of limited resources for children from birth through age 8 has been a consistent feature of the landscape of early care and education for decades. These resource limitations constrain the compensation of educators, the resources available to them for their work with children, the recruitment of capable and motivated individuals into this workforce, the training they can obtain, and other essential features of building a high-quality system that best serves young children. Recognizing this shortfall, many cities and states have embarked on locally initiated, innovative funding strategies to provide capital for investment in young children. Examples of innovative funding strategies under way in many communities, described briefly here, are detailed further in Appendix G.

Targeted public investments are designed to provide specific resources for improving workforce training or infrastructure to enhance quality. Such strategies include

- subsidies to improve professional training, services, and compensation, which can occur through individual or program grants from public funds (e.g., the Vermont Early Education Initiative Grants, Wisconsin's REWARD program, and the Professional Development System administered by the state of Washington);

BOX 12-7 Continued

- refundable tax credits to early childhood programs, funders, and/or providers based on quality improvement metrics (e.g., Louisiana's School Readiness Tax Credits and Maine's Child Care Investment Tax Credit programs);
- local or state tax initiatives to improve early care and education services (e.g., those approved by voters in Seattle, San Antonio, and elsewhere, and California's First 5 initiative, which has provided hundreds of millions of dollars in enhanced funding for early childhood programs since 1998 through a voter-approved tobacco tax); and
- revenues from lottery or gaming activities devoted to supporting high-quality early care and education programs (e.g., in Georgia and Missouri).

Public–private partnerships aim to improve the quality or accessibility of early care and education programs by pooling public and private resources in local communities through

- program development, with combined contributions from local business leaders, public officials, local and national philanthropies, and other groups (e.g., Boston's Thrive in Five program, the contributions of the George Kaiser Family Foundation to expanding high-quality early education programs in Tulsa, and the Educare program);
- loan subsidies that enable early education programs to obtain funds for program improvement at significantly reduced cost (e.g., through qualified section 501(c)(3) bonds and general credit enhancement strategies);
- redevelopment funding, such as through developer impact fees or Tax Increment Financing districts created by local governments; and
- public land trust revenue (e.g., an initiative approved by Nebraska voters in 2006 to create the Nebraska Early Childhood Education Endowment through a combination of public funding from allocated public land trusts and private-sector funds).

Business investments used as seed funding can spur public support through demonstration projects that enhance the quality of early care and education programs. One example is the Minnesota Early Learning Foundation/St. Paul Early Childhood Scholarship Pilot, which was funded with $20 million in corporate donations to support scholarships for young children from low-income families to attend high-quality early education programs. The Minnesota legislature subsequently expanded the scholarship program.

Social impact contracts or bonds entail public or private investments in the development of high-quality early care and education programs that are later repaid by the return on those investments in the form of reduced special education costs, higher tax revenues, or other benefits.

Shared service systems enable local early care and education programs to create economies of scale by collaborating on infrastructure costs, professional development, and other shared concerns, often with the assistance of public agencies. Examples can be found in Fairfax, Virginia, and Seattle, Washington.

and analysis of financing options, and evidence currently is insufficient to warrant specific conclusions and recommendations about which options to employ under what local circumstances. Nonetheless, local communities can examine the examples provided in considering how they might mobilize the necessary resources to improve the quality of the care and education of young children. These examples could be considered as ways to improve the salaries and benefits of care providers, to strengthen infrastructure and improve practice environments, to fund or subsidize the costs of professional learning, and to support efforts for collective action to achieve systems change.

FINAL THOUGHTS

The professionals who care for and educate children from birth through age 8 have an enormous influence on their lifelong success. Thanks to significant advances in understanding of child development, the idea that "the early years matter" is becoming more widely accepted. In the meantime, however, workforce policies have lagged behind the science and the growing consensus on the importance of fostering development and early learning for young children from infancy through early elementary school. Implementing the committee's recommendations will produce substantive changes that elevate the perception of the professionals who work with children from birth through age 8 and improve the quality of professional practice, the quality of the practice environment, and the status and well-being of the workforce—and ultimately, outcomes for children.

Changes to the Workforce: Necessary But Not Sufficient

This report focuses on recommendations related to the workforce, especially on changes to professional learning and other supports that contribute to the quality of professional practice. However, it is important to note that to promote the development and early learning of all children, it will not be sufficient to change how the workforce is developed and supported. Other factors that influence child development include, for example, the availability of and equitable access to services and programs for children and their families; the funding and financing that affect the allocation of resources to and among those services and programs; the quality of implementation on a large scale; the policies for oversight, evaluation, and accountability for those services and programs; and the facilitation of interactions across settings and sectors.

Many of the same principles articulated in this report with respect to supporting the workforce apply not only to systems components that affect the quality of professional practice but also across the rest of the elements that make up the landscape of policies, resources, systems, and stakeholders affecting young children. For change to be successful, relevant stakeholders and leaders in federal, state, and local governments; in the philanthropic sector; in the corporate and business sector; and in nongovernmental organizations will need not only to improve support for the professional workforce but also to comprehensively review and reform their portfolio of investments, policies, programs, and services to align with the principles of child development and early learning set forth in this report. This effort will reflect the recognition that a healthy, well-educated population is important to the economic and social prosperity of local communities and the nation, which in turn requires successful investments in getting and keeping the care and education of young children on the right track.

A Call to Action

Many of the challenges discussed in this report are not new. For too long, the nation has been making do with the systems and policies for the care and education workforce that *are* rather than envisioning the systems and policies that are *needed*, and committing to the strategies necessary to achieve them. The committee hopes that this report will move practitioners, leaders, policy makers, and other stakeholders to make that commitment. Comprehensive implementation of these recommendations will not happen quickly and will not come cheaply. It will require a strategic, progressive trajectory of change over time to transform the professional landscape, accompanied by significant commitment and investment of financial and other resources. Yet persisting with the status quo for the professionals who do this important, complex work will only perpetuate today's fragmented approach. The ultimate result will be inadequate learning and development of young children, especially among the nation's most vulnerable families and communities. Devoting attention to the adults who work with young children is one of the most important channels available for improving the quality of their care and education.

The committee expects that building on a unified foundation, driven by the science of child development and early learning, will introduce a self-perpetuating cycle of excellence, supported by policy makers and a society that recognize the complex and important role of early care and education professionals; the intellectually, physically, and emotionally challenging nature of their work; and the deep, extensive, and ongoing professional learning required for them to be successful. These changes hold promise for helping to retain highly effective practitioners in these professional roles and to bolster the recruitment of a robust and viable pipeline of new professionals. It is through the quality work of these adults that the nation can make it right from the very beginning for all of its children.

Appendixes

Appendix A

Biosketches of Committee Members and Staff

COMMITTEE MEMBERS

LaRue Allen, Ph.D. (*Chair*), is Raymond and Rosalee Weiss Professor of Applied Psychology and Chair of the Department of Applied Psychology in the Steinhardt School of Culture, Education, and Human Development at New York University. She also directs the Child and Family Policy Center, which focuses on bringing social science knowledge to policy makers and practitioners concerned with children and their families. Her research interests include urban preschool, adolescent and emerging adult development; impact of social, cultural, and ecological factors on human development; issues in cross-cultural and cross-national research methods and design; civic engagement; and financial literacy. Dr. Allen was visiting professor at the Centre de Recherche de l'Education Spécialisée et de l'Adaptation Scolaire in Paris, France, where she collaborates on research on preventing school failure through interventions with young children, their families, and the community structures that support them. She was also a Visiting Scholar at the American University of Paris from 2006 to 2010. She was a member of the 1991 National Research Council committee that produced the report *Work and Family: Policies for a Changing Work Force*. Dr. Allen received her Ph.D. in Clinical/Community/Developmental Psychology from Yale University and her A.B. from Harvard University.

W. Thomas Boyce, M.D., is Distinguished Professor in the Division of Developmental-Behavioral Pediatrics, Department of Pediatrics at the University of California, San Francisco (UCSF). Before moving to UCSF in

565

2013, he was the Sunny Hill Health Centre/BC Leadership Chair in Child Development at the University of British Columbia. As a social epidemiologist and a developmental-behavioral pediatrician, his research addresses how genetic, neural, and psychosocial processes work together to produce inequalities in childhood health and disease across different socioeconomic groups. His work has shown how psychological stress and neurobiological reactivity to aversive social contexts interact to produce disorders of both physical and mental health in populations of children. He serves as co-director of the Experience-Based Brain and Biological Development Program of the Canadian Institute for Advanced Research and is a past member of Harvard University's National Scientific Council on the Developing Child. Dr. Boyce was elected to the Institute of Medicine (IOM) in 2011 and currently serves on the IOM–National Research Council Board on Children, Youth, and Families. Dr. Boyce received his M.D. from Baylor College of Medicine and completed pediatric residency training at UCSF. Following residency, he was named a Robert Wood Johnson Foundation Clinical Scholar at the University of North Carolina at Chapel Hill.

Joshua L. Brown, Ph.D., is an Associate Professor of Applied Developmental Psychology in the Department of Psychology at Fordham University. His research focuses on the design and evaluation of programs to support urban public schools and teachers in promoting the social-emotional and academic development of children from diverse backgrounds and socioeconomic conditions. His research is conducted in collaboration with urban school districts and community-based partners and has been supported by grants from federal and private organizations including the National Institute of Mental Health, the Institute of Education Sciences, and the William T. Grant Foundation. His current research projects involve (1) a long-term follow-up study of an elementary school social-emotional learning intervention on youth health risk behaviors across middle and high school transitions; (2) conducting among the first federally funded randomized controlled trials of a mindfulness-based professional development program designed specifically for public school teachers; and (3) the development and evaluation of a school-based social-emotional learning and literacy intervention integrated with an intensive video-based teacher coaching model. Dr. Brown has served as a principal scientific review panel member for the Institute of Education sciences and an invited panel reviewer for the National Institute on Minority Health and Health Disparities. He has been a recipient of a William T. Grant Scholars Award and is currently a senior representative on the Steering Committee for the University-Based Child and Family Policy Consortium. Dr. Brown earned his doctorate in human development from Teachers College, Columbia University.

Douglas H. Clements, Ph.D., is a Kennedy Endowed Chair in Early Childhood Learning, Professor, and Executive Director of the Marsico Institute of Early Learning and Literacy at University of Denver's Morgridge College of Education. Previously, Dr. Clements worked as a kindergarten teacher for 5 years and a preschool teacher for 1 year, and he has since conducted research and published widely in the areas of (1) the learning and teaching of early mathematics; (2) computer applications in mathematics education; (3) creating, using, and evaluating a research-based curriculum and in taking successful curricula to scale using technologies and learning trajectories; and (4) development and evaluation of innovative assessments of mathematics achievement, as well as mathematics teaching. Prior to his appointment at the University of Denver, Dr. Clements was a State University of New York (SUNY) Distinguished Professor at the University of Buffalo. He was a member of President Bush's National Math Advisory Panel and served on the National Research Council Committee on Early Childhood Mathematics. Dr. Clements received his Ph.D. in elementary education from SUNY at Buffalo.

Fabienne Doucet, Ph.D., is Associate Professor and Content Area Director of the Program in Early Childhood Education in the Department of Teaching and Learning at the New York University (NYU) Steinhardt School of Culture, Education, and Human Development. Her research program addresses how immigrant and U.S.-born children of color and their families navigate education in the United States. A critical ethnographer, Dr. Doucet studies how taken-for-granted beliefs, practices, and values in the U.S. educational system position children and families who are linguistically, culturally, and socioeconomically diverse at a disadvantage, and her work seeks active solutions for meeting their educational needs. Her primary line of inquiry is a critical examination of how family involvement in schools is framed in the United States. This work forcefully argues that traditional constructions of family involvement often obscure and disempower families, particularly those coming from less privileged positions. One overarching goal of this work has been to build a new imagination for family involvement. Dr. Doucet is Chair of the Haiti Working Group at the NYU Steinhardt Institute for Human Development and Social Change and an affiliated faculty member of the NYU Center for Latin American and Caribbean Studies. Dr. Doucet received her Ph.D. in human development and family studies from the University of North Carolina at Greensboro and was a postdoctoral fellow at the Harvard Graduate School of Education with fellowships from the National Science Foundation and the National Academy of Education/Spencer Foundation.

John C. Duby, M.D., is Director of Developmental-Behavioral Pediatrics and Medical Director of the Family Child Learning Center at Akron Children's Hospital. He is also Professor of Pediatrics at Northeast Ohio Medical University. Previously, he worked as a general pediatrician in private practice. He is a member of the Sub Board in Developmental-Behavioral Pediatrics of the American Board of Pediatrics. He is President-elect of the Society for Developmental and Behavioral Pediatrics. Dr. Duby has served in a number of leadership roles, including President of the Ohio Chapter of the American Academy of Pediatrics (AAP), President of the Ohio AAP Foundation, and Chair of the AAP Task Force on the Vision of Pediatrics 2020. He is currently Chair of the AAP Mental Health Leadership Work Group. He has led statewide quality improvement initiatives in Ohio focused on early identification and management of emotional, developmental, and behavioral issues in primary care. In 2009, he received the Elizabeth Spencer Ruppert Ohio AAP Outstanding Pediatrician award. In 2011, he was honored as 1 of the 100 Buckeyes You Should Know by the Ohio State University Alumni Association. Dr. Duby received his M.D. from the Ohio State University College of Medicine and completed his pediatric training at Baylor College of Medicine and fellowship in developmental-behavioral pediatrics at Boston University.

David N. Figlio, Ph.D., is the Orrington Lunt Professor of Education and Social Policy and Director of the Institute for Policy Research at Northwestern University. Dr. Figlio conducts research on a wide range of educational and tax issues from school accountability and standards to welfare policy and policy design. His current research projects involve evaluating the Florida Corporate Tax Credit Scholarships Program, the largest school-voucher program in the United States; conducting a large-scale study of school accountability in Florida; identifying intergenerational effects in health and education; and examining student learning outcomes. Dr. Figlio is also a Research Associate at the National Bureau of Economic Research and a member of the Executive Board of the National Center for the Analysis of Longitudinal Data in Education Research. Dr. Figlio served as the inaugural Editor of the Association for Education Finance and Policy's journal, *Education Finance and Policy* (MIT Press), and currently serves as co-editor of the *Journal of Human Resources* and Associate Editor of the *American Economic Journal: Economic Policy, Journal of Urban Economics, Education Finance and Policy*, and *Public Finance Review*. He has been part of many national education task forces and panels, such as the National Research Council Committee on Test Design for K-12 Science Achievement, and advised several U.S. states and foreign nations on the design, implementation, and evaluation of educational policies. He also serves as co-director of the National Science Foundation's network of scholars, policy makers, and practitioners to make use of linked administrative data to improve education scholarship, policy, and practice. Dr. Figlio received his Ph.D. in economics from the University of Wisconsin.

Jana Fleming, J.D., Ph.D., has extensive experience evaluating the quality of early education programs and services, training teachers on best practices in early education, studying means of financing services for children and families, and advising policy makers on strategies to improve educational and social services for young children and their families. In early 2015 she moved to Abu Dhabi, United Arab Emirates, to direct the Salama bint Hamdan Al Nahyan Foundation's Center of Excellence in Early Childhood Development. Prior to assuming this position, she served as Director of the Herr Research Center for Children and Social Policy at Erikson Institute (Chicago, Illinois) where she directed research, evaluation, and public outreach projects to inform and support effective early childhood public policy development and implementation. While at Erikson, she also directed two professional learning programs aimed at preparing leaders from diverse ethnic and racial backgrounds to work effectively in early childhood policy making and systems building. Prior to joining Erikson, Dr. Fleming was at the City Colleges of Chicago, the largest urban community college system in the United States, where she launched and directed a system-wide effort to overhaul its child development degree programs and earn national accreditation, as well as transform five childcare centers into functioning laboratory preschools. Dr. Fleming worked for 16 years at the Frank Porter Graham Child Development Institute (FPG) at the University of North Carolina at Chapel Hill. At FPG, she served as a research investigator managing large-scale research and evaluation projects, as well as co-director of the Early Childhood Leadership Development Program, providing graduate-level education and training for early childhood professionals in health services, education, social welfare, childcare, and family protective services. She also has experience as a policy analyst in state government and was a consultant to the Chicago-based Joyce Foundation directing its grant making in early education. Dr. Fleming holds a Ph.D. from the University of North Carolina at Chapel Hill, a law degree from Duke University, and a B.A. degree from Cornell University.

Lisa Guernsey, M.A., is Director of the Early Education Initiative and Director of the Learning Technologies Project at New America, a nonpartisan think tank in Washington, DC, where she focuses on how to scale up high-quality learning environments for young children, birth through age 8. She is the lead author of *The Next Social Contract for the Primary Years of Education* (New America, 2010) and *Watching Teachers Work: Using Observation Tools to Promote Effective Teaching in the Early Years and*

Early Grades (New America, 2011). A journalist by training, Ms. Guernsey has been a technology and education writer at the *New York Times* and the *Chronicle of Higher Education* and has written about technology, education, and social science issues for a wide variety of publications, including *Newsweek*, *Time.com*, *Consumer Reports*, *Ladies Home Journal*, *The Washington Post*, the *Los Angeles Times*, *The American Prospect*, and others. She contributes to the Ed Central blog, which includes a subsection built on the previously named Early Ed Watch focusing on policy and research in early learning, and she writes regularly for Slate magazine's Future Tense blog. Ms. Guernsey's most recent book is *Screen Time: How Electronic Media—From Baby Videos to Educational Software—Affects Your Young Child* (Basic Books, 2012). The book is an update to *Into the Minds of Babes: How Screen Time Affects Children from Birth to Age 5*, published in 2007. She contributed a chapter to *Mobile Technology for Children: Designing for Interaction and Learning* (Morgan Kaufman, 2009) and wrote one of the first Internet handbooks focused on education: *College.Edu: A Guide for the Cyber-Savvy Student* (1997-2010). She received her M.A. in English/American studies from the University of Virginia.

Ron Haskins, Ph.D., is a Senior Fellow in Economic Studies at the Brookings Institution, where he co-directs both the Center on Children and Families and the Budgeting for National Priorities Project. He is also a senior consultant at the Annie E. Casey Foundation. He is the author of *Work Over Welfare: The Inside Story of the 1996 Welfare Reform Law* (2006), co-author of *Creating an Opportunity Society* (2009), and Senior Editor of *The Future of Children*. In 2002 he was the Senior Advisor to the President for Welfare Policy at the White House. Previously, he spent 14 years on the staff of the House Ways and Means Human Resources Subcommittee, serving as the subcommittee's Staff Director after Republicans took control of the House in 1994. In 1997, Dr. Haskins was selected by the *National Journal* as 1 of the 100 most influential people in the federal government. He holds a Ph.D. in developmental psychology from the University of North Carolina at Chapel Hill.

Jacqueline Jones, Ph.D., is the President and CEO of the Foundation for Child Development. During the first term of the Obama Administration she served as Senior Advisor on Early Learning to Secretary of Education Arne Duncan and as the country's first Deputy Assistant Secretary for Policy and Early Learning in the U.S. Department of Education. Prior to federal service Dr. Jones was the Assistant Commissioner for the Division of Early Childhood Education in the New Jersey State Department of Education. For over 15 years she served as a Senior Research Scientist at the Educational Testing Service in Princeton, New Jersey. Dr. Jones has been a faculty member at the

City University of New York and a visiting faculty member at the Harvard Graduate School of Education. She received both M.A. and Ph.D. degrees from Northwestern University.

Marjorie Kostelnik, Ph.D., is Dean of the College of Education and Human Sciences at the University of Nebraska–Lincoln (UNL). She came to UNL in 2000 as Dean of the College of Human Resources and Family Sciences. In 2004, Human Resources and Family Sciences partnered with Teachers College to become the College of Education and Human Sciences. Receiving a bachelor of science degree in child development from the University of Pittsburgh, Dr. Kostelnik began her career working with Head Start before receiving her master's and doctoral degrees in human development and family studies from the Pennsylvania State University. She was on faculty at Michigan State University for 22 years, serving first as program supervisor of the Child Development Laboratories and then as chair of the Department of Family and Child Ecology. During her time in Michigan, she worked with educators in more than 100 programs inside and outside the United States designing developmentally appropriate curricula, enhancing children's school readiness, and working with teachers to develop positive child guidance strategies. An author of 18 books, Dr. Kostelnik has also taught a variety of classes at both the undergraduate and graduate levels, and her research focuses on early childhood education and community coalition building. She currently serves on the Lincoln Public Schools Community Learning Centers Advisory Board (focused on before and after-school education), the Malaika Foundation Board (focused on global education), and the Dimensions Foundation Board (focused on nature education). Nationally, Dr. Kostelnik has served as vice president of the National Association for the Education of Young Children, treasurer and board of directors member for the Board on Human Sciences, and chair for the Great Plains Interactive Distance Education Alliance Cabinet, a consortium of universities engaged in distance education. Most recently, she was awarded the Nebraska Association for the Education of Young Children Outstanding Service to Children award.

Nonie K. Lesaux, Ph.D., is Juliana W. and William Foss Thompson Professor of Education and Society at the Harvard Graduate School of Education, where she leads a research program that focuses on increasing opportunities to learn for students from diverse linguistic, cultural, and economic backgrounds. Dr. Lesaux's research and teaching focus primarily on the cognitive and linguistic factors that enable children and adolescents to read effectively. Her research has included longitudinal studies investigating reading and language development among English language learners as well as experimental evaluations of academic vocabulary instruction. She is currently a principal investigator of a longitudinal study investigating the interrelated dimensions of linguistically diverse children's cognitive, socio-emotional, and literacy development, and co-directs a project focused on building capacity in the early education workforce. Dr. Lesaux authored a state-level literacy report which forms the basis for a Third Grade Reading Proficiency bill passed in the Massachusetts House of Representatives. The legislation established an Early Literacy Expert Panel, which Dr. Lesaux co-chairs, charged with developing new policies and policy-based initiatives in a number of domains that influence children's early literacy development. From 2002 to 2006, Dr. Lesaux was senior research associate of the National Literacy Panel on Language Minority Youth and from 2007 to 2009, she was a member of the Reading First Advisory Committee for the Secretary of Education in the U.S. Department of Education. Dr. Lesaux's scholarship has resulted in two prestigious early career awards—the William T. Grant Foundation Faculty Scholars Award and a Presidential Early Career Award for Scientists and Engineers from the U.S. government.

Ellen M. Markman, Ph.D., is Senior Associate Dean for the Social Sciences and the Lewis M. Terman Professor in the Department of Psychology at Stanford University. She was on the faculty at the University of Illinois before joining the Stanford faculty in 1975. Dr. Markman was Chair of the Department of Psychology from 1994 to 1997 and served as Cognizant Dean for the Social Sciences from 1998 to 2000. In 2003 she was elected to the American Academy of Arts and Sciences, in 2004 she was awarded the American Psychological Association's Mentoring Award, in 2011 she was elected to the National Academy of Sciences, and in 2013 she was awarded the American Psychological Society's William James Lifetime Achievement Award for Basic Research. Dr. Markman's research has covered a range of issues in cognitive development including work on comprehension monitoring, logical reasoning, and early theory of mind development. Much of her work has addressed questions of the relationship between language and thought in children focusing on categorization, inductive reasoning, and word learning. One current research project aims to lay the groundwork for a preschool curriculum on nutrition. Dr. Markman received her Ph.D. in developmental psychology from the University of Pennsylvania.

Rollanda E. O'Connor, Ph.D., is Professor and holds the Eady/Hendrick Endowed Chair in Learning Disabilities in the Graduate School of Education at the University of California, Riverside. Her research focuses on increasing the responsiveness of children to reading interventions in grades K-4, including the effects of tier 2 intervention for English learners across their first 5 years of reading development. She currently leads a research team to develop interventions to improve academic vocabulary and reading comprehension of students with disabilities. A former editor of the *American Educational Research Journal* and President of the Division for Learning Disabilities of the Council for Exceptional Children (CEC), Dr. O'Connor was awarded the Jeanette E. Fleischner Career Leadership Award from the CEC in 2015 to recognize her lifelong contributions to the field of learning disabilities. Her research has been funded by the U.S. Department of Education's Office of Special Education Programs and the Institute of Education Sciences. Dr. O'Connor received her Ph.D. in education, special education, and reading from the University of Washington.

Cheryl Polk, Ph.D., is President of the HighScope Educational Research Foundation. Dr. Polk previously served as the Executive Director of the Lisa and John Pritzker Family Fund. She is a noted leader in the child and family services field with a wealth of experience as a clinical psychologist, academic, and civic volunteer. She has worked closely with children and families to promote healthy child development for more than 25 years. Through her leadership at the Mimi and Peter Haas Fund and as Commissioner of the San Francisco Children and Families Commission, Dr. Polk has led major support for early childhood programs. She served as President of the Board of Directors of Zero to Three: National Center for Infants, Toddlers and Families and has been a board member of that organization for more than 10 years. Dr. Polk has received many citations, recognitions, and awards, including the prestigious National Leadership Fellowship from the Kellogg Foundation, as well as being a Salzburg Fellow for Early Childhood Development. She was named San Francisco Outstanding Advocate for Children in 2003 and received the Shining Star Award for Leadership and Dedication to the Children of San Francisco in 2000. She received her Ph.D. in psychology from the Alliant International University-San Francisco Bay.

P. Fred Storti, Ed.S., is the recently retired Executive Director of the Minnesota Elementary School Principals' Association in St. Paul, Minnesota. Prior to assuming this position of statewide and national advocacy, Mr. Storti gained 27 years of experience as a principal/superintendent in Minnesota urban, suburban, and rural schools. In his broad stewardship for children and elementary and middle-level principals, Mr. Storti served on the Alliance for Student Achievement, the P-20 Education Committee, the National Association of Elementary School Principals' (NAESP's) Pre K-3 Task Force, and the Ready 4K Board, and convened the Minnesota PreK-3 Summit. He also served as the Chair of the NAESP Executive Directors for 4 years. Mr. Storti received his M.S. and educational specialist degrees from Winona State University.

Ross A. Thompson, Ph.D., is Distinguished Professor of Psychology at the University of California, Davis. Dr. Thompson's research focuses on early parent–child relationships, the development of emotion understanding and emotion regulation, conscience development, and the growth of prosocial motivation in young children. He also studies the applications of developmental research to public policy concerns, including school readiness and its development, early childhood investments, and early mental health. Dr. Thompson received the Ann Brown Award for Excellence in Developmental Research in 2007, and the University of California, Davis, Distinguished Scholarly Public Service Award in 2011. He was a member of the 2000 Board on Children, Youth, and Families committee that produced the report *From Neurons to Neighborhoods: The Science of Early Childhood Development*. He is a member of the Board of Directors of Zero to Three, and the Scientific Advisory Board of the National Institute for Early Education Research. His books include *Preventing Child Maltreatment Through Social Support: A Critical Analysis* (Sage, 1995), *The Postdivorce Family: Children, Families, and Society* (co-edited with Paul Amato) (Sage, 1999), *Toward a Child-Centered, Neighborhood-Based Child Protection* (co-edited with Gary Melton and Mark Small) (Praeger, 2002), and *Socioemotional Development* (University of Nebraska Press, 1990). Dr. Thompson received his Ph.D. in psychology from the University of Michigan.

Albert Wat, M.A., is a Senior Policy Analyst in the Education Division of the National Governors Association. Mr. Wat provides state policy makers with analyses and information on promising practices and the latest research in early childhood education policy, from birth through third grade. His work focuses on preschool education systems and alignment of early childhood and early elementary practices and policies, including standards, assessments, and data systems. Mr. Wat's previous experience includes Research Manager, Senior Research Associate, and State Policy Analyst for Pre-K Now, a project of The Pew Charitable Trusts' Pew Center on the States. He served on the board of directors of Great Start DC and on the board of advisors for the Student Coalition for Action on Literacy Education at the University of North Carolina at Chapel Hill. His publications include co-author of *A Governor's Guide to Early Literacy: Getting All Students Reading by Third Grade* (National Governors Association, 2013); *Governor's Role in Aligning Early Education and K-12 Reforms: Challenges, Opportunities, and Benefits for Children* (National Governors Association, 2012); *Transforming Public Education: Pathway to a Pre-K-12 Future* (Pew Center on the States, 2011); *Why Pre-K for All* (Phi Delta Kappan, 2010); *The Case for Pre-K in Education Reform: A Summary of Program Evaluation Findings* (Pew Center on the States, 2010); *Beyond the School Yard: Pre-K Collaborations with Community-Based Partners* (Pew

Center on the States, 2009); and *Pre-K Pinch: Early Education and the Middle Class* (Pre-K Now, 2008). Mr. Wat received his M.A. in education policy from George Washington University and an M.A. in education, with a focus in social sciences in education, from Stanford University.

PROJECT STAFF

Bridget B. Kelly, M.D., Ph.D., is a Senior Program Officer with the Board on Children, Youth, and Families and Board on Global Health and works on a range of topics in health and education. In addition to serving as the study director for the Committee on the Science of Children Birth to Age 8: Deepening and Broadening the Foundation for Success, she is also director of the Collaborative on Global Chronic Disease Prevention and Control and a co-organizer of the annual Public Health Case Challenge for university student teams in the Washington, DC, area. Most recently she was the study co-director for the *Evaluation of PEPFAR*, an evaluation of U.S. global HIV/AIDS programs, and the project co-director for the workshop *Evaluation Design for Complex Global Initiatives*. Previously she was the study director for the report *Promoting Cardiovascular Health in the Developing World*, and a series of related follow-up activities on global chronic diseases, including the workshop *Country-Level Decision Making for Control of Chronic Diseases*. She has also worked for projects on strengthening the use of economic evidence to inform interventions for children and families; prevention of mental, emotional, and behavioral disorders among children, youth, and young adults; and depression, parenting, and child development. She was a 2007 Christine Mirzayan Science and Technology Policy Graduate Fellow at the National Academies. She holds both an M.D. and a Ph.D. in neurobiology, which she completed through the Medical Scientist Training Program at Duke University. She received her B.A. in biology and neuroscience from Williams College, where she was also the recipient of the Hutchinson Fellowship in fine arts. In addition to her background in science and health, she is a dancer and choreographer with many years of experience in grassroots arts administration and production.

Sheila A. Moats is a program officer with the Institute of Medicine and the National Research Council's Board on Children, Youth, and Families (BCYF). She has been on the National Academies' staff for 13 years and has worked on studies for both BCYF and the Food and Nutrition Board. In addition to her work with the Committee on the Science of Children Birth to Age 8: Deepening and Broadening the Foundation for Success, Ms. Moats is working with the Committee on Fostering School Success for English Learners: Toward New Directions in Policy, Practice, and Research. She has been the project director for several workshops, most recently *Nutrition*

Education in the K-12 Curriculum: The Role of National Standards and *An Update on Research Issues in the Assessment of Birth Settings*. She has assisted with overseeing numerous consensus studies, including *School Meals: Building Blocks for Healthy Children* and *Child and Adult Food Program: Aligning Dietary Guidance for All*. Prior to joining the National Academies, she worked for the American Diabetes Association and the University of Colorado Health Sciences Center. She received a B.S. in nutrition science from Pennsylvania State University.

Wendy E. Keenan is a Program Associate for the Board on Children, Youth, and Families at the Institute of Medicine (IOM). She helps organize planning meetings and workshops that cover current issues related to children, youth, and families, and provides administrative and research support to the Board's various program committees. Ms. Keenan has been on the National Academies' staff for 15 years and has worked on studies for both the IOM and the National Research Council (NRC). As a senior program assistant, she worked with the NRC's Board on Behavioral, Cognitive, and Sensory Sciences. Prior to joining the National Academies, she taught English as a second language for Washington, DC, public schools. She received a B.A. in sociology from Pennsylvania State University and took graduate courses in social and public policy at Georgetown University.

Sarah M. Tracey, M.A., joined the Board on Children, Youth, and Families in September 2013. She currently provides research support to the Committee on the Science of Children Birth to Age 8, the Committee on Supporting Parents of Young Children, and the Forum on Investing in Young Children Globally. Prior to joining the National Academies, Ms. Tracey taught academic and survival English courses to adults in Portland, Oregon. In 2010-2011, she assisted the Haiti Working Group at New York University's Institute of Human Development and Social Change (IHDSC) on research projects and grant proposals. In this role, she also helped plan the IHDSC's 2010 conference on children, families, and disasters in Haiti. Outside of her work at the IHDSC, Ms. Tracey assisted with communication efforts for the nonprofit Partners for a Bright and Healthy Haiti. In 2006-2007, Ms. Tracey taught the English language arts program for grades 3 through 8 at Southwest School in La Esperanza, Honduras. Ms. Tracey received her M.A. in international education from New York University in 2011, and her B.A. in English literature from the University of Washington in 2004.

Allison L. Berger is a Senior Program Assistant for the Board on Children, Youth, and Families and the Food and Nutrition Board at the Institute of Medicine (IOM) of the National Academies. She currently provides administrative and meeting planning support for the Committee on the Science of Children Birth to Age 8: Deepening and Broadening the Foundation for Success, and the Committee on a Framework for Assessing the Health, Environmental, and Social Effects of the Food System. Ms. Berger joined the IOM staff in 2002 and has provided assistance on various consensus studies and workshops during her tenure. Most recently, she provided support for the IOM Committee on Physical Activity and Physical Education in the School Environment, the Committee on National Nutrition Education Curriculum Standards: A Workshop, and the Committee on Fitness Measures and Health Outcomes in Youth, just to name a few. She also served as the administrative assistant for the IOM Board on Global Health. Prior to joining the IOM, Ms. Berger served as administrative assistant at the American Psychological Association, where she worked on programs that promote psychological science in the academic and scientific arenas. She is currently pursuing a professional certification in meeting and convention planning.

Kimber Bogard, Ph.D., is the Director of the Board on Children, Youth, and Families at the Institute of Medicine and the National Research Council of the National Academies. In this role, she directs a range of activities that address emerging and critical issues in the lives of children, youth, and families. Recently released reports include *The Cost of Inaction for Young Children Globally; Considerations in Applying Benefit-Cost Analysis to Preventive Interventions for Children, Youth, and Families; Sports-Related Concussions in Youth: Improving the Science, Changing the Culture; Confronting Commercial Sexual Exploitation and Sex Trafficking of Minors in the United States; New Directions for Research on Child Abuse and Neglect;* and *Investing in the Health and Well-Being of Young Adults*. She was previously the Associate Director of the Institute of Human Development and Social Change at New York University where she managed a portfolio of domestic and international grants and contracts that examined child development within a changing global context. A developmental psychologist by training, Kimber has worked with numerous organizations that support children's cognitive, affective, and behavioral development in early childhood education through the high school years, including the Foundation for Child Development, W.K. Kellogg Foundation, the Center for Children's Initiatives, and Partners for a Bright and Healthy Haiti. Kimber often speaks to various audiences about child development in the context of families and schools, with a keen focus on how policies influence developmental, educational, and health trajectories. In 2006, she received her Ph.D. from Fordham University in applied developmental psychology, and she also holds a master's degree from Columbia University-Teachers College where she studied evidence-informed risk and prevention strategies for children, youth, and families.

Appendix B

Public Session Agendas

PUBLIC INFORMATION-GATHERING SESSION
February 28, 2014
National Academy of Sciences
Lecture Room
2101 Constitution Avenue NW
Washington, DC 20418

AGENDA

8:30 am   **Welcome and Goals of the Public Session**
LaRue Allen, New York University, Committee Chair

8:40 am   **PANEL 1: Perspectives from Example Initiatives on Opportunities and Challenges for a Birth Through 8 Continuum**

Moderator: *P. Fred Storti, Executive Director Emeritus, Minnesota Elementary School Principals' Association, Committee Member*

Initiatives and Panelists:

GREAT START DELAWARE
Harriet Dichter, Executive Director, Delaware Office of Early Learning
Daphne Y. Evans, Lead Facilitator, Delaware Readiness Teams

INVEST EARLY MINNESOTA
Kelly Chandler, Manager, Itasca County Public Health Division
Amy Galatz, Principal, King Elementary School, Deer River
Mary Kosak, Program Officer, Blandin Foundation

HARTFORD BLUEPRINT FOR YOUNG CHILDREN
Jane Crowell, Assistant Director, Hartford Department of Families, Children, Youth and Recreation

10:15 am   **Break**

10:30 am   **PANEL 2: Perspectives on the Workforce for Birth Through 8**

Moderator: *Ron Haskins, The Brookings Institution, Committee Member*

Panelists:
Peter Mangione, Center for Child and Family Studies, WestEd
Sharon Ritchie, Frank Porter Graham Child Development Institute, University of North Carolina
Frances O'Connell Rust, Teacher Education Program, University of Pennsylvania
Teri N. Talan, McCormick Center for Early Childhood Leadership and National Louis University
Marcy Whitebook, Center for the Study of Child Care Employment, University of California, Berkeley

12:00 pm   **Lunch**

1:00 pm   **Introduction to Afternoon Session**
LaRue Allen, New York University, Committee Chair

1:10 pm   **Perspectives from Stakeholders**

Moderator: *LaRue Allen, New York University, Committee Chair*

Question to be addressed: From your perspective, how can children be supported to move more seamlessly through the birth through age 8 continuum?

Deborah Adams, National Association of Early Childhood Specialist in State Departments of Education
Lindsey Allard Agnamba, School Readiness Consulting
Elena Bodrova, Tools of the Mind
Kimberly Boller, Mathematica Policy Research
Brandi Cage, Council for Professional Recognition
Cindy Cisneros, Committee for Economic Development
Anne Douglass, University of Massachusetts Boston
Marcy Guddemi, Gesell Institute of Child Development
Diane Horm, Early Childhood Education Institute, University of Oklahoma–Tulsa
Sue Russell, T.E.A.C.H. Early Childhood National Center and Child Care Services Association
Barbara Sawyer, National Association for Family Child Care
Malik Stewart, Red Clay Consolidated School District, Wilmington, Delaware
Grace Whitney, Connecticut Head Start State Collaboration Office
Barbara Willer, National Association for the Education of Young Children
Noreen Yazejian, Frank Porter Graham Child Development Institute, University of North Carolina at Chapel Hill

2:30 pm   **Break**

2:45 pm   **Project Dissemination and Communications: Discussion with Stakeholders**
                 Abbey Meltzer, Director, Institute of Medicine Office of Communications

3:45 pm   **Closing Remarks and Adjourn**
                 LaRue Allen, New York University, Committee Chair

PUBLIC INFORMATION-GATHERING SESSION
Panel Discussion on Higher Education for the Birth Through 8
Continuum
April 22, 2014
Erikson Institute
Chicago, IL

AGENDA

1:00 pm   **Welcome**
            LaRue Allen, New York University, Committee Chair

1:10 pm   **Panel Discussion**

            Moderator: *Jana Fleming, Committee Member,*
                Erikson Institute

            Panelists:
            Barbara Bowman, Erikson Institute
            Johnna Darragh Ernst, Heartland Community College
            Susan Fowler, University of Illinois at Urbana-Champaign
            Chris Maxwell, Erikson Institute
            Carrie Nepstad, Harold Washington City College
            Steve Tozer, University of Illinois at Chicago

2:20 pm   **Open Discussion**

            Moderator: *Jana Fleming, Committee Member,*
                Erikson Institute

2:55 pm   **Closing Remarks and Adjourn**
            LaRue Allen, New York University, Committee Chair

PUBLIC INFORMATION-GATHERING SESSION
April 29, 2014
Arnold and Mabel Beckman Center of the National Academy of Sciences
100 Academy Drive
Irvine, CA

AGENDA

9:00 am   **Welcome and Goals**
LaRue Allen, New York University, Committee Chair

9:10 am   **PANEL 1: Higher Education Preparation**

Moderator: *Jana Fleming, Erikson Institute,*
Committee Member

Panelists:
Betsy Cahill, Professor and Director of Early Childhood
Teacher Education, New Mexico State University
Judy Gump, Department Chair, Early Childhood Education,
Aims Community College, Greeley, Colorado
Michelle J. Sobolak, Assistant Clinical Professor, College of
Education, University of Pittsburgh
Susan Thompson, Professor, Department of Elementary and
Early Childhood Education, University of Northern
Colorado

10:20 am   **Break**

10:40 am   **PANEL 2: Professional Development for the Birth Through**
Age 8 Workforce

Moderator: *Jacqueline Jones, Independent Consultant,*
Committee Member

Panelists:
Chip Donohue, Dean of Distance Learning and Continuing
Education and Director, Technology in Early Childhood
Center, Erikson Institute
Jason Downer, Director, The Center for Advanced Study of
Teaching and Learning and Research Associate Professor,
University of Virginia

*Claire Dunham, Senior Vice President, Programs and
    Training, Ounce of Prevention Fund*
*Kristie Kauerz, Research Assistant Professor, University of
    Washington*
*Sarah LeMoine, Project Director, National Center on
    Child Care Professional Development Systems and
    Workforce Initiatives, ZERO TO THREE*
*Teajai Anderson Schmidt, Supervisor of Literacy PreK-12,
    Saint Paul Public Schools Office of Teaching, Learning,
    and Leading*

12:30 pm   **Lunch**

1:30 pm   **PANEL 3: Perspectives of Employers and Employees in the
            Workforce for the Birth Through Age 8 Continuum**

            Moderator: *Marjorie Kostelnik, University of Nebraska–
            Lincoln, Committee Member*

            Panelists:
            *Laura Butler, Owner, Imagination Island Family Child
                Care, Milton, Vermont*
            *Hannah Griffith, Public Preschool Teacher, Papillion-La
                Vista School District, Nebraska*
            *Stacey Kadrmas, Principal, Frost Lake Elementary School,
                St. Paul Public Schools*
            *Margaret Mahoney, Clinical Director, Thom Anne Sullivan
                Center Early Intervention*
            *Barbara Mayfield-Coatney, Executive Director, Gulf Coast
                Community Action Agency, Mississippi*

3:10 pm   **Break**

3:30 pm   **PANEL 4: Intersecting Professions in the Birth Through
            Age 8 Continuum**

            Moderator: *John Duby, Northeast Ohio Medical University,
            Akron Children's Hospital, Committee Member*

            Panelists:
            *Tumaini Rucker Coker, Pediatrician, Mattel Children's
                Hospital, David Geffen School of Medicine, University
                of California, Los Angeles*

Peggy Gallagher, Professor and Coordinator, Early Childhood Special Education, Georgia State University
Jisela Hernandez, Resource Specialist, Children's Social Worker, Magnolia Place Family Resource Center
Kresta Horn, Director of Children and Youth Services, UMOM New Day Centers, Phoenix
Lisa Kelly-Vance, Director of School Psychology, University of Nebraska–Omaha
Melinda Landau, School Nurse, San José Unified School District

5:30 pm   **Closing Remarks and Adjourn**
             LaRue Allen, New York University, Committee Chair

PUBLIC INFORMATION-GATHERING SESSION
Panel Discussion on Envisioning the Future for
Children Birth Through Age 8 in Oklahoma
May 7, 2014
Founders Hall
University of Oklahoma–Tulsa

AGENDA

2:00 pm   **Welcome**
Bridget Kelly, Institute of Medicine and National Research Council, Study Director

2:10 pm   **Panel Remarks**

Moderator: *LaRue Allen, New York University, Committee Chair*

Panelists:
Keith E. Ballard, Tulsa Public Schools
Gerard P. Clancy, University of Oklahoma–Tulsa
Steven Dow, Community Action Project (CAP) Tulsa
Annie Koppel Van Hanken, George Kaiser Family Foundation
Paige Whalen, Child Care Resource Center (CCRC), Tulsa

3:15 pm   **Open Discussion**

Moderator: *LaRue Allen, New York University, Committee Chair*

3:55 pm   **Closing Remarks and Adjourn**
LaRue Allen, New York University, Committee Chair

PUBLIC INFORMATION-GATHERING SESSION
Panel Discussion on Policies for Bridging
Early Childhood Education to Early Elementary School:
From the State Level to the School Level
May 29, 2014
Blackriver Conference Center
Renton, WA

AGENDA

3:00 pm   **Welcome**
                 Bridget Kelly, Institute of Medicine and National Research
                 Council, Study Director

3:10 pm   **Panel Discussion**

                 Moderator: *Albert Wat, National Governors Association,*
                 Committee Member

                 Panelists:
                 Angelica Alvarez, Board Member, Highline Public Schools
                 Robert Butts, Assistant Superintendent for Early Learning,
                 State of Washington Office of Superintendent of Public
                 Instruction
                 Lorna Spear, Executive Director of Teaching and
                 Learning Services, Spokane Public Schools
                 Sam Whiting, President & CEO, Thrive by Five
                 Washington

4:20 pm   **Open Discussion**

                 Moderator: *Albert Wat, National Governors Association,*
                 Committee Member

4:55 pm   **Closing Remarks and Adjourn**
                 Albert Wat, National Governors Association,
                 Committee Member

Appendix C

Information-Gathering from the Field

SITE VISITS

During the course of the study, committee members and staff gathered information through site visits and interviews in three locations, Chicago, Illinois; Tulsa, Oklahoma; and Washington State. The purpose of the site visits and interviews was to explore topics and issues relevant to the study charge from the perspective of stakeholders familiar with the pragmatic realities of local environments, including the policies, systems, and services or programs that relate to both children ages birth through 8 and the adults who provide for them. They informed the committee's deliberations by eliciting insight from those with policy, practice, and implementation experience, including examples of successes and challenges.

The site visits and interviews were an opportunity to provide the committee with information that cannot be readily obtained through documentation and other means. The locations, specific sites to visit, and interviewees were chosen by the committee and staff using purposeful sampling. The selections were based on the topics identified as priorities to explore using this approach and were designed to include a range of perspectives and experiences, example approaches, practice settings, and professional roles covering the range from infancy through the early elementary years. The selections do not reflect any conclusions the committee drew about best practices or exemplars. The site visits and interviews were not intended to be a comprehensive research effort, but served as an important complement to the committee's many other information-gathering activities and approaches.

A list of participating organizations and individual participants is provided below. This is followed by highlights of key themes from the information gathered.

Participating Organizations

Bremerton Early Childhood Care and Education—Birth to Five Collaborative
Child Care Resource Center (CCRC) Tulsa
Children's Home + Aid
Collaboration for Early Childhood
Community Action Project (CAP) Tulsa
De Diego Community Academy, Chicago Public Schools
Educare Chicago
Educare Seattle
Educare Tulsa
Erikson Institute
Everett Public Schools
George Kaiser Family Foundation
Harold Washington College, City College of Chicago
Healthy Families Chicago
Illinois Action for Children
Illinois State Family and Parent Association
Illinois State Governor's Office of Early Childhood Development
Infant Welfare Society of Evanston
National Louis University McCormick Center for Early Childhood
    Leadership
Naval Avenue Early Learning Center, Bremerton School District
Oklahoma Early Childhood Program
Ounce of Prevention
Rosa Parks Early Childhood Education Center, Union Public Schools
Rosa Parks Elementary School, Union Public Schools
Rosia's K T C Family Childcare
Spokane Public Schools
Tulsa Public Schools
University of Oklahoma–Tulsa Early Childhood Education Institute
University of Washington College of Education
Washington State Department of Early Learning
Washington State Educational School District 105
Washington State Educational School District 189
Washington State Legislature, 16th District
Washington State Legislature, 32nd District
Washington State Legislature, 48th District
Washington State Office of Superintendent of Public Instruction

Wee Are the World Home Daycare
White Center Heights, Highline Public Schools

Individual Participants

Faith Arnold
Tracy Bayles
Michelle Boatright
Celeste Bowen
Juliet Bromer
Brendan Bulger
Caren Calhoun
Lexi Catlin
Patricia Ceja-Muhsen
Christi Chadwick
Gerard P. Clancy
Steven Dow
Monique Draper
Claire Dunham
Libby Ethridge
Amy Fain
Donna Gearns
Leslie Gilbert
Linda Gilkerson
Linda Hamburg
Theresa Hawley
Jessica Hollingsworth
Diane Horm
Holly Householder
Ross Hunter
Cynthia Jones
Gail Joseph
Ruth Kagi
Kristie Kauerz
Karen Kiely
Susan Knight
Chris Koch
Lynn Lahey
Vickie Lake
Tom Layman
Chris Maxwell
Dona Maye

Diana McClarien
Lynn McClure
Andrew McKenzie
Kellie Morrill
Juliet Morrison
Teresita Patino
Vickie Pendleton
Anne Reece
Rosario Rodriguez
Deborah Rogers-Jaye
Diana Rosenbrock
Elizabeth Rothkopf
Michelle Saddler
Diane Scruggs
Ruth Slocum
Julie Smith
Lorna Spear
Amanda Stein
Linda Sullivan-Dudzic
Sharon Syc
Teri Talan
Kathe Taylor
Pat Twymon
Annie Van Hanken
Karen Vance
Jaclyn Vasquez
Erin Velez
Maureen Walsh
Rosia Watson
John Welsh
Paige Whalen
Maria Whelan
Shanel Wiley
Amy Williamson
Cass Wolfe
Vicki Wolfe

Key Themes from Site Visits

Overall Key Messages[1]

- Importance of strong, supportive, and strategic *leadership* throughout systems that support care and education—leaders who understand and value early childhood, are reflective and intentional, and understand and value the importance of building relationships.
- Importance of establishing a *common language* or other ways of supporting communication and understanding across systems and roles.
- Importance of communicating the value of a birth through third grade continuum to everyone in the community, including administrators, educators, parents, and policy makers.
- Strengths in *higher education* programs include
  - Exposure to practice opportunities, especially those with diverse populations of children.
  - All classes in the program addressing diversity and cultural sensitivity, but field placements in diverse settings seen as the best way to train for this.
  - Exposure to engaging directly with families (e.g., learning to do home visits)—especially families from different socioeconomic and cultural backgrounds than the practitioners.
  - Establishing a cohort who are available to each other as a support once they enter practice.
  - Training for advocacy.
  - Focusing support and professional development in the first year of professional practice.
  - Alignment with alumni networks.
  - Evaluation/accountability system for gauging whether students are graduating with the necessary knowledge/skills, including three components: knowledge, practice (self-assessment, site supervisor rating), and reflection (seminars, video project).
- Combined education and professional learning for early care and education and early elementary practitioners is seen as beneficial to achieving a birth through age 8 continuum. A joint professional development system that is organized across content knowledge, cuts across ages, and allows educators to share content knowledge and discuss pedagogy. This also provides a clearer "line of site" on where the child has been and is heading.

---

[1] These overall messages represent themes that emerged across all types of stakeholders interviewed during site visits.

- Absence of a *fundamental knowledge of child development* among educators.
  - Early childhood/preschool educators were described as needing to learn more about direct, standards-based instruction in content areas and using data to inform instruction, while K-3 educators were described as needing to learn more about child development, socioemotional development, comprehensive services, and observational assessments.
- The K-12 field has competing priorities that sometimes trump incorporating a developmental framework in its curriculum—and also trump developing meaningful partnerships and collaborations with the early care and education field. This is an issue of time as much as it is about (real and perceived) conflicting approaches (e.g., developmentally appropriate practice and Common Core, educator evaluation).
- Family engagement and supporting parents comprehensively and as a partnership are critically important.
  - Difficulty transmitting developmental science knowledge to families.
  - Importance of addressing the empathy gap between practitioners and families.
  - Doulas and home visitors work with families as a way to promote linkages/continuity.
- *Reflective and intentional practice* (individual and facilitated) was seen as important.
- Professional learning systems should be designed to accommodate the needs of the learners.
- Increased salaries and *professionalism* of the early childhood workforce are viewed as necessary to raise the perceived value of the field. Salaries are also seen as an obstacle to creating any sort of comprehensive system, because noncompetitive salaries are linked to the continuity issue. Early childhood practitioners are leaving the jobs because of low pay. Promoting the professionalism of the workforce by using science to drive an understanding of their value would be beneficial.
- Strong reliance on philanthropic *funding* was seen in most examples. However, one school district exemplified an alignment effort with minimal additional external funding. Initial early learning funding from a private foundation served as a catalyst in this district; otherwise it uses existing federal/state funding streams for early childhood and public school.
- Challenge of *coverage and access* (promising programs and good opportunities, but not reaching all the children).

Policy/Governance/Infrastructure/Systems

- Collaborative arrangements among government agencies are key to a state's ability to share information and develop cohesive plans and initiatives through the various systems. Despite these partnerships, however, there is still a need for better communication between state legislators, government agencies, administrators, and districts before decisions are made. Examples were seen of the departments of health and child and family services, and the state education agencies forming partnerships.
- Layers of leadership within community: government, philanthropy, university. An example was seen of a community that has been galvanized around an issue that key leaders support (philanthropists, university president).
- Quality Rating Improvement Systems (QRISs) are seen as way to help with continuity of learning and focus on development across the birth through age 8 continuum.
- Plurality and layers of schools (e.g., neighborhood, charter, private, special/magnet schools), which have varying policies and systems that affect student pipelines, make alignment challenging.
    - Aligning private schools/programs with public schools can be difficult because rules and regulations are less forgiving (often due to collective bargaining agreements). Aligning to charter schools has its own challenges.
    - Different types of institutions are working together to develop a common language/framework for working with children from birth through age 8 but need to traverse differences in teaching and learning approaches (e.g., developmentally appropriate practice versus standards-based instruction).
- In a school district where a birth through third grade system is in place, every time a new school board member is elected, school administrators need to reeducate him/her on its value.
- Subsidy eligibility requirements for specialized programs make families very vulnerable to displacement from the program due to changes to income or circumstances, e.g., employment. This poses a problem for continuity of services as children cycle in and out of program eligibility. Administrators are exploring strategies to provide a better safety net for families, for example, providing 12-month eligibility for subsidy recipients.
- Policy makers need to be persuaded by the science.
- Myriad policies and reforms across federal, state, and local governments and school districts make alignment difficult, e.g., Common Core, curriculum requirements. There is inconsistency between

policy and practice. In an effort to ameliorate these misalignments, in one site new age 0-3 year guidelines are being cross-walked with age 3-5 year guidelines, which are being cross-walked with Common Core.

- Networks of peer support are developing, especially among family childcare educators, such as cohorts and communities of learners. Regional early learning coalitions that are made up of health care professionals, social workers, etc., have been set up in one site.
- Efforts are being made to incorporate early care and education perspectives/practices into state educator evaluation and coaching systems for public schools. Also an effort is under way to align licensure/credentialing and policies for higher education programs with early care and education standards and competencies. There is a need to determine what education, professional development, and certifications are needed to support quality programs and services. Legislators in one state were not interested in requiring bachelor's degrees at this point.
- Legislators attempted to target quality of early childhood education by tying subsidies to educators meeting quality standards, but the bill did not pass. There was pushback from educators because many feel they are experienced, having provided services for a long time, and do not have the means or time to pursue further education.
- Legislators believe they have no way to leverage changes in K-12 school systems, because there is district-level control.
- Articulation agreements between 2- and 4-year institutions of higher education are seen as a system that should be made stronger.
- A main challenge is the capacity to serve children and families who experience trauma. This is recognized at the level of governance.
- Major needs:
  - Time/money/facilities.
  - To see early care and education connected to K-12 schools.
  - To cross over the focus of early childhood practitioners on child development with the K-12 practitioners focus on instruction so that both systems come together.
  - To establish a common way of knowing and assessing across birth through age 8—this is a systems issue if it is to work across birth to age 5 and K-12 schools.
- Challenges to greater commonality are a product of having different funding streams, historical practices, and disparate goals.

Program/Initiative Implementation

- Head Start critiques are around program's administration, coverage, and reach, not programming. Untapped potential to serve the poor was attributed to regulations and administrative requirements, e.g., paperwork.
- It was noted that a large number of children are not served by formal programs.
- Transportation is an issue for access for children to programs and for engaging families.
  - Families do not all have cars.
  - Public transportation is limited or time consuming.
  - Young children in one location visited cannot ride the bus due to seatbelt laws.
- Characteristics of an example birth through third grade public school setting:
  - Infant, toddler, preschool, Head Start, and kindergarten through third grade located on the same campus.
  - Selection of high-quality educators.
  - A grant from a private foundation for early learning support was obtained, as well as the support of the superintendent and school board.
  - Lack of space is an issue, have a kindergarten overflow classroom.
  - Support for children and parents transitioning from preschool to kindergarten:
    - Visits from children and parents in Head Start program and other preschools in the community to kindergarten classes, so that preschoolers could learn about kindergarten activities from the current kindergarten students.
    - Kindergarten educator goes to Head Start classroom to work with children that will be coming to kindergarten the following year.
  - Preschool educators and kindergarten educators share some trainings and mesh expectations and negotiate targets for the transition from prekindergarten to kindergarten.
  - Kindergarten educators hold parent meetings to provide home activities to help with literacy and math skills.
  - Kindergarten through third grade educators meet regularly, which helps with continuity across the elementary grades.
  - A district joint early care and education/early elementary professional development was an impetus for the elementary educators to incorporate more socioemotional skills in their instructional activities.

- Early Head Start/Head Start on site
  - Head Start educators go to school district-wide training once per month.
  - Look at data for third graders to assess what to change in programs for ages birth to 5 to improve scores over time.
  - If child is having difficulty, a 2-week transition program is available in the summer in the kindergarten classroom before the school year starts.
  - Most educators have a B.A. or an A.A. degree, teaching assistants have an A.A. degree or are working on it.
  - Flexibility is practiced in ages of children transitioning from infant room to Early Head Start and Head Start.
  - All children get vision and hearing testing.
- A program is in place that attempts to reach parents who do not have children in preschool:
  - Offered for 1.5 hours once per month to about 10 parents each time.
  - Most parents are families in which the children do not qualify for Head Start but their families cannot afford preschool.
  - Staff provide children and their parents with learning activities to do at home.
  - Support is provided through funding an educator on special assignment.
- A childcare company connects principals/elementary schools with childcare educators:
  - Professional development is provided quarterly for educators.
  - A grant to pay educators to attend professional development meetings in hopes of building relationships that will show the importance of continuing education.
- Characteristics of an example community linkages approach:
  - A building design that is developmentally appropriate for children:
    - Windows are built at the child level, magnets on classroom doors to make it harder for young children to open them; bathrooms are built inside the classroom for young children; easy access to outdoor space with greenery and appropriate manipulatives.
    - Connected to elementary schools to facilitate transitions.
    - Co-location (early childhood program as part of the public school).
  - Two-generation focus that engages parents and families
    - Career advancement program: Education courses for parents which enters them into the health care pipeline.

- A challenge was that the entering skill levels were lower than anticipated; therefore a developmental education piece was added.
  - Family engagement
    - Educators visit parents and families at their home at the beginning of the year.
    - Structured drop-off routine for families and children because it is not developmentally appropriate for young children to ride the bus.
    - At the Early Childhood center, they have family support specialists/liaisons who are available to speak with families/parents as they arrive during child drop-off.
  - Community schools and wraparound services
    - They have a variety of services: dental, health, social service collocation; a continuum of services under the roof of one school.
    - The Community School Coordinator coordinates partnerships and communication (learning to speak the same language among all practices); this cannot fall solely on the principal of the school.
  - Assessments
    - No formative assessment exists to determine why there is a gap in scores for children in grades 1-3.
    - Prekindergarten screening exists, but no district-wide assessment for grades 1-3.
  - Special needs
    - Young children are served in 10 programs in the district, and when they turn 5, they transition to the neighborhood school.
- Characteristics of an example birth to 5 public–private program:
  - Working to enhance academic programming while still strongly supporting socioemotional learning.
  - Attempting to map Common Core backwards to provide what children need along the way.
  - Access to comprehensive services and family advocates, who help families access services outside of the school.
- Major needs/opportunities:
  - Encouraging intentionality
    - Do the programs have a plan, goals, or are they just collecting fees for childcare?
    - Do they know they are more than just glorified babysitters?
  - Programs need to be culturally relevant, embracing the diversity of communities, including economically diverse and diversity of ability.

Resources

- Time is sometimes the most limited resource, especially for people already working in the field.
- State funding for universal prekindergarten based on a weighted formula related to the number of children served and their daily attendance.
- Universal voluntary prekindergarten is not covering all 4-year-olds.
- Although public–private partnerships are a source of funds, the commitment of government agency support was seen as critical to development.
- Head Start and non–Head Start funds blended in some centers, but centers are not able to share/redistribute resources equally (e.g., Head Start children take one school bus, non–Head Start children take another).
- Partnerships are an important factor in providing services for children.
- A need was expressed to release money from the silos and braid Head Start and childcare funding.
- Because of the increase in early childhood programs and QRISs, there is an increased demand for highly qualified educators, but the supply does not meet the demand.
- Because Race to the Top funds have been used to scale up professional development, there is concern about what will happen when that funding goes away.
- A concern was voiced by practitioners that resources are being taken away from K-12 because the focus is now on early childhood.
- If financial incentives are in place to encourage staff with higher quality, programs will adjust themselves.
- Major needs/opportunities:
  - Increase in consistency of funding, K-12 system has consistent source of funding versus early learning which has subsidies that come and go.
  - Getting entire taxpayer community support.

Higher Education

- Certification exam is used as a measure but has no relation to whether a person is a good educator. Educators should have to demonstrate competence as done in other fields, e.g., doctors, lawyers.
- The issue of faculty quality in institutions of higher education. One institution of higher education described a project that helped

faculty become updated on the growing research on brain development and how it affects their instruction.

- There is a lack of continuity in educator preparation programs.
- The question about what is more valuable: B.A. degree or experience
  - The reflection of executive functioning and life skills of those who earn a B.A. is important to recognize.
  - There is an association between a B.A. and quality but it is not direct.
- In order to serve diverse populations, a core skill is to be able to develop relationships with the families.
  - Students who show knowledge of developmentally appropriate practices and of how to work with and talk to parents and families are stronger.
  - Many educators do not know how to work with families; there is an empathy barrier. Specifically, educators do not understand poverty.
    - An example was given of Head Start educators going on home visits as a way to overcome this barrier.
- Field training experiences, both independent and embedded in courses, were seen as a vital component of higher education programs.
- Use of technology seen as an asset to providing quality education, e.g., guest lecturers via video, videotaping educators in training to provide feedback.
- Use of intentional teaching framework—identify best evidence-based practices and develop a shared language of practice.
- Support should be provided to students who may be returning to school later in life or are new to online learning. An example was given of two beginning courses to build confidence and skills in students:
  - Technology (using videos and digital cameras, uploading information online).
  - Resilient Educator (stress management, caring about one's health and well-being).
- Higher education opportunities for leadership
  - Participants described benefits of a leadership program as
    - Networking/establishing partnerships.
    - Having a safe space to have difficult conversations and reflection on putting what has been learned into practice.
    - Value in having a framework to build a P-3 system, learning how to cut across the different systems, and learning the prioritization of the steps to take.

- Provides assistance with knowing how to communicate the value of a P-3 system to educators, district administrators, and the community.
- Building leadership skills to bridge the communities, interpersonal communication skills, and advocacy skills.
- Will increase the level of professionalism of leadership in early childhood.
- Data sharing is uneven in implementation, so participants can assist each other with that issue.
- Appreciate new information about brain development and family engagement.
- Most participants did not see the P-3 Leadership program as an impetus for a career change, but said it will change the nature of their position to be more effective at what they do.
- Value in discussion to stimulate shared language across levels of programs these individuals lead.
- Gaps in training
  - Educators in K-3 programs are not trained sufficiently on knowledge and skills around child development (psychological and cognitive) nor on developmentally appropriate programming.
  - K-8 license may be too broad, options for endorsement types are being considered.
  - There is a need to help early care and education professionals navigate pathways to further their education and credentials; for example, articulation is a challenge.
- Major needs/opportunities:
  - Coordination between 2- and 4-year colleges; development of meaningful articulation agreements.
  - Focus on training educators together in birth through age 8 continuum.

Professional Learning During Ongoing Practice

- An example of a statewide professional development system included a registry of providers, professional development advisers, core competencies, credentials, scholarships/wage supplements, and processes for approving training programs/trainers.
  - One challenge reported is that higher education institutions are not required to align themselves to the professional development system.
- The importance of focusing on support in the first year of teaching was emphasized.

- Compare/contrast community college to 4-year college graduates as potential hires
  - When 4-year college students graduate, they are beginners.
  - When students graduate from community college, often they are mid-career (because many times they are going back for degree after already being in the field).
  - It was suggested, as potential employers, public schools should support the workforce from the community college because they are more seasoned.
- Leadership/administration layer is seen as critical lever for change—responsible for day-to-day support of and environment for educators.
- One school system received philanthropic funding to reinvent professional development, which is currently called professional learning.
  - Nine-week themed modules and school system offers time for educators to participate.
- In one school district, educators discuss what gaps in knowledge exist to determine what professional development is needed. New educators are assigned mentors.
- Educators feel it is valuable to learn from other schools in district-wide professional development.
- Professional learning communities, which include activities such as book reading, peer-to-peer learning, and joint professional development, were reported to be used in several school districts to align across preschool and elementary school.
- Learning to use the data to improve instruction is new to the field.
- The quality of online learning varies drastically but the potential is vast.
- Professional development needs to be ongoing, linked to classroom practice, provide opportunities to reflect and check for understanding, and linked to a P-3 continuum, allowing educators to see backward and forward.
- Professional development is embedded in the QRIS in one state. Coaching is provided by a state agency for 3-4 star rated programs. Childcare resource and referral agencies also provide additional coaching.
- Practice is not keeping up with the science of adult learning—one-shot, 2-day workshops are useless.
- Need better assessment of professional development workshops: no way of knowing whether or not anyone learned anything—there is a satisfaction survey, not an exam.
- Major needs/opportunities

- Bring professional development courses to educators.
  - An example was seen of a child parent center working with a local university on professional development for educators, but it is only a thin slice of professional development that seeks to build capacity of the lead educator.
- Aligning funds for professional development—the funding for professional development is about the most flexible funding and least regulated there is—looking to mandate an integrated approach to professional development.
- Fully funded high quality preservice education and professional development.
- Time for early care and education and K-12 collaboration, professional development.

Practitioners

Knowledge/preparation of workforce
- Knowledge gaps in the workforce:
  - Fundamental knowledge of child development was identified as a knowledge gap in childcare educators.
  - Classroom practices not aligned to development (e.g., 2-year-olds being asked to write their names, etc., versus exploration and play).
  - Educators are not trained to be child psychologists, so they do not know how to deal with behavioral issues. It is a challenge to teach all students in a class when a few need special attention because of behavioral issues.
  - Educators are not prepared to deal with increased diversity and do not understand what it means to be in poverty.
- Increase in understanding of the science of child development will help others to understand the importance of early learning.
- Must acknowledge the power that parents have.
  - Recognition of parents as the first educators and the need to involve families.
  - Parent education on the value of early learning.
  - Pressure on educators from parents, directors, etc., to change practices so childcare is more convenient for adults (e.g., accelerating potty training for very young children). An educator in an ideal situation could explain to a parent that these things are not developmentally appropriate for a 2-year-old.
- Suggestions for workforce development:
  - Child development course in high schools.

– Begin recruiting bilingual speakers in elementary and middle schools to view their future as a care and education professional.

Well-being of workforce

- The health and well-being of the workforce affects children.
  – Becoming a "resilient learner" includes educators' care for their own health and well-being.
  – Family childcare educators networks: especially active in taking care of each other and advocating for legislative changes to benefit profession.
  – Group professional development was seen in some centers that have a "support system" through regular meetings within the professional development framework.
- Self-care is often neglected. For doulas/home visitors it was noted that to help with this issue includes persuading directors/practitioners to recognize the stress of their jobs and teach about self-care so that they are more effective. Additional opportunities for helping with educator stress and burnout included providing scheduled leave time, yoga/fitness programs, coaching and mentoring, and peer support.

Professionalism

- Increase pay and respect for early childhood field. Working with young children is a profession, but the workforce is not adequately paid.
  – There is a need to dramatically change the way people view early care and education and professionalize it; this will help build a quality workforce.
  – The need to elevate position of educators who work with 1- and 2-year-old children so that educators are paid equally to that of the public school educators.
  – In one school system they are trying to reenvision how to support elementary educators, even in the face of salaries that cannot compete with nearby states.
- High turnover of staff in Head Start was reported.

Relationships

- Relationships are important.
  – Mixed-aged classrooms benefit the students and the educator.
  – Looping grades to establish continuity of educators.

- Continuity of leaders/trainers of the educator.
- Continuity of the educator and family relationships.
- In one school district, monthly meetings between preschool and kindergarten through third grade educators promote collaboration. Elementary school educators have more respect for what preschool does, kindergarten educators have a better understanding of "what they are getting" and preschool educators understand what the kindergarten educators need.
- Diverse populations
  - Family childcare educators discussed working with cultural diversity, religious diversity—no preparation but they had their resource network (among family childcare educators) which helped, along with developing a good relationship with the families.

Leadership/Management of Practitioners

- Challenges for leadership (directors/principals) described at one site:
  - "Birth to College"—the leaders among all institutions need to coordinate what they are doing and come together around common understanding (principals, center director).
  - Leaders do not pay attention to their own development because there are few incentives to improve.
  - Sometimes few incentives to offer professional development to educators; do not want to offer professional development to educators because they might lose them.
  - If society does not value the early childhood workforce, why should directors care about investing in developing staff?
  - Fractured communication that can be very political; however, there are initiatives to connect with principals and early childhood network leaders.
- Lack of clarity in early childhood programs about expectations for knowledge and competencies in early care and education directors and educators.
- Possible solutions
  - Starting early with leadership development and identification.
  - Incorporating early care and education content into principals' preparation programs; administrators need a stronger understanding of child development.
  - Developing a common vision/language/approach among different sectors.

- In one school district, there are three principal licenses, and only 3 of the 54 elementary school principals knew anything about early childhood.
- A birth to age 5 public–private program that was visited uses an assessment for hiring leaders that evaluates leadership potential, stress management, core competencies and values.
- Dedicated time for reflective practice, reflective leadership, and reflective supervision.
  - Supportive supervision: recognizing and correcting in real time: moving from theory to daily practice.
- A core competency for leaders includes the ability to talk to staff about things they might be lacking, in other words, the ability to have crucial conversations.
- Administrators struggle with how to connect to the community.

Evaluation and Assessment

- What is being assessed?
  - Assessment of children birth to age 5 is about development; assessment of children 5 years old and up is about content.
  - The assessment of family childcare educators measures the impact of their work as reflected in the children (e.g., "Is the child comfortable in her skin? Social competence and self-regulation? What are the child's study skills like?").
- QRIS is an important component in requiring educators to meet standards.
  - QRIS will drive education requirements.
  - Governance interviewees talked about QRIS applying the same standards to early care and education programs across settings, including public schools. The current system makes some differentiation between settings and allows for different kinds of evidence.
- In one example, a birth to age 5 public–private program is trying to introduce its assessment tools to the public school, but it is challenging because it is another language.
- In another example, a performance evaluation advisory council has asked for guidance from early childhood to evaluate prekindergarten through grade 3 educators.
- Privacy concerns about data: one school that was visited asks direct parent permission to share data.
- Ambivalence/mixed reactions were reported toward a kindergarten entry assessment (KEA) used in one state.

- Educators and administrators like the family engagement piece of the KEA. However, home visits by educators are costly; two people are needed for safety purposes.
- They do not like the observational techniques used.
- They feel that the assessment may be missing children that need help due to score inflation. Twenty percent of children that need help are left out.
- Some perceive the KEA as a way to get kindergarten educators to bear the burden of showing the effectiveness of early childhood programs, and to demonstrate the need for more support for early childhood programs.
- Some have seen the KEA improve shared understanding between early childhood educators and elementary school educators.
- The KEA requires a "cultural transformation" about teaching, learning, and assessment. The concept of observation assessment can be foreign to educators.
- The KEA can be an entry point for improving early elementary instruction. Educators may know how to differentiate children within a continuum (as opposed to assessing children against standards), how to scaffold children's' learning, and view learning and development comprehensively.
- There was concern about using the KEA for educator evaluation.
- In one state, a teacher–principal evaluation model has focused modules (one of five categories) each year, but every 4 years a comprehensive evaluation is conducted.
  - More focus is on the quality of teaching and instructional practice versus being evaluated on keeping the class quiet, for example.
  - The district can choose among three frameworks for instructional evaluation. The district uses an evaluation, which is based on what children are doing versus collecting "artifacts," e.g., lesson plans.
- Major gaps reported in knowledge and assessments:
  - Instructional support.
  - Building critical thinking skills.
  - Ensuring that materials are available.
- A hybrid assessment tool, that combines the best parts of the KEA with content assessments, is reportedly being used in one state.
- Major needs/opportunities:
  - Optimism that QRIS can be a lever of change. If it were to achieve some of its goals—and serve as an opportunity for reflection and continuous improvement versus being a checklist—

it could be more of an opportunity to ensure that best practices are actually happening more.

- Create longitudinal data system—an integrated data system that tracks children over time to show how children are progressing and the impact of interventions.
- Ideal would be for demographic characteristics not to be a predictor of success.

Continuity and Linkages

Interprofessional

- Need to integrate the health system into the education system. Medical information needs to reach educators. Educators need to be able to identify hungry children, find where disabilities are, and identify what struggles they are experiencing outside of school.
- Community school model partners with after-school programs, service providers, the department of health, and the department of child and family services.
  - Clinics are on site and for anyone in the community.
- At one point, one city had 40 co-located school health clinics, but as a result of the state legislature rejecting Medicaid expansion under the Affordable Care Act, the number has decreased to 4.
- Interconnection between social services and education
  - Improving computer system so that information can be shared across agencies.
  - Currently about 20 percent of children move in and out of social service programs due to income eligibility. Would like to have 1-year eligibility for programs.
  - Legislators expressed the desire to turn state funded childcare from a welfare program into an education program.
  - Contrast seen between a birth to age 5 center funded through a public–private partnership, which provides access to social services, and the public elementary school, which does not provide similar services.
- Examples of roles that work between sectors
  - A doula works from prenatal care through child birth. As someone who works with the health system, one doula described how important it is to develop relationships and how that made her feel competent.
  - Faculty from an institution of higher education described the role of child life specialists, who work in a health care setting to help children cope with hospital experience.

- How do you train people to work across sectors and ages?
  - Educators are talking with other educators across the continuum, but not across sectors—"lip service" given to continuity and linkages.
  - Embedding early childhood in different professions and sectors
    - One institution of higher education now has a Master's of Social Work with early childhood embedded.
    - Intersector collaboration is also an important part of the training for its Early Childhood Special Education program and the infant/toddler program (e.g., training as Child Life Specialists in hospitals).
    - One participant proposed putting home visitors with a pediatrician.
  - Home visitor and doula interviewees described the need for more consistent vision/language/approach when interacting with other professions.
- Major needs/opportunities:
  - Transform schools into centers for families providing a full continuum of services.
  - Have a "family navigator" to help with consistency.

Within education systems

- Importance of relationships between early care and education settings and elementary schools—a challenge can be when an elementary school does not have a clear feeder program.
- Several examples were seen of practitioner continuity for the child over years of education (mixed age classes in birth to age 3 and ages 4/5; looping of educators in K-1 and 2-3).
- Other examples were seen of educators and children doing classroom visits across ages (e.g., educators of children birth to age 3 visit 4-year-old classrooms at a center serving birth to age 5).
- Community school model:
  - Before students enter the first grade, the first grade educators visit the preschool program to meet the children to prepare for the transition.
  - K-1 is looped, 2-3 is looped, and 4-5 is looped.
  - The classes are situated next to one another (intentional space organization).
- The need for a common language was a reoccurring theme.
  - Not only for early care and education and K-12 professionals but also policy makers and other community leaders.

- Coaching—One state agency that provides coaching to K-12 educators is exploring ways to imbed early childhood elements in the system.
- The importance of getting the birth to age 3 population involved in the continuum was mentioned, i.e., not just prekindergarten through third grade.
- Home visits are known to be important, but educators still feel unsupported or unsure of how to make this part of their job.

MAPPING OF SYSTEMS AND EXPLORATION OF PROFESSIONAL LEARNING SYSTEMS

Additional interviews with thought leaders and practitioners were conducted by a consultant team to inform a mapping of professional stakeholders, systems, and professional roles in care and education and related sectors (see also Chapters 1 and 2) and to explore professional learning systems in greater depth from a range of perspectives across professional roles in the birth through age 8 continuum. Interviewees were selected through purposeful sampling by the committee, project staff, and consultants.

A list of interviewees and organizational affiliations is provided below. This is followed by highlights of key themes from the information gathered, including a brief summary of major overall themes, profiles of professional learning supports by professional role, and ideas for reenvisioning professional learning.

Interviewees

Anna Arlotta-Guerrero
Faith Arnold
Stephanie Byrd
Jaya Chatterjee
Sherry Cleary
Ida Rose Florez
Lynette M. Fraga
Saundra Harrington
Elizabeth Heidemann
Michelle N. Hutson
Elizabeth M. Hyde

Marilou Hyson
Marica Mitchell
Carrie A. Nepstad
Kelly Pollitt
Valerie Preston
Malik J. Stewart
Megan Stockhausen
Heidi Sullivan
Heather Taylor
Marcy Whitebook
Marty Zaslow

Organizational Affiliations

American Federation of Teachers
Center for the Study of Child Care Employment
Child Care Aware of America
Child Trends
Cushing Community School
George Mason University
Gulf Coast Community Action Agency Head Start
Harold Washington College, City Colleges of Chicago
Infant & Toddler Connection of Norfolk
LifePoint Solutions
National Association for Elementary School Principals
National Association for the Education of Young Children
New York City Department of Education
New York City Early Childhood Development Institute/New York State
    Early Childhood Advisory Council
Red Clay Consolidated School District
Service Employees International Union
Success by 6 (Greater Cincinnati)
Sun Children's Inc.
University of Pittsburgh
Virginia Home Visiting Consortium
Washington State Department of Early Learning
WestEd/First 5 California Early Education Effectiveness Exchange

Key Themes from Interviews

Overall Themes: Current State of Professional Learning Supports

A number of the interviewees commented about the "nonsystem" that is birth through age 8. These interviewees mentioned the need for a fundamental rethinking, and even creation of a birth through age 8 system.

Barriers to quality practice and professional learning
- The main barriers mentioned by most interviewees were:
    - Lack of time to pursue professional learning.
    - Lack of available professional learning opportunities during nonwork hours.
    - Lack of funds to pay for professional learning.
- Many interviewees also mentioned lack of a professional community with whom to learn and sympathize. This isolated feeling is present especially in those working in systems serving children birth to age 5, and in small organizations.

- Other barriers mentioned include
  - Staff turnover and the need to constantly retrain.
  - K-12 union contracts that limit flexibility of professional learning spending.
  - Availability of trainings, especially in rural and resource-constrained geographies, and for specialized training.
  - Competition for "clients" between school district-run prekindergarten and center-based prekindergarten, which can get in the way of shared professional learning.

Role of organizational leadership in professional learning

- In general, interviewees emphasized the importance of leadership in incentivizing staff to seek professional learning supports. Interviewees also emphasized leadership's role in encouraging and allowing staff to seek supports that are tailored to individual needs.

Profile of Professional Learning Supports for a Home Visitor

The degree of sophistication and amount of home visitors' professional learning varies widely depending on the employing organization and the home visitor's career track (e.g., social worker, nurse, high school graduate). The skills needed to be a home visitor are very diverse, ranging from developing relationships with parents to connecting families with other social services. Coaching and mentoring are seen as effective ways to improve practice, particularly independent problem-solving for clients. Paying for professional learning is very difficult for home visitors in agencies that are budget constrained.

What do professional learning supports look like for this role?

- Home visiting is a service delivery method, and the majority of training occurs in existing professional pathways (e.g., as a licensed clinical social worker or nurse) instead of being designed specifically for home visiting. In addition, home visitors possess a wide range of qualifications, from a high school diploma to master's degrees, and the amount and type of formal coursework received by home visitors depends on their level of education.
- The degree of availability and sophistication of ongoing professional learning depends on the employing organization. It can range from a well-functioning professional learning support system for its employees, to only basic training. While mentoring and coaching seems to be an acknowledged best practice, the degree to which they are offered varies depending on the employer.

What skills, knowledge, or other supports are most needed in this role?
- The skills needed to be a home visitor are very diverse, ranging from developing relationships with parents to connecting families with other social services.
- Coaching can be very helpful in order to train employees to problem solve independently. The lack of independent problem solving can increase attrition rates.

What motivations or incentives to access professional learning supports exist for this role?
- Home visitors are incentivized by their organizations' requirements for competence, and motivated by wanting to learn. For example, for home visitors who are held accountable for seeing a minimum number of families, there is motivation to improve her practice, or risk losing clients.

Are they aware of the professional learning supports available to them?
- Although there are listservs for trainings, one home visitor said that staying aware of training opportunities is very haphazard.

How are professional learning supports funded for this role?
- Paying for ongoing professional learning is increasingly difficult, according to one interviewee. However, some specialized trainings (e.g., how to serve populations with special needs, mental health issues) are available and paid for through programs.

Profile of Professional Learning Supports for a Licensed Family Childcare Educator

Family childcare educators face a fairly challenging professional learning environment, both in terms of the professional learning supports made available to them and their ability to access those supports. While the training and experience with formal coursework varies by individual, family childcare educators are generally required to have less formal coursework than other practitioners in the early care and education field. They are also not required to have any prior training or experience to open their own childcare business beyond the standards they need to meet to be licensed.

Among the menu of professional learning supports, family childcare educators are most consistently accessing licensure and credentialing, and to some extent, participating in state quality assurance programs or going through an accreditation process. The most common ongoing professional supports are in the form of trainings and workshops that are often made available through childcare resource and referral networks or state agen-

cies. Several gaps exist in their professional learning and have been identified as important to improving quality of practice: mentoring, coaching,
and opportunities for reflective practice and peer learning. Generally, family
childcare educators are not receiving any type of supervision and evaluation beyond participating in assessments through a state quality assurance
program or accreditation process.

What do professional learning supports look like for this role?

- Because family childcare educators are a heterogeneous group from
  varied professional backgrounds, experience with formal coursework varies tremendously both by state, depending on the licensing requirements, and individually, depending on an individual's
  previous career path or desire to pursue formal coursework once
  in the role. In general, when compared to other professional roles
  in the early childhood care and education field, family childcare
  educators have less experience with formal coursework as a result
  of the licensing requirements that in many cases have no formal
  coursework or degree requirements. However, beyond licensing requirements, many family childcare educators pursue formal coursework either as standalone credits or toward a degree, certificate, or
  credential. One interviewee had just completed her master's degree
  with 90 percent of her tuition funded from the state professional
  development system. However, she was quick to note that pursuing
  formal coursework while working as a family childcare educator
  with long days and the responsibilities of owning and operating
  your own business is not without challenges.
- Credentialing/Licensure: Credentialing and licensure are the most
  consistently available professional learning supports for family
  childcare educators/owners/operators. Every state has specific credentialing and licensure requirements, and the rules on who must
  obtain a license based on the number of children they care for and
  the training they need to have differ from state to state. Similar to
  center-based childcare educators, credentialing is considered the
  "next step" beyond licensing, with a common credential being the
  Child Development Associate (CDA) credential. The credentialing
  and licensure processes require specific standards to be met within
  the home setting along with trainings and workshops (often referred to as "clock hours") that in some states may be aligned with
  state quality assurance programs (e.g., QRIS).

  Beyond the training or "clock hour" requirements for licensing,
  there are safety and health guidelines that need to be met. In the
  state of Illinois, for example, the person who does the licensing of
  family childcare educators in their homes may be a potential pro-

fessional learning resource for family childcare educators beyond ensuring the standards are met.

- Professional Practice Quality Components Within Systems for Program Accreditation and Quality Assurance: Program accreditation and participation in quality assurance programs such as the state QRIS are generally available to family childcare educators/owners/operators. Beyond credentialing and licensure, accreditation and quality assurance programs are voluntary and each provide different mechanisms to improve a family childcare educator's quality of practice and the quality of the care setting. Training connected to QRIS or other state quality assurance systems may not be reaching home-based childcare educators. One interviewee noted that there was confusion around program quality assurance and accreditation programs among family childcare educators (presumably related to the different criteria required to participate). While the interviewee described the process of entering the quality rating system as a "little daunting," she described it as a "wonderful" experience that provided her a "framework on which to build." Another interviewee noted that motivation to pursue accreditation for family childcare educators who largely rely on private funds (as opposed to public funds or clients paying with public subsidies) may have a lot to do with the parents creating a market demand for family childcare educators to be accredited. One interviewee noted that while quality rating systems are helping to put some language around quality standards, there is still inconsistency across states. To the extent that quality assurance programs or quality rating systems rely on assessments for quality improvement, there are limited opportunities for childcare educators to reflect and engage in quality improvement processes beyond the act of being assessed.
- Ongoing Professional Support: Ongoing professional supports for family childcare educators largely exist in the form of trainings or workshops that are required to maintain their license or credential, or are required as part of an accreditation program or state quality assurance system. Major resources for trainings are local childcare resource and referral networks or state agencies (e.g., licensing or early learning agencies). Because family childcare educators are often owners of their own business, work long hours, and do not have someone to substitute for them, they face significant barriers in accessing trainings and workshops even when they are made available. Additionally, the content of trainings are often redundant and do not necessarily build on each other. For the most part, family childcare educators are the most isolated of their peers and thus do not have access to the "built in" professional supports

that come with working with other educators in a center-based setting. However, three interviewees mentioned that family childcare educators rely on ad hoc childcare educator networks in the form of informal family childcare associations or community-based networks where educators can go to get support, receive training hours, or reflect. Similar to their peers in center-based childcare settings, family childcare educators are generally missing the critical formal mentoring and coaching support that allows them to apply what they may have learned in formal coursework, trainings, or workshops to their own practice. Opportunities for reflective practice or reflective supervision are extremely limited for family childcare educators as they are often the only adults in their setting. Opportunities for mentoring and coaching are often informal and depend on the individual educator's professional peer network.

- Supervision/Evaluation: Supervision and evaluation were described as "nonexistent" for family childcare educators. There are no formal mechanisms for supervision and evaluation beyond the quality assessments that may occur if a family childcare educator participates in a quality assurance system or an accreditation program. One interviewee noted that because family childcare educators are usually small business owners, the reflection and supervision pieces are missing. As an alternative, some family childcare educators may seek the reflection component through informal networks, but they are unlikely to receive true supervision and evaluation that supports quality improvement.

What skills, knowledge, or other supports are most needed in this role?

- Family childcare educators more often than not are playing the role of practitioner, owner, and operator of their own small business. As such, they require a very broad and often complex set of skills. While some family childcare educators may specialize in a particular age group, many often care for children of different ages at the same time and thus require knowledge of child development across the age spectrum.
- Beyond needing to know the "basics" (health, safety, nutrition, and basic child development), family childcare educators often serve as connectors between families and other resources. Family childcare educators need to be able to engage families effectively, understand family dynamics, and understand the context of the community they work in. As owners of their own business, they also require general business management and administrative skills (e.g., budgeting, completing business documentation). Like many other professional roles in the early care and education field, and

perhaps even more so due to the individual and isolated nature of their work, family childcare educators can benefit from the ability to self-reflect and to maintain a "learning mindset" throughout their career.

How are professional learning supports funded for this role?

- Generally speaking, family childcare educators are able to leverage some amount of public funds, or they use their own funds to pay for professional learning supports. In most states, a combination of federal and local funds go to a state agency in which a portion of the funds are dedicated to quality improvement and may be used to support professional learning for family childcare educators. Often, federal and state funds come through childcare resource and referral networks who provide trainings and other resources to childcare educators for free or at a low cost. The amount of public funds available specifically for family childcare educators varies state to state. Key sources of federal funding include the Childcare Development Block grant and Race to the Top, which recently expanded to include early learning settings. Some states (e.g., Illinois) have a professional development system that allows family childcare educators to pursue formal coursework by paying all or a portion of their tuition. There are also grants and scholarships available to apply toward credentials or accreditation, though this varies by state.

What are the challenges or barriers to accessing professional learning supports for this role?

- Family childcare educators/owners/operators face significant barriers to accessing professional learning supports, mainly time and resource constraints and the isolated nature of their work. Family childcare educators work long hours usually by themselves, do not have access to substitutes who can care for children in their setting while they access professional learning, and are often paid very low wages. On top of that, family childcare educators are often owners of their own business, playing the dual function of administrator and practitioner, leaving little time and space for professional learning.

Profile of Professional Learning Supports for a Center-Based Childcare Educator

Availability of and access to professional learning supports for center-based childcare educators varies widely and depends on the individual center's funding streams, size, level of resources, and center leadership. Additionally, formal coursework and degree requirements vary largely by state. The major avenues that govern quality in center-based childcare settings and support professional learning for educators are credentialing/licensing and program accreditation (e.g., the NAEYC accreditation) and quality assurance systems (e.g., state QRIS). A critical gap in the professional learning supports available for center-based childcare educators is a focus on mentoring, coaching, and reflective supervision that helps educators to apply theory to practice, ultimately changing their behaviors. Another gap is support for educators for whom English is a second language.

What do professional learning supports look like for this role?

- Formal Coursework: Requirements for formal coursework vary by state and can range from less than an associate's degree, to a bachelor's degree in an unrelated field, to a master's degree (in one state). Many center-based childcare educators may pursue formal coursework toward a degree or a credential while working in childcare centers.

- Credentialing/Licensure: Credentialing and licensure were said by one respondent to be the "most consistently available supports" for center-based childcare educators. The employer would need a license to operate the center. Beyond that, individual educators might need or want to pursue a credential such as the CDA, though requirements to have a credential vary by state and within states depending on the individual center. Credentials come with their own competencies and requirements for training that often serve as ongoing professional supports (e.g., trainings, workshops) while the educator is working. In many states, credentialing and licensing requirements are aligned with the state quality assurance systems (e.g., a state QRIS) to ensure consistency in content and competencies.

- Professional Practice Quality Components Within Systems for Program Accreditation and Quality Assurance: Program quality assurance systems (e.g., a state QRIS) are one of the main avenues through which training and other ongoing professional learning supports are delivered to center-based childcare educators. As such, quality assurance systems like QRIS can be an important lever for improving the quality of practice for center-based childcare educators. However, it is important to note that training connected to QRIS or other state quality assurance systems may not be reaching all centers, especially smaller, lower-resourced centers.

- Ongoing Professional Support: Trainings and workshops seem to be the most commonly available ongoing professional learning supports for center-based childcare educators and are often required to maintain center licensing, accreditation, or certain rankings within a program quality assurance system. Center-based childcare educators have more access to trainings and workshops compared to their home-based/family childcare educators who cannot rely on their employer to provide access to or funding for trainings that may require time away from their classroom. In addition to what is provided via center employers, childcare resource and referral networks are central access points for ongoing professional learning, though availability of quality resources seems to vary. While trainings and workshops may be common, one interviewee identified mentoring, coaching, and reflective supervision for center-based childcare educators as gaps to fill in order to help them translate theory into practice. Another interviewee confirmed the variance across centers, noting that mentoring support may be happening in some centers but not others.

- Supervision and Evaluation: There are more opportunities for supervision and evaluation for center-based childcare educators compared to their counterparts in family or home-based settings.

What skills, knowledge, or other supports are most needed in this role?

- Interviewees emphasized the importance of moving beyond the "basics of health, safety, and basic child development," to having skills around developing relationships with children and the ability to "integrate knowledge on brain development into ongoing curricula that is responsive to children." Similar to the knowledge and skills needed for family childcare educators, center-based educators need to know how to navigate parent and family relationships, how to effectively navigate group care, and understand the context of the community they are working in. While conducting training for childcare educators on screenings and autism, one interviewee noted that there was much more knowledge needed around child development and communicating effectively with parents.
- Beyond content knowledge, center-based childcare educators also need content to be delivered in a way that allows them to learn skills to apply theory to their day-to-day practice.

How are professional learning supports funded for this role?

- Similar to center-based prekindergarten educators, center-based childcare educators in centers that are participating in state quality assurance programs (e.g., QRIS) can often access low-cost or free trainings that are required as training hours. However, the quality of these trainings may be inconsistent. Professional learning budgets for center-based childcare educators are determined by leadership and can vary center by center. One respondent who works in an administrative role in a school district mentioned that childcare centers generally do not have major resources to devote to professional learning, thus there is a need for them to be creative when trying to maintain the training hours required by quality assurance and accreditation programs.

What are the challenges or barriers to accessing professional learning supports for this role?

- Center-based childcare educators face barriers to accessing professional learning supports such as lack of funding, lack of time, trainings not at a convenient location. One interviewee also mentioned a childcare educator's low sense of self-worth when it comes to their profession. If similar perceptions of childcare educators exist in the field, this may result in underutilizing the skills and values that childcare educators can bring to a team of adults (e.g., parents, physicians) who are working to support a child's development.

Profile of Professional Learning Supports for a Center-Based Prekindergarten Educator

The professional learning environment for center-based prekindergarten educators is largely dependent on the center's funding streams and the center's leadership, resulting in wide ranging requirements and opportunities for professional learning. Similar to center-based childcare educators, formal coursework requirements for center-based prekindergarten educators and credentialing/licensing requirements at the center level vary both by state and within states depending on the type of organization (e.g., Head Start center, state prekindergarten, private prekindergarten) or whether the center is accredited or participates in a state quality assurance system. Additionally, access to ongoing professional supports such as training, mentoring, or coaching vary tremendously from center to center.

What do professional learning supports look like for this role?

- Formal Coursework: Similar to center-based childcare educators, requirements for formal coursework vary by state and can range from a high school diploma or GED (General Educational Development) certification, to a small number of college credits, to a college degree. Requirements for formal coursework vary from state to state and within states vary depending on the type of prekindergarten program (e.g., Head Start center, state prekindergarten, private prekindergarten) and whether that program is accredited. There are also a number of different roles in prekindergarten centers that are referred to as "teacher" (teacher aid, teacher assistant, lead teacher), so experience with formal coursework may also vary significantly within individual centers. Center-based prekindergarten educators may also be pursuing formal coursework in the community colleges or universities toward a degree, credential, or certification while working. However, one interviewee noted that formal coursework specific to center-based prekindergarten educators at community colleges are fairly limited.

- Credentialing/Licensure: Similar to center-based childcare centers, a prekindergarten center needs to be licensed in the state it is operating in, which generally comes with some requirements for ongoing professional learning among prekindergarten educators. There is no consistent requirement for a credential or individual license across states for center-based prekindergarten educators. That said, minimum educational standards are increasing; for example, Head Start has a goal of having 50 percent of their educators possessing bachelor's degrees.

- Professional Practice Quality Components Within Systems for Program Accreditation and Quality Assurance: Beyond licensing requirements for prekindergarten centers, centers can voluntarily undergo an accreditation process (e.g., the NAEYC accreditation) or may participate in a state quality assurance system (e.g., the Pennsylvania Stars program). Both processes may hold both formal degree requirements and requirements for ongoing professional learning among center-based prekindergarten educators and may open up opportunities for supports like mentoring, evaluation, or peer-learning opportunities.

  Two interviewees noted that the accreditation process is a big step that requires time and resources that may deter some centers from starting the process. However, an additional motivation for prekindergarten centers and their educators to pursue accreditation or participate in a quality assurance program may be the market demand from parents and families who are discerning about a center's quality and the access to professional learning for educators.

- Ongoing Professional Support: Ongoing professional supports beyond "single-shot" trainings and workshops that may be required through licensing standards, quality assurance systems, or accreditation programs are generally limited and highly dependent on the type of organization and the discretion of the center's leadership. For national programs like Head Start, workshops and trainings and professional learning resources are provided through the national office and thus have more consistency across centers in terms of content when compared to ongoing professional supports provided to or accessed by other center-based prekindergarten educators. However, they may not necessarily provide the content sought by the educators. For example, one Head Start educator was disappointed with the content available through Head Start and state trainings and turned to her own self-directed learning largely through free courses offered by universities online or by reading up on relevant articles.

- Mentorship, coaching, reflective supervision, and peer learning for center-based prekindergarten educators seem to be missing but needed. One Head Start educator noted that she has never had a coach in her classroom and that she was looking forward to a new "teacher-mentor" program about to be implemented in her center.

What skills, knowledge, or other supports are most needed in this role?

- Center-based prekindergarten educators need a wide-ranging set of knowledge and skills that go beyond child development content, though child development content remains foundational to their practice. Critical skills and qualities for a center-based prekindergarten educator include having "appropriate dispositions, interpersonal and inter-professional competencies," and the ability to communicate and advocate on behalf of early childhood development to a variety of audiences, including center directors, parents and families, or even a reporter. There is a need for educators to understand child development at a level that would enable them to serve as advocates for early childhood development within their organizations and their communities.
- Additionally, a critical skill for center-based prekindergarten educators, and educators in all settings, is the ability to apply what was learned in formal coursework or in trainings to real-world classroom settings. This necessary skill highlights the importance of integrating field experiences throughout formal education or certification programs.

How are professional learning supports funded for this role?

- Funding of professional learning supports for center-based prekindergarten educators depends on the type of organization they are working in. In general, funding may be more variable by center and more inconsistent over time when compared to their school-based counterparts whose funding largely comes through the school district. Center-based prekindergarten educators generally rely on funding provided by their center's budget for professional learning or may end up paying for their own professional learning depending on the center's level of resources. State quality assurance programs often offer free or subsidized professional learning opportunities in addition to free online materials, though the quality of these supports vary.

What are the challenges or barriers to accessing professional learning supports for this role?

- Lack of funding provided by the employer for professional learning supports is a major barrier to professional learning for center-based prekindergarten educators. Budgets for professional learning can be slim and may vary year to year which can make planning to meet certain requirements difficult for low-wage childcare educators who may have to pay their own way.
- A Head Start educator described another barrier within her organization as unnecessary siloes between the different roles within her organization (i.e., assistant teacher, teacher, center manager, education specialist). These siloes prevented her from accessing information or learning skills beyond the scope of her individual role.
- The Head Start educator also felt that avenues for professional learning beyond what was mandated and offered through Head Start were not made available to her, resulting in gaps in her professional learning.
- A lack of support to navigate one's career (from ongoing professional learning to higher education) hinders professional development.

Profile of Professional Learning Supports for an Elementary School Educator[2]

Elementary school educators are, in general, ill prepared in the area of child development through the available formal coursework and licensure requirements. Certification requirements vary from state to state, and even when requirements include early learning years (i.e., birth to age 5), the content focuses more on the older years. In addition, ongoing professional learning generally focuses on core subjects like math and reading, instead of broader child development topics.

---

[2] The profile for this role encompasses school-based prekindergarten educators through grade 3.

What do professional learning supports look like for this role?
- Formal Coursework: Coursework on developmentally appropriate teaching is severely lacking.
- Credentialing/Licensure: The ages for which educators become credentialed varies from state to state. Despite being a high leverage point, credentials generally do not lead to knowledge of child development.
- Ongoing Professional Support: For elementary school educators, ongoing professional support is often determined by teachable subjects (such as math and reading), and not broader child development issues. One interviewee mentioned that the majority of her ongoing learning is self-directed, and comes from articles and online resources. Supervision from principals was noted as important by interviewees; supervision and evaluation in early elementary settings is a complex subject and has been well documented.

What skills, knowledge, or other supports are most needed in this role?
- Early childhood practices, such as individualization of instruction and active learning, are important. But, educators are currently not prepared to gain these skills.
- In addition, being able to know what other resources are available for children and families is important, as educators are often an important point of contact to those systems.

Are they aware of the professional learning supports available to them?
- While educators are aware of basic certifications, they are less aware of alternative certifications.

What motivations or incentives to access professional learning supports exist for this role?
- Incentives in K-12 settings are gaining adequate tests scores at the end of third grade. However, one interviewee notes that there are some unintended consequences of the focus on test scores.

What are the challenges or barriers to accessing professional learning supports for this role?
- One interviewee noted that even in large teacher's colleges, courses focused on child development are not widely available. In addition, school districts may be overly allocating funds to workshops, at the expense of mentoring and coaching.

Profile of Professional Learning Supports for an Early Care and Education Center Director

Experiences with formal preparation prior to entering the role and access to professional learning supports once in the role vary widely for center directors and are not necessarily focused on meeting their specific needs as a director, e.g., effective supervision of staff and the ability to create a quality learning environment for their staff to improve their practice. Given the importance of their role as one who directs and determines what professional learning supports are available and accessed by their staff, improving the systems of professional learning supports for center directors may be a key leverage point for improving the overall quality of practice for practitioners working in early care and education centers.

What do professional learning supports look like for this role?

- Credentialing/Licensure: Credentialing and licensure requirements for center directors vary by state. In some states it is left to the individual to pursue additional formal coursework or credentialing credits in states when a director's credential is encouraged but not required. As a result, some center directors may have more formal preparation either through formal coursework or by completing a credential, while others transition into the director role from another early care and education role (e.g., a childcare or prekindergarten educator) without direct experience in or preparation for a director's role.
- Professional Practice Quality Components Within Systems for Program Accreditation and Quality Assurance: Program quality assurance systems (e.g., a state QRIS) were viewed by an interviewee as an essential component to ensure quality for the early care and education system as a whole, and also as an "extra support" for improving the quality of a center director's own practice.
- Ongoing Professional Support: Generally, access to ongoing professional supports for center directors seems ad hoc and depends on the state or locale within a state. While mentoring and coaching seem to be happening in some places, generally speaking there is a gap in this kind of support. Some states may host leadership institutes and directors may also form their own support groups to coach each other. Some directors, depending on the type of center they are in, may belong to a national organization such as the National Coalition of Campus Children Centers through which they might receive coaching and other ongoing professional supports.

What skills, knowledge, or other supports are most needed in this role?

- Center directors require a very broad skill set and are often required to wear many hats depending on the size and resources of their particular center. Most importantly, a large part of their job is the supervision of staff and being responsible for their staff's own professional learning which one interviewee noted as an area where directors need a lot of support.

How are professional learning supports funded for this role?

- Center directors are responsible for budgeting funds for professional learning among staff which also includes budgeting funds for themselves. While it varies from state to state, in some cases there may be funds available (federal or state) through program quality assurance systems (e.g., QRISs). Generally, there is a broad range of how center directors might allocate funds for their staff or pay for their own professional learning supports.

What are the challenges or barriers to accessing professional learning supports for this role?

- Many center directors, especially those new to the role, may lack a formal system of professional learning supports that are focused on their specific needs as directors. For example, one interviewee stated that the National Association for the Education of Young Children does not "have a lot for directors." Furthermore, a director's role can be lonely and isolating, especially in rural locations that lack the systems to connect directors to professional learning resources. While technology may play an important role in improving access to professional learning supports for director's who cannot get away from their center or who are in more isolated areas, the quality of those supports varies.

Profile of Professional Learning Supports for an Elementary School Principal

Elementary school principals have an opportunity to connect the prekindergarten and elementary school systems. A principal's job is multifaceted, and requires instructional and operational leadership capabilities. The specific role of being a "hub" between early childhood systems is a particularly important one that principals can play, but requires that principals learn competencies that they currently do not have en masse, and that they receive support and are incentivized by district leadership to make connections with prekindergarten leaders.

What skills, knowledge, or other supports are most needed in this role?
- The National Association for Elementary School Principals (NAESP) identifies six competencies for effective principal practice:
  - Embrace the prekindergarten to third grade early learning continuum.
  - Ensure developmentally appropriate teaching.
  - Provide personalized, blended learning environments.
  - Use multiple measures to guide student growth.
  - Build professional capacity across the learning community.
  - Make schools the hub of prekindergarten to third grade learning for families and communities.
- Of these competencies, the first and the last explicitly encourage principals to make connections with the "feeder system" for elementary schools. Elementary school principals are well positioned to be an important linkage between these systems. Principals need the skills to bridge the systems. Principals need to understand developmentally appropriate practice and connect with other organizational leaders in the prekindergarten space. For example, principals need competencies to interact with leadership of prekindergarten childcare agencies and also with other sectors, such as health. It is worth noting that NAESP does not currently recommend that principals connect with the birth to age 3 system, largely because principals have difficulty conceiving what coordinated activities would look like, given the distance between the two age groups.
- Principals do not receive enough early childhood training. While elementary school principals receive generalized training, what they need is specialized training for leading elementary schools. However, principals' priorities, as dictated by district leadership and incentives, often do not encourage learning developmentally appropriate practice. Therefore, district leadership has a role to play in providing the space for such training.

What motivations or incentives to access professional learning supports exist for this role?
- District leadership needs to incentivize and provide the space for principals to bring together the elementary and prekindergarten systems.

Reenvisioning Professional Learning Supports: What Could Be?

Following a discussion of the current state of professional learning supports for various roles within the birth through 8 workforce, interviewees were asked a series of questions about what could make for ideal professional learning supports in terms of availability, accessibility and the financing of those supports, or in other words, "What could be?" Interviewees were also asked to reenvision the professional learning support system either for specific professional roles or for the birth through age 8 workforce as a whole, with specific attention paid to key leverage points that could be used to create a more ideal professional learning support system.

The following are themes on "what could be" for professional learning supports among the birth through age 8 workforce.

What are the opportunities for intersection of professional learning across the birth through age 8 workforce?

- Across the board, interviewees recognized the importance of shared, interdisciplinary professional learning experiences across the birth through age 8 workforce. Joint professional learning among a variety of roles were mentioned by several interviewees as important opportunities to improve quality practice for front-line roles up to leadership. For example, joint professional learning might take place between
  - Family childcare educators and center-based childcare educators.
  - Public prekindergarten educators and Head Start educators.
  - Prekindergarten educators and K-3 educators.
  - Family childcare educators and K-3 educators.
  - Early care and education center directors and elementary school principals.
  - Center directors and mental health professionals.
- These opportunities for shared learning could come in a variety of formats and serve different purposes. The opportunities would ideally recognize and accommodate the issues of hierarchy among different professional roles by recognizing that all practitioners have something to teach and learn from one another. For example, practitioners who work with the same age group of children (e.g., public prekindergarten educators and Head Start educators) might attend a shared training on brain development or join a peer learning collaborative where they share resources and do group problem solving. This type of joint learning and collaboration could be thought of as "horizontal integration."
- Opportunities for practitioners who work at different points along the birth through age 8 continuum (e.g., prekindergarten educators and kindergarten educators) to learn together can be termed "vertical integration." Vertical integration could occur through joint transition planning for students, or observation of colleagues. For example, one interviewee spoke of the importance of "pushing up" early childhood professional development to the early grades.

- One interviewee noted that the vertical integration is much harder than horizontal integration of professional learning.
- Cross-disciplinary learning among leadership roles and among staff was also mentioned as an important opportunity.
- It is important to note that leadership (e.g., center directors, elementary school principals) is critical to enabling shared learning opportunities among their employees. Leaders may have to get creative with funding mechanisms or with their traditional professional learning offerings.
- One interviewee described district plans to repurpose some Title 1 funds (meant to establish transition plans for students coming into kindergarten) into joint trainings with district educators and Head Start agencies, including Head Start parent councils and staff. This intersection of professional learning provides benefits for both parties. Districts might also provide coursework or other professional learning for their elementary school educators that support their licensure or credentialing in early care and education as a way to achieve some of the benefits of cross-disciplinary learning.

How might the availability, accessibility, and financing of professional learning supports be improved to better meet the needs of the birth through 8 workforce?

Interviewees often spoke of availability, access, and financing as different sides of the same coin, all being key leverage points that need to be addressed in concert to produce the desired results.

- Improving the Availability of Professional Learning Supports: While the availability of specific professional learning supports (e.g., coursework or trainings or mentoring) varies tremendously, there are some common themes in terms of the content and skills covered that would ideally be available to the birth through age 8 workforce.
  - One key improvement would be to make the available professional learning supports as flexible and as responsive as possible to the needs of the practitioner. Professional learning needs not only vary by locale (e.g., from neighborhood to neighborhood), but they vary significantly within the birth through age 8 workforce depending on the background of the individual and the setting they work in. For example, an ideal professional learning support system "does not assume that [the world of] childcare educators is a homogenous world."
  - Interviewees also mentioned content, skills, or opportunities that would ideally be made more available:

- A foundational knowledge of child development that spans ages birth through 8, regardless of the practitioner's role.
- National standards for licensing/credentialing/certifications to promote a consistent level of quality across states.
- Training on how to work collaboratively and effectively in team settings.
- Mental health consultation services and support for behavioral issues.
- Opportunities that help people to make connections with others who serve children birth through age 8 and to navigate community resources through locally based collaboratives.
- Ongoing learning supports like mentoring and coaching across the birth through age 8 workforce.
- Career advising and counseling that walks care and education professionals through different career options.

  – Another improvement would be a centralized clearinghouse of evidence-based practices, covering both content and process (e.g., how to do reflective supervision). The clearinghouse would also list professional learning opportunities available to all practitioners working across the birth through age 8 continuum (e.g., a childcare educator can go to one place and see a training that is being provided by a home visiting agency).

- Improving the Accessibility of Professional Learning Supports: Even when professional learning supports are made available, there are often many barriers to accessing those supports. Accessibility is determined by a number of different factors: where, when, and how professional learning is delivered; cost; the incentives tied to accessing the support; and awareness. The more learning supports are designed to address the common barriers (time, cost, location) faced by practitioners, the more accessible professional learning becomes. Interviewees offered several ideas for improving the accessibility of professional learning supports for the birth through age 8 workforce.

  – Deliver professional learning supports in a variety of formats and in different settings to address the needs of an extremely diverse workforce. Different formats might include in-person learning, online learning, or blended learning. One interviewee suggested that community colleges are particularly well suited to serve as a "hub for professional learning" both for formal coursework and other professional learning supports.

  – A significant barrier for practitioners that work outside of the school district system is not having the infrastructure to support time away from their classrooms for professional learning. Family and center-based childcare and prekindergarten educators have difficulty accessing professional learning supports when there are no substitutes made available to care for their children while they are out. The idea of "substitute pools" was suggested by a few interviewees as a promising way to improve access to professional learning for this group of practitioners.

– Adjust the adult working environment to allow space for more ongoing practice supports like mentoring, coaching, and reflective practice to take place in a meaningful way.

• Improving the Financing of Professional Learning Supports: Many interviewees identified funding as a key lever for improving access to professional learning supports. In an ideal world, professional learning would be funded by the organizations/programs/agencies practitioners work in. While funding for professional learning supports seems to be slightly better for practitioners working in early elementary settings compared to those in early care and education settings, both face funding challenges. Many practitioners, especially family childcare educators and smaller, center-based childcare and prekindergarten educators, are paying out of pocket for professional learning supports beyond any state-subsidized learning opportunities. Government and private funders have an important opportunity to support professional learning by providing much needed funding for supports identified as critical to improving practice among birth through age 8 practitioners.

– Grants, scholarships, and tuition and loan forgiveness programs are key to making formal coursework in a higher education setting more accessible to larger portions of the birth through age 8 workforce. Ideally, employers or outside funders would also make funding available to practitioners to pursue additional coursework beyond their existing degree or coursework as a way to continue learning and stay updated on new developments in the field.

– Beyond the funding needed to support a practitioner's pursuit of higher education, one interviewee called for more funding to be allocated to "on-site practice supports" like mentoring and coaching on the implementation of specific practices. While a lot of funding goes toward trainings and workshops, not enough resources are devoted to learning how to apply what was learned in those trainings to a real world context. Tying monetary incentives or other types of awards or recognition to professional learning opportunities like the National Board Certification process for elementary educators might also improve the uptake of existing supports.

- In order to address the quality of practice in a comprehensive way, funding must be allocated to policies and practices that produce supportive learning environments and compensation that provides for the economic well-being of practitioners. Transforming the adult learning environment and adult well-being in the care and education workforce is critical to seeing the kinds of improvements professional learning supports are meant to produce.

How else might it look to reenvision professional learning for the birth through age 8 workforce?

- There is an opportunity to think beyond improving the learning for the paid birth through age 8 workforce so that everyone gets critical information about child development regardless of their profession. Interviewees want to get information into the hands of the families and communities who are raising children and to build their knowledge and skills around the science of child development. One Head Start educator described engaging in learning alongside the family as akin to "treating the source of the problem, not just the symptoms." Another interviewee discussed ways to incentivize learning opportunities for family, friend, and neighbor caregivers and family childcare educators who tend to have less access to professional learning supports such as conducting community learning events while providing food, free toys, and free childcare during the event.

- Create a system that incentivizes the professional learning processes that are known to make a difference in the quality of practice. One interviewee noted that while our evidence for whether certifications or having a bachelor's degree result in stronger child gains and stronger practice is mixed, the strongest body of evidence is around the ongoing professional learning "processes" such as mentoring and coaching. As such, systems should be designed to incentivize or give "credit" to the processes that achieve stronger practice.

Appendix D

Historical Timeline:
Preparation for the Care and Education Workforce in the United States

	Nursery School	Childcare	Kindergarten	Elementary School
Early 1800s			Kindergarten, developed in the early 1800s by Friedrich Froebel, was grounded in the belief that children learned best through supervised play. The design of training for kindergarten teachers occurred in tandem with the development of kindergarten. Froebel's ideas and methods quickly spread throughout Europe and to the United States. In the United States, kindergarten teacher training involved visiting Germany to observe kindergartens and to participate in in-service workshops conducted by Froebel. Magazines and literary periodicals also informed professional practice.	The first formal teacher training was conducted in academies beginning in the 1800s, the 2-year equivalent of today's secondary schools. Teachers had previously been predominately male, but by the 1820s, men were leaving lower school teaching for higher paying professions. It then became more common for women to become teachers in the early grades. The first private "normal school," developed as a 2-year institute for training elementary school teachers, was opened in 1823 by Samuel R. Hall. In 1834, Pennsylvania became the first state to require prospective teachers to pass an exam focusing on reading, writing, and math. The first state-funded normal school was founded in 1839 by Cyrus Pierce in Massachusetts, with the help of Horace Mann.

continued

| Mid- to late 1800s | Settlement Houses, which provided social services to immigrant, poor, and working class people, were founded in the late 1800s and early 1900s. Services included childcare, youth activities, and family support.

Day nurseries protected children from harm and helped assimilate immigrant children into American culture. Child "minders" were from local communities and had not received formal education. No education requirements existed for caregivers in day nurseries. | German-trained kindergarten teacher educators migrated to the United States to provide 26-week formal training programs.

By the 1880s, 2-year kindergarten training programs included courses in child study, psychology, child hygiene, sociology, children's literature and storytelling, public speaking, philosophy of education, school management, and kindergarten principles and practices, among others, as well as the study of Froebel's theories. Practical experiences with children were central to all aspects of the training.

As kindergartens became more prevalent in the public schools, kindergarten training was added to many normal school programs, often in a department of its own. | Licensure exams permitted teachers to teach in particular schools. The exams required showing high moral character and general knowledge.

There was rapid growth in the number of normal schools (2-year programs) with an emphasis on training elementary school teachers.

Preparation for secondary-school teaching, which was treated as requiring a larger academic component than necessary for elementary education, was left to 4-year liberal arts colleges.

By 1867, most states required teachers to pass a locally developed test to get a state certificate that expanded upon the basic skills, to include U.S. history, geography, spelling, and grammar. |

Nursery School	Childcare	Kindergarten	Elementary School
		The International Kindergarten Union (IKU) was founded in 1892 to promote appropriate classroom curricula and kindergarten teacher preparation.	Alternative teaching programs included "county normals" and summer teaching institutes. These programs supplemented normal schools and offered free training opportunities to aspiring teachers who could not afford normal school.
			Universities began adding chairs in pedagogy to the liberal arts faculty. Chairs of pedagogy could grant state teaching certificates.
			In 1890, the National Education Association (NEA) issued a *Statement of Policy for the Normal Schools*, calling them to be the main agents for teacher certification.

By the 1890s, more than 100 normal schools were in operation. These schools expanded their curricula beyond elementary to include secondary education as well. Demand for teachers was high and "mass production" was needed.

Credentials from normal schools were considered professional licenses by state governments. By 1897, 28 states accepted normal diplomas as licenses.

In 1896 John Dewey founded the University of Chicago Laboratory School, the first school for experimenting and researching new methods in a university setting.

continued

	Nursery School	Childcare	Kindergarten	Elementary School
1900s-1920s	In 1911, Margaret and Rachel McMillan opened the Open-Air Nursery School and Training Centre in London, in an effort to prevent the physical and mental health problems they observed in poor communities. This program provided children with nutritious food, regular health inspections, planned activities, and support from attentive teachers.		A third-year course was added to the curricula of several "kindergarten" normal school programs to allow kindergarten teachers to teach at the primary level, too. By 1913, 147 institutions of higher education offered kindergarten teacher preparation courses. As normal school kindergarten teacher training increased, the 2-year courses of study offered by freestanding kindergarten-training schools declined. This period saw an increased focus on kindergarten theory and practice, through coursework, publications, and the development of professional organizations for kindergarten teachers and teacher educators.	Longer training and specializations were recommended in the 1900s, resulting in the reorganization of normal schools into 4-year teaching programs.

| 1920s-1930s | The nursery school movement migrated from England to the United States in the 1920s. By 1924 there were 28 nurseries in 11 states. The first American nursery school teachers traveled to England to study and work under Margaret McMillan. | New York City public schools offered free professional training and preparation for the teacher's license examination in teacher training schools, leading the way to obtaining trained kindergarten teachers.

Wheelock College, founded in 1889, was devoted solely to kindergarten education in its early years. In 1925, Wheelock instituted a 3-year teacher preparation program that became a model for other schools across the country. The third year focused on the skills and knowledge to qualify students for kindergarten director positions.

By the 1930s kindergarten teacher training had spread around the United States. | By 1921, all states accepted graduation from a normal school or a university as qualification for certification. However, 30 states still had no prior schooling requirement for initial certification.

By 1930, 31 states required a high school diploma and some professional training.

Between 1920 and 1940, normal schools became state teachers colleges. As a result, teacher education at these state colleges became more marginalized. |

continued

	Nursery School	Childcare	Kindergarten	Elementary School
1930s–1940s	The nursery school movement in the United States was associated with the public's scientific interest in child development and learning. By the mid-1930s, there were approximately 200 nursery schools in the United States, and more than half were affiliated with colleges and universities. Leaders of the nursery school movement advocated 4 years of college as the appropriate background for nursery school teachers so that they could interact effectively with specialists in the fields of nutrition, psychology, psychiatry, and pediatrics. Nursery school teacher education programs often required pedagogical trainings as well as a knowledge base that encompassed chemistry, biology, case study methods, educational measurements, and record keeping.	In the 1930s, Works Progress Administration (WPA) programs, which included early care and education programs for low-income children, were founded in response to unemployment during the Great Depression. Programs were federally funded and designed to reemploy teachers, nurses, and janitors who had worked in rural elementary schools that had closed due to a lack of local funding. Most of these teachers held certificates from academies and normal schools based on their previous employment.	Through the 1930s admission to kindergarten teacher training required candidates to be of "good character," good health, to be generally "refined," and able to demonstrate musical ability. Native ability and a love of children were other essential criteria for admission. Demonstration of these criteria was determined via essays, interviews, and observations of adult–child interactions.	

continued

Women applied to nursery education programs with the backgrounds in kindergarten and primary teaching, liberal arts, and home economics, among other areas. Criteria for entry to nursery school education programs included "a definite interest in young children," good health, adequate fundamental preparation, superior scholarship, good native ability, and fine character.

	Nursery School	Childcare	Kindergarten	Elementary School
1940s-1950s	The U.S. Office of Education's 1943 pamphlet titled *Nursery Schools Vital to the War Effort* indicated that skilled teachers with specialized training in nursery school education were essential to the war effort. After the war, nursery school teacher education included an emphasis on democratic principles and teaching techniques. Programs also encompassed a variety of fields concerned with human development and social progress, individualized instruction, child guidance, multiple theories of child development, expressive activities, and student teaching in community schools.	The Lanham Act, passed in 1940, authorized federal grants to public or private agencies to operate childcare facilities for working mothers in war-affected areas. No regulations, such as teacher preparation requirements, accompanied the federal funds. Following the war, this funding ceased and most centers closed. Child Service Centers, illustrated by the Kaiser Centers in California, provided full-day childcare programs during World War II. Education requirements for center directors and teachers included a master's degree and bachelor's degree, respectively, as well as specialized training in early childhood education for assistant teachers. Centers also employed nutritionists, pediatricians, registered nurses, and social workers. Employees were recruited from colleges and universities. These programs were closed following the war.		A movement toward establishing professional standards began, laying the groundwork for the formation in 1952 of the National Council for Accreditation of Teacher Education (NCATE). In 1948, the American Association of Colleges for Teacher Education (AACTE) was formed. By 1953, 23 states required a 4-year degree for elementary teachers; 40 states required a 4-year degree for high school teachers.

The Forty-Sixth NSSE Yearbook decried the lack of training and curricula available in normal schools and state colleges for adults caring for young children.

1960s-1980s	Nursery school education continued to be the purview of private colleges and home-economics departments at state colleges and universities. Few state teacher's colleges or normal schools addressed the early years as part of their mission. Nursery school teacher training institutions experimented with varying models of teacher preparation based on differing philosophies. Nursery schools in the community were largely replaced with full-day childcare or Head Start programs. Many nursery schools began to call themselves preschools, or early education programs.	The Office of Economic Opportunity's Community Action Program initiated Project Head Start as an 8-week summer program to promote healthy development and learning for low-income children between the ages of 3 and 5 years. At its inception, Head Start was often staffed by teachers off for the summer; however formal training in early education was not required for employment.	The Child Development Associate (CDA) National Credentialing Program was implemented, and was conceived as applicable to the entire early childhood field, although Head Start was the prime audience for the program in its early days.	Kindergarten training came under the umbrella of state certification. By 1988, 32 states had some type of certification for the preparation of kindergarten teachers, often consisting of an additional endorsement to an elementary education certificate. Criteria for kindergarten teacher candidates began to mirror that of the elementary grades, including a minimum grade point average, certain prerequisite general education courses, and sometimes a preliminary practicum during which behavioral suitability of teacher candidates was assessed.	Teacher education became more fully integrated into the university setting under the leadership of professors in a school or college of education. This evolution was due in part to the need for local, affordable, and accessible forms of higher education. National Commission on Teacher Education and Professional Standards suggested 5th year training and alternative routes. Teacher Corps was founded (from the Higher Education Act of 1965) in which higher education and districts partner for training teachers for high poverty schools.

continued

	Nursery School	Kindergarten	Childcare	Elementary School
1960s-1980s			The first CDA was awarded in 1975. It was administered by the CDA Consortium until 1979, then Bank Street College until 1985. In 1985 the National Association for the Education of Young Children (NAEYC) created a nonprofit organization, the Council for Professional Recognition, to administer the CDA Credential. A Position Paper titled *Guidelines for Early Childhood Education Programs in Associate Degree Granting Institutions* was published by the NAEYC in 1985. This document has been updated three times and currently consists of six professional standards.	Practical experience in schools became a more predictable and integrated part of the teacher education curriculum, especially at the elementary education level. *A Nation at Risk* criticized teacher education for an emphasis on methods over subject matter. The Carnegie Task Force on Teaching as a Profession published *A Nation Prepared: Teachers for the 21st Century*. Holmes Groups published *Tomorrow's Teachers*. Both call for the elimination of undergraduate teacher certification and for researched-based teaching practice. Holmes Group proposed the "professional development school" and a National Board for Professional Teaching Standards. Teach For America was founded in 1989.

	Childcare, Preschools, and Early Education Programs	Kindergarten	Elementary School
1990s-2000s	By the 1990s a variety of nonbaccalaureate teacher education programs were available, including the CDA credential, associate degrees, vocational programs, and continuing education programs. In 1997, the NAEYC published new guidelines to establish standards for associate degrees in early childhood education. States developed requirements for early childhood teacher preparation for children ages 3-5; these vary significantly from state to state. Project T.E.A.C.H. (Teacher Education and Compensation Helps), a scholarship program that assists childcare and early learning practitioners to pursue professional development and higher education options, was initiated through the U.S. Department of Education. In 1997, 34 percent of Head Start teachers held an associate's degree in early childhood education.		Holmes Groups published *Tomorrow's Schools*, formalizing principles for professional development schools. All but one state established detailed content standards in core subject areas. These content standards were reflected in the teacher preparation requirements and certification standards within those states.

continued

	Childcare, Preschools, and Early Education Programs	Kindergarten	Elementary School
2000s-2010s	In 2001, the NAEYC approved standards for early childhood professional preparation initial licensure programs. In 2002, the NAEYC approved standards for early childhood professional preparation advanced degree programs, and also established the Commission on Early Childhood Associate Degree Accreditation. In 2003, the NAEYC approved standards for early childhood professional preparation associate degree programs. Congress mandated that 50 percent of Head Start teachers hold B.A. or A.A. degrees by 2003. The NAEYC adopted a position statement titled *NAEYC Standards for Early Childhood Professional Preparation* in 2009.		The Western Governors University (WGU), a nonprofit online institution created by governors of nine states in 1998, opens a teachers college that grants teaching degrees based on demonstrated competencies, rather than a final exam, and received NCATE approval in 2006 (http://www.wgu.edu/about_WGU/ncate_accreditation_11-1-06, accessed March 24, 2015).
Today	Teacher education continues to be addressed in some universities and colleges. The Commission on Early Childhood Associate Degree Accreditation (ECADA) currently accredits more than 150 institutions in 31 states.	Kindergarten teachers are required to hold a 4-year teaching degree in elementary education or early childhood education. Teacher candidates are required to take courses related to child development, curriculum planning, and assessment, as well as gain practical experience in the classroom.	The Common Core State Standards addresses standards in English language arts and math for K-12, prompting many teacher education programs to align their curricula with these standards.

Requirements for teachers are covered by state licensing/regulations for childcare centers rather than state mandated licenses for teachers. In many states, requirements are governed by Departments of Social Services, not Departments of Education, for nursery school teachers.

More than 300,000 individuals have earned the CDA.

Federal regulations call for half of Head Start lead teachers nationwide to have bachelor's degrees by fall 2013.

Individuals who have earned a bachelor's degree in a field other than education may pursue alternative certification routes.

State licenes are required for all teachers in public schools, though reqruiements vary by state.

Each state has its own requirements for teacher certification. There is no single early childhood, elementary or special education certification that transfers to all states.

REFERENCES

Almy, M., and A. Snyder. 1947. The staff and its preparation. In *The forty-sixth yearbook of the National Society for the Study of Education, Part II: Early childhood education*, edited by N. B. Henry. Chicago, IL: University of Chicago Press. Pp. 224-242.

Barnett, W. S. 2004. *Better teachers, better preschools: Student achievement linked to teacher qualifications*. Preschool Policy Matters, Issue 2. New Brunswick, NJ: National Institute for Early Education Research.

Beatty, B. 1995. *Preschool education in America: The culture of young children from the colonial era to the present*. New Haven, CT: Yale University Press.

Beck, R. 1973. The White House Conference on Children: An historical perspective. *Harvard Educational Review* 43(4):653-668.

Berry, B. 2013. Good schools and teachers for all students. In *Closing the opportunity gap: What America must do to give every child an even chance*, edited by P. L. Carter and K. G. Welner. Oxford, UK: Oxford University Press. Pp. 181-192.

Borrowman, M. L. 1971. Teachers, education of: History. In *Encyclopedia of education*. Vol. 9, edited by L. C. Deighton. New York: Macmillan. Pp. 71-79.

Bredekamp, S., and S. G. Goffin. 2013. Making the case: Why credentialing and certification matter. In *Handbook of early childhood education*, edited by R. Pianta. New York: Guildford Press. Pp. 584-604.

Cahan, E. 1989. *Past caring: A history of U.S. preschool care and education for the poor, 1620-1965*. New York: National Center for Children in Poverty.

Cohen, A. J. 1996. A brief history of federal financing for child care in the United States. *The Future of Children* 6(2):26-40.

Council for Professional Recognition. 2014. *History of Child Development Associate (CDA) credential*. Washington, DC: Council for Professional Recognition. http://www.cdacouncil. org/the-cda-credential/about-the-cda/history-of-the-cda (accessed August 14, 2014).

Darling-Hammond, L., A. Pacheco, N. Michelli, P. LePage, and K. Hammerness. 2005. Implementing curriculum renewal in teacher education: Managing organizational and policy change. In *Preparing teachers for a changing world: What teachers should learn and be able to do*, edited by L. Darling-Hammond and J. Bransford. San Francisco, CA: Jossey Bass. Pp. 442-479.

Drury, D., and J. Baer. 2011. *The American public school teacher: Past present & future*. Cambridge, MA: Harvard Education Press.

Early, D., and P. Winston. 2001. Preparing the workforce: Early childhood teacher preparation at 2- and 4-year institutions of higher education. *Early Childhood Research Quarterly* 16(3):285-306.

Feiman-Nemser, S. 2012. *Teachers as learners*. Cambridge, MA: Harvard Education Press.

Hammerness, K., L. Darling-Hammond, and J. Bransford. 2005. How teachers learn and develop. In *Preparing teachers for a changing world: What teachers should learn and be able to do*, edited by L. Darling-Hammond and J. Bransford. San Francisco, CA: Jossey Bass. Pp. 390-441.

Hart, K., and R. Schumacher. 2005. *Making the case: Improving Head Start teacher qualifications requires increased investment*. Head Start Series Paper No. 1, July. Washington, DC: Center for Law and Social Policy. http://www.leg.state.vt.us/PreKEducationStudy Committee/Documents/hs_policy_paper_1.pdf (accessed August 14, 2014).

Herbst, J. 1989. *And sadly teach: Teacher education and professionalization in American culture*. Madison: University of Wisconsin Press.

Hewes, D. W. 1990. *Historical foundations for early childhood teacher training: The evolution of kindergarten teacher preparation*, edited by B. Spodek and O. N. Saracho. New York: Teachers College Press.

History of Education. 2013. *History of teacher training.* http://historyeducationinfo.com (accessed August 14, 2014).

Hymes, J. L. 1970. Industrial day care's roots in America: Proceedings of the conference on industry and day care. In *Sources: Notable selections in early childhood education,* 2nd ed., edited by K. M. Paciorek and J. H. Munro. Guilford, CT: Dushkin/McGraw-Hill. Pp. 101-112.

IOM (Institute of Medicine) and NRC (National Research Council). 2012. *The early childhood care and education workforce: Challenges and opportunities. A workshop report.* Washington, DC: The National Academies Press.

Kopp, W. 2003. *A chance to make history: What works and what doesn't in providing an excellent education for all.* Cambridge, MA: Public Affairs.

Labaree, D. F. 2004. *The trouble with ed schools.* New Haven, CT: Yale University Press.

_____. 2008. An uneasy relationship: The history of teacher education in the university. In *Handbook of research on teacher education: Enduring issues in changing contexts.* 3rd ed., edited by M. Cochran-Smith, S. Feiman-Nemser, and J. McIntyre. Washington, DC: Association of Teacher Educators. Pp. 290-306.

Lagassé, P. 2012. *The Columbia electronic encyclopedia.* 6th ed. New York: Columbia University.

Lascarides, V. C. 1989. *The role of the United States government in early education during the depression of the 1930s.* Paper presented at International Conference for the History of Education, August 11, Oslo, Norway.

Lascarides. V. C., and B. S. F. Hinitz. 2011. *History of early childhood education.* Abington, UK: Routledge.

Liston, D. P., and Kenneth M. Zeichner. 1991. *Teacher education and the social conditions of schooling.* New York: Routledge.

McCarthy, J. 1988. *State certification of early childhood teachers: Analysis of the 50 states and the District of Columbia.* Washington, DC: National Association for the Education of Young Children.

McMillan, M. 1919. *The nursery school.* New York: E. P. Dutton.

Meisels, S. J., and J. P. Shonkoff. 2000. Early childhood intervention: A continuing evolution. In *Handbook of early childhood intervention.* 2nd ed., edited by J. P. Shonkoff and S. J. Meisels. Cambridge, UK: Cambridge University Press. Pp. 3-31.

Milton Friedman Foundation. 2010. *A brief history of education in America.* http://www.cblpi.org/ftp/School%20Choice/EdHistory.pdf (accessed August 14, 2014).

NAEYC (National Association for the Education of Young Children). 2001. *NAEYC at 75.* Washington, DC: NAEYC.

National Committee on Nursery Schools. 1927. *Conference on nursery schools: Report of the second conference of those interested in nursery schools, held at the Majestic Hotel in New York City, April 22-23, 1927.* Washington, DC: National Committee on Nursery Schools.

_____. 1929. *Third conference of nursery school workers.* Chicago, IL: National Committee on Nursery Schools.

NRC (National Research Council). 2001. *Eager to learn: Educating our preschoolers.* Washington, DC: National Academy Press.

NSSE (National Society for the Study of Education). 1929a. *The twenty-eighth yearbook of the National Society for the Study of Education: Preschool and parental education.* Vol. 28, Issue 1. Bloomington, IL: Public School Publishing Company.

_____. 1929b. *Yearbook of the National Society for the Study of Education: Research and method.* Vol. 28, Issue 2. Bloomington, IL: Public School Publishing Company.

Osborn, K. 1965. Project Head Start: An assessment. *Educational Leadership* 23(2):98-102.

Paciorek, K. M., and J. H. Munro. 1999. *Sources: Notable selections in early childhood education.* Guilford, CT: Dushkin Publishing Group.

Powell, D. R., and L. Dunn. 1990. Non-baccalaureate teacher education in early childhood education. In *Early childhood teacher preparation,* edited by B. Spodek and O. N. Saracho. New York: Teachers College Press. Pp.45-66.

Ravitch, D. 2003. *A brief history of teacher professionalism.* White House Conference on Preparing Tomorrow's Teachers. http://www2.ed.gov/admins/tchrqual/learn/preparing teachersconference/ravitch.html (accessed August 14, 2014).

Saracho, O. N. 1993. Preparing teachers for early childhood programs in the United States. In *Handbook of research on the education of young children,* edited by B. Spodek. New York: Macmillan Publishing. Pp. 412-425.

Shonkoff, J. P., and S. J. Meisels. 2000. *Handbook of early childhood intervention.* Cambridge, UK: Cambridge University Press.

Spodek, B. 1972. Staff requirements in early childhood education. In *The seventy-first year-book of the National Society of the Study of Education: Early childhood education,* edited by I. J. Gordon. Chicago, IL: University of Chicago Press. Pp. 358.

U.S. Bureau of Labor Statistics. 2014. *Occupational outlook handbook.* http://www.bls.gov/ooh/education-training-and-library/kindergarten-and-elementary-school-teachers.htm. http://www.bls.gov/ooh/education-training-and-library/kindergarten-and-elementary-school-teachers.htm (accessed August 14, 2014).

U.S. Department of Education. 2014. *Education resource organizations directory.* http://wdcrobcolp01.ed.gov/Programs/EROD/org_list.cfm?category_cd=SEA (accessed August 14, 2014).

U.S. Office of Education. 1943. *Nursery schools vital to the war effort.* School children and war series. Washington, DC: Federal Security Agency.

Vanderwalker, N. C. 1917. *The kindergarten in American education.* New York: The Macmillan Company.

Whitebook, M., D. Gomby, D. Bellm, L. Sakai, and F. Kipnis. 2009. *Preparing teachers of young children: The current state of knowledge and a blueprint for the future.* Berkeley: University of California, Berkeley, Center for the Study of Child Care Employment.

Appendix E

Credentials by Setting and State

State	Credentials for Early Childcare Providers	Certificate/Endorsements for Early Childhood Education	Certificate/Endorsements for Early Elementary Education
Alabama[a]	• Child Development Associate (CDA) Credential • Certified Child Care Professional	• Early Childhood: P-3 • Early Childhood Special Education: Birth Through Age 8	• Collaborative Special Education: K-6 • Elementary: K-6 • Elementary-Secondary: P-12 • Special Education: P-12
Alaska[b]	• Child Development Associate Credential • Certified Child Care Professional • Licensed Child Care Homes • Licensed Child Care Group Homes • Licensed Child Care Centers	• Type E Early Childhood Certificate • Limited Type I Certificate for Instruction Aides	• Elementary Education (K-6)
Arizona[c]	• Certified Child Care Professional • Child Development Associate	• Provisional Early Childhood Certificate: Birth-Third Grade • Standard Early Childhood Certificate: Birth-Third Grade	• Provisional Elementary Education Certificate: First-Eighth Grade

[a] Alabama Department of Human Resources. n.d. *Child care quality enhancement training.* http://dhr.alabama.gov/services/child_care_services/Schedule_Training.aspx (accessed January 16, 2015); Alabama State Department of Education. 2014. *To approve teacher education programs; The University of Alabama.* http://www.alsde.edu/sites/boe/_bdc/ALSDEBOE/BOE%20-%20Resolutions_4.aspx?ID=1657 (accessed January 16, 2015); Care Courses School Inc. 2014. *Child care training information by location.* http://www.carecourses.com/PublicPages/StateInformation.aspx (accessed January 16, 2015).

[b] Alaska Department of Health and Social Services Division of Public Assistance. 2012. *Child care program office: Information for parents. Eligible provider types.* http://dhss.alaska.gov/dpa/Pages/ccare/eligible-providers.aspx (accessed January 16, 2015); Care Courses School Inc. 2014. *Child care training information by location.* http://www.carecourses.com/PublicPages/StateInformation.aspx (accessed January 16, 2015).

[c] Arizona Department of Education Certification Unit. 2014. *Requirements for Early Childhood Education, Birth through Age 8 or Grade 3 Endorsement.* http://www.azed.gov/educator-certification/files/2011/09/requirements-for-early-childhood-endorsement.pdf20140523 (accessed January 16, 2015).

continued

State	Credentials for Early Childcare Providers	Certificate/Endorsements for Early Childhood Education	Certificate/Endorsements for Early Elementary Education
Arkansas[d]	• Child Development Associate • Certified Child Care Professional • Caregiver Certificate (CC) • Early Care and Education (ECE) Specialist Certificate	• Special Education Early Childhood Instructional Specialist: Birth-Fourth Grade	• Elementary Education: K-Sixth Grade
California[e]	• Child Development Associate Teacher Permit • Certified Child Care Professional • Child Development Teacher Permit • Child Development Master Teacher Permit • Child Development Site Supervisor Permit • Child Development Program Director Permit	• Early Childhood: Preschool-Third Grade • Kindergarten-Primary: K-third grade	• Elementary: K-Ninth Grade

[d] Arkansas Department of Education. 2014. *Additional Licensure Plans (ALP)*. http://www.arkansased.org/divisions/human-resources-educator-effectiveness-and-licensure/educator-licensure-unit/add-licensure-area-to-license/additional-licensure-plans-alp (accessed January 16, 2015); Arkansas Department of Human Services. n.d. *Arkansas early childhood professional development system: SPECTRUM*. http://humanservices.arkansas.gov/dccece/documents/spectrum.pdf (accessed January 16, 2015); Care Courses School Inc. 2014. *Child care training information by location*. http://www.carecourses.com/PublicPages/StateInformation.aspx (accessed January 16, 2015).

[e] Care Courses School Inc. 2014. *Child care training information by location*. http://www.carecourses.com/PublicPages/StateInformation.aspx (accessed January 16, 2015); State of California Commission on Teacher Credentialing. 2013. *Child development permits*. http://www.ctc.ca.gov/credentials/leaflets/cl797.pdf (accessed January 16, 2015); TK California. n.d. *TK roadmap: Credential requirements*. http://www.tkcalifornia.org/tk-roadmap/operations/the-tk-teacher.html (accessed January 16, 2015).

State	Credentials for Early Childcare Providers	Certificate/Endorsements for Early Childhood Education	Certificate/Endorsements for Early Elementary Education
Colorado[f]	• Child Development Associate • Certified Child Care Professional	• Early Childhood Entry Certificate • Preschool Early Childhood Teacher Certificate • Infant/Toddler Early Childhood Teacher Certificate	
Connecticut[g]	• Child Development Associate • Certified Child Care Professional	• Integrated Early Childhood/Special Ed., N-K-Elem. 1-3 (ECE)	• Elementary: 1-6
Delaware[h]	• Child Development Associate • Certified Child Care Professional	• Early Childhood: Birth to Grade 2	• Elementary Education: Grades K-6
Florida[i]	• Florida Child Care Professional Credential • Child Development Associate • Certified Child Care Professional	• Prekindergarten Primary: Age 3-Grade 3	• Elementary Education: Grades K-6

[f] Care Courses School Inc. 2014. *Child care training information by location.* http://www.carecourses.com/PublicPages/StateInformation.aspx (accessed January 16, 2015); Red Rocks Community College. n.d. *Preschool early childhood teacher certificate.* http://www.rrcc.edu/catalogs/13-14/preschool-early-childhood-teacher-certificate.htm (accessed January 16, 2015).

[g] Care Courses School Inc. 2014. *Child care training information by location.* http://www.carecourses.com/PublicPages/StateInformation.aspx (accessed January 16, 2015); Eastern Connecticut State University Department of Education. *Frequently asked questions about undergraduate programs leading to teaching certification in the education unit at Eastern Connecticut State University.* http://www.easternct.edu/education/faq.html#questionOne (accessed January 16, 2015).

[h] Care Courses School Inc. 2014. *Child care training information by location.* http://www.carecourses.com/PublicPages/StateInformation.aspx (accessed January 16, 2015); Miller, R. n.d.-a. *How to become a teacher in Delaware.* http://www.degreetree.com/resources/how-to-become-a-teacher-in-delaware (accessed January 16, 2015).

[i] Care Courses School Inc. 2014. *Child care training information by location.* http://www.carecourses.com/PublicPages/StateInformation.aspx (accessed January 16, 2015); Florida Department of Education. 2015. *NBPTS certificate subjects and corresponding subjects in Florida.* http://www.fldoe.org/teaching/certification/pathways-routes/nbpts-certificate-subjects-correspondi.stml (accessed March 24, 2015).

State	Credentials for Early Childcare Providers	Certificate/Endorsements for Early Childhood Education	Certificate/Endorsements for Early Elementary Education
Georgia[j]	• Child Development Associate Credential • Certified Child Care Professional • Technical Certificate of Credit (TCC) (PDR Career Level 5) in — Early Childhood Education — Child Development — Infant and Toddler — Program Administration — School Age and Youth Care • Technical College Diploma (TCD) in Early Childhood Education or Child Development • Associate's degree in Early Childhood Education or Child Development • Current PSC Paraprofessional Certificate	• Early Childhood Education (pre-kindergarten through fifth grade) • Preschool Through Grade 12	
Hawaii[k]	• Child Development Associate • Certified Child Care Professional	• Early Childhood Education	• Elementary Education

[j] Care Courses School Inc. 2014. *Child care training information by location.* http://www.carecourses.com/PublicPages/StateInformation.aspx (accessed January 16, 2015); Education-Colleges.com. n.d. *Georgia, GA teacher certification.* http://www.education-colleges.com/georgia-teacher-certification.html (accessed October 20, 2014); Georgia Department of Early Care and Learning. 2014. *Bright Start: Professional Development Registry (PDR) for early childhood professionals.* http://www.decal.ga.gov/Bfts/ProfessionalDevelopmentRegistry.aspx (accessed October 20, 2014).
[k] Care Courses School Inc. 2014. *Child care training information by location.* http://www.carecourses.com/PublicPages/StateInformation.aspx (accessed January 16, 2015); Miller, R. n.d.-b. *How to become a teacher in Hawaii.* http://www.degreetree.com/resources/how-to-become-a-teacher-in-hawaii#areas (accessed October 20, 2014).

continued

State	Credentials for Early Childcare Providers	Certificate/Endorsements for Early Childhood Education	Certificate/Endorsements for Early Elementary Education
Idaho[l]	• Child Development Associate • Certified Child Care Professional	• Early Childhood Education: 3-8 Years • Early Childhood Special Education	• Elementary Education: Grades K-6

Illinois[m]	• Child Development Associate
	• Certified Child Care Professional
	• ECE Credentials
	  — Level 1
	  — Levels 2-5
	• Illinois Director Credential (IDC)
	• Infant Toddler Credential (ITC)
	• School-Age and Youth Development Credential (SAYD)
	  — Level 1
		• Early Childhood Certificate: Birth-Grade 3
		• Special Preschool through Age 21 Certificate
			• Elementary Certificate: Grades K-9
			• Secondary Certificate: Grades 6-12
			• Special Certificate: Grades K-12

Indiana[n]	• Child Development Associate • Certified Child Care Professional	• Pre-Kindergarten Education	• Kindergarten Education • Elementary Education

[l] Care Courses School Inc. 2014. *Child care training information by location.* http://www.carecourses.com/PublicPages/StateInformation.aspx (accessed January 16, 2015); Teachingcertification.com. 2012f. *Types of teaching certifications.* http://www.teaching-certification.com/types-of-teaching-certifications.html (accessed October 20, 2014).

[m] Care Courses School Inc. 2014. *Child care training information by location.* http://www.carecourses.com/PublicPages/StateInformation.aspx (accessed January 16, 2015); Gateways to Opportunity Illinois Professional Development System. n.d. *Gateways ECE credential level 1.* http://www.ilgateways.com/en/ece-level-1-components (accessed October 20, 2014); Northern Illinois University. 2014. *Educator licensure and preparation formerly known as teacher certification.* http://www.niu.edu/teachercertification/statecert/scr_stc.shtml#10 (accessed October 20, 2014).

[n] Care Courses School Inc. 2014. *Child care training information by location.* http://www.carecourses.com/PublicPages/StateInformation.aspx (accessed January 16, 2015).

State	Credentials for Early Childcare Providers	Certificate/Endorsements for Early Childhood Education	Certificate/Endorsements for Early Elementary Education
Iowa[o]	• Child Development Associate • Certified Child Care Professional	• Early Childhood Special Education-PK-K • Early Childhood SPED-PK-K • Early Childhood Teacher-Pre K-K	• Teacher Elem Classroom-K-6
Kansas[p]	• Child Development Associate • Certified Child Care Professional	• Early Childhood Unified: Birth-Kindergarten	• Elementary K-6
Kentucky[q]	• Child Development Associate • Certified Child Care Professional	• Interdisciplinary Early Childhood Education: Birth to Primary	• Elementary School: Primary to Grade 5
Louisiana[r]	• Child Development Associate • Certified Child Care Professional	• Early Childhood: Grades PK-3	• Elementary Education: Grades 1-5

[o] Care Courses School Inc. 2014. *Child care training information by location.* http://www.carecourses.com/PublicPages/StateInformation.aspx (accessed January 16, 2015); Iowa Board of Educational Examiners. n.d. *Endorsement numbers.* http://www.boee.iowa.gov/endnos.html (accessed October 20, 2014).

[p] Care Courses School Inc. 2014. *Child care training information by location.* http://www.carecourses.com/PublicPages/StateInformation.aspx (accessed January 16, 2015); Kansas State University. 2014. *Licensing information.* https://coe.k-state.edu/departments/csps/licensure (accessed October 20, 2014).

[q] Teachingcertification.com. 2012a. *Kentucky teaching certification.* http://www.teaching-certification.com/kentucky-teaching-certification.html (accessed October 20, 2014).

[r] Care Courses School Inc. 2014. *Child care training information by location.* http://www.carecourses.com/PublicPages/StateInformation.aspx (accessed January 16, 2015).

continued

State	Credentials for Early Childcare Providers	Certificate/Endorsements for Early Childhood Education	Certificate/Endorsements for Early Elementary Education
Maine[s]	• Child Development Associate • Certified Child Care Professional	• Early Childhood Teacher: Birth-5 Years	• Early Elementary Teacher: K-Third Grade • Elementary Teacher endorsement: K-Eighth Grade
Maryland[t]	• Child Development Associate • Certified Child Care Professional	• Early Childhood Education: PreK-Third Grade • Special Education: Infant/primary: Birth-Third Grade	• Elementary Education: First-Sixth Grade • Special Education: Elementary/Middle: First-Eighth Grade
Massachusetts[u]	• Infant Toddler Certification • Child Development Associate • Certified Child Care Professional	• Early Childhood: PreK-Second Grade	• Elementary: First-Sixth Grade
Michigan[v]	• Child Development Associate • Certified Child Care Professional	• Early Childhood-General and Special Education	• General Elementary: Grades K-Fifth

[s] Care Courses School Inc. 2014. *Child care training information by location.* http://www.carecourses.com/PublicPages/StateInformation.aspx (accessed January 16, 2015); University of Maine at Augusta. 2012. *Teacher preparation programs.* http://www.uma.edu/elementaryeducation.html (accessed October 20, 2014).

[t] Care Courses School Inc. 2014. *Child care training information by location.* http://www.carecourses.com/PublicPages/StateInformation.aspx (accessed January 16, 2015); Miller, R. n.d.-c. *How to become a teacher in Maryland.* http://www.degreetree.com/resources/how-to-become-a-teacher-in-Maryland#areas (accessed October 20, 2014).

[u] Care Courses School Inc. 2014. *Child care training information by location.* http://www.carecourses.com/PublicPages/StateInformation.aspx (accessed January 16, 2015); Mass.gov Executive Office of Education. n.d. *EEC Professional Certification.* http://www.mass.gov/edu/birth-grade-12/early-education-and-care/workforce-and-professional-development/educator-certifications/early-education-care-professional-certification/eec-professional-certification.html (accessed October 20, 2014); Miller, R. n.d.-d. *How to become a teacher in Massachusetts.* http://www.degreetree.com/resources/how-to-become-a-teacher-in-massachusetts (accessed October 20, 2014).

[v] Care Courses School Inc. 2014. *Child care training information by location.* http://www.carecourses.com/PublicPages/StateInformation.aspx (accessed January 16, 2015).

State	Credentials for Early Childcare Providers	Certificate/Endorsements for Early Childhood Education	Certificate/Endorsements for Early Elementary Education
Minnesota[w]	• Child Development Associate • Certified Child Care Professional	• Preprimary Endorsement License: Age 3 to 5/Grade K • Early Childhood: Birth to Age 8 (Grade 3) • Special Education: — Blind or Visually Impaired: Birth-Grade 12 — Deaf or Hard of Hearing: Birth-Grade 12 — Oral/Aural Education: Birth-Grade 12 — Developmental Adapted Physical: Pre K–Grade 12 — Developmental Disabilities: K-12 — Early Childhood: Birth to Age 6 — Emotional Behavioral Disorders: K-12 — Learning Disabilities: K-12 — Physical and Health Disabilities: Pre K-12	• Elementary Education: Grades K-6
Mississippi[x]	• Child Development Associate • Certified Child Care Professional	• Child Development: Pre K-K	• Elementary Education: K-6 • Special Education: K-12

[w] Care Courses School Inc. 2014. *Child care training information by location.* http://www.carecourses.com/PublicPages/StateInformation.aspx (accessed January 16, 2015); Teachingcertification.com. 2012b. *Minnesota teaching certification.* http://www.teaching-certification.com/minnesota-teaching-certification.html (accessed October 20, 2014).

[x] Care Courses School Inc. 2014. *Child care training information by location.* http://www.carecourses.com/PublicPages/StateInformation.aspx (accessed January 16, 2015).

continued

State	Credentials for Early Childcare Providers	Certificate/Endorsements for Early Childhood Education	Certificate/Endorsements for Early Elementary Education
Missouri[y]	• Child Development Associate • Certified Child Care Professional	• Early Childhood: Birth-Third Grade • Education of Young Children • Early Childhood Special Education: Birth-Third Grade • Special Education: Preschool/Early Childhood	• Elementary: First-Sixth Grade
Montana[z]	• Child Development Associate • Certified Child Care Professional		• Elementary K-8
Nebraska[aa]	• Child Development Associate • Certified Child Care Professional	• Early Childhood Inclusive: Birth-Third Grade • Special Education-Early Childhood Special Education: Birth-Kindergarten	• Elementary Education: K-6
Nevada[bb]	• Child Development Associate • Certified Child Care Professional	• Early Childhood: Birth-Second Grade • Early Childhood Developmentally Delayed: Birth-7 Years	• Elementary: K-Eighth Grade

[y] Care Courses School Inc. 2014. *Child care training information by location.* http://www.carecourses.com/PublicPages/StateInformation.aspx (accessed January 16, 2015).
[z] Care Courses School Inc. 2014. *Child care training information by location.* http://www.carecourses.com/PublicPages/StateInformation.aspx (accessed January 16, 2015); Teachingcertification.com. 2012c. *Montana teaching certification.* http://www.teaching-certification.com/montana-teaching-certification.html (accessed October 20, 2014).
[aa] Care Courses School Inc. 2014. *Child care training information by location.* http://www.carecourses.com/PublicPages/StateInformation.aspx (accessed January 16, 2015); http://www.education.ne.gov/legal/webrulespdf/pdfCLEANRule24_2014 (accessed June 21, 2015).
[bb] Care Courses School Inc. 2014. *Child care training information by location.* http://www.carecourses.com/PublicPages/StateInformation.aspx (accessed January 16, 2015).

continued

State	Credentials for Early Childcare Providers	Certificate/Endorsements for Early Childhood Education	Certificate/Endorsements for Early Elementary Education
New Hampshire[cc]	• Child Development Associate • Certified Child Care Professional	• Early Childhood: N-3 • Early Childhood Special Education: N-3	• Elementary Education: K-Sixth Grade
New Jersey[dd]	• Child Development Associate • Certified Child Care Professional	• Early Childhood Education: Preschool-Third Grade	• Elementary Education: Kindergarten-Sixth Grade • Special Education: Kindergarten-Twelfth Grade
New Mexico[ee]	• Child Development Associate • Certified Child Care Professional	• Early childhood: B-3	• Elementary: K-8 • Special education teacher: K-12

[cc] Care Courses School Inc. 2014. *Child care training information by location.* http://www.carecourses.com/PublicPages/StateInformation.aspx (accessed January 16, 2015); New Hampshire Department of Education. 2014. *Code list of endorsements.* http://www.education.nh.gov/certification/documents/codelist.pdf (accessed October 20, 2014).

[dd] Bloomfield College. 2014. *Traditional teacher education: Elementary education (K-6).* http://www.bloomfield.edu/academics/degrees-programs/education/post-bacc-k5 (accessed March 24, 2015); Care Courses School Inc. 2014. *Child care training information by location.* http://www.carecourses.com/PublicPages/StateInformation.aspx (accessed January 16, 2015).

[ee] Care Courses School Inc. 2014. *Child care training information by location.* http://www.carecourses.com/PublicPages/StateInformation.aspx (accessed January 16, 2015); New Mexico Public Education Department Professional Licensure Bureau. n.d. *Endorsement areas.* http://www.sde.state.nm.us/Licensure/dl08/ENDORSEMENT%20AREAS.pdf (accessed October 20, 2014).

State	Credentials for Early Childcare Providers	Certificate/Endorsements for Early Childhood Education	Certificate/Endorsements for Early Elementary Education
New York[ff]	• Infant Toddler Care & Education Credential • Child Development Associate • Certified Child Care Professional	• Early Childhood: Birth-Second Grade • Student with Disabilities: Birth-Grade 2	• Childhood Education: First-Sixth
North Carolina[gg]	• Infant/Toddler Credential • Child Development Associate • Certified Child Care Professional	• Elementary: Birth Through Kindergarten	• Elementary: K-6 • Exceptional children: K-12
North Dakota[hh]	• Child Development Associate • Certified Child Care Professional	• Early Childhood Education • Special Education: Early Childhood	• Kindergarten Endorsement • Elementary Education

[ff] Care Courses School Inc. 2014. *Child care training information by location.* http://www.carecourses.com/PublicPages/StateInformation.aspx (accessed January 16, 2015); New York Early Childhood Professional Development Institute. n.d.-a. *The NYS Infant Toddler Care and Education Credential (ITCEC).* http://www.earlychildhoodnyc.org/education/ITCEC.cfm (accessed October 20, 2014); New York Early Childhood Professional Development Institute. n.d.-b. *NYS teacher certification for early childhood educators.* http://www.earlychildhoodnyc.org/education/teacher certification.cfm#generalNYS (accessed October 20, 2014).

[gg] Care Courses School Inc. 2014. *Child care training information by location.* http://www.carecourses.com/PublicPages/StateInformation.aspx (accessed January 16, 2015); Miller, R. n.d.-e. *How to become a teacher in North Carolina.* http://www.degreetree.com/resources/how-to-become-a-teacher-in-north-carolina (accessed October 20, 2014); North Carolina Department of Health and Human Services. 2014. *North Carolina infant-toddler program guidance for personnel certification.* http://www.beearly.nc.gov/data/files/pdf/ITPGuidePersonnelCert.pdf (accessed October 2014, 2014).

[hh] Care Courses School Inc. 2014. *Child care training information by location.* http://www.carecourses.com/PublicPages/StateInformation.aspx (accessed January 16, 2015); North Dakota State Government Education Standards and Practices Board. n.d. *Licensure.* http://www.nd.gov/espb/licensure/types.html (accessed October 20, 2014); Teachingcertification.com. 2012d. *North Dakota teaching certification.* http://www.teaching-certification.com/north-dakota-teaching-certification.html (accessed October 20, 2014).

State	Credentials for Early Childcare Providers	Certificate/Endorsements for Early Childhood Education	Certificate/Endorsements for Early Elementary Education
Ohio[ii]	• Child Development Associate • Certified Child Care Professional	• Birth to Age 3 Early Intervention Specialist license	• Early Childhood Education license: Pre-K-Third Grade • Early Childhood Intervention Specialist license: Pre-K-Third Grade
Oklahoma[jj]	• Child Development Associate • Certified Child Care Professional	• Certificate to Teach 4-Year-Olds and Younger • Certificate to Teach Infants, Toddlers, and 3-Year-Olds	• Early Childhood-Grades Pre-Kindergarten (PK)-3
Oregon[kk]	• Child Development Associate • Certified Child Care Professional	• Early Childhood Authorization Level: Age 3-Fourth grade	• Elementary Authorization Level: Third-Eighth Grade
Pennsylvania[ll]	• Child Development Associate • Certified Child Care Professional	• PreK-4 Teacher Certificate • Special Education PreK-8 with Dual Certification in Early Childhood, Elementary/Middle, or Reading Specialist	

[ii] Bowling Green State University. n.d. *Inclusive early childhood education.* https://www.bgsu.edu/education-and-human-development/school-of-teaching-and-learning/inclusive-early-childhood-education.html (accessed October 20, 2014); Care Courses School Inc. 2014. *Child care training information by location.* http://www.carecourses.com/PublicPages/StateInformation.aspx (accessed January 16, 2015).

[jj] Care Courses School Inc. 2014. *Child care training information by location.* http://www.carecourses.com/PublicPages/StateInformation.aspx (accessed January 16, 2015); The State of Oklahoma. 2015. *Oklahoma State Department of Education.* http://ok.gov (accessed January 16, 2015).

[kk] Care Courses School Inc. 2014. *Child care training information by location.* http://www.carecourses.com/PublicPages/StateInformation.aspx (accessed January 16, 2015); Teachingcertification.com. 2012e. *Oregon teaching certification.* http://www.teaching-certification.com/oregon-teaching-certification.html (accessed October 20, 2014).

[ll] University of Pittsburgh School of Education. 2014. *Early childhood education.* http://www.education.pitt.edu/AcademicDepartments/InstructionLearning/Programs/EarlyChildhoodEducation.aspx (accessed October 20, 2014).

continued

State	Credentials for Early Childcare Providers	Certificate/Endorsements for Early Childhood Education	Certificate/Endorsements for Early Elementary Education
Rhode Island[mmm]	• Child Development Associate • Certified Child Care Professional	• Early Childhood Education: PK-2nd Grade	• Elementary Education: 2nd-6th Grade
South Carolina[nnn]	• Infant/Toddler Credential • Child Development Associate • Certified Child Care Professional	• Early Childhood Education: K-Third Grades	
South Dakota[ooo]	• Infant/Toddler Certificate • Child Development Associate • Certified Child Care Professional	• Birth Through Preschool Special Education Endorsement • Birth Through Preschool Endorsement	• Kindergarten Endorsement Special Education Endorsement
Tennessee[ppp]	• Child Development Associate • Certified Child Care Professional	• Early Childhood: Birth Through Third Grade • Special Education-Early Childhood (infants through third grade)	• Elementary: Grades K-6

[mmm] Care Courses School Inc. 2014. *Child care training information by location.* http://www.carecourses.com/PublicPages/StateInformation.aspx (accessed January 16, 2015); Teachingcertification.com. 2012. *Rhode Island teaching certification.* http://www.teaching-certification.com/rhode-island-teaching-certification.html (accessed March 24, 2015).

[nnn] Care Courses School Inc. 2014. *Child care training information by location.* http://www.carecourses.com/PublicPages/StateInformation.aspx (accessed January 16, 2015); South Carolina Center for Child Care Career Development. 2014. *South Carolina's early care and education credentialing system.* http://sc-ccccd.net/Credentialing/Credentialing.html (accessed March 24, 2015); TEACH.com. 2014. *Become a teacher in South Carolina.* http://teach.com/states/become-a-teacher-in-south-carolina (accessed March 24, 2015).

[ooo] Care Courses School Inc. 2014. *Child care training information by location.* http://www.carecourses.com/PublicPages/StateInformation.aspx (accessed January 16, 2015); South Dakota Department of Education. 2015. *Special education endorsement.* http://doe.sd.gov/oatq/spedendorcement.aspx (accessed March 24, 2015).

[ppp] Care Courses School Inc. 2014. *Child care training information by location.* http://www.carecourses.com/PublicPages/StateInformation.aspx (accessed January 16, 2015).

State	Credentials for Early Childcare Providers	Certificate/Endorsements for Early Childhood Education	Certificate/Endorsements for Early Elementary Education
Texas[qq]		• Early Childhood to Sixth Grade Certification	• All-Level (Early Childhood through 12th Grade) Teacher Certification
Utah[rr]	• Child Development Associate • Certified Child Care Professional	• Early Childhood (K-3) License Area • Special Education License (K-12) with Endorsements in Early Childhood Disabilities • Early Childhood Special Education License (Pre K-3)	• Elementary (1-8) License Area
Vermont[ss]	• Child Development Associate • Certified Child Care Professional	• Early Childhood Birth-Grade 3 • Early Childhood Special Education Birth-Age 6	• Elementary K-Grade 6
Virginia[tt]	• Child Development Associate • Certified Child Care Professional	• Early Education: PreK-Third Grade	• Elementary Education: PreK-Sixth Grade

[qq] Study.com. 2015. *Texas teacher certification program requirements and information.* http://education-portal.com/texas_teacher_certification.html (accessed March 24, 2015).

[rr] Care Courses School Inc. 2014. *Child care training information by location.* http://www.carecourses.com/PublicPages/StateInformation.aspx (accessed January 16, 2015); Utah State Office of Education. 2010. *Endorsements and early childhood education (ECE) license area.* http://www.schools.utah.gov/cert/Endorsements-ECE-License.aspx (accessed March 24, 2015).

[ss] Care Courses School Inc. 2014. *Child care training information by location.* http://www.carecourses.com/PublicPages/StateInformation.aspx (accessed January 16, 2015); University of Vermont. *College of education and social services.* http://www.uvm.edu/~cess/?Page=services/licensure.html&SM=servicesmenu.html (accessed March 24, 2015).

[tt] Care Courses School Inc. 2014. *Child care training information by location.* http://www.carecourses.com/PublicPages/StateInformation.aspx (accessed January 16, 2015); Teachingcertification.com. 2012. *Virginia teaching certification.* http://www.teaching-certification.com/virginia-teaching-certification.html (accessed March 24, 2015).

continued

State	Credentials for Early Childcare Providers	Certificate/Endorsements for Early Childhood Education	Certificate/Endorsements for Early Elementary Education
Washington[uu]	• Child Development Associate • Certified Child Care Professional	• Early Childhood Education (P-3) • Early Childhood Special Education (P-3)	• Elementary Education (K-8)
West Virginia[vv]	• Child Development Associate • Certified Child Care Professional		• Elementary Education (PreK-12th)
Wisconsin[ww]	• Infant/Toddler Credential • Child Development Associate • Certified Child Care Professional	• Early Childhood: Birth to Age 8 • Early Childhood Through Middle Childhood: Birth to Age 11 • Early Childhood Through Adolescence: Birth to Age 21	
Wyoming[xx]	• Child Development Associate • Certified Child Care Professional	• Early Childhood Birth to Eight Endorsement • Early Childhood Birth to Five Endorsement • Early Childhood Special Education	

[uu] Care Courses School Inc. 2014. *Child care training information by location.* http://www.carecourses.com/PublicPages/StateInformation.aspx (accessed January 16, 2015).
[vv] Care Courses School Inc. 2014. *Child care training information by location.* http://www.carecourses.com/PublicPages/StateInformation.aspx (accessed January 16, 2015).
[ww] Care Courses School Inc. 2014. *Child care training information by location.* http://www.carecourses.com/PublicPages/StateInformation.aspx (accessed January 16, 2015). *Wisconsin teaching certification.* http://www.teaching-certification.com/wisconsin-teaching-certification.html (accessed March 24, 2015).
[xx] Care Courses School Inc. 2014. *Child care training information by location.* http://www.carecourses.com/PublicPages/StateInformation.aspx (accessed January 16, 2015).

SOURCE: Compiled by University of Nebraska–Lincoln, 2014.

Appendix F

Tools and Examples to Inform Collaborative Systems Change

This appendix provides some examples of tools and resources that may be useful for implementing collaborative systems change. These include tools for systems change as a process in general, as well as tools that are specific to systems change in care and education. Finally, some additional examples of existing illustrative initiatives using collaborative approaches at different levels and in different localities are provided as a complement to the examples found in Chapter 5's discussion of continuity (see Boxes 5-1 and 5-2). The tools and resources do not represent a comprehensive review, and the committee did not draw conclusions to select best practices or endorse particular exemplars. They are included as a prompt to explore available options and resources that can assist in collaborative systems change efforts.

GENERAL TOOLS FOR COLLABORATIVE SYSTEMS CHANGE

Collective Impact

- Collective Impact—Five core conditions of Collective Impact (Kania and Kramer, 2011).
- Channeling Change: Making Collective Impact Work—Detailed guidance on how to implement the principles of collective impact, using three successful initiatives as examples (Hanleybrown et al., 2012).

- Understanding the Value of Backbone Organizations in Collective Impact—Role of backbone organizations in supporting collective impact (Turner et al., 2012).
- Embracing Emergence: How Collective Impact Addresses Complexity—How the rules of interaction defined in a collective impact process yield solutions to complex problems (Kania and Kramer, 2013).

Getting to Outcomes® Toolkit

Free how-to manuals developed for coalitions to work through 10 key steps for sustainable results, including process evaluation and outcome evaluation (RAND Corporation, 2015).

Evaluating Community Change: A Framework for Grantmakers

A framework of measures and potential indicators to help evaluate and ultimately improve complex, long-term, place-based initiatives that involve multiple partners joining together to tackle pressing community-wide issues (Grantmakers for Effective Organizations, 2014).

Guide to Evaluating Collective Impact

This three-part guide offers detailed advice on how to plan for and implement effective performance measurement and evaluation activities in the context of collective impact and evaluating complex systems change (Preskill et al., 2014). Part Two includes four case studies and Part Three includes sample evaluation questions, samples outcomes, and more than 150 sample indicators of progress.

TOOLS FOR CARE AND EDUCATION SYSTEMS CHANGE

Planning, Implementing, and Evaluating Prekindergarten-Third Grade Approaches

The Framework for Planning, Implementing, and Evaluating PreK-3rd Grade Approaches was developed over a 2-year period, the process of which involved an extensive literature review, pilot testing, and peer review. This framework focuses on several important issues encountered by those who are developing a prekindergarten-third grade approach, including identifying components of a comprehensive approach, understanding what is meant by alignment and what needs to be aligned, and understanding what shared roles and responsibilities exist between the birth to 5 and K-3 sectors and what behaviors in adults benefit children. Users of this framework include schools, district leaders, and early care and education programs (Kauerz and Coffman, 2013).

The report *PK-3: What Is It and How Do We Know It Works?* provides recommendations for state Departments of Education and local school boards and school districts to incorporate approaches to better align pre-kindergarten and early elementary schools in existing programs at relatively low cost. The report bases these recommendations on evidence from studies of the Carolina Abecedarian Project, the Chicago Child-Parent Center and Expansion Program, the U.S. Department of Education's Early Childhood Longitudinal Study-Kindergarten Cohort (ECLS-K), and the National Head Start/Public School Early Childhood Transition Demonstration Project (Graves, 2006).

BUILD Initiative

The BUILD Initiative, a foundation-funded multi-state effort to support comprehensive and coordinated early childhood programs, policies, and services, has several resources to inform efforts to improve early childhood systems (BUILD Initiative, 2015). Among these are BUILD's Theory of Change, which helps describe and connect the diverse processes and actions that are needed to build an early childhood system (BUILD Initiative, 2005) and a framework for evaluating systems initiatives (Coffman, 2007).

The Early Childhood Higher Education Inventory

The Center for the Study of Child Care Employment at the University of California, Berkeley, created the Early Childhood Higher Education Inventory, which is a mechanism to help detail the landscape of care and education programs in higher education at the associate's, bachelor's, master's, and doctoral levels. This inventory describes program goals, content, and characteristics such as faculty composition and course and field-based learning requirements. Policy makers, institutions of higher education, and other stakeholders can use this inventory as a guide to help build a coordinated and comprehensive preparation and professional learning system by assessing the landscape, identifying gaps, and recognizing opportunities for improvement (Center for the Study of Child Care Employment, 2015a).

In 2013, the Center released an inventory of higher education in New Hampshire, New Jersey, and Rhode Island. Each inventory lists the higher education programs available in each state and their goals, services and supports available to teacher candidates, and characteristics of courses, fieldwork experiences, and professional development opportunities. They also provide recommendations for improving higher education systems for educators of young children (Austin et al., 2013; Kipnis et al., 2013a,b).

Supportive Environmental Quality Underlying Adult Learning (SEQUAL)

The SEQUAL tool assesses the policies and practices in the workplace that support the professional learning of educators. It is administered to educators directly to evaluate five areas: teaching supports, learning community, job crafting, adult well-being, and program leadership (Center for the Study of Child Care Employment, 2015b).

Guidebook for Community Schools

Community schools, a research-based strategy of promoting student achievement through the collaboration of communities and their resources, consists of high-quality instructional programs and practices, an enriching learning environment for students and families, and health services that foster student well-being. Community schools provide smooth transitions between early childhood and elementary settings due to co-location of programs; encourage out-of-school experiences with children and families; and address both academic and nonacademic needs for students, such as social, emotional, and physical health. Partnerships are essential to the community school strategy, and involve school leadership and faculty, parents, and organizations and leaders within the community. Additionally, the role of site coordinator is crucial to the effectiveness of the community school. They coordinate planning, manage partnerships and resources, and facilitate recruitment. The National Center for Community Schools created a guidebook which provides a framework for the community school model accompanied by case studies. It also includes tools and guides for lead partners and site coordinators as well as resources on theory of change and stages of developing a community school (Lubell, 2011). In addition, examples and key features of community school models in Cincinnati, Ohio; Evansville, Indiana; Multnomah County, Oregon; and Tulsa, Oklahoma, can be found in a 2012 report by the Coalition for Community Schools (Jacobson et al., 2012).

Aligning Policies for Childcare

The report *Confronting the Child Care Eligibility Maze*, from the Work Support Strategies initiative, provides a framework for simplifying and aligning childcare subsidy policies and supports and facilitating access to other benefits. The report offers policy strategies, with examples from existing state efforts, to minimize burdensome administrative processes, improve service delivery, and address challenges to families in accessing and maintaining benefits (Adams and Matthews, 2013).

Transitioning to Kindergarten: A Toolkit for Early Childhood Educators

The National Center for Learning Disabilities and the America Federation of Teachers created a toolkit for school administrators, early childhood professionals, childcare providers and kindergarten teachers that provides materials to help children transition into kindergarten (National Center for Learning Disabilities, 2006).

EXAMPLES OF COLLABORATIVE SYSTEMS CHANGE EFFORTS[1]

Campaign for Grade-Level Reading

The Campaign for Grade-Level Reading is an effort to ensure that more children "succeed in school and graduate prepared for college, a career, and active citizenship." The benchmark used as a predictor for graduation is grade-level reading by the end of the third grade, as this prepares students for the more advanced and complex work they will encounter in the later elementary grades. This program is an effort to provide support in particular to low-income students who are currently not reading at grade level.

The Campaign recognizes that ensuring children's success is a collaborative effort, and brings together partners from various sectors, including foundations, nonprofit organizations, businesses, government agencies, and states and local communities. Alongside addressing the reading gap, the Campaign also focuses on issues of chronic absence and the loss of reading over the summer months. They also promote core strategies to encourage parent engagement in schools; the physical, social and emotional, cognitive, and verbal development of young children; and collaboration with state advocacy networks (The Campaign for Grade-Level Reading, 2015).

Transforming Early Childhood Community Systems

The Center for Healthier Children, Families, & Communities, a community-based research, policy, and training center at the University of California, Los Angeles, and the United Way Worldwide partnered to establish the Transforming Early Childhood Community Systems Initiative. This initiative uses a community engagement tool to map school readiness of young children, specifically assessing children's physical health, socio-emotional competence and maturity, language, cognitive development, and communication skills. Data collected by kindergarten teachers are collected along with available health, economic, and resource availability data. With

---

[1] Additional examples can be found as part of the discussion of continuity in Chapter 5 (see Boxes 5-1 and 5-2).

the resulting neighborhood-level data and mapping results, the Initiative helps communities assess needs in a highly localized way and take action to improve outcomes for young children. This is accompanied by regular monitoring and reassessment to identify challenges that emerge, promote accountability, and continuously guide local strategic planning, resource allocation, and systems improvement efforts. Participating communities form part of a network that offers mechanisms to share effective approaches. This Initiative also assists with establishing or improving local coalitions. Supported by the W.K. Kellogg Foundation, the Initiative has spread to more than 30 participating communities (Center for Healther Children Families & Communities, n.d.).

Cincinnati Strive Together

StriveTogether is a cradle-to-career effort to improve student outcomes that is strengthened by four pillars: a shared vision among community members; evidence-based decision making; collaborative action; and sustainability. The first cradle-to-career networks brought together representatives from across sectors: school leadership, nonprofit practitioners, community and business leaders, and university presidents. Together, these networks collaborated to create a set of indicators and benchmarks, or a roadmap to success, across the age continuum. As a part of StriveTogether, community networks provide a community report card, which tracks student- and community-level outcomes. Currently, 55 community networks across 28 states share the commitment of ensuring opportunities for academic achievement and lifelong success (StriveTogether, 2014).

StrivePartnership, the first cradle-to-career network, is implemented in Cincinnati, Ohio, and Newport and Covington, Kentucky. It has identified eight benchmarks for students to achieve between birth through college (StrivePartnership, 2015c). Three initiatives have been implemented which help to achieve these goals: quality continuous improvement; the Talent Pipeline Initiative; and the Read On! Venture Fund (StrivePartnership, 2015a). StrivePartnership recognizes the strength of community improvement, and builds upon strategies, infrastructures, and resources used by the Cincinnati Children's Hospital and Medical Center in health care improvement. The Talent Pipeline Initiative establishes relationships between students and employers in order to provide students starting in grade 4 with enriching career-based experiences. Finally, Read On! is an initiative with the goal of ensuring that every third grader is reading at grade level by 2020. More than 70 partners are engaged in this campaign, which is based around six evidence-based strategies. StrivePartnership, as a guiding principle, measures its achievements by assessing progress based on a number of different outcomes and reviewing how funding aligns with action (StrivePartnership, 2015b).

First 5 California

First 5 California, adopted by California voters through Proposition 10 in 1998, recognizes that children's health and education in the early years are a priority, especially during the first 5 years and prenatally. First 5 California, in collaboration with its partners and through local First 5 county commissions, includes comprehensive programs focused on the child, parent, and teachers with the aim of achieving optimal childhood outcomes. Focus areas include health, nutrition, language and literacy development, childcare, and smoking cessation. Additionally, efforts to build public engagement, increase investment, and influence policy change are intended to help to develop a sustainable and effective early childhood system (First 5 California, 2010).

Early Head Start Partnerships

Early Head Start–Child Care Partnerships are formally arranged collaborations between Early Head Start programs and providers at childcare centers or family childcare homes (providers must meet standards set by Head Start). This partnership program is funded by the Administration for Children and Families (ACF) and is part of President Obama's Early Learning Initiative. These partnerships are an effort to expand high-quality early learning experiences to infants and toddlers from low-income families, as well as support working families by providing full-day care for children. These programs provide services for education and child development, health and mental health, nutrition, community partnerships, family and parent involvement, and disabilities (HHS and ACF, 2014).

Professional learning resources for educators that complement such efforts are also available through the Early Childhood Learning & Knowledge Center, covering topics such as effective practice; practice-based coaching; working with students with disabilities; transitions to kindergarten, and teacher development (HHS and Office of Head Start, 2015).

Gateways to Opportunity: Illinois Professional Development System

Gateways to Opportunity, developed by the Professional Development Advisory Council in Illinois, is a statewide, integrated professional learning system that provides support, guidance, and information to professionals in the early care and education field. This online system provides access to resources and information regarding credentialing, professional learning, training, career guidance, and scholarships. The purpose of this system is to promote professionalism among those in the early care and education field, as well as to provide affordable and accessible opportunities for additional education and training (Gateways to Opportunity, n.d.).

Great Expectations for Teachers, Children, and Families: United Way of Tucson and Southern Arizona

Great Expectations for Teachers, Children, and Families, funded by First Things First and United Way, is a professional learning system that seeks to improve the knowledge and competencies of those working in early childhood care and education. Ten learning communities were established that focus on specific areas related to developmentally appropriate practices, early childhood degree completion, instructional support, and the quality of early childhood settings, among others. The aim of Great Expectations is to achieve a prepared workforce by building pathways to higher education, and ensuring high-quality experiences for young children (United Way, 2015).

REFERENCES

Adams, G., and H. Matthews. 2013. *Confronting the child care eligibility maze.* Washington, DC: Work Support Strategies Initiative and Center for Law and Social Policy, Inc.

Austin, L. J. E., F. Kipnis, L. Sakai, M. Whitebook, and S. Ryan. 2013. *The state of early childhood higher education in Rhode Island: The Rhode Island early childhood higher education inventory.* Berkeley, CA: Center for the Study of Child Care Employment.

BUILD Initiative. 2005. *The Build Initiative's Theory of Change.* http://www.buildinitiative. org/Portals/0/Uploads/Documents/TheoryofChangeExecutiveSummary.pdf (accessed May 31, 2015).

———. 2015. *Resource Center.* http://www.buildinitiative.org/Resources.aspx (accessed May 31, 2015).

The Campaign for Grade-Level Reading. 2015. *3rd grade reading success matters.* www. gradelevelreading.net (accessed February 26, 2015).

Center for Healther Children Families & Communities. n.d. *Systems innovation & improvement: Transforming Early Childhood Community Systems (TECCS).* http://www.healthy child.ucla.edu/ourwork/teccs (accessed March 20, 2015).

Center for the Study of Child Care Employment. 2015a. *Early childhood higher education inventory.* http://www.irle.berkeley.edu/cscce/2013/early-childhood-higher-education-inventory (accessed March 18, 2015).

———. 2015b. *Supportive Environmental Quality Underlying Adult Learning (SEQUAL).* http://www.irle.berkeley.edu/cscce/2014/sequal (accessed March 18, 2015).

Coffman, J. 2007. *A framework for evaluating systems initatives.* Boston, MA: Build Initiative.

First 5 California. 2010. *Welcome to First 5 California.* http://www.first5california.com (accessed March 20, 2015).

Gateways to Opportunity. n.d. *Gateways overview.* http://www.ilgateways.com/en/gateways-overview (accessed March 20, 2015).

Grantmakers for Effective Organizations. 2014. *Evaluating community change: A framework for grantmakers*. http://docs.geofunders.org/?filename=geo2014_indicators_framework. pdf (accessed December 18, 2014).

Graves, B. 2006. *PK-3: What is it and how do we know it works? FCD policy brief no. 4*. New York: Foundation for Child Development.

Hanleybrown, F., J. Kania, and M. Kramer. 2012. Channeling change: Making collective impact work. In *Stanford Social Innovation Review*. Stanford, CA: Leland Stanford, Jr. University.

HHS (U.S. Department of Health and Human Services) and ACF. 2014. *Early Head Start—child care partnerships*. http://www.acf.hhs.gov/programs/ecd/early-learning/ehs-cc-partnerships (accessed March 24, 2015).

HHS and Office of Head Start. 2015. *Early Childhood Learning and Knowledge Center (ECLKC): Engaging interctions and environments*. http://eclkc.ohs.acf.hhs.gov/hslc/tta-system/teaching/practice/engage/engage.html (accessed March 20, 2015).

Jacobson, R., L. Jacobson, and M. J. Blank. 2012. *Building blocks: An examination of the collaborative approach community schools are using to bolster early childhood development*. Washington, DC: Coalition for Community Schools, Institute for Educational Leadership.

Kania, J., and M. Kramer. 2011. Collective impact. In *Stanford Social Innovation Review*. Stanford, CA: Stanford University.

———. 2013. *Embracing emergence: How collective impact addresses complexity*. Stanford, CA: Stanford University.

Kauerz, K., and J. Coffman. 2013. *Framework for planning, implementing, and evaluating preK-3rd grade approaches*. Seattle: University of Washington, College of Education.

Kipnis, F., L. J. E. Austin, L. Sakai, M. Whitebook, and S. Ryan. 2013a. *The state of early childhood higher education in New Hampshire: The New Hampshire early childhood higher education inventory*. Berkeley, CA: Center for the Study of Child Care Employment.

Kipnis, F., M. Whitebook, L. Austin, and S. Ryan. 2013b. *The state of early childhood higher education in New Jersey: The New Jersey early childhood higher education inventory*. Berkeley, CA: Center for the Study of Child Care Employment.

Lubell, E. 2011. *Building community schools: A guide for action*. New York: National Center for Community Schools, Children's Aid Society.

National Center for Learning Disabilities. 2006. *Transitioning to kindergarten: A toolkit for early childhood educators*. New York: National Center for Learning Disabilities.

Preskill, H., M. Parkhurst, and J. Splansky Juster. 2014. *Guide to evaluating collective impact: Assessing progress and impact*. Washington, DC: Collective Impact Forum and FSG.

RAND Corporation. 2015. *Getting to outcomes® improving community-based prevention: Toolkit to help communities implement and evaluate their prevention programs*. http://www.rand.org/health/projects/getting-to-outcomes.html (accessed March 24, 2015).

StrivePartnership. 2015a. *Capacity building*. http://www.strivepartnership.org/our-priorities-2 (accessed March 20, 2015).

———. 2015b. *Data driven*. http://www.strivepartnership.org/education-results-resource (accessed March 20, 2015).

———. 2015c. *Who we are*. http://www.strivepartnership.org/about-the-partnership (accessed March 20, 2015).

StriveTogether. 2014. *The strivetogether story*. http://www.strivetogether.org/vision-roadmap/strivetogether-story (accessed March 20, 2015).

Turner, S., K. Merchant, J. Kania, and E. Martin. 2012. *Understanding the value of backbone organizations in collective impact*. Stanford, CA: Stanford University.

United Way. 2015. *Great expectations*. http://www.unitedwaytucson.org/content/great-expectations (accessed March 20, 2015).

Appendix G

Funding and Financing Examples

T here are a number of good examples and promising strategies for how to generate resources to invest in strengthening the quality of early care and education (ECE) programs. The examples collected here reflect innovative funding mechanisms for improving the quality of ECE programs. In different ways, they could be used to improve the salaries and benefits of care providers, to strengthen infrastructure and improve practice environments, to fund or subsidize the costs of professional learning, and to support efforts for collective action to achieve systems change. The committee did not conduct a comprehensive review and analysis of financing options, and evidence evaluating the following strategies currently is insufficient to warrant specific conclusions and recommendations about which to employ under what local circumstances. Nonetheless, local communities can examine these examples in considering how they might mobilize the necessary resources to improve the quality of the care and education of young children.

As described in Chapter 2, although there are a wide range of federal programs focused on quality supports for child development and early learning, much of the funding invested in the care and education of children from birth through age 8 comes from state and local sources and from sources outside of government, including philanthropic investments, employer-based childcare benefits, and out-of-pocket payments by families. This reinforces one of the central messages of this report, that stakeholders interested in improving the availability of a highly qualified workforce for children birth through age 8 need not only focus on influencing federal and other national efforts, but also develop concerted strategic systems change—including financing reforms and resource mobilization—at the state and local levels.

PUBLIC INVESTMENTS

One pathway for increasing funding is to increase allocations to existing public funding streams at local, state, and federal levels, or to expand the scope and mandate of universally available publicly financed education to extend to children at birth. Some expansion of this kind is occurring with the implementation of publicly funded preschool in many states and municipalities, including in some cases the integration of preschool into a state's school funding formula. However, this is unlikely to be implemented nationwide at the level of investment necessary, especially given how much of current care and education for children is financed through out-of-pocket payments by families or employer subsidies, costs that would be difficult to absorb through public investments alone. That said, there are some examples to consider to increase or more efficiently use public investments to support high-quality professional practice.

Subsidies to Improve Professional Training, Services, and Compensation

Subsidies to improve professional training, services, and compensation can occur through individual or program grants from public funds to support further education of ECE providers, recruitment of new providers, improvement of services, or subsidy of provider income.

- The Washington State Professional Development System is administered by the Department of Early Learning and provides significant financial incentives for several aspects of professional development, including (a) scholarships for educators to extend their training related to child development, and (b) a career lattice program offering financial incentives to educators to advance their training. The lattice program also requires enrollment of educators in a registry permitting professional networking and data gathering (Washington State Department of Early Learning, 2010).
- The REWARD Wisconsin stipend program provides income supplements to early care and education providers based on levels of education and experience (Wisconsin Early Childhood Association, 2015). Similar programs can be found in North Carolina (WAGE$ initiative) and other states.
- Vermont Early Education Initiative Grants provide funds from $10,000 to $30,000 to support the development of early education programs for children between ages 3 and 5 who are at risk of edu-

cational delays (Vermont Agency of Education, 2015). The state also has a program of income subsidies (bonuses) for ECE providers who achieve specific educational or training requirements, and other financial incentives for ECE programs to obtain national accreditation (Vermont Department for Children and Families, 2015).

- The Delaware Office of Early Learning, in cooperation with the Delaware Association for the Education of Young Children, administers a Compensation, Retention, and Education (CORE) awards program through its Race to the Top–Early Learning (RTT–ELC) grant. The purpose of the program is to provide financial incentives to individuals and programs to attract, train, reward, and retain educators participating in state Quality Rating Improvement System (QRIS) centers. CORE awards are particularly targeted to programs serving large populations of at-risk children. There are a variety of CORE awards associated with improving educational attainment, strengthening retention, and enhancing recruitment (Delaware Association for the Education of Young Children, 2015).

Incentives to Collaboratively Blend Funding Streams

Incentives to collaboratively blend funding streams to support ECE programs by combining resources and personnel across programs can increase efficiencies and potentially improve quality. The success of these collaborative initiatives requires genuine and continuing support from federal and state administrative agencies and their leadership. Examples can be found in the Illinois Preschool for All (Illinois State Board of Education, n.d.) and Illinois Early Childhood Collaboration (Illinois Early Childhood Collaboration, 2015) programs. In each case, funding for pre-K and preschool programs administered by the Illinois State Board of Education are in grants that follow 3- to 5-year-olds to the blended programs that serve them, whether based in local school districts, community-based programs, family childcare programs, and Head Start/Early Head Start programs or some combination of them.

Expansion of Performance Partnership Pooled Funding Pilots

Performance Partnerships are a new federal pilot program, building on a strategy implemented by the Environmental Protection Agency, that is designed to pilot better ways of using federal resources and to reduce administrative and reporting burden by allowing additional flexibility in using discretionary funds across multiple federal programs. Initial pilots in

2013 allow states, regions, localities, or federally recognized tribes to consolidate federal funds for program objectives related to disconnected youth and distressed neighborhoods, two areas recognized as potentially benefiting from greater flexibility and coordination across federal programs. With the flexibility to pool funds comes greater accountability. The partners must enter into an agreement which identifies the funds, programs, and services involved in the pilot; the population to be served; oversight procedures; methodology for outcome-measurement; and the consequences and corrective actions to be made if expected outcomes are not achieved (Readyby21. org, n.d.; U.S. Department of Education, n.d.). Given the cross-sectoral nature of care and education for children birth through age 8 and the major current challenges with diverse funding streams, it is a policy area that may be a natural candidate for expansion after the pilot phase.

Tax and Revenue Initiatives

Refundable Tax Credits

Refundable tax credits can be used to directly subsidize high-quality ECE programs and/or providers working in those programs, and are often tied to quality measures of program performance. Such a strategy, which requires legislative action, provides incentives for increased quality of early care and education and can also provide income support for providers. Besides the two programs described following, Colorado and Oregon offer other examples of innovative tax credit programs to support investments in ECE programs and their quality (Blank and Stoney, 2011).

- Louisiana School Readiness Tax Credits (SRTC) have benefitted both ECE providers and the centers in which they work since 1987 (Department of Children & Family Services, 2010). The SRTC for centers requires participation in the state QRIS system, and the amount of the credit is based on the number of stars (i.e., level of quality) of the center and the number of children served from the foster care or family assistance systems. (Centers also receive a reimbursement bonus from the state for serving these special populations depending on the number of stars they have received in the QRIS system.) The SRTC for providers (teachers and directors) requires that they work at a center in the QRIS system and enroll in a provider registry, and is based on the provider's level of education and length of experience. In each case, this is a refundable tax credit that is not limited by income, although a tax return must be filed. There is also a parent SRTC that increases the parent's Louisiana Child Care Tax Credit by a percentage amount based on the number of stars of the child's ECE program. In addition, there is also a business SRTC based on (a) a percentage of the "eligible expenses" incurred in support of ECE programs participating in the state QRIS (e.g., costs for construction or renovation; purchase of equipment; costs in the maintenance or operation of the program), (b) payments to a QRIS program for childcare services to support employees, and/or (c) donations made to Child Care Resource and Referral Agencies, with the amount of the credit also depending on the number of stars of the relevant program. Both for-profit and nonprofit businesses are eligible (presumably including ECE programs themselves), and this is also a refundable tax credit.

- Maine Child Care Investment Tax Credit subsidizes costs for the improvement of centers or homes that provide early care and education (Maine Department of Health and Human Services, 2012). Individuals receive the credit as the result of contributing $10,000 or more to quality improvement in 1 year, and it provides a $1,000 annual tax credit for 10 years followed by a $10,000 credit at the end of this period. Businesses receive a credit of 30 percent of their investments in quality improvement up to a $30,000 investment. The investment tax credit can be carried-over to a subsequent year.

Local or State Tax Initiatives

Local or state tax initiatives have received voter support in several regions to support the development of high-quality ECE programs. Besides these examples there are many others, including San Francisco's Children's Fund that has been resourced through property taxes, approved by voters, since 1991 (Ballotpedia, 2014).

- In 2005, a property tax was implemented in Summit County, Colorado, with the aim of supporting ECE programs. Funds from this initiative support the Right Start Project (Early Childhood Options, n.d.), which provides (a) salary supplements for ECE providers earning low income, (b) scholarships to support further training or education by ECE providers, (c) support for a shared services alliance among local providers, (d) parenting classes, and other initiatives.
- In 2011, voters in Seattle, Washington, approved a property tax levy for a period of 7 years to support educational achievement (Department of Education and Early Learning, 2015). The Families and Education Levy earmarked $61 million for early childhood programs that year, including (a) the development of Preschool for All, a voluntary, high quality preschool for 3- to 4-year-olds,

(b) a parent–child home-visitation program for 2- to 3-year-olds, and (c) a training program for birth-to-third grade educators and home-based childcare practitioners.

- In 2012, Mayor Julián Castro convinced voters in San Antonio, Texas, to approve a one-eighth cent sales tax increase to fund several programs to enhance the quality of early care and learning for young children in the city under the Pre-K 4 SA program. The centerpiece of Pre-K 4 SA is the establishment of a network of full-day pre-K programs for 4-year-old children.

- First 5 in California was inaugurated by a voter-approved tobacco tax in 1998 through Proposition 10 (Children and Families Initiative) to generate funds for supporting and improving the development of children from birth through age 5. The initial revenue of more than $700 million led to the creation of statewide (20 percent of revenues) and county-level (80 percent) First 5 Commissions to identify local needs and support a wide range of projects to support families with young children. Many of these projects are devoted to improving quality and access to high-quality ECE programs. Over time, the revenues yielded by the tobacco tax have declined, resulting in refinement and prioritizing among supported activities.

Revenues from Lottery or Gaming Activities

Several states have designated revenues obtained from state-supported lotteries, gambling, or other gaming activity to support improvements in the quality and accessibility of high-quality ECE programs. The Missouri Early Childhood Development, Education, and Care Fund annually provides tens of millions of dollars to the startup, expansion, and improvement of programs serving children from birth to kindergarten age and their families, drawing on state revenues from gambling fees (Missouri Legislature, 2014). The Georgia Lottery for Education provides more than $900 million annually to educational activities, of which a statewide voluntary pre-kindergarten program is a major component (Raden, 1999).

Anticipated Cost Savings from the Effects of High-Quality Childcare and Education

Some of the most recent widely discussed approaches seek to recover and reallocate the cost savings to other social institutions that are anticipated as the result of young children's participation in high-quality ECE programs. Those social institutions can include schools (such as reduced special education costs), public systems (such as reduced welfare expenditures and enhanced tax revenues from greater employment), and other social institutions. These anticipated cost savings are based on longitudinal studies documenting the later public (as well as individual) benefits deriving from young children's participation in high-quality programs.

Social impact contracts/bonds Social impact bonds provide for the use private funds (from individuals or corporations) to implement high-quality ECE programs. These funds are repaid by the government if the intended results are met. They may be contingent on performance outcomes or on revenue outcomes (such as reduced public spending) (Nonprofit Finance Fund, 2013). Pay for Success, one type of social impact bond, aims to improve early childhood outcomes and reduce government costs. ReadyNation has used this strategy to use special education cost savings to pay for prekindergarten programs in Salt Lake City, Utah, as well as for prenatal health care and counseling in Virginia financed through savings from Medicaid cost avoidance (ReadyNation, 2015a).

Reallocation of special education funds At present, federal and most state statutes provide special education funding based on the number of children directly receiving such services. Advocates associated with the Granite School District in Utah have proposed that if one of the outcomes of investments in high-quality ECE programs is a reduction in special education enrollments in the school district, those cost savings should be reinvested in strengthening and expanding those programs. The expected result would be progressive improvements in quality preschool program access over time and comparable decreases in special education enrollments (Voices for Utah's Children, 2013). Implementing such a strategy would require statutory changes at the federal and, possibly, state levels to enable such redirection of cost savings.

PRIVATE INVESTMENTS IN IMPROVING THE QUALITY OF ECE PROGRAMS

There has been some interest in the business community in investing in education, including early learning. One avenue is investment in early childhood care and education through childcare benefits or subsidies for their employees or through directly providing childcare services. Another avenue is through business leaders engaging in advocacy to foster greater government investment (for example, the use of business leaders in the advocacy efforts of the Pew Charitable Trusts campaign for prekindergarten education and the efforts of ReadyNation [2015b], a national business advocacy group that is also focused on increasing public investments in early learning).

In some cases businesses and corporations invest directly to improve the availability and quality of care and education programs in their communities, in part motivated as a business investment in local workforce preparation. This may not be as widespread as it could be because of barriers to direct investment strategy that include (a) the return on this investment is not business specific but rather a shared social good from which businesses benefit very indirectly, and (b) the time horizon for the return on this investment is a long one, by contrast with many other kinds of business investment. Some businesses, however, do see the value of these long-term investments in the less direct social and human capital. In addition, an alternative view is that such business and corporate investment could be viewed as part of the business community's return for the public investment in infrastructure from which business entities directly benefit.

Corporate Philanthropy Used as Seed Funding

The Minnesota Early Learning Foundation/St. Paul Early Childhood Scholarship Pilot was funded with $20 million in private (primarily corporate) funding to provide seed money for a variety of programs to support early childhood education, including (a) parenting mentoring, especially through home visitation, (b) 2-year scholarships for 3- to 4-year-old children coming from lower-income families (i.e., <185 percent of the federal poverty level) to attend high-quality ECE programs, and (c) systematic evaluation of childcare quality through a program called "Parent Aware." Funding came primarily through philanthropic donations from corporate sponsors throughout Minnesota, with a focus on the Minneapolis–St. Paul region. The program lasted from 2006 to 2011 and yielded promising results suggesting that there were increases in the quality of childcare programs serving lower-income children and improvements in the school readiness of scholarship recipients, and the Minnesota legislature subsequently significantly expanded the scholarship program (Minnesota Department of Education, 2015; Minnesota Early Learning Foundation, 2011; Schwartz and Karoly, 2011; Think Small, 2013).

PUBLIC–PRIVATE PARTNERSHIPS

Program Development

Program development is the most direct and visible form of public–private partnership to contribute to the creation, improvement, or enhancement of ECE programs. This can occur on a statewide level but is most often local, resulting from the direct collaboration of local business leaders, public officials, and local and national philanthropies to pool resources to create changes that none would have been capable of doing alone. Several examples were also described in Chapter 3:

- Boston's Thrive in Five program began with initial funding from local foundations, local health care organizations, the city, and United Way to pay for planning and infrastructure. The W.K. Kellogg Foundation provided much of the implementation funding. State funding also contributes to Thrive in Five (National League of Cities, 2012).
- Educare also illustrates public–private partnership both in the initial development of the Educare model in Chicago and in its extension to other regions throughout the country (Educare Schools, 2015).
- The involvement of the George Kaiser Family Foundation in expanding access to high-quality early education programs in Tulsa is a further illustration of how private funds in league with public agencies can result in systems change (GKFF, 2015).

Loan Subsidies

One general public–private strategy is to provide avenues for nonprofits that run ECE programs to obtain loan revenues at lower cost from private and public sources that can be used for a variety of purposes. One of the problems of this strategy is the difficulty that many ECE providers are likely to encounter in paying back the loan amount, which is why programs that provide loan guarantees or subsidies can be most useful.

- *Qualified section 501(c)(3) bonds* are typically used to help non-profits finance capital improvements, but they can also provide a general mechanism by which capital from private investors can be made available to improve the quality of ECE programs run by nonprofit agencies. The state or local government issues the bonds, with funds provided by private investors. The nonprofit agrees to pay back the debt over time. Interest on the bond is tax exempt, which lowers the cost of the financing, but one problem with this strategy is that it may be difficult for nonprofits to identify or create revenue sources for bond repayment. The Illinois Finance Authority (2012) and the Indiana Economic Development Corporation (n.d.) are two state agencies that have used such instruments for funding early education programs. The Connecticut Child Care Facility Loan Fund (Connecticut Health and Educational Facilities Authority, 2015) offers three programs, including one with subsidized interest rates (according to one source, the Connecticut program also paid 80 percent of debt service, with Temporary Assistance for Needy Families [TANF] funds used to help repay loans; see Zeidman and Scherer, 2009).

- *General credit enhancement* is often needed by directors of ECE programs to make program improvements, and various mechanisms can enhance the credit-worthiness of an ECE program through the assistance of a public or private entity: a line of credit, liquidity enhancement, or even a loan guarantee. Credit enhancement, provided either privately (such as a philanthropy) or publicly, can significantly lower the cost of financing, especially if the approach includes partial subsidy of interest and/or principal payments or a loan guarantee if the borrower defaults. Because of the importance of high-quality ECE programs to public welfare, public credit enhancements are more likely. As one example, the Division of Child Care and Early Childhood Education of the Arkansas Department of Human Services has created a Child Care Facilities Guaranteed Loan Program that includes a guarantee to reimburse up to 80 percent of the principal of the loan amount up to a $25,000 maximum (Arkansas Department of Human Services, 2011). Eligible loan projects include "any aspect of establishing or expanding a childcare facility," including classroom and playground equipment, training expenses, construction costs, and temporary financial support. Other states (including Connecticut, Maryland, Tennessee, and West Virginia) have similar programs.

General Redevelopment

Another strategy is to leverage funds from private sources to enhance the quality of early care and education programs. San Francisco, for example, has such an investment program (Low Income Investment Fund, 2014). Other examples illustrate the use of public mechanisms to leverage such finds:

- *Tax Increment Financing (TIF) districts* are created when a local government designates a large or small geographical region as a "TIF district" and freezes the tax rate in this region. The bonds or loans that are issued to fund redevelopment projects in that district are repaid from the increased tax revenue that is expected to occur as a result of the redevelopment activity. TIF funding is often used for expenses related to land acquisition, public works construction or improvement, capital construction, and financing costs, but some states have included childcare costs for families living in the district as a TIF expense. TIF funds can also be used to finance improvements in the facilities or operating costs of ECE programs within the district as part of the redevelopment effort. Enabling legislation by the state may, however, be necessary for this to occur. Other problems with this strategy are similar to those of social impact bonds (e.g., crediting local tax revenue increases specifically to the improvement in the local ECE infrastructure), although the TIF strategy is based on an assumption that any revenue increases will be allocated to bond/loan repayment.

- *Developer impact fees* are often required of real estate developers by state and local governments to offset the costs resulting from the impact of their activities on the community (e.g., necessary public works improvements). Some cities have allocated developer impact fees to improve childcare and education programs deriving from the expected increase in demand for these programs resulting from real estate construction. For example, commercial developers in Palm Desert, California, are required to pay a Child Care Facilities Impact Mitigation Fee for new developments (City of Palm Desert, 2015).

Public Land Trust Revenue

Public land trust revenue is typically used to fund public institutions, including schools. In 2006, Nebraska voters passed a constitutional amendment to allow revenue generated from public land trusts to be used for early childhood education, with a focus on birth to three (Stebbins, 2010). These funds provided the basis for the development of the Nebraska Early Childhood Education Endowment, created from the public commitment of $40 million from the Educational Lands and Trust Fund and a commitment from the private sector of an additional $20 million raised over a 5-year period. In this respect, the Nebraska model is a public–private partnership because of how the public investment was used to leverage a private match. The Nebraska Department of Education administers these funds under a program called Sixpence to provide grants to school districts who work with local agencies to provide high-quality birth-to-three programs, with a 100 percent local match to statewide funds. The programs supported by this program include parent support initiatives to teenage parents, home visitation, and other programs.

SHARED SERVICES

It is common that several agencies, organizations, or businesses work together to share overhead costs and provide services in a more efficient manner. The general goal is that by collaborating on infrastructure costs (particularly capital management and improvement costs, financial accounting, human resources, billing, staff management, and other administrative services), professional development, and other common concerns, each agency can gain cost savings, notwithstanding the other potential benefits of collaboration. Sound Child Care Solutions in Seattle is one example of a shared services organization consisting of seven childcare programs in that region (Sound Child Care Solutions, 2012). Another example is Infant/Toddler Family Day Care in Fairfax, Virginia, that serves family childcare programs serving very young children (Infant Toddler Family Day Care, n.d.).

REFERENCES

Arkansas Department of Human Services. 2011. *Arkansas child care facilities guaranteed loan program.* http://humanservices.arkansas.gov/dccece/Pages/ChildCareFacilities GuaranteedLoanProgram.aspx (accessed August 21, 2014).

Ballotpedia. 2014. *City of San Francisco "Children and Families First" city funds, tax and administration proposal, proposition C.* http://ballotpedia.org/City_of_San_Francisco_%22Children_and_Families_First%22_City_Funds,_Tax_and_Administration_Proposal,_Proposition_C_%28November_2014%29#cite_note-Public-1 (accessed May 30, 2015).

Blank, S., and L. Stoney. 2011. *Tax credits for early care and education: Funding strategy in a new economy.* http://opportunities-exchange.org/wp-content/uploads/OpEx_Issue Brief_Tax_Final1.pdf (accessed May 30, 2015).

City of Palm Desert. 2015. *Fees.* http://www.cityofpalmdesert.org/Index.aspx?page=40 (accessed August 21, 2014).

Connecticut Health and Educational Facilities Authority. 2015. *Programs.* https://www.chefa.com/products/childcare (accessed August 21, 2014).

Delaware Association for the Education of Young Children. 2015. *Core.* http://www.daeyc.org/core (accessed August 21, 2014).

Department of Children & Family Services. 2010. *School readiness tax credits.* http://www.qrslouisiana.org/child-care-providers/school-readiness-tax-credits (accessed August 22, 2014).

Department of Education and Early Learning. 2015. *About the families and education levy.* http://www.seattle.gov/education/about-us/about-the-levy (accessed August 22, 2014).

Early Childhood Options. n.d. *Right Start Project.* http://www.earlychildhoodoptions.org/right-start (accessed August 22, 2014).

Educare Schools. 2015. *What is Educare?* http://www.educareschools.org/about/pdfs/What-is-Educare.pdf (accessed May 30, 2015).

GKFF (George Kaiser Family Foundation). 2015. *Early childhood learning.* http://www.gkff.org/areas-of-focus/education/early-childhood-learning (accessed June 8, 2015).

Illinois Early Childhood Collaboration. 2015. *About us.* http://ilearlychildhoodcollab.org/about (accessed August 21, 2014).

Illinois Finance Authority. 2012. *Education.* http://www.il-fa.com/programs/education (accessed August 21, 2014).

Illinois State Board of Education. n.d. *Early childhood education.* http://www.isbe.net/earlychi/preschool/default.htm (accessed August 21, 2014).

Indiana Economic Development Corporation. n.d. *Indiana.* http://iedc.in.gov (accessed August 21, 2014).

Infant Toddler Family Day Care. n.d. *Infant toddler family day care.* http://www.infanttoddler.com (accessed August 22, 2014).

Low Income Investment Fund. 2014. *Child care facilities fund.* http://www.liifund.org/products/grants/grants-for-child-care/ccff (accessed August 21, 2014).

Maine Department of Health and Human Services. 2012. *Child and family services: Business support.* http://www.maine.gov/dhhs/ocfs/ec/occhs/businesssupport.htm (accessed August 22, 2014).

Minnesota Department of Education. 2015. *Early learning scholarships program.* http://www.education.state.mn.us/MDE/StuSuc/EarlyLearn/EarlyLearnScholarProg/index.html (accessed March 17, 2015).

Minnesota Early Learning Foundation. 2011. *Early education reform blueprint.* Minneapolis, MN: Minnesota Early Learning Foundation.

Missouri Legislature. 2014. *Missouri revised statutes. Chapter 161: State department of elementary and secondary education.* http://www.moga.mo.gov/mostatutes/stathtml/16100002151.html (accessed August 23, 2014).

National League of Cities. 2012. *Educational alignment for young children: Profiles of local innovation.* Washington, DC: National League of Cities.

Nonprofit Finance Fund. 2013. *Pay for success learning hub.* http://payforsuccess.org (accessed August 24, 2014).

Raden, A. 1999. *Universal prekindergarten in Georgia: A case study of Georgia's lottery-funded pre-k program.* New York: Foundation for Child Development.

Readyby21.org. n.d. *Section 737: Performance partnerships.* http://www.readyby21.org/sites/default/files/Performance%20Partnerships%20Fact%20Sheet.pdf (accessed January 16, 2015).

ReadyNation. 2015a. *Pay for success.* http://www.readynation.org/pfs (accessed March 10, 2015).

———. 2015b. *Readynation.* http://www.readynation.org (accessed August 24, 2014).

Schwartz, H. L., and L. A. Karoly. 2011. *Cost study of the Saint Paul Early Childhood Scholarship Program.* Santa Monica, CA: RAND Corporation.

Sound Child Care Solutions. 2012. *Sound child care solutions.* http://soundchildcare.org (accessed August 22, 2014).

Stebbins, H. 2010. *Dedicating trust land revenue for early care and education.* Boston, MA: HMS Policy Research, Partners in Early Childhood & Economic Development.

Think Small. 2013. *Report to the community 2013: A year of breakthroughs: Preparing children for school and life.* http://www.thinksmall.org/files/pdf/2013_TS_AnnReport_forDA.pdf (accessed March 17, 2015).

U.S. Department of Education. n.d. *Performance partnerships for disconnected youth.* http://www.ed.gov/blog/wp-content/uploads/2014/03/2014-PPPs-Fact-Sheet.pdf (accessed January 16, 2015).

Vermont Agency of Education. 2015. *Early education.* http://education.vermont.gov/early-education (accessed August 21, 2014).

Vermont Department for Children and Families. 2015. *Grants.* http://dcf.vermont.gov/cdd/grants (accessed August 21, 2014).

Voices for Utah's Children. 2013. *A sustainable financing model for high quality preschool for at-risk children: Results from the granite school district in Utah.* http://www.utahchildren.org/issues/early-care-and-pre-k-education (accessed August 18, 2014).

Washington State Department of Early Learning. 2010. *Washington state professional development system.* http://www.del.wa.gov/requirements/professional/Default.aspx (accessed August 21, 2014).

Wisconsin Early Childhood Association. 2015. *Reward Wisconsin.* http://wisconsinearlychildhood.org/programs/reward/ (accessed August 21, 2014).

Zeidman, B., and J. Scherer. 2009. *Innovative financing strategies for early childhood care.* Washington, DC: The Pew Center on the States.